MW01055825

Introduction to Ethnic Studies

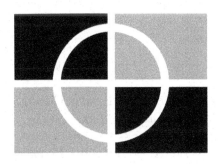

THIRD EDITION

EDITED BY

Brian Baker ■ **Julie López Figueroa** ■ **Boatamo Mosupyoe**
■ **Gregory Yee Mark**

California State University—Sacramento

Kendall Hunt
publishing company

Front cover image: "Dream Songs" copyright © Frank Lapena. Used with permission. Back cover photos courtesy of James Sobredo.

Copyright © 2004 by Brian Baker, Boatamo Mosupyoe, Robert Muñoz, Jr., Wayne Maeda, Eric Vega, Gregory Mark

Copyright © 2007 by Julie López Figueroa, Boatamo Mosupyoe, and Brian Baker

Copyright © 2011 by Brian Baker, Julie López Figueroa, Boatamo Mosupyoe and Gregory Ye Mark

ISBN: 978-0-7575-9412-0

Printed in the United States of America
10 9 8 7 6 5 4 3 2

Contents

RACE, CLASS AND GENDER

IDENTITY AND INSTITUTIONS

RESPONSE AND RESPONSIBILITY

Dedication

In honor of the memory of Dr. Alexandre Kimenyi and his contribution to Linguistics, African Studies, Social Justice and Human Rights.

Photo courtesy of California State University, Sacramento.

Introduction to Ethnic Studies

Brian Baker and Julie López Figueroa

Between December 15 and 28, 2003, a group of 72 Lakota people traveled more than 300 miles on horseback in the cold South Dakota winter weather.[1] Why did they do this at this time of year? These *Future Generations Riders* of Lakota traversed the same path taken by Chief Bigfoot whose goal was to find refuge among relatives on the Pine Ridge Indian Reservation. On foot, and carrying only what they could take with them, Chief Bigfoot and over 350 Lakota, mostly women, children, and elders, made this journey in 1890. Many of the Lakota were weak due to illness and hunger; Chief Bigfoot himself was ill with pneumonia. Despite this, they continued walking through the winter snow because they had fled and were in search of safety.

Eventually, the U.S. Calvary caught up with this so-called band of *renegade Indians* at Wounded Knee Creek on the Pine Ridge Reservation. Completely surrounded by American troops, without weapons, and exhausted from their 300 mile trek on foot, the Indians wondered what would happen next on the morning of December 28. When a single gun shot was heard, the soldiers commenced shooting indiscriminately. The Lakota dispersed and ran in every direction. Unarmed, they were chased by soldiers on horseback. When the shooting stopped, more than a few hundred Lakota people were on the ground in an area that stretched nearly four square miles. Following this tragedy a blizzard set in and the Lakota who were not already dead were left there to die by the American military. For the Lakota who survived as witnesses to this act of terror, they had no choice but to follow a life defined by the laws and policies dictated by the American government toward American Indians.

In 2003, the descendants of those who survived the Wounded Knee massacre followed in the footsteps left by their relatives under the leadership of Chief Bigfoot in 1890. Along the way, the Lakota riders on horseback could feel the presence of their ancestors who lost their lives. The *Future Generations Riders* has become an annual journey of discovery and healing for many contemporary Lakota since 1986, an important event that includes many children. This event not only reflects the relevance of historical memory and grief to contemporary identity; it is also an example of how an ethnic group asserts identity and culture.[2] According to Ron His Horse Is Thunder, president of Sitting Bull College, and one of the event organizers:

For 100 years, our young people have been taught that they needed to forget about being Indian in order to succeed. Today we're trying to reverse that by letting them know that our culture is important and that being Indian is a great thing. The ride is part of that process.[3]

For the Lakota, the massacre continues to be an important memory and marker of their history and identity, and it has come to symbolize ethnic persistence and cultural pride.

Along with Lakota honoring of their ancestors, there are other examples of movements that have elicited controversy. A Day Without Immigrants March that occurred all over the United States on May 1, 2006, in which over one million Latinos from such cities as New York, Los Angeles, Sacramento, and Chicago, demonstrated for better immigration reform to challenge, contest, and recover lost, marginalized, and distorted histories. More specifically, this was a national grassroots movement intended to bring public attention to the presence and contribution of immigrant workers in the U.S. economy.[4] Cities like Chicago and New York were especially important cities because they attempted to disrupt the practice of ascribing immigrant workers solely to Latinos. Non-Latino immigrant workers from Europe, Asia, and Africa marched in solidarity given their own understanding of how the same issues impact their quality of life differently. Anti-immigrant sentiments largely inform this nation's identity and process when confronting a new people. Tactics of intimidation against Latinos continue beyond the issue of the border to most recently include the dispersal of thousands of letters written in Spanish to Hispanics in Orange County, California, warning that immigrants could be sent to jail for submitting a ballot in the upcoming governor's election between Arnold Schwarzenegger and Phil Angelides.[5] No doubt a response to public acts of intimidation will forge a new beginning and bring an added complexity to the way we celebrate and practice culture.

These actions open up a public space to gain visibility in a world where these communities and its heroes and heroines are diminished into small paragraphs or conveniently lost in the history textbooks. When communities choose to respond, that is a prime opportunity to recover the truth and share a piece of shelved U.S. history. Ethnic Studies unapologetically puts forth the campaign that we must have a better and more accurate view of history in order to claim to truly be a United States. Beyond holidays and other significant events that define our culture and national identity as Americans, a number of unique and culturally specific ethnic events are held around the country. In fact, it would be impossible to list all of the cultural events that acknowledge and/or celebrate various aspects of the history, culture, and identity of all ethnic groups in America. Once subject to more extreme discrimination at the institutional and individual level in American history, contemporary African Americans, Asian Americans, Latino Americans, and Native Americans continue to assert their ethnic identities and play an important role in the remaking of contemporary American identity and culture. While America has always been a nation marked by racial and ethnic diversity, the difference in the contemporary world is that this diversity is now recognized and sanctioned as a vital and vibrant dimension of American society. America's future seems to be one that will be more multicultural and multilingual.

The Dynamics of Ethnicity, Ethnocentrism, and Racism

The 1960s and 1970s were important for many reasons, particularly due to the politics around race, class, and gender. Before the 1960s, *institutionalized racism,* supported by law and politics, defined and structured race relations in America. For example, it was *politically correct* for African Americans to sit in the back of the bus or eat at separate lunch counters before the civil rights movement in the American South. Americans of Asian, Latino, and Native (indigenous) descent were also the targets of such racism that shaped and limited their life opportunities in terms of education, housing, and occupation, among other things. In fact, dominant ethnocentric justifications played a key role in explaining and perpetuating racial and ethnic inequality. Dominant sentiments expressed in American culture defined Native Americans as ignorant and lazy people in need of protection, a powerful idea that was sanctioned in the historical development of Federal Indian law and policy under the guise of a *guardian* to *ward* relationship. Through the Bureau of Indian Affairs, Americans presumed that dominant society was burdened with the responsibility to care for American Indians because they could not do so on their own. In fact, the *white man's burden* and *manifest destiny* were the basic tenets of American political culture that also adversely impacted the daily lives of African Americans, Asian Americans, and Latinos. However, in the face of exclusion and oppression, and even under conditions of powerlessness, ethnic minorities survived and have successfully continued to define and assert their ethnic identity.

In a society where income and occupation continue to be important factors in how Americans gain access to health, housing, and education, to name but a few, socioeconomic status plays a central role in determining quality of life. Despite positive changes in recent decades, such as the implementation of Affirmative Action law and policy, to reconfigure race and ethnic relations in the United States, the fact is that racial socioeconomic inequality remains the reality. For example, the median family income for Hispanic ($26,502) and African American ($32,180) men was far below that for white men ($44,525) in 2001.[6] Do these income differences reflect something about the continuing role of race and ethnicity in the United States? How can we explain these differences? Further, while the median family income for white women ($31,575) is above that for Hispanic ($26,502) and African American women ($27,335), comparatively, women overall still earned less when compared to men in 2001. Do the differences in median family income between men and women reflect something about the continuing significance of gender inequality in the United States? How can we account for the differences? To what extent have the dynamics of ethnic and gender inequality been altered?

Culture, Experience and Contributions

The historical experience of African, Asian, Latino, and Native Americans relative to U.S. society is necessary to sufficiently understand current events and circumstances in the dynamics of ethnic relations. Due to their own unique historical circumstances and contributions to the making of America, each group possesses its own unique culture and historical memory. At the same time, we must take note of the fact that these groups are pan-ethnic identities. For example, the Asian American population as a group reflects something about dominant ideas regarding a race while simultaneously including distinct groups. Asian American as a category of ethnicity encompasses groups that have their own culture and identity, as in the case of people of Asian Indian, Japanese, Filipino, Korean, or Chinese descent. While this is not an exhaustive representation of all the distinct ethnic groups that come under the category of Asian American, there is something about American society that brings them together on some level *as* Asian American. While there is an element of experience and culture that brings a people together as Asian American on some level, it is also important to pay attention to the fact that there is diversity in the identities of the various groups that make up Asian Americans in the United States. This is also true for African Americans, Latino Americans, and Native Americans.

Through an understanding of their historical experience, we can also highlight the contributions that African Americans, Asian Americans, Latino Americans, and Native Americans have made to America. For example, although Japanese Americans were ousted from their homes and pushed out of their businesses to live in *evacuation camps,* and while Filipinos in America had the status of noncitizens, adult males from both groups joined the military and fought for the United States during World War II. Thus, while subject to conditions of oppression in the United States, Filipino and Japanese Americans made a positive contribution to the American war effort. In fact, a closer and more inclusive examination of American history reveals that Asian Americans, African Americans, Latino Americans, and Native Americans have all made a number of important contributions to the United States in addition to their own ethnic communities.

What Is Ethnic Studies?

The *National Ethnic Studies Association* defines Ethnic Studies as an "interdisciplinary forum for scholars and activists concerned with the national and international dimensions of ethnicity."[7] Given the politics of the 1960s and 1970s, coupled with the emergence of a vocal and visible population of African American, Asian American, Latino American, and Native Americans students attending colleges and universities, Ethnic Studies came into existence as an outcome of activism during this time period. As a discipline, Ethnic Studies has consciously cut across traditional academic disciplines as a necessary strategy to highlight the unique experiences of ethnic communities, and to build and strengthen connections with those communities outside of the academic institution. As a result, the voices and ideas of ethnic peoples, scholars and nonscholars alike, have changed academic institutions and affected the production of knowledge and ideas.

This volume, *Introduction to Ethnic Studies,* is designed to reflect the interdisciplinary nature of Ethnic Studies – the readings are drawn from academic fields in the humanities and social sciences. A few first-person narratives are also included, so we can get a sense of how individuals experience their ethnic group status. Overall, the readings in this book are meant to provide students with a foundation in ethnic studies.

This book is divided into five sections. The first section, "Perspectives," is intended to provide students with theoretical concepts to foster critical view on the way U.S. society is constructed. This section openly invites the reader to examine and reexamine not just individual roles, beliefs, attitudes, and actions, but how the collective gathering of those individual voices can either lead to experiencing greater freedoms or can collective mislead us into thinking that a particular situation is normal because of the peer pressure of maintaining the status quo. The readings are meant to incite critical reflection to recognize the tensions of living within the United States given its ideal way of life versus the actual realities. In order to fully understand the significance of ethnic identity, we need to pay attention to the fact that ethnic identity is fluid and dynamic, subject to external and internal ethnic group pressures. Why do you believe what you believe about the world? In what ways is your world socially constructed that your perspective is justified?

The second section, "History," is intended to provide students with a basic understanding of the distinct histories of Asian Americans, African Americans, Latino Americans, and Native Americans. Comparatively, how are these histories similar on the one hand and dissimilar on the other? What can we learn from these histories?

The third section addresses the intersection of "Race, Class, and Gender" as the primary dimensions of stratification in the United States. The purpose of this section is not only to provide students with an understanding of how individuals and groups gain access to valued resources in society, but also to demonstrate that race, class, and gender play a key role in that process. In what ways do race, class, and gender continue to be important dimensions of inequality in the United States? In what ways do race, class, and gender intersect and why are those intersections important?

The purpose of the fourth section, "Identity and Institutions," is to demonstrate the various circumstances under which ethnic groups not only define themselves on their own terms, but also show how external conditions affect this process. This section helps bring complexity to the ongoing debate of explanations that want to relegate racial/ethnic issues to the category of cultural problems to resolve. Not only does this section highlight the coercive means by which institutions shape identity, but there is an example that illuminates how, even after institutions are physically dismantled, the psychological impact in terms of our own colonization is still in the process of recovery. How were communities racialized in order to justify the social workings of our society?

The final section, "Response and Responsibility," addresses the question, given that American society continues to manage and deal with politics relating to ethnic identity: What are the responsibilities of Americans as citizens? To what extent do Americans contribute to problems relating to ethnicity by participating in and accepting popularized images and stereotypes? For example, one issue has to do with the use of Native Americans as mascots in sports. Why is this a problem and what should be the appropriate response by society? Another issue has to do with the problem of gender inequality within social movement organizations during the Civil Rights movement of the 1960s. Why was gender inequality a problem in a movement that emphasized racial equality?

[1] Fedarko, Kevin (2004, May 16). This ride is about our future. *The Sacramento Bee,* Parade section, pp. 4–6.

[2] Yellow Horse Brave Heart, Mara, & DeBruyn, Lemyra (2000). The American Indian holocaust: Healing historical unresolved grief. *American Indian and Alaska Native Mental Health Research,* 8(2), 60–62.

[3] Fedarko, p. 5.

[4] Keen, Judy, & Kasindorf, Martin (2006, May 1). 1 million rally for immigrants. *USA Today.*

[5] Marquez, Jeremiah (2006, October 17). Intimidating voting letter to U.S. Hispanics investigated. *Herald Tribune.*

[6] Feagin & Feagin, page 82.

[7] National Ethnic Studies Association, http://www.ethnicstudies.org.

Questions for Introduction to Ethnic Studies

The questions are intended to support the fostering of critical and engaged readers. Each section offers a set of framing questions and reflection questions. Framing questions are meant to prepare the reader for the coming section and invite world experiences while reflection questions at the end of each section inquire about what they learned, invite the reader to question what else could be learned from the experience, and assist in the transition to the following section.

Suggested questions have been identified to initiate a personal and classroom dialogue. Students are encouraged to address those questions for which space was provided. Faculty and students are invited to use these questions to build a rich discussion in reference to the readings. Faculty and students are invited to consider addressing optional questions to build upon personal and class discussions. Please select the questions that support students to become critical thinkers as well as skilled readers. All questions are meant to address the blank spots and blind spots as well as to maximize the instrumental value of this book.

Pre-Book Exercise

Framing Questions

1. What do you know or what have you heard about Ethnic Studies? Turn to a neighbor and share your impressions. Jot down three adjectives or thoughts.

2. What might be some assumptions made either by you or someone you know regarding who might best relate to this book? Please jot down at least two examples to discuss in class.

3. Upon reviewing the table of contents, the readings are combined historical and narrative accounts. Do you know the difference? Why do you think the editors offered this combined reading? Provide a brief explanation. (Optional)

4. Referencing the table of contents, which are the readings you think you might know something about and why? What are the readings you might know less about and why? Do the selected titles prompt images, sounds, stories, or adjectives? What are they?

5. Setting aside for one moment the question regarding familiarity with the readings, consider yourself a member within this society. How do you think you could use these readings to enrich your own life experiences as a member of this society and/or relate to someone you know nothing about? Turn to a partner and together come up with a list of four ways you could use the readings. (Optional)

◗ Framing Questions

1. What is the value of telling and listening to history within family, among your friends, or people you consider to be important in your life? What is the role of history? Please share a piece of history that has influenced who you are today.

2. What are the various kinds of resources used to tell history? Do you rely on books, newspapers, oral traditions, movies, pictures? What is your cultural practice for learning and building knowledge? (Optional)

3. To what degree do you think not knowing about your history influences how you hear, interpret, and appreciate someone else's history? (Optional)

4. To what degree do you understand that how you speak or what is referred to as everyday discourse reflects your gender, race, class, and ethnicity? (Optional)

5. To what degree do you understand that your gender, race, class, and ethnicity influence how you interpret the readings in this particular kind of book? Please provide some examples to illustrate your point.

6. To what degree can you recognize that how you are perceived and treated in the world is mediated by gender, race, class, and ethnicity? (Optional)

Reflection Questions

1. Given the definition of Ethnic Studies, was it similar to or different from what you discussed prior to the introduction? (Optional)

2. To what extent do you think it is important for you to know the background of the author who writes about the history you read? (Optional)

3. Do you think any and all information is value-free? (Optional)

4. What is the process you employ to differentiate between biased and unbiased information? Provide a brief explanation to explain the process you employ to discriminate between biased and unbiased information.

5. To what extent do you know about the racial/ethnic history of your own community compared to the history of other racial/ethnic communities? What either facilitated or hindered your knowing more or less given your experience in school prior to college? Provide a brief explanation.

Perspectives

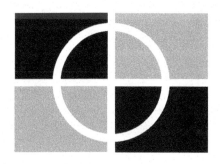

◆ Framing Questions

1. How do you define perspectives? What is important about having a perspective? (Optional)

2. When you think of the elderly, the young, the poor, the wealthy, the college educated, which perspectives are valued more than others? Who gets to determine which perspectives are valuable and which can be dismissed?

3. What might be the reasons that some people have more than one perspective on the world versus others who do not? Do you think culture, language, age, generational differences, and so forth have anything to do with having multiple perspectives?

4. What are the elements that shape your perspective? Has your perspective changed with age and what are the positive sides and down sides of having a perspective? (Optional)

Framing the Value and Purpose of Perspectives

Julie López Figueroa

This section represents an opportunity to explore why you believe what you believe and consider deconstructing why your perspective at times strongly resonates with us while other times perspectives unintentionally cause eyebrows to be raised in disagreement or peak from curiosity.

By using a process commonly referred to as critical reflection, the collection of readings is fundamentally intended to have "learners begin to re-evaluate their lives and to re-make them" (Mezirow, 1990). Why? More than fulfilling an intellectual exercise, critically reflecting on perspectives in the United States enables a practice of accountability to insure that freedom operates in a contemporary and responsive manner in relationship to its ever-changing populations. The readings offer analytical and theoretical perspectives to frame the chapters in the other sections as well as broadly introduce an Ethnic Studies perspective to conceptualize the world in ways we might not otherwise consider. Because the quality of our questions is a measure of our critical thinking (Paul & Elder, 2005), the format of this section is guided by a series of basic questions that will hopefully prompt a journey of self-reflection and self-discovery.

What are perspectives and where do perspectives originate? We are not born with perspectives, but rather socialized into having perspectives. In the United States, the two most influential institutions that socialize and define our early perspectives in life are home and school (Bowles & Gintis, 1976). Even with the transcendence of these sociocultural spaces, school and home continue to serve as touchstones from which to compare and contrast other perspectives. No matter our backgrounds, we are all exposed to a variety of perspectives broadly classified as radical, liberal, progressive, mainstream, moderate, and conservative. For instance, presidential and gubernatorial platforms are public mediums that embody some of these perspectives. Though these perspectives are itemized, some people's perspectives blend together to become progressive conservative, or as moderately liberal. This kind of discourse signals that perspectives can be multidimensional but also that life is more complex than our language can even capture.

In the case of Ethnic Studies, an Ethnic Studies perspective emerged in response to the unquestioned academic practice of solely functioning from a Eurocentric male perspective to examine all other experiences. These academic blinders would cast any lived experience that was non-eurocentric male as being deficient or inferior. Beginning in the late 1960s, Ethnic Studies amplified the rigor of analytical frameworks by centering the intersectionality race, class, gender, and sexual orientation issues. Ethnic Studies questions those ideas we take for granted for the purpose of creating a more equitable society. On this note Mark's chapter, *"We're Going Out. Are You With Us?" The Origins of Asian American Studies*, provides a first hand account regarding the experiences and conversations that led to what is historically known as the 'Third World Strike' at UC Berkeley. From this strike, Ethnic Studies as a discipline was born. What were the perspectives that needed to be challenged in order for true democracy to equally exist for all communities in this nation? Almost as an answer to this question, Chavez, a former undergraduate with an Ethnic Studies major, offers a contemporary perspective as to the personal and professional benefits of selecting an Ethnic Studies major in her chapter titled, *Why Ethnic Studies was Meant for Me*. Appropriately following the personal and professional accounts by Mark and Chavez, Kimenyi's chapter helps us understand how culture shapes our perspectives to reflect appropriate attitudes, practices, values, beliefs, traditions, and norms. With a clear discussion by Kimenyi's chapter, *Anatomy of Culture*, Omi and Winant's chapter, *Race and Ethnicity*, brings to light how a process of racialization steadily occurs in our society. To create an inclusive intellectual journey, Sue's chapter, *White and Ethnicentric Monoculturalism*, challenges the idea that one perspective can possibly offer a complete way to assess the world around us given the diversity that exists in our nation. This book is an invitation to juxtapose an Ethnic Studies perspective with your own perspectives to encourage a greater understanding about the way prejudice and discrimination formulate perspectives.

What role and function does our cultural practice of individualism play in shaping our perspective? Although we see the world through our individual perspectives, we also need to remember that our individual perspectives are porous to larger social perspectives. Another way of talking about perspectives is to consider the terms, micro and macro. Micro perspecties are individual whereas macro perspectives speak to societal or to a global level influence. Micro perspectives are always couched in macro perspectives therefore our individual perspectives are permeated by society's messages. Certainly, we have choices to believe certain things or see the world in a particular way but this is not always constant. For example, in my courses white and non-white students often demonstrate great apprehension to develop or let go of perspectives because changing perspectives somehow threatens family loyalty and/or they do not want to risk losing social acceptance among peers. In this way, students will distance themselves from critically thinking about the world and yet recognize that injustice is being experienced or do not want to think of injustice as working in their favor. Even though we live in a democratic nation, we make no apologies for not equally valuing and marginalizing the perspective of various communities throughout history. Because our perspectives are shaped by lived experiences, sometimes those lived experience are perceived to be the same or different. When individual differences are very different, that difference can either surface that harm of traditional practices or confirm the value of traditional practices.

Perspectives that operate at a macro level publicly declare and delineate appropriate social and cultural standards for viewing, framing, and engaging in a particular society. To insure macro perspectives are firmly interwoven in the society's structure, macro perspectives must permeate and define cultural norms and traditions in order to organize and regulate human behavior to insure "identity" is sustained, or socially reproduced throughout many generations (Bowles & Gintis, 1976). For example in a social and cultural context like the United States, the mainstream perspective is expressed in the commonly known phrase, the American Dream. The American Dream is nominally associated with being White and middle class, living a heterosexual lifestyle where father works and mother (assuming they are married) takes care of children in their purchased home where English is the preferred language. Collectively, these items represent a standard or ideal way of life indicating success. More often than not these standards are detached from the everyday realities that confront single mothers, single fathers, divorced parents, unmarried parents, gay and lesbian parents, gay and lesbian communities, grandparents raising grandchildren, adopted children, the homeless, adoptive parents, active racial/ethnic enclaves, and working poor. Having an ideal life identified creates the temptation to readily sort our lifestyles and perspectives into mainstream or non-mainstream bins. There is a real danger in oversimplifying how life happens. When we have an ideal by which to measure our level of success, very few people actually stop to consider what it takes to live up to the American Dream.

For example, in the United States where mainstream perspectives are intimately linked with representing good American traditional values and the norm, the majority of folks in this country can never be allowed to achieve the American Dream. Why? Our social outlook and cultural practice explicitly confirms that Americans in the United States revere and admire what cannot be commonly attained. In other words, the notion of exclusivity assigned to an experience or owning a rare material good is highly prized and admired in our nation. Maintaining glamour in practical terms requires that the common person not have full access to that particular experience or item. That is, inequality is a required condition that must exist in order for the American tale of meritocracy to exist.

The language of meritocracy rationalizes the exclusive experiences as an outcome of working harder and having more ability than others to achieve. Wing Sue defines and illustrates with examples how meritocracy can be the greatest American myth to shroud privilege and entitlement. Meritocracy, of course, assumes a level playing field and institutions are inherently fair. Because meritocracy is not only a cornerstone of our American identity, but a cultural ideology that informs our practice, we fail to critically recognize that inequality must exist in order for meritocracy to keep operating. That is, meritocracy cannot exist without making sure there is a group of folks that can be referenced as having less so the story of people pulling themselves up by the boot straps does not lose its luster. The earlier discussion of home and school is another example of how meritocracy emerges based on inequality and notions of neutrality. Home and school are social and cultural contexts that may or may not always coincide with one another (Delgado-Gaitan, 1992; Erickson, 1987; Villegas, 1994). When the home culture and school culture coincide, the experience of individuals for whom it coincides (Phelan, Davidson & Yu, 1993) very rarely is framed as unearned privilege. Instead, we continue to push the idea that everyone has a fair chance and that education is the great equalizer. No one stops to consider the differences in access to resources and opportunities (Oakes, 1994; Rios, 1996), the varying degrees in quality of schooling (Kretovics & Nussel, 1994), the lack of qualified teachers being directed to poor schools (Payne, 1994), or the fact that networks and mentoring can hugely make a difference in the lives of students (Stanton-Salazar, 1997). The tensions that centrally inform our lives hopefully inspires some realization that the ideal way of life can be detached from the complex realities through which life happens. While we need to celebrate our individuality, we also need to recognize our failures and successes are not solely determined by sheer will but are also mediated by active social structures.

What purpose does having a perspective serve in shaping identity? We must have the courage to contemplate the role of privilege when we cannot find value in one another's perspectives or essentialize someone else's experience. Privilege can be a hard term to apply to ourselves mostly because we do not set out to purposefully diminish or under value people. Yet, historically we can point to proccesses like assimilation, genocide, colonization, and conquest that occurred like slavery, Boarding Schools, and Manifest Destiny that violently divided communities. Generations later, some of us benefited from this outlook whereas others folks were severely disenfranchised. Certainly the progress in our communities releases us from having to live in the binary of winners and losers even though society insists that we all live in the binary to measure progress and tell stories of then and now.

How can social movements help us evaluate our individual perspectives? When individual perspectives are reticent to change, social movements are critical sites of accountability that keep inclusion and social justice as a priority. Social movements remind us that mainstream American perspectives have the inability to progressively transform given that they are color-blind, male-centric, and class-blind, among other things. While social movements may not entirely abolish the issues targeted, social movements invite us to recognize that working collectively rather than individually can transform our world. Without different civil right and social movements the once normal American traditions of slavery, conquest, colonization, segregation, xenophobia, denying a woman's rights to vote, eugenics, anti-miscegenation laws, and anti-Semitism might not otherwise be disrupted at a monumental scales. In some instances, communities are still surviving and/or recovery from these life changing events. We have to make more responsible choices no matter the level of fear that overcomes us and no matter the threat of social alienation. I want to invite you to sit in silence to contemplate what you contribute to the world around you and what kind of movement you belong to by virtue of your (un)conscious choices, or rather your individual perspectives.

I recently attended a speaking engagement in which Dr. Angela Davis (2006) was the featured speaker. Dr. Davis reflected on growing up during segregation in Birmingham, Alabama and shared how her mother would tell her at a very young age, "Things aren't suppose to be this way, this is not how things are supposed to be." I have to believe that there are more people in the world who would agree with this but perhaps feel it is enough to live comfortably and conveniently as long as one's needs are addressed and success is happening.

When we cling to our beliefs or become apprehensive to evaluating our perspectives, we do not build new knowledge or become critical thinkers. While it is important to celebrate what we know, it is even more essential to surface those power dynamics that refrain us from thinking there is nothing wrong or worse yet we cannot do anything to make substantive changes. If we feel at all inspired by Martin Luther King Jr., Dolores Huerta, Mahatma Gandhi, Jimmy Carter, Barbara Jordan, Gloria Anzaldúa, let us remember feeling inspired by these and other folks happens not just because we stand in agreement for what they do but I want to suggest that it is also because a part of us potentially recognizes our capacity to have the same courage. We need multiple voices and multiple perspectives to bring the same perspective of social justice to build awareness.

The collection of authors in this section invites readers to consider their outlook on society. More specifically, the readings examine the role and purpose of culture, the organizational structure of society, the intersection of race, class, and gender, the nature and purpose of meritocracy, the role of heterosexism, and the workings of racial formation. The readings refute the notion that perspectives emerge in happenstance way, and instead highlight the processes that silently inform but explicitly influence our perspectives. To this end, it is the hope of this author that these readings synergistically foster a habit of critical reflection among its readers to imagine a world where diversity is not viewed as a threat to American life, but gives life to Americans in the United States.

References

Bowles, S. and Gintis, H. (1976). *Schooling in capitalist America: Educational reform and contradictions of economic life*. New York: Basic Books.

Davis, Angela. (2006). *Making Real Change*. (Talk given at the University of California at Davis on October 10, 2006)

Delgado-Gaitan, C. (1992). School matters in the Mexican-American home: Socializing children to education. *American Educational Research Journal*, *29*(3), pp. 495–513.

Erickson, F. (1987). Transformation and school success: The politics and culture of educational achievement. *Anthropology and Education Quarterly*, *18* (4), 335–356

Hurtado, A., Haney, C and Garcia, E. (1999). Becoming the mainstream: Merit, changing demographics and higher education in California. *La Raza Law Journal*, *10*(2), 645–690.

Mezirow, J. (1990), "How critical reflection triggers transformative learning", in Mezirow, J. (Eds), *Fostering Critical Reflection in Adulthood. A Guide to Transformative and Emancipatory Learning* (pp.1–20). Jossey-Bass, San Francisco, CA.

Neill, D. M. & Medina, N. J. (1994). Standardized testing: harmful to educational health. In J. Kretovics & E. J. Nussel (Eds.) *Transforming urban education* (pp. 128–145). Boston: Allyn and Bacon.

Oakes, J. (1994). Tracking, inequality, and the rhetoric of reform: Why schools don't change. In J. Kretovics & E. J. Nussel (Eds.), *Transforming urban education* (pp.146–164). Boston: Allyn and Bacon.

Paul, R. & Elder, L. (2005). *Critical thinking: Concepts and tools*. Dillion Beach: Foundation for Critical Thinking.

Payne, R. S. (1994). The relationship between teacher's beliefs and sense of efficacy and their significance to urban LSES minority students. *Journal of Negro Education*, *63* (2), 181–196.

Phelan, P., Davidson, A. L., & Yu, H. C. (1993). Students' multiple worlds: Navigating the borders of family, peer, and school cultures. In P. Phelan & A. L. Davidson (Eds.), *Renegotiating cultural diversity in American schools*, (pp. 52–88). New York: Teachers College Press.

Rios, F. (1996). Teachers' principles of practice for teaching in multicultural class-rooms. In F. Rios (Ed.) *Teacher thinking in cultural contexts* (pp.129–148). Albany, NY: State University of New York Press.

Stanton-Salazar, R. D. (1997). A social capital framework for understanding the socialization of racial minority children and youths. *Harvard Educational Review*, *67* (1), 1 – 39.

Villegas, A. M. (1994). School failure and cultural mismatch: Another view. In J. Kretovics and E. Nussel (Eds.), *Transforming urban education* (pp. 347–359). Boston: Allyn and Bacon.

"We're Going Out. Are You with Us?" The Origins of Asian American Studies

By Gregory Yee Mark

Introduction

Scholars trace back the beginning of Ethnic Studies in the United States to the student led strikes at San Francisco State College, now San Francisco State University (November 1968), and University of California, Berkeley ("Berkeley") (January 1969). At most universities and colleges, Asian American Studies (AAS) is one of the major components of Ethnic Studies. I grew up in Berkeley and Oakland, California, and the beginning for me was the summer of 1968. I was a student at UC, Berkeley and majored in Criminology. Earlier that year, I had transferred from Merritt Community College which was on Grove Street (now Martin Luther King, Jr. Way) in Oakland. Three events that summer played key roles in creating and defining the Asian American Movement and my own lifelong interest and commitment to Ethnic Studies.

The first was a family generational journey that I still travel today. From age six to 19, I lived in Berkeley and my grandparents lived two blocks away on California Street. One day, in June 1968, my grandmother, Violet Wong, asked me to go downstairs with her to the basement and she pulled out an old film canister which contained three reels of 35mm film. As she was pointing to the canister, Grandmother told me "Gregory, you do something with this." I took the film to Palmer's in downtown Berkeley to a childhood friend and from the decaying reels he saved 30 minutes of film and transferred it to 16 mm film. Five years later, at our 1973 family Christmas party, 60 family members viewed the showing of the very first Asian American film, the 1916 silent movie, Curse of Quon Gwon. Grandmother starred in the black/white film which co-starred her sister-in-law, Marion Wong. Marion played the villainess but, most importantly, Curse of Quon Gwon was her project. A unique perspective about the film is that the key actors and people behind the scenes were Chinese American women. In fact, three generations of women in my family are in Curse of Quon Gwon. Aunt Marion conceived of the idea, raised the money, wrote the script, and directed the film. Today, I am

Dr. Mark teaching "Introduction to Ethnic Studies," Spring 2011 (photo courtesy of James Sobredo).

still "doing something with it." In 2006, <u>Curse of Quon Gwon</u> was selected to the Library of Congress' National Film Registry. I am doing research on this pioneering film, and I hope to make the remnants of the film into an educational tool to examine the early Asian American community via film.

The second historical event was the founding of the Asian American Political Alliance (AAPA) in Berkeley by Yuji Ichioka and Emma Gee. I attended AAPA meetings and activities, and considered myself a fringe member. The Asian American Political Alliance became the major political organizing arm of a large contingent of UC, Berkeley's Asian American students and represented the Asian Americans student contingent in the UC, Berkeley Third World Liberation Front. The AAPA played a key role for Asian American visibility and leadership to the University administration and the public at large.

The third historical event was the August 17, 1968 demonstration in San Francisco Chinatown (Umemoto: 33). The purpose of this demonstration, which was my first demonstration/protest, was to bring attention to the numerous social problems that plagued San Francisco Chinatown. We wanted to push the Chinatown establishment to action and make the public, especially government agencies, aware of these hidden social issues. I remember the sign that I carried; it said, "Look around You, Chinatown Is a Ghetto." This peaceful demonstration was especially important because it brought together community folks, university students (primarily from UC, Berkeley and San Francisco State), and even AAPA members.

The 1968 San Francisco Chinatown demonstration for the first time brought together Asian American community members and student activists advocating for their communities. Many of these students later became leaders in community mobilization efforts such as the International Hotel (I-Hotel) Struggle, Oakland Chinatown youth organizations, and Japanese American senior citizen programs in the cities of Berkeley and San Francisco. These community service projects have left their legacies through an extensive network of community-based organizations and created a pipeline for young Asian Americans to become involved in today's social justice issues and social services. For example, the multi-service Asian Health Services in Oakland Chinatown can trace its origins to the '60s and young Asian American activists.

The Asian Experience in America: Yellow Identity Symposium

In November 1968, three months after the San Francisco Chinatown demonstration, I was talking to five other Asian American students in the Chinese Students Club (CSC) office, on campus in Eshleman Hall. At that time, I was President of the CSC. In 1968-69, Asian American students made up 10% of UC, Berkeley's student population. There were four major Asian American student organizations: the CSC, (American born Chinese); the Chinese Students Association (CSA, Chinese Foreign and immigrant students); the Nisei Students Club (NSC, Japanese American students); and Pi Alpha Phi (the Asian American fraternity). The first three organizations had offices on the fifth floor of Eshleman Hall.

On that November Friday afternoon, six male members from CSC, CSA and NSC were talking about campus life. We started to talk about dating and one of the men, Gary, talked about a beautiful Asian American woman on campus who was from Sacramento. All the men knew who she was because she truly stood out on campus. In a dejected fashion, Gary told us that he had asked her out but she said a firm "no." He then asked her why she wouldn't go out with him. Gary said that she told him, "I only go out with White men." Then the six men let out a spontaneous groan. For the next two hours, I led my first discussion dealing with Asian American men and their relationships with Asian American women. A significant part of our discussion was about a topic which later became known as "Asian American Identity." After our impromptu discussion, Gary and another friend said that they really enjoyed the discussion and gained a lot from it. As I was going down the elevator, I thought to myself, "Why not expand the discussion beyond the six of us?"

As President of the CSC, I called together a cabinet meeting and asked the members what they thought about the Club organizing a conference about Asian Americans. At the first planning meeting, about ten people attended; the next meeting, about 20, and by December 1968, there were 60 people on the conference planning/implementation committee.

On January 9, 1969, CSC and some of the other Asian American clubs hosted the "Asian Experience in America: Yellow Identity Symposium" which was attended by 800 Asian Americans from around the United States but mainly from California. The symposium was the first national conference that was organized by Asian Americans, was about Asian Americans, and was for Asian Americans. I served as the symposium's emcee and we had three keynote speakers. They were Dr. Paul Takagi, Isao Fujimoto and Dr. Stanford Lyman. The topics ranged from Asian American history to the socio-economic political status of Asian Americans. Many of the Asian Americans who helped plan the conference and attended the meeting, later also participated in the Berkeley Third World Strike.

From that November, Friday afternoon to the day of the conference, I knew the conference was very important. I just did not realize how timely and important it really was. In fact, noted criminologist and Asian American scholar-activist Takagi, the symposium's lead keynote speaker, today often laughs, "Can you believe that?" regarding my 'boldness' in using the term "Yellow" for "Asian Americans," since it was not commonly used at the time. When Dr. Takagi was asked in May 2011 to reflect on his life's work, he wrote, "Perhaps Greg Mark asking me to keynote an event that he titled, The Yellow Symposium, was the beginning of my career!" Here, Takagi is referring to his criminology career that took a significant turn from traditional criminology to Asian American scholarly activism. To Dr. Takagi, the Yellow Identity Symposium was so significant, that he often humbles me by crediting me with founding Asian American Studies. By this he means the symposium was a primary catalyst in initiating the formation of the field of Asian American Studies. Just before he passed away in May 2009, the noted "Dean" of Chinese American Studies, historian Him Mark Lai, who attended the symposium, said regarding the symposium, "It was an awakening."

The Sacramento Connection-full Circle

Another Asian American activist who attended the "Yellow Identity Symposium" was California State University, Sacramento (Sac State) student Wayne Maeda. In May 2011, Maeda stated that:

> Sac State 42 years ago was a place that had its political awareness shaped by the Civil Rights Movement, the war in Vietnam and the Black Power movement. It was, after all, in Sacramento in 1967, that Black Panthers carried guns into the Capitol. However, it was events in 1968 that shaped many of us who were just students then. 1968 began with the Tet offensive where the Viet Cong attacked across Vietnam with impunity, followed by revelation of Mai Lai massacre cover up, assassinations of Martin Luther King and Robert Kennedy, Mayor Daly's thugs turned loose at the Democratic conventions in Chicago and San Francisco State and UC Berkeley campuses shut down in a push for Ethnic Studies. So there was a core of us becoming politically aware of issues of social justice and inequalities. But it was not until the 'Asian American in Experience: Yellow Identity Symposium' held in January 1969 that we began to think in terms of Asians in American and our identity. A number of us came back from this first ever conference on Asian Americans even more focused and dedicated to push for Ethnic Studies at Sac State. We consolidated a coalition of Black, Chicano, Native American and white radical students to push for hiring minority, women faculty and fundamental change in curriculum.

The timing of the "Yellow Identity Symposium" was significant for another reason. During the symposium's lunch break, my fellow classmate in Criminology,

Maurice Williams, came by to see me. Maurice was a good friend who took me to African American parties and restaurants, and likewise I took him to Asian American parties and restaurants. Originally, he was a student athlete recruited to play football at Cal (UC, Berkeley). Maurice was the Black Student Union (BSU) liaison with other student groups. So Maurice told me that at last night's (Friday, January 8, 1969) BSU meeting, **"We met last night and decided that we are going out. Are you with us?"** I told Maurice, "Yes, we are with you." In other words, I was telling him that the Cal Asian Americans students would be part of the Strike, too. Ten days later, on January 19, 1969 the Third World Liberation Front began the Third World Strike at the University of California, Berkeley.

The Fight for Ethnic Studies: The Third World Liberation Front

The Third World Liberation Front students went on strike for the creation of a Third World College that would incorporate four programs: Asian American Studies, Black Studies, Chicano Studies and Native American Studies. A significant part of the strike agenda was to achieve individual and community self-determination and to end racism. Third World (TW) was a term adopted from Frantz Fanon's book, The Wretched of the Earth. To the strikers, TW meant not only the underdeveloped countries of the world but also the working class people of color in the United States.

In the first two weeks of the Strike, it was exciting: peaceful picketing, marching around campus, listening to speeches from community folks and older student leaders, and handing out leaflets in front of classroom and administrative buildings. We had to have moving picket lines and not block the entrance to any buildings. We held our signs up proudly and over and over again shouted, "On Strike, Shut It Down, On Strike, Shut It Down!" and "Power to the People!" I remember the Asian American contingent holding long planning meetings to plan for the next day's strike events, sometimes meeting virtually the whole night. Then our representatives had to meet with the other Coalition members to agree on the days and even the week's strategies. As the Strike progressed, there was an increasing law enforcement presence. In the first week or so, it was the campus police and folks from the Dean of Students Office who monitored our activities. Next came the City of Berkeley Police Department, then a consortium of local police departments to augment the Berkeley Police Department, such as departments from Oakland and San Leandro, and then they were joined by the California Highway Patrol. Then the TWLF strategy changed from moving picket lines to what we called the "snake" which consisted of strikers moving around campus, making noise and disrupting classes that still met. As the number of student strikers declined from the daily grind and stress, the "snake" tried to avoid law enforcement and be moving targets. As the Strike progressed, the Alameda County Sheriffs or the "Blue Meanies" escalated the tension and violence even more. By the last few weeks of the Third World Strike, the National Guard was brought in with fixed bayonets attached to their rifles, and physical, violent confrontation became the daily standard mode of operation. They used tear gas and even brought in helicopters to tear gas us. Of course, tear gas did not know the difference between a striker and a student going to class. The end result was the campus being shut down because of the increasingly heavy-handed law enforcement presence.

For the students the strike was very trying. In week six, I remember going to Cowell Hospital, the University student hospital, for treatment and the waiting area was filled with strikers. Everyone was just so tired, run down, and suffered from a lack of sleep and fatigue. I remember several personal low points in the strike for me.

The first low point was the increasing violence. I personally believed in non-violence and I still do. However, the Strike was becoming increasingly more violent. Two major contributors were the "Blue Meanies" and the National Guard. One day, from the fifth floor of Eshleman Hall, I looked down from the outdoor stairways balcony at the role of baton-carrying Sheriffs and fixed bayonets Guards trying to stare down protesters on the other side of Bancroft Ave. For some reason, one of the Sheriffs looked up and fired what I thought was a tear gas canister at me. I was not doing anything wrong or illegal, yet this man – this stranger – felt that he had the right to take a shot at me. It took all my self-control not to throw a chair down at him.

The second low point was a rumor that the strike was going to end. . . . that the University Administration was going to meet our demands. One of the members of the Black Student Union, Charles wanted to celebrate on the steps of Sproul Hall (the Administration Building). He brought some watermelon and then he asked me if I had any opium. (And no, he wasn't joking about stereotypes of Blacks and Asian Americans.) I was so disappointed in Charles that he, a fellow striker, negatively stereotyped me with the old images of Chinese Americans as opium addicts and dealers. He thought that because I was Chinese American that I had access to opium.

During the Nineteen Century, the early Chinese pioneers to the United States were frequently accused of smuggling opium into the U.S., operating opium dens and exposing/polluting White Americans to the drug. Actually, in the late 1700s, the British, French, Americans and most of the European powers smuggled opium into China and by 1900 essentially 27 percent of China's adult male population were opium addicts. So when Charles asked me if I had any opium, I was really disappointed in him.

By week eight of the strike, the end of the Winter 1969 quarter, on March 15, 1969, the UC, Berkeley Third World Strike ended. The TWLF and the University negotiated a compromise. The main demand was the creation of a Third World College. Instead we ended up with four separate Ethnic Studies programs which combined and became one Department. Somehow, Black Studies worked out an independent arrangement with the administration and they became a separate Black Studies Program. I could not believe this – after this intense Strike, a significant component of Ethnic Studies went off on its own.

By the end of the Strike, I was getting tired from the daily demands to sustain the strike but also I was getting upset with outside elements in the UC, Berkeley street community. As the Strike progressed they felt entitled to become involved with the TWLF strike. In the Strike's last month, they used it as an excuse for violence and trashing the University. I felt that this outside element and law enforcement moved the Strike more towards the confrontation mode than the Strikers. I learned a lesson from this. . . . six years later at San Jose State University, I was the Director of the Asian American Studies Program. I led a takeover of President John Bunzel's office because he was threatening to take away some of the meager resources from Asian American Studies. During the takeover, in the late afternoon, non-Asian Americans came to me and one of them said, "Let's break some windows and trash the administration building." I told them something to the effect of, "You don't tell us Asian Americans what to do. We determine our own strategies and our own destiny, and if you want, you can support us, but you don't tell us what to do." I never saw him or his friends again.

Sac State was highly impacted by the two Third World Strikes. Professor Wayne Maeda recalled that:

> *Beginning an Ethnic Studies program, hiring faculty, developing curriculum, and the general demand for fundamental change at the campus level was made infinitely less confrontational by enormous sacrifices of students and faculty at both SF State and UC Berkeley. Moreover, they provided us models for classes, curriculum, and they even came to Sac State to provide guidance and inspiration to us. Thus, we were able to institute the first Asian American course in the Fall 1970 which was team taught.*

The Very First Asian American Studies Course in the United States

During the first week of the Winter 1969 quarter, we went "On Strike" and on Wednesday nights, the first ever Asian American Studies course, Asian American Studies 100X, met. Since we were "On Strike," we had to meet in one of the off campus university's residence halls. Of course, we could not violate our own Strike by going to class on campus. There were 150 students enrolled in the class – and I was one of them. Professor Paul Takagi was the instructor of record. However, it was a team taught class that also included graduate students such as Floyd Huen, Ling Chi Wang, Bing Tom, Alan Fong and Richard Aoki. Class meetings were electric. There was this positive tension in the air that for the first time we were all meeting to learn about ourselves. Most students had attended Asian American weddings, baby parties, dances and even funerals but now we were studying "Our History, Our Way" (the slogan for the University of Hawai'i at Manoa Ethnic Studies Department).

We students networked, studied and discussed issues/topics that were relevant to our lives, and were simply awed by having the opportunity to validate our own and our family's lives. Since this was the first Asian American Studies class ever, there were no textbooks. Therefore, each week, we had lectures and frequently guest speakers were brought in such as Edison Uno who talked about the World War II Internment of Japanese Americans. Another time, a European American Anthropologist, George DeVos, was brought to the class to speak. He came in with an arrogant attitude and was challenged by several students. The students questioned him regarding what gave him the right to tell us who we were. One of these students, Danny Li, is one of my close friends. He objected to the lecturer's "holier-than-thou" tone and questioned "whether a non-Asian would have the insights of people of color who had experienced racial discrimination firsthand. "

Danny later moved to Hawai'i in the fall of 1971 to continue graduate studies in Chinese History and he was involved in community-base organizations in Honolulu's Chinatown, whose multi-ethnic residents were also facing 'urban development' relocations, just like elderly Chinese American & Filipino American residents in the International Hotel (I-Hotel) in San Francisco's Chinatown. As with other involved Asian Americans, the Strike and the Movement provided Danny and many others a beginning of a lifelong commitment to end racism, social injustice and improve society.

Another friend who was involved in the Strike and AAS 100X was my close childhood and adult friend, Floyd Huen, M.D. Floyd was one of the early leaders for Asian American Studies. He wrote the first proposal for Asian American Studies, and represented AAPA on the TWLF Central Strike Committee. This Committee made the long- and short-run decisions for the Strikers and negotiated with the university administration. After Asian American Studies became a program at UC, Berkeley, Floyd became the first program administrator. He was the AAS Coordinator from 1969-70 and taught the pioneering courses "Introduction to Asian American Studies" and the "Pacific Rim Seminar."

Floyd had been one of the hardest working members of the Asian American student contingent. Prior to the Strike, Floyd felt in love with another student activist who was deeply involved in the Strike, AAS 100X and in general the creation of Asian American Studies. Her name was Jean Quan. Jean was an undergraduate student in charge of communiquè during the TWLF strike. At UC, Berkeley, she co-taught the first Asian American Women's course with Emma Gee and edited and wrote the Asian Women's Journal. Later, in the mid-1980s, Quan was the Western Regional Coordinator of the Justice for Vincent Chin campaign.

January 1969 was truly a highpoint for me personally and for the Asian American Movement. "The Asian Experience in America: Yellow Identity Symposium" was not only successful but also the first national Asian American conference ever, anywhere in the U.S. Asian American Studies 100X was an amazing experience. . . . it was very dynamic, exciting and historical because it was the nation's first Asian American Studies class. At that time, where else did Asian Americans teach a course about their own history and social issues affecting our own communities? The course even served as an integral part of the recruitment of students into the

Asian American component of the Third World Liberation Front Coalition. I served as a volunteer Teaching Assistant (TA) for AAS 100X. In my section, I had 30 students. A group of the students and I compiled a resource directory, conducted an informal needs assessment survey, and started to network with individuals and organizations in Oakland Chinatown.

◑ Service to the Community: Oakland Chinatown

During the middle of the Strike, around February 1969, I started to reflect more about the roles that we, as Asian American students, should play to improve the quality of life in our communities. I assessed the needs in my own community – the community that had been a major part of my life – and what I could do as "an insider" to work on behalf of my own community. As a result, I started community service projects in the Oakland Asian American community or specifically in the City's Chinatown. I was born in Oakland and raised in both the cities of Oakland and Berkeley. As a child and young adult, my father frequently took me to Chinatown to visit with friends, eat Chinese food, and visit Chinese societies such as the Suey Sing Tong. As a young boy, I got haircuts from the barber on 8th street, and this old Chinese woman barber gave us lollipops. I remember the corner (8th/Webster) grocery store whose owners, Mr. and Mrs. Gee gave me soda and crack seed. As a part of the Asian American Movement, I felt that I could use my education to better serve my community. In fact, at this time, I decided to apply to the School of Criminology graduate program because I thought that I could be more effective in my community work with an advanced degree.

In 1965, Oakland began to experience what many major U.S. cities experienced as a result of the change in United States immigration policy created by the Civil Right movement inspired-1965 Immigration Reform Act. This dramatic increase in the Asian American population, in particular, initially impacted the Chinese American and Filipino American populations. As a result, by 1969, Oakland's Asian American community was undergoing a dramatic transition. Many new immigrants, especially Chinese, were moving into the Bay Area. Oakland Chinatown attracted many newcomers as demonstrated in the three Chinatown-serving neighborhood schools: Lincoln Elementary School; Westlake Junior High School; and Oakland Technical High School. As with San Francisco Chinatown, there was a critical need for bilingual education, job training, and bilingual services such as in health, affordable housing, and youth programs. Inspired by the Civil Rights movement, the Asian American Movement, and the Third World Strike, community based organizations were created as early as the mid-1960s to address these needs.

During the last month of the Strike, I went out into the community and networked with Oakland Chinatown organizations such as the Chinese Presbyterian Church. I also attended board meetings of the Oakland Chinese Community Council (OCCC), which at that time was the primary social service organization in Chinatown, and served as their youth representative.

Lincoln's principal, Mr. Moynihan, was on the OCCC board. At that time approximately two-thirds of Lincoln School students were Asian American, primarily Chinese American, many of whom were immigrants. At board meetings, Moynihan expressed his concern regarding the difficulties faced by these non-English speaking, new arrivals from Asia, and how these students needed special assistance. I volunteered to help, thinking of the many Asian American students involved in the emerging Asian American Movement who would likely answer to such a call for service.

In AAS 100X, I had worked with a small group of students from one of its sections. These students and I did a preliminary needs assessment of Oakland Chinatown. One of the greatest needs was for the community's youth. The three primary public schools serving Chinatown expressed their concern for their recent Asian American immigrant students and there was a growing youth violence and gang problem in this community.

In the Spring 1969 quarter, three new additional Asian American Studies courses were offered. One of the courses was the "Asian American Communities" course which was also referred to as the "Asian American Field Work" class. I was a TA for one of the sections which was called the "Oakland Chinatown" section. There were 40 students in my section. In this course, we assessed the needs in Oakland Chinatown even more extensively, researched this community's history, and started a community service project. In this needs assessment as well, it was clear that one of the community's greatest needs was in its youth. At the time, there were no social services targeting the youth.

Considering the needs of Oakland Chinatown based on our needs assessments, coupled with Moynihan's appeal for help at Lincoln, I recruited students from the AAS Field Work course to tutor at Lincoln, and the Lincoln Elementary School Tutorial Program was born.

The Program was geared toward all Lincoln students, and its goals included improving their reading and writing proficiency. However, for those students with limited English speaking abilities (primarily Asian American immigrant children), the program also aimed to improve their English verbal skills.

In this way, the AAS Field Work course served as a direct pipeline to the Lincoln School Tutorial Program. My section of the Field Work course supplied the majority of the 35 tutors in the program. The program was a success, and continued for at least for four more years. According to Moynihan, the immigrant children's English proficiency scores dramatically improved. Furthermore, this project was a manifestation of one of the first times an AAS course was directly involved with local Asian American communities and literally applied theory and research to direct practice. In addition, it helped to jumpstart a new community based organization focused on Asian American youth in Oakland.

In August 1969, I founded the East Bay Chinese Youth Council, Inc. This wouldn't have been possible without my having roots in this community, the partnerships that I had developed with youth in the community, and with the support from Reverend Frank Mar of the Oakland Chinese Presbyterian Church.

The East Bay Chinese Youth Council, Inc.

The East Bay Chinese Youth Council (EBCYC) was formed to improve the quality of education, provide employment training and opportunities, prevent youth violence, and provide recreational activities for Asian American youth in the East Bay. From 1969-1973, it ran an impressive array of youth programs and simultaneously sought to empower these Asian American youth. We were able to obtain funding via sub-grants from the Oakland Model Cities Program and the Oakland Unified School District, two recipients of a federal program called Neighborhood Youth Corps (NYC).

With this funding, one of EBCYC's programs was the summer Neighborhood Youth Corps that in 1970 and 1971 employed 133 and 230 Asian American youth respectively between the ages of 14 and 18. Some of these programs were: a community school for immigrant youth; community celebrations; film festivals; and medical needs assessment; and general community outreach.

In 1973, the youth council changed its location and name but continued many of the initial programs. The name changed to East Bay Asians for Community Action (EBACA). EBACA continued the medical outreach program, and in 1974 expanded to a one-room clinic.

The clinic is now called Asian Health Services (AHS), and it has become one of the region's primary community health centers. AHS is an ever-expanding center which offers primary health care services to 21,000 adults and children and offers over 101,000 patient visits annually. Occupying a three-story building in the heart of Oakland Chinatown, AHS has 36 examination rooms and also has a dental clinic with seven chairs. Its staff is fluent in English and nine Asian languages (Cantonese, Vietnamese, Mandarin, Korean, Khmer (Cambodian), Mien, Mongolian, Tagalog and Lao) (Asian Health Services: 2011).

The I-Hotel

One of the founding principals of Ethnic Studies was a commitment to service to our communities and "to do community work," which later also became known as "community service." For the past 20 years, this model of bridging the community with mainly higher education has been more popularly called Service-Learning. Yet little acknowledgment is given to the contributions of Ethnic Studies to the development of the Service-Learning paradigm. Service-learning in its purest form — community service — was actually a critical part of the original mission of Ethnic Studies, and was in fact practiced as early as 1969 with the formation of Ethnic Studies.

The UC, Berkeley Asian American Studies students focused their community work (service) on five projects in Berkeley, Oakland, and San Francisco. In Berkeley the project centered upon the Issei (first generation Japanese Americans). In San Francisco, students worked with Issei in Japantown (J-Town), Chinatown with garment workers, a book store, and the International Hotel (I-Hotel).

The most immediate and high impact project was "Save the I-Hotel." In 1969, the Hotel was home to manongs (first generation Filipino American farmworkers) and elderly Chinese. One of the leaders to emerge from the struggle to save the I-Hotel and also, a key participant in the Berkeley Third World Strike, was Emil DeGuzman. DeGuzman was born and raised in San Francisco. In April 2011, he said:

My father would take me down to Kearny Street as a little kid along with my younger brother. I had a godfather who had his photography shop under the Palm Hotel near Washington and Kearny Street. The Palm went down in 1968 and the I-Hotel was next. So I was very familiar with Manilatown growing up. When the fire happened that killed three manongs in March 1969, the Third World strike had just concluded . . . and we had fought so hard and learned so much, we were ripe to battle in the community. . . . Fortunately, my roommate Dwight Scott and myself organized students both from the strike and non-strikers who were anxious to be active to make a difference in the lives of their people. We did community work but it allowed us to join with the United Filipino Association representing the tenants to fight the owners. The success of the struggle which is true even today is the intergenerational unity where the young people unite with the elderly was the winning combination that drove the fight for eight years to stop eviction of the tenants at the I-Hotel.

In the summer of 1969, I had a wonderful work study job working for the Dean of Students at the University of California, Berkeley . . . Our proposal was an Asian American Film Festival (Asian films for Asian American audiences) in several Bay Area Asian American communities.

It was the one of the best times in my early student years because the summer was hot and the campus was bustling with activity. The Third World Strike had ended months prior after the Winter of 1969. This long fought struggle opened doors for minority students in the university. The victory to open an Ethnic Studies department was a major concession from the University Of California Board Of Regents. The TWLF movement had achieved new respect in persevering in the fight for the principle of self determination in higher education.

The summer was a time when the university was transforming and a new era was emerging. Our positions and the film festival was a new direction the university had taken at the time. The creation of Ethnic Studies created new dimensions and opportunities that had a rippling effect outside the university. Nationwide other students of color were making the same demands and receiving concessions by their universities and colleges for Ethnic Studies. Communities gladly accepted our invitations to promote the film festival in their community centers. We chose four communities: San Francisco Chinatown, Manilatown, Japantown and Oakland Chinatown. (The screenings happened in the summer of 1969.) The films that were chosen were from Japan and China. Our budget allowed us to produce fliers and print posters to publicize the movies. In Manilatown, it was shown in the International Hotel. The films chosen were mainly

Japanese films since there were none found with English sub-titles from China and the Philippines. The directors were all famous: Akira Kurosawa, Kenji Mizoguchi and Yasujiro Ozu.

Dwight and I had no experience organizing a festival . . . (and furthermore, we were not that) familiar with Asian films. Through the outreach and contacts, we were encouraged to make the University of California, Berkeley serve our communities which never could be imagined one year before. The film festival was a success. Many hundreds of young and elderly came to see the films with translators there to speak if the audience was monolingual speaking.

By the summer of '69, the Asian American population was 3,089,932 (U.S. Department of Commerce: 1973). This represented a significant increase from the previous decade. The three major Asian American groups were: Japanese (591,290), Chinese (435,062), and Filipino (343,060). The war in Southeast Asia was reaching a peak with the Tet Offensive just the year before. The Asian American Anti-War Movement was just beginning to take form and become visible in certain cities and campuses. This movement peaked a year later in April 1970 with the United States invasion of Cambodia and the increased intensity of the larger Anti-War Movement. At UC, Berkeley, Asian Americans as a united group were highly visible in the Anti-War demonstrations and marches. I remember at a planning meeting (April 1970) at the YMCA on Bancroft Avenue for one of the marches, there was a childhood friend who was attending this meeting. Ron, a Japanese American, was a Black Belt in Karate and a City of Berkeley Police Officer. I asked Ron, "Are you working now?" He embarrassingly said that he was working. We kind of laughed because it was obvious that he was working undercover to gather intelligence information on the pending march.

The summer of '69 symbolized a critical time for the United Farm Workers Union (UFW) and their link to the Asian American Movement. Early Union leaders such as Larry Itlong, Philip Vera Cruz, and Cesar Chavez were utilizing Gandhi's tactics of non-violence. Itlong and Vera Cruz, both Filipino Americans, also represented an important part of the 1969 Asian American population. This group was the manongs. Many manongs were farmworkers who worked in the fields with their Chicano counterparts. In order to improve farm workers' wages and work conditions, the UFW utilized numerous non-violent methods to achieve their goals such as strikes against non-union farms, boycotts of supermarkets such as Safeway that sold grapes and lettuce from non-union growers, a march to Sacramento, Chavez's well known hunger strikes. A short time after the TWLF Strike, Professor Takagi organized of a car caravan of Berkeley Asian American students and UFW supporters to go to the UFW headquarters in Delano to show our support for the Union and delivered carloads of bags of rice. I remember arriving in Delano and going with Professor Takagi and a small group of students into the UFW headquarters and walking into a back room. In this room, in a hospital bed, was Cesar Chavez.

He waved to us to come closer to him. My impressions for those five minutes were how kind he was, passionate about his cause, humble, and angelical. Although Chavez was weak and in poor health from his hunger strike, there was a peacefulness about this experience that I will never forget. This experience has left a lasting impression on me. To move people, to move mountains, one can do it with the positive, unflinching attitude of "Si, se puede (Yes, we can)."

The Third World Strike to establish Ethnic Studies at UC, Berkeley was a hard fought battle to establish a new discipline in higher education, but also in K-12. The College of Ethnic Studies was established at San Francisco State University, and Ethnic Studies Departments and Programs flourished at universities such as Sacramento State and the University of Hawai'i at Manoa. Ethnic Studies and related race and ethnicity courses sprang up all over the United States. Just as important was a new generation of community organizers and community-based organizations that for the past 42 years have truly impacted the communities they were meant to serve.

Today, 42 years later, in 2011:

I am a Professor of Ethnic Studies and the Director of Asian American Studies at California State University, Sacramento. My community service work in Oakland was followed by decades of service in Honolulu, and, even today, I'm engaged in community service programs I have created in Sacramento. I continue to work for a more just and fair society for all.

Dr. Paul Takagi is retired and continues to write about, reflect on, and be a strong advocate for social justice. For over 43 years, he has been my mentor and friend.

Him Mark Lai passed away May 2009. His research, publications, and mentoring of students of Chinese American history lives on.

Danny Li is semi-retired on the Big Island of Hawai'i. He continues to fight for social justice and equality.

Floyd Huen, M.D. is Medical Director at Lifelong Medical Care and Over Sixties Health Center in Berkeley and Oakland. He continues to organize communities for social justice.

Jean Quan is the Mayor of the City of Oakland. She is the City's first woman mayor and its first Asian American mayor. Mayor Quan brings her decades of training in the Civil Rights Movement to build a better and stronger Oakland.

Emil DeGuzman is the City and County of San Francisco Human Rights Commission Fair Housing & Public Accommodations Investigator & Mediator. He continues to fight for social justice and is an activist in the Filipino American community.

Dwight Scott passed away November 2008. I have never forgotten his commitment and friendship.

Sac State is fortunate to have Wayne Maeda going into his 43rd year of teaching in the Ethnic Studies Department. Since its inception, Wayne has been the foundation for Asian American Studies at Sacramento State.

References

Asian Health Services Website, 2011.

Fanon, Frantz, <u>The Wretched of the Earth</u>, Grove Press, 2004.

Umemoto, Karen, "'On Strike!' San Francisco State College Strike, 1968-1969: The Role of Asian American Students" in Zhou & Gatewood (eds.), <u>Contemporary Asian America</u>, (2nd ed.), New York University Press: 2007.

U.S. Department of Commerce, Japanese, Chinese, and Filipinos in the United States: 1970 Census of Population, A United States Department of Commerce Publication, Washington DC: July 1973.

Wei, William, <u>The Asian American Movement</u>, Temple University Press/Philadelphia, 1993.

Interviews

DeGuzman, Emil, April 2011.

Huen, Floyd, April 2011.

Li, Danny, August 2010.

Maeda, Wayne, May 2011.

Takagi, Paul, March 2011 and April 2011.

Why Ethnic Studies Was Meant for Me

Rosana Chavez, M.S.

My Golden Moment

I remember my graduation as if it were yesterday. Stepping foot into this huge stadium where the lights were so bright, all I could hear was the roaring crowd. I was instructed to move forward to take my photo, and then was hooded. I find myself standing next to these strong bronze women sharing this celebratory moment together. Everything is happening so fast and it's all just a huge blur. Then I hear my name being called into the mike, "Rosaaannna Chaveeeez". What! They said my name correctly! This was the first thought that rushed into my head. My goodness they actually said my God-given name the way it was meant to be pronounced! I shook the hand of the College of Education and my paper diploma was handed to me. This is it? I thought to myself out loud. This is truly it! I did it! I felt this huge sense of accomplishment take over my entire body. I felt as if I could fly and a huge weight had been lifted from me. Tears rolled down my cheeks as I looked for my family in the sea of people. With my diploma in hand, I waved it in the direction of my family. I yelled to my family, "This is for you!" This was my golden moment that I owned and that no one could take from me. I worked for the past seven years beginning with my undergraduate and ending with my graduate degree with fierce determination. Logistically, I earned a piece of paper that the University likes to call a Master's degree. But, oh boy, was it more than just a piece of paper with fancy writing. This was a piece of paper that symbolized much more.

Receiving this diploma embodied all of my and my family's hard work. Receiving this diploma represented overcoming many struggles and barriers that I had faced in addition to those that my family had endured. This piece of paper represented the blood and sweat of my Chicano gente involved in the Chicano Movement and the many educational struggles it took before my time for me to be able to experience my golden moment. This piece of paper represented far more than what words can express. Receiving this diploma symbolized my new beginning as a first generation college graduate. I became the first woman in my entire family to earn a bachelor of arts degree, let alone a master of science degree. I reflect on my degrees hanging in my bedroom wall and relive the moment as much as possible. I relieve them to appreciate the past and present efforts to make education accessible. Sharing the graduation experience serves as a benchmark to remember that moment strongly influenced by my decision to major in Ethnic Studies as an undergraduate. Selecting the right major as an undergraduate is never an easy experience, especially a major few people generally understand. Just because people did not understand Ethnic Studies as a discipline did not deter me. In fact, the more I took courses in Ethnic Studies the more I recognized its universal applied value. I want to share my proud experiences for the sole purpose of educating those who are considering majoring in Ethnic Studies. However, my positive feelings about being an Ethnic Studies major also meant confronting many hurdles in order to experience academic success. But in order to understand my reflections I must rewind and share what life was like before my college journey began.

Where My Journey Began

What do you want to be when you grow up is a common question that many children have been asked while in grade school. Right? Some children might respond with wanting to be a doctor, a lawyer, an astronaut, or even a teacher. As very young children, our range of career choices are framed by the exposure we receive through school, in our home or even through our television sets. Although we might not realize at the time we are asked such questions as children, but those messages are informing part of our career development process. I am sure no child would answer (at least that I am aware of) that they want to major in Ethnic Studies and study social justice in a modern day society. As a child, I was definitely not the exception. However, I will tell you this: ever since I can remember I wondered why history books presented in classes always seemed to cover the same topics over and over and at the same time could never seem to locate my cultural history, or see people who looked like me, represented in my history books. As this learning experience continued, I became more eager and curious to learn and discover what was being hidden from me and why.

As an adult, I remember being in the second grade and the first book I checked out from my school's library was a book titled, Cesar Chavez. I did not know who he was or the history of the United Farm Workers Movement at age eight, but I choose this book because I read my last name "Chavez" on the front cover. I was so excited because my very own last name was written on a book. Now was this a coincidence? Or was I actually beginning the planning of my future major in Ethnic Studies? Reflecting on this experience helps me to reinforce that even as a child I was eager to learn about socio-culture history. I was captivated by the title of this book simply because I could relate. These feelings I was exposed to at such a young age were the same feelings I felt as I discovered Ethnic Studies as a major.

My curiosity of my culture did not end in elementary school, but it definitely transferred into my high school years. I was a sophomore and I attended my first MEChA (Movimiento Estudiantil Chicano de Aztlan) Youth Conference at Sacramento State University. This was my first time stepping foot on to a college campus and I instantly fell in love. The campus felt welcoming and it was covered with many trees and buildings. There were many people walking from class to class and I remember seeing all the diverse faces. It was such a foreign world to me but all I knew was that I wanted to be part of it. This is when I first set the goal of graduating from high school and making college a part of my future plans. I did my research; I spoke with counselors and did everything possible in my power to make sure that I was eligible to apply for college. I was determined to attend Sacramento State even though my high school counselors told me that I was not university bound.

College Can Come True

In the fall semester of 2001 my dream became a reality when I began my college career at Sacramento State. I was a first-time freshman and scared out of my mind. I moved from a small local high school to this city size campus of 28,000 people overnight. I only knew one person from my high school that also began that same semester. Not knowing many people at the university was scary and I felt alone. I needed to make connections with students and the best way to do so was through my major. Initially I was majoring in apparel marketing and design. I wanted to be a fashion designer which in my mind translated into becoming rich and famous just like on television. This is what sounded good to me at the time because I had no other perception of what else was out there. I took classes in this major but did not find a personal connection. Before I discovered Ethnic Studies as a major I felt this huge emptiness and confusion about who I was as a person of color and where I was going with my life. I needed to find a major that matched my intellectual talents with my personal values and beliefs. A connection similar to the one I experienced as a child when I read my first book on Cesar Chavez. I knew that I had some type of purpose and mission to fulfill, but at the moment I was lost like many college students are during their first and even their sophomore year in college. What am I going to do with my life? I put this huge pressure on myself because it took so long for me to get into college and now I had no plan.

It was not until my beginnings of junior year at Sac State that I decided to take a class called Ethnic America with Professor Wayne Maeda. I chose this class because the description spoke to me. It was as follows: "Through an interdisciplinary approach, introduces the four major American ethnic groups – Black, American Indian, Chicano, Asian American. Focuses on themes common to all four groups (racism, economic and political oppression) and demonstrates the varied contributions of each culture to American social and economic life". Achieving my educational goal of beginning college also meant I could further educate myself on my culture, and I felt this class was my opportunity to do so. Since my ideas about having a career in fashion was steadily becoming uninteresting, I figured I had nothing to lose by exploring my personal interest. Little did I know that making this one simple decision, I was about to embark on a life changing experience that would impact my life path forever.

I still remember my first day of class. I couldn't find the building, I was late. I had to beg Professor Maeda to add me into his section. Luckily he did! Taking this course made me feel as if I was opening my eyes for the first time. Professor Maeda kept true to the description of the course. Learning about racism, oppression, and the various social justice movements of the four ethnic groups was empowering. Empowering in that I was learning about how and why these terms came into existence. My consciousness was being expanded. I stepped foot into this course that I was able to grasp an intellectual understanding and put into context how my own socially-lived experiences related to my history in the United States. My life began to make sense. Hearing what I like to call the other half of history made me feel complete. Like Professor Maeda would say "I was given a new pair of lenses to see the world through!" This statement carries so much meaning. Taking this course was like having a new pair of eyes and I could see life so clearly. My experiences as a woman of color began to make more sense to me. During that class Professor Maeda became a great mentor and actually convinced me in changing my major to Ethnic Studies. That is exactly what I did!

In the Process

Changing your major is not always the easiest process. Sure all it takes is a piece of paper with a few signatures, but there are social obligations and responsibilities that come along with receiving an education. Even though I found my calling and I knew Ethnic Studies was for me, I now had the duty to explain to my family and my peers what this major entailed. When asked what my major was going to be, my family and peers always responded with: "What are you going to do with that major?" Sound familiar? At the moment, I could honestly say I did not know how to answer that question. Or what was to become of me majoring in this field, but all I knew is that it felt right! With this deep-seated conviction, all I needed to know to keep moving forward without regret or doubt. I remember when I told my dad what I was studying he responded "Que es eso?" ("What is that)? I slowly explained Ethnic Studies, but all he would ask is if I was going to make good money and if I was going to graduate fast. My mother, on the other hand, did not question me at all, she was just happy to see her daughter follow her path. My parents never really knew what this major was about, and I am not too sure if they still fully understand, but they were definitely proud of my renewed confidence as a student and daughter. My parents realized that selecting a major with this much enthusiasm meant I had direction to accomplish not just graduating from college but obtain a career that was personally and professionally fulfilling.

My Experience Matters

Ethnic Studies has built a strong foundation for my career and my everyday life. Learning about my cultural background in the classroom has been empowering to me. It was not until I stepped foot into an Ethnic Studies classroom that I was told my experience matters. One course in particular helped me conceptualize what it meant to be a woman of color and has facilitated my understanding of my different life roles. The course titled La Mujer Chicana (The Chicana Woman) taught by

Dr. Julie Figueroa was a course where I literally studied and was invited to reflect on myself and the life I was living. In this course, the bar was consistently set to a high standard. Some of the most sensitive culturally taboo topics were addressed and it brought me out of my comfort zone. Topics included identity, feminism, sexuality, cultural tradition, language, religion, and art – just to name a few. Studying these types of topics in a classroom setting was mind blowing. It was through this course where I was able to ethnically identify myself through studying my own identity. I was never too sure how to ethnically define myself on campus until I meet Dr. Figueroa. I knew that I was a hybrid of different cultures and that I was more than a person who was born in the United States, of Mexican descent. Like many first generation college students I struggled to understand my identity on a college campus and in my home. At home I was Mexicana, even though my aunt from Mexico begged to differ. She said I was a gringa with Mexican parents. On campus I did not identify as an American because this term did not embrace the whole me. This is when I decided that I was to reject the pre-determined labels that were given to me and that I was going to take charge on how to ethnically identify myself. I was then able to link my two worlds and make it into my one entity. I identify as a Chicana woman because it personifies the full me and it represents my experience best in the United States. Overall this course supported my critical thinking skills and challenged what I thought I knew about myself and taught me what I needed to know. More importantly, it helped me understand where I wanted to go in life and how I was going to get there. Dr. Figueroa constantly pushed me towards academic success and she succeeded as a professor. My experience truly matters and I do have something worth sharing. Just as you do too.

My experiences with Dr. Maeda and Dr. Figueroa's courses illustrate how Ethnic Studies supported my critical thinking skills. I was able to develop this newfound consciousness and understanding of who I am as a Chicana woman. In respects to learning about myself, I also became aware of the diverse cultural backgrounds that surround me. I experienced various courses that shared the socially-lived experiences of a wide range of ethnic groups. Learning about social justice made me aware that different ethnic groups share a commonality with one another. We all faced and continue to face different oppressive social issues and struggles. Learning that when we unite as a people we can overcome hardships that cross our paths. This has enlightened me. More importantly, it has taught me the importance of celebrating diversity and as humans we actually have a lot more in common than what we think. Ethnic Studies has humbled me to appreciate not only myself, but the experiences of others. This is what Ethnic Studies can offer you.

Lessons Learned:

I currently work as a full time counselor for the College Assistance Migrant Program here at Sacramento State. I work with first year students who mostly are first generation college students just like me. Having Ethnic Studies as my foundation not only allowed me to understand my student's socio-cultural backgrounds, but I am able to share and relate my own experiences with them. As my students are going through their own self-exploration process I teach them to refuse what society has made of us and to become trend-setters within their families and communities. In so doing, they will find their purpose in life through fulfilling their own dreams. There are many lessons I learned while going through my college journey. They are the same lessons I pass down to my own students and that I will like to pass on to you. Lesson number one: follow your heart. Nowadays people seem to focus too much on their external influences and forget to give themselves permission to explore their likes and interest. It is through exploring yourself that you will find what is meant for you. Even though you may not know your calling it will shine through if you accept the exploration process. Lesson number two: trust yourself. It is completely natural to experience self-doubt and ask what I am doing? However, sometimes it takes this self-doubt to help you open your eyes and see what is truly right for you. Embrace this self-doubt and make it into a positive. How you may ask? Use this self-doubt as a motivator to do some of your own research as you are shopping for a major. Trust this process. Lesson number three: never settle for less. Don't go for the major that you randomly select with closed eyes, or the major your family and peers tell you to follow. Don't settle for what you think will be the easiest. You will not be fully satisfied with your career in the long run if you opt to take a short cut. Lesson number four: discover who you are through understanding were you come from. This has always been my motto. This helps keep you focused and humble. It will help you keep your priorities lined up and it will remind you why you are here in the first place? Coming to your realization and following these lessons will help you achieve academic and career success at Sacramento State.

The Journey Continues

As a counselor I enjoy working with first time freshmen and being part of their exploration process for my students. I am happy to give back and share what Ethnic Studies has given me. Over the years I have refused to be another negative statistic and decided to become a trend-setter for my family and my community. I decided to follow my dreams which created my path of success. I continue to give myself permission to explore for this process does not necessarily end once you graduate. I challenge you all to make similar efforts and create your path towards success. Refuse to be a negative statistic and create your own destinies and become trend-setters. Fulfill your life destinies so you too can experience your own golden moment. When in doubt follow your heart and your instincts and you will find that things will naturally unfold. Remember your experience does matter and you have a lot to share. You will come across your own lessons learned in your college careers that you too can share with future generations. Remember the journey still continues after you graduate, but it is up to you how you decide to navigate it. If you are deciding to purse Ethnic Studies and the next time someone asks you what can you do with that major, I would like for you all to please respond "What can you NOT do with that major" Now give yourself permission and go explore!

Anatomy of Culture

Alexandre Kimenyi

Culture is the subject of inquiry of different disciplines such as anthropology, sociology, linguistics, economics, geography, psychology, history, philosophy, and political science. Each discipline has its own definition. This is not a ground-breaking essay on the subject of culture, nor is it reinventing the wheels since culture is the most studied subject in all academic fields. It only offers a new look, perspective and interpretation. The views that are expressed in the present article are based on my own studies but they are also supported by data. Culture is not an abstraction. Thus any assumptions, presuppositions about culture to be valid, have to undergo the scrutiny of empirical investigation. The goal of this article is not only to present a fresh look but also to renew a high level debate on the subject and to show its importance especially in social sciences and more importantly for students of ethnic studies.

1. Explaining the Title of the Essay

The two nouns which make up the title of this essay are metaphors. Although anatomy is recognizable as a dead metaphor from biology, very few people are aware of the fact that culture is a metaphor as well. It has been part of the unconscious mind. Etymologically, it comes from Romance languages as a conceptual metaphor from plantation, meaning 'cultivation'. In French, a learned person is called "cultivée" cultivated. The word culture falls thus in the general category of visual metaphors, in which light is used as the embodiment of knowledge and lack of it as ignorance as shown in Kimenyi (2003). A non-cultivated area such as a forest lacks light whereas a cultivated area does. Hence the expression "It is a jungle out there" meaning total darkness, thus ignorance. Synonymous conceptual metaphors are journey metaphors, as "advanced" versus "backward" or "retrograde," food metaphors, such as "seasoned" versus "raw" or tectile metaphors such as "polished" versus "rough." The onomatopeic word "barbarians" which etymologically means people who speak an incomprehensible language was extended to mean people "without culture" because they do things differently. The name Berber which refers to the indigenous people of Northern Africa who waged many wars with both Greeks and Romans is clearly a phonetic variation of "barbare."

Some social scientists equate culture with civilization which implies a people or society that have made a specific and significant contribution to humanity in science, technology, arts, religion and ideas. It is the reason why for instance, the Southeast Native American groups namely Cherokees, Choctaws, Chicasaws, Creeks and Seminoles were labeled the *Five Civilized Nations* by the first European settlers when other groups were called savages and primitive. The new settlers were impressed by this Native American group because they were advanced in agriculture and had everything Europeans wanted namely tobacco, cotton, indigo and corn. This group was, unfortunately the first one to be affected by the 1830 Removal Act which is responsible for the creation of Indian reservations that inspired the building of "bantustans" or "homelands" for blacks in South Africa by the white apartheid regime. The journey to the new territory is referred to, in history books, as the Trail of Tears because thousands of people: children, old people, the sick, pregnant women, who were forced to walk on foot thousands of miles under harsh conditions to the Indian Territory, the present-day Oklahoma, died along the way, before reaching their destination.

This etymological definition of culture is not only eurocentric and elitist but wrong. There is no society without culture. Even today, some scientists continue to reference African, American Indian and Asian languages as "dialects," ethnic groups as "tribesmen," rebel leaders in developing countries as "war lords," and traditional healers, as "witch doctors." These labels are used because of eurocentrism. Those who use these expressions believe that their respective cultures are not as advanced as the Western culture. In the former African Belgian colonies, for instance, Africans who were educated in European schools were called "evolués," evolved in the Darwinian sense and the rest *indigènes,* indigenous, a term which had a negative connotation that time. There is no primitive language, however. All languages have rules and all have dialects, which are either regional, socio-economical or ethnic. The so called high culture and low culture are also found in all hierachical societies of both city-states and nation-states.

The anatomy metaphor is used to illustrate that even though it is abstract, culture like the human body, is indeed biological and can also be dissected and analyzed to study its structure which consists of components with their respective formal and functional properties.

2. The Importance of Culture

Culture is a very important driving force. It is the reason why, together with space, it is the major cause of conflict in all pluralistic societies and colonized countries. The dominant group not only removes the minority from the most desirable space and creates spatial segregation but it also always imposes its culture on subordinate groups and occupied territories. The minorities resist the assimilation because they consider their culture not only as their character, personality and identity but mostly as their "soul". It is the reason why even here in the United States, against all odds the Amish culture of Pennsylvania and the black Gullah or Geeche culture of South Carolina have been able to survive. The cultural conflict also exists at the global level. The cold war between the Soviet Union and the United States which have fought in proxy developing countries was largely ideological. The US and European military interventions in Asia and the Middle East as well as the treatment of people in the Middle East in the West have prompted scholars to coin the terms *Orientalism* and *Occidentalism*. Orientalism was created by the late Columbia University Professor Edward Said to refer to the negative stereotypes that Europeans have of Asians and Occidentalism was conceived by Ian Buruma and Margalit Avishal (2004) to refer to the caricatural view that people have of Europe which is seen as materialistic, spiritually wanting and morally bankrupt. Culture is a collective behavior, a code of conduct or societal attitudes.

3. Components of Culture

All cultures consist of concepts, values, customs, systems, icons, symbols, rituals, aesthetics and entertainment. What makes cultures distinct from each other is either the maximization or the variation of the properties of these components.

3. 1. Concepts

Concepts have to do with how we conceive and perceive both physical and metaphysical phenomena. Depending on our cultural background the same "reality" may be perceived or conceived differently or may not be perceived and conceived at all. For instance, even though death is universal, there are societies in which it is viewed as the end of life but there are others where it is seen as the beginning of life. The concept of beauty not only varies from culture to culture but also shifts from generation to generation. Natural gaps between teeth and black gum are signs of beauty in Rwanda but in the US gaps have to be filled. Fat is seen today as a sign of poverty and bad eating habits and slimmess as a symbol of wealth and aristocracy, but it used to be the opposite. Time also has been found to be conceived differently. Among Anglo-Saxons, time is objective, unidirectional and seen as a commodity, hence the saying "Time is money". It has very much affected their lives. Among the Latins (French, Italians, Portuguese, Spaniards) time can be subjective as demonstrated by their languages: thus morning is either *le matin* or *la matinée,* day is *le jour* or *la journée,* evening *le soir* or *la soirée,* year *l'an* or *l'année.* The masculine form shown by the article *le* is objective whereas the feminine form marked by the article *la* is subjective. Among Rwandans, however, and some other Bantu groups, time is both phenomenological and cyclical. It is phenomenological because it is produced by events and activities. If the events that produce it such as change of seasons, sunset, sunrise, or moonlight, fail to materialize, time doesn't take place either. This is seen in the language use, thus hour is "watch" *isáahá,* month is "moon" *ukwéezi,* year "crop" *umwáaka* and a political regime "drum" *ingoma.* These temporal expressions are metonymically related to the meanings of the primary plane of expression. A watch is used to show the time, a new month is shown by a new moon in the sky, crops are planted once a year and traditionally before colonialism the symbol of authority was the drum during the monarchy. Time is also elastic. It can be short or long depending on the length of the event. Among the Bantu time is also cyclical. It comes back. For instance, "soon" is seen as "recently", "tomorrow" as "yesterday" and "distant future" as "far past." The expression for "soon" and "recently" is the same in Kinyarwanda *vuba,* for "tomorrow" and "yesterday" it is *ejo,* whereas "the distant future" and "the far past" it is *kera.*

That people don't see or understand the same reality the same way even in the same culture is demonstrated by language use. Thus a city may be seen as "sitting," "standing," "lying," "spreading," "stretching," "sprawling," or "rolling." In all cultures, all people also intuitively know that the same reality may be seen and understood differently. This is again shown by linguistic expressions such as "to see through the lens of" or "to see the bottle half-full or half-empty."

The classical example mentioned in anthropological linguistics literature about differences in cultural perceptions and conceptions, although some scientists think it is a hoax, is the concept of snow in Eskimo (Inuit-Aleut). Apparently, the Inuit-Aleut have an analytic view rather than a synthetic view of snow. Twelve terms are used to refer to different types of snow whereas English uses one word to refer to all of them.

3. 2. Values

Values are things that matter for the society and play a very important role in its members' behavior. They are not innate and don't have any intrinsic value. Like many other components of culture, they are conventional because what is important for one culture may not have any value whatsoever in other societies.

In the Western culture, for instance, flowers, especially roses, are very much valued. They have inspired great poets and painters. Flowers are appreciated as presents by girls and women from their lovers. Some cultures don't understand why people would be excited by flowers as presents when they can be picked up for free from the bush. In Rwanda, on the other hand, the great present that people give to the ones they love, admire, or are grateful to is a cow. During the monarchy, cows were given as gifts to visiting heads of states, and there were both military and cow parades everywhere in all regions when the king was touring the country. This cow parade called *kubyukurutsa* still takes place at weddings.

It is not flowers that inspire artists but cows. For instance, pastoral poetry (cow praise-poems) called *amazina y'inka* in Kinyarwanda ranks first among the three traditional elite poetic genres. The other two are dynastic poetry (praise-poems for kings) *ibisigo* and panegyric poetry (praise-poems for national heroes and great warriors) *ibyivugo*. Female folk dances imitate the cow's elegance and its beautiful long horns. Not only are cow songs a genre of folk music that are sung by herders when they take them to graze, to drink or in the evening when they return home, but are also motifs in other music folk genres and modern music as well. The popular stone game, called *igisoro*, which some people call the African chess game consists of capturing the adversary's cows (game stones) and children have cow dolls.

The cow is the icon par excellence of the Rwandan society. It is seen as the quintessential paradigm of beauty, elegance and grace. In the Rwandan culture it is thus a great complement to tell a woman that she has cows' eyes or walks like a cow.

The cow has been integrated into the whole culture. It has also affected the language. Many Rwandan names are related to cows, people swear by the name of the person from whom they received cows, greeting expressions are about cows and many metaphors come from cow vocabulary. The cow plays in Rwanda the same role that the buffalo did among Great Plains Indian (Sioux, Cheyenne, Comanche, Kiowa, Apache, Blackfeet, Osage, Arapaho, Crow, Ojibwa, Omaha, Hidatsa, Wichita, Pawnee, etc). There is a symbiotic relationship between cows and Rwandans. It is a gift to them from the country's founding father, Gihanga, who the legend says created both cows and drums (*Gihanga cyahanze inka n'ingoma*). Everything from the cow whether it is its product, waste, body part, has a use and value. Nothing from the cow is wasted.

In the Western culture youth is prized and celebrated and old people feel good when they are told that they look young. In other cultures, however, it would be an insult to call an adult young, since old age is respected as a sign of experience and wisdom.

Individualism and mobility are some of the main characteristics of American culture and are very much idealized. People don't owe any loyalty to any place or institution. Americans can change jobs, religions, political parties any time they want. They can move from one city to another or from one state to another state. A house is not a home but a piece of real estate that can be sold any time when its value has gone up. People here can marry or divorce many times, choose not to marry or have children. In other societies, however, the community comes first. For this reason, the mobility found in the United States is inexistent, because of the loyalty to one's birth of place, employer and other institutions. If I have turned down job offers from other universities with better pay and I have been teaching at the same university for more than a quarter of a century it is because of my culture which has followed me. I would feel guilty if I left.

3. 3. Customs and Traditions

Customs are recurrent activities or events in which actions, actors and stages are predictable. Greetings, eatings, naming ceremonies, dating systems, weddings, funerals, rite of passage are examples of customs. Eating habits are part of the customs.

The society decides how many meals are eaten a day and what is eaten at each meal. The naming system differs from culture to culture. In some societies, naming ceremonies take place several days after the baby is born. The Some cultures give only one name. In others, there are two names, the first name and the last name whereas Americans have a first name, a middle name and a last name. Europeans and Americans think that Alexandre is my first name and Kimenyi is my last name. In Rwanda we don't have the concept of first name and last or family name. We just have a name. Everybody has his or her own name. Children have their individual names. Wives don't take their husbands' names. Those who become Christians, however, get a Christian name when they get baptized. It is embarrassing to me when my wife's students and friends call me Mr. Mukantabana. They assume that Mathilde is her first name and Mukantabana is my name. But Mukantabana is clearly a female name for Kinyarwanda speakers because of the onomastic prefix *muka-* found in many female names. There are, of course, some Westernized Rwandans who have adopted the European system but they are still a minority. I got the name Alexandre when I started school, because to be admitted everybody had to get a European name since all the schools belonged to the European missionaries. Since in the American customs names are monosyllabic, such Joe for Joseph, Dick for Richard, Bob for Robert, Fred for Frederick, Greg for Gregory, Ted for Edward, Bill or Will for William, Tom for Thomas . . . those who think that Alexandre is my first call me Alex whereas others call me Kim.

3. 4. Systems

Systems, institutions or societal organizations are the pillars on which the society is built. Some of these institutions are the family structure, government system, economy, justice, religion, and education.

Family Structure

Families in various societies are either nuclear or extended, patriarchal or matriarchal. For a family to be nuclear or extended seems to be dictated by economics. During the agricultural period and the industrial revolution, America had an extended family system, because of the share of labor for each member of the family. In the computer age, however, any individual can be self-sufficient. Because of this, the size of the family has shrunk and many single families with single mothers or single fathers have increased exponentially.

In patriarchal societies, the father is the head of the family, children receive the last name of the father, boys are the ones who inherit the family property and in case of divorce, the wife goes back to her parents. A matriarchal system is the mirror image of the former, the children get the mother's last name, only girls inherit the family property, in the case of divorce, the husband is sent back to his parents but the head of the family in many cases that have been reported so far is not the mother but one of her brothers.

The family structure in some cultures dictates the rules of exogamy and endogamy. In the Middle East, for instance, people marry parallel cousins (father's brother's child) whereas in others it is cross cousins (father's sister's child or mother's brother's child).

Economy

Economy has to do with wealth production and distribution and ownership. The society decides who should participate in the work force, what and how much should be produced. These policies are the ones which are responsible for the existence of subsistence economies and consumer economies, capitalist economies like the United States and welfare states like Western Europe and Canada. In some societies, the land belongs to the state or the community like in many African, Asian and American Indian nations before colonialism, in others it belongs to the aristocracy, the landlords, like in Medieval Europe. It is unthinkable and uncomprensible in many societies how an individual can own a river, a lake, a forest or an island. They believe that like the sun, the moon, the sky, and the air, all natural resources, should be public.

The 1887 Indian Allotment Act also known as the Dawes Act was detrimental to Native Americans. Not only did it steal 90 million acres from them from the 138 previously allocated, but did it destroy their culture as well. By giving 164 acres to one family, the extended family structure was destroyed and so was the community because what united them was the communal property, the sharing of space and their traditional leaders.

Government

All societies, besides hunter-gather and nomadic ones, have a system of government. It can be the council of elders, monarchy, theocracy, plutocracy, gerontocracy, etc. The monarchy can be constitutional or absolute. A government can be a presidential system like the US and France or parliamentary system like the majority of European countries. Democratic governments also differ from one another. They can be ethnic democraties, liberal democraties, consociative democraties. The concept of federal government applied here in the United States and which European countries have started adopting was borrowed from the Iroquois Confederacy also known as the League of Six Nations, namely Seneca, Mohawk, Cayuga, Onondaga, Oneida and Tuscarora. The reason why there is political instability in many developing nations, it is because of the importation or the experimentation of alien systems of government by the Western-educated elite in which the majority of the people especially the traditional wise elders don't have a voice.

A new term, *kleptocracy,* has been recently introduced to refer to some of the regimes of corrupt leaders such as the late dictator of the Democratic Republic of Congo, Mobutu Sese Seko, Sani Abacha of Nigeria, Marcos of the Philippines, Charles Taylor of Liberia, because these leaders are more interested in stealing their countries' resources than managing them for the interest of the people.

Justice

To service and keep a social balance and harmony, all societies have a system of law and order. Some societies put more emphasis on the protection of community rights than on individual rights. Each society defines what is a crime and implements its own system of handling these crimes. Some African countries are undergoing turmoil because of the conflict between the application of Western law brought in during colonialism, the traditional legal system and Islamic law, called *Shariah.* In the United States, many immigrants find themselves in legal trouble when they try to use the system of their home country to punish their children. "It takes a whole village to raise a child" is not a slogan in Africa. Any adult who is not related to the child can reprimand a child, spank him/her or use any other means if s/he is misbehaving or doing things which are not acceptable.

The Rwandan government is going back to the traditional justice system called *gacaca,* which handled petty crimes, to judge Hutu responsible of genocide. The outcome of this system which, in a sense looks like the American jury system, was always reconciliation. Survivors of genocide, however, see the reintroduction of *gacaca* as a travesty of justice by the government because traditionally it dealt with small problems existing between neighbors whereas murders were handled by the Royal Court, because all Rwandans considered themselves *rubanda rw'umwami,* the king's people.

When the Southwest was taken from Mexico after its defeat in the 1846–48 American-Mexican war by the United States after the signing of the Treaty of Guadalupe Hidalgo in 1848, Mexicans living in those territories lost their properties to the Anglos and the US government because of the Anglo-Saxon law which required titles and property taxes for all owners of businesses, houses, land and ranches. This is how important individuals of that time such Salvador Vallejo of Napa and the Swiss-born immigrant John Augustus Sutter got ruined.

Religion

All societies have their own religions and spiritual values. Many African religions, for instance, have the same concept of God as Christians do. They are monotheistic. God is conceived as transcendent, omnipresent, omnipotent, and omniscient. The only difference is how they relate to him and the fact they respect other people's religions, practice ancestor worship and don't try to prosetylize. To European missionnaries, however, these religions are not religions but paganism. In many cases, messianic religions in their holy wars, evangilizing and proselytizing, have done more harm than good, by prosecuting those who don't believe in their dogmas or refuse to convert to their religions.

Education

The educational system is there to maintain the society's values and the status quo. Many European countries practice an elitist education, meaning that many students fail to go to high school or the university. These educational systems are mostly by-products of economics. The governments make sure that those who graduate have jobs. The US has a similar system. Since agriculture is done by Mexicans and migrant workers, children of migrant workers end up becoming migrant workers as well, thus creating a caste system, because they cannot attend regular schools which would allow them both socio-economical vertical and horizontal mobility.

People who rule the US such as senators, CEOs of big companies, university presidents come from the elite universities, mostly private ones such as Stanford, the University of Chicago or Ivy League schools. In France, however, public schools are more prestigious and the majority of important personalities are graduates of *Les Grandes Ecoles.*

Although he meant well, as recounted in the video *In the White Man's Image,* Richard Henry Pratt is also responsible for the destruction of Native Americans' culture by forcibly taking children from their parents to the Carlisle Indian School thus missing their parents' education. The 1934 Indian Reorganization Act was too late since separating children from parents had created a new generation of Indians who were alienated, unable to live either in the White world or the Indian world because they had lost their language and culture.

3. 5. Icons

All societies have objects or people that everybody identifies with which become a unifying factor. They can be national heroes, religious leaders, intellectuals, or pop stars such as athletes, musicians, actors, and products. Landmarks such as rivers, mountains, and cities and monuments, even buildings can be icons as well. Examples of rivers which have become icons are for instance, the Mississippi river for Americans, the Seine for French, the Nile for Egyptians, the Yangtze for Chinese, Nyabarongo for Rwandans. Examples of mountains are Mount Shasta for Shasta Indians, Wintu, Tolowa, Karok, Yurok, Hupa, Chilula, Whilikut, Wiyot, Chimariko, and others, Mount Kenya for the Kikuyu and Mount Kilimanjaro for Tanzanians. The Statue of Liberty and Eiffel Tower are examples of monuments which are icons for Americans and French respectively. The Taj Mahal, in Agra, is not only a tourist attraction but the national icon of India. McDonalds, Coca-Cola, etc. are icons of the United States abroad. Not only do these icons inspire artists but they are part of collective heritage.

One of the major sources of conflicts between Native Americans and the U.S. government is that the government is destroying these icons or desecrating important landmarks such burial sites, or sacred areas.

3. 6. Symbols

Symbols are objects which have a conventional meaning for a society. In semiotics, however, the science of signs in general, linguistic and non-linguistic, it has a specific meaning. A symbol means a sign whose relationship with the object it stands for has become opaque. There are two semiotic systems depending on how much information they can convey: namely macrosemiotic systems or speech surrogates and microsemiotic systems. Microsemiotic systems such as uniforms, body wear, highway code, . . . give a very much limited information such as profession, gender, religion or age for the uniform, social status for bodywear, and driving information for the latter. Macrosemiotic systems such as language, writing, sign language . . . don't have any constraints on what can be communicated. It is the reason why sign language was the lingua franca of Great Plains Indians, since coming from many different linguistic backgrounds, it was the only way they could communicate.

Semiotics classifies signs defined as "something which stands for something else" into three categories, namely icons, indices and symbols. Icons which are either images, metaphors, and diagrams have a similarity either physical or functional with objects they stand for. Indices namely signals and symptoms have an association with the objects they refer to such as cause and effect, content and container, possession and possessor, part and whole, product and producer, whereas symbols as said earlier fail to show any connection with their referrents. Like linguistic signs, the majority of signs in all cultures belong to the last category. The majority of words are symbols. Their etymological history shows, however, that they initially started as either icons or indices. It is the same for non-linguistic communication systems as well. We are born in a society with symbols without any knowledge of their genesis and history.

Whether these signs are icons, indices or symbols, however, they all can be polysemous or homonymous and this shows clearly that they are conventional. Homonymy, the use of signs which look alike but have different meanings or functions occur by accident. Polysemy, the use of the same sign for different meanings or functions is very common because of the asymmetry which exists between symbols and the real world. The real world is infinite but the number of signs is very much limited. Within the same culture, the same object can be assigned different meanings or functions such as the ring in the Western culture but it is also possible for two or many objects which look similar but are not related to function as symbols. This is referred to as homonymy. The cross, for instance, may show that somebody is a Christian but it is also a luxury jewerly for others.

The society thus decides which objects will be used as symbols. Uniforms, headwear, chestwear, bracelets, medals can give information about profession, religion, social status. In Rwanda for instance, before colonization, married women and unmarried women dressed differently and had a different hair style. Mothers also, in formal ceremonies, have to wear a maternity crown called *urugore*. Symbols may be icons of companies or organizations such as logos and mascots for schools and sports teams. There are national symbols as well. Before the late nineteenth century partition of Africa by European powers at the Berlin Conference, many countries had drums with specific names as national emblems instead of flags as in Europe. The capture of these drums was also a national defeat.

Although symbols seem to be arbitrary, anthropologists have found out that totems are not. Clans in all societies are characterized by the existence of totems and taboos. Clans are still found in Africa, Asia and among Native Americans. I belong to the *Abazirankende* clan and our totem is *inyamanza,* a wagtail. The majority of totems happen to be plants and animals. Totems grew out of the necessity to protect the environment, explain the experts. The clan whose totem is a certain plant or animal is assured protection. The animal totem cannot be killed by the clan and the plant cannot be cut down either.

3. 7. Rituals

Like symbols, rituals also have conventional meanings. They differ from the former in that symbols are objects sometimes frozen in space and time whereas the latter are actions or activities. They usually accompany customs and ceremonies like greetings, eating, weddings, funerals, the rite passage, the transfer of power, naming ceremonies, farewell, etc. Libation in Africa to thank the ancestors at all important ceremonies, the 21-gun salute for visiting foreign dignataries in the Western culture, the Japanese tea ceremony, the Ethiopian coffee ceremony, the breaking of kola nuts among the Igbos of Nigeria and the Wolof of Senegal in various ceremonies, or in time of war the tying of yellow ribbons in the United States and the wearing of the leaf from the plant *impumbya* by Rwandan women are examples of rituals.

3. 8. Entertainment

To survive, members of the society are busy, each, depending on age, gender, or experience assigned a specific task. For a better performance, time for leisure and relaxation is also put aside. For instance, in France, people work 35 hours instead of 40 hours like here in the United States. The society decides the number of work days a week and how many hours people have to work. The American concept of weekend is now being adopted by many countries. In Europe, it used to be half-days. The work would stop at noon on both Wednesdays and Saturdays. In France and Italy, for instance, all activites including banks, schools, and hospitals, stop for lunch and nap from twelve to two in the afternoon. I made a mistake once of going to Paris in the month of August. Many businesses including hotels and restaurants were closed for a month because everybody had gone on vacation!

It is the society which also decides how its members are going to kill the time during this period of relaxation and which games and sports to play. It is the reason why some games and sports such as soccer, cockfighting, bullfighting, cricket, rugby, or hockey, become popular in some countries but not in others. In Japan, sumo wrestlers are treated like Hollywood movie stars, but the late satirist Mike Royko compared sumo wrestler stars with fat babies wearing diapers. When Americans talk about the "world series," non Americans get confused because they are expecting a real world competition and not about U.S. baseball teams.

There is a ranking and hierarchy in sports and games as well. If African-Americans outnumber whites in football, basketball and boxing, it is not because of their ethnicity which makes them superior athletes but because of the deliberate decision of the establishment. Even in Ancient Rome, entertaining sporting events such as the gladiators were performed by slaves. Elite sports and games such as golf, tennis, horse riding, car racing, swimming, pheasant hunting, chess . . . are the monopoly of the elite.

3. 9. Aesthetics

All societies express their aesthetic experiences through the same mediums and genres. These are visual (paintings, sculpture, decoration, graphics, photography, ceramics), aural (music, poetry), kinetic (dancing and gymnastics), and multimedia (theater, cinema, opera). Each culture maximizes or selects these genres found in the different mediums. It also ranks which ones are more important. In the visual arts, for instance, calligraphy is very highly valued in both Islamic and Japanese art. In Rwanda it is decoration whereas in West Africa it is masks and figurines. In paintings and decorations, some socities prefer certain colors and certain shapes. The appreciation of musical melodies differs from culture to culture even musical instruments. The piano is the instrument of choice in the Western culture, but in Rwanda it is the cithare *inanga*.

The tastes in rhythm, movement, body parts in dancing performance are also culturally conditioned. The Middle East is the birth place of belly dancing. In Ethiopia, dancing consists of lifting and moving shoulders. Among the Banyankore, women dance while sitting. Among the Maasai dancing consists of jumping rhythmically as high as they can without moving any other parts of the body. Congolese dance moving hips whereas Rwandan women dance with their arms arched like horns of Tutsi cows.

Visual arts of non-Western countries are collectively referred to as craft and other genres such as music, dance, poetry, oral literature . . . as folklore. These artistic objects are not considered as art because they are utilitarian, their creators are not known, and are not housed in museums and galleries. To consider them as craft, however, is a manifestation not only of lack of knowledge of local cultures and history but what true art is as well. In Africa, both high art and folk art existed before colonialism. Individual painters and sculptors were known and their work was sometimes commissioned by the king or the chiefs. Although literature was oral, there was a distinction also between elite literature namely court literature in Rwanda and folk literature. These composers, poets, singers, were also known by everybody in the country. The griots in West Africa in the countries of Mali, Guinea, Senegal and Gambia, who were poets, story tellers, oral historians belonged to this high culture and still do.

Art is an aesthetic experience that the artist tries to share with the community through creation using any of the mediums of expression. The perfect art is the one which is able to bring the three types of pleasure: sensual pleasure, intellectual pleasure and spiritual pleasure. So, whether the object is utilitarian, the author is anonymous, or is not housed in the museum, doesn't matter, as long as the target consumers like it.

Because of other cultural contacts and new experiences aesthetics in all cultures always keeps changing as shown by the influence of raggae and rap on world music today or the history of Western visual arts, which from the 16th century went through the Italian Renaissance, Classism, Baroque, Rococco, Dutch art, Romanticism, Impressionism, Expressionism, Fauvism, Cubism, Surrealism, and Minimalism.

It is interesting to note that these universal cultural components are also found in animals' cultures. All species have their symbols to communicate information, they have their own rituals and their social organization is similar to that of humans. Some animals are monogamous whereas others are polygamous. Some are patriarchal when others like the bonobos of Congo are matriarchal. Some practice endogamy while others practice exogamy. The only difference between the two species is probably the last component. Are they capable of sharing their aesthetic experience through visual, aural, kinetic and multimedia creativity? This is what I think should be the first priority of scientists to find out. Research in further cultural studies should also shed more light on why the Batwa and Pygmies of Central Africa and Gypsies (Bohemians) of Europe are natural born artists.

4. Nature and Nurture

The debate as to whether culture is natural, thus innate, being part of our biological make-up or whether it is man-made, manufactured by societies has not been settled yet. The proponents of culture as nurture advance five main arguments to support their view: (a) culture is not connected to language, race or ethnicity; (b) some aspects of culture are arbitrary, (c) there exist societies with evidence of clearly manufactured cultures, (d) some individuals find their culture to be unnatural and exile themselves to societies which have cultures in which they feel less alienated and (e) finally, culture is learned. In Central Africa, for instance, the Pygmies and the Batwa don't have a language of their own but speak languages of the Bantu groups with whom they live. Here in the United States, African Americans are Anglo-Saxon culturally and linguistically. Arbitrariness of culture is used in Saussurian sense to mean conventional. This arbitrariness is not only limited to symbols and rituals but to all components of the society as the section on cultural components shows. The society arbitrarily decides what is important for its members. This is indeed supported by the fact that what is important and meaningful for one culture may not mean anything in other cultures. Even body gestures such as finger pointing, handshaking, head bowing, head shaking, head scratching, shoulder shrugging, throat clearing, and whistling. While these seem to be universal forms of behaviors, they do not have the same meanings in all societies.

Pidgins and creoles found mostly on coasts and islands are also recent phenomena, thus hybrids of languages and cultures of new immigrants who come from different linguistic backgrounds. It is also true that counterculture movements and intergenerational conflicts exist in all societies and migration has been occuring since times immemorial not only to run away from bad economies but also from oppressive regimes and oppressive cultures as well.

That culture is learned from both informal and formal education is also a fact. Abandoned wild children have never acquired neither culture or language. This has pushed behaviorists led by B. E. Skinner to claim that children are born with blank slates, *tabula rasa,* and that both culture and language are learned through the process of stimulus-response.

For a culture to grow it has to have a proper soil the way an infant cannot survive without its mother. The proponents of culture as a social construction miss the point, however, because these phenomena emerge as a result of language death, cultural destruction, cultural contact and forced assimilation. Human behavior is what distinguishes the homo sapiens from other species. All species have strategies which help them to keep the balance and ensure their survival: how they relate to each other, the protection of both private and public space, mating practices, means of communication, social hierachy. This behavior is hard-wired. It is part of the genetic evolution. The human culture is different from that of animals in only that it is more elevated due to the fact that the human brain has more genes than animals.

The studies of language, the existence of cultural universals and current research in evolutionary biology and neuroscience support the biological basis of culture.

Language, a component of culture, through which culture is communicated and transmitted is biological (Chomsky, Kimenyi). It is located in the brain. When this location is damaged language is affected. All children from different linguistic backgrounds are preprogrammed to master it within a specific time. There is a critical stage as well. If the language is not acquired by the age of seven, the child is doomed not to develop it. Linguists have also found out that rules that govern language are so elegantly mathematically formulated that the child and the average native speaker cannot make them themselves. Suprasegments such as stress rules or tone rules are out of control of the conscious mind. Studies also show that native speakers of tone languages are tone deaf. They are unaware of tone rules and cannot tell which syllables have tones and which ones don't. For instance, although I am a professional linguist and Kinyarwanda is my mother tongue, it has taken me years to be able to understand, describe and explain the tone patterns of this language. Cognitive linguists (George Lakoff & Mark Johnson; Alexandre Kimenyi) also have found that speakers of all languages use conceptual metaphors without being aware that they are metaphors. All this suggests that there is a software in the human mind which is responsible for formal linguistic rules of encoding, processing and decoding. Many rules happen also to be universal. Because of their universality, cultures have the same deep structure and differ only on the surface structure in Chomskian sense with their diverse physical manifestations or parametric variations due to societies' individual environmental and experiential factors.

Evolutionary biologists have also found similarities between biological systems and cultural systems such as common ancestry, adaptation and transmission. Death and hybridity are also found in both. Studies of autism, a social learning disorders disease, have found it to be caused by specific genes.

Although culture is biological, it is not genetically connected to race. Cultural diversity is due environmental factors, cultural dynamism and people's different existential experiences. The négritude poets, Léopold Sédar Senghor, the late president of Senegal and the Caribbean poets Aimé Césaire and Léon Damas who were influenced by the Harlem Renaissance, a group of African-American artists, poets and writers such as Langston Hughes, Claude McKay, Richard Wright, Countee Cullen, Irving Miller, Anne Spenser, Jean Turner and James Weldon Johnson, were wrong when they attributed the difference between African culture and European culture to race, a perspective that ignores geography, history and experience.

With their stereotypes and preconceived ideas that all Africans were primitive and savages, European scientists came out also with the so-called Hamitic Hypothesis when they found out that some Africans such as the Tutsi had a very advanced culture. To the Europeans, African societies which impressed them were their distant cousins who came before them to colonize the continent.

5. Archetype and Stereotype

Although national character or identity is a reality, it is impossible to find any single individual who is the exemplar, the embodiment of this culture because of the existence of subcultures. Some of these subgroups are regional, ethnic, socio-economic, educational, generational and gender related.

A society is characterized by members occupying the same space, although it can be discontinuous like in the case of Alaska and Hawaii which are distant American territories. All physical cultural spaces have subregions: a north, a south, an east, a west, a center and peripheries. These regions do not only have a physical character they also a subcultural identity in terms of dialect, architecture, food, and customs. People at the periphery have more in common with neighboring cultures than their cultural center. The rural and urban population, the elite and the masses differ everywhere mostly in values, and lifestyles. Although, the US dominant culture is historically Anglo-Saxon, not only have other European ethnicities and racial minority groups namely Native Americans, African Americans, Asian Americans and Latinos, contributed to it but do they still practice their respective ethnic cultures as well. Upper classes, middle classes and lower classes are defined by specific lifestyles and values. Men and women, children and adults are supposed to behave differently in some situations. All these factors make it impossible to find any individual in any society who is a prototype of the culture. Culture is real but abstract. Because of this abstractness and dynamism, it becomes very difficult to find the right metaphor, for instance, which describes ethnic and race relations in the United States. The ones that have been proposed such as melting pot, salad bowl, kaleidoscope, quilt, fabric, grocery bag, or mosaic, all capture some of the defining characteristics of the American culture but fail, unfortunately to account for others.

6. The Sapir-Whorf Hypothesis

In cultural anthropology and anthropological linguistics, the Sapir-Whorf hypothesis corresponds to both cultural relativity and cultural determinism. Edward Sapir was the father of American linguistics and Benjamin Whorf his student. They were specialists of American Indian languages. Their research and studies of these languages convinced them that indeed language reflects and affects people's view of the world and their behavior. Cultural relativity entails the fact that there is no superior or inferior culture. It is thus against ethnocentrism, the tendency to judge other cultures using the standard of one's own. In cultural relativity there are no absolutes. There is no one way of looking or evaluating things. This article has given abundant examples from all the components of culture which show this to be the case. Cultural determinism implies that we are products of our culture. The culture shapes our conception of the world. Our tastes, smells, visions, sounds are acquired from it. We are freed from this determinism through cultural dynamism which is caused by environmental changes, cultural contact, and systemic changes.

It is from the Sapir-Wholf hypothesis that the concept *moral relativism* developed. What is considered morally wrong for one culture, may be morally good for another. For instance, polygamy which is condemned in the West was universally practiced in Africa. This practice emerged for both religious and practical reasons: the desire for immortality and to give status to unmarried women with fatherless children. Africans obtain immortality through ancestor worship. This can be achieved only if the deceased has many offspring. In the African mind, people die only when they are not remembered. It also happens that everywhere, not only in Africa, women outnumber men. Studies show that there is a higher male infant mortality than female. Because of gender behavior, more boys die in their teen years than girls. And when there are wars, men are the ones who are sent to the front. Monogamy thus prevents many women from finding husbands. In many African countries single mothers are treated as prostitutes and their children become outcasts. Polygamy gives a status to the women and makes children legitimate. Celibacy for priests, nuns or other individuals might be a virtue in Europe but is incomprehensible to the Africans. Africans believe that all individuals have a responsibility to keep both the family and the community alive through marriage and procreation. It is also common to find bare-breasted women in all African countries and to breast-feed babies in public. This is seen by Westerners as indecency. These opposing views show that morality is indeed in some cases culturally constructed.

When ANC led by Nelson Mandela was fighting against the supremacist regime of South Africa, it was called a terrorist organization by the government and its allies but hailed by the rest of the world as freedom fighters. When the Contras financed by the U.S. government trying to topple the Sandinista's regime, they were called by the Reagan administration freedom fighters but to others they were just criminals.

There are times when moral relativism is misused to condone flagrant violations of universal inalienable human rights, to refuse to condemn them or to remain inactive. In 1959 thousands and thousands of tutsi were massacred and others sent into exile with the blessing of the archbishop André Perraudain and the assistance of the Belgian government, because this was not a genocide but a revolution. The late colonial Belgian governor of Rwanda, Jean-Paul Harroy, stated in his memoirs that he was proud to have "assisted the Hutu Revolution." International organizations stationed in Kigali and churches didn't do anything to plead for mercy for the victims of this pogrom. Apparently killing thousands of innocent civilians is justified if it is done in the name of the Revolution. The non-intervention in 1994 Tutsi in Rwanda although it was broadcast live in people's homes everywhere in the world because according to the pundits, there was a deep-hatred between Hutu and Tutsi and that they had been fighting each other for centuries. This "root cause" explanation is of course both a cliché and a myth.

Conclusion

Cultures are means by which societies ensure their survival and create societal balance and harmony. Because of the diversity of cultural spaces due to different landscapes, fauna and flora, histories and experiences, each culture obviously has a better way than others of seeing and understanding certain phenomena and reacting in a more appropriate way to them. For instance, some societies which have undergone certain universal experiences before others know how to handle better the same situations when they reoccur. Like academic fields, some societies are experienced and specialized in certain areas. Therefore other cultures have to learn from them. In Rwanda, before colonialism, the only meat that was eaten was beef, although there was plenty of fish, chickens, goats, pigs and sheep. Chickens were used only for divination purposes. Eggs were not eaten. Sheep were sacred animals. Only the Batwa, the pariah of the society like the Burakumin in Japan and the Dalit or Untouchables in India, ate lamb. The only use of sheep was their skins, which were used to carry babies. A Hutu or a Tutsi who ate lamb became automatically an outcast. Pork was eaten for the first time in the late 1950's by the European educated elite. This action caused such a sensation and scandal that a very popular satiric poem by the Rwandan scholar Alexis Kagame, called *Indyohe-shabirayi,* meaning "what makes potatoes taste better" is still the most popular written work among Rwandans inside the country and in the diaspora. It is from Congolese also that Rwandans learned that cassava leaves make a delicious relish called *isombe* and that when pounded these roots produce a flour from which a dough called *ugari* is eaten with all types of sauces. There are certain plants which are found in all parts of the world whose parts such as barks, roots, leaves, and seeve, are used as medicine or food but whose use other cultures are not aware of even if they are found in their ecosystem. For instance, gum arabic, a sap from acacia trees, which is used in soft drinks, beauty products, and pharmaceuticals is the lifeblood of Sudan's economy. Many African countries in the tropics, however, which also have these types of acacia trees, are not aware of this use. It was discovered recently, as reported in the New York Times issue of April 1, 2003, that the !Kung (also known as the San) of the Kalahari desert have a plant called *hoodia* which cures impotency and functions like Viagra and that they have been using it for centuries. This plant was recently bought by the giant pharmaceutical company, Pfizer. These examples support the concept of cultural relativity and cultural complementarity. No culture holds the monopoly on truth, knowledge and wisdom. Cultures need to borrow from each other. It is also evident that what works for one culture may not necessarily be prescribed as the right medicine for another. The attempt, for instance, by the US government to impose the American type of democracy in the Middle East is already dead on arrival because of different respective history and experience. The American type of government was not imported; it was created from the botton up.

Globalization and nationalism are both a threat to cultural pluralism. Globalization is seen by its critics not only as an attempt to prevent developing countries from being able to compete in the world market but mostly as the McDonaldization and Hollywoodization of the world, that is flooding the world with fast food, cheap products and loosened morals. It is viewed as neo-colonialism of developing countries with a different face and a different approach. Not only should the majority group allow minority cultures to exist because of cultural complementarity but members of the majority should also be tolerant of cultural pluralism. Multiculturalism should not be confused or equated with symbolic ethnicity which only allows ethnic groups to celebrate their heritage once a year, as in the case of Cinco de Mayo for Mexicans, or Ockoberfest for Germans. The majority should make a more concerted effort to understand other cultures.

Nationalism is not the best way to protect the culture. Purists, assimilationists and nativist movements can succeed in destroying minority cultures but they cannot prevent the majority culture from changing. The French Academy should serve as a lesson. This institution was created in the 17th Century to protect the purity of the French language but it has not succeeded.

In California navitist movements have been trying to make English the only official language. Although this is against the spirit and the letter of the text of the Treaty of Guadalupe Hidalgo, there is no reason for Anglos to panick. Similarly, assimilationists such as the Harvard professor Samuel P. Huntington should not be afraid that the new immigrants especially Hispanics are going to affect the core of the American culture namely individualism and work ethic as he states. Both "work ethic" for Anglo-Saxons and "the culture of poverty" for Hispanics and African-Americans are myths and clichés that have already been debunked. If the majority of Hispanics live in poverty it is not because they come from "a culture of poverty" background. Their work ethic is also demonstrated by the fact that they work hard to feed their families and contribute to the economy of this country. An effort should be made instead to explain the so-called "Hispanic Paradox". Scientists have found that even though the majority of Hispanics live in poverty, they have less health problems and chronic diseases than middle class whites who have better education and income.

There is no mechanism which will stop the change of the American culture, since all cultures are dynamic. Insular cultures are the ones that die. Even though, for instance, English is an Anglo-Saxon language, its vocabulary in great majority is French not only in the area of superstratum such as administration, justice, army, science, religion, art, but in the substratum as well including even kinship terms such as *family, grandparents, uncle, aunt, cousin*. The borrowing has not affected the English language identity, but it has made it richer. There is anxiety and fear among many European countries right now because countries of East Europe, former states of the Soviet Union are going to be integrated into the European Union. Although many European countries share many cultural elements such as religion, traditions and values, some members of the European Union are afraid that their culture might be affected. These fears are unfounded because the borrowings make the culture stronger and richer without losing its identity. And since today many individuals, organizations and groups with similar interests live in "a world without borders", in virtual spaces, all attempts to protect national cultures will fail.

Multiculturalism and multilingualism make people more complete. Learning other cultures opens our eyes, makes us hear new sounds, helps us develop new tastes and expand our horizons and allows us to have different world views with a magnifying glass. Our knowledge becomes richer, deeper and broader.

Many cultures, unfortunately, have become extinct because of colonialism, invasion, and genocide. Policy makers and the elite have a responsibility to make sure that endangered cultures do not disappear. All of us in privileged positions have a responsibility to protect these cultures. Failing to do so will be not only be a disservice to humanity but will make us willing participants in ethnocide.

References

Buruma, Ian & Avishal Margalit. (2004). Occidentalism: The West in the Eyes of the Enemy. Penguin Press.

Harmon, Amy. (2004). *An answer, but not a cure, for a social disorder.* New York Times, Vol. CLIII: No.52, 834.

Harris, Lee. (2004). Civilization and Its Enemies: The next stage of history. New York: The Free Press.

Huntington P. Samuel. (1993). *The clash of civilizations.* Foreign Affairs Vol.72, No. 3, pp. 22–28.

Kagame, Alexis. Indyoheshabirayi. www.kimenyi.com/indyohesha-birayi.php

Kimenyi, Alexandre. Cow metaphor in Kinyarwanda. www.kimenyi.com/cow-metaphors.php

Kimenyi, Alexandre. The Role of Symbols in Nation Building: The Case of Rwanda. www.kimenyi.com/the-role-of-symbols-in-nation-building-the-case-of-rwanda.php

Kimenyi, Alexandre. Clichés: a Window to the Mind. www.kimenyi.com/cliches.php

Kimenyi, Alexandre. Umuco karande. UKURI and www.kimenyi.com/umuco-karande.php/

Kimenyi, Alexandre. Body Metaphors in Kinyarwanda. www.kimenyi.com/the-body-as-a-human-experience-metaphor-in-kinyarwanda.php

Lakoff, Georges & Mark Johnson. (1980). Metaphors we live by. University of Chicago Press.

Lakoff, Georges & Mark Johnson. (1999). A philosophy in the flesh. New York: Basic Books.

Said, Edward. (1978). Orientalism. New York: Pantheon Books; London: Routledge and Kegan Paul.

Thompson, Ginger. (2003). *Bushmen squeeze money from a humble cactus.* New York Times April 1.

Werthein, Margaret. (2004). *Bursts of Cornets and Evolution Bring Harmony to Night and Day.* New York Times. March 9, 2004.

Dane Morrison

American Indian Studies: An Interdisciplinary Approach to Contemporary Issues New York: Peter Lang Publishing 1997.

Race and Ethnicity

Michael Omi and Howard Winant

Racial Formations

In 1982–83, Susie Guillory Phipps unsuccessfully sued the Louisiana Bureau of Vital Records to change her racial classification from black to white. The descendant of an eighteenth-century white planter and a black slave, Phipps was designated "black" in her birth certificate in accordance with a 1970 state law which declared anyone with at least one-thirty-second "Negro blood" to be black. The legal battle raised intriguing questions about the concept of race, its meaning in contemporary society, and its use (and abuse) in public policy. Assistant Attorney General Ron Davis defended the law by pointing out that some type of racial classification was necessary to comply with federal record-keeping requirements and to facilitate programs for the prevention of genetic diseases. Phipps's attorney, Brian Begue, argued that the assignment of racial categories on birth certificates was unconstitutional and that the one-thirty-second designation was inaccurate. He called on a retired Tulane University professor who cited research indicating that most whites have one-twentieth "Negro" ancestry. In the end, Phipps lost. The court upheld a state law which quantified racial identity, and in so doing affirmed the legality of assigning individuals to specific racial groupings.[1]

The Phipps case illustrates the continuing dilemma of defining race and establishing its meaning in institutional life. Today, to assert that variations in human physiognomy are racially based is to enter a constant and intense debate. *Scientific* interpretations of race have not been alone in sparking heated controversy; *religious* perspectives have done so as well.[2] Most centrally, of course, race has been a matter of *political* contention. This has been particularly true in the United States, where the concept of race has varied enormously over time without ever leaving the center stage of US history.

From *Racial Formations in the United States: From the 1960s to the 1980s* by Michael Omi and Howard Winant. Reprinted by permission of Taylor and Francis.

⊕ What Is Race?

Race consciousness, and its articulation in theories of race, is largely a modern phenomenon. When European explorers in the New World "discovered" people who looked different than themselves, these "natives" challenged then existing conceptions of the origins of the human species, and raised disturbing questions as to whether *all* could be considered in the same "family of man."[3] Religious debates flared over the attempt to reconcile the Bible with the existence of "racially distinct" people. Arguments took place over creation itself, as theories of polygenesis questioned whether God had made only one species of humanity ("monogenesis"). Europeans wondered if the natives of the New World were indeed human beings with redeemable souls. At stake were not only the prospects for conversion, but the types of treatment to be accorded them. The expropriation of property, the denial of political rights, the introduction of slavery and other forms of coercive labor, as well as outright extermination, all presupposed a worldview which distinguished Europeans—children of God, human beings, etc.—from "others." Such a worldview was needed to explain why some should be "free" and others enslaved, why some had rights to land and property while others did not. Race, and the interpretation of racial differences, was a central factor in that worldview.

In the colonial epoch science was no less a field of controversy than religion in attempts to comprehend the concept of race and its meaning. Spurred on by the classificatory scheme of living organisms devised by Linnaeus in *Systema Naturae,* many scholars in the eighteenth and nineteenth centuries dedicated themselves to the identification and ranking of variations in humankind. Race was thought of as a *biological* concept, yet its precise definition was the subject of debates which, as we have noted, continue to rage today. Despite efforts ranging from Dr. Samuel Morton's studies of cranial capacity[4] to contemporary attempts to base racial classification on shared gene pools,[5] the concept of race has defied biological definition. . . .

Attempts to discern the *scientific meaning* of race continue to the present day. Although most physical anthropologists and biologists have abandoned the quest for a scientific basis to determine racial categories, controversies have recently flared in the area of genetics and educational psychology. For instance, an essay by Arthur Jensen which argued that hereditary factors shape intelligence not only revived the "nature or nurture" controversy, but raised highly volatile questions about racial equality itself.[6] Clearly the attempt to establish a *biological* basis of race has not been swept into the dustbin of history, but is being resurrected in various scientific arenas. All such attempts seek to remove the concept of race from fundamental social, political, or economic determination. They suggest instead that the truth of race lies in the terrain of innate characteristics, of which skin color and other physical attributes provide only the most obvious, and in some respects most superficial, indicators.

Race as a Social Concept

The social sciences have come to reject biologistic notions of race in favor of an approach which regards race as a *social* concept. Beginning in the eighteenth century, this trend has been slow and uneven, but its direction clear. In the nineteenth century Max Weber discounted biological explanations for racial conflict and instead highlighted the social and political factors which engendered such conflict.[7] The work of pioneering cultural anthropologist Franz Boas was crucial in refuting the scientific racism of the early twentieth century by rejecting the connection between race and culture, and the assumption of a continuum of "higher" and "lower" cultural groups. Within the contemporary social science literature, race is assumed to be a variable which is shaped by broader societal forces.

Race is indeed a pre-eminently *sociohistorical* concept. Racial categories and the meaning of race are given concrete expression by the specific social relations and historical context in which they are embedded. Racial meanings have varied tremendously over time and between different societies.

In the United States, the black/white color line has historically been rigidly defined and enforced. White is seen as a "pure" category. Any racial intermixture makes one "nonwhite." In the movie *Raintree County*, Elizabeth Taylor describes the worst of fates to befall whites as "havin' a little Negra blood in ya'—just one little teeny drop and a person's all Negra."[8] This thinking flows from what Marvin Harris has characterized as the principle of *hypo-descent:*

> *By what ingenious computation is the genetic tracery of a million years of evolution unraveled and each man [sic] assigned his proper social box? In the United States, the mechanism employed is the rule of hypo-descent. This descent rule requires Americans to believe that anyone who is known to have had a Negro ancestor is a Negro. We admit nothing in between. . . . "Hypo-descent" means affiliation with the subordinate rather than the superordinate group in order to avoid the ambiguity of intermediate identity. . . . The rule of hypo-descent is, therefore, an invention, which we in the United States have made in order to keep biological facts from intruding into our collective racist fantasies.[9]*

The Susie Guillory Phipps case merely represents the contemporary expression of this racial logic.

By contrast, a striking feature of race relations in the lowland areas of Latin America since the abolition of slavery has been the relative absence of sharply defined racial groupings. No such rigid descent rule characterizes racial identity in many Latin American societies. Brazil, for example, has historically had less rigid conceptions of race, and thus a variety of "intermediate" racial categories exist. Indeed, as Harris notes, "One of the most striking consequences of the Brazilian system of racial identification is that parents and children and even brothers and sisters are frequently accepted as representatives of quite opposite racial types."[10] Such a possibility is incomprehensible within the logic of racial categories in the US.

To suggest another example: the notion of "passing" takes on new meaning if we compare various American cultures' means of assigning racial identity. In the United States, individuals who are actually "black" by the logic of hypodescent have attempted to skirt the discriminatory barriers imposed by law and custom by attempting to "pass" for white.[11] Ironically, these same individuals would not be able to pass for "black" in many Latin American societies.

Consideration of the term "black" illustrates the diversity of racial meanings which can be found among different societies and historically within a given society. In contemporary British politics the term "black" is used to refer to all non-whites. Interestingly this designation has not arisen through the racist discourse of groups such as the National Front. Rather, in political and cultural movements, Asian as well as Afro-Caribbean youth are adopting the term as an expression of self-identity.[12] The wide-ranging meanings of "black" illustrate the manner in which racial categories are shaped politically.[13]

The meaning of race is defined and congested throughout society, in both collective action and personal practice. In the process, racial categories themselves are formed, transformed, destroyed and reformed. We use the term *racial formation* to refer to the process by which social, economic and political forces determine the content and importance of racial categories, and by which they are in turn shaped by racial meanings. Crucial to this formulation is the treatment of race as a *central axis* of social relations which cannot be subsumed under or reduced to some broader category or conception.

Racial Ideology and Racial Identity

The seemingly obvious, "natural" and "common sense" qualities which the existing racial order exhibits themselves testify to the effectiveness of the racial formation process in constructing racial meanings and racial identities.

One of the first things we notice about people when we meet them (along with their sex) is their race. We utilize race to provide clues about *who* a person is. This fact is made painfully obvious when we encounter someone whom we cannot conveniently racially categorize—someone who is, for example, racially "mixed" or of an ethnic/racial group with which we are not familiar. Such an encounter becomes a source of discomfort and momentarily a crisis of racial meaning. Without a racial identity, one is in danger of having no identity.

Our compass for navigating race relations depends on preconceived notions of what each specific racial group looks like. Comments such as, "Funny, you don't look black," betray an underlying image of what black should be. We also become disoriented when people do not act "black," "Latino," or indeed "white." The content of such stereotypes reveals a series of unsubstantiated beliefs about who these groups are and what "they" are like.[14]

In US society, then, a kind of "racial etiquette" exists, a set of interpretative codes and racial meanings which operate in the interactions of daily life. Rules shaped by our perception of race in a comprehensively racial society determine the "presentation of self,"[15] distinctions of status, and appropriate modes of conduct. "Etiquette" is not mere universal adherence to the dominant group's rules, but a more dynamic combination of these rules with the values and beliefs of subordinated groupings. This racial "subjection" is quintessentially ideological. Everybody learns some combination, some version, of the rules of racial classification, and of their own racial identity, often without obvious teaching or conscious inculcation. Race becomes "common sense"—a way of comprehending, explaining and acting in the world.

Racial beliefs operate as an "amateur biology," a way of explaining the variations in "human nature." Differences in skin color and other obvious physical characteristics supposedly provide visible clues to differences lurking underneath. Temperament, sexuality, intelligence, athletic ability, aesthetic preferences and so on are presumed to be fixed and discernible from the palpable mark of race. Such diverse questions as our confidence and trust in others (for example, clerks or salespeople, media figures, neighbors), our sexual preferences and romantic images, our tastes in music, films, dance, or sports, and our very ways of talking, walking, eating and dreaming are ineluctably shaped by notions of race. Skin color "differences" are thought to explain perceived differences in intellectual, physical and artistic temperaments, and to justify distinct treatment of racially identified individuals and groups.

The continuing persistence of racial ideology suggests that these racial myths and stereotypes cannot be exposed as such in the popular imagination. They are, we think, too essential, too integral, to the maintenance of the US social order. Of course, particular meanings, stereotypes and myths can change, but the presence of a *system* of racial meanings and stereotypes, of racial ideology, seems to be a permanent feature of US culture.

Film and television, for example, have been notorious in disseminating images of racial minorities which establish for audiences what people from these groups look like, how they behave, and "who they are." The power of the media lies not only in their ability to reflect the dominant racial ideology, but in their capacity to shape that ideology in the first place. D. W. Griffith's epic *Birth of a Nation*, a sympathetic treatment of the rise of the Ku Klux Klan during Reconstruction, helped to generate, consolidate and "nationalize" images of blacks which had been more disparate (more regionally specific, for example) prior to the film's appearance. In US television, the necessity to define characters in the briefest and most condensed manner has led to the perpetuation of racial caricatures, as racial stereotypes serve as shorthand for scriptwriters, directors and actors, in commercials, etc. Television's tendency to address the "lowest common denominator" in order to render programs "familiar" to an enormous and diverse audience leads it regularly to assign and reassign racial characteristics to particular groups, both minority and majority.

These and innumerable other examples show that we tend to view race as something fixed and immutable—something rooted in "nature." Thus we mask the historical construction of racial categories, the shifting meaning of race, and the crucial role of politics and ideology in shaping race relations. Races do not emerge full-blown. They are the results of diverse historical practices and are continually subject to challenge over their definition and meaning.

Racialization: The Historical Development of Race

In the United States, the racial category of "black" evolved with the consolidation of racial slavery. By the end of the seventeenth century, Africans whose specific identity was Ibo, Yoruba, Fulani, etc., were rendered "black" by an ideology of exploitation based on racial logic—the establishment and maintenance of a "color line." This of course did not occur overnight. A period of indentured servitude which was not rooted in racial logic preceded the consolidation of racial slavery. With slavery, however, a racially based understanding of society was set in motion which resulted in the shaping of a specific *racial* identity not only for the slaves but for the European settlers as well. Winthrop Jordan has observed: "From the initially common term *Christian,* at mid-century there was a marked shift toward the terms *English* and *free.* After about 1680, taking the colonies as a whole, a new term of self-identification appeared—*white.*"

We employ the term *racialization* to signify the extension of racial meaning to a previously racially unclassified relationship, social practice or group. Racialization is an ideological process, an historically specific one. Racial ideology is constructed from pre-existing conceptual (or, if one prefers, "discursive") elements and emerges from the struggles of competing political projects and ideas seeking to articulate similar elements differently. An account of racialization processes that avoids the pitfalls of US ethnic history remains to be written.

Particularly during the nineteenth century, the category of "white" was subject to challenges brought about by the influx of diverse groups who were not of the same Anglo-Saxon stock as the founding immigrants. In the nineteenth century, political and ideological struggles emerged over the classification of Southern Europeans, the Irish and Jews, among other "nonwhite" categories. Nativism was only effectively curbed by the institutionalization of a racial order that drew the color line *around,* rather than *within,* Europe.

By stopping short of racializing immigrants from Europe after the Civil War, and by subsequently allowing their assimilation, the American racial order was reconsolidated in the wake of the tremendous challenge placed before it by the abolition of racial slavery. With the end of Reconstruction in 1877, an effective program for limiting the emergent class struggles of the later nineteenth century was forged: the definition of the working class *in racial terms*—as "white." This was not accomplished by any legislative decree or capitalist maneuvering to divide the working class, but rather by white workers themselves. Many of them were recent immigrants, who organized on racial lines as much as on traditionally defined class lines. The Irish on the West Coast, for example, engaged in vicious anti-Chinese race-baiting and committed many pogrom-type assaults on Chinese in the course of consolidating the trade union movement in California.

Thus the very political organization of the working class was in important ways a racial project. The legacy of racial conflicts and arrangements shaped the definition of interests and in turn led to the consolidation of institutional patterns (e.g., segregated unions, dual labor markets, exclusionary legislation) which perpetuated the color line *within* the working class. Selig Perlman, whose study of the development of the labor movement is fairly sympathetic to this process, notes that:

> The political issue after 1877 was racial, not financial, and the weapon was not merely the ballot, but also "direct action"—violence. The anti-Chinese agitation in California, culminating as it did in the Exclusion Law passed by Congress in 1882, was doubtless the most important single factor in the history of American labor, for without it the entire country might have been overrun by Mongolian [sic] labor and the labor movement might have become a conflict of races instead of one of classes.

More recent economic transformations in the US have also altered interpretations of racial identities and meanings. The automation of southern agriculture and the augmented labor demand of the postwar boom transformed blacks from a largely rural, impoverished labor force to a largely urban, working-class group by 1970. When boom became bust and liberal welfare statism moved rightwards, the majority of blacks came to be seen, increasingly, as part of the "underclass," as state "dependents." Thus the particularly deleterious effects on blacks of global and national economic shifts (generally rising unemployment rates, changes in the employment structure away from reliance on labor intensive work, etc.) were explained once again in the late 1970s and 1980s (as they had been in the 1940s and mid-1960s) as the result of defective black cultural norms, of familial disorganization, etc. In this way new racial attributions, new racial myths, are affixed to "blacks." Similar changes in racial identity are presently affecting Asians and Latinos, as such economic forces as increasing Third World impoverishment and indebtedness fuel immigration and high interest rates, Japanese competition spurs resentments, and US jobs seem to fly away to Korea and Singapore. . . .

Once we understand that race overflows the boundaries of skin color, super-exploitation, social stratification, discrimination and prejudice, cultural domination and cultural resistance, state policy (or of any other particular social relationship we list), once we recognize the racial dimension present to some degree in *every* identity, institution and social practice in the United States—once we have done this, it becomes possible to speak of *racial formation*. This recognition is hard-won; there is a continuous temptation to think of race as an *essence*, as something fixed, concrete and objective, as (for example) one of the categories just enumerated. And there is also an opposite temptation: to see it as a mere illusion, which an ideal social order would eliminate.

In our view it is crucial to break with these habits of thought. The effort must be made to understand race as *an unstable and "decentered" complex of social meanings constantly being transformed by political struggle.*

Notes

[1]*San Francisco Chronicle,* 14 September 1982, 19 May 1983. Ironically, the 1970 Louisiana law was enacted to supersede an old Jim Crow statute which relied on the idea of "common report" in determining an infant's race. Following Phipps's unsuccessful attempt to change her classification and have the law declared unconstitutional, a legislative effort arose which culminated in the repeal of the law. See *San Francisco Chronicle,* 23 June 1983.

[2]The Mormon church, for example, has been heavily criticized for its doctrine of black inferiority.

[3]Thomas F. Gossett notes:

Race theory . . . had up until fairly modern times no firm hold on European thought. On the other hand, race theory and race prejudice were by no means unknown at the time when the English colonists came to North America. Undoubtedly, the age of exploration led many to speculate on race differences at a period when neither Europeans nor Englishmen were prepared to make allowances for vast cultural diversities. Even though race theories had not then secured wide acceptance or even sophisticate formulation, the first contacts of the Spanish with the Indians in the Americas can now be recognized as the beginning of a struggle between conceptions of the nature of primitive peoples which has not yet been wholly settled. (Thomas F. Gossett, Race: The History of an Idea in America (New York: Schocken Books, 1965), p. 16)

Winthrop Jordan provides a detailed account of early European colonialists' attitudes about color and race in *White Over Black: American Attitudes Toward the Negro, 1550–1812* (New York: Norton, 1977 [1968]), pp. 3–43.

[4]Pro-slavery physician Samuel George Morton (1799–1851) compiled a collection of 800 crania from all parts of the world which formed the sample for his studies of race. Assuming that the larger the size of the cranium translated into greater intelligence, Morton established a relationship between race and skull capacity. Gossett reports that:

In 1849, one of his studies included the following results: The English skulls in his collection proved to be the largest, with an average cranial capacity of 96 cubic inches. The Americans and Germans were rather poor seconds, both with cranial capacities of 90 cubic inches. At the bottom of the list were the Negroes with 83 cubic inches, the Chinese with 82, and the Indians with 79. (Ibid., p. 74)

On Morton's methods, see Stephen J. Gould, "The Finagle Factor," *Human Nature* (July 1978).

[5]Definitions of race founded upon a common pool of genes have not held up when confronted by scientific research which suggests that the differences *within* a given human population are greater than those between populations. See L. L. Cavalli-Sforza, "The Genetics of Human Populations," *Scientific American* (September 1974), pp. 81–89.

[6]Arthur Jensen, "How Much Can We Boost IQ and Scholastic Achievement?", *Harvard Educational Review,* vol. 39 (1969), pp. 1–123.

[7]Ernst Moritz Manasse, "Max Weber on Race," *Social Research,* vol. 14 (1947), pp. 191–221.

[8]Quoted in Edward D. C. Campbell, *Jr, The Celluloid South: Hollywood and the Southern Myth* (Knoxville: University of Tennessee Press, 1981), pp. 168–70.

[9]Marvin Harris, *Patterns of Race in the Americas* (New York: Norton, 1964), p. 56.

[10]Ibid., p. 57.

[11]After James Meredith had been admitted as the first black student at the University of Mississippi, Harry S. Murphy announced that he, and not Meredith, was the first black student to attend "Ole Miss." Murphy described himself as black but was able to pass for white and spent nine months at the institution without attracting any notice (ibid., p. 56).

[12]A. Sivanandan, "From Resistance to Rebellion: Asian and Afro-Caribbean Struggles in Britain," *Race and Class,* vol. 23, nos. 2–3 (Autumn–Winter 1981).

[13]Consider the contradictions in racial status which abound in the country with the most rigidly defined racial categories—South Africa. There a race classification agency is employed to adjudicate claims for upgrading of official racial identity. This is particularly necessary for the "coloured" category. The apartheid system considers Chinese as "Asians" while the Japanese are accorded the status of "honorary whites." This logic nearly detaches race from any grounding in skin color and other physical attributes and nakedly exposes race as a juridicial category subject to economic, social and political influences. (We are indebted to Steve Talbot for clarification of some of these points.)

[14]Gordon W. Allport, *The Nature of Prejudice* (Garden City, New York: Doubleday, 1958), pp. 184–200.

[15]We wish to use this phrase loosely, without committing ourselves to a particular position on such social psychological approaches as symbolic interactionism, which are outside the scope of this study. An interesting study on this subject is S. M. Lyman

Whiteness and Ethnocentric Monoculturalism: Making the "Invisible" Visible

Derald Wing Sue

Whiteness and ethnocentric monoculturalism are powerful and entrenched determinants of worldview. Because they are invisible and operate outside the level of conscious awareness, they can be detrimental to people of color, women, and other marginalized groups in society. Both define a reality that gives advantages to White Euro American males while disadvantaging others. Although most Americans believe in equality and fairness, the inability to deconstruct these 2 concepts allows society to continue unjust actions and arrangements toward minority groups. Making the "invisible" visible is the major challenge to liberating individuals and society from the continued oppression of others.

The American Psychological Association's "Ethical Principles of Psychologists and Code of Conduct" (APA, 2002) states explicitly that psychologists must attend to cultural, individual, and role differences related to age, gender, race, ethnicity, and national origin if they are to provide appropriate services to a culturally diverse population. In 2002, the APA took a historic step when the Council of Representatives endorsed the "Guidelines on Multicultural Education, Training, Research, Practice, and Organizational Change for Psychologists" (APA, 2003).[1] Whereas these multicultural guidelines pertain primarily to racial/ethnic minority groups, it is among several major documents (APA, 1993, 2000; Sue et al., 1982, 1998) that has challenged the profession of psychology as being culture-bound and potentially biased toward racial/ethnic minorities, women, and gay men and lesbians.

Given that there is increasing recognition of the potentially biased nature of the science of human behavior and that there are calls to attend to important sociodemographic variables, I have often wondered why psychologists as a group continue to ignore these important dimensions of the human condition in practice, research, education, and training (Sue, 2001; Sue, Bingham, Porché-Burke, & Vasquez, 1999). What makes some psychologists so reluctant or resistant to implementing multiculturalism in their research and practice? Why have APA accreditation criteria not been used more firmly to enforce multicultural standards? I realize that these are strong allegations that may not be shared by the majority of psychologists—and therein lies the problem.

The racial/cultural reality or worldview of many persons of color differs from that of their White colleagues and perhaps from that of the profession at large (Guthrie, 1997). Although White colleagues perceive positive change and movement by the profession in becoming more multicultural (Fowers & Richardson, 1996), people of color continue to see "cultural malpractice" and the growing obsolescence of psychology (Hail, 1997; Sue et al., 1999).

What accounts for this major difference in worldview? Are the majority of psychologists resistant to change because they are simply bigots, racists, sexists, and homophobes? Do they intentionally mean to ignore the concerns of people of color? Isn't the profession of psychology supposed to be dedicated to improving the lives and life conditions of the people whom psychologists hope to serve? If so, why has it been so hard to get colleagues to understand and change the field and psychological practice?

The Invisibility of Whiteness: A Clue to the Problem

Strangely enough, it has been through my study of racism and "Whiteness" that I have gained clues to the problem (Sue, 2003; Sue et al., 1999). I have come to realize that most of my colleagues are well-intentioned and truly believe in equal access and opportunity for all but have great difficulty freeing themselves from their cultural conditioning (Dovidio & Gaertner, 2000; Hodson, Dovidio, & Gaertner, 2002; Sue, 1999). They are, in essence, trapped in a Euro American worldview that only allows them to see the world from one perspective. To challenge that worldview as being only partially accurate, to entertain the notion that it may represent a false illusion, and to realize that it may have resulted in injustice to others make seeing an alternative reality frightening and difficult. Although using the terms *Whiteness* and *Whites* may perpetuate the inaccurate notion that these terms describe a racial group (Jones, 1997), little doubt exists that skin color in this society exposes people to different experiences. Being a White person means something quite different from being a person of color (Sue, 2003). I use one particular example here to illustrate how Whiteness and its invisibility serve as a default standard that makes it difficult to see how it may unfairly intrude into the lives of racial/ethnic minority groups (Fine, Weiss, Powell, & Wong, 1997).

The Color-Blind Phenomenon

Commonly known as the "Race Information Ban," Proposition 54 on the 2003 ballot in California attempted to forbid the government form collecting demographic information on the basis of race, ethnicity, color, or national origin in public education, employment, and contracting. The polls taken at that time showed that the initiative, under the guise of moving the United States to a color-blind society that facilitates antidiscrimination, was supported by a majority of California voters. From my perspective, I saw the proposition as potentially dangerous, with devastating consequences for people of color. Rather than preventing disparities, it would prove to have precisely the opposite effect—lessening the ability to monitor inequities and encouraging greater discrimination. As others have warned banning racial and ethnic statistics would blind people to real, meaningful differences that exist between groups in educational opportunities, civil rights protections, race specific medical conditions, and so forth. Agencies, for example, would be unable to determine and rectify health care disparities and racial/ethnic disease patterns important for medical treatments ("Health Disparities Report at Center of Controversy," 2004; Jones, 1997; U.S. Department of Health and Human Services, 2001, 2003). Worse yet, it would undermine accountability for civil rights violations such as hate crimes, discrimination in the workplace, and biased racial profiling. I was concerned that despite the defeat of Proposition 54, so many misguided voters supported the legislation.

After some 35 years of work on diversity and multiculturalism, I continue to be baffled by how difficult it is for many White Americans to see the false promises of the "color-blind society." When I testified before President Clinton's Race Advisory Board in 1997 and participated in a congressional briefing on the myth of a color-blind society, for example, I tried to point out how it had a detrimental impact on racial minorities and White Americans (President's Initiative on Race, 1998). Some White Americans who watched and listened to my testimony on C-SPAN reacted with considerable anger and defensiveness. One person accused me of being a racist of a different color and of supporting "preferential treatment" for minorities, whereas others made actual threats on my life. The reactions of White viewers made me realize that I had pushed powerful buttons in their psyche that aroused strong and negative emotions to my message. Since that testimony, I have often asked myself why some viewers reacted so strongly. Why were they so upset that they needed to threaten me in such a vehement fashion? What was the source of their anger? What raw nerve had I touched? Could it be that I challenged their view of the United States as a fair and just society? More important, could it be that they saw my testimony as potentially truthful about their own biases and prejudices?

◈ Masking Disparities

Martin Luther King once advocated judging people not by the color of their skin but by their internal character. On the surface, such a statement from a renowned civil rights advocate seems to reinforce the concept of a color-blind society as an answer to discrimination and prejudice. Unfortunately, many proponents of this concept have failed to understand the context of King's statement and/or have co-opted it for their own ends. For all groups to have equal access and opportunity assumes that a level playing field exists and that everyone, regardless of race, ethnicity or national origin, has an equal chance of success. Although many White Americans may believe that discrimination has been minimized or even eliminated, research clearly indicates that equity currently does not exist in U.S. society (Crosby, Iyer, Clayton, & Downing, 2003; Jones, 1997).

Let me use some statistics to illustrate my point. If one compares the distribution of White Euro American men in certain high-level positions with that of other groups, some very puzzling disparities appear. For example, White men occupy approximately 80% of the tenured positions in higher education and 92% of the Forbes 400 executive/CE)–level positions; they constitute 80% of the House of Representatives, 84% of the U.S. Senate, 99% of athletic team owners, and 100% of U.S. Presidents (Sue, 2003). These statistics are even more disturbing when one sees that White men comprise only 33% of the U.S. population! Where, I ask, are the persons of color, and where are the women? If one assumes that people of color and women are equally capable and qualified, the disparity can only be caused by an uneven playing field favoring White men. Ironically, these statistics would not even exist to gauge civil rights progress if society were, indeed, color blind.

In my research on the causes and effects of bias and discrimination, I have come to realize that color blindness uses "Whiteness" to mimic the norms of fairness, justice, and equality by "whiting" out differences. It is a default key that perpetuates the belief in sameness and equality. In essence, color blindness is really a denial of differences. A denial of differences is really a denial of the unfair power imbalance that exists in society. A denial of power imbalance allows Whites to deny their unearned privilege and advantage in society. And by couching racial discrimination in the rhetoric of equal treatment and opportunity, White Americans perpetuate the false illusion that equality exists and that they serve no role in the oppression of others (Dyer, 2002).

In my work on racism awareness training, I have come to realize that many of my White students pretend not to see color because, whether consciously or unconsciously, the are motivated by the need to appear unbiased and by fears that what they say or do may appear racist (Rothenberg, 2002). Whether knowingly or not, color blindness allows Whites to deny the experiential reality of minorities by minimizing the effects of racism and discrimination in their day-to-day lives. It further allows many Whites to deny how they benefit from their own Whiteness and how their Whiteness intrudes upon persons of color.

I have often heard, for example, White teachers express resentment toward African American students who engage in Black cultural expressions in the classroom. Black students are frequently admonished to "leave your cultural baggage at home and don't bring it into the classroom." Many educators possess little awareness that they also bring their own Whiteness into the classroom and operate from a predominantly White ethnocentric perspective. I wonder how they would respond if they were to be asked, "Why don't you leave your White cultural baggage at home when teaching?"

Several years ago, during my sabbatical, I field tested a study on "The Invisibility of Whiteness" (Sue, 2003). I would approach White strangers in the middle of downtown San Francisco and ask them the following question: What does it mean to be White?" Their responses were interesting, to say the least. Many respondents did not seem to understand my question, seemed to become annoyed, or said they had never thought about it. When asked "why," the most prevalent response was, "It's not important to me or it doesn't affect my life." Others, however, became quite irritated, angry, and defensive. They seemed to believe that I was accusing them of being racist or bigoted, and they found the question offensive. A significant number of respondents denied being White by saying "I'm not White; I'm [Irish], [Italian], [Jewish], [German]. . . ." It was obviously easier for them to acknowledge their ethnicity than their skin color.

Perpetuating the Illusion of Fairness

From my interviews, I concluded that White respondents would rather not think about their Whiteness, are uncomfortable or react negatively to being labeled White, deny its importance in affecting their lives, and seem to believe that they are unjustifiably accused of being bigoted by virtue of being White. Those who were most uncomfortable with the question generally ended the conversation with statements like "people are people," "we are all Americans," or "we are all the same under the skin." It was clear that their discomfort led them to desire eliminating racial differences form the conversation or diluting them. To persons of color, "Whiteness" is most visible when it is denied, evokes puzzlement or negative reactions, or is equated with normalcy. Few people of color react negatively when asked what it means to be Black, Asian American, Latino, or a member of their race. Most could readily inform the questioner about what it means to be a person of color.

It appears that the denial or mystification of White Euro Americans regarding the issue of Whiteness has a significant underlying reason. Whiteness is transparent precisely because of its everyday occurrence. It represent institutional normality, and White people are taught to think of their lives as morally neutral, average, and ideal. As a person of color, however, I do not find Whiteness to be invisible because I do not fit many of the normative qualities that make Whiteness invisible.

The deception of Whiteness as a universal identity has a monumental hidden meaning—that is, being a human being is being White! Elsewhere, I have stated that the invisible veil of Whiteness inundates the definitions of such expressions as "human being," being "just a person," and being an "American." The speaker is usually saying something like this: "Differences are divisive, so let's avoid acknowledging them and seek out our commonalities. I'm uncomfortable with racial differences, so let's pretend they don't exist."

It suddenly dawned on me that the invisibility of Whiteness is motivated by the denial of the advantages associated with being White or what some now call "White privilege." White privilege can be defined as the unearned advantages and benefits that accrue to White people by virtue of a system normed on the experiences, values, and perceptions of their group (McIntosh, 2002; Sue, 2003). Because of its invisibility, White privilege is seen as a source of strength, and it provides Euro Americans with permission to deny its existence and use it to treat persons of color unfairly. I realized the insidious and seductive nature of White privilege on White Euro Americans. The benefits that accrue to them by virtue of their Whiteness serve to keep them satisfied and enlist their unwitting complicity in maintaining unjust social arrangements.

The Invisibility of Ethnocentric Monoculturalism

It was the recognition of the invisibility of Whiteness that provided the clue to another form of invisibility that may be much more damaging and problematic: *ethnocentric monoculturalism.* This is a term used to describe the invisible veil of a worldview that keeps White Euro Americans from recognizing the ethnocentric basis of their beliefs, values, and assumptions (Sue et al., 1999; Sue & Sue, 2003). Because of its lack of visibility, it is a worldview that is imposed on all culturally diverse groups in this society. Although Whiteness is not identical to ethnocentric monoculturalism, the psychological dynamics related to the denial of differences, that is, equating it with normalcy and not understanding how it intrudes on the life experiences of those who do not share its worldview—are similar. Ethnocentric monoculturalism shares features of what Wrenn (1962, 1985) called "cultural encapsulation" and Jones (1972, 1997) called "cultural racism." It is characterized by five major attributes that potentially result in cultural oppression (Sue et al., 1998; Sue & Sue, 2003).

Belief in Superiority, "Choseness," and Entitlement

Ethnocentric monoculturalism creates a strong belief in the superiority of one group's cultural heritage, history, values, language, beliefs, religion, traditions, and arts and crafts. The collective sense of superiority leads to a sense of "choseness" and entitlement that has been described as a dangerous belief that may lead to conflict with out groups (Eidelson & Eidelson, 2003). In the United States, this component of ethnocentric monoculturalism is manifested in the value of individualism, the Protestant work ethic, capitalism, the desirability of certain physical features (blond hair, blue eyes, and fair-skin), monotheism (Christianity), monolingualism (English), and a written tradition (Katz, 1985). People who possess or adhere to these characteristics are often allowed easier access to the rewards of the society; their validation in society makes them feel special, chosen, and entitled. Their "superior" status in society also makes them prone to believing that their definitions of problems and solutions are the right ones. In many respects, the belief in individual or group superiority often results in an inability to empathize or understand the viewpoints or experiences of other individuals who are different from them (Eidelson & Eidelson, 2003; Hanna, Talley, & Guindon, 2000; Keltner & Robinson, 1996).

In the field of psychology, the belief in superiority is often translated into an inflexible assumption of possessing the absolute truth that defines the profession. Some psychologists of color, for example, point out that the original definition of *psychology* arose from African–Egyptian civilization and was considered the study of the "soul or spirit" rather than the mind or behavior (Parham, 2002). Yet it is a strong Western belief that the latter definition is more valid and scientific (Parham, White, & Ajamu, 1999). Likewise, in the West, scientific empiricism is considered a superior means of asking and answering questions about the human condition (Seligman & Csikszentmihalyi, 2001). Western science remains skeptical of non-Western and indigenous methods that relate to spirituality in ascribing causation.

Definitions of appropriate and therapeutic behavior on the part of clinicians are also manifested in the profession's code of ethics and standards of practice. These form the basis of accreditation and licensure criteria. It is interesting that framing some of these guidelines into therapeutic taboos (truths) is very revealing about the reality of Western mental health. In the field of clinical practice, for example, therapists are admonished generally not to (a) self-disclose their thoughts and feelings, (b) give advice and suggestions, (c) engage in dual role relationships, (d) accept gifts from clients, and (e) barter services (APA, 2002; Sue & Sue, 2003). These taboos are grounded in beliefs that the therapeutic relationship should not foster dependency, should be free of potential conflicts of interest, and should maintain the objectivity of the helping professional. Although I have obviously simplified the complexity of these guidelines, the question I ask is this: What if other culturally diverse groups consider these behaviors or alternative roles to be qualities of the helping relationship? Indeed, work on indigenous healing and explorations on culture-specific therapeutic approaches indicate precisely this fact (Parham, 2002; Sue & Sue, 2003).

Belief in the Inferiority of Other Groups

History is replete with examples of Western attempts to civilize the "heathens," have them adopt a single-god concept, and bring a Western way of life to "less developed" and "primitive" cultures (Hanna et al., 2000). Behind these actions and descriptors are intrinsic beliefs of no only the superiority of one group but the inferiority of the customs, norms, traditions, religions, and lifestyles of other groups (Jones, 1997). Such a determination of inferiority or even pathology is strongly linked to differences from the mainstream culture. Elsewhere, we (Sue & Sue, 2003), concluded the following about the inferiority component of ethnocentric monoculturalism:

> Other societies or groups may be perceived as less developed, uncivilized, primitive, or even pathological. The group's lifestyles or ways of doing things are considered inferior. Physical characteristics such as dark complexion, black hair, and brown eyes; cultural characteristics such as belief in non-Christian religions (Islam, Confucianism, polytheism, etc.), collectivism, present time orientation, and the importance of shared wealth; and linguistic characteristics such as bilingualism, non-standard English, speaking with an accent, use of nonverbal and contextual communications, and reliance on the oral tradition are usually seen as less desirable by the society. (p. 70)

This perception means that people of color, for example, are prone to being seen as less qualified, less capable, unintelligent, inarticulate, unmotivated, lazy, and as coming from broken homes. Little doubt exists that the perception of inferiority can be translated into unequal access and opportunities in education, career options, employment, hiring practices, housing, and so on. In mental health practice, it may mean pathologizing the lifestyles or cultural values of clients who do not share characteristics of the mainstream.

The Power to Define Reality

In truth, all major groups and societies are ethnocentric. They believe strongly in the superiority of their own group and the inferiority of other groups. Anyone who has spent significant times in China and Japan, for example, has been exposed to the Asian cultural belief that the Chinese or Japanese come from a superior culture and history (Chu, 1991; Gao, 1991). The distinguishing characteristic between ethnocentrism and ethnocentric monoculturalism, however, is power—one group's ability to impose its reality and beliefs upon another group (Sue, 2001). Although power is often associated with economic and military might, I submit that true power resides in a group's ability to define and impose that reality upon others.

Several years ago, a Native American colleague asked an audience, "Who owns history?" The answer to that question is precisely answered by the title of Robert Guthrie's book, *Even the Rat Was White* (Guthrie, 1976, 1997). The extreme bias in knowledge construction from a Euro American perspective means that the history taught to children is at best incomplete, and at worse, inaccurate and distorted (Banks, 2004). When children are told, for example, that "Columbus discovered America," teachers are not only perpetuating an ethnocentric illusion of superiority for the mainstream group but are engaging in cultural oppression of Native Americans. Native American children who are told this falsehood know a different reality (Columbus was lost and thought he had discovered the continent of India). This reality, however, is tested further when teachers give a "true/false" test with the statement, "Columbus discovered America." To answer "true" means the youngster actually believes the statement or "sells out." To answer "false" is to get the answer wrong. The Native American student is caught in a catch-22.

In conclusion, it appears that the group who "owns" history also controls the gateway to knowledge construction, truth and falsity, problem definition, what constitutes normality, and abnormality, and ultimately, the nature of reality. When those in the social sciences use terms and concepts for racial/ethnic minorities like "genetically inferior," "culturally deficient," or "culturally deprived" (Hernstein & Murray, 1994; Riessman, 1962), they set in motion a whole set of interlocking systems grounded in a false reality that is detrimental to persons of color; it privileges one group and oppresses another (Samuda, 1998).

Manifestation in Institutions

Although institutional structure, programs, policies, and practices are developed to regularize procedures, increase efficiency of operation, and allow for fairness in application, they often contribute to inequities and oppression. Laws, public policy, rules, and regulations endorsed by American society have a long history of bias and discrimination. They are often overt, intentional, and obvious—for example, (a) the Constitutional provision defining Blacks as three fifths of a man; (b) the "separate but equal doctrine" in *Plessy v. Ferguson;* (c) laws forbidding Native Americans to practice their religions; and (d) laws forbidding Asians to own land. Institutional racism continues to this day in the form of criteria (high membership fees and select attributes) to exclude certain "undesirable" groups in private clubs and organizations, real estate associations, and bank lending practices (Jones, 1997; Sue, 2003).

More damaging, however, are the insidious and invisible programs and policies that represent ethnocentric values and beliefs. Because most institutional systems are monocultural in nature, they represent a potential source of cultural oppression for racial/ethnic minorities and women. Standard operating procedures demand compliance and a way of operation that may deny equal access and opportunity (Sue, 1995). Performance appraisal systems, for example, often use criteria for hiring, retention, and promotion that are culture-bound. Some time back, a major multinational corporation contacted me about doing leadership training for Asian American employees whom they believed lacked managerial skills. Apparently, in a survey conducted by the company, Asian Pacific Americans expressed unhappiness with their status in the company, felt they were not being promoted when they were otherwise qualified, and many indicated that they intended to leave the company and seek employment elsewhere. Because the company valued the technical competence of the Asian American workforce and knew that replacement costs in rehiring and training would be great, the solution they proposed was assertiveness training. Because of my work with Asian Americans, I immediately suspected that the company might be operating from stereotypes—that is, that Asian Americans are good in math and sciences but poor in "people skills," make poor leaders, and are relatively passive and nonverbal (Sue, 1999). I was able to get the company to acknowledge several observations: (a) The definition of a good leader among traditional Asian societies is an individual who is subtle and able to work behind the scenes to obtain group consensus, (b) the criteria used by the company for managerial positions were primarily Western and masculine in orientation (competitive, dominating, and aggressive), and (c) the criteria were not predictive of leadership effectiveness for many Asian Americans (Levinson, 1994). In Asian societies, effectiveness of a leader is judged by team productivity instead of individual achievement. Thus, Asian American employees were being denied promotions on the basis of criteria that were unrelated to their productivity. I am sad to say that although the company has acknowledged these conclusions, it has not changed its performance appraisal criteria.

Institutional bias is often reflected in management systems, communication systems, chain-of-command systems, and performance appraisal systems (promotion and tenure in academia). In academia, for example, a university often mirrors the nature of race and gender relations in the wider society. The university culture may create culture conflicts for students, staff, and faculty of color, leading to alienation, loss of productivity, and problems with retention, graduation, and promotion.

The Invisible Veil

The fourth-century Chinese sage Chang-Tsu often asserted that "how we view the world is not only about what we see, but about what we do not see." What Americans consciously see and what they are explicitly taught are grounded in basic democratic ideals of equality, justice, fairness, respect, and dignity for the worth of all citizens. These are taught to Americans through the Bill of Rights, the U.S. Constitution, and the Declaration of Independence. What one does not see is the invisible veil of personal and institutional injustice that operates outside the level of conscious awareness (Dovidio & Gaertner, 2000; Sue, 2001). The invisible veil is a product of cultural conditioning; individuals are taught not only the prejudices and biases of society but also the many myths that serve to guide the interpretation of events. Three of these are (a) the myth of meritocracy (the cream of the crop will rise to the top), (b) the myth of equal opportunity (everyone has a chance to succeed in this society), and (c) the myth of fair treatment (equal treatment is fair treatment).

The myth of meritocracy operates from the dictum that there is a strong relationship between ability, effort, and success. Those who are successful in life are more competent, capable, intelligent, and motivated. Those who fail to achieve in society are less capable, intelligent, and motivated. The myth of equal opportunity assumes that everyone encounters the same obstacles in life and that the playing field is a level one. Thus, everyone has an equal chance to succeed or enjoy the fruits of their labor. The myth of fair treatment equates equal treatment with fairness, whereas differential treatment is considered discriminatory or preferential. All three often act in unison to mask disparities and inequities and to allow actions that oppress groups that are not in the mainstream. I use several examples to illustrate this invisible dynamic.

During President George W. Bush's first run for presidency, syndicated columnist Molly Ivins noted something along the lines of "George Bush was born on third base and believes he hit a triple." The ultimate illusion of meritocracy allows people to believe that their favored position in life is the result of superior aptitude and hard work rather than privilege and favoritism. Using the baseball analogy, one can say that many people of color and women work equally hard or harder and are equally qualified or more so but seldom make it even to the batter's box. The illusion that the field is level and wide open—that merit alone is all that is needed— denies the reality of persons of color and women. It dismisses or dilutes the importance of individual, institutional, and cultural racism that places barriers in the way of achievement for these groups. Furthermore, the belief that "you are the master of your own fate" unfairly blames people of color for their inability to achieve more in this society.

Likewise, the backlash against affirmative action is in part due to the public's perception that equal access and opportunity already exist and that any treatment that uses "race" as one criterion is discrimination because it gives advantages to people of color (Crosby et al., 2003). It is harder for White Americans to see, however, that affirmative action already exists for White males (à la George W. Bush). The affirmative action example also challenges another myth or illusion—that equal treatment is fair treatment, whereas differential treatment is preferential treatment. There is a common belief that if everyone is treated the same, racial or gender discrimination is not possible. Many organizations' standard operating procedures are developed to apply equally to everyone, thereby avoiding charges of discrimination. What is less visible, however, is that equal treatment can be discriminatory treatment, and differential treatment is not necessarily preferential. Earlier, I used the example of performance appraisal systems to indicate how such a system discriminated against Asian Americans by keeping them from being promoted. Institutions often claim that they do not discriminate because they use the same standards to hire, retain, or promote their employees. Institutions of higher education make a similar claim: If students obtain above a certain grade point average or Scholastic Aptitude Test standard, they can gain admission. The problem is that such "equal" treatment has unfavorable outcomes highly correlated with the racial and gender identity of employees and students.

It is difficult for the majority culture to understand that marginalized groups are not necessarily asking for equal treatment. Rather, they desire equal access and opportunity. Ironically, achieving that end often dictates differential treatment. The blind application of a single policy or standard by institutions may not only be unfair but oppressive as well.

Conclusion

Whiteness and ethnocentric monoculturalism, culturally conditioned in all individuals from the moment of birth, maintain their power through their invisibility. On a personal level, people are conditioned and rewarded for remaining unaware and oblivious of how their beliefs and actions may unfairly oppress people of color, women, and other groups in society. On an institutional level, people fail to recognize how standard operating procedures serve to deny equal access and opportunities for some while providing advantages and benefits for others. If the profession of psychology and society in general truly value diversity and multiculturalism, and if this is to be a nation that achieves the democratic ideals it professes, then they very difficult process of deconstructing Whiteness and ethnocentric monoculturalism must begin. To do so, however, requires us to realize that our reality is only one of many others. The monocultural curriculum of psychology that reflects only one perspective must be deconstructed and reconstructed to include a multicultural perspective (Banks, 2004). Formal education is one of the primary mechanisms by which misinformation and biases are transmitted to children. Multicultural educators have made clear the revolutionary steps that need to be undertaken in kindergarten through Grade 12 and in higher education to achieve this end (Banks, 2004; Gay, 2004; Ladson-Billings, 2004).

For the profession of psychology, this means realizing that explanations of human behavior may be culture-bound and potentially limited in inapplicability to an increasingly diverse population. It means realizing that the knowledge base comes from only one perspective and that there is a great need to develop a truly multicultural psychology that recognizes important dimensions of the human condition such as race, culture, ethnicity, gender, religion, sexual orientation, and other sociodemographic variables. A psychology that does not recognize and practice diversity is a psychology that is truly bankrupt in understanding the totality of the human condition. It will forever perpetuate a false reality that provides advantages for certain groups while disadvantaging and oppressing others. As long as the invisible is not visible, the profession of psychology may continue to operate from monocultural theories and practices that deny the rights and privileges due to all individuals and groups.

Author's Note

Correspondence concerning this article should be addressed to Derald Wing Sue, Department of Counseling and Clinical Psychology, Box 36, Teachers College, Columbia University, 525 West 120th Street, New York, NY 10027, E-mail: dw2020@columbia.edu

References

American Psychological Association. (1993). Guidelines for providers of psychological services to ethnic, linguistic, and culturally diverse populations. *American Psychologist, 48,* 45–48.

American Psychological Association. (2000). Guidelines for psychotherapy with lesbian, gay, and bisexual clients. *American Psychologist, 55,* 1440–1451.

American Psychological Association. (2002). Ethical principles of psychologists and code of conduct. *American Psychologist, 57,* 1060–1073.

American Psychological Association. (2003). Guidelines on multicultural education, training, research, practice, and organizational change for psychologists, *American Psychologist, 58,* 377–402.

Banks, J. A. (2004). Multicultural education. In J. A. Banks & C. A. McGee Banks (Eds.), *Handbook of research on multicultural education* (2nd ed., pp. 3–29). San Francisco: Jossey-Bass.

Chu, C.-N. (1991). *The Asian mind game.* New York: Macmillan.

Crosby, F. J., Iyer, A., Clayton, S., & Downing, R. A. (2003). Affirmative action: Psychological data and policy debates, *American Psychologist, 58,* 95–115.

Dovidio, O. F. & Gaertner, S. L. (2000). Aversive racism and selective decisions: 1989 and 1999. *Psychological Science, 11,* 315–319.

Dyer, R. (2002). The matter of whiteness, In P. S. Rothenberg (Ed.). *White privilege: Essential readings on the other side of racism* (pp. 9–14). New York: Worth.

Eidelson, R. J., & Eidelson, J. I. (2003). Dangerous ideas: Five beliefs that propel groups toward conflict. *American Psychologist, 58,* 182–192.

Fine, M., Weiss, L., Powell, L. C., & Wong, L. M. (1997). *Off White: Readings on race, power, and society.* New York: Routledge.

Fowers, B. J., & Richardson, F. C. (1996). Why is multiculturalism good? *American Psychologist, 51,* 609–621.

Gao, Y. (1991). *Lure the tiger out of the mountains.* New York: Simon & Shuster.

Gay, G. (2004). Curriculum theory and multicultural education. In J. A. Banks & C. A. McGee Banks (Eds.), *Handbook of research on multicultural education* (2nd ed., pp. 30–49). San Francisco: Jossey-Bass.

Guthrie, R. V. (1970). *Even the rat was White.* New York: Harper & Row.

Guthrie, R. V. (1997). *Even the rat was White: A historical view of psychology* (2nd ed.), New York: Harper & Row.

Hall, C. C. I. (1997). Cultural malpractice. *American Psychologist, 52,* 642–651.

Hanna, F. J., Talley, W. B., & Guindon, M. H. (2000). The power of perception: Toward a model of cultural oppression and liberation. *Journal of Counseling & Development, 78,* 430–446.

Health disparities report at center of controversy. (2004, February 12). *Black Issues in Higher Education,* p. 6. Retrieved July 17, 2004, from www.findarticles.com/p/articles/mi_m0DXK/is_26_20/ai-113759288

Hernstein, R., & Murray, C. (1994). *The bell curve: Intelligence and class structure in American life.* New York: Free Press.

Hodson, G., Dovidio, J. F., & Gaertner, S. L. (2002). Processes in racial discrimination: Differential weighting of conflicting information. *Personality and Social Psychology Bulletin, 28,* 460–471.

Jones, J. M. (1972). *Prejudice and racism.* New York: McGraw-Hill.

Jones, J. M. (1997). *Prejudice and racism.* (2ne ed.) New York: McGraw-Hill.

Ladson-Billings, G. (2004). New directions in multicultural education. In J. A. Banks & C. A. Banks (Eds.). *Handbook of research on multicultural education* (2nd ed., pp. 50–63). San Francisco: Jossey-Bass.

Levinson, H. (1994). Why the behemoths fell: Psychological roots of corporate failure. *American Psychologist, 49,* 428–436.

Katz, J. H. (1985). The sociopolitical nature of counseling, *The Counseling Psychologist, 13,* 615–624.

Keltner, D., & Robinson, R. J. (1996). Extremism, power, and imagined basis of social conflict. *Current Directions in Psychological Science, 5,* 101–105.

McIntosh, P. (2002). White privilege: Unpacking the invisible knapsack. In P. S. Rothenberg (Ed.), *White privilege: Essential readings on the other side of racism* (pp. 97–102). New York: Worth.

Parham, T. A. (2002. *Counseling persons of African descent.* Thousand Oaks, CA: Sage.

Parham, T. A., White, J., & Ajamu, A. (1999). *The psychology of Blacks: An African-centered perspective.* Thousand Oaks, CA: Sage.

President's Initiative on Race. (1998). *On America in the 21st century,* Washington, DC: U.S. Government Printing Office.

Riessman, F. (1962). *The culturally deprived child.* New York: Harper & Row.

Rothenberg, P. S. (2002). *White privilege.* New York: Worth.

Samuda, R. J. (1998). *Psychological testing of American minorities.* Thousand Oaks, CA: Sage.

Seligman, M. F. P., & Csikszentmihalyi, M. (2001). Reply to comments, *American Psychologist, 56,* 89–90.

Sue, D. W. (1995). Multicultural organizational development. In J. G. Ponterotto, J. M. Casas, L. A. Suzuki, & C. M. Alexander (Eds.), *Handbook of multicultural counseling* (pp. 474–492). Thousand Oaks, CA: Sage.

Sue, D. W. (1999). Creating conditions for a constructive dialogue on "race": Taking individual and institutional responsibility. In J. Q. Adams & J. R. Welsch (Eds.),

Cultural diversity: Curriculum, classroom, and climate (pp. 15–20). Chicago: Illinois Board of Higher Education.

Sue, D. W. (2001). Multidimensional facets of cultural competence. *The Counseling Psychologist, 29,* 790–821.

Sue, D. W. (2003). *Overcoming our racism: The journey to liberation.* San Francisco: Jossey-Bass.

Sue, D. W., Bernier, J. B., Durran, M., Feinberg, L., Pedersen, P., Smith, E., & Vasquez-Nuttall, E. (1982). Position paper: Cross-cultural counseling competencies. *The Counseling Psychologist, 10,* 45–52.

Sue, D. W., Bingham, R. P., Porché-Burke, L., & Vasquez, M. (1999). The diversification of psychology: A multicultural revolution. *American Psychologist, 54,* 1061–1069.

Sue, D. W., Carter, R. T., Casas, J. M., Fouad, N. A., Ivey, A. E., Jensen, M., et al. (1998). *Multicultural counseling competencies: Individual and organizational development.* Thousand Oaks, CA: Sage.

Sue, D. W., & Sue, D. (2003). *Counseling the culturally diverse: Theory and practice* (4th ed.). New York: Wiley.

U.S. Department of Health and Human Services. (2001). *Mental health: Culture, race, and ethnicity* (Supplement to *Mental Health: A Report of the Surgeon General*). Washington, DC: Author.

U.S. Department of Health and Human Services. (2003). *National healthcare disparities report.* Washington, DC: Author.

Wrenn, C. G. (1962). The culturally-encapsulated counselor. *Harvard Educational Review, 32,* 444–449.

Wrenn, C. G. (1985). Afterward: The culturally encapsulated counselor revisited. In P. B. Pedersen (Ed.), *Handbook of Cross cultural counseling and therapy.* (pp. 323–329). Westport, CT: Greenwood Press.

 Note

[1] See www.apa.org/pi/multiculturalguidelines.pdf

Reflection Questions

1. How can we use some of the concepts to evaluate the perspectives we hold to be true? (Optional)

2. What aspects of the readings do you agree or disagree with and why?

3. Reflecting on the readings, what are the perspectives that dominate and define our life in the United States? (Optional)

4. What are the solutions and challenges we can draw from the readings to positively influence our quality of life?

5. Which perspectives do you hold on to and which have you let go of at this point in your life? What process or guidelines did you apply to negotiate your perspectives? Do you think these readings can enrich this process?

History

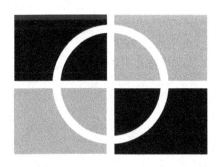

Framing Questions

1. What is the purpose of Ethnic Studies given the author's discussion? Provide a brief explanation using two examples to illustrate your viewpoint.

2. Do you believe the law is objective? If so, what are the strengths and limitations of a color-blind law given the diversity in our society?

3. Have you ever read history books by scholars who are nonwhite? If not why, not? If so, then explain what were the circumstances. (Optional)

4. Do you think that reading focused on the lived experiences written by nonwhite scholars might be different or the same as those written by white scholars? Provide a brief explanation. (Optional)

5. If you consider the works of white scholars and nonwhite scholars to be similar, how might you explain that in college the preferred way of telling history is often through the perspective of white scholars? (Optional)

Introduction

Wayne Maeda

Ethnic Studies as a program and as a field of study was really born during the Third World Liberation strikes at San Francisco State College from November 1968 to March 1969 and University of California, Berkeley from January 1969 to March 1969.[1] African American, Chicano, Asian American, Native American and other students demanded, among other things, that institutions of higher learning provide access to poor and minority students, hiring minority faculty, administrators, and provide relevant curriculum. For those in the burgeoning field of ethnic studies, relevant curriculum broadly meant developing new perspectives, different methods of analysis, reconsidering what constituted "facts" and "interpretations" that shaped social realities for America's racial groups.

One of the most important functions envisioned over four decades ago in the field of ethnic studies was to provide a scholarly critique of the methods, theories, and practices of framing "the minority" experience by mainstream disciplines. This new breed and generation of historians challenged the notion that interpretation of history rested on dates, great men, and that "facts" speak for themselves in this grand narrative that passed as "the" definitive national history of America. In reality, the actual interpretation of history is affected by which facts are used, omitted, falsified, distorted, and known by the historian. More importantly, historical interpretation depends as much on the historian's own assumptions, biases, and agendas as it does on "facts." Because student activists of the late 1960s realized that the facts in the histories of African, Asian, Chicano, and Native Americans were often distorted, buried or simply "MIH" (missing in history) they argued that it was necessary to recover, re-interpret, and revise those histories. Ethnic Studies still commits itself to the goal of recovering, re-interpreting, and revising our past so that we can make sense of the present in order to prepare for the future that will become even more diverse.

The problem of the twentieth century is the problem of the color line. Although this prophetic statement made by W.E. B. Du Bois in 1903 reflected concerns and ideas of student activists in the 1960s, it still resonates even in this "post-Obama" era and remains one of the most salient and intractable issues facing America in the twenty-first century. When he published *The Soul of Black Folks* in 1903, Du Bois was well aware of the Chinese who journeyed to "Gold Mountain" in the 1850s were denied naturalization rights and prevented from intermarrying with whites.

In fact, the Chinese held the distinction of being the first ethnic group in the United States to be persecuted and excluded from immigration based on race in 1882. The Japanese, who followed the Chinese immigrants beginning in 1880s, not only inherited the anti-Asiatic sentiment but also faced the same fate of denial of citizenship and ownership of land, as well as ultimate exclusion in 1924. Moreover, by the time Du Bois's book was published, America was on the verge of concluding its first imperialistic venture into Asia with the military conquest and occupation of the Philippines. Under the guise of "benign assimilation," American imperialistic policy brought civilization to the "brown monkeys," "savages," and Filipino "niggers" in the Philippines. Du Bois recognized the depth, complexities and nuances of navigating the issue of the "color line" across the color spectrum: the challenge for all of us in the twenty-first century remains . . . *the problem of the color line-the relationship of the darker to the lighter races of men in Asia and Africa, in America and the islands of the sea.*[2]

To begin this section on history, Charles Roberts provides a different perspective of early pre-California, Gold Rush, and ensuing statehood. In *California Indian History, 1846 to 1862*, Roberts explores in great detail what happened to the various Native American people in California from American occupation, the Gold Rush, and subsequent American take-over. While the mission period has been viewed as a romantic era of haciendas, priests, missions, and sweeping cattle ranching, this period was the beginning of devastation for Native Americans in what was to become California. Along with diseases, racist attitudes and practices brought by various groups including vigilantes, state militias, and federal troops proved devastating to the California Indians. But in the end this story, like many other stories of oppressed groups in America, is about adaptation and survival.

Cruz Reynoso, in *Ethnic Diversity*, examines religious, linguistic, and historical diversity through his own personal reflections of being a Mexican American. Reynoso incorporates his legal expertise and reflects on his role as a justice on the California Supreme Court. With his legal knowledge and insight Reynoso helps shed light on divisive "hot button" issues from segregation in public schools, to what language we use in the public, to who is an American these issues still resonates across the country today.

Steven Crum provides the reader with a focus on broad federal policies that impacted the Native American people from the nineteen-century to recent times. While these federal policies may be familiar to many, Crum explores the complexities of Native Americans as not merely victims but agents. Native Americans in the past have been constructed as one-dimensional "savages" or as victims of federal policies. Crum demonstrates that Native Americans responded, reacted, and, even more importantly in the processes became actors forcing the federal government to become the "reactors."

Timothy Fong, in *The History of Asians in America* demonstrates with a grand sweep, the diversity that makes up this group labeled "Asian Americans" and divides them into four general historical epochs. In doing so, Fong situates various Asian

American groups throughout our history beginning in 1840s, through War World II, to Southeast Asian refugee groups fleeing the effects of Vietnam War, and the "new immigrants" who have invigorated the pre-1965 Asian American communities. Asian Americans, with changes in immigration laws and growth of globalization, are now posed to become, in more urban and suburban cities in California, the majority population.

In *Recent African Immigration History*, Boatamo Mosupyoe illuminates little known or understood immigration from Africa and the Caribbean. So much emphasis has been focused on Asian immigration and their growth in America that recent immigrants from Africa and the Caribbean have not been on our radar. Even with President Barack Obama's father, a Kenyan, our simplistic view of "the" African American experience continues. Mosupyoe, however, examines the complex relationships of identity formation of these recent immigrants from Africa and the Caribbean, as well as the nuances between the new immigrants and the long-established African American communities.

This introductory section on history is meant to be just that — an introduction. There are many more areas to be studied, explored, recovered, re-interpreted, and even continually re-written. It is hoped that the seed of curiosity, a desire to question, and the valuing of a critical approach have been sown, for there is much work to be done in all fields of ethnic studies to be engaged in by future generations of historians, researchers, and writers.

Notes

[1] William Wei, *The Asian American Movement* (Philadelphia: Temple University Press, 1993), 15.
[2] Du Bois, 23.

California Indian History, 1846 to 1862

Charles Roberts

California Indians suffered greatly in the two decades after the United States' occupation in 1846. Their population declined precipitously, and their access to the spiritual world of their progenitors was shattered. On the eve of the occupation, the native Indian population numbered approximately 150,000. Some 14,000 lived in Southern California, and the remainder resided in the north. Since 1769, when the Spanish established a mission and presidio on the San Diego River, this population had declined from an estimated 350,000, primarily from such diseases as dysentery, syphilis, and malaria. The 1833 epidemic of malaria alone killed some 30,000 Indians in the Central Valley, devastating especially the Wintun and Maidu. Such a catastrophic loss of life, together with Spanish and Mexican policies of missionization and dispossession, disrupted native societies in much of California south of San Francisco. The secularization of the missions after 1832 induced many Indians to work for a rapidly expanding rancho system. Northern California was less affected, but the colonization of Russians along the Mendocino Coast and up the Russian River, the efforts of British and American fur trappers, and the establishment of John Sutter's New Helvetia in 1839 also caused fissures in the native way of life. The results of the United States takeover were even more disastrous. Between 1846 and 1860, the native population plummeted to barely 30,000. Although diseases continued to kill large numbers, these years witnessed a widespread assault upon the Indians by vigilantes, state militia, and federal troops.[1]

When the United States military took over California in the summer of 1846, it was faced with a fervent plea by landowners to protect their property against Indian raiders. Indians, including many former Mission neophytes, had for years been making raids on the missions and ranchos, taking cattle, sheep, horses, and mules for consumption or trade. On July 24, Thomas O. Larkin, the American consul to Mexican California and the owner of land in the Sacramento Valley, asked Commodore Robert F. Stockton to send a "force of horsemen" to contain the raiding and punish the perpetrators. On August 15, Walter Colton, alcalde of Monterey, pleaded with Stockton "to protect the property of citizens from the depredations of wild Indians." Stockton's response was fateful, anticipating the course of Indian policy in California for the next two decades. On August 17, he agreed to use volunteers "to prevent and punish any aggression by the Indians . . . upon the property of individuals, or the peace of the Territory. . . ." In addition, Stockton required vagrant Indians to labor at public works and for all Indians to carry permits that allowed them to be absent from their places of employment. Stockton's policies were continued by his successor, Brigadier General Stephen W. Kearny. On February 28, 1847, Kearny received a petition from fifteen Sacramento Valley ranchers, who declared that, without assistance, they would be forced to abandon their "farms and leave our property to the Marcy of the Indians perhaps something worse." On April 7, Kearny appointed John Sutter as subagent for the Indians of the Central Valley and ordered him to persuade them to cease their raiding. If the Indians persisted, Kearny told Sutter, "they will most assuredly be punished by an armed force which I will send among them. . . ." Two weeks later Kearny appointed Mariano Vallejo as subagent for the Indians north of San Francisco, including Clear Lake and Cache Creek, with the same authority. Stockton's and Kearny's proclamations, appointments, and actions clearly upheld Mexican policy toward Indians. They established a punitive policy that assumed Indians were guilty and privileged the interests of whites in real property and livestock.[2]

The discovery of gold at Coloma, a Nisenan village site on the American River, on January 24, 1848, set off a massive intrusion of emigrants from all parts of the globe. At this time California was still part of Mexico. The Treaty of Guadalupe Hidalgo, signed in early February, would not be officially ratified and proclaimed until July. Only then would California officially be a part of the United States. California Indians, especially in the gold rush regions, were in no position to cope with such a flood. For them, what ensued was a decade and more of death, dispossession, and cultural loss. Their ability, through prayer and dance, to renew the earth was nearly lost. Many were forced to relocate out of their own homelands and into other parts of the state. By 1860, the native population was roughly 30,000, a scant 20 percent of what it was in 1846. This diminution continued for years, reaching its nadir at the end of the century. The United States census of 1880 enumerated 16,277 California Indians and that of 1900 only 15,377.[3]

As the gold rush commenced, the federal government scurried to obtain information about the territory obtained from Mexico. On July 17, 1848, Congress asked the Commissioner of Indian Affairs to report on the number of Indians in Oregon, California, and New Mexico. After a cursory investigation, the Commissioner admitted that his knowledge of "the various tribes, within these territories, is too limited to justify it in making any specific recommendations" regarding policy. With such vague information, he estimated the California Indian population at 16,390. More precise knowledge was imperative. In April, 1849, the Secretary of State sent Thomas Butler King to investigate conditions among the California Indians, especially in the gold regions. A few months later, the Secretary of the Interior directed William Carey Jones to report on the legal rights that California Indians had under Spain and Mexico. King's report of March 26, 1850, anticipated a reservation policy. He recommended that Indians be collected at specific locations where they would be taught the "arts and habits of civilization." On April 10,

Jones reported that Mexican law recognized two categories of Indians, those who were "wild" and those who were "domesticated." For the former, he asserted, Mexico had not recognized "any title whatever to the soil." But, the others had the right to as much land as was necessary for "tillage, habitation, and pasturage." Jones declared that Mexican law "always intended the Indian of the missions . . . to have homes upon the mission grounds." Significantly, he added that these same rights "may be said of the larger ranchos . . . and of the Indian settlements or rancherias upon them." These reports, however, came too late to protect the rights of California natives.[4]

In 1848, Indians were prominent as workers in the gold fields. It was common for nearby ranchers to bring their work force into the placers, and for some to make a considerable profit. Usually the Indians were paid in food, clothing, and medicine. Colonel Richard Mason reported that William Daylor and Perry McCoon, employing four white men and about a hundred Indians, extracted $17,000 in gold in a week's time. Mason also reported that John Sinclair employed fifty Indians and netted around $16,000. Another rancher, John M. Murphy, employed six hundred Indians at what became Murphy's Camp in Calaveras County. An important factor in Murphy's success was his marriage to a daughter of a local Miwok headman. John Bidwell, using Mechoopda workers, took out approximately $100,000 in gold from the Feather River, making it possible for him to purchase the land that became Rancho Chico. In July, 1848, Pierson B. Reading employed a work force consisting of three whites, one Delaware, one Walla Walla, one Chinook, and about sixty Wintun on the Trinity River. In December, James Clyman estimated that two thousand whites were working in the gold fields "and more than double that number of Indians." As the gold rush continued, many of the Indians worked for themselves, including entire families, and traded gold dust for merchandise and food. Some worked for wages. James Delevan noted that Indians "were for a long time employed to gather for the ranchos, until they became wise enough to set up for themselves. . . ."[5]

Indians in Southern California were also deeply affected by the gold rush. Large numbers of miners crossed into California at the juncture of the Gila and Colorado Rivers. In 1849, an estimated 12,000 Americans and 6,000 Mexicans, mostly from Sonora, took this route. By the end of 1851, some 60,000 had done so. This area of the Colorado was lush with cottonwood and mesquite on both sides of the river. The local Quechan people cultivated extensive fields of beans, corn, melons, and other crops. They harvested large quantities of mesquite beans. With the arrival of soldiers and miners, the Quechan traded their crops for clothing, tools, horses, and other animals. They charged the emigrants for ferrying services, especially the swimming of animals across the river. However, as the newcomers passed through in larger numbers, the ecosystem was disrupted by overuse and severely damaged. Theft, on the part of the miners and the Quechan, became common. A group of whites, led by John J. Glanton, preempted the ferrying business and refused to allow the Indians to participate. As a result, a war broke out between the Quechan and the emigrants that lasted for two years, ending with the establishment of Fort Yuma. In the coastal region, Indians provided most of the manual labor. A few owned their own farms and ranches. As the ranchos expanded their livestock production to meet the demands of the miners in the north, Indians took jobs as vaqueros, teamsters, skilled craftsmen, and domestics. They built fences, dug ditches and canals, erected walls and buildings, tended horses and other livestock, and cultivated and harvested a wide diversity of crops. For example, the Los Angeles basin in 1850 had 125 vineyards and twelve vintners, and nearly all the workers were Indians. Los Angeles produced 500,000 gallons of wine and brandy annually, with most of it sent to San Francisco and the gold region. One of the vintners, John Frohling, hired over 150 Indians at harvest time, and 60 worked for William Wolfskill's winery in twelve hour shifts for two weeks. As another example, Henry Dalton employed twenty Indians as a permanent work force on his 19,975 acre Rancho Azusa, but he also hired a migrant group of nearly a hundred Cahuilla from Agua Caliente when needed for harvesting.[6]

This early stage, characterized by extensive use of Indian labor, did not last. By the spring of 1849 war had broken out between whites and Indians along the American River and quickly spread to other parts of California. This conflict had many causes. The coming of whites greatly reduced the Indians' means of subsistence. The miners destroyed the Indians' fish dams and interrupted their seasonal round of collecting food. The miners stripped riverbanks of their covering, created barriers to the annual migrations of salmon, and destroyed spawning beds. The whites killed large numbers of deer, elk, and other animals. They cut down trees that protected the rivers and provided acorns for native consumption. Their livestock overran the grasslands. As a result, Indians were compelled to seek employment on valley ranches or to beg or simply to starve. Many of the Indian women were forced into concubinage or prostitution. Indians frequently complained of these injustices and sought compensation. The *Sacramento Union*, on February 5, 1853, reported that Indians on the lower Mariposa and Chowchilla Rivers "complain that the Americans have cut off their supply of fish, destroyed their acorn trees, and have killed or driven away the deer from their hunting grounds, and that they are in a state bordering on actual starvation."[7]

By 1850, the Indians were in large part driven from the gold fields and their trade had collapsed. From this date miners, vigilantes, and state militia engaged in a war of predation on the native population. The onset of this conflict can be traced to events in late March, 1849. A party of miners from the Oregon territory attacked a village of Maidu on the North Fork of the American River at a time when most of the Indian men were absent. The Oregonians raped many of the Indian women and young girls and killed older men and boys who tried to protect them. After the Maidu retaliated and killed five Oregonians, a vigilante group was formed in Coloma and in turn destroyed a Maidu village near Weber's Creek, killing a dozen Indians and capturing many more. Seven of these captives were executed after the drunken miners returned to Coloma, despite the protest of James Marshall. The consequences of these actions were momentous. Afterwards, as pointed out by William M'Collum in his book *California As I Saw It* (1850), the Oregonians "hunt them as they would wild beasts." Theodore Johnson, in *Sights in the Gold Region* (1849), reported that, since the first attacks, relations with the Indians had changed for the worse. "The late emigrants from across the mountains, and especially from Oregon," he wrote, "had commenced a war of extermination upon them, shooting them down like wolves, men and women and children, wherever they could find them." Johnson realized that harmony with the Indians and the profitable trade with them had "been utterly sacrificed by this extensive system of indiscriminate revenge." M'Collum's and Johnson's views, however, were in the minority. Majority opinion was more clearly expressed by an emigrant, Charles Ferguson: "I do not believe in wanton cruelty to the Indian, but when you are in a country where you know he is your enemy, and is not only waiting his chance but looking out for his opportunity, why not cut him down as he most surely will you."[8]

Warfare and homicide spread rapidly throughout northern California. One of the most heinous examples of this violence occurred at Clear Lake in 1850. In the summer of 1848, a group of twenty eight Pomo men were taken to the Feather River by Benjamin Kelsey from a ranch on Clear Lake owned by Benjamin's brother Andrew and Charles Stone. Andrew, in particular, was notorious for his abuse of Indians who worked for him. In a month's time the party amassed a "bag of gold as long as a man's arm." For their labor each of the Pomo received "a pair of overalls, a hickory shirt, and a red handkerchief." Kelsey and Stone used their profits to buy an additional 1,000 head of cattle, more than doubling their herd. The next year Kelsey, Stone and others organized another expedition, again led by Benjamin, of one hundred Pomo workers. Rather than mine for gold, Benjamin sold provisions intended for the Pomo to other miners and returned to Clear Lake. He left the Pomo to fend for themselves, and most of them succumbed to malaria. No more than ten managed to make their way home. In their grief, and angered by persistent mistreatment at the hands of Andrew Kelsey and Stone, the Pomo killed the two men in late December. These killings provoked a violent reaction by vigilantes and the United States Army. Shortly after discovering the bodies, Benjamin Kelsey organized volunteers to avenge his brother's death. Instead of going to Clear Lake, however, he began an indiscriminate slaughter of Indians who worked on farms and ranches closer to Sonoma. In one night they killed twenty Indians but were, according to Peter Campbell, "prevented by the citizens from utterly annihilating them, and most of them arrested by order of the Government, but no further proceedings initiated." Subsequently, the United States Army took charge. In late January, 1850, troops under Lieutenant J. W. Davidson went to Clear Lake and conducted a hasty investigation. Instead of identifying the Pomo who were involved, Davidson concluded that "all the Indian tribes upon the lake are more or less concerned in this atrocious murder." As a second expedition under Captain Nathaniel Lyon reached Clear Lake on May 11, the Pomo fled to an island in the northern part of the lake. On the 14th, the soldiers attacked a village on the western shore, killing four and capturing a headman. The next day the troops attacked the island and killed between sixty and one hundred Indians. The soldiers proceeded to the Russian River, where Lyon suspected that local villages were harboring refugees from Clear Lake. On the 19th, the troops attacked the Yohaiyake Pomo and killed some 75 to 150. In these forays, none of the soldiers were killed and only two were wounded. To Lyon and his superiors, the deaths of nearly two hundred Indians were justified for the deaths of two white men.[9]

California became a state on September 9, 1850. As a result of this premature entry into the union, lines of authority over Indian affairs became increasingly blurred. Under normal conditions, the federal government was obligated to negotiate treaties that would draw clear lines between Indian country and the United States and determine relations between them. The Northwest Ordinance of 1786 set up a procedure that first required treaties, surveys, and a territorial status before statehood. Until treaties were ratified, any entry into Indian country without consent was illegal. Under terms of the 1834 Trade and Intercourse Act, trespassers were subject to eviction and arrest. Secretary of War, George W. Crawford, concerned with violence in California, acknowledged that, without treaties, miners were violating federal laws that denied access to Indian lands. In a letter to General Persipher F. Smith, Crawford argued that "the necessary control which the United States exercise over all savage tribes in their territory cannot be diminished or exposed to the hazard of diminution by permitting foreigners to enjoy an unrestricted intercourse with them." The state, however, refused to comply with federal control over the Indians. California's constitution did not recognize the property rights of the Indians nor their citizenship as provided in the treaty with Mexico. California did, however, on April 22, 1850, pass "an Act for the Protection of the Indians" that reflected the state's agricultural and ranching interests. This act established a system of indenture and debt peonage for Indians deemed vagrants, immoral, or profligate. Such vagrants could be sold at public auction under the supervision of local mayors or justices of the peace. It allowed the adoption of Indian children, if they were orphans or their parents voluntarily agreed, until they reached the age of majority. As many as four thousand Indian children were compelled to labor under this provision by the time the law was rescinded in 1863, at a time when the United States was consumed by a war over slavery. Many were stolen in the north and sold in southern counties. Thousands of adults were arrested and charged with vagrancy. The state legislature also enacted laws that denied Indians the right to testify against whites in both criminal and civil cases, denied ownership of firearms, and forbid access to public schools. Most tellingly, the state frequently authorized the use of militia to fight Indians. In January, 1851, Governor Peter Burnett predicted that "a war of extermination will continue to be waged between the races until the Indian race becomes extinct." Colonel J. Neely Johnson, commander of the state militia, insisted that a war upon the Indians "would of necessity be one of extermination to many of the tribes." On March 15, 1851, Governor John McDougall, who believed that California was being "ravaged by hordes of savages," declared that 100,000 Indian warriors were fighting whites in the gold regions and pleaded for federal assistance.[10]

In late September, 1850, Congress belatedly authorized treaty negotiations. President Millard Fillmore ordered commissioners Redick McKee, Oliver Wozencraft, and James Barbour to "examine the condition, habits, and circumstances" of the Indians and to make "such treaties and compacts" with them as they deemed necessary. The commissioners soon became aware of how violent the war against the Indians had become and how culpable the whites were. In early March, 1851, they were present when the Mariposa Battalion of volunteers, led by Major James Savage, destroyed many Indian villages, killed many of the Indians, and forcibly relocated others to a site on the Fresno River. Savage, who had married several Indian women, employed over a thousand Indians. For him the war was a way of protecting his livelihood. Wozencraft estimated that Savage's workers had produced some $400,000 to $500,000 in gold for him. The commissioners were appalled by the mistreatment of Indians throughout California. Their perspective, however, was rife with fatalism. McKee concluded, early in 1851, that "the General Government not the people of California have but one alternative in relation to these remnants of once numerous and powerful tribes, viz: extermination or domestication." As a result the commissioners decided on a policy that would segregate Indians from whites by placing them on reservations. From March 9, 1851, to January 7, 1852, the commissioners negotiated eighteen treaties wherein California natives ceded approximately 64,000,000 acres to the United States and reserved 8,516,900 acres in seventeen reservations. Only the treaty signed at Clear Lake did not provide for a reservation. Many of the tribes were not treated with, especially those in the far eastern parts of California and along the coast south of San Francisco. The treaties also had provisions for the relocation and subsistence of the Indians. They promised thousands of pounds of flour, more than one thousand mules and horses, nearly twelve thousand beef cattle, twenty medical doctors, teachers, schools, farmers, and tools. Dr. W. M. Ryerson was contracted to vaccinate Indians against smallpox at $2 apiece. On September 26, 1851, he reported that he had travelled 1,500 miles and billed the government for $13,402. Because of time constraints and the large number of tribes, the commissioners exceeded the $50,000 authorized for negotiation and indebted the United States to a sum of $779,796.79. They defended their efforts as the best way to protect the Indians and bring peace to the gold regions. In a letter to Commissioner of Indian Affairs, Luke Lea on May 14, 1851, Barbour argued that "you will probably think that the amount agreed to be given to these tribes with whom we have treated too great; but when you take into consideration their poverty, the country they surrender, and particularly the expense of a war with them that would necessarily last for years, to say nothing of the gold mines which they give up, I do not think you will conceive that we have given them too much."[11]

The final two treaties were negotiated in San Diego County in early January, 1852, by Commissioner Wozencraft. When he arrived in December, Wozencraft witnessed the last stages of a revolt led by Antonio Garra of the Cupa, whose ancestral homeland was largely subsumed in a ranch owned by John J. Warner. Garra, baptized as a Catholic and reared at Mission San Luis Rey, had become an influential headman among his people after secularization. The revolt was sparked by San Diego County's levy of property taxes upon Christian Indians "owning ranches." The previous year $600 had been paid by Indians. But, in 1851, General Joshua Bean advised the Indians not to pay taxes and wait for the arrival of the treaty commission to resolve the issue. However, the state Attorney General ruled that "there is no doubt that the possessions, real and personal, of Christianized Indians, are taxable." When Garra refused to pay taxes, Sheriff Agoston Haraszthy threatened to confiscate the Indians' cattle. Garra sent messages to all the tribes in the region, but most refused to join any military alliance. On November 21, Garra's forces killed four whites at Agua Caliente and the next day sacked Warner's ranch. Whites succumbed to hysteria and feared a general uprising. State militia and volunteers soon brought the fighting to an end. On December 21, five leaders of the revolt, including Antonio Garra, Jr., were captured. Three days later, they were summarily executed. In early January, Garra himself was turned over to the militia by Juan Antonio, a headman of the Cahuilla who had earlier refused to assist Garra. On January 8, Garra was tried for treason, murder, and robbery. Two days later he was convicted of murder and ordered to be shot. His sentence was carried out three hours later in Old Town, San Diego. Although the revolt began as a refusal to pay taxes, Garra's motives are best explained in a letter he sent to Juan Antonio on December 2. "My will is for all, Indians and whites," he wrote, "since by the wrongs and damages they have done, it is better to end us at once . . . If we lose this war, all will be lost—the world if we gain this war, then it is forever; never will it stop, this war is for a whole life."[12]

As the contents of the treaties leaked out, Californians quickly objected. Many of the ranchers and farmers argued that the treaties would deny them access to Indian labor. John Bidwell, for example, insisted that conditions in California were unique because the Indians were "all among us, around us, with us—hardly a farm house—a kitchen without them." Instead of reservations, he proposed a system of Indian labor supervised by whites. His position was upheld by members of the state legislature. On February 12, 1852, the state Senate Committee on Public Lands opposed reservations because they "would withdraw a large body of Indians who are now semi-civilized, from the locations, which they peaceably occupy under the paternal protection of the old residents of the country." This committee proposed a "system of missions for the Indians," where they would be subsisted and taught to cultivate the soil. Indians who were already working on ranches and farms would not be disturbed since they were "already in the best school of civilization." Other motives were at play. Most whites did not want Indians to control what might be valuable land and resources. On March 13, 1852, the *Los Angeles Star* averred: "To place upon our most fertile soil the most degraded race of Aborigines upon the North American continent, to invest them with the rights of Sovereignty, and teach them that they are to be treated as powerful and independent nations, is planting the seeds of future disaster and ruin. . . ." Congressman James McCorkle shared the paper's views. "Could the treaties have been carried out," he declared, "some of what are now the most populous and prosperous regions of California would have been today peopled by a few undeveloped natives."[13]

On March 3, 1852, Congress created the California Superintendency of Indian Affairs. A day later the President appointed Edward F, Beale as its first superintendent. On July 8, the eighteen treaties were rejected by the United States Senate, despite endorsements by Beale, the Commissioner of Indian Affairs, the Secretary of the Interior, and the President. On December 6, Fillmore lamented this failure to set apart lands for the Indians. In California and Oregon," he stated, "there has been no recognition by the government of the exclusive right of the Indians to any part of the country. They are, therefore, mere tenants at sufferance, and liable to be driven from place to place at the pleasure of the whites." Nonetheless, Fillmore— and his successors— decided not to resume treaty negotiations. After the rejection of the treaties, Beale was ordered to devise a plan for California's Indians. On October 29, 1852, he proposed what he called "military reservations." Indians would be invited to reside on them and their labor would subsist them and the troops stationed there. His plan was endorsed by General Ethan A. Hitchcock, who held that it was "the only one calculated to prevent the extermination of the Indians." A year later, on March 3, Congress passed a law that established no more than five reservations, none of which could be larger than 25,000 acres and none established on lands potentially valuable to whites. The act also provided $250,000 for removal and subsistence of the Indians. The first of these reservations was established in November in the Tejon Pass, a curious choice since the greater need was in the gold regions and this area had already been set aside by Mexican land grants. Beale argued that this site was necessary to keep Indians from cutting off the beef supply to the northern mines. Tejon was the only reservation established by Beale, but he added a farm of 350 acres on the Fresno River. This farm was leased from a local resident and attached administratively to the Tejon Reservation. Commissioner of Indian Affairs George W. Manypenny removed Beale from office on May 29, 1854, for fraud and malfeasance. An act of Congress on July 31, 1854, allowed three more reservations, but these were to be no larger than 5,000 to 10,000 acres. Under its authority Beale's replacement, Thomas J. Henley, established a reservation, Nome Lackee, in Tehama County in September, 1854, and one on the Mendocino Coast in March, 1855. He created another reservation on the lower Klamath River in September, 1856. Henley also created farms on the King's River, the Tule River, and in Round Valley, the first two by leasing land from settlers and the latter in a part of Mendocino County recently occupied by whites.[14]

This system was too flawed and too limited to benefit the Indians. They were reluctant to leave their own homes for the promises of a distant reservation. Many were forcibly taken to the reservations. In 1855, for example, Maidu from Nevada County were taken to the Nome Lackee Reservation, and the next year some of them were relocated to Round Valley. In 1859, large numbers of Paiutes from

Owens Valley were taken to the Tejon. In all, few Indians were gathered on the reservations and farms, and many of them soon left. Those who remained were frequently victimized by white vigilantes and kidnappers of their children. On May 5, 1855, the *Humboldt Times* reported that the price of an Indian child old enough to work ranged from $50 to $250. In 1856, Henley, describing this "infamous practice," said that "hundreds of Indians have been stolen and carried into the settlements and sold; in some instances entire tribes were taken en masse, driven to a convenient point, and such as were suitable for servants, selected from among them, generally the children and young women, while the old men and the infirm were left to starve or make their way back to their mountain homes. . . ." In many cases, he declared, "the fathers and mothers have been brutally killed when they refused assistance to the taking away of their children." The system was riddled with corruption. Investigations by J. Ross Browne of the Treasury Department in 1857 and by Goddard Bailey in 1858 discovered numerous instances of fraud. Bailey's report of November 4 concluded, "at present the reservations are simply government alms-houses, where an inconsiderable number of Indians are insufficiently fed and scantily clothed, at an expense wholly disproportionate to the benefit conferred. There is nothing in the system, as now practiced, looking to the permanent improvement of the Indian. . . ." Commissioner of Indian Affairs A. B. Greenwood forced Henley to resign on April 4, 1859. He was replaced by James Y. McDuffie, whose duty was to administer a policy that had clearly failed the Indians. In September McDuffie submitted a detailed report and inventory that declared all of the reservations, except Klamath, were in a state of debilitation. Greenwood recommended abandonment of the system. In June, 1860, California was divided into two districts, and only $57,000 was appropriated to manage both.[15]

As the reservation system collapsed, the federal government was unable to bring conflict to an end and could not ameliorate the privations suffered by California natives. From 1853 into the 1860s, Indians who escaped removal to the reservations were hunted down with increasing vigor by white vigilantes. In particular, whites sought to avenge losses of livestock by taking Indian lives. Nowhere was this response more brutal than in northeastern Mendocino County. Believing that Yuki and others had killed large numbers of cattle and horses, vigilantes took the offensive in the summer of 1859. In September, Walter S. Jarboe was appointed commander of a state militia unit. He later boasted, as reported in the *San Francisco Bulletin* on February 24, 1860, that he had "fought them twenty-three times, killed 283 warriors, the number of wounded was not known, took 292 prisoners, and sent them to the Reservation." Although Jarboe's group was disbanded, attacks upon the Indians continued. The *Bulletin* on January 21, 1860, pointed out that on December 19, "the settlers turned out, and attacking the enemy succeeded in killing 32 and taking two prisoners." By the time this onslaught sputtered to an end in 1864, the Yuki, who numbered over 12,000 in 1846, had been reduced to a population of less than one hundred. Another example of this violence occurred at Humboldt Bay on February 25, 1860, when whites made a coordinated attack at three locations. Their motive again was the alleged theft of cattle by the local Wiyot people. The *San Francisco Bulletin* reported on March 13 that vigilantes had brutally killed 55 natives on Indian Island, 58 on South Beach, and 40 on the South Fork of the Eel River. Major G. J. Raines, in command at Fort Humboldt, visited Indian Island and saw a "scene of atrocity and horror," involving the death of mostly women and children and committed "without cause or the authority of law." As war continued on the Klamath and Eel Rivers, Colonel Francis Lippitt reported on March 5, 1862, that in this state of things no Indian can ever show his head anywhere without being shot down like a wild beast. The women and children," he asserted, "are considered good game, not only in the mountains but here all around us. . . ."[16]

With the onset of the Civil War, the federal government paid little attention to California Indians and allowed the reservation system to shrivel. By the end of 1862, all four reservations and the farms on the King's and Fresno Rivers had been abandoned. In their stead, a new reservation was created on the Smith River, especially designed to harbor refugees from the disastrous floods on the Klamath in the winter of 1851-1852. Southern California Indians were greatly neglected. They only received a modicum of federal support, there were no reservations for them, and their land rights were largely unrecognized. In his annual report for 1862, Commissioner of Indian Affairs William F. Dole lamented the dispossession of the California Indians from their lands and the failure of the United States to protect them. "Despoiled by irresistible force of the land of their fathers; with no country on earth to which they can migrate; in the midst of a people with whom they cannot assimilate," he concluded, "they have no recognized claims upon the government, and are compelled to become vagabonds—to steal or to starve."

Dole's lament did not tell the whole story. Despite the tremendous toll in lives and the abject failure of the federal government to provide assistance, California Indians slowly adjusted to the tsunami that had engulfed them. Some isolated themselves in the mountains and deserts, but most survived by attaching themselves to farms, ranches, and businesses, working for subsistence or wages. John Bidwell employed fifty two Maidu on his ranch near Chico. In Butte County, as well, J. A. Keefer had twelve Indian men and four women working for him, and R. W. Durham employed twenty one vaqueros, farm workers, and a cook. Indian labor was essential to the growth of the grain industry in the Central Valley and the potato industry in the Bay Area. Indians from Round Valley became famous for their skills with livestock and were widely sought as sheepshearers. Pomo along the Russian River provided labor for hops farms, vineyards, and fruit orchards. Yurok became commercial fishers and many were employed in fish canneries at the mouth of the Klamath. In 1886 John Bomhoff started a cannery at Requa and reserved all the fishing and canning jobs for them. Wintu on the McCloud River worked at a fish hatchery started by Livingston Stone. Indian women took jobs as domestics on farms and ranches, and some moved into Los Angeles or San Francisco to find work. California Indian labor was indispensable until replaced by Chinese, Japanese, Mexican and other emigrant workers. Even so, their employment was subject to the vagaries of the economy and subject to the racism that surrounded them. Because they did not have title, for the most part, to their homes, they were often evicted by state and county officials and forced to relocate. Their working and living conditions reflected a poverty that barely permitted them to survive. From their nadir in the 1890s, California natives began a slow trajectory of demographic and cultural recovery. In 2004, the United States Census Office identified 687,400 Indians living in California, of whom roughly one third were California natives. Nonetheless, the world which California natives once occupied was seriously disrupted by the gold rush and cannot be restored.[17]

Notes

[1]These population numbers for 1769 and 1846 are generally used by students of California Indian history and are based on the work of Sherburne Cook. See his *The Population of California Indians, 1769–1970* (Berkeley: University of California, 1976). His number for 1769, however, is highly problematic since he underestimates the impact of disease in the early contact era. William Preston posits a much larger number in two articles, "Serpent in Eden: Dispersal of Foreign Diseases into Pre-Mission California," *Journal of California and Great Basin Anthropology*, 18, No. 1 (1996), 2–37; and "Portents of Plague from California's Protohistoric Period," *Ethnohistory*, 49, No. 1 (2002), 69–121. A more conservative approach is taken by Lisa Kealhofer, "The Evidence for Demographic Collapse in California," in *Bioarchaeology of Native American Adaptation in the Spanish Borderlands*, eds. Brenda J. Baker and Kealhofer (Gainesville: University Press of Florida, 1996), 56–92. See also Kathleen L. Hull, *Pestilence and Persistence: Yosemite Indian Demography and Culture in Colonial California* (Madison: University of Wisconsin, 2009).

[2]The United States takeover of California and the actions of its first military governors are discussed in many sources. Among the most informative are George Harwood Phillips, *Indians and Intruders in Central California, 1769–1849* (Norman: University of Oklahoma, 1993); Albert L. Hurtado, *Indian Survival on the California Frontier* (New Haven: Yale, 1988); and Hurtado, "Controlling California's Indian Labor Force: Federal Administration of California Indian Affairs During the Mexican War," *Southern California Quarterly*, 61, No. 3 (September, 1979), 217–238. For general overviews of United States policy in California, *see* Jack Forbes, *Native Americans in California and Nevada* (Healdsburgh, CA: Naturegraph Publications, 1969) and Robert Heizer and Alan Almquist, *The Other Californians: Prejudice and Discrimination Under Spain, Mexico, and the United States to 1920* (Berkeley: University of California, 1977).

[3]For information on the effects of the gold rush on California natives, *see* Hurtado, *Indian Survival on the California Frontier*; Hurtado, "Clouded Legacy: California Indians and the Gold Rush," in *Riches for All: The California Gold Rush and the World*, ed. Kenneth Owens (Lincoln: University of Nebraska, 2002), 90–117; James Rawls, "Gold Diggers: Indian Miners in the California Gold Rush," *California Historical Quarterly*, 55 (Spring, 1976), 28–45; and Rawls, *Indians of California: The Changing Image* (Norman: University of Oklahoma, 1976).

[4]These earliest responses by the federal government to conditions in California are analyzed by Hurtado, *Indian Survival on the California Frontier*; Phillips, *Indians and Intruders in Central California*; Phillips, *Indians and Indian Agents: The Origins of the Reservation System in California, 1848-52* (Lincoln: University of Nebraska, 1997); and William Ellison, 'The Federal Indian Policy in California, 1846–1860," *Mississippi Valley Historical Review*, 9 (June, 1922), 37–67.

[5]See the above mentioned works by Hurtado and Rawls. Also, *see* Hurtado, "California Indians and the Workaday West: Labor, Assimilation, and Survival," *California History*, 69, No. 1 (1990), 2–11.

The environmental impact on the gold rush country is discussed by Andrew C. Isenberg, *Mining California: An Ecological History* (New York: Hill and Wang, 2005).

[6]The impact of the gold rush on Southern California Indians is found in numerous sources. See especially George Harwood Phillips, *Vineyards & Vaqueros: Indian Labor and the Economic Expansion of Southern California, 1771–1877* (Norman, OK: Arthur H. Clark, 2010), and Richard Steven Street, *Beasts of the Field: A Narrative History of California Farmworkers, 1769–1913* (Stanford: Stanford University, 2004). See also Michael Magliari, ""Free Soil, Unfree Labor: Cave Johnson Couts and the Binding of Indian Workers in California, 1850–1867," *Pacific Historical Review*, 73 (August, 2004), 349–389; Richard L. Carrico, *Strangers in a Stolen Land: American Indians in San Diego, 1850–1880* (Newcastle, CA: Sierra Oaks, 1987); and Sheldon G. Jackson, *A British Ranchero in Old California: The Life and Times of Henry Dalton and the Rancho Azusa* (Glendale, CA: Arthur H. Clark, 1977). For accounts of events on the Colorado River, *see* David P. Robrock, "Argonauts and Indians: Yuma Crossing, 1849," *Journal of Arizona History*, 32 (Spring, 1991), 21–40; and Edgar C. Smith, "Massacre on the Colorado River," *Overland Journal*, 21 (Spring, 2003), 10–21.

[7]See the works by Isenberg, Hurtado, and Rawls.

[8]The events on the American River are mentioned in many contemporary sources and in the secondary accounts by Hurtado and Rawls. The matter of warfare in Northern California has been the subject of much study in recent years. For example, *see* Brendan Charles Lindsay, "Naturalizing Atrocity: California's Indian Genocide, 1846–1916," Ph.D. dissertation, University of California, Riverside, 2007. The older work by Sherburne Cook, originally published in 1943, remains the starting point, *The Conflict Between the California Indian and White Civilization* (Berkeley: University of California, 1976).

[9]Robert F. Heizer, ed., *Collected Documents on the Causes and Events in the Bloody Island Massacre of 1850* (Berkeley: Archaeological Research Facility, Department of Anthropology, University of California, 1973).

[10] See the works by Hurtado and Phillips. Contemporary documents on California Indians in the 1850s and 1860s have been collected in Robert F. Heizer, ed., *The Destruction of California Indians: A Collection of Documents From the Period 1847 to 1863 In Which Are Described Some of the Things that Happened to Some of the Indians of California* (Santa Barbara: Peregrine Smith, 1974); Heizer, ed., *They Were Only Diggers: A Collection of Articles from California Newspapers, 1851–1866, On Indian and White Relations* (Ramona, CA: Ballena, 1974); and Clifford E. Trafzer and Joel R. Hyer, eds., *Exterminate Them!: Written Accounts of the Murder, Rape, and Enslavement of Native Americans During the California Gold Rush* (East Lansing: Michigan State, 1999).

[11]Much has been written about the treaty negotiations, the eighteen treaties, and their rejection by the United States Senate. Among the most informative are Hurtado, *Indian Survival on the California Frontier* and Phillips, *Indians and Indian Agents*. See also Ray Raphael, *Little White Father: Redick McKee on the California Frontier* (Eureka, CA: Humboldt County Historical Society, 1993); Michelle Stover, "John Bidwell and the Rancho Chico Indian Treaty of 1852: Seduction, Betrayal, and Redemption," *California Territorial Quarterly*, Issue 42 (June, 2000); and George E. Anderson and Robert F. Heizer, "Treaty-making by the Federal Government in California, 1851–52," in *Treaty Making and Treaty Rejection by the Federal Government in California, 1850–1852*, eds., George E. Anderson, William E. Ellison, and Robert F. Heizer (Socorro, NM: Ballena Press, 1978), 1–36. Primary sources may be found in Heizer, ed., *George Gibbs' Journal of Redick McKee's Expedition Through Northern California in 1851* (Berkeley: University of California, 1972), and his *The Eighteen Unratified Treaties of 1851–1852 Between the California Indians and the United States Government* (Berkeley: Archaeological Research Facility, University of California, 1972).

[12]Accounts of the Garra Revolt are found in George Harwood Phillips, *Chiefs and Challengers: Indian Resistance and Cooperation in Southern California* (Berkeley: University of California, 1975) and in Richard Alan Hanks, "'This War Is for a Whole Life': The Culture of Resistance Among Southern California Indians, 1850-1966," Ph.D. dissertation, University of California, Riverside, 2006. Contemporary newspaper accounts are found in Trafzer and Hyer, *Exterminate Them!*, 94–116.

[13]See Hurtado, *Indian Survival on the California Frontier*; Raphael, *Little White Father*; and Phillips, *Indians and Indian Agents.*

[14]See the works by Phillips and Hurtado. The most insightful study of Beale is in Phillips, *"Bringing Them Under Subjection": California's Tejon Indian Reservation and Beyond, 1852-1864* (Lincoln: University of Nebraska, 2004). Other important studies of Beale are Gerald Thompson, *Edward F. Beale and the American West* (Albuquerque: University of New Mexico, 1983); and Carl Briggs and Clyde Francis Trudell, *Quarterdeck and Saddlehorn: The Story of Edward F. Beale, 1822–1893* (Glendale, CA: Arthur H. Clark, 1983).

[15]The collapse of the reservation system is discussed in many sources. The most important studies are the works of Hurtado and Phillips, listed above. See also William B. Secrest, "The Rise and Fall of Thomas J. Henley in California," *The Californians*, 6 No. 6 (1988), 23–29; Michael A. Sievers, "Malfeasance or Indirection? Administration of the California Indian Superintendency's Business Affairs," *Southern California Quarterly*, 56 (September, 1974), 273–294; and Richard Dillon, *J. Ross Browne, Confidential Agent in Old California* (Norman: University of Oklahoma, 1965). Primary sources attesting to the corruption of the California Superintendency may be found in Lina Ferguson Browne, ed., *J. Ross Browne: His Letters, Journals, and Writings* (Albuquerque: University of New Mexico, 1969).

[16]The study of the Yuki and Round Valley has received considerable attention in recent years. Among these are William J. Bauer, Jr., *We Were All Like Migrant Workers Here: Work, Community, and Memory on California's Round Valley Reservation, 1850–1941* (Chapel Hill: University of North Carolina, 2009); Bauer, "'We Were All Migrant Workers Here': Round Valley Indian Labor in Northern California, 1850–1929," *Western Historical Quarterly*, 37 (Spring, 2006), 43-63; Benjamin Madley, "California's Yuki Indians: Defining Genocide in Native American History," *Western Historical Quarterly*, 39 (Autumn, 2008), 303–332; Jason Charles Newman, "'There Will Come a Day When White Men Will Not Rule Us': The Round Valley Indian Tribe and Federal Indian Policy, 1856–1934," Ph.D. dissertation, University of California, Davis, 2004); Virginia Miller, *Ukomn'm: The Yuki Indians of Northern California* (Socorro, NM: Ballena Press, 1979); Linda Pitelka, "Mendocino: Race Relations in a Northern California County," Ph.D. dissertation, University of Massachusetts, Amherst, 1994; Lynwood Carranco and Estle Beard, *Genocide and Vendetta: The Round Valley Wars of Northern California* (Norman: University of Oklahoma, 1981); and William B. Secrest, "Jarboe's War," *The Californians*, 6 No. 6 (1988), 16–22.

[17]Following the example of Hurtado's *Indian Survival on the California Frontier*, recent scholarship on California natives has focused on their survival and adaptation to the cultures that invaded their homelands. The best examples of such scholarship are Bauer, *We Were All Like Migrant Workers Here* and Joel Hyer, *"We Are Not Savages": Native Americans in Southern California and the Pala Reservation, 1840–1920* (East Lansing: Michigan State University, 2001).

Iu Mien – We the People

Fahm Khouan Saelee and Muey Ion Saetern

When people ask what ethnicity we are, we say, "I am Iu Mien". Since most people are unfamiliar with the name, they then ask who are the Iu Mien and where are we from? Our response is "we do not have a country of our own but we originate from China." Often times this response is enough to satisfy their curiosity. However, for many Iu Mien Americans, this answer does not suffice.

The Iu Mien immigrated to the United States over 30 years ago. There are limited resources available to the public about Iu Mien people and our culture. As we explore our identities, we begin to realize that as Iu Mien Americans, we are the ones who need to create and provide these resources. This article examines Iu Mien history, statistical data regarding the Iu Mien, and includes personal experiences from two Iu Mien Americans, Farm Khouan Saelee and Muey Ion Saetern.

Iu Mien History and Background

The Iu Mien are one of "the smallest major refugee groups in the U.S. and the least known in the refugee literature" (Macdonald, 1997, p. 3). Historically, the Han Chinese used the term "Man" (蛮) to identify various groups of southern ethnic minorities, including the Iu Mien. "Man" is derived from the ancient Chinese word for "barbarian" (Fortune, 1939; Eberhard, 1982; Wiens, 1967). In modern China, the Iu Mien are more commonly known as "Yao" (瑶). "Yao" is a government classification given to ethnic minority groups in China. In the United States as well as other parts of the Western world, we call ourselves Iu Mien.

Due to the Sinocentric biases of the mostly Chinese records, the early history of the Iu Mien is obscure and unclear. There is no reliable history of the Iu Mien before the tenth century A.D. (Macdonald, 1997, p. 70). This is because – before this time – the Han did not distinguish among different ethnic minorities. They labeled all Southern China ethnic minorities "Man". "Although many modern Western and Chinese scholars have tried to unravel the ethnohistory of the Yao" from that of the "Man," their conclusions are mostly based upon assumptions and theories, which can never be fully proved" (Macdonald, 1997, p. 70).

Origin of Iu Mien Surnames

"The Iu Mien have various myths concerning the origin of the world, of the gods, of the Iu Mien, and other humans." Influences from the highland cultures and Han Chinese culture have contributed to the various versions that exist (Macdonald, 1997, p. 75).

A popular myth alludes that the Iu Mien's 12 surnames are derived from the sons and daughters of Bienh Hungh, the Iu Mien totemic ancestor. The first six clans descend from the six sons of Bienh Hungh. The surnames are: Saephan (Bienh), Saelaw (Lorh), Saelee (Leiz), Saechou (Zuagv), Saetern (Dangc), and Saeyang (Yangh). The other six clans descend from the six daughters of Baeng Hung, which include Saechao (Zeuz), Saelio (Lio), Saefong (Bungz), Saezaanh (Zaanh), Saechin (Chin), and Saeseao (Siaau). Moreover, there are two additional clans, Saetong (Dorngh) and Saepao (Bao), which are derived from second sons-in-law of Bienh Hungh's daughters.

Iu Mien men served as U.S. allies during the Vietnam War. When U.S. forces withdrew from Southeast Asia, the Iu Mien were left at the mercy of the communists in Laos. To avoid persecution, the Iu Mien fled to refugee camps in Thailand. Thai authorities added "Sae" as the prefix to all Iu Mien last names. Today it is more difficult to distinguish Iu Mien from other ethnicities solely based on their surnames since many Iu Mien Americans are changing their last names by dropping the prefix "Sae".

Iu Mien Migration to Southeast Asia

Many Iu Mien migrated across national boundaries long ago. Records indicate that the first southward migration from China to Vietnam occurred during the 17th and 18th centuries. Throughout the late 19th and early 20th centuries, the Iu Mien migrated into Laos, Burma, and Thailand. Many believe these migrations were due to Han encroachments, Yao's refusal to pay additional taxes, and the search for fertile land among other reasons (Saeteurn).

A large number of Iu Mien families settled in the mountains of northern and central Laos. Here, the Iu Mien practiced slash and burn agriculture, which involves cutting down trees and brush, burning the area to clear it, and then planting. They grew rice and other crops such as squash, beans, and poppies. The men crafted beautiful silver jewelry and the women embroidered intricate designs on clothing and accessories (Gogol, 1996, p. 20).

The simple and serene lives of the Iu Mien were abruptly interrupted by a civil war. From 1945 to 1954, the French struggled to re-establish control over Vietnam, Laos, and Cambodia. In 1958, the Central Intelligence Agency (CIA) began heavy recruitment among the hill tribes in order to counteract the Chinese, Vietnamese, and Laotian communists (Gross). By early 1960s, a full-fledged civil war broke out in Laos. This war in Laos "quickly became part of a larger regional conflict known in the United States as the Vietnam War. Supported by the United States, the Royal Laotian government opposed Communist forces. An anti-Royalist group in Laos known as the Pathet Lao received military aid from North Vietnam, a neighboring Communist country" (Gogol, 1996, p. 20).

The Vietnam War is known by many Iu Mien as the "Secret War". During this war "Iu Mien men were recruited as anti-guerrilla forces by the CIA" (Macdonald, 1997, p. 88). In the documentary, Voices from the Mountains, Eric Crystal stated, "the United States dropped more conventional bombs in Laos that has ever been dropped in any country in the history of warfare, more than were dropped in Japan in World War II" (Saeliew, 2007). Many hill tribes including the Iu Mien fought a bloody secret war for the United States. Led by Generals Chow Mai Saechao, Chow Lah Saechao, and Vern Chien Saechao, Iu Mien men and teenage boys fought bravely and suffered many casualties.

In 1975, Pathet Lao forces won the war in Laos. Because the Iu Mien fought along side the United States, they became targets for persecution. "Over 70% of the Iu Mien in Laos were forced to leave, abandoning their livelihood and walking two to three months to settle in large camps where they survived on the limited supplies provided by the American army" (Moore-Howard, 1989, p. 75.) To escape danger, many families and even entire villages began to flee Laos. The majority of the Iu Mien population fled to Thailand resettling in refugee camps. "After several years, the United States returned to fulfill their contract made with the ethnic minorities. They offered a refugee rescue program, which gave the Iu Mien and other groups the choice to resettle in the United States" (Saeteurn). U.S. residents aided by sponsoring Iu Mien and other hill tribe families from the refugee camps. In 1976, the first Iu Mien families reached the United States settling in Portland, Oregon.

Iu Mien Migration to United States

The first significant group of Iu Mien arrived in the United States during the late 1970s. "As their numbers grew in the 1980s, the majority of the Iu Mien settled in California, Oregon, and Washington. A smaller number settled in Alabama, North Carolina, Illinois, Minnesota, Kansas, Texas, and Oklahoma. Between 1980 to 1982, approximately seven families settled in Sacramento, California" (Saechao, 1992).

Although the Iu Mien community grew significantly since their first arrival, the U.S. Census fails to recognize them as a separate ethnic group. The U.S. government includes the Iu Mien in the subgroups, "Laotian" and "Other Asian." One main reason why the Iu Mien are not recognized as an independent group is due to the fact that the Iu Mien community has yet to establish a consensus on one particular spelling of Iu Mien. The spelling of Iu Mien include: Iu Mien, Iu-Mien, Iu Mienh, Iu-Mienh, Yiu Mienh, Mienh and Mien. Since the Iu Mien remain aggregated under the "Laotian" and "Other Asian" categories, exact numbers for the Iu Mien population are unknown. Estimates vary from as little as 30,000 to as much as 150,000 Iu Mien residing in the United States.

Muey Ion Saetern's Personal Experiences

The 1.5 generation are "immigrants who come at a young age who retain their ability to speak, if not always read and write the ancestral language as well as Asian values and norms" (Chan, 2006, pg. xiv). Iu Mien Americans who belong to this generation must retain the Iu Mien culture while at the same time learn to embrace the mainstream American society. Growing up as an Iu Mien American, Muey Ion Saetern faced many challenges. A major challenge for her today is teaching her own children Mien. The following is an example of how quickly the Iu Mien language and culture can disappear in just one generation.

An eight-year-boy stands in front of his class and begins to share with his peers who he is. "My name is Kai Saetern. I am Iu Mien." Up to this moment, his classmates thought Kai was Chinese. Kai himself believed he was Chinese.

Earlier that week, my son Kai approached me with a class project. He asked, "Mommy can you help me? I have to tell my friends in my class who I am." My response was, "You're Iu Mien". He responded, "No, I'm Chinese". Kai did not want to tell his classmates he was Iu Mien.

My name is Muey Ion Saetern. I was born in Thailand but raised in the United States. As an Iu Mien American, I strongly believe in maintaining a connection to our Iu Mien heritage. In our current community, there is a huge disconnect between the older and younger generations. This disconnect comes from the burgeoning language barrier among these two generations. I believe the only way to bridge this gap is through communication yet so many of the Iu Mien youth today struggle to speak and understand Mien. This is the community's biggest obstacle to overcome as we try to preserve our culture.

My family and I relocated to the United States in the summer of 1988 with the help of organizations such as the International Rescue Committee (IRC). IRC is a leading non-sectarian, non-governmental international relief and humanitarian aid organization based in the United States, with operations in over 40 countries (International Rescue Committee, 2011). I grew up speaking Mien and learned to speak, read and write English as I assimilated into the American culture. As I learned English in the public school system – at home – I communicated with my parents and older relatives solely in Mien. Because of this, I remain bilingual today. Now that I have children of my own, I encourage them to speak Mien and embrace their culture though with much difficulty and little success. I can only hope as my children learn more about their heritage, they are interested and motivated to continue Iu Mien traditions and keep our unique culture alive.

Farm Khouan Saelee's Personal Experiences

I, Farm Khouan Saelee was born in Ban Vinai refugee camp located in Loei, Thailand. On June 26, 1988, at the age of two, my family and I migrated to the United States. My parents, Wern Khouan Lee and Khae Luang Saelee, raised their children with traditional Iu Mien values and norms. They could only communicate to their children in Mien. My parents expect my siblings and I to understand, participate, and respect Iu Mien traditions. We retain the ability to speak Mien today.

While studying abroad at Peking University (北京大学) in Beijing, China from August 2006 to July 2007 I encountered many people who asked what nationality I am. Very few thought I was Chinese, most assumed I was Korean or Japanese. When I told them I was American, some were immediately surprised and asked how that could be since I have the black hair, a petite stature, and the face of someone from the East, not the West. If I told them I was Thai, I would be lying. Sure, I was born in Thailand, but I left the country at age two and never learned the language or culture. I couldn't tell them I was Chinese. I knew my ancestors descended from China, but how long ago and exactly from where, I wasn't sure. I realized my uncertainty about my identity was why I was in China. I wanted to explore who I am and research where I came from.

After a few months in China, I began to seek out Iu Mien living in China. I contacted an Iu Mien woman, Li Shaomei, a professor at the Central University for Nationalities (CUN) (中央民族大学). I was also fortunate enough to meet her father-in-law, Pan Cheng Qian, a retired Associate Professor of CUN. To my surprise, Mien literacy classes are offered at this university. I also discovered the Museum for Nationalities of CUN. This museum, created in 1951, is a professional museum that collects, displays, and researches the culture relics of 56 ethnic groups in China (Beijing). I was both astonished and excited that I was surrounded by an abundance of resources that could help me find answers I have been searching for about my identity. I realized this trip would be the first of many to China. My experience in China was a huge contribution to my knowledge about the Iu Mien. My discoveries there have lead to my aspirations of researching even more about my people, the Iu Mien.

Survey on Iu Mien Language conducted by Farm Khouan Saelee in 2007

When the Iu Mien fled China, they brought with them "an Iu Mien spoken dialect, which had no written characters, and Mandarin, which was both spoken and written by a select, male, educated elite" (Egert, 2009, pg. 5). Today the Iu Mien language, Mien, has a form of Romanized transliteration that was developed in the late 20th century. Mandarin survives among the Iu Mien only as written characters of texts for ceremonies, which can be interpreted by shamans (Egert, 2009, pg. 5).

In November 2007, shortly after returning from China, I surveyed 135 Iu Mien currently living in California. The results indicate that the majority of Iu Mien Americans cannot speak Mien. Eighty-six percent of those surveyed have lived in the U.S. for less than 25 years. Fourteen percent have been in the U.S. for over 25 years. The data shows half are fluent in Mien, and 92 percent are fluent in English. Eighty-two percent feel most comfortable speaking English, while only 18 percent indicate that they feel most comfortable speaking in Mien. Within just a few decades, the Iu Mien language is on the brink of extinction in California. The relevance of learning Mien has been replaced by the need to learn English. Many Iu Mien, especially the 1.5, 2nd and 3rd generation Iu Mien Americans are losing their ancestral language despite the fact that 99 percent of first generation Iu Mien Americans are fluent in Mien.

As alarming as these survey results are, Iu Mien Americans show an interest in preserving their language. Many are not fluent in Mien, but are interested in learning the language. The survey asks, "If Mien language courses are offered at a community college, a university, or a place nearby you, will you consider taking a course?" Seventy one percent responded yes. Twenty-two percent were unsure and only seven percent responded no. Ninety-seven percent believe it is important for Iu Mien people to be able to speak their ethnic language. One particular individual stated, "Language is one of the most critical factors for ethnic association. Without our language, we essentially would lose part of our identity. Further, our future generations need to be able to speak Mien to prevent our own extinction. Once a language is extinct, it is impossible to revive it as we have seen with many other extinct languages." He also feels it is important for Iu Mien to read and write Mien. It is important for the Iu Mien to learn the Romanized script "because of the nature of societal changes that necessitate us to have our language in a written form to make it useful. Furthermore, that would be one way of trying to increase usage and perhaps preserve what is left of our language." The overall consensus is it is important to take measures in preserving the Mien language. The Iu Mien have concerns about the availability of resources for them to maintain and learn the language. Ninety-one percent of the Iu Mien surveyed don't think there are enough learning materials available.

Iu Mien continue to struggle to maintain our community and culture in the United States. It is our responsibility as Iu Mien and Iu Mien Americans to preserve our identity. We need to contribute to the resources by doing academic research and oral history projects. Websites such as immien.com, iumien.com, and imanc.org have contributed to the preservation of our Iu Mien heritage. With our combined efforts, future Iu Mien Americans can more accurately define who we are. Until then, there are more questions to be explored and more research to be done.

References

Beijing Museum for Nationalities of Central University for Nationalities, Beijing Museums - Beijing China Travel Agency. (n.d.). *Beijing Tours, Beijing Tour, Beijing China Tours - Beijing Travel Agency and China Tour Operator*. Retrieved May 18, 2011, from http://www.tour-beijing.com/museums_guide/museum_for_Nationalities _of_central_university_for_nationalities.php

Chan, S. (2006). *The Vietnamese American 1.5 generation: stories of war, revolution, flight, and new beginnings*. Philadelphia, PA: Temple University Press.

Cushman, R. D. (1970). *Rebel haunts and lotus huts: problems in the ethnohistory of the Yao*. Unpublished Ph.D. dissertation, Cornell University.

Eberhard, W. (1982). *China's Minorities: Yesterday and Today*. Belmont, CA: Wedsworth Publishing Co.

Egert, N. (2009). A place where the wind blows: Mien women plant new roots at Oakland's original rancho: a photographic. Oakland, Calif.: Vinapa Foundation.

Fortune, R. (1939). *Yao society: a study of a group of primitives in China*. Canton [China: Department of Sociology, Lingnan University.

Gogol, S. (1996). *A Mien family*. Minneapolis: Lerner Publications Co.

Gross, M. (n.d.). Wildflowers Institute - Iu Mien Community Portrait. *Wildflowers Institute HomePage*. Retrieved May 18, 2011, from http://www.wildflowers. org/community/IuMien/portrait2.shtml

International Rescue Committee. (2011). International Rescue Committee: definition. Retrieved May 18, 2011, from http://www.rescue.org/

MacDonald, J. L. (1997). *Transnational aspects of Iu-Mien refugee identity*. New York: Garland Pub.

Moore-Howard, P. (1989). *The Iu Mien: tradition and change*. Sacramento, CA: Patricia Moore-Howard.

Saechao, S. (1992). *The Iu Mien community*. Sacramento, CA: Asian Community Center of Sacramento Valley, Inc.

Saeliew, J. (n.d.). Voices From The Mountain by Jai Saeliew | IMMIEN - Connecting Iu Mien with the world. IMMIEN.com - Connecting Iu Mien people with the world. Retrieved May 18, 2011, from http://www.immien.com/entertainment/arts-and-entertainment/videos/voices-from-the-mountain-by-jai-saeliew-2/

Saeteurn, F. F. (n.d.). United Iu-Mien Community, Inc. - Iu-Mien History. *United Iu-Mien Community, Inc*. Retrieved May 18, 2011, from http://www.unitediumien. org/MienHistory.php

Sarayote. (n.d.). What's Iu-Mien? . *Angelfire: Welcome to Angelfire*. Retrieved May 18, 2011, from http://www.angelfire.com/ca6/tomswebpage/Mien.html

Wiens, H. J. (1967). *Han Chinese expansion in South China*, Hamden, Conn.: Shoe String Press.

Ethnic Diversity: Its Historical and Constitutional Roots

Cruz Reynoso

I want to talk with you about the law and ethnic diversity in our country. Since the birth of our nation, we Americans have been in an evolutionary process of defining who we are as Americans, what the American community is, and who belongs to it. In that regard, the American experience has been a great historical experiment, successful sometimes, but not successful other times. The experience we have had as a people is intertwined with out Constitution and the principles that the Constitution has established. The basic question we have to ask ourselves is the following: How can we as a people, or as peoples of diverse religions, races and ethnicities live together and prosper together?

Before the birth of our nation, and sadly it continues today, some of the great wars in this world have come about due to the hatred toward those who are different—by religion, race or ethnicity. We see what is happening in the former Soviet Union, Eastern Europe, the Middle East, Africa and even such places as South America. These hatreds are live issues, traumatic issues that have brought a great deal of suffering to the human family. When we as Americans came together to form our nation, I think we asked the same basic question: Can we have a nation, can we have a people, who can live together and consider themselves as one, and yet be as different as the peoples of this world?

One of America's experiments was in religion. Even though the Constitution declares that the federal government shall not establish religion, we understood early that the essence of that constitutional mandate was a concern about our right, as individual Americans, to practice our own religion. Those who penned the Constitution had in mind the great wars of Europe and the Middle East which had killed so many and had brought so much suffering. So they concluded that the new country had to be one in which folk of different religions could live together. The living together by those who practice different religions has not been all that easy. Books have been written about the "other Americans," Americans who were not of European,

From *Villanova Law Review,* 1992 by Cruz Reynoso. Copyright © 1992 Villanova Law Review. Reprinted by permission of the Law Review.

Protestant ancestry. Fred Hart, former Dean of the University of New Mexico, and still a professor there, tells that his dad remembers when they were growing up in Boston. Signs in some establishments that hired workers would read something like, "Help wanted: Irish and Dogs need not apply." That reaction of prejudice and hatred by some of the owners of those plants was based on religion as well as ethnicity. Indeed, it was not until John Kennedy's presidential campaign that the nation said, "We have matured enough that we can see a Catholic in the White House." That is a long time—from the inception of our country until 1960.

We have succeeded in creating an American culture wherein folk of different religions can live together and consider themselves one people. We appear to have reached a relatively satisfactory solution, at least for a while, because the issue of religion does not come up all the time. There is a fellow you may have heard of by the name Pat Buchanan. He is described by some as a conservative, a right winger, a racist, and by others as a great American. Never is he described as "the Catholic candidate." Yet he is a Catholic, and he often cites his Catholicism to reject the accusation that he is a racist. To me, it is an evolution in the public life of our country that we have a person running for president whose Catholicism hardly gets mentioned.

Others have also suffered. Non-Christians, particularly Jewish people, as well as Hindus and Native Americans have suffered from exclusion. A few years ago, the Alaska Supreme Court issued, I thought, a moving opinion about the rights of a Native American to kill a moose because it was part of the religion of that particular tribe.[1] The Alaska Supreme Court was balancing the right of the state to protect the environment with the right of that particular tribe to exercise its own religion, and, in a sensitive opinion, tried to balance those interests. Thus, the historic process continues.

Issues of religion will always be with us, because who we are religiously is so important to each of us. Yet, we have made so much progress. That is our success story. In America we have been able to live together and consider ourselves as one people, though a people of great religious diversity.

The next area in which we as a nation have worked so hard has been that of race, particularly pertaining to African-Americans. We succeeded so poorly that we experienced here what had happened in other countries—a great war, a great civil war. A larger percentage of Americans were killed and maimed during that war than any other war, over something called race. The Civil War is just a reminder of how important and divisive issues of diversity can be. But from the suffering of this nation in that great war, which pitted brother against brother and sister against sister, came an important amendment to the Constitution—the Fourteenth Amendment. Some post-Civil War amendments, like the Thirteenth, are easily understood. The more difficult Fourteenth Amendment provided the source for a redefinition of who we are as Americans. The constitutional notions of equality and due process found within the pre-Civil War Fifth Amendment were incorporated into the post-Civil War amendments. With the Fourteenth Amendment our country was saying, "We meant what we said in the original Ten Amendments." We redefined ourselves as a people to include African-Americans, including former slaves. While many African-Americans had lived as freed men and women before the Civil War we had not previously succeeded in dealing with the issue of race.

You recall that in the Lincoln-Douglas debates Abraham Lincoln argued that the Constitution set forth the ideal of equality. Those who signed the Constitution understood that we would not meet that ideal immediately, but that we as Americans had a duty to work day in and day out to get the reality of our country a little bit closer to that ideal. To me, and this may sound strange to you, we reached a new public understanding of the reality that we as Americans are of many races, when we built the Vietnam Veterans Memorial in Washington, D.C., and included a black soldier among the soldiers represented. I think we recognized publicly that all races have sacrificed to make this nation great.

Native Americans, like African-Americans, have suffered because of race. Our country originally dealt with Native Americans through the War Department. We viewed Native Americans as the enemy—they were to be killed or captured. Since then American history has evolved to a better understanding between the Indian and non-Indian.

In recent years, the issue of ethnicity and language has come into the forefront. Ethnicity and language, like religion and race, define us. Are we as Americans, or should we be, a people of one language and one ethnicity? In many states there is what is called the English-only movement. A friend of mine from New England, with whom I have served on several committees of the American Bar Association, came up to me one day and said, "Cruz, I know an elderly couple, friends of mine, who went from New England to Florida, and when they came back they said that they were taken aback. They found portions of Miami where everybody spoke Spanish. Only when the couple explained that they did not speak Spanish was English spoken." My friend said, "Cruz, we must do something about this; we must have one language for all of us." I responded: "You are absolutely right. When are you learning Spanish?"

We have struggled with the issue of language and ethnicity throughout our national life. I do not think that we have yet decided what our national ideal is in that regard. My own view is that we Americans are now, and have historically always been, a people of many languages and many ethnic groups. I mentioned the Native Americans, who were here before the European-Americans, and who enjoyed great civilizations and who created marvelous works of art. Somehow we look at the Native Americans of Mexico and the Latin Americans as being those who created great civilizations and great art. The reality is that Native Americans who have lived in what we now call the United States also had that great creativity. We can look to the great irrigation system constructed in New Mexico, or we can look to the political organization of the Navajo nation. Other ethnic groups, such as the Spanish-speaking, came to this land over a hundred years before the English-speaking. Travel in New Orleans or Florida, certainly in Puerto Rico and the Southwest, demonstrates their influence. Sante Fe, New Mexico claims to be the longest standing city that has been a seat of government in what is now the United States. It goes back to the mid-sixteenth century. So folk of different languages and different ethnics groups have been here for a long time.

In the seventeenth century, when the English-speaking Europeans came to the eastern shores of the United States, so did those who spoke French and German and other languages. Indeed, in his autobiography, Benjamin Franklin spoke about how the United States Constitution was translated into the German language during the political debates about whether or not the Constitution should be approved by the people of this country. It seems to me that we have always recognized the importance of people who are of different ethnic groups and tongues.

Take a look at the history of my own state of California. While I spent four years in New Mexico, and I tell folks that I consider myself part manito (a New Mexican is a manito), I was born in California. First came the Native Americans, then the Mexicans and Spaniards who came and settled that land well before the Americans got there. Then came groups from South America, particularly the Chilean community in San Francisco, in large parts because they were fishermen and traders who sailed up and down the Pacific coast. In the middle of the last century, the Americans came to California, and about the same time came many Chinese, followed by Japanese and Filipinos. Currently we have great influxes of people from Southeast Asia and Central America. In Los Angeles, I see whole communities change in a matter of few years. I used to stay in a certain part of Los Angeles which a few years ago was mostly Mexican-American (Chicano) and Anglo-Americans. Now it is mostly Central Americans.

We have seen these great historical changes in our country. It seems to me that we have the political foundation and the ideals of our Constitution to help us meet those realities. Those ideals will help us craft a country in which we consider ourselves as one people, while continuing to enjoy the strength which comes from different religions, races, languages and ethnicities.

We start with basics. The Constitution states that all of us, all the "persons" in this country, enjoy constitutional protections; it is not "citizens," the "English-speaking" or the "Spanish-speaking," who are protected, but all of us as "persons." The United States Supreme Court had occasion to deal with the issue of ethnicity and language in a case that came before it in 1923. You may have read about it in your Constitutional Law classes, *Meyer v. Nebraska*.[2] You may remember that it is a case that dealt with a state statute enacted around 1919 during the First World War.[3] There was a strong anti-German feeling during that time in America. I recall older persons I knew, who were adults during that war, telling me that in their schools, German books and music were destroyed. If they were German, they could not be good. At the time, the Nebraska legislature enacted a criminal statute that prohibited the teaching of German to youngsters before they had graduated from the eighth grade.[4] There was a parochial school in Nebraska called the Zion Parochial School where youngsters were taught in English and in German.[5]

A young teacher by the name of Meyer, despite the law, continued to teach in German. He was arrested and convicted.[6] Here is what the statute said:

> No person individually or as a teacher, shall, in any private, denominational, parochial or public school, teach any subject to any person in any language other than the English language. . . . Languages, other than the English language, may be taught as languages only after a pupil shall have attained and successfully passed the eighth grade as evidenced by a certificate of graduation issued by the county superintendent of the county in which the child resides.[7]

Meyer appealed his conviction, but the courts in Nebraska upheld the constitutionality of the statute.[8] Interestingly, court decisions in Nebraska excluded the "dead languages,"—Latin, Greek and Hebrew—from this statute.[9] The legislature, according to the state supreme court, did not mean that students could not study dead languages, only that they could not study certain "live" languages.[10] Eventually the case reached the United States Supreme Court, and the Court looked at the facts and asked itself whether the statute could be constitutional. The Court tried to define what "liberty" meant under the Fourteenth Amendment.[11]

Although the Justices did not talk about it, I think they were also concerned about the Ninth Amendment. When the first Ten Amendments were introduced, an important political debate took place regarding the question of whether those protections that we receive from the first ten amendments were exclusive. In many states, many people said, "No, we want to make clear that those protections are by way of description, for there are many other rights that we have as Americans that government does not have the right to take away." That conclusion was echoed in the *Meyer* case:

> While this Court has not attempted to define with exactness the liberty thus guaranteed [by the Fourteenth Amendment], the term has received much consideration and some of the included things have been definitely stated. Without a doubt, it denotes not merely freedom from bodily restraint but also the right of the individual to contract, to engage in any of the common occupations of life, to acquire useful knowledge, to marry, to establish a home and bring up children, to worship God according to the dictates of his own conscience, and generally to enjoy those privileges long recognized at common law as essential to the orderly pursuit of happiness by free men.[12]

Notice that none of these protections mentioned are found in the Constitution. The Court was saying that surely the right to marry, the right to have children, the right to bring up your family have to be so fundamental that Congress and the states cannot monkey around, if you will, with those rights. Those unstated rights include the right to worship God according to the dictates of a person's own conscience, and generally to enjoy those privileges long recognized at common law as essential to the orderly pursuit of happiness by free men and women. The Court then went on to discuss the importance of language to an individual.[13] The Court ruled that the Nebraska statute was unconstitutional, and that the state had to have an overwhelmingly important reason to prohibit a youngster from learning German, or a teacher from teaching German.[14] The state, the Court wrote, clearly may go very far in order to improve the quality of its citizens, physically, mentally and morally.[15] The individual, however, has certain fundamental rights which must be respected and that includes the right of languages.[16] It seems to me that such a right includes the right of ethnicity. The right to one's own language was recognized as fundamental within our constitution.

The Court had another occasion to look at the issue of ethnicity in a case from the state of California. We produce a great deal of constitutional law from the state of California. A case came up in 1947, if I remember correctly, called *Oyama v. California*.[17] California had passed a statute that prohibited aliens from owning land in California.[18] The breadth of the statute had been narrowed by court decisions; by the 1940s the statute had been interpreted to mean that Japanese could not own land in California. A Japanese immigrant had bought and paid for some land and then put the title in the name of his son, so the son was the legal owner.[19] The father then filed in court to become the guardian, and, in fact, was the child's actual guardian.[20] The statute declared that if a person, who could not legally become a citizen, paid for the land, it would be presumed that such payment was an effort to get around the statute.[21] In that event, the land would escheat to the state.[22] Interestingly, it was the Attorney General of California who brought the action against Mr. Oyama. The only person who testified was the person in charge of the land.[23] The Oyamas did not testify because the hearing took place during the Second World War, when the Oyamas were confined in a concentration camp.[24]

The trial court decided against the Oyamas, and the case was appealed in the California courts.[25] The courts found that the father had paid for the land, and that the Oyamas were clearly trying to get around the statute, and, therefore, the land properly escheated to the state.[26]

The United States Supreme Court looked at the case from the point of view of the little boy, Fred Oyama, and said, "Wait a minute. We are looking at the rights of a citizen, Fred Oyama."[27] Another contemporaneous statute in California permitted parents to make a gift of land to a child by paying for the land.[28] The Court underscored that an American citizen, the child, was being treated differently because of who his parents were.[29] This case presented a conflict between a state's right to formulate a policy in land holding within its boundaries and the right of American citizens to own land anywhere in the United States.[30] The Court concluded that when these two rights clash, the rights of a citizen may not be subordinated merely because of his father's country of origin (that is, the ethnicity of the citizen).[31]

So we start to see a constitutional pattern which protects persons from discrimination on the basis of ethnicity. And I just want to remind us that the Constitution so often deals in the negative, that is, "You can't do A, B, and C," but what it really means is that people have certain rights. While the Court ruled that the Constitution provided protection from discrimination, it really was defining the right of Americans to their own language and ethnicity.

When I was a youngster in Orange County, California, we still had segregated schools. For several years I was sent to a public grammar school referred to as "The Mexican School." There were other schools called "The American Schools." I was born in the then-little town of Brea; Orange County was rural in those pre-Disneyland days. I had gone to school in Brea for a couple years and then my family moved to the nearby community of La Habra. There were a lot of folks in La Habra of Mexican ancestry. When September came, we looked for a school and found a place that looked like a school we were used too—it was built with bricks, it was two stories and had a playground in the back. My brothers and I went there to sign up, and the school officials said, "No, you don't go to this school, you go to another, the Wilson School." So we went to Wilson School. We noticed that all the youngsters there were Latinos and Chicanos, and we asked why we were being sent to this school. We were told that we were being sent to this school to learn English. Since my brothers and I already knew English, we were a little bit suspicious that maybe that was not the reason. After a few months a black family with two youngsters moved into our barrio. They did not speak a word of Spanish; they only spoke English. Nonetheless, they were sent to our school. So we got doubly suspicious. Incidentally, educationally-speaking, it was not a lost cause at all. You may have heard of the "immersion system" of learning a language other than your own; those black youngsters were speaking Spanish as well as we in about six months. Meanwhile, we noticed that there were Anglo-American families whose houses literally abutted on Wilson School, and they were being sent to distant schools. After a while we recognized that, in fact, ours was a segregated school.

A few years after I "graduated" from Wilson (grades kindergarten through sixth), the school was integrated. A lawsuit was filed challenging the segregation of Mexican-American school children in a nearby school district. A federal judge ruled that under California law, school segregation was unlawful.

Related issues reached the United States Supreme Court. It was in a different context that the case of *Hernandez v. Texas*[32] came before the high Court in 1954. A Texan who was Mexican-American had been convicted of murder and appealed.[33] He was unhappy that there had been no Latinos, Chicanos or Mexican-Americans on the jury.[34] The county in Texas where he was tried was fourteen percent Mexican-American, yet for twenty-five years there had not been one Latino on a jury commission, a grand jury or a petit jury.[35] During that time apparently 6,000 persons had been called to serve on one of those commissions or juries and not one had a Spanish surname.[36] Indeed, the Court also pointed out that there were some suspicious matters in that community. In the courthouse, there were two bathrooms, one unmarked, and the other with a sign that read "Colored Men" and then below it "Hombres Aqui" (Men Here). That made the Court a little bit suspicious.[37] There was at least one restaurant in town, the Court said, that had a sign in front that read, "No Mexicans Served." Until very recently the public schools had been segregated.[38] There was extensive testimony in the record by the authorities arguing that they had never discriminated against Latinos; all they tried to do was to find the best possible people to serve.[39] The Supreme Court concluded that despite the generalized denial, it was very difficult to believe that out of 6,000 people, they had not been able to find one qualified Latino.[40] The Court noted that "[t]he state of Texas would have us hold that there are only two classes—white and Negro—within the contemplation of the Fourteenth Amendment,"[41] even as late as 1954. Incidentally, you will find *Hernandez v. Texas* reported just before a case that may sound familiar to you, *Brown v. Board of Education of Topeka.*[42] The Court was busy in those days. The Court rejected the Texas notion out of hand. "The Fourteenth Amendment," the Court said, "is not directed solely against the discrimination due to a 'two-class theory'—that is, based upon differences between 'white' and Negro."[43] The Court went on to say that the Constitution indeed protects everybody:

> *The exclusion of otherwise eligible persons from jury service solely because of their ancestry or national origin is discrimination prohibited by the Fourteenth Amendment. The Texas statute makes no such discrimination, but the petitioner alleges that those administering the law do.*[44]

And, in fact, the Court was convinced that that is exactly what had happened. So again we have a confirmation by the Court that ethnicity is protected.

For those of you who might be concerned about the current Supreme Court, I just want to tell you that the following is written by a distinguished observer of the court:

> *Even Justice Rehnquist, the modern Justice who takes the least interventionist view of equal protection and who is the strongest opponent of the expansion of "suspect classification" jurisprudence, acknowledged in Trimble v. Gordon . . . that classifications based on "national origin, the first cousin of race" . . . were areas where "the Framers obviously meant [equal protection] to apply."*[45]

So apparently even those who take lightly the post-Civil War amendments are convinced that in this area, in the area of ethnicity, there is no question that it is protected by the Constitution.

Finally, I want to mention a case decided by the California Supreme Court called *Castro v. California.*[46] It is one of my favorite cases, maybe because I was the director of a legal services group called California Rule Legal Assistance (CRLA) which filed this action on the behalf of its clients. The challenged California constitutional provision read: "[N]o person who shall not be able to read the Constitution in the English language, and write his or her name, shall ever exercise the privileges of an elector in this State."[47] That constitutional provision was passed in 1891, and I will come back to that fact in a few minutes.[48]

Our clients were able to show that in Los Angeles County where they lived, there were seventeen newspapers published in Spanish, eleven magazines, many radio and television stations, and through these, they were able to know exactly what the public issues of the day were and were able to cast a vote that was educated.[49] The California Supreme Court, analyzing the state constitutional provision by the standards of the federal Constitution, said, in essence, "It cannot stand. We consider the right of citizens. The right to vote is very important." The court determined that the state could not take away the right to vote unless there was a very important reason to do so, and here the court simply did not find that reason. These voters, by reading and hearing, could, in fact, educate themselves.[50] Then, at the end of the opinion, the court added one of my favorite paragraphs in American jurisprudence. Writing for the court, Justice Raymond Sullivan said:

> We add one final word. We cannot refrain from observing that if a contrary conclusion were compelled it would indeed be ironic that petitioners, who are the heirs of a great and gracious culture, identified with the birth of California and contributing in no small measure to its growth, should be disenfranchised in their ancestral land, despite their capacity to cast an informed vote.[51]

So we have come a long way—in California and in the nation.

In *Castro,* the court reviewed the history of constitutional and statutory changes in California, and in one of the footnotes it cited to a case called *People v. Hall.*[52] It is one of my favorite cases in California jurisprudence for a reason opposite that of *Castro v. California.* Let me tell you about the *Hall* case. When California was first formed into a state, the English-speaking and the Spanish-speaking worked cooperatively. They got together in the constitutional convention of 1849 and agreed upon a constitution, even though some who were at that convention spoke no English, and others spoke no Spanish. Yet they got together and created a constitution that was published in both English and Spanish.

But then, sadly, the atmosphere started changing in California, and the case of *People v. Hall,*[53] decided in 1854, gives you a sense of how much change had come about. The legislature had passed a statute that prohibited any testimony against a white person in court if the testimony came from a black, mulatto or an American Indian.[54] A white man was convicted of murder by the testimony of a Chinese man.[55] At that time we had no intermediate court, so the lawyers for the convicted appealed directly to the California Supreme Court.

The California Supreme Court was composed of three members at that time, and it wrote an opinion that is great fun to read in its historical context. The court pointed out that the Native Americans are part of the Mongoloid races and that eons ago, the Mongoloid races from Asia had travelled over the Bering Straits and through Alaska. In the course of many thousands of years these migrants ended up in the lands we now call the United States. The Indians and the Chinese were of the Mongoloid race. When the legislature said Indians could not testify, it obviously meant to include anybody of the Mongoloid race.[56] Since Chinese belong to the Mongoloid race, the court reasoned, they obviously cannot testify against a white man, and so the court reversed the murder conviction.

The *Hall* court described the Chinese people as a "distinct people . . . whose mendacity is proverbial; a race of people whom nature has marked as inferior, and who are incapable of progress or intellectual development beyond a certain a point, as their history has shown. . . ."[57] This quote does not include another discussion in which the court noted that if allowed to testify against a white person, the Chinese would soon want to vote, want to be lawyers, and would even want to sit on the bench.[58] The court ruled on the basis of clear statutory construction. The court seemingly asked, "How could anybody disagree that Indian means Chinese." Indeed, the court wrote: "[E]ven in a doubtful case we would be impelled to this decision on the grounds of public policy."[59]

Sadly, just a few years thereafter, Manuel Dominguez, who had been at the California constitutional convention, and had signed the constitution, was not permitted to testify in a court of law in San Francisco in 1857 because he was of Indian ancestry. That is part of the history of California. To look at the *Castro* decision and see how the law has evolved is a matter of great satisfaction to me.

Incidentally, I have always been interested in Los Angeles. If you visit Los Angeles, go down to the area where Los Angeles was first founded, La Placita (the little plaza). There is a plaque there which has the names of all of the people who helped found Los Angeles. The Spaniards were great record keepers. The records identify people by race and by occupation as well as other characteristics. That plaque identifies the race of the original settlers. I have a book here[60] which published a census taken about the time Los Angeles was founded. Let me just go down the line; you will see the great variety of people that founded California. The reality contrasts with the early romanticized movies that came out of Hollywood portraying Spanish vaqueros as typical. Here are the real Californios: Josef de Lara, Spaniard; his wife Maria, india sabina; Josef Navarro, mestizo; his wife Maria, mulata; Basil Rosas, indian; a husband, indian; his wife, indian; another husband Alejandro Rosas, indian; his wife Juana, coyote indian—mixture of pure Indian and mestizo; Pablo Rodriguez, indian; wife Maria Rosalia, indian; Manuel Camero, mulato; his wife Maria Tomasa, mulata; Luis Quintera, negro; his wife Maria Petmulata; Jose Moreno, mulato; Antonio Rodriguez, chino (Chino—a person who has negroid features, but was born of white parents).[61] That is the real mixture of Los Angeles from whence many of us come.

Let me just read you a passage from that same book. A very distinguished early Californio, Pablo de la Guerra, who was late as state senator, is quoted. The title of the book was FOREIGNERS IN THEIR NATIVE LAND, taken from a speech he delivered in the California legislature in 1856:

> It is the conquered who are humble before the conqueror asking for his protection, while enjoying what little their misfortune has left them. It is those who have been sold like sheep—it is those who were abandoned by Mexico. They do not understand the prevalent language of their native soil. They are foreigners in their own land. I have seen seventy and sixty year olds cry like children because they have been uprooted from the lands of their fathers. They have been humiliated and insulted. They have been refused the privilege of taking water from their own wells. They have been denied the privilege of cutting their own firewood.[62]

This is our history.

Yet we have struggled. As the cases from the California and the United States Supreme Courts indicate, we have indeed made a great deal of progress. The struggles continue. Issues like education and political empowerment create conflict. As we all know, progress does not come overnight. My hope is that as we struggle with these issues, we will also struggle with that notion of how can we be diverse and yet be one people.

For myself, I have enjoyed that diversity. I have a friend by the name of Bill Ong Hing, a professor at Stanford. He invited my family and me to go to his church where a Chinese play was presented. We enjoyed tremendously seeing a culture that my family and I had not seen before. I remember walking down the streets of San Francisco and a gentleman coming up to Bill. The two of them chatted for a couple of minutes in Chinese and then spoke in English. I did not feel that they were talking about me during that time. So often we reject folk who speak a language other than our own, because we think, "Well, they must be talking about me." I never thought that any one person was that important. I would hope that we learn to enjoy the reality that other people are different and that they have a language, a cultural richness, if you will, that we can enjoy. Indeed, I really do give thanks for the fact that we have people in this country who speak different languages and come from different cultures who will make our country far stronger economically and far stronger politically.

I always think of the advertising that we as Americans do. I am told that there was a time when General Motors was advertising in Latin America for their then-new car called the Nova. Apparently nobody had told them that "Nova" in Spanish is "Nova," which means "It won't go." It was not a successful advertising campaign. Or another time when my former colleague, Justice Joseph Groden of the California Supreme Court, came back from a long trip in China, and he told me there were Coca-Cola signs all over China. I asked about Pepsi-Cola because I had read that Pepsi had a contract with the Chinese government. At that time Pepsi-Cola had a little ditty, you may remember many years ago, that went something like, "Pepsi, come alive with Pepsi." Unfortunately, it had been mistranslated in Chinese, to read, "Pepsi brings your ancestors back to life," and the Chinese, with their respect for their ancestors, were not amused. Pepsi apparently lost its contract.

I also remember reading an article by a German industrialist who said basically, "You know, I speak English, and I go to all of these gatherings where folk come from all over the world selling their high-tech equipment. I go and look at all that and I see that the Americans make very good equipment, and the Japanese have very good equipment, as do other nationals. They all look very good. Then afterwards, though I speak English, I socialize with folks generally in the German language, because I feel more comfortable in German. All I can tell you is that in Germany, you'll sell in the German language."

I think that our diversity will indeed bring strength to us, and I think that we can profit from it. But more importantly, we need to continue working with the reality that we are a very diverse people, ethnically and linguistically. Despite those differences, as with differences of race and religion, we ought to look at what unites us, what makes us all Americans. We need to look at our history, at the land, at the suffering we have been through as a people. We need to examine the ideals that we find in the Constitution, those very ideals that have brought the California and the United States Supreme Courts to declare that there are those rights so important that government can not take them away from us. If nobody can take those rights away from us, we need to rejoice in those rights, to rejoice in our differences, to appreciate those differences, and to profit one from another.

Notes

[1] Frank v. State of Alaska, 604 P.2d 1068 (Ala. 1979).

[2] 262 U.S. 390 (1923).

[3] *Id.* at 397 (citing NEB LAWS 1919, ch. 249 (entitled "An act relating to the teaching of foreign languages in the State of Nebraska" (approved April 9, 1919))).

[4] *Id.* (citing NEB. LAWS 1919, ch. 249, § 2).

[5] *Id.* at 396–97.

[6] *Id.* at 396.

[7] *Id.* at 397 (quoting NEB LAWS 1919, ch. 24, §§ 1–2).

[8] *Id.*

[9] *Id.* at 400–01.

[10] *Id.* at 401.

[11] The Fourteenth Amendment states, in pertinent part: "No State shall . . . deprive any person of life, liberty, or property, without due process of law; nor deny to any person within its jurisdiction the equal protection of the laws." U.S. CONST. amend. XIV, § 1.

[12] *Meyer,* 262 U.S. at 399.

[13] *Id.* at 400–03.

[14] *Id.* at 402–03.

[15] *Id.* at 402.

[16] *Id.* at 400–01.

[17] 332 U.S. 633 (1948).

[18] *Id.* at 635–36 & nn. 1 & 3 (citing Alien Land Law, 1 CAL. GEN. LAWS, Act 261 (Deering 1944 & Supp. 1945)).

[19] *Id.* at 636–37.

[20] *Id.*

[21] *See id.* at 636 (citing Alien Land Law, 1 CAL. GEN. LAWS, Act 261, § 9(a)).

[22] *Id.*

[23] *Id.* at 638. The witness, John Kurfurst, had been left in charge of the Oyama property when the Oyama family was evacuated in 1942 as part of the evacuation of persons of Japanese descent during World War II. *Id.* at 637–38.

[24] *See id.* at 638.

[25]*See id.* at 639.

[26]*Id.* at 639–40.

[27]*See id.* at 640.

[28]*Id.* at 640 & n. 16 (citing CAL., PROB. CODE ANN. § 1407).

[29]*Id.* at 640–41.

[30]*Id.* at 647.

[31]*See id.* at 646–47.

[32]347 U.S. 475 (1954).

[33]*Id.* at 476.

[34]*Id.* at 476–77.

[35]*Id.* at 480–81 & n. 12.

[36]*Id.* at 482.

[37]*Id.* at 479–80.

[38]*Id.* at 479.

[39]*Id.* at 481.

[40]*Id.* at 482.

[41]*Id.* at 477.

[42]347 U.S. 483 (1954).

[43]*Hernandez,* 347 U.S. at 478.

[44]*Id.* at 479.

[45]CONSTITUTIONAL LAW 624 n.3 (Gerald Gunther ed., 11th ed. 1985) (citing Trimble v. Gordon, 430 U.S. 762, 777 (1977) (Rehnquist, J., dissenting)).

[46]466 P. 2d 244 (Cal. 1970).

[47]*Id.* at 245 (quoting CAL. CONST. art. 2, § 1).

[48]*Id.* The English literacy requirement was proposed in 1891 by a California state assembly-man, A. J. Bledsoe, who in 1886 had been part of a committee that expelled all persons of Chinese ancestry from Humboldt County, California. *Id.*

[49]*Id.* at 254–55.

[50]*See, e.g., id.* at 254–57.

[51]*Id.* at 259.

[52]*Id.* at 248 n.11 (citing People v. Hall, 4 Cal. 399 (1854)).

[53]4 Cal. 399 (1854).

[54]*Id.* at 399 (quoting Act of April 16, 1850 (regulating California criminal proceedings)).

[55]*Id.*

[56]*Id.* at 400–04.

[57]*Castro,* 466 P.2d at 248 n.11 (quoting *Hall,* 4 Cal. at 404–05.

[58]*Hall,* 4 Cal. at 404–05.

[59]*Id.* at 404.

[60]FOREIGNERS IN THEIR NATIVE LAND 33 (David J. Weber ed., 1st ed. 1973).

[61]*Id.* at 34–35.

[62]*Id.* at vi (quoting Pablo de la Guerra, Speech to the California Senate (1856)).

Understanding the Black Collective Will through Black Music

Ricky Green

> *Soul-force in "Black talk" describes that quality of life that has enabled Black people to survive the horrors of their Diaspora. Soul signifies the moral and emotional fiber of the Black man that enables him to see his dilemmas clearly and at the same time encourages and sustains him in his struggles. Force connotes strength, power, intense effort and a will to live. The combined words "soul-force"—describes the racial inheritance of the New World African; it is that which characterizes his life-style, his world view and his endurance under conflict.[1]*

Black music is historically the vehicle through which the strength of the Black soul in both its collective and individual dimensions is best expressed, developed and given function. Other discourses such as those developed in the Black church and Black literature are utilized; however, through Black music a discourse has developed which functions as the least constrained, most expressive and most functional discourse conveying the strength and contours of the Black soul. It has consistently demonstrated, in W.E.B. Du Bois' words, the "dogged strength" necessary to keep the Black soul whole even under the pressure of an extremely hostile environment. As we may understand soul-force as essential to the Black collective will, music becomes an essential discourse through which the Black collective will is developed and expressed.

As a discourse it consistently draws on as many voices as possible distributed throughout all levels and areas of the community in its preparation, development and dissemination. Music in this sense is the most participatory discourse within the community. Historically it has been both ancient and contemporary, a discourse that has not only kept understandings of its African roots but constantly delves deeper to reconstruct more of its African essence. Still, this discourse has pushed into the future, both immediate and far, in an attempt to inform an identity that is often well removed, in time and space, from those African roots. Perhaps just as essential, music is the one discourse the Black collective brought

---

[1]Barrett, 1974: 1–2.

from Africa, could sustain throughout the Diaspora, and could articulate the experience of the three dimensions of Black new world existence (African antecedents, middle passage horrors and "new world" development). Hence it is the discourse most utilized and arguably most trusted by Black people throughout the Diaspora.

It is only through an analysis of music that we can sufficiently reconstruct the development of Black political and cultural norms. For most Diaspora populations which have been historically oppressed such analyses produce a fragmented and artificially homogenized analysis of political and cultural norms—most of the political and cultural discourse is not analyzed and given this glaring omission, that which is analyzed is done so incorrectly. For most Diaspora populations such analyses have favored populations who are upwardly mobile *within the constraints of the historically oppressive population.* This also holds true in the sense of resistance. Black music has historically maintained a strong connection to the masses. While there exists an obvious bias towards youth in the popular music industry, music within the Black community and especially working class communities tends to unite across generations. Since the spirituals, music within the Black community has functioned to address the major conflicts amongst the various sub groups within the community especially in terms of class, gender and generation.

In our inquiry into the function of music in concerns to the collective will, we need to explore not only the function, form and method of the music but through those three features we must also reconstruct its development in order to understand the development of soul-force. In its development Black music is inherently pluralistic, fiercely independent and a strong, consistent, if intermittingly accepted, participant in nearly every society which exhibits a significant Diaspora population. Still it has functioned most consistently attempting to bridge the disparities between certain groups within Diaspora communities. While other commentators recognize the contribution of Black music to democracy, I believe such arguments are too general and do not fully articulate the form, function, method and development of Black music and the Black collective will throughout the Diaspora. Only through understanding the development of Black music as a pluralistic phenomenon can we truly understand the development of the Black collective will. Like the form, function and method of the music this pluralistic development is complex, both historically and analytically. Through a reconstruction of that complexity, Black political thought and action can be better understood and reconstructed. To begin that reconstruction we will begin to look at essential concepts within the development of Black music.

While most commentary on Black Diaspora music has concentrated on distinct musical forms such as the Blues, Reggae, Jazz or Rap, this inquiry will focus on the function of the music. Despite their focus on form most commentators agree that Black music is primarily functional, similar to folk music in this aspect, even in its popular expression. Organizing our inquiry along the lines of function allows us to better reconstruct the development of the collective will of any particular Diaspora group. A functional analysis of the music allows us to reconstruct the contours of the various conflicts and compromises within the Diaspora community that were recorded through the music. A functional analysis also may afford us the ability to perceive the subtle connections in the music between form and method and apply those connections to the political and cultural context. Finally a functional analysis may even reveal that particular conflicts within the community have been mediated primarily through music and that through understanding music's mediation function we can develop a particular insight into mediation on the cultural and political level.

> *Scholars seem to agree that the aim of African music has always been to translate the experiences of life and of the spiritual world into sound, enhancing and celebrating life...*[2]

> *This notion of sacredness gets at the essence of the spirituals, and through them at the essence of the slave's world view. Denied the possibility of achieving an adjustment to the external world of the antebellum South which involved meaningful forms of personal integration, attainment of status, and feelings of individual worth that all human beings crave and need, the slaves created a new world by transcending the narrow confines of the one in which they were forced to live. They extended the boundaries of their restrictive universe backward until it fused with the world of the Old Testament and upward until it became one with the world beyond.*[3]

There was initially very little difference in the general function of music in the life of the African and the life of those taken from the continent. Change of environment appears to have had a greater affect on the form and methods of music. I would add, too, that in Africa a variety of self-determinant art forms existed through which the more general functions of music were dispersed, since the general function of African music listed above is really a general function of all art. For most Black people throughout the Diaspora the diversity of art was nowhere as great as in Africa. Given the paucity of available art forms, music throughout the Diaspora becomes much more heavily relied upon as a discourse to express and develop those general functions. Also it is one of the few art forms which could have been sufficiently practiced and developed from initial capture to auction block. Due to this greater stress a heightened intensity has been placed upon music in fulfilling these general functions throughout the Diaspora. Where in Africa there is much more of an equal footing amongst the arts in the discourse concerning the general

---

[2]Floyd, 1995: 32.
[3]Levine, Lawrence, 1977: 32–33.

function of art, throughout the Diaspora and in particular in the United States music historically dominates that discourse. Obviously there are consequences attached to this dominance.

The particular functions that we will examine during the course of this inquiry include: trust, catharsis, voice, activism, amalgamation (humanism and syncretism), and worship (faith, transcendence and discipline). It is hard to argue that even the specific functions of Black music have changed from their African roots. I do believe however, that the functions of activism, voice, catharsis, trust and especially amalgamation have been historically pursued with a greater intensity in Black music than in African music. Our focus in this work is primarily concerned with functional categories that are directly connected to the development of the Black collective will; however an analysis of entertainment as a function of Black music will reveal the contours of some essential conflicts within the community, especially those surrounding the genre of rap.

The Pluralistic Foundation of Black Music

While it is difficult to envision pluralism as a function or even as a goal of early African music there is a clear distinction between African music and the music that emerged in communities throughout the Diaspora. There is also a clear distinction between European music forms and the spirituals and work songs which developed within communities held in bondage. Black pluralism, wherever it appears throughout the Diaspora, developed not as a political system but as a mass based humanistic movement of African peoples attempting to transform the fundamental conditions of their new environment. European definitions of pluralism do not and cannot fully encompass the scope and depth of Black pluralism neither can European systems of pluralism.

While on an institutional level this has always appeared a tentative argument, especially in the United States, one must remember that most Africans lived their understandings, expressed them through their daily actions. It is due to this holistic nature that so much of the African experience found function in the lives of so many people of African descent throughout the Diaspora generations beyond those initially captured. The oral tradition that was integral to the development of African culture was also instrumental to this development and survival, in its retention by Blacks and in its obliviousness (primarily through misinterpretation) to European Americans. Black pluralism then developed as a direct response of African understandings to a new environment.

Music ever present in African life became the foundation upon which the experiences of the new environment were developed, understood and interpreted by those held in bondage. Music also became the strainer through which new intellectual constraints were siphoned and music became the strength with which those held in bondage pushed everything and everyone around them attempting to move themselves by moving others. The most obvious and frequent direction in which they pushed was towards Africa. The music of those held in bondage in the United States differed from African music in a few essential ways, mostly in form if not in entirely function and method. The spirituals incorporated European American religiosity. However, that religiosity as Levine's passage above indicates was fundamentally altered to reflect African understandings within their new environment. The work day songs were much more guided by African understandings than the spirituals because they were much more spontaneous and in that spontaneity subject more to African holism:

> This material is far more fragmentary than the spirituals, but being a combination of folk poetry and folk music, the words are welded closer to the music than in the case of spirituals. For they were more of a direct improvisation than the spirituals, which in thought were too influenced by the evangelical hymns after which they were originally modeled.[4]

However, even Locke's excellent distinction between the spirituals and work songs may be slightly misleading since Frederick Douglass informs us that this distinction was never made by the composers of the music themselves.[5] The amalgamation of African and European elements is evident in both forms to various degrees.

Syncretism always a strong possibility in most African cultures, becomes much more of a necessity in the new environment. The spirituals and the work songs brought together two of the most disparate cultural and intellectual paradigms. There were obvious methodological differences, the signifying and call and response, allowed Black music to continue to develop itself as a mass participatory art form, while European music stressed elitism and individualism for centuries and the methodology reflected such a paradigm. The community building functions of the spirituals had no parallels in European music which had nearly reduced the function of music to aesthetics and sensuality. The practical nature of the American strain of European philosophy had further reduced art in general and music in particular to special events and placed it as background to more "serious" discourses. Beyond the music the philosophical and political traditions and experiences of both groups moved in very different if not opposing directions.

In the area of spiritualism the differences may have been most striking. The developing Black spiritualism throughout most of the Diaspora including the United States mirrored through the development of "attitude" the holistic nature of African spiritualism. Black people held in bondage lived their spiritualism, it emanated from

---

[4]Locke, 1936: 28.
[5]Douglass, 1845: 57–58.

every pore in their being. This totality of belief, this spiritual strength, as Frederick Douglass informs us, was the essence of the spirituals:

> They told a tale of woe which was then altogether beyond my feeble comprehension; they were tones loud, long, and deep; they breathed the prayer and complaint of souls boiling over with the bitterest anguish.[6]

In contrast the United States was a nation led by agnostics. Spiritualism had a place just not in every facet of life, most importantly it could not truly be acted upon, could not be lived. The compartment of American life that spiritualism was afforded properly reduced it to a religion that was intermittently practiced—purely ceremonial for many adherents and only useful on the collective level when it enhanced or brought moral legitimacy to a particular aggregated self-interest. Maybe most revealing of the difference is that spiritual conflicts in the American mainstream are translated into moral conflicts as they become part of the political discourse and the mediation of them are severely constrained by the myriad of interests within political and economic arenas the least of which are spiritual.

From the perspective of those held in bondage, a decidedly communal and holistic perspective, the spirituals developed as a humanistic and pluralistic force within a dehumanizing caste system. The spirituals were developed through a methodology that was often in direct opposition to a primarily amoral system, prioritizing spiritualism within Black communities and in the American mainstream (which they understood in terms of the southern plantation community). Spiritualism became the force through which they attempted to constrain the political and economic forces proscribing their oppression. Pluralism became both a way of understanding these forces and overcoming them:

> Into all of their songs they would manage to weave something of the Great House Farm. Especially would they do this, when leaving home. They would then sing most exultingly the following words:—"I am going away to the Great House Farm! O, yea! O, yea! O!" This they would sing, as a chorus, to words which to many would seem unmeaning jargon, but which, nevertheless, were full of meaning to themselves.[7]

Once again we have to turn to the concept of holism—they composed as they lived, and how they lived—two disparate even warring understandings informing their actions. Black music became the vehicle through which they mediated the conflict—first amongst themselves and then between themselves and external communities. It is at this moment in this context that we begin to see significant divergence within the collective Black consciousness. Locke is correct in recognizing a significant difference in the work songs and the Spirituals. That difference is indicative of the way

---

[6]Douglass, 1845: 57–58.
[7]Douglass, 1845: 57.

in which European understandings are incorporated into the holistic lives of those held in bondage. We might even recognize a third strain in the development of the cakewalk, Black minstrels of the European American plantation owning class. All strains are in fact represented in present-day Black music and within the consciousness of the Black community. All of these strains have been afforded significant voice within the community and all form resources for Black development within the community. I will also state here that these strains are not mutually exclusive.

As Black collectivity developed without significant self determinant mediating institutions (besides music) in most areas syncretism and pluralism became essential within the community as components of Black resistance and the attempt to reacquire and redevelop humanism on the collective level. Syncretism and pluralism develop, as have many Black artifacts, as a lived attitude, part of the cultural consciousness. It is evident in all forms of Black music throughout the Diaspora. Through the various African fragments in the music we can begin to reconstruct the development of a particular Diaspora spiritualism. The specifics of this spiritualism in the U.S. is reconstructed by writers such as Lawrence Levine, in Jamaica, Leonard Barrett, in Haiti, Gerdes Fleurant. It is from this spiritualism that pluralism within the Black community develops. This then is both its oppositional nature to and compatibility with American liberalism.

It is interesting that Douglass in a passage that is written to place the spirituals within the context of resistance to the dehumanization of slavery begins the passage by placing the creation and development of the spirituals within what can only be described as one of the least resistive contexts of Black existence:

> *The slaves selected to go to the Great House Farm, for the monthly allowance for themselves and their fellow slaves, were peculiarly enthusiastic. While on their way, they would make the dense old woods, for miles around, reverberate with their wild songs, revealing at once the highest joy and the deepest sadness.*[8]

On the other hand Douglass argues that the essence of the spirituals was resistance to the dehumanization of slavery:

> *...they breathed the prayer and complaint of souls boiling over with the bitterest anguish. Every tone was a testimony against slavery and a prayer to God for deliverance from chains.*[9]

There is this particular irony in Douglass' writing. It is an irony deep within the essence of his subject—a population of slaves honoring the master (at least the ideal of the master) even as they resist and attempt to destroy the system. However, we must understand that the reconstruction of the humanity of our ancestors was a complex undertaking.

---

[8]Douglass, 1982: 57.
[9]Douglass, 1982: 58

As Levine argues Black people within these communities of bondage developed a spiritualism based primarily upon Old Testament understandings and African spiritual fragments—amalgamating the two into Black religion. But the truth of this amalgamation is that they only had access to fragments of protestant Christianity which itself was formed as sort of a synthesis of two people's disparate histories—Hebrew and European. The captured African had little to no access to either of these histories only imaginings of both through fragments that reconstructed them as ideals. The fragments of their African past were much more immediate, realistic, sobering, and quite frankly because of the holistic nature of Black life *much more numerous and complete.* Consequently a new spiritualism was constructed from the amalgamation of these disparate fragments of spiritual paradigms and the religions that were attached. Both Douglass' writings and the words of the spirituals attest to this amalgamation. As we shall discuss in detail in the next chapter the resultant spiritualism and the religion that developed held the early contradictions of its constituent parts despite the skill of the amalgamators. Douglass' writing bears witness to these difficulties from an intimate sympathetic perspective. Despite the contradictions apparent we can also see in Douglass' passages the roots of pluralism developing as this initial morality develops.

Pluralism, I will argue at this moment of the inquiry and throughout is a complex attitude both in the Black psyche and in Black music. It is in fact mediation between various often competing attitudes within the Black community and within Black music. Those competing attitudes are obviously at the core of the development of Black people throughout the Diaspora and are specific to each area and each community. I have previously listed those areas of mediation as follows: trust, catharsis, voice, activism, amalgamation, worship and entertainment. It is by looking at the development of music in those specific areas and understanding such development as interactive and interrelated that we will begin to envision the development of a conscious collective pluralistic will throughout the Diaspora and within specific areas of the Diaspora.

While it is not possible given current space constraints to fully develop each area it is possible to develop a specific area from which an understanding of Black pluralism can be derived. I have chosen this particular area because it is essential to the development of Black identity in both the degree to which it was shattered as Africans were removed from the continent and in its nature of being foundational— a necessary underpinning to the other areas which follow.

The Development of Black Trust

Black trust, to say the least, came to the new world as a shattered concept and developed on the collective level slowly from a deeply fragmented essence. This fragmentation began at every level in Africa. At every level of the slave trade and at most levels of African society there was complicity, individually and collectively, despite the fact that very few Africans were actually involved in the slave trade.

Also, unlike conventional knowledge holds, it is most likely at this stage that Africans, especially those captured by slave traders, began to distinguish between European and African. Because of the slave trade within various regions and the continent itself distinctions also began to be made on a scale different than that which had produced the various African ethnic groups. Such distinctions included those Africans engaged in the slave trade. Trust like nearly every other component of African identity underwent significant transformation before the captives ever left the continent. The horrors of the middle passage further eroded concepts of human trust as individuals were assaulted on all levels, starved, abused and murdered by their captors. What undoubtedly also began to develop were understandings of a new collective trust based on collective catharsis and the pooling of resources, mostly intellectual and spiritual, to at least endure at most overcome a hostile environment. However, this newly developing trust must have been extremely tentative. This pre new world development of trust is well documented by historians. Alex Haley's work, *Roots*, based upon his compilation of various oral histories, records the development of both the Black mindset prior to and during the middle passage, and the development of trust on the collective level. Works such as Lerone Bennett's *Before the Mayflower*, recorded the results of that trust in the development of uprisings and revolts during the marches to various sites of departure, within the forts of departure, and on the ships during the Atlantic crossing. While the movie *Amistad* focused on the development of levels of trust between Cinque and European Americans the greater significance of the event lay in the development of levels of trust among the middle passage Africans who liberated the ship. This development proceeded from the remains of a trust that was severely shattered.

The question of the function of music in the development is complex. We know that music was at the core of African life and we also know that those captured engaged in music during every phase of the experience. We even know that during particular phases of the experience their captors encouraged the Africans to engage in their music. The specifics however are unknown. No one with intimate knowledge of any particular African culture or any specific African identity recorded the experience in the western tradition and that which was recorded in the African tradition is obscured and most likely lost to Western thought. We can however, draw parallels to analogous experiences that have had the type of historic preservation that we seek.

The most analogous would be the various acts of resistance of African peoples in the various areas of destination for those held in bondage following the middle passage. In nearly every area at nearly every phase of resistance music was essential. The drums beat in the hills of Saint Domingo for days calling the rebels to action as a precursor to the Haitian revolt. The music served not just a communicative function but also served an organizing function and a cathartic function. Organization centered on movement of individuals and groups into vital areas of preparation (the initial revolt plan was one of mass poisoning). The cathartic function centered on the development of the "attitude" of revolt which included charms and protections for the rebels against their oppressors and an attempt to instill fear and doubt within the enemy. Trust is deeply embedded in all functions and the drums functioned as the best instrument to purvey the deepness of this trust in the Black psyche. It is well documented how music was utilized in the work fields and later in spaces where Black people were afforded what leisure they could in between work and exhaustion. In the fields African rhythms through the medium of the Black voice (replacing the outlawed drum) found its initial arbitrative function, setting the pace for the day's labor—a compromise amongst the workers themselves.

The methodology developed in communities of bondage along with the various African methods of music development including call and response stressed an essential level of secrecy. That secrecy resulted in the development of hidden transcripts as a methodology. These had all been traditional within African societies, music as a functioning component of not only rituals and ceremonies but as vital to everyday activities. Alongside of that development was the development of excellence in Africa through the use of secret societies. The methods of institutions which had been developing for centuries in Africa were successfully adapted within the Diaspora. The most essential adaptation within the Diaspora for purposes of our immediate inquiry is the degree of inclusiveness. The degree of inclusiveness which was unprecedented for most African societies developed in large part due to the straightforwardness that became more essential in most Diaspora communities such as in the United States.

The forms and methodology of Black music were essential to the development of collective trust. Not only did the trust amongst individuals and various groups in the community develop but as the forms developed and the methodology proved successful trust of music to express and develop general and more specific functions also increased. Essential to our inquiry is the common sense observation that music became more trusted than the various European American institutions and institutional discourses:

> I have sometimes thought that the mere hearing of those songs would do more to impress some minds with the horrible character of slavery, than the reading of whole volumes of philosophy on the subject could do.[10]

> I know that these songs are the articulate message of the slave to the world.[11]

In his initial manuscript, *Narrative of the Life and Times of Frederick Douglass*, Fredrick Douglass develops a brief philosophical inquiry into Black music. This inquiry as part of his overall critique of slavery takes place on just three pages out of 151. Those three pages however are profound especially in their connection to Black political thought. In the brief passage Douglass refers to the spirituals as "sorrow

---

[10]Douglass, 1982: 57.
[11]Du Bois, 1898: 207.

songs," a reference which W.E.B. Du Bois picks up as the last chapter to his work, *The Souls of Black Folk*. Douglass accomplishes two things of importance within the brief passage. Born bonded to a European American in Maryland, Douglass' analysis is one of the few if not the only one proffered by a Black held in bondage during the period when the spirituals were developed. From Douglass we get both text and context from the perspective and understanding of the people who created the music.

> *They would compose and sing as they went along, consulting neither time nor tune. The thought that came up, came out—if not in word, in sound; —and as frequently in the one as in the other. They would sometimes sing the most pathetic sentiment in the most rapturous tone, and the most rapturous sentiment in the most pathetic tone. Into all of their songs they would manage to weave something of the Great Farm House.*[12]

Douglass' inquiry gives us a few insights on the question of trust development amongst those Blacks held in bondage. The first is imbedded in the music and composers relationship to the community. Despite the continuing importance of music in fulfilling those general functions discussed above in Douglass' passages we can envision the more solitary and melancholy development of the spirituals than its African predecessors. The new environment was compartmentalized to a degree that was alien to the African mind. The child occupied not only a distinct physical compartment from parent but a spiritual and intellectual one as well. Child from parent, field worker from house worker, male from female, African from European, free from slave, poor from rich, all of these compartmental distinctions were essential in the American mind. The spirituals developed in this alien environment as a moderating factor to this hyper compartmentalization.

The spirituals sought to unify through the analogy of God's children in Israel and the war against dehumanization. The spirituals also sought to maintain the practice of holism. The methodology used in the construction of the music allowed the development of these sub functions of trust. The music became much more impromptu; the newly forming Black community trusted the formal much less than their ancestors. We see in Douglass' analysis, the initial development of a trust wary of so much, still most wary by far of outside voices. Within their own voices the emotive is given priority over the formal, rational and traditional. Even as they trust almost exclusively their own voice they do not trust others to understand them through the hearing. They are misunderstood and mischaracterized in their music. The spirituals become a moderating factor against the compartmentalization, the disunity, and ethnocentricity of the new environment and in doing so sets Black music and Black thought upon a specific course of collective development. These moderating factors form the basis of the development of trust within the Black community.

There are four distinct themes which are essential to the development of trust amongst Black people—righteousness, emotive unity, secrecy, and self-determination.

---

[12]Douglass, 1986: 57.

All are themes within the Douglass' inquiry which have been further developed by other philosophical inquiries into Black music. These four themes aggregated are the foundation for the development of Black spiritualism throughout the Diaspora. One may argue that the development of Black trust reaches its apex throughout the Diaspora with the development of holistic understandings of Black spiritualism and that these understandings are essential to the development of trust on a level required for significant political action, specifically for our concern the development of a collective will. Black music fueled that development through the spirituals.

As a witness who "was within in the circle" Douglass points us to the most essential themes of the spirituals in his passage on music and the rest of his work supports these themes as essential. Douglass' work also through both substance and method imparts something just as essential, the holistic nature of Black spiritualism and Black life. For even as commentators have attempted to categorize both Douglass argues the artificialness of this even during his lifetime which begins in 1818 less than fifty years before the end of the Civil War. The pathetic, rude and incoherent found expression alongside the most rapturous sentiment and highest joy according to Douglass. The spiritualism that was constructed in these communities was lived, holistic and the distinction between secular and spiritual was foreign to those within the community. I would argue that this is only revealed through an analysis of Black music that is thorough. By thorough I mean not simply an analysis that traverses through the culture but one that understands the subtle nature of the culture through living. Douglass' analysis though brief fell into the latter category. Understanding this holistic nature of Black spiritualism is key to understanding the collective Black consciousness at the time of the early development of the Black collective will.

> *The thought that came up, came out—if not in the word, in the sound—and as frequently in the one as the in the other.*[13]

> *...they were tones loud, long, and deep: they breathed prayer and complaint of souls boiling over with the bitterest anguish. Every tone was a testimony against slavery....*[14]

Righteousness, more than the other three were at the heart of Douglass' work. Our other most immediate witness to the strength of the spirituals, Du Bois echoes though briefly Douglass' analysis:

> *Through all the Sorrow Songs there breathes a hope—a faith in the ultimate justice of things. The minor cadences of despair change often to triumph and calm confidence. Sometimes it is faith in life, sometimes a faith in death, sometimes assurance of boundless justice in some fair world beyond.*[15]

---

[13]Douglass, 1982: 57.

[14]Douglass, 1982: 57–58.

[15]Du Bois, 1898: 213–214.

This concept of righteousness lay at the core of the slaves world view. Levine argues that it was a complex concept grounded in a specific environment.

> *Similarly, the folk beliefs of slaves were expressed on different but complimentary levels. The unremitting system of slavery made its subjects not merely idealists who created a sacred universe which promised change and triumph, allowed them to reach back to relive the victories of the past, and drew them into the rich future where justice and goodness that had been experienced before would exist again; it also made them realists who understood the world as it operated in the present. To have acculturated their children exclusively to a world view proclaimed by their religion would have signified an impracticality that slaves rarely showed. The universe held promise and hope, but it was also dominated by malevolence, injustice, arbitrary judgment, and paradox which had to be dealt with here and now.*[16]

For my part I will argue that it is not a passive concept of justness and goodness in the sense of being just and good within oneself. It could not have been it could not be. The slave who stole himself from his master was righteous, more so if spirited himself and others away in his former master's carriage. Righteousness was not only about justice and goodness but it had a leveling effect—pulling Blacks up from an assigned inferiority and sub humanness while simultaneously pulling Whites down from an argued superiority and super humanness. Righteousness was a direct involvement in the conflict between good and evil represented specifically in the conflict between European American oppressors and the Black oppressed. Simply to be Black was not enough, simply to wish for one's own freedom was not enough. Righteousness required direct action, direct opposition to the system of oppression—in most Black communities throughout the United States it still holds this requirement. Not surprisingly, for Douglass the self-liberated slave who both physically and intellectually fought for his freedom righteousness lies at the core of his narrative and at the core of his analysis of the spirituals:

> *In coming to a fixed determination to run away, we did more than Patrick Henry, when he resolved upon liberty or death. With us it was a doubtful liberty at most, and almost a certain death if we failed.*[17]

We can begin with a list of all the secret meetings held outside the purview of the slave system. These would encompass most Black activities during the period from intimate, to spiritual, to rebellion. All of these types of activities prohibited within the slave system entailed various degrees of severe punishment up to death and in most Black music played an essential part. Only the trusted were invited and information was guarded closely even within the circle. Righteousness was at the

[16]Levine, 1977: 134.
[17]Douglass, 1982: 124.

core of this trust for anyone found out could easily cause terrible problems for any other member of the group.

> *The frequency of this has had the effect to establish among the slaves the maxim, that a still tongue makes a wise head. They suppress the truth rather than take the consequences of telling it, and by doing so prove themselves a part of the human family.*[18]

The righteous took their punishment and implicated as few others as humanly possible—hopefully no one else besides themselves. Those less so revealed essentials. Leaders obviously were required to exhibit this quality of righteousness, which we must now begin to understand as both spiritual and practical. This particular concept has survived centuries from the earliest slaves in the field to the inner city streets. I can, at least, bear witness for many within my generation. Most of us, young Blacks between the ages of fifteen and twenty-five, saw Malcolm and Martin as righteous men, not because of their religion but because of their life. Emmett Till, Stokely Carmichael, Tommie Smith and John Carlos all exhibited righteousness through their sacrifice to give the most disempowered Black people a voice. Many in my generation abandoned traditional institutions even the Black church imitating this righteousness in every manner possible, we lived it and in us it became an attitude. As Kelley notes this type of political development for oppressed populations is not possible within traditional institutions. While commentators such as Adolph Reed may look at this attitude in working class Black youth as primarily superficial I would tend to disagree. As Black music guides and informs so much within Black working class life the imitative, without premature termination, becomes a strive for excellence.[19] This movement is due in part to the holistic nature which is still very much in evidence in working class Black life almost exclusively due to Diaspora music.

The flip side of the discussion of the development of trust between members of Black Diaspora communities is the development and sustenance of mistrust between those communities and the European communities in which they were imbedded. Douglass commits significant energy to this inquiry:

> *I have often been utterly astonished, since I came to the north, to find persons who could speak of the singing, among slaves, as evidence of their contentment and happiness. It is impossible to conceive of a greater mistake. Slaves sing most when they are most unhappy. The songs of the slave represent the sorrows of this heart; and he is relieved by them, only as an aching heart is relieved by its tears.*[20]

While Douglass' analysis may appear completely innocuous, for commentators who followed, particularly Du Bois and Alain Locke, it forms an essential

---

[18]Douglass, 1982: 62.

[19]Reed, 1999: 197–224.

[20]Douglass, 1982: 58.

theme of their analysis. For both Du Bois and Locke it forms the foundation for their attempt to categorize the spirituals, and reconstruct true forms of early Black music. In that development it moves from the astonishment based upon European American faulty analysis to directly addressing "the debasements" of the spirituals in many of their manifestations:

> Side by side, too, with the growth has gone the debasements and imitations— the Negro "minstrel" songs, many of the "gospel" hymns, and some of the contemporary "coon" songs, --a mass of music in which the novice may easily lose himself and never find the real Negro melodies.[21]

Underlying this is the fundamental assertion that most European Americans cannot be trusted to truly understand honest expressions of Black consciousness. The core of this misunderstanding is the prevalent exploitation of the Black population as a labor intensive population by a leisured or leisure aspirant economic class or those sympathetic to such a class. For Du Bois the various debasements of the spirituals inhibited not only the expression of Black consciousness but as they competed unfairly with the true spirituals placed various obstacles in the path of the Black collective consciousness. Alain Locke who becomes our first major political thinker to develop an entire treatise on Black music, *The Negro and His Music*, develops a very similar analysis to Du Bois in this area concerning himself with the classification of different forms of Black music. Locke who wrote a generation following the publication of Du Bois' *Souls* focused more on achievement as opposed to the predominate theme of resistance found in both Douglass and Du Bois. His main concern with Black music was its development on a larger scale, or, more precisely, on a more refined scale. Locke is looking to develop the beauty held within true Black folk music into music on the classical level. Primarily for Locke this meant the institutionalization of Black folk music in its true form. In passing it is worth mentioning that Locke's separation of minstrel music from the spirituals is especially harsh and in its harshness revealing of this developing mistrust based upon the European skewing of musical expressions of the Black consciousness. For Locke the minstrel was "no lyric troubadour, but an improvising clown."[22] This is important to note that this was the original point of access to Black music for most European Americans. Such a point of entry ironically placed ass backwards both the truest medium of Black consciousness and its content in the American mainstream mind.

It is within Amiri Baraka's work, *Blues People* that trust primarily through the concept of righteousness achieves the next level of development in Black music. Baraka, then LeRoi Jones, develops the first argument which incorporates

---

[21]Du Bois, 1898: 209.
[22]Locke, 1936: 43.

Black music as a fundamental aspect of Black political thought. Indeed Baraka's political analysis proceeds from an understanding of the development of Black music:

> The Negro as slave is one thing. The Negro as American is quite another. But the path the slave took to "citizenship" is what I want to look at. And I make my analogy through the slave citizen's music—through the music that is most closely associated with him: blues and a later, but parallel development, jazz.[23]

Later works developed upon Baraka's thesis include Robin Kelley's *Race Rebels* and Angela Davis' *Blues Legacies and Black Feminist Thought* and on a broader cultural scope than just music Lawrence Levine's *Black Culture and Black Consciousness*. Baraka's goal was nothing less than to find the essence of Black political thought and action through an analysis of Black music. Douglass while seemingly sharing this belief never attempts to develop it beyond an initial observation. Writing in a Christian context he left many Black/African artifacts displayed on various shelves such as his allusion to the function and success of his friend's Sandy root. Du Bois nor Locke centered their works on such a radical argument even though they developed acute understandings of Black music.

It is not sufficient to say that given Baraka's argument that one can understand the political will of African Americans. Given the complexity of the collective understandings of people of African ancestry in the United States, Baraka's argument justifies nothing less than the following correlative—contained in an understanding of Black music is a map of the contours of the political discourse of the Black community including the conflicts between various competing understandings. In terms of Black trust Baraka's work combines both the resistance of Douglass and the achievement orientation of Locke. More importantly the discussion of righteousness, so essential for Douglass and his time, is developed simultaneously with its flipside discourse of European mistrust.

> "Blues, had, and still has, a certain weight in the psyches of its inventors. What I am proposing is that the alteration or repositioning of this weight in those same psyches indicates changes in the Negro that are manifested externally."[24]

For Baraka the sorrow songs become the Blues. The blues…the music of a Black Diaspora population battling racial and economic based oppression that resonated deep within the political, social and cultural systems and institutions of oppressive nations. The defining moments of the blues are those in which systems and cultures of oppression are directly addressed or alternatively Black culture and political systems are directly developed. These systems and cultures are directly addressed by giving voice, strong voice, to Black emotional expression within context. That voice is the foundation of the collective will because music within the African

---

[23]Jones, 1963: ix.
[24]Jones, 1963: x.

Diaspora cannot properly function without significant participation from within the Black community. While Locke's understanding of cultural pluralism sought to elevate Black folk music specifically the blues and spirituals to a classical level, Baraka understood Black music as, at least the representation, at most the essence, of Black political pluralism at least a century old in its development.

> *Jazz, as it emerged and as it developed, was based on this new widening of Afro-American culture. In the best of jazz, the freedman citizen conflict is most nearly resolved, because it makes use of that middle ground, the space that exists as the result of any cleavage, where both emotional penchants can exist as ideas of perhaps undetermined validity, and not necessarily as "ways of life."[25]*

And while Baraka may seem to disavow the holism of Black life and music in the passage, to make such a conclusion may be premature. For Baraka may well be indicating jazz as the first articulated step of Black pluralism and its development through a resultant mediation between two previously conflicting ways of life. But whatever the initial state of pluralism in jazz (as pure thought and/or reconciled emotions) it must sooner or later in Black music become holistic, a way of life.

For Baraka righteousness becomes a holistic experience weaving through the very fabric of Black culture. It is so essential to Black music at that particular historic moment that Baraka develops it as an attitude:

> *Music, as paradoxical as it might seem, is the result of thought. It is the result of thought perfected at its most empirical, i.e., as attitude, or stance...If Negro music can be seen to be the result of certain attitudes, certain specific ways of thinking about the world (and only ultimately about the ways in which music can be made), then the basic hypothesis of this book is understood. The negro's music changed as he changed, reflecting shifting attitudes or (and this is equally important) consistent attitudes within changed contexts. And it is why the music changed that seems most important to me.[26]*

At the essence of bebop jazz lay the various components of Black righteousness, truth and straightforwardness (telling it like it is, keepin' it real), imploding myths and the distrust of formality. This is and has always been labeled in U.S. society as non conformity. And Blacks have historically been understood in the United States as the most consistently non conformist group. This righteousness was at the core of bebop because of the early jazz/blues period. For Baraka bebop emerges from the early exploitation of the Black jazz musician by his white counterpart. In its creation, context, and content it fulfills and develops the Black understanding of righteousness.

Without delving too extensively into the history of the exploitation of Black music we need to understand that exploitation as systemic and a function of European American understandings of ethnocentrism and racial superiority. We must also be

---

[25]Jones, 1963: 140.
[26]Jones, 1963: 152–153.

cognizant of the Blues' connection to black face minstrelsy. For each form of Black music Black artists stood at the apex of its creation and development but European American artists co-opted the apex of its excellence both in terms of artistry and economic benefit—Al Jolson, Elvis Pressley, Benny Goodman, etc. Black music was seen as an inferior art form, if art at all. Likewise any musical excellence possessed came from an innate ability and was developed, if at all, because of the same. Black music was credited with nothing that went beyond this innate ability, particularly thought. Therefore quite insidiously European Americans argued that Black music had no function for Black people, artist and audience, beyond its sensuality and seductiveness. It took the European American mind to give it a function beyond, even if that function was purely recreational. The Jolson's, Pressley's and Goodman's provided that excellence to Black music through the least essential of all art's functions—entertainment. Arguably this history formed the motivation for Locke's belief that Black music needed to be elevated to a level synonymous with Europe's classical music.

Enter into this melodrama Louis Armstrong, Charlie Parker, Dizzy Gillespie and other Beboppers. Jazz as an African American art form was perceived very differently by European Americans. According to Baraka it becomes the first genre of Black music to which European Americans have true access. That access is achieved through aesthetics (mastering the methodology) as opposed to (understanding and developing) function. The movement of the Black population from slave to citizen had caused the function of music (always the most essential component from its original African origins) to be balanced by aesthetic concerns which were primarily driven by African American concerns of legitimacy in European American institutions in particular classical music. At as the Blues and later jazz produced written forms European American access to these forms on the aesthetic level became possible.

> But blues is an extremely important part of jazz. However, the way in which jazz utilizes the blues "attitude" provided a musical analogy the white musician could understand and thus utilize in his music to arrive at a style of jazz.

> This development signified also that jazz would someday have to contend with the idea of its being an art (since that was the white man's only way into it). The emergence of the white player meant that Afro-American culture had already become the expression of a particular kind of American experience, and what is most important, that this experience was available intellectually, that it could be learned.

And as it became accessible at the level of art, European American institutions with their wealth of resources attempted to assume control over its development and excellence. It is through those two levels, access and resource control that European Americans began to exploit Black music and Black musicians in a more insidious way than previously achieved, even beyond that of the Black faced minstrels. But maybe more importantly the concentration on aesthetics began to erode the prominence historically held by function within Black music.

> *The white musician understood the blues first as music, but seldom as an atti-*
> *tude, since the attitude, or world-view, the white musician was responsible to*
> *was necessarily quite a different one. And in many cases, this attitude, or world-*
> *view, was one that was not consistent with the making of jazz.*

For Blacks aesthetics without attitude was discourse without context. It operated much like European American law—application of a standardized formula to each situation without adequate contextual understanding. Yet the European American argument surrounding aesthetics in Black music had worn so long Black musicians had begun to incorporate such arguments in their world view, their musical attitude. Jazz as it became self-conscious in terms of removing the marginalization from Black music in the United States sought to bridge the wide gap between the Black musical experience and the European musical experience. To do so without an assumed inferiority during the period in question in the U.S. was extremely difficult, if not impossible.

Louis Armstrong, as much as his contemporary, the actor Lincoln Perry, traversed that space, cultural purgatory, in which the European American artistic experience attempted to simultaneously control and understand the Black artistic experience. Perry never had a chance outside Stepin Fetchit—the ideology surrounding entertainment of European Americans controlled the image of Blacks in Hollywood. The artistic excellence for which Perry strived peeks through its constraints every once in a blue moon. Satchmo traversed an area of that purgatory which in many ways was much less constraining. Like Perry, Armstrong despite being the pioneer of jazz, had a very problematic relationship with the Black community especially amongst younger members within the jazz artist community. Many saw the strained smile that seemed to perpetually don his face in public performances as the most obvious part of the minstrel mask. As Black culture, influenced by Garvey's popular Black Nationalist movement in the 1920's, moved closer to the Black power and consciousness movement of the 1960's black artists struggled to divorce themselves and their art from the derogatory images of its minstrel background. Armstrong represented for the emerging beboppers the socially constructed happy go lucky naturally talented coon image that most of America was still trying to force upon them. The image was simple, undisciplined, an image driven by the basest of desires and pleasures. Still it was much more conducive to profit than the other popular images with which the American populace constrained Black males.

> *Armstrong was not rebelling against anything with his music. In fact, his music*
> *was one of the most beautiful refinements of Afro-American musical tradition,*
> *and it was immediately recognized as such by those Negroes who were not busy*
> *trying to pretend that they had issued from Beiderbecke's culture. The incredible*
> *irony of the situation was that both stood in similar places in the superstructure*

of American society: Beiderbecke, because of the isolation any deviation from mass culture imposed upon its bearer: Armstrong, because of the socio-historical estrangement of the Negro from the rest of America. Nevertheless the music that two made was as dissimilar as possible within jazz.[27]

But for the Beboppers, Sacthmo was not quite Black enough, or more precisely coming from a cultural context in which they had learned of and chosen to address and resist the base exploitation of Black art this generation envisioned Blackness in different terms. And while the world view had not changed drastically for Black people between the two generations it had significantly developed.

Trust was no longer determined as it had in rural times during segregation in terms of resistance (ironically resistance had developed by appeasing and attempting to confuse oppressors). As more Blacks moved to the city and began to recognize their strengths in terms of accomplishment (aggregation of numbers and cultural development), trust became more aggressive, more grounded in achievement and resistance became more overt, less constrained and more spontaneous. Self-definition, self-determination now centered community understandings of trust, still both of these communal concepts were predicated upon one of the oldest of Black experiences—righteousness. It is hard to explain the complexity of this new spiritualism, specifically within a society which constantly simplifies its morality tales and so often relates those tales within its historically favorite White/Black dichotomy. Robin Kelley in his work on Black urban culture, *Race Rebels,* understood part of this new spiritualism through the development of "political space."[28] Political space was much more easily developed in Black urban areas than in the rural south due to the aggregation of Blacks and the resultant diversity within these developing communities. Part of this greater diversity included the aggregation of more militant elements within the community. Radicalism always a possibility within the Black community was much more readily camouflaged within the urban environment. Urban streets provided the bulk of that security until particular organizations such as Garvey's UNIA and the Nation of Islam began to institutionalize Black radicalism. The result was the development of a radical Black spiritualism on the urban streets. As I have alluded to at the beginning of this paragraph this new spiritualism in particular dimensions turned aspects of the old spiritualism upon it head. Perhaps of more importance is the related movement of that traditional concept of righteousness moving into the streets. Urban streets provided the context within which this traditional experience, severely constrained and marginalized within southern rural settings, could develop and later be institutionalized.

While Garvey and Elijah Mohammad developed institutions which partially appealed to the new spiritualism, jazz had long held this possibility. Armstrong

---

[27]Jones, 1974: 153–154.

[28]Kelley, 1997: 6-13, 35–53.

himself had been born into the Black working class urban context. His formal schooling ended at the age of seven, Louis learned his music on the streets of New Orleans. However, Armstrong's experiences were steeped in Du Bois double consciousness which was tethered by southern segregation. Running the streets as a pre-teen, his consciousness formed through the experience of righteousness, Armstrong not unexpectedly experienced a youth that was both within and outside of the American mainstream. That duality followed him into his adult life and despite the oppression experienced by Armstrong his love of America, was always apparent. Armstrong purposely changed the date of his birthday from August 4th to July 4th to demonstrate that duality. And while the generation before them would have perceived the shrewdness of this action regardless whether or not they believed it to be sincere, the beboppers perceived such acts as conciliatory and too much of a concession to an exploitive oppressor.

Kelley in his analysis of Malcolm X looks at this development of the beboppers in its political dimensions as a conflict between Blacks and European Americans. In the passage below he quotes Gillespi:

> *Well, look at this time, at this stage in my life here in the United States whose foot has been in my ass? The white man's foot has been in my ass hole buried up to his knee in my ass hole!...Now you're speaking of the enemy. You're telling me the German is the enemy. At this point, I can never even remember having met a German. So if you put me out there with a gun in my hand and tell me to shoot at the enemy, I'm liable to create a case of "mistaken identity," of who I might shoot.[29]*

Kelley also speaks of the holistic nature of this political attitude:

> *While the suit itself was not meant as a direct political statement, the social context in which it was created and worn rendered it so. The language and culture of zoot suiters represented a subversive refusal to be subservient. Young black males created a fast-paced, improvisational language which sharply contrasted with the passive stereotype of the stuttering, tongue-tied Sambo; in a world where whites commonly addressed them as "boy," zoot suiters made a fetish of calling each other "man." Moreover, within months of Malcolm's first zoot, the political and social context of war had added an explicit dimension to the implicit oppositional meaning of the suit: it had become an explicitly un-American style.[30]*

Still the key to this change in paradigm was not in its political dimensions despite the essential nature of the development of this political attitude. Instead the key lay within it spiritual dimensions. Into Armstrong's generation there was still, as Dubois argued "a hope—a faith in the ultimate justice of things," not separable from I will argue a hope and faith that this could be achieved in America. So

---

[29]Kelley, 1997: 171–172.
[30]Kelley, 1997: 166.

Armstrong and his generation developed a much more conciliatory and racially inclusive understanding of righteousness. The following generations moved differently, their inner ear attuned to a different rhythm. Young urban Blacks embraced their marginalization in the U.S. (and more thoroughly as a Diaspora population); indeed they sought to further alienate the mainstream population as the two quotes immediately above illustrate.

As young Blacks they tapped into the old concept of righteousness not moderated by what Baraka describes as the attempt to become American. That concept of righteousness had afforded slaves the argument that slave owners were evil and had been extended to those who justified any form of dehumanization. This argument as part of the Black collective experience had moved into the urban context with the descendants of those Blacks held in bondage. A much more radical argument it explains much of the attraction of urban Black males and females to the early argument of the Black Muslims that Europeans were a race created in a test tube by an evil Black scientist. While the Black Muslim argument was much too simplistic to be taken seriously by most urban Blacks the argument did turn upon its head the argument initiated by slave owners and white clergy in both the north and the south that Black Africans were the sons of Ham. That juxtaposition did indeed resonate within the Black consciousness and became a fundamental element of bebop jazz as understood within Black urban communities.

Ironically this new spiritualism which had come up from the south and developed through the urban context became the second wave of Black political movement during the Civil Rights Era. The Black power and consciousness movement through Garveyism and Black Islam, interpreted and introduced to the Black masses primarily through Malcolm X, rested and developed upon that understanding of righteousness. Black trust became centered on the experience of militancy and power, Black achievement.

It is easy to mistake this new spiritualism, in its militancy and its aggregation of power as purely political, many have attempted such simplifications of Black development. Empowerment had been a goal of the population for most of its existence. Such a mistake could easily be made if one does not look at the complexity of the Black experience. Empowerment as an experience had grown out of the Black attempt to gain respectability, to be truly accepted as a human, as much as a need for self determination. The key to that change from Armstrong to the Beboppers was that Europeans were no longer placed at the epitome of human development. This required a diminishing of the European experience as it dealt with Africans and other non-European peoples, it also brought many European values and traditions into severe scrutiny, constraining most of these in the Black collective mindset. To achieve this level of Black trust, a significant degree of marginalization had to be accepted, at the least, expected.

The struggle against dehumanization, to have our labors respected and properly valued, to achieve human dignity as a Black Diaspora population, in terms of Black music took an ironic turn:

No jazzman, not even Miles Davis, struggled harder to escape the entertainer's role than Charlie Parker. The pathos of his life lies in the ironic reversal through which his struggles to escape what in Armstrong is basically a make-believe role of clown resulted in Parker's becoming something far more "primitive"; a sacrificial figure whose struggles against personal chaos, onstage and off, served as entertainment for a ravenous, sensation-starved, culturally disoriented public which had only the slightest notion of its real significance.[31]

While this part of the analysis focuses on the individual struggles of the artist and the constant need of European Americans to recast musicians and especially the human discourse into terms necessary for serving specific functions of American society, much of Ellison's analysis concentrates on the collective aspects of this struggle and places them within a particular historical context.

The thrust toward respectability exhibited by the Negro jazzmen of Parker's generation drew much of its immediate fire from their understandable rejection of the traditional entertainer's role—a heritage from the minstrel tradition—exemplified by such an outstanding creative musician such as Louis Armstrong... By rejecting Armstrong they thought to rid themselves of the entertainer's role. And by way of getting rid of the role, they demanded, in the name of their racial identity, a purity of status which by definition is impossible to the performing artist.... The result was a grim comedy of racial manners, with the musicians employing a calculated surliness and rudeness, treating the audience very much as many white merchants in poor negro neighborhoods treat their customers, and the white audiences were shocked at first but learned quickly to accept such treatment as evidence of "artistic" temperament. Then comes a comic reversal. Today the white audience expects the rudeness as part of the entertainment.... For the jazzmen it has become a proposition of the more you win the more you lose.[32]

The conflict between, what at the time where, the two largest ethnic groups in the U.S., their respective cultures, and respective forms of music, had never been quite as acute. The movement towards Black autonomy was no less acute in music and in some ways much more. However the attitude was classified, it was a small part of a much larger and more essential discourse, a discourse grounded in the Black community and much more concerned about the development of that community than even Ellison gives credit. Admittedly, the break was hard, and admittedly, individuals such as Armstrong suffered from this hard break—still it was necessary. And in its rudeness it most likely changed the dynamics of the policy of integration in the perception of African Americans, pushing it towards pluralism and away from assimilation.

As much as one perceives the new spiritualism as a movement away from the Black church and during the movement the Black church did suffer a significant

---

[31]Ellison, Ralph, 2001: 71.

[32]Ellison, 2001: 69–70.

loss of influence among Black youth, or a symptom of urbanization, one must also look through the lens that Baraka offers us, understanding the early Christianization of most Blacks as a movement towards assimilation, or at least away from African roots. Given the nationalistic rhetoric, the rhetoric which placed the European Christian church as an active oppressor, and the budding realization of Diaspora Blacks that the Christianity to which they were introduced was not simply a moral argument but inseparable from the European historical experience, the numbers of Blacks leaving the church many in emulation of Malcolm, must also be seen as a reaction against assimilation.

The further development in Black music which took hold in Black urban areas records much of this reaction. The innovation popular within the community during the period (the 70's and 80's) traced its lineage, not from gospel, but from the Blues through jazz and soul music, Funk music picked up all the elements of this new spiritualism particularly the marginalization, even the drug culture associated with bebop. But this drug culture was not a new artifact of the music or the Blues attitude, it simply reflected the harsh replacement of the rural segregation context with an inner city institutionalized racism context. As movement to the city occurred parallel movement from alcohol to more harsh drugs took place. Funk music eventually spurs the development of rap and gangsta rap music and in its watered down version hip hop culture. All genres have struggled with marginalization as much if not more so as did bebop. Most have embraced the marginalization under the same terms as did bebop, with the exception of hip hop which glorifies marginalization as a way into mainstream privilege. The degree to which these particular genres are constrained through the concept of righteousness is a strong indication of their ability to contribute to the development of trust within Black communities.

References Works

Barrett, Leonard E (1974). Soul-Force: *African Heritage in Afro-American Religion.* Garden City: Anchor Press/Doubleday.

Douglass, Frederick (1845). *Narrative of the Life of Frederick Douglass: An American Slave.* Reprinted with an introduction by Houston A. Baker, Jr. New York: Penguin Books, 1986.

Du Bois, W.E.B. (1903). *The Souls of Black Folk.* Reprinted with introduction by Donald B. Gibson. New York: Penguin Classics, 1989.

Ellison, Ralph (2001). *Living With Music.* New York and Toronto: Modern Library (Random House).

Fleurant, Gerdes (1996). *Dancing Spirits: Rhythms and Rituals of Haitian Vodun,* the Rada Rite. London: Greenwood Press.

Jones, Leroi (1963). *Blues People: Negro Music in White America:* Edinburgh: MacGibbon and Kee.

Kelley, Robin (1994). *Race Rebels: Culture, Politics & the Black Working Class.* New York: The Free Press.

Levine, Lawrence (1977). *Black Culture and Black Consciousness: Afro-American Folk Thought from Slavery to Freedom.* New York: Oxford University Press.

Locke Alain (1925). *The New Negro.* New York: Touchstone Rockefeller Center, Simon and Schuster Inc. (1992)

Locke Alain. (1936). *The Negro and His Music.* New York: Arno Press and *The New York Times* (1969).

Reed, Adolph (1999). *Stirrings In the Jug: Black Politics in the Post-Segregation Era.* London: University of Minnesota Press.

Native Americans and the United States, 1830–2000 Action and Response

Steven J. Crum

Introduction

In this chapter, I will focus on federal government policies toward Native American people from the early nineteenth century forward. Although this story has been told numerous times, and scholars have called it an old-fashioned historical approach to the writing of Indian history–an assessment I agree with–I will work hard not to repeat the same examples others have given over the years. Instead, I will provide some new examples as much as possible. My main argument is that the history of federal government policy toward Indian people is one of action on one side and response and reaction on the other. More often than not, the federal government initiated the action and the Indians responded or reacted to it. At times, however, the Indians served as actors and persuaded the federal government what to include in its interactions with tribal people, including treaty provisions of the nineteenth century.

Indian Removal

In 1830, Congress passed the Indian Removal Act, which paved the way for the mass-scale physical removal of thousands of Native Americans who lived east of the Mississippi River. In the southeast alone, the federal government moved roughly 60,000 tribal people to the area we now call eastern Oklahoma (Indian Territory up to 1907). Those of us who study Native American history know the historical accounts of the removed Cherokee, Choctaw, Creek, Chickasaw, and Seminole. We are fully aware of the Trail of Tears of 1838 in which thousands of Cherokee died en route from their former homeland.[1]

Although Indian removal was a case of the American government having its way, at the same time, some of the tribes made certain that favorable provisions ended up in the removal treaties. In the Treaty of Dancing Rabbit Creek of 1830, negotiated with the Choctaw of Mississippi, the Choctaw leadership persuaded the government to include a provision for the education of Choctaw people. The tribe viewed education as a means of "survival" and a way of dealing with the white Americans. With the funds coming from the treaty, the tribe eventually created the Forty Youth Fund, which helped several Choctaws pursue a higher education. Some earned college and university degrees from eastern postsecondary institutions and returned home to help maintain their Choctaw Nation. Concerning the educational provision of the 1930 treaty, it was a case of the Choctaw leadership calling the action and the treaty negotiators responding.[2]

When we read about Indian removal of the nineteenth century, we typically think about eastern Indians being removed west of the Mississippi River. What we seldom read about are the number of far western tribes who were also subjected to the same policy. In the state of California alone, the government applied its removal policy to the tribes of this state, especially in the 1860s. In 1863, California state troops gathered up roughly 400 Concow Maidu of Butte County (about 100 miles north of Sacramento) and marched them across the Sacramento Valley, over the coastal range, and placed them on the Round Valley Reservation in Mendocino County. The descendants of the Maidu still live at Round Valley.[3] In another case, the military gathered up 800 Owens Valley Paiute from eastern California and placed them at Fort Tejon in the mountains overlooking the San Joaquin Valley. Because the military did not have the strength to manage the Paiutes, every one of them eventually escaped and most returned to Owens Valley. A few ended up on the Tule River Reservation between Fresno and Bakersfield.[4]

Along with these actual removal cases in California, there were also removal proposals made by federal officials. In 1862, Senator Milton Latham of the state submitted a bill into Congress which, if passed, would have paved the way for the tribes of the state to be removed over the Sierra Nevada Mountains and placed in Owens Valley. This bill never made it out of Congress. There was also a removal proposal to colonize the tribes of California on some of the off-shore islands near Santa Barbara.[5]

The Reservation Policy

Around the mid-nineteenth century, the government created a new policy called the reservation policy. Its objective was to gather up the tribes of the North American continent and place them on reserves where they could be managed and controlled. Under the supervision of federal agents, the tribes could slowly be subjected to so-called American "civilization" since the white Americans viewed Indians as savages. The new reservation policy did not replace the earlier removal policy entirely. Instead, the federal sector carried out both simultaneously, with the tribes being removed to reservations. The only noticeable difference was that the government did not move the eastern tribes farther west.[6]

Some tribal individuals showed their extreme dislike of the reservation policy by eventually rejecting reservation life. The Office of Indian Affairs (today's BIA), the federal agency given the responsibility to run Indian affairs, required the Modoc of extreme northern California to move across the state line and settle on the newly established Klamath reservation of southern Oregon in the 1860s. At first the tribe went along with the plan. However, the Modoc felt uncomfortable living in a foreign area. Not willing to face confined reservation life, the Modoc left and returned to their ancestral homeland in northern California. The government branded the Modoc as lawbreakers and declared war against them. This led to the well-known Modoc War of 1873 in which the American military finally won.[7]

To punish the Modoc, the government carried out three forms of punishment. In the first instance, it hung the major leaders and sent their skulls to Washington, D.C., for so-called scientific study. Next, it confined two leaders on Alcatraz Island as prisoners. Third, it removed the larger number of Modoc to eastern Indian Territory, where they remained as prisoners of war of the government until 1909. Removal thus became a form of punishment for tribes that did not accept the reservation policy.[8]

Other Native Americans refused to move to newly established reservations when asked. For example, in 1877, the government created the Duck Valley Reservation, which straddles the Idaho-Nevada border. The plan was to induce all the Western Shoshones of the Great Basin region to move there in the years immediately thereafter. But this effort was largely a failure, for only one-third of the tribe moved, those tribal groups and bands that lived closest to Duck Valley. The other two-thirds publicly refused to move and used the aboriginal argument of their deep attachment to particular valleys and mountain ranges where their ancestors had lived "since time immemorial." Their form of punishment was deliberate indifference; that is, the government largely pretended that nonreservation Indians did not exist in the Basin area. Thus they received little or no services from the Indian bureau. Not until the 1930s would the BIA give these Shoshones consistent federal attention.[9]

Assimilation

Around 1880, the American government came up with a third generalized Indian policy called assimilation with the objective to Americanize those Indians living on reservation land. The assimilation campaign had several components. The Indian bureau created on-reservation police forces and tribal courts to make adult Indians give up their native ways. The police forces consisted of tribal members who were bought off by BIA agents. Agents provided them various benefits and services, which included wood-frame houses, firewood, and extra food provisions. Under the supervision of the agent, the police tried to make their own kind surrender their Indian ways and become good Americans.[10]

Many tribal individuals outsmarted the assimilation plan by pretending to become responsible Americans. They joined Christian churches, learned rudimentary

English, and displayed different forms of American patriotism. Some reservation Indians organized Fourth of July Grounds where they camped out for days to celebrate American independence and democracy. But in reality these encampments were a way for the Indians to create underground cultures that allowed the participants to perpetuate native dances and social practices, including indigenous forms of gambling. To this day, the descendants of the nineteenth-century reservation Indians still remain native to varying degrees.[11]

One of the most visible forms of assimilation for young Indians was formal schooling. The government developed three kinds of schools in the last quarter of the nineteenth century: reservation day schools, reservation boarding schools, and off-reservation boarding schools. Typically, the youngest children started their schooling in the reservation schools. As they became older, the bureau removed them from their families, kinship groups, and tribes and sent them to large off-reservation schools located hundreds or even thousands of miles away from home. In other instances, very young children spent all their schooling in distant off-reservation boarding schools.[12]

In the government schools, the government subjected the students to a detribalization process. It stripped them of their native dress and issued military uniforms for young boys and Victorian dresses for the girls. It suppressed tribal languages and required the students to speak and read English. It made the students follow American values and practices, which included the puritanical work ethic, Christian values, and die-hard individualism.[13]

As for the students, they reacted to forced schooling by expressing various forms of resistance, which can be classified as "overt" and "covert." Perhaps the most popular form of overt resistance was running away. Unable to cope with institutionalized schooling, an unspecified number of students ran away with the objective of returning home. Most were captured, but some succeeded in returning to their families and tribes. Covert forms of resistance included "work slow down," talking tribal languages behind the scenes, and stealing food from the cafeteria.[14]

Although the vast majority of students ended up learning English and wearing American clothing, they still remained native to varying degrees, and most returned home to their Indian communities. There they lived out their lives by being both American and native. They built wood-frame houses and acquired horses and cattle. Yet, at the same time, they continued to speak their native languages and relied on indigenous medicinal remedies. In short, their schooling was only a partial success.[15]

Another form of assimilation was the breaking apart of Indian reservation land. To carry out this initiative, Congress passed the Dawes Act (General Allotment Act) of 1887, which allowed the federal sector to subdivide reservation land and issue individual allotments to the tribal members. For the most part, adult heads of households received 160 acres of land since this specific acreage represented the size of a nineteenth-century American homestead. The BIA expected the Indian allottees to farm the land and become American-style homesteaders. Once the government surveyed and allotted a reservation, it sold any remaining surplus land. By carrying out these initiatives, it hoped to destroy the tribal way of life and make Indians think and act individualistically rather than communally or tribally.[16]

Many tribal people did not passively accept the allotment process. They expressed their dislike in a number of ways. One person, Lone Wolf of the Kiowa tribe in Indian Territory, took the American government to court because of his opposition to the 1887 act. In the Supreme Court decision *Lone Wolf v. Hitchcock* (1903), Lonewolf argued that the Dawes Act could not be applied to the Kiowa because of prior treaty rights. He was correct, for some years earlier, under the Medicine Lodge Treaty of 1867 made with the Kiowa and other tribes of the southern Great Plains area, the treaty specified that the only way the government could alter the landbase of the reservation given to the Kiowa was if the majority of adults agreed to any form of alteration. But years later, the Kiowa never agreed in the majority to have their reservation subdivided by the Dawes act. Thus the act violated Kiowa treaty rights. However, the Supreme Court disregarded treaty rights and argued that the federal government had superior power over Indian tribes.[17] Therefore, Congress could apply an act to Native Americans, regardless of prior treaty rights.

To show their anger over the Dawes Act, which of course led to substantial land loss, other Native Americans considered leaving the United States completely in the late nineteenth and early twentieth centuries and moving to Mexico. Several tribal individuals from Indian Territory made trips to Mexico between 1890 and 1938 to look for a new homeland where Indian tribes could be free from negative governmental laws and policies. In the opening decade of the twentieth century, Crazy Snake and his followers of Creek Indians of eastern Oklahoma talked about moving to Mexico. As late as the 1930s, some Seminoles of Oklahoma met with the president of Mexico to discuss Mexico as a future home. In the end, these delegations chose to remain in the U.S.[18]

Other aspects of the overall assimilation policy surfaced after the turn of the century. One was the BIA's in-house regulation called Circular 1665 of 1921 and 1923. This BIA regulation either suppressed or prohibited Native American religious practices. It allowed Indians to have only one monthly traditional dance, which could be held from September to February. No dances could be held from March to August. Moreover, the monthly dance could take place only during the day time. No nighttime dance could take place. Only those fifty years and older could participate in the monthly daytime dance. Lastly, Indians could no longer carry out their traditional giveaways.[19]

Most Native American people rejected Circular 1665 and found ways to maneuver around the regulation. Some tribal individuals held dances in remote areas where BIA agents could not find them. Some joined the dances of other tribes held in outlying areas where agents would not or could not visit. Others practiced public exhibition dancing for white audiences, thus enabling them to practice traditional dances throughout the year. The BIA did not prohibit exhibition dances because these dances were nonthreatening and pleased the white crowds that wanted to observe what it labeled "exotic" Indians. Some Indians performed popular forms of white dances and entertainment during early evening hours to convince watchful agents that they were becoming good Americans. Once the officials left, and late at night, the Indians resorted to their traditional dances. All these tactics allowed tribal individuals to outwit the BIA in the early years of the twentieth century.[20]

Cultural Pluralism and the Indian New Deal

As time moved forward in the twentieth century, some white people realized that the government's campaign to assimilate the Indians had largely failed. Native Americans simply could not be completely transformed because of their deep-rooted cultures and traditional beliefs. White reformists advanced the argument that because the U.S. was a democracy where people are given choices, then Indian people must be given the choice to remain native if they wanted. One of the noted reformers was non-Indian John Collier who created the American Indian Defense Association in 1923 with a two-fold purpose: that Indians must be given their religious freedom and that the Indian landbase must be preserved. Besides private individuals such as Collier, even some federal officials concluded that the BIA needed to change some of its policies toward Indian people. In response, Hubert Work, the Secretary of the Interior in 1926, authorized the establishment of a ten-member team to study the "so-called Indian problem" and make recommendations in a published report of how the BIA could be improved.[21]

In 1928, the Meriam team released its lengthy study called *The Problem of Indian Administration,* or popularly known as the Meriam report. The report pointed out the serious problems within Indian affairs, including the substantial land loss of Indian people since the passage of the Dawes Act in 1887, poor health care, and the poor quality of education and life students had received in the BIA boarding schools. At the same time, the report team made positive recommendations of how life could be improved for Native Americans. The federal government needed to provide improved health care for Indians, Indian students needed to be given a quality education in the Indian schools, and the Indian students needed to be taught native subject matter. Here was a case of reformists rejecting the half-century assimilationist policy.[22]

One of the ten members of the Meriam team was Henry Roe Cloud of the Winnebago tribe in Nebraska. After experiencing the boarding school process as a youngster, Cloud made the decision to go to college. He earned more than one college degree, including the bachelor's degree from Yale in 1910. Aware that the BIA did not give Indian students a full high school education in the early twentieth century, he established the American Indian Institute, an all-Indian high school in Wichita, Kansas, for those students who aspired to a full secondary education. Cloud encouraged his students to appreciate their Indianness, and it became obvious why the Meriam report favored the teaching of native subject matter in the Indian schools.[23]

One important end result of the reform sentiment of the 1920s and early 1930s was the Indian Reorganization Act (IRA) of 1934. The provisions of this congressional act were largely the work of John Collier, who became the new commissioner of the BIA in 1933. As a federal official, Collier put his reformist ideas into action by making sure Congress passed the IRA. Some of the provisions of the act were as follows: it ended any further allotment of Indian reservations; it returned to reservation status any remaining surplus land; it allowed tribes to organize politically with tribal constitutions and charters, or it gave tribes a kind of quasi-sovereign status; it provided loans so that tribal individuals could create business enterprises and become better off economically; it provided loans so that Indian students could pursue a college or university education; and it introduced "Indian preference," which was a measure to employ qualified Indians to work in the BIA.[24]

The majority of Indian tribes voted to become IRA tribes since they liked the provisions of the act. Specifically, 181 of them voted in favor of the act. However, 77 tribes voted against it for their own reasons.[25] As a case in point, the Paiutes of Owens Valley voted against the act in large numbers, not because they disliked the act, but because of the BIA's recent rhetoric of Indian removal. Both before and at the time of the act's passage, the BIA had considered removing the Owens Valley Paiutes completely from their ancestral valley in eastern California. The bureau used the argument that the Indians could not really make a living there because the city of Los Angeles had taken much of the water from the Owens River for its California Aquaduct, channeling the river water across the desert to Los Angeles. Thus the BIA wanted the Paiutes to move either to the Walker River Reservation in western Nevada or to move over the Sierra Nevada Mountains and settle down near Merced in the San Joaquin Valley. Insecure about possible removal, the Paiutes voted against the act. In the end, the bureau backed away from removal, allowed the Paiutes to remain, and even created three small reservations for them in the second half of the 1930s: Bishop, Big Pine, and Lone Pine.[26]

The Hupa of northern California also voted against the IRA. Unlike the Paiutes of Owens Valley, the Hupa voted against the act for completely different reasons. First, the tribal leaders favored land allotment, which the IRA ended. Secondly, the Hupa already had a tribal council in operation for some years before Congress passed the act. Thus, there was no need to create a new one under the IRA. Lastly, the Hupa, as well as other tribes of California, had impending claims against the American government. This claims matter was rooted in the eighteen treaties that the Senate did not ratify in the mid-nineteenth century, which would have set aside over seven million acres of land for California Indians. Six years before Congress passed the IRA, it had approved the California Indian Jurisdiction Act of 1928 to allow the California tribes to file suit for past injustices, including the unratified treaties. The Hupa in the mid-1930s felt that the IRA might somehow disrupt the current claims case even though the act itself specified that cases would not be affected.[27] Here was a case of government action and tribal reaction.

Since the passage of the IRA in 1934, tribal individuals have expressed a wide range of views about the act. Some leaders pointed out that despite the act's limitations, it still had some good outcomes. Tim Giago (Lakota), former editor of *Indian Country Today,* stressed that "there wouldn't be any reservations left today if it wasn't for the IRA."[28] Another Lakota, Pat Spears, leader of the Lower Brule Sioux, stated.: "It's better than what it replaced. . . . I don't think we're better off by the IRA. . . . It's been the only vehicle we had, but I think it's time we trade it in."[29] Webster Two Hawk, chairperson of the Rosebud Sioux Tribe, expressed a similar view: "I have mixed opinions regarding the IRA. I have to support it because I work for an IRA government. . . . The IRA was a child of the federal government and did not really contain Indian ideas. . . . In redoing it, I would remove many of the restrictions."[30] Some Lakota leaders were much more critical of the IRA. Robert Fast Horse, tribal judge from Pine Ridge, stressed that the IRA "wouldn't recognize our traditional form of government."[31] Bertha Chasing Hawk of Cheyenne River argued that "the tribal court is useless to us because the [IRA] tribal council can overrule the tribal court's decisions."[32] All of the above individuals are from reservations in North and South Dakota.

Regardless of the IRA's shortcomings, it did create some new directions. The Indian preference clause made it possible for more Indians to be employed by the BIA, especially those who were college educated. By the mid-1940s, the following individuals were superintendents of BIA agencies and reservations: Henry Roe Cloud (Winnebago), Kenneth Marmon (Laguna Pueblo), George LaVatta (Shoshone), Archie Phinney (Nez Perce), Frel Owl (Cherokee), and Gabe Parker (Choctaw).[33]

Termination

In the late 1940s and early 1950s. the BIA inaugurated a new Indian policy called Termination. Its basic purpose was the end of the "long-term historic relationship" the Indian tribes had with the American government. The government wanted Indians to assimilate into the larger dominant society. To carry out the new policy, the BIA and other branches of the government came out with several components of termination. The first was the congressional Indian Claims Commission Act of 1946. Under it, the government wanted to compensate the Indian tribes for all unjust acts committed against Indian people. The tribes would be given the opportunity to develop shopping lists and submit documented examples of injustices before the Indian Claims Commission. If a tribe won suit, it was awarded a monetary settlement or claims money. The BIA distributed this money in the form of per capita payments.[34]

Another component was House Concurrent Resolution (HCR) 108 in 1953, which paved the way for the elimination of various Indian reservations across the country. Under HCR 108, the Indians lost 1.3 million acres of land in the postwar period. The BIA wanted the more successful tribes to be terminated first, including the Menominee of Wisconsin and the Klamath of Oregon. But in the end, most of the tribes terminated were small and defenseless. This included forty small Indian rancherias of California and four Southern Paiute bands of southwestern Utah.[35]

Another component of termination was Operation Relocation (1952) in which the BIA induced reservation people to leave their respective reservations and move to urban areas. The BIA provided incentives, including paid transportation; rent money for the first few months; short-term educational training that included auto mechanics, welding, licensed practical nursing, and dental assistant training; and the overall promise of a better way of life, which included jobs, education, and recreation.[36]

From a statistical standpoint, relocation was extremely successful, for thousands of Indians across the nation moved to various big cities that had BIA-run relocation centers. Some of the cities included Chicago, Dallas-Fort Worth, Denver, Detroit, Los Angeles, Oakland, San Francisco, and San Jose. As a result of relocation, Native Americans became markedly urbanized from the 1950s forward. In 1950, only 13.4 percent of the Indian population lived in cities, whereas by 1980, fifty percent of them were urbanites. The Indian population of California alone skyrocketed after 1950. In 1950, only 19,000 Indians lived in the state. By 1960, it was 39,000. By 1980, it stood at 200,000 with relocation being the huge factor.[37]

The relocation component was both a success and a failure. On the success side, if the BIA's plan was to amalgamate Indians into the overall population in urban America, this effort led to urban Indians having one of the highest out-marriage rates in the nation. Those in the cities have a 50/50 chance of marrying non-Indians. On the failure side, many urban Indians did not melt into urban white America. Instead, they looked for ways to remain native. Some worked hard to live in certain neighborhoods so that families could visit one another. Christian Indians established all-Indian churches in the inner city. Those who were more traditional held sweat ceremonies in their backyards and carried out Peyote ceremonies.

Most attended intertribal pow wows. Others sponsored all-Indian sports, which included basketball and softball tournaments. Others gathered at intertribal urban Indian centers that provided various services, including job referral and social gatherings. In short, urban Indians reacted and created ways to remain native and never surrendered their identities, both tribal and intertribal.[38]

Self-Determination

After 1960, the American government came up with still another Indian policy called self-determination. This policy in certain ways was the opposite of termination. The government encouraged Indians to remain on reservations if they chose. The BIA wanted the tribes to become involved in running their own affairs with federal financial support. Like termination, self-determination had a number of components. The Department of Housing and Urban Development (HUD) helped tribal families build "self-help" houses to replace the older substandard houses that lacked indoor running water and other basic necessities. These new houses of the 1960s forward eventually became known as HUD houses, named after the federal department.[39]

Reservation Indians also benefitted from aspects of the Office of Economic Opportunity (OEO) which was intended for poor people in general, regardless of race. Young Indian students entered preschool programs called Headstart, and high school students lived on college campuses during summer months under Upward Bound. This latter program sought to encourage the high school students to consider higher education after graduating from high school.[40]

The BIA also encouraged the teaching of Indian languages and culture in reservation-based schools run by the tribes themselves. The Rough Rock Demonstration School of the Navajo reservation in Arizona was an example of the Navajos creating their own school to emphasize native culture. The school received financial support from the BIA. Several other tribes would also build their own tribally run schools to provide elementary and secondary education. These schools received support from the congressional Indian Self-Determination and Education Assistance Act of 1975.[41]

Self-determination also encouraged tribal people to develop reservation-based higher education programs because of the shortcomings of mainstream higher education. The Navajo Nation established its Navajo Community College in 1968 (renamed Dine College in 1997). This tribally controlled college inspired dozens of other tribes also to establish tribal colleges.[42] As of 2000, thirty-three tribally run colleges existed throughout the U.S. They are run largely by college-educated tribal people, and they offer Indian courses to the students. The colleges receive funding from a number of sources, including the congressional Tribally Controlled Community College Act of 1978.

Congress supported the notion of self-determination in the late 1960s and 1970s by passing more than one act. The Indian Civil Rights Act of 1968 applied certain aspects of the U.S. Bill of Rights to Indian reservations. This meant that reservation-based Indian people possessed certain constitutional guarantees, including the freedom of religion, the freedom of the press, and the right to assemble. The Indian Child Welfare Act of 1978 provided a preference of who could adopt Indian children. First preference is given to the child's extended family, second to other members of the child's tribe, third to members of other tribes, and fourth to non-Indians if no one adopted from the three higher categories. Congress passed this law to make sure an adopted Indian child would remain connected to his native culture. In the same year, Congress passed the American Indian Religious Freedom Act which allowed Indian people to possess sacred objects (e.g., eagle feathers), overall freedom to practice traditional religions both on and off reservation, and the right to practice ceremonies at traditional places.[43]

Self-Governance

The most recent federal Indian policy is self-governance, which emerged in the late 1980s. For the most part, self-governance is an extension of self-determination but with some big differences. Under it, the BIA wants to shift its long-term functions over to the tribes themselves. One example of this action is higher education, which has been a BIA function since the early 1930s. From the 1950s forward, the BIA's regional area offices administered higher education grants and loans to Indian students pursuing a postsecondary education. But under self-governance, the tribes themselves receive BIA funds to run their own higher education programs. The BIA is no longer involved except to channel funds.[44]

Conclusion

In this brief account of the history of Indian policy, we have looked at the pattern of government action and native responses and reactions. Although this has been the prevalent pattern for almost two centuries, there are also times when the process is reversed with the Indians as actors and the government as the reactor. For example, in 1916, the BIA began to add the higher high school grades to its off-reservation boarding schools, which went only to the eighth grade. This BIA action was in response to the Indian members of the intertribal organization Society of American Indians, which asserted that Indians should be given more education instead of being educated as simple laborers in the Indian schools.[45] More recently, in 1988, Congress passed the Indian Gaming Regulatory Act, which determines what tribal nations can do in the domain of gaming. The act designates three classes of gaming: (1) traditional gaming, which tribes can carry out without restriction; (2) gaming such as bingo and card games, which Indian tribes can have in their casinos but would be regulated by a national Indian gaming commission; and (3) Nevada-styled gaming, which the tribes can carry out but only if these forms are legal within a given state where the Indian casino is located. Congress passed the law because it wanted to regulate the rising tide of Indian gaming that started in 1979 with the Seminole tribe in Florida. As of the late 1990s, 148 tribal groups had casinos with class three gaming. They introduced them for two reasons in the 1980s. The first was to move away from the state of poverty that many tribes had lived in for decades. Second, in the early 1980s, President Reagan's administration reduced substantially federal funds for poverty programs. The tribes sought new sources of funding for tribal survival, and one means was the revenue from new casinos. But when casinos started to become too numerous, the government stepped in with its regulations.[46] Here was a case of Indian action and government reaction.

◆ Notes

[1]Philip Weeks, *Farewell My Nation: The American Indian and the United States, 1820–1890* (Arlington Heights, IL: Harlan Davidson, Inc., 1990), 22–23; Francis Paul Prucha, *The Great Father: The United States Government and the American Indians,* abridged edition (Lincoln: University of Nebraska Press, 1984), 64–93.

[2]7 Stat. 315; Grayson B. Noley, "The History of Education in the Choctaw Nation from Precolonial Times to 1830," (Ph.D. dissertation, Pennsylvania State University, 1976), 172; Clara Sue Kidwell, *Choctaws and Missionaries in Mississippi, 1818–1918* (Norman: University of Oklahoma Press, 1995), 96; 136; James D. Morrison, *Schools for the Choctaws* (Durant, OK: Choctaw Bilingual Education Program, 1978), 240.

[3]Dorothy Hill, *The Indians of Chico Rancheria* (Sacramento, CA: Department of Parks and Recreation, 1978), 39–42.

[4]Steven Crum, "Deeply Attached to the Land: The Owens Valley Paiutes and Their Rejection of Indian Removal, 1863 to 1937," *News From Native California,* 14 (summer 2001): 18.

[5]"A bill . . ." *The Visalia (Weekly) Delta,* 5 June 1862, p. 2; "About Indian Affairs," *The Visalia (Weekly).Delta,* 17 December 1983, p. 2; James J. Rawls, *Indians of California: The Changing Image* (University of Oklahoma, 1984), 169.

[6]Prucha, *The Great Father,* 116, 129–132, 181–197; Weeks, *Farewell My Nation,* 60, 159, 170, 178, 208.

[7]Lucille J. Martin, "A History of the Modoc Indians: An Acculturation Study," *The Chronicles of Oklahoma,* 47 (winter 1969–70): 398–417.

[8]Ibid., 420–421, 441.

[9]Steven Crum, *The Road on Which We Came* (Salt Lake City: University of Utah Press, 1994), 43–84.

[10]Prucha, *The Great Father,* 195–197, 218–219; Weeks, *Farewell My Nation,* 217–232.

[11]Crum, *The Road,* 52.

[12]David Wallace Adams, *Education for Extinction: American Indians and the Boarding School Experience, 1875–1928* (Lawrence: University Press of Kansas, 1995), 21–24, 28–59.

[13]Ibid., 97–163.

[14]Ibid., 232–238; K. Tsianina Lomawaima, *They Called It Prairie Light: The Story of Chilocco Indian School* (University of Nebraska Press, 1994), 115–126.

[15]Adams, *Education for Extinction,* 273–306.

[16]Prucha, *The Great Father,* 224–228.

[17]Blue Clark, *Lone Wolf v. Hitchcock: Treaty Rights and Indian Law at the End of the Nineteenth Century* (University of Nebraska, 1994).

[18]Steven Crum, " 'America, Love It or Leave It': Some Native American Initiatives to move to Mexico, 1890–1940," *The Chronicles of Oklahoma,* 79 (winter 2001–02): 408–429.

[19]Peggy V. Beck and Anna L. Walters, *The Sacred: Ways of Knowledge, Sources of Life* (Tsaile: Navajo Community College Press, 1977), 158–161.

[20]Annette Louise Reed, "Rooted in the Land of Our Ancestors, We Are Strong: A Tolowa History," (Ph.D. dissertation, University of California, Berkeley, 1999), 155–163.

[21]Kenneth R. Philp, *John Collier's Crusade for Indian Reform, 1920–1954* (Tucson: University of Arizona Press, 1977), 55–91; Peter Iverson, *'We Are Still Here,' American Indians in the Twentieth Century* (Wheeling, IL: Harlan Davidson, Inc., 1998), 58–76.

[22]Prucha, *The Great Father,* 277–279; Iverson, *'We Are Still Here,'* 75.

[23]Steven Crum, "Henry Roe Cloud: A Winnebago Indian Reformer: His Quest for American Indian Higher Education," *Kansas History,* 11 (autumn 1988): 171–184.

[24]Prucha, *The Great Father,* 311–339; Philp, *John Collier's Crusade,* 135–186; Iverson, *'We Are Still Here,'* 77–102.

[25]Philp, *John Collier's Crusade,* 163; Prucha, *The Great Father,* 324.

[26]Crum, "Deeply Attached to the Land," 19.

[27]Joachim Roschmann, "No 'Red Atlantis' on the Trinity: Why the Hupa Rejected the Indian Reorganization Act," paper presented at the Sixth Annual California Indian Conference, 27 October 1990; George H. Phillips, *The Enduring Struggle: Indians in California History* (San Francisco: Boyd & Fraser Publishing Company, 1981), 50, 69.

[28]Quoted in "Lakotas Have Different Views on Indian Reorganization Act," *Lakota Times,* 28 November 1984, 7.

[29]Ibid.

[30]Quoted in "Fifty Years of IRA–Working or Not?" *Lakota Times,* 4 July 1984, 1.

[31]"Lakotas Have Different Views," 7.

[32]Ibid.

[33]*Interior Department Appropriation Bill for 1947,* 97th Congress, 2nd session, Part I (Washington, D.C.: Government Printing Office, 1946), 822.

[34]Donald L. Fixico, *Termination and Relocation: Federal Indian Policy, 1945–1960* (Albuquerque: University of New Mexico Press, 1986), 3–21; Larry W. Burt, *Tribalism in Crisis: Federal Indian Policy, 1953–1961* (UNM, 1982); Prucha, *the Great Father,* 340–356; Iverson, *'We Are Still Here,'* 103–138.

[35]Fixico, *Termination and Relocation,* 91–110; Prucha, *The Great Father,* 340–356.

[36]Ibid., 137–157; Donald L. Fixico, *The Urban Indian Experience in America* (University of New Mexico, 2000), 8–25.

[37]Prucha, *The Great Father,* 394; Francis Paul Prucha, *Atlas of American Indian Affairs* (University of Nebraska Press, 1990), 142; Russell Thornton, *American Indian Holocaust and Survival: A Population History Since 1492* (University of Oklahoma, 1987), 227.

[38]Thornton, *American Indian Holocaust,* 236; Fixico, *The Urban Indian Experience,* 74, 80, 125, 127, 133.

[39]George Pierre Castile, *To Show Heart: Native American Self-Determination and Federal Indian Policy, 1960–1975* (University of Arizona Press, 1998), 23–42.

[40]Ibid, 35–42.

[41]Margaret Connell Szasz, *Education and the American Indian: The Road to Self-Determination,* 3rd ed. (University of New Mexico, 1999), 169–187.

[42]Wayne J. Stein, *Tribally Controlled Colleges: Making Good Medicine* (New York: Peter Lang, 1992).

[43]Iverson, *'We Are Still Here,'* 170–171; Prucha, *The Great Father,* 379.

[44]David E. Wilkins, *American Indian Politics and the American Political System* (New York: Rowman & Littlefield Publishers, Inc., 2002), 105, 117–118.

[45]"Editorial Comment," *Quarterly Journal of the Society of American Indians,* 2 (April–June 1914): 99; *Annual Report of the Department of the Interior, 1915, Vol. II: Indian Affairs and Territories* (Washington, D.C.: GPO, 1916), 7.

[46]W. Dale Mason, *Indian Gaming: Tribal Sovereignty and American Politics* (University of Oklahoma, 2000), 44, 47, 64–65; Wilkins, *American Indian Politics,* 164–172.

The History of Asians in America

Timothy Fong

Visibility and Invisibility

On October 14, 2000, Miss Hawaii, Angela Perez Baraquio, was crowned Miss America 2001, becoming the first Filipino American and Asian American ever to hold the title. Miss California, Rita Ng, the first Asian American to hold that state's beauty title, was selected as the second runner-up. This seemingly innocent historical event was not lost to many Asian Americans, especially Filipino Americans. "After years of invisibility in the mainstream and being seen as inferior to accepted standards of beauty, we now have a sudden validation of the multicultural in America," beamed *Asian Week* columnist Emil Guillermo. Despite his celebratory mood, Guillermo also touched on an important irony. Baraquio was never referred to as Filipino American or Asian American. Instead, she was referred to as Hawaiian. On the surface, this would seem to make sense because she is from Honolulu. "So what explains Miss Louisiana being reported as 'black' . . . and Baraquio's Hawaiian?" Guillermo asked incredulously. "The significance is that since their arrival on the scene in America at the turn of the century, Filipinos have toiled quietly and invisibly. It seems when they get face time, they don't get the credit they deserve."[1]

Guillermo's observation speaks loudly to the fact that Asian Americans are at once visible, yet invisible. This is particularly true with regards to the history of Asians in the United States. The historical experience of Asian Americans is not at all atypical of other minority groups. As a distinct racial minority group, and as immigrants, Asian Americans faced enormous individual prejudice, frequent mob violence, and extreme forms of institutional discrimination. But Asian Americans have not merely been victims of hostility and oppression; indeed, they have also shown remarkable strength and perseverance, which is a testimony to their desire to make the United States their home.

Fong, Timothy P., *Contemporary Asian American Experience, The: Beyond The Model Minority,* 2nd Edition, © 2002, pp.15–35. Reprinted by permission of Pearson Education, Inc., Upper Saddle River, NJ.

Immigration

Between 1848 and 1924, hundreds of thousands of immigrants from China, Japan, the Philippines, Korea, and India came to the United States in search of a better life and livelihood. Although this period represents the first significant wave, these immigrants were by no means the very first Asians to come to America. Recent archaeological finds off the coast of Southern California have led to speculation that the West Coast may have been visited by Buddhist missionaries from China in the fifth century. Direct evidence of this claim is still being debated, but it is known that the Spanish brought Chinese ship-builders to Baja California as early as 1571, and later Filipino seamen were brought by Spanish galleons from Manila and settled along the coast of Louisiana. Chinese merchants and sailors were also present in the United States prior to the discovery of gold in California in 1848. Most people are unaware that Asian Indians were brought to America during the late eighteenth century as indentured servants and slaves.[2]

The California gold rush did not immediately ignite a mass rush of Chinese immigrants to America. In fact, only a few hundred Chinese arrived in California during the first years of the gold rush, and most of them were merchants. However, large-scale immigration did begin in earnest in 1852 when 52,000 Chinese arrived that year alone. Many Chinese came to the United States not only to seek their fortunes but also to escape political and economic turmoil in China. As gold ran out, thousands of Chinese were recruited in the mid-1860s to help work on the transcontinental railroad. Eventually more than 300,000 Chinese entered the United States in the nineteenth century, engaging in a variety of occupations. During this same period Chinese also immigrated to Hawaii, but in far fewer numbers than to the continental United States.[3]

Large capitalist and financial interests welcomed the Chinese as cheap labor and lobbied for the 1868 Burlingame Treaty, which recognized "free migration and emigration" of Chinese to the United States in exchange for American trade privileges in China. As early as 1870 Chinese were 9 percent of California's population and 25 percent of the state's work force.[4] The majority of these Chinese were young single men who intended to work a few years and then return to China. Those who stayed seldom married because of laws severely limiting the immigration of Chinese women and prohibiting inter-marriage with white women. The result was the Chinese were forced to live a harsh and lonely bachelor life that often featured vice and prostitution. In 1890, for example, there were roughly 102,620 Chinese men and only 3,868 Chinese women in the United States, a male to female ratio of 26:1.[5] Despite these conditions, Chinese workers continued to come to the United States.

Following the completion of the transcontinental railroad in 1869, large numbers of unemployed Chinese workers had to find new sources of employment. Many found work in agriculture where they cleared land, dug canals, planted orchards, harvested crops, and were the foundation for successful commercial production of many California crops. Others settled in San Francisco and other cities to manufacture shoes, cigars, and clothing. Still others started small businesses such as restaurants, laundries, and general stores. Domestic service such as house boys, cooks, and gardeners were also other areas of employment for the Chinese. In short, the Chinese were involved in many occupations that were crucial to the economic development and domestication of the western region of the United States.[6] Unfortunately, intense hostility against the Chinese reached its peak in 1882 when Congress passed the Chinese Exclusion Act intended to "suspend" the entry of Chinese laborers for ten years. Other laws were eventually passed that barred Chinese laborers and their wives permanently.[7]

The historical experience of Japanese in the United States is both different yet similar to that of the Chinese. One major difference is that the Japanese immigrated in large numbers to Hawaii, and they did not come in large numbers to the United States until the 1890s. In 1880 only 148 Japanese were living in the U.S. mainland. In 1890 this number increased to 2,000, mostly merchants and students. However, the population increased dramatically when an influx of 38,000 Japanese workers from Hawaii arrived in the U.S. mainland between 1902 and 1907.[8] The second difference was the fact the Japanese were able to fully exploit an economic niche in agriculture that the Chinese had only started. The completion of several national railroad lines and the invention of the refrigerator car were two advancements that brought tremendous expansion in the California produce industry. The early Japanese were fortunate to arrive at an opportune time, and about two thirds of them found work as agricultural laborers. Within a short time the Japanese were starting their own farms in direct competition with non-Japanese farms. By 1919 the Japanese controlled over 450,000 acres of agricultural land. Although this figure represents only 1 percent of active California agricultural land at the time, the Japanese were so efficient in their farming practices that they captured 10 percent of the dollar volume of the state's crops.[9]

The third major difference was the emergence of Japan as a international military power at the turn of the century. Japan's victory in the Russo-Japanese War (1904–1905) impressed President Theodore Roosevelt, and he believed a strategy of cooperation with the Japanese government was in the best interest of the United States. Roosevelt blocked calls for complete Japanese exclusion and instead worked a compromise with the Japanese government in 1907 known as the "Gentleman's Agreement." This agreement halted the immigration of Japanese laborers but allowed Japanese women into the United States. With this in mind, the fourth difference was the fact that the Japanese in the United States were able to actually increase in population, start families, and establish a rather stable community life.[10]

Filipino immigration began after the United States gained possession of the Philippines following the Spanish-American War in 1898. The first Filipinos to arrive were a few hundred *pensionados,* or students supported by government scholarships. Similar to the Japanese experience, a large number of Filipinos went directly to Hawaii before coming to the U.S. mainland. Between 1907 and 1919 over 28,000 Filipinos were actively recruited to work on sugar plantations in

Hawaii. Filipinos began to emigrate to the United States following the passage of the 1924 Immigration Act, which prohibited all Asian immigration to this country, and there was a need for agricultural and service labor.[11]

Because Filipinos lived on American territory, they were "nationals" who were free to travel in the United States without restriction. In the 1920s over 45,000 Filipinos arrived in Pacific Coast ports, and a 1930 study found 30,000 Filipinos working in California. These Filipinos were overwhelmingly young, single males. Their ages ranged between 16 and 29, and there were 14 Filipino men for every Filipina. Sixty percent of these Filipinos worked as migratory agricultural laborers, and 25 percent worked in domestic service in Los Angeles and San Francisco. The rest found work in manufacturing and as railroad porters. Unlike the Japanese, Filipinos did not make their mark in agriculture as farmers, but as labor union organizers.[12] Both Filipino farm worker activism and Japanese farm competition created a great deal of resentment among white farmers and laborers.

Koreans and Asian Indians slightly predated the Filipinos, but arrived in much smaller numbers. Between 1903 and 1905 over 7,000 Koreans were recruited for plantation labor work in Hawaii, but after Japan established a protectorate over Korea in 1905, all emigration was halted.[13] In the next five years, Japan increased its economic and political power and formally annexed Korea in 1910. Relatively few Koreans lived in the United States between 1905 and 1940. Among those included about 1,000 workers who migrated from Hawaii, about 100 Korean "picture brides," and a small number of American-born Koreans. The Korean population in the United States during that time was also bolstered by roughly 900 students, many of whom fled their home country because of their opposition to Japanese rule. Like other Asian immigrant groups, Koreans found themselves concentrated in California agriculture working primarily as laborers, although a small number did become quite successful farmers.[14]

The first significant flow of Asian Indians occurred between 1904 and 1911, when just over 6,000 arrived in the United States. Unlike the other Asian groups, Asian Indians did not work in Hawaii prior to entering the American mainland, but they worked primarily in California agriculture. Similar to the Chinese, Filipinos, and Koreans, they had an extremely high male to female ratio. Of the Asian Indians who immigrated to the United States between 1904 and 1911, there were only three or four women, all of whom were married.[15] Eighty to ninety percent of the first Asian Indian settlers in the United States were Sikhs, a distinct ethnoreligious minority group in India. Despite this fact, these Sikhs were often called Hindus, which they are not. Sikhs were easily recognizable from all other Asian immigrant groups because of their huskier build, their turbans, and their beards. But like other Asians in the United States at the time, they also worked primarily in California's agricultural industry. Asian Indians worked first as farm workers, and like the Japanese, they also formed cooperatives, pooled their resources, and began independent farming.[16] Immigration restrictions, their relatively small numbers, and an exaggerated male to female ratio prevented Asian Indians from developing a lasting farm presence. One major exception can be found in the Marysville/Yuba City area of Northern California, where Asian Indian Sikhs are still quite active in producing cling peaches.[17]

Anti-Asian Laws and Sentiment

The United States is a nation that claims to welcome and assimilate all new-comers. But the history of immigration, naturalization, and equal treatment under the law for Asian Americans has been an extremely difficult one. In 1790 Congress passed the first naturalization law limiting citizenship rights to only a "free white person."[18] During the period of reconstruction in the 1870s following the end of the Civil War, Congress amended the law and allowed citizenship for "aliens of African nativity and persons of African descent."[19] For a while there was some discussion on expanding naturalization rights to Chinese immigrants, but that idea was rejected by politicians from western states.[20] This rejection is exemplary of the intense anti-Chinese sentiment at the time.

As early as 1850 California imposed the Foreign Miners Tax, which required the payment of $20 a month from all foreign miners.[21] The California Supreme Court ruled in *People v. Hall* (1854) that Chinese could not testify in court against a white person. This case threw out the testimony of three Chinese witnesses and reversed the murder conviction of George W. Hall, who was sentenced to hang for the murder of a Chinese man one year earlier.[22] In 1855 a local San Francisco ordinance levied a $50 tax on all aliens ineligible for citizenship. Because Chinese were ineligible for citizenship under the Naturalization Act of 1790, they were the primary targets for this law.[23]

The racially distinct Chinese were the primary scapegoats for the depressed economy in the 1870s, and mob violence erupted on several occasions through to the 1880s. The massacre of 21 Chinese in Los Angeles in 1871 and 28 Chinese in Rock Springs, Wyoming, in 1885 are examples of the worst incidents. It is within this environment that Congress passed the 1882 Chinese Exclusion Act. The act suspended immigration of Chinese laborers for only ten years, but it was extended in 1892 and 1902. The act was eventually extended indefinitely in 1904.[24] The intense institutional discrimination achieved the desired result: The Chinese population declined from 105,465 in 1880 to 61,639 in 1920.[25]

Anti-Chinese sentiment easily grew into large-scale anti-Asian sentiment as immigrants from Asia continued to enter the United States. During the same period that the Chinese population declined, the Japanese population grew and became highly visible. As early as 1910 there were 72,157 Japanese Americans compared to 71,531 Chinese Americans in the United States.[26] Japanese farmers in California were particularly vulnerable targets for animosity. One of the most sweeping anti-Asian laws was aimed at the Japanese Americans but affected all other Asian American groups as well. The 1913 Alien Land Law prohibited "aliens ineligible to citizenship" from owning or leasing land for more than three years. Initially the

Japanese Americans were able to bypass the law primarily because they could buy or lease land under the names of their American-born offspring (the Nisei), who were U.S. citizens by birth. The law was strengthened in 1920, however, and the purchase of land under the names of American-born offspring was prohibited.[27]

Several sweeping anti-immigration laws were passed in the first quarter of the twentieth century that served to eliminate Asian immigration to the United States. A provision in the 1917 Immigration Act banned immigration from the so-called "Asian barred zone," except for the Philippines and Japan. A more severe anti-Asian restriction was further imposed by the 1924 National Origins Act, which placed a ceiling of 150,000 new immigrants per year. The 1924 act was intended to limit eastern and southern European immigration, but a provision was added that ended any immigration by aliens ineligible for citizenship.[28]

Asian Americans did not sit back passively in the face of discriminatory laws; they hired lawyers and went to court to fight for their livelihoods, naturalization rights, and personal liberties. Sometimes they were successful, but oftentimes they were not. In the case of *Yick Wo v. Hopkins* (1886), Chinese successfully challenged an 1880 San Francisco Laundry Ordinance, which regulated commercial laundry service in a way that clearly discriminated against the Chinese. Plaintiff Yick Wo had operated a laundry service for 22 years, but when he tried to renew his business license in 1885 he was turned down because his storefront was made out of wood. Two hundred other Chinese laundries were also denied business licenses on similar grounds, although 80 non-Chinese laundries in wooden buildings were approved. The Supreme Court ruled in favor of Yick Wo, concluding there was "no reason" for the denial of the business license "except to the face and nationality" of the petitioner.[29]

The inability to gain citizenship was a defining factor throughout the early history of Asian Americans. The constitutionality of naturalization based on race was first challenged in the Supreme Court case of *Ozawa v. United States* (1922). Takao Ozawa was born in Japan but immigrated to the United States at an early age. He graduated from Berkeley High School in California and attended the University of California for three years. Ozawa was a model immigrant who did not smoke or drink, he attended a predominantly white church, his children attended public school, and English was the language spoken at home. When Ozawa was rejected in his initial attempt for naturalization, he appealed and argued that the provisions for citizenship in the 1790 and 1870 acts did not specifically exclude Japanese. In addition, Ozawa also tried to argue that Japanese should be considered "white."

The Court unanimously ruled against Ozawa on both grounds. First, the Court decided that initial framers of the law and its amendment did not intend to *exclude* people from naturalization but, instead, only determine who would be *included*. Ozawa was denied citizenship because the existing law simply didn't include Japanese. Second, the Court also ruled against Ozawa's argument that Japanese were actually more "white" than other darker skinned "white" people such as some Italians, Spanish, and Portuguese. The Court clarified the matter by defining a "white person" to be synonymous with a "person of the Caucasian race." In short, Ozawa was not Caucasian (although he thought himself "white") and, thus, was ineligible for citizenship.[30]

Prior to the *Ozawa* case, Asian Indians already enjoyed the right of naturalization. In *United States v. Balsara* (1910), the Supreme Court determined that Asian Indians were Caucasian and approximately 70 became naturalized citizens. But the Immigration and Naturalization Service (INS) challenged this decision, and it was taken up again in the case of *United States v. Thind* (1923). This time the Supreme Court reversed its earlier decision and ruled that Bhagat Singh Thind could not be a citizen because he was not "white." Even though Asian Indians were classified as Caucasian, this was a scientific term that was inconsistent with the popular understanding. The Court's decision stated, "It may be true that the blond Scandinavian and the brown Hindu have a common ancestor in the dim reaches of antiquity, but the average man knows perfectly well that there are unmistakable differences between them today."[31] In other words, only "white" Caucasians were considered eligible for U.S. citizenship. In the wake of the *Thind* decision, the INS was able to cancel retroactively the citizenship of Asian Indians between 1923 and 1926.

Asian Americans also received disparate treatment compared to other immigrants in their most private affairs, such as marriage. In the nineteenth century, antimiscegenation laws prohibiting marriage between blacks and whites were common throughout the United States. In 1880 the California legislature extended restrictive antimiscegenation categories to prohibit any marriage between a white person and a "negro, mulatto, or Mongolian." This law, targeted at the Chinese, was not challenged until Salvador Roldan won a California Court of Appeals decision in 1933. Roldan, a Filipino American, argued that he was Malay, not Mongolian, and he should be allowed to marry his white fiancée. The Court conceded that the state's antimiscegenation law was created in an atmosphere of intense anti-Chinese sentiment, and agreed Filipinos were not in mind when the initial legislation was approved. Unfortunately, this victory was short-lived. The California state legislature amended the antimiscegenation law to include the "Malay race" shortly after the Roldan decision was announced.[32]

World War II and the Cold War Era

For Asian Americans, World War II was an epoch, but the profound impact was distinct for different Asian American groups. For over 110,000 Japanese Americans, World War II was an agonizing ordeal soon after Japan's attack of Pearl Harbor on December 7, 1941. The FBI arrested thousands of Japanese Americans who were considered potential security threats immediately after the Pearl Harbor bombing raid. Arrested without evidence of disloyalty were the most visible Japanese American community leaders, including businessmen, Shinto and Buddhist priests, teachers in Japanese-language schools, and editors of Japanese-language newspapers. Wartime hysteria rose to a fever pitch, and on February 19, 1942, President Franklin Roosevelt issued Executive Order 9066. This order established various military zones and authorized the removal of anyone who was a potential threat. Although a small number of German and Italian aliens were detained and relocated, this did not compare to the mass relocation of Japanese Americans on the West Coast of the United States.[33]

The order to relocate Japanese Americans because of military necessity and the threat they posed to security, was a fabrication. Even military leaders debated the genuine need for mass relocation, and the government's own intelligence reports found no evidence of Japanese American disloyalty. "For the most part the local Japanese are loyal to the United States or, at worst, hope that by remaining quiet they can avoid concentration camps or irresponsible mobs," one report stated. "We do not believe that they would be at least any more disloyal than any other racial group in the United States with whom we went to war."[34] This helps explain why 160,000 Japanese Americans living in Hawaii were not interned. More telling was the fact that Japanese Americans in the continental United States were a small but much resented minority. Despite government reports to the contrary, business leaders, local politicians, and the media fueled antagonism against the Japanese Americans and agitated for their abrupt removal.[35]

With only seven days notice to prepare once the internment order was issued, and no way of knowing how long the war would last, many Japanese Americans were forced to sell their homes and property at a mere fraction of their genuine value. Japanese Americans suffered estimated economic losses alone of at least $400 million. By August 1942 all the Japanese on the West Coast were interned in ten camps located in rural regions of California, Arizona, Utah, Idaho, Wyoming, and Arkansas. Two thirds of the interned Japanese American men, women, and children were U.S. citizens, whose only crime was their ancestry; even those with as little as one-eighth Japanese blood were interned. The camps themselves were crude, mass facilities surrounded by barbed wire and guarded by armed sentries. People were housed in large barracks with each family living in small cramped quarters dubbed "apartments." Food was served in large mess halls, and toilet and shower facilities were communal. Many of the camps were extremely cold in the winter, hot in the summer, and dusty all year round. The camps remained open for the duration of the war.[36]

After the first year of the camps, the government began recruiting young Japanese American men to help in the war effort. The military desperately needed Japanese Americans to serve as interpreters for Japanese prisoners of war and translators of captured documents. But to the military's incredulity, most American-born Japanese had only modest Japanese-language skills and needed intense training in the Military Intelligence Service Language School before they could perform their duties.[37] It was, however, the heroic actions of the 100th Infantry Battalion, which later merged with the 442nd Regimental Combat Team, that stand out the most among historians. The two segregated units engaged in numerous campaigns and served with distinction throughout Europe. By the end of the war in Europe, for example, the Nisei soldiers of the 442nd suffered over 9,000 casualties, and earned over 18,000 individual decorations of honor. The 442nd was the most decorated unit of its size during all of World War II.[38]

Compared to the Japanese American experience, other Asian American groups fared far better during and after World War II. Changes for Chinese Americans were particularly dramatic. Prior to the war, the image of the Chinese was clearly negative compared to the Japanese. A survey of Princeton undergraduates in 1931 thought the top three traits of the Chinese were the fact they were "superstitious, sly, and conservative," whereas Japanese were considered "intelligent, industrious, and progressive."[39] Immediately after the bombing of Pearl Harbor, Chinese store owners put up signs indicating they were not Japanese, and in some cases Chinese Americans wore buttons stating, "I am Chinese." To alleviate any further identification problems. *Time* magazine published an article on December 22, 1941, explaining how to tell the difference between Chinese and "Japs." The article compared photographs of a Chinese man and a Japanese man, highlighting the distinguishing facial features of each.[40] Just months later, a 1942 Gallup Poll characterized the Chinese as "hardworking, honest, and brave," and Japanese were seen as "treacherous, sly, and cruel."[41]

Employment opportunities outside of the segregated Chinatown community became available to Chinese Americans for the first time during the war and continued even after the war ended. Chinese Americans trained in various professions and skilled crafts were able to find work in war-related industries that had never been open to them before. In addition, the employment of Chinese American women increased threefold during the 1940s. Leading the way were clerical positions, which increased from just 750 in 1940 to 3,200 in 1950. In 1940 women represented just one in five Chinese American professionals, but by 1950 this increased to one in three. On another level, Chinese actors suddenly found they were in demand for film roles—usually playing evil Japanese characters. Shortly after the war, writers such as Jade Snow Wong and Pardee Lowe discovered the newfound interest and appreciation of Chinese Americans could be turned into commercial success through the publication of their memoirs.[42]

On the military front, Asian Americans also distinguished themselves. Over 15,000 Chinese Americans served in all branches of the military, unlike the Japanese Americans who were placed only in segregated infantry units and in the Military Intelligence Service. Similarly, over 7,000 Filipino Americans volunteered for the army and formed the First and Second Filipino Infantry Regiments. About 1,000 other Filipino Americans were sent to the Philippines to perform reconnaissance and intelligence activities for Gen. Douglas MacArthur.[43] Equally significant was the War Bride's Act of 1945, which allowed war veterans to bring wives from China and the Philippines as non-quota immigrants. This resulted in a rapid and dramatic shift in the historic gender imbalance of both groups. For example, between 1945 and 1952, nine out of ten (89.9 percent) Chinese immigrants were female, and 20,000 Chinese American babies were born by the mid-1950s.

Similarly, between 1951 and 1960 seven out of ten (71 percent) Filipino immigrants were female.[44]

On the broad international front, alliances with China, the Philippines, and India eventually began the process of changing the overtly discriminatory immigration laws against Asians. The Chinese Exclusion Law was repealed in 1943, and an annual quota of 105 immigrants from China was allotted. In 1946 Congress approved legislation that extended citizenship to Filipino immigrants and permitted the entry of 100 Filipino immigrants annually. Also in 1946, the Luce-Cellar Act ended the 1917 "Asian barred zone," allowed an immigration quota of 100 from India, and for the first time permitted Asian Indians to apply for citizenship since the *United States v. Thind* case of 1923. Although these changes were extremely modest, they carried important symbolic weight by helping create a favorable international opinion of the United States during and immediately after the war.[45]

Geopolitical events during the Cold War era of the 1950s and 1960s immediately following World War II continued to have important ramifications for Asian Americans. After the 1949 Communist Revolution in China, about 5,000 Chinese students and young professionals were living in the United States. These "stranded" individuals were generally from China's most elite and educated families and not necessarily anxious to return to China because their property had already been confiscated and their livelihoods threatened. They were eventually allowed to stay in the United States.[46] Several other refugee acts in the late 1950s and early 1960s allowed some 18,000 other Chinese to enter and also stay in the United States. Many of these refugees were well-trained scientists and engineers who easily found jobs in private industry and in research universities. These educated professionals were quite distinct from the vast majority of earlier Chinese immigrants because they usually were able to integrate into the American mainstream quickly, becoming the basis of an emerging Chinese American middle class.[47]

The Cold War affected immigration from Asian countries as well, but in a very different fashion. During and after the Korean War (1950–1953), American soldiers often met and married Korean women and brought them home to the United States. Between 1952 and 1960 over 1,000 Korean women a year immigrated to the United States as brides of U.S. servicemen. At the same time, orphaned Korean children, especially girls, also arrived in the United States in significant numbers. Throughout the 1950s and up to the mid-1960s, some 70 percent of all Korean immigrants were either women or young girls. Korea was the site of the actual conflict, but large numbers of troops were also stationed in nearby Japan. Even higher numbers of Japanese women married American soldiers, left their home country, and started a new life in the United States. Roughly 6,000 Japanese wives of U.S. servicemen annually immigrated to the United States between 1952 and 1960, which was over 80 percent of all immigrants from Japan. These Korean and Japanese war brides and Korean orphans were spread throughout the United States and, as a result, had very little interaction with other Asian Americans already living in this country.[48] These war bride families were, however, a significant part of the biracial Asian American baby boom that is discussed in greater detail in Chapter 7.

Post-1965 Asian Immigrants and Refugees

A number of factors have clearly influenced Asian immigration and refugee policies, including public sentiment toward immigrants, demands of foreign policy, and the needs of the American economy. World War II and the Cold War years were epochal for Asian Americans, but the period since the mid-1960s has proven to be even more significant. An overview of U.S. immigration statistics shows just how important recent immigration reforms and refugee policies have affected Asian Americans.

Official records on immigrants entering the United States did not exist before 1820, but since that time it is quite obvious that the largest number of immigrants come from European countries. Between 1820 and 1998 over 38.2 million Europeans immigrated to the United States (see Table 1-1). In contrast, only 8.3 million immigrants came from Asia during the same period of time. Looking at this figure more closely, however, we find over 6.6 million immigrants from Asia arrived in the United States in the period between 1971 and 1998. Although the Chinese and Japanese have the longest histories in the United States, the largest group of Asian immigrants since 1971 has come from the Philippines. Over 1.4 million Filipino immigrants entered the United States between 1971 and 1998. It is also significant to note that over 90 percent of Filipino, Asian Indian, Korean, and Vietnamese have entered the United States since 1971.

This next section focuses on three broad events that have directly influenced both the numbers and diversity of Asians entering the United States since 1965: (1) the passage of the 1965 Immigration Reform Act, (2) global economic restructuring, and (3) the Vietnam War.

The 1965 Immigration Reform Act

Why did the dramatic increase in Asian immigration take place? What changes in the law or public attitudes facilitated such a rapid influx of immigrants from Asia? One important reason was the civil rights movement of the 1960s, which brought international attention to racial and economic inequality in the United States—including its biased immigration policies. This attention is the background for the passage of the 1965 Immigration Reform Act, the most important immigration reform legislation. This act, along with its amendments, significantly increased the token quotas established after World War II to allow the Eastern Hemisphere a maximum of 20,000 per country, and set a ceiling of 170,000.

This act created the following seven-point preference system that serves as a general guideline for immigration officials when issuing visas: (1) unmarried children of

Region	Total 1820–1998	1971–1998	% of Immigrants Since 1971
All countries	64,599,082	18,836,444	29.2
Europe	38,233,062	2,693,920	7.0
Asia	8,365,931	6,673,085	79.7
China*	1,262,050	818,747	64.9
Hong Kong†	398,277	298,129	74.9
India	751,349	710,553	94.6
Japan	517,686	152,302	29.4
Korea	778,899	738,305	94.8
Phillippines	1,460,421	1,337,519	91.6
Vietnam	699,918	692,243	98.9
North America			
Canada and Newfoundland	4,453,149	484,441	10.9
Mexico	5,819,966	4,115,959	70.7
Caribbean	3,525,703	1,435,703	40.7
Central America	1,242,394	985,240	79.3
South America	1,693,441	1,200,740	70.9
Africa	614,375	537,902	87.6
Oceana	250,206	132,031	52.8
Not specified	290,679	24,264	.8

*Beginning in 1957, China includes Taiwan.
†Data not reported separately until 1952.
Source: U.S. Immigration and Naturalization Service, 1998 Statistical Yearbook of the Immigration and Naturalization Service (Washington, DC: U.S. Government Printing Office, 2000), Table, pp. 8–10.

U.S. citizens who are at least 21 years of age; (2) spouses and unmarried children of permanent resident aliens; (3) members of the professions, scientists, and artists of exceptional ability; (4) married children of U.S. citizens; (5) brothers and sisters of U.S. citizens who are at least 21 years of age; (6) skilled or unskilled workers who are in short supply; and (7) non-preference applicants.

U.S. immigration policy also allowed virtually unrestricted immigration to certain categories of people including spouses, children under 21, and parents of U.S. citizens. These provisions served to accelerate immigration from Asia to the United States. The primary goal of the 1965 Immigration Reform Act was to encourage family reunification, however, a much higher percentage of Asian immigrants initially began entering the United States under the established occupational and nonpreference investment categories. In 1969, for example, 62 percent of Asian Indians, 43 percent of Filipinos, and 34.8 percent of Koreans entered the United

TABLE 1-2 Percentage of Immigrants Admitted by Region, Fiscal Years 1901–1998

Decade	Europe	Asia	North America	South America	Africa
1901–10	91.6	3.7	3.2	.2	.1
1911–20	75.3	4.3	19.2	.7	.1
1921–30	60.0	2.7	35.9	1.0	.2
1931–40	65.8	3.1	28.8	1.5	.3
1941–50	60.0	3.6	32.2	2.1	.7
1951–60	52.7	6.1	36.0	3.6	.6
1961–70	33.8	12.9	43.9	7.8	.9
1971–80	17.8	35.3	37.5	6.6	1.8
1981–90	10.4	37.3	43.0	6.3	2.4
1991–98	14.9	30.9	43.8	5.8	3.7

Source: U.S. Immigration and Naturalization Service, *Naturalizations, Fiscal Year 1998* (Washington, DC: U.S. Government Printing Office, 2000), Chart B, p. 4.
Note: Figures may not add to 100 due to rounding. Oceana and unspecified regions represent no more than 1 percent of legal immigration each decade.

States under the occupational and investor categories. By the mid-1970s, however, 80 to 90 percent of all Asian immigrants entered the United States through one of the family categories.[49] Studies clearly show that most post-1965 Asian immigrants tend to be more middle-class, educated, urbanized, and they arrive in the United States in family units rather than as individuals, compared to their pre-1965 counterparts.[50]

The framers of the 1965 law did not anticipate any dramatic changes in the historical pattern of immigration, but it is clear Asian immigrants have taken advantage of almost every aspect of the 1965 Immigration Reform Act. Asians were just 6.1 percent of all immigrants to the United States between 1951 and 1960; this rose to 12.9 percent between 1961 and 1970, and increased to 35.3 percent between 1971 and 1980. The percentage of Asian immigrants peaked at 37.3 percent between 1981 and 1990 but declined to 30.9 percent by the 1990s (see Table 1-2). This decline was due to the sudden increase of mostly Mexicans who were able to apply for legal status following the passage of the Immigration Reform and Control Act of 1986 (IRCA). By the late 1990s, about 3 million aliens received permanent residence status under IRCA.[51]

This "amnesty" provision was only a part of IRCA, which was fully intended to control illegal immigration into the United States. IRCA also required that all employers verify the legal status of all new employees, and it imposed civil and criminal penalties against employers who knowingly hire undocumented workers.[52] While IRCA closed the "back door" of illegal immigration, another reform, the Immigration Act of 1990, was enacted to keep open the "front door" of legal immigration. Indeed, this law actually authorizes an *increase* in legal immigration to the United States. In response to uncertain economic stability at home, growing global economic competition abroad, and the dramatically changed face of immigration, the 1990 law sent a mixed message to Asian immigrants.

First of all, the law actually authorized an increase in legal immigration, but at the same time placed a yearly cap on total immigration for the first time since the 1920s. For 1992 to 1995, the limit was 700,000 and 675,000 thereafter. This appears to be an arbitrary limit, but it still allows for an unlimited number of visas for immediate relatives of U.S. citizens. This may not have a negative effect on Asian immigration because, as a group, Asians have the highest rate of naturalization compared to other immigrants.[53] Second, the law encourages immigration of more skilled workers to help meet the needs of the U.S. economy. The number of visas for skilled workers and their families increased from 58,000 to 140,000, and the number for unskilled workers was cut in half to just 10,000. This may prove to be a benefit to Asians who, since 1965, have been among the best educated and best trained immigrants the United States has ever seen. Third, the 1990 immigration law also seeks to "diversify" the new immigrants by giving more visas to countries who have sent relatively few people to the United States in recent years. This program has been popular with lawmakers who want to assist those from Western European countries at the expense of Asians. For example, up to 40 percent of the initial visas allocated for the diversity category were for Ireland. Noted immigration attorney Bill Ong Hing found sections of the Immigration Act of 1990 "provide extra independent and transition visas that are unavailable to Asians."[54]

The lasting legacy of the civil rights movement on immigration policy was the emphasis on fairness, equality, and family reunification. But the increased emphasis on highly skilled immigrants found in the 1990 immigration law indicates some loosening of those ideals and priorities. It is clear from the descriptions of Asian American history here that the conditions for the post-1965 Asian migrants are quite distinct from pre-1965 migrants. This seemingly obvious observation reflects the fact that international migration is not a simple, stable, or homogeneous process. Even with this in mind, the most popular frame of reference for all movement to the United States continues to be the European immigrant experience throughout the nineteenth and early twentieth centuries. The popular European immigrant analogy is highlighted in the words of welcome written on the Statue of Liberty:

> Give me your tired, your poor
> Your huddled masses yearning to breathe free
> The wretched refuse of your teeming shore.
> Send these, the homeless, tempest-tost to me,
> I lift my lamp beside the golden door!

The European immigrant experience, however, is by no means universal, and it is only part of what scholars today see as a much broader picture of the international movement of people and capital. Understanding the broader dynamics of global economic restructuring is useful in comparing and contrasting post-1965 Asian immigrants with other immigrants and minority groups in the United States.

Global Economic Restructuring

What makes people want to leave their home country and migrate to another country? The most commonly accepted answer is found within what is known as the push-pull theory. This theory generally asserts that difficult economic, social, and political conditions in the home country force, or push, people away. At the same time, these people are attracted, or pulled, to another country where conditions are seen as more favorable. On closer examination, however, this theoretical viewpoint does run into some problems. Most significantly, the push-pull theory tends to see immigration flows as a natural, open, and spontaneous process, but it does not adequately take into account the structural factors and policy changes that directly affect immigration flows. This is because earlier migration studies based on European immigration limited their focus on poor countries that sent low-skilled labor to affluent countries with growing economies that put newcomers to work. The push-pull theory is not incorrect, but is considered to be incomplete and historically static. Recent studies have taken a much broader approach to international migration and insist that in order to understand post-1965 immigration from Asia, it is necessary to understand the recent restructuring of the global economy.[55]

Since the end of World War II, global restructuring has involved the gradual movement of industrial manufacturing away from developed nations such as the United States to less developed nations in Asia and Latin America where labor costs are cheaper. This process was best seen in Japan in the 1950s through 1970s, and accelerated rapidly in the 1980s to newly industrialized Asian countries, namely Taiwan, Hong Kong, Singapore, and South Korea. Other Asian countries such as India, Thailand, Indonesia, Malaysia, and the Philippines also followed the same economic course with varying degrees of success. In the 1990s mainland China increased its manufacturing and export capacity dramatically and was steering on the same economic path of other Asian nations.

Among the effects of global restructuring on the United States is the declining need to import low-skilled labor because manufacturing jobs are moving abroad. At the same time, there is an inclining need to import individuals with advanced specialized skills that are in great demand. According to research by Paul Ong and Evelyn Blumenberg (1994), this phenomena is evidenced in part by the increasing number of foreign-born students studying at U.S. colleges.[56] In the 1954–1955 academic year the United States was host to just 34,232 foreign exchange students; this number increased to over 440,000 in 1994.[57] Today over half of all foreign students in the United States are from Asian countries, and most major in either engineering, science, or business. In 1997 foreign students earned 53 percent of the doctorates in engineering, 50 percent of doctorates in mathematics, and 49 percent of doctorates in computer science.[58] Many of these foreign graduate students planned to work in the United States and eventually gained permanent immigrant status. Companies in the United States have, of course, been eager to hire foreign-born scientists and engineers. Not only are highly skilled immigrants valuable to employers as workers, but many also start their own high-tech businesses. For example, Vinod Khosla is the co-founder of Sun-Microsystems, and Gururaj Deshpande is co-founder of a number of high-tech businesses worth around $6 billion.[59]

The medical profession is another broad area where Asian immigrants have made a noticeable impact. Researchers Paul Ong and Tania Azores (1994) found that Asian Americans represented 4.4 percent of the registered nurses and 10.8 percent of the physicians in the United States in 1990. Ong and Azores estimate that only a third of Asian American physicians and a quarter of Asian American nurses were educated in the United States. Graduates of overseas medical and nursing schools have been coming to the United States since the passage of the 1946 Smith-Mundt Act, which created an exchange program for specialized training. Although this exchange was intended to be temporary, many medical professionals were able to become permanent immigrants. A physician shortage in the United States during the late 1960s and early 1970s, coupled with the elimination of racial immigration quotas in 1965, brought forth a steady flow of foreign-trained medical doctors from Asian countries. A 1975 U.S. Commission on Civil Rights report found 5,000 Asian medical school graduates entered the United States annually during the early 1970s. But, under pressure from the medical industry, Congress passed the 1976 Health Professions Educational Act, which restricted the number of foreign-trained physicians who could enter the United States. Despite the passage of this law, almost 30,000 physicians from Asia immigrated to the United States between 1972 and 1985, and data up to 1990 show roughly half of all foreign-trained physicians entering the United States have come from Asia.[60]

Asia is also the largest source for foreign nurses. In particular, over half of all foreign-trained nurses come from the Philippines. One 1988 study conservatively estimated 50,000 Filipino nurses were working in the United States at the time. Filipino nurses find work in the United States attractive because they can earn up to 20 times the salary they can make in the Philippines, and their English-speaking abilities make them highly desired by employers. Filipino nurses are also attracted to the United States because of liberal policies that eventually allow them to stay permanently. Most foreign-trained nurses are brought to work initially on a temporary basis, but the passage of the Immigration Nursing Relief Act of 1989 allows nurses to adjust to permanent status after three years of service.[61]

The general explanations for the origins of migration found that the push-pull theory continues to have some value today. Opportunities for large numbers of professionals in Asian countries are still difficult and limited, and opportunities and relatively high salaries are available in the United States. Political instability throughout Asia also continues to be an important push factor for Asian immigrants and refugees. At the same time, this immigration process is not totally natural or spontaneous, as witnessed by foreign student and immigration policies encouraging well-trained individuals to come to the United States. Overall, the changing character of the push and pull in terms of the types of immigrants entering the United States and the new skills they bring are very much a result of dynamic global economic restructuring. Global economic restructuring is an important context for understanding not only why Asian immigrants have come to the United States but also how well they have adjusted and been accepted socially, economically, and politically. Note that not all Asian immigrants are middle-class and successful professionals; a sizable number of other Asian immigrants, especially refugees, have also found their lives in America extremely difficult. The extreme diversity among Asian Americans is due in large part to the third major event affecting migration from Asia—the Vietnam War.

The Vietnam War and Southeast Asian Refugees

Since 1975 large numbers of Southeast Asian refugees have entered the United States, and today California is the home for most of them (see Table 1-3). Roughly three quarters of all Southeast Asian refugees are from Vietnam, with the rest from Laos and Cambodia. Unlike most other post-1965 Asian immigrants who came to the United States in a rather orderly fashion seeking family reunification and economic opportunities, Southeast Asian refugees arrived as part of an international resettlement effort of people who faced genuine political persecution and bodily harm in their home countries. Southeast Asian refugees to the United States can be easily divided into three distinct waves: the first arrived in the United States in 1975 shortly after the fall of Saigon; the second arrived between 1978 and 1980; and the third entered the United States after 1980 and continues to this day. The United States has accepted these refugees not only for humanitarian reasons but also in

TABLE 1-3	States with the Largest Southeast Asian Populations, 1990				
State	**Vietnamese**	**Cambodian**	**Laotian**	**Hmong**	**Total**
Washington	18,696	11,096	6,191	741	36,724
California	280,223	68,190	58,058	46,892	453,363
Texas	69,634	5,887	9,332	176	85,029
Minnesota	9,387	3,858	6,381	16,833	36,459
Massachusetts	15,449	14,050	3,985	248	33,732
Virginia	20,693	3,889	25,899	7	27,178
Pennsylvania	15,887	5,495	2,048	358	23,788
Wisconsin	2,494	521	3,622	16,373	23,010
New York	15,555	3,646	3,253	165	22,619
Florida	16,346	1,617	242	7	20,379

Source: U.S. Bureau of the Census, *1990 Census of the Population, General Population Characteristics, United States Summary* (Washington, DC: U.S. Government Printing Office, 1993), CP-1-1, Table 262.

recognition that U.S. foreign policy and military actions in Southeast Asia had a hand in creating much of the calamity that has befallen the entire region.

U.S. political interests in Southeast Asia actually began during World War II, although for years efforts were limited to foreign aid and military advisers. Direct military intervention rapidly escalated in 1965 when President Lyndon B. Johnson stepped up bombing raids in Southeast Asia and authorized the use of the first U.S. combat troops in order to contain increasing communist insurgency. The undeclared war continued until U.S. troops withdrew in 1973 at the cost of 57,000 American and 1 million Vietnamese lives. The conflict also caused great environmental destruction throughout Southeast Asia and created tremendous domestic antiwar protests in the United States.[62]

As soon as the U.S. troops left, however, communist forces in Vietnam regrouped and quickly began sweeping across the countryside. By March 1975 it was clear that the capital of South Vietnam, Saigon, would soon fall to communist forces. As a result, President Gerald Ford authorized the attorney general to admit 130,000 refugees into the United States.[63] In the last chaotic days prior to the fall of Saigon on April 30, 1975, "high-risk" individuals in Vietnam, namely high-ranking government and military personnel, were hurriedly air-lifted away to safety at temporary receiving centers in Guam, Thailand, and the Philippines. This group marked the first wave of Southeast Asian refugees, who would eventually resettle in the United States. The first wave is distinct in that they were generally the educated urban elite and middle class from Vietnam. Because many of them had worked closely with the U.S. military, they tended to be more westernized (40 percent were Catholics), and a good portion of them were able to speak English (30 percent spoke English well). Another significant feature is the fact that roughly 95 percent of the first wave of Southeast Asian refugees were Vietnamese, even though the capitals of Laos and Cambodia also fell to communist forces in 1975.[64]

Once these first-wave refugees came to the United States, they were flown to one of four military base/reception centers in California, Arkansas, Pennsylvania, and Florida. From these bases they registered with a voluntary agency that would eventually help resettle them with a sponsor. About 60 percent of the sponsors were families, while the other 40 percent were usually churches and individuals. Sponsors were responsible for day-to-day needs of the refugees until they were able to find jobs and become independent. The resettlement of the first wave of refugees was funded by the 1975 Indochinese Resettlement Assistance Act and was seen as a quick and temporary process. Indeed, all the reception centers closed by the end of 1975, and the Resettlement Act expired in 1977.

The second wave of Southeast Asian refugees was larger, more heterogeneous, and many believe even more devastated by their relocation experience than the first wave. The second wave of refugees were generally less educated, urbanized, and westernized (only 7 percent spoke English and only about 7 percent were Catholic) compared to their predecessors; at the same time they were much more ethnically diverse than the first wave. According to statistics, between 1978 and 1980, about

55.5 percent of Southeast Asian refugees were from Vietnam (including many ethnic Chinese), 36.6 percent from Laos, and 7.8 percent from Cambodia. The second wave consisted of people who suffered under the communist regimes and were unable to leave their countries immediately before or after the new governments took power.[65]

In Vietnam, the ethnic Chinese merchant class was very much the target of resentment by the new communist government. Many of the Chinese businesses in Vietnam were nationalized, Chinese language schools and newspapers were closed, education and employment rights were denied, and food rations were reduced. Under these conditions, about 250,000 escaped North Vietnam, seeking refuge in China. Roughly 70 percent of the estimated 500,000 boat people who tried to escape Vietnam by sea were ethnic Chinese. The treacherous journey usually took place on ill-equipped crowded boats that were unable to withstand the rigors of the ocean or outrun marauding Thai pirates. The U.S. Committee for Refugees estimates at least 100,000 people lost their lives trying to escape Vietnam by boat.[66] Along with the Chinese, others in Vietnam, particularly those who had supported the U.S.-backed South Vietnamese government and their families, were also subject to especially harsh treatment by the new communist leadership. Many were sent to "reeducation camps" and banished to work in rural regions clearing land devastated by 30 years of war.

The holocaust in Cambodia began immediately after the Khmer Rouge (Red Khmer) marched into the capital city of Phnom Penh on April 17, 1975. That same day the entire population of the capital was ordered to the countryside. After three years it has been broadly estimated between 1 and 3 million Cambodians died from starvation, disease, and execution out of a population of less than 7 million. In 1978 Vietnam (with support from the Soviet Union) invaded Cambodia, drove the Khmer Rouge out of power, and established a new government under its own control. Famine and warfare continued under Vietnamese occupation, and by 1979 over 600,000 refugees from Cambodia fled the country, mostly to neighboring Thailand. In Laos, the transition from one government to another was initially rather smooth compared to Vietnam following the fall of Saigon. After over a decade of civil war, a coalition government was formed in April 1974 that included Laotian communists, the Pathet Lao. But shortly after communists took power in Vietnam and Cambodia, the Pathet Lao moved to solidify its full control of the country. It was at this time that troops from both Laos and Vietnam began a military campaign against the Hmong hill people, a preliterate ethnic minority group that lived in the mountains of Laos who were recruited by the U.S. government to serve as mercenaries against communist forces in the region. The Hmong were seen as traitors to the communist revolution, and massive bombing raids were ordered against them that included the dropping of napalm and poisonous chemicals. Thousands of Hmong were killed in these fierce assaults, and those who remained had little choice but to seek refuge in neighboring Thailand. The Hmong were not the only people in Laos who were persecuted. By 1979 roughly 3,000 Hmong were entering Thailand every month, and as late as 1983 an estimated 75 percent of the 76,000 Laotians in Thai refugee camps were Hmong people.[67]

The world could not ignore this massive outpouring of refugees from Southeast Asia, and in 1979 President Jimmy Carter allowed 14,000 refugees a month to enter the United States. In addition, Congress passed the Refugee Act of 1980, which set an annual quota of 50,000 refugees per year, funded resettlement programs, and allowed refugees to become eligible for the same welfare benefits as U.S. citizens after 36 months of refugee assistance (this was changed to 18 months in 1982).

Many of the Southeast Asians who came in the third wave are technically not considered refugees, but are in actuality immigrants. This has been facilitated by the 1980 Orderly Departure Program (ODP), an agreement with Vietnam that allows individuals and families to enter the United States. ODP was a benefit for three groups: relatives of permanently settled refugees in the United States, Amerasians, and former reeducation camp internees. By the end of 1992, over 300,000 Vietnamese immigrated to the United States, including 80,000 Amerasians and their relatives, as well as 60,000 former camp internees and their families.[68] The resettlement experience, the development of Southeast Asian communities, as well as the influx of Amerasians to the United States are respectively discussed in greater detail in Chapters 2 and 7.

It is obvious that Southeast Asian refugees/immigrants have been a rapidly growing and extremely diverse group. According to the 1990 census, there were 1,001,054 Southeast Asians in the United States, or 13 percent of the total population of Asian Americans. Individually, the census counted 614,547 Vietnamese, 149,014 Laotians, 147,411 Cambodians, and 90,082 Hmong. Some have argued that these census figures are an undercount of the actual numbers of people from Southeast Asian countries. Researchers point to the fact that the total number of arrivals to the United States from Southeast Asia is roughly the same as census figures. This is an anomaly because the census figure should be about 20 percent larger to reflect the number of American-born Southeast Asians. There are, however, several reasons for this disparity. First of all, new arrivals from Southeast Asia who have little knowledge of the English language may simply not have responded to census questionnaires. This certainly is a general concern for all Asian American groups. Second, and probably most important, an estimated 15 to 25 percent of those from Vietnam, Cambodia, and Laos are actually ethnic Chinese. It is quite possible that many ethnic Chinese from Southeast Asia answered the appropriate census question of ethnicity without regard to their nationality. Third, no one is exactly sure how Amerasians identified themselves on the 1990 census or if they even participated at all. Although a factor, note that most of the Amerasians from Vietnam did not actually enter the United States until after the 1990 census was taken. In all references to the Southeast Asian population, keep these considerations in mind.[69]

Conclusion

This chapter briefly describes the history and recent growth of the Asian population in the United States. It also highlights the significance of the 1965 Immigration Reform Act, global economic restructuring, and the Vietnam War as three broad events that profoundly impacted both the number and type of migrants who have come to the United States from Asian countries. In order to examine post-1965 Asian Americans comprehensively, it is particularly important to look at the rapid growth of the population, personal history, nativity, length of time in the United States, premigration experiences and traumas, education, socioeconomic class background, and gender. Chapter 2 details the social and economic diversity of immigrant and American-born Asians, as well as their settlement patterns and impact on various communities across the United States.

Notes

[1] Emil Guillermo, "From Miss America to Mr. President," *Asian Week,* October 19, 2000.

[2] Shih-shan Henry Tsai, *The Chinese Experience in America* (Bloomington: Indiana University Press, 1986), p. 1; also see Stan Steiner, *Fusahang: The Chinese Who Built America* (New York: Harper & Row, 1979), pp. 24–35; Elena S. H. Yu, "Filipino Migration and Community Organization in the United States," *California Sociologist 3:2* (1980): 76–102; and Joan M. Jensen, *Passage from India: Asian Indian Immigrants in North America* (New Haven: Yale University Press, 1988), pp. 12–13.

[3] Sucheng Chan, *Asian Californians* (San Francisco: MTL/Boyd & Fraser, 1991), pp. 5–6.

[4] Ronald Takaki, *Strangers from a Different Shore* (Boston: Little, Brown, 1989), pp. 79, 114.

[5] Stanford Lyman, *Chinese Americans* (New York: Random House, 1974), pp. 86–88.

[6] Chan, *Asian Californians,* pp. 27–33.

[7] Lyman, *Chinese Americans,* pp. 63–69.

[8] Yuji Ichioka, *The Issei: The World of the First Generation Japanese Immigrant's, 1885–1924* (New York: Free Press, 1988), pp. 64–65.

[9] Roger Daniels, *Concentration Camps: North American Japanese in the United States and Canada During World War II* (Malabar, FL: Robert A. Kreiger, 1981), p. 7.

[10] Bill Ong Hing, *Making and Remaking Asian America Through Immigration Policy, 1850–1990* (Stanford, CA: Stanford University Press, 1993), pp. 28–30.

[11] Chan, *Asian Californians,* p. 7.

[12] Edwin B. Almirol, *Ethnic Identity and Social Negotiation: A Study of a Filipino Community in California* (New York: AMS Press, 1985), pp. 52–59; and H. Brett Melendy, "Filipinos in the United States," in Norris Hundley, Jr. (ed.), *The Asian American: The Historical Experience* (Santa Barbara: Cleo, 1977), pp. 101–128.

[13] Takaki, *Strangers from a Different Shore,* pp. 53–57.

[14] Chan, *Asian Californians,* pp. 7, 17–19, 37; and Warren Y. Kim, *Koreans in America* (Seoul: Po Chin Chai, 1971), pp. 22–27.

[15] Joan M. Jensen, *Passage from India: Asian Indian Immigrants in North America* (New Haven: Yale University Press, 1988), pp. 24–41; and Rajanki K. Das, *Hindustani Workers on the Pacific Coast* (Berlin and Leipzig: Walter De Gruyter, 1923), p. 77.

[16]Das, *Hindustani Workers*, pp. 66–67.

[17]Bruce La Brack, "Occupational Specialization Among Rural California Sikhs: The Interplay of Culture and Economics," *Amerasia Journal* 9:2 (1982): 29–56.

[18]Naturalization Act of 1790, I Stat. 103 (1790).

[19]Act of 14 July 1870, 16 Stat. 256.

[20]Roger Daniels, *Asian Americans: Chinese and Japanese in the United States* (Seattle: University of Washington Press, 1988), p. 43.

[21]Chan, *Asian Californians*, p. 42.

[22]Robert F. Heizer and Alan F. Almquist, *The Other Californians: Prejudice and Discrimination Under Spain, Mexico, and the United States to 1920* (Berkeley: University of California Press, 1971), p. 129.

[23]Takaki, *Strangers from a Different Shore*, p. 82.

[24]Lyman, *Chinese Americans*, pp. 55–85.

[25]Takaki, *Strangers from a Different Shore*, pp. 111–112.

[26]Juan L. Gonzales, *Racial and Ethnic Groups in America*, 2nd ed. (Dubuque, IA: Kendall/Hunt, 1993), p. 136; and Juan L. Gonzales, *Racial and Ethnic Families in America*, 2nd ed. (Dubuque, IA: Kendall/Hunt Publishing Co., 1993), p. 3.

[27]Chan, *Asian Californians*, pp. 44–45.

[28]Hing, *Making and Remaking Asian America*, pp. 32–39.

[29]*Yick Wo v. Hopkins*, 118 U.S. 356 (1886); and Lyman, *Chinese Americans*, p. 79.

[30]*Takao Ozawa v. United States*, 260 U.S. 178 (1922); Heizer and Alquist, *The Other Californians*, pp. 192–193; and Ichioka, *The Issei*, pp. 210–226.

[31]*United States v. Bhagat Singh Thind*, 261 U.S. 204 (1923); Jensen, *Passage from India*, pp. 255–260; and Gurdial Singh, "East Indians in the United States," *Sociology and Social Research* 30:3 (1946): 208–216.

[32]Megumi Dick Osumi, "Asians and California's Anti–Miscegenation Laws," in Nobuya Tsuchida (ed.), *Asian and Pacific American Experiences: Women's Perspectives* (Minneapolis: Asian/Pacific American Learning Resource Center, University of Minnesota, 1982), pp. 1–37; and Takaki, *Strangers from a Different Shore*, pp. 330–331.

[33]William Petersen, *Japanese Americans* (New York: Random House, 1971), pp. 66–100; Roger Daniels, *Concentration Camps, U.S.A.* (New York: Holt, Rinehart & Winston, 1971), pp. 75, 81–82; and Jacobus tenBroek, Edward N. Barnhart and Floyd W. Matson, *Prejudice, War, and the Constitution* (Berkeley: University of California Press), pp. 118–120.

[34]Cited in Commission on Wartime Relocation and Internment of Civilians, *Personal Justice Denied* (Washington, DC: U.S. Government Printing Office, 1982), pp. 52–53.

[35]Takaki, *Strangers from a Different Shore*, pp. 379–392.

[36]Commission on Wartime Relocation and Internment of Civilians, *Personal Justice Denied*, p. 217; tenBroek, Barnhart, and Matson, *Prejudice, War, and the Constitution*, pp. 155–177, 180–181; and Daniels, *Concentration Camps: North America*.

[37]Chan, *Asian Californians*, p. 101.

[38]Petersen, *Japanese Americans*, p. 87.

[39]Cited in Marvin Karlins, Thomas L. Coffman, and Gary Walters, "On the Fading of Social Stereotypes: Studies of Three Generations of College Students," *Journal of Personality and Psychology* 13 (1990): 4–5.

[40]*Time*, December 22, 1941, p. 33.

[41]Cited in Harold Isaacs, *Images of Asia: American Views of China and India* (New York: Harper & Row, 1972), pp. xviii–xix.

[42]Chan, *Asian Californians,* pp. 103–104; and Lyman, *Chinese Americans,* pp. 127, 134.

[43]Takaki, *Strangers from a Different Shore,* pp. 357–363, 370–378; Manuel Buaken, "Life in the Armed Forces," *New Republic* 109 (1943): 279–280; and Bienvenido Santos, "Filipinos in War," *Far Eastern Survey* 11 (1942): 249–250.

[44]Harry H. L. Kitano and Roger Daniels, *Asian Americans: Emerging Minorities,* 2nd ed. (Upper Saddle River, NJ: Prentice Hall, 1995), p. 42, Table 4–2; and Monica Boyd, "Oriental Immigration: The Experience of Chinese, Japanese, and Filipino Populations in the United States," *International Migration Review* 10 (1976): 48–60, Table 1.

[45]Chan, *Asian Californians,* pp. 105–106.

[46]Diane Mark and Ginger Chih, *A Place Called Chinese America* (San Francisco: The Organization of Chinese Americans, 1982), pp. 105–107.

[47]Chan, *Asian Californians,* pp. 108–109.

[48]Ibid., pp. 109–110.

[49]Hing, *Making and Remaking Asian America,* Appendix B, pp. 189–200; Table 9, p. 82.

[50]Hing, *Making and Remaking Asian America,* pp. 79–120; Luciano Mangiafico, *Contemporary American Immigrants: Patterns of Filipino, Korean, and Chinese Settlement in the United States* (New York: Praeger, 1988), pp. 1–26; James T. Fawcett and Benjamin V. Carino (eds.), *Pacific Bridges: The New Immigration from Asia and the Pacific Islands* (Staten Island, NY: Center for Migration Studies, 1987); and Herbert R. Barringer, Robert W. Gardner, and Michael J. Levine (eds.), *Asian and Pacific Islanders in the United States* (New York: Russell Sage Foundation, 1993).

[51]U.S. Immigration and Naturalization Service, *Statistical Yearbook of the Immigration and Naturalization Service, 1993* (Washington DC: U.S. Government Printing Office, 1994), p. 20.

[52]Roger Daniels, *Coming to America* (New York: HarperCollins, 1990), pp. 391–397.

[53]U.S. Immigration and Naturalization Service, *Statistical Yearbook of the Immigration and Naturalization Service, 1994* (Washington, DC: U.S. Government Printing Office, 1996), p. 126, Chart O.

[54]Hing, *Making and Remaking Asian America,* pp. 7–8.

[55]Paul Ong, Edna Bonacich, and Lucie Cheng (eds.), *The New Asian Immigration in Los Angeles and Global Restructuring* (Philadelphia: Temple University Press, 1994), pp. 3–100; and Edna Bonacich, Lucie Cheng, Norma Chinchilla, Nora Hamilton, and Paul Ong (eds.), *Global Production: The Apparel Industry in the Pacific Rim* (Philadelphia: Temple University Press, 1994), pp. 3–20.

[56]Paul Ong and Evelyn Blumenberg, "Scientists and Engineers," in Paul Ong (ed.), *The State of Asian Pacific America: Economic Diversity, Issues & Policies* (Los Angeles: LEAP Asian Pacific American Public Policy Institute and UCLA Asian American Studies Center, 1994), pp. 113–138. Note that I am distinguishing between foreign exchange students who are overseas nationals from Asian American students who happen to be foreign born.

[57]Ibid., p. 173; and U.S. Department of Commerce, *Statistical Abstract of the United States, 1995* (Washington, DC: U.S. Government Printing Office, 1995), p. 188, Table 295.

[58]U.S. Department of Commerce, *Statistical Abstract of the United States, 1999* (Washington, DC: U.S. Government Printing Office, 2000), p. 625, Table 1004.

[59]"The Golden Diaspora: Indian Immigrants to the U.S. Are One of the Newest Elements of the American Melting Pot—and the Most Spectacular Success Story," *Time Select/Global Business,* June 19, 2000, pp. B26–27.

[60]Paul Ong and Tania Azores, "Health Professionals on the Front-Line," in Paul Ong (ed.), *The State of Asian Pacific America: Economic Diversity, Issues & Policies,* pp. 139–164.

[61]Paul Ong and Tania Azores, "The Migration and Incorporation of Filipino Nurses," in Ong et al. (eds.), *The New Asian Immigration in Los Angeles and Global Restructuring,* pp. 166–195; and Mangiafico, *Contemporary American Immigrants,* pp. 42–43.

[62]Literature on the Vietnam conflict is voluminous. For an excellent and readable overview, see Stanley Karnow, *Vietnam: A History* (New York: Penguin, 1991).

[63]The quota for refugees under the 1965 Immigration Reform Act was only 17,400, so President Gerald Ford instructed the attorney general to use his "parole" power to admit the 130,000 refugees. The use of parole power was also used to bring European refugees to the United States during the 1950s. For more detail, see Hing, *Making and Remaking Asian America,* pp. 123–128; and Paul J. Strand and Woodrow Jones, Jr., *Indochinese Refugees in America: Problems of Adaptation and Assimilation* (Durham, NC: Duke University Press, 1985).

[64]Chan, *Asian Californians,* p. 128; and Chor-Swan Ngin, "The Acculturation Pattern of Orange County's Southeast Asian Refugees," *Journal of Orange County Studies* 3:4 (Fall 1989–Spring 1990): 46–53.

[65]Ngin, "The Acculturation Pattern of Orange County's Southeast Asian Refugees," p. 49; and Ngoan Le, "The Case of the Southeast Asian Refugees: Policy for a Community 'At-Risk,'" in *The State of Asian Pacific America: Policy Issues to the Year 2020* (Los Angeles: LEAP Asian Pacific American Public Policy Institute and UCLA Asian American Studies Center, 1993), pp. 167–188.

[66]For more details, see Strand and Jones, *Indochinese Refugees in America;* Barry L. Wain, *The Refused: The Agony of Indochina Refugees* (New York: Simon & Schuster, 1981); and U.S. Committee for Refugees, *Uncertain Harbors: The Plight of Vietnamese Boat People* (Washington, DC: U.S. Government Printing Office, 1987).

[67]Chan, *Asian Californians,* pp. 121–138; Kitano and Daniels, *Asian Americans: Emerging Minorities,* pp. 170–191; U.S. Committee for Refugees, *Cambodians in Thailand: People on the Edge* (Washington, DC: U.S. Government Printing Office, 1985); and U.S. Committee for Refugees, *Refugees from Laos: In Harm's Way* (Washington, DC: U.S. Government Printing Office, 1986).

[68]U.S. Committee for Refugees, *Uncertain Harbors,* pp. 19–20; and Ruben Rumbaut, "Vietnamese, Laotian, and Cambodian Americans," in Pyong Gap Min (ed.), *Asian Americans: Contemporary Trends and Issues* (Thousand Oaks, CA: Sage, 1995), p. 240.

[69]Ruben Rumbaut and J. R. Weeks, "Fertility and Adaptation: Indochinese Refugees in the United States," *International Migration Review* 20:2 (1986): 428–466; and Rumbaut, "Vietnamese, Laotian, and Cambodian Americans," pp. 239–242.

Recent African Immigration

Boatamo Mosupyoe

Introduction

Current immigration policy in the United States and the manner in which it has operated have created more opportunities for citizens of other nations to immigrate into the country (Nag, 2005), which has manifested in an increasing number of immigrants since the 1970s as natives from other countries continue to migrate to the United States. The immigrants often arrive in search of opportunities to improve their standard of living (Lee, Myers, Ha & Shin, 2005; Nag, 2005). Many of these immigrants are well-educated, holding managerial and professional positions in their native country prior to immigrating (Buzdugan & Halli, 2009; Nag, 2005). On their arrival in the United States, some of these professionals are forced to take on jobs that are considered "low skill" in spite of their educational background (Adamuti-Trache & Sweet, 2005).

While this article draws from my unpublished research of recent African immigrants in Washington State and the San Francisco Bay area of California and the state's capitol, Sacramento, my discussion also draws from other sources. The article should not be seen as a report on my research, since it just borrows and does not even begin to give an exhaustive account of the research.

Areas of focus are the lives and experiences of recent African immigrants entering the United States of America relative to the following issues:

- the immigration pattern of Africans in the United States
- the motivations for immigrating to the United States
- collective and multiple identities (e.g., how and to what extent ties to the African continent affect the group's identity; the extent to which their views converge and diverge with their children's; their respective achievements and failures and the extent to which these are ideological or structural; issues like school performance are considered as well as the relevance of Ogbu's theory of voluntary and involuntary minority)
- the assertion that recent African immigrants are favored by institutions and are benefiting from Affirmative Action more than African American descendants of former enslaved people

- the relationship of African Americans with their recent African counterparts
- the challenges that recent African immigrants face, including domestic violence
- an overview of their contribution of to the U.S. economy

Immigration Patterns

The United States is always defined as a country of immigrants. Native Americans have been very generous in accommodating people from different countries, a point never acknowledged. The United States immigration pattern reveals a historical preference towards European immigration into the United States and varied degrees of less preference towards immigrants from other parts of the world, including Africa. Salih Omar Eissa (2005) accurately observes that the 19th and 20th century immigration policy was discriminatory and heavily Eurocentric, despite the migration of Black Cape Verdean mariners to Massachusetts during this period.

Even when the McCarran-Walter Act of 1952 eliminated all racially specific language from the Immigration and Nationality Act (INA), and the Hart-Cellar Act of 1965 passed, national quotas remained and migration from the African continent was set at the lowest quota of 1,400 annually. Eissa (2005) further argues that of all people admitted to the United States between 1990 and 2000 only ten percent were Africans. This notwithstanding, the number of Africans in the United States has been increasing. An examination of immigration figures show that 30,000 Africans came legally into the United States in the 1960s, 80,000 in the 1970s, and 176,000 in the 1980s (Khalid El-Hassan, 2005). Since the 1980s the number has more than quadrupled. The figures from the Immigration and Naturalization Services (INS) reveal that between 1981 and 2000 the number stood at 531,832. It is important to note that some scholars, including myself, believe the U.S. Census Bureau 2000 report fails to capture the actual number of recent African immigrants. The possibility exists that the report underreported the number of Africans by hundreds of thousands. Africans who are in the country illegally exhibit the same behavioral pattern as other immigrants. They would not participate in the census exercise or even seek government help in other matters. At all costs they avoid authorities since they seek to hide their statuses.

Motivations for Immigrating to the United States

U.S. Census 2000 show that most recent African immigrants come from West Africa at 35 percent a year, 26 percent from East Africa, 20 percent from North Africa, seven percent from South Africa, and less than two percent from Central Africa. They are found in major metropolitan cities as well as in small towns and are not necessarily clustered in one part. The reasons for their immigration to the United States are varied and will be discussed. However, to give a context to the many issues that the recent Africans face, a very brief overview of the first African immigrants and their contribution is in order. We all know that the majority of first people of African descent to come into the United States came as people who were later enslaved. Any account about African immigrants that fails to acknowledge the foundation laid by these first Africans would be disingenuous (Mosupyoe, 2005).

Europeans traded with Africans as early as 1450. In the 17th century the British started transporting Africans to North America. They were also captured from different parts of Africa, including Bight of Benin, Senegambia, and the Gold Coast in West Africa, Angola, et al. Their labor and presence transformed the sociocultural and economic patterns of the United States. By the mid 1800s the positions they occupied and the kind of work they performed varied to include teamsters, porters, domestics, and plantation workers. At this time European immigration was encouraged and favored. European immigrants were also granted citizenship, a right that was denied to Africans, through the 1857 Dred Scott decision (Mosupyoe, 2005).

The decision declared Africans as "beings of an inferior order," and therefore deserving to be denied rights by the Constitution, including the right of citizenship. In addition, many other laws denied Africans their basic human rights. Although January 1, 1808, became the date designated for the prohibition of trade with African people, the capture and enslavement of African people continued well into the mid-19th century. The Emancipation Proclamation of 1863 permanently ended enslavement of African people. Thereafter, in 1868, the 14th amendment to the U.S. Constitution guaranteed citizenship, due process, and equal protection under the law for people of African descent, thereby overturning the Dred Scott decision (Mosupyoe, 2005).

In spite of all these gains, discrimination against African Americans continued in various ways, Jim Crow laws in the South being one of those. Through different organizations, such as the National Association for the Advancement of Colored People (1909), National Urban League (1911), and United Negro Improvement Association (1916), African Americans and institutions such as Howard University, Morehouse College, and Spelman University, African Americans were able to secure for themselves their rightful place in the U.S. landscape.

These remarkable people and their descendants, who have endured tremendous adversity and displayed admirable temerity, unquestionably laid the foundations of opportunity for a new wave of immigration after slavery and desegregation. Their struggles against and triumphs over slavery, Jim Crow, and segregation, through the civil rights movement and other means have been instrumental in transforming the sociopolitical climate in the United States. Pertinent to this discussion is the 1965 Hart-Cellar Immigration Act. The act advocates admission of immigrants based on their skills, professions, and familial relations.

The ideology of the act, in origin, substance, and final passage as law, mirrors the spirit of the civil rights movement as well as the thoughts of other Pan African activist who preceded the movement. Moreover, the African American involvement could be attributed to the direct success of a series of post-1965 immigration policy shifts that opened the doors to a steady increase in African immigration in the latter part of the 20th century. African Americans, descendants of enslaved Africans, created benefits through their struggle, which recent African immigrants like me enjoy. They produced an environment far more accepting of new immigrants. Today, approximately 50,000 Africans arrive annually from different parts of Africa for different reasons (Mosupyoe, 2005).

The post-enslavement period migration of Africans falls within the purview of Ogbu's voluntary immigrants' classification (Ogbu, 1993). The voluntary African immigrants came to the United States for many different reasons. In the 1950s and 1960s many Africans migrated to Europe; however, during the 1970s and 1980s most European countries experienced recessions that went along with aversion to immigration and culminated in the tightening of immigration laws. Meanwhile with the passage of the 1965 Hart-Cellar Immigration Act the U.S. immigration policies became somewhat liberalized. The United States then became the country of choice for Africans to immigrate to.

The push to immigrate stems from various factors. In the 1970s high unemployment and devalued currencies in most African countries resulted from failed economic policies engendered by poor management and "structural adjustment" programs demanded by the World Bank and International Monetary Fund. These conditions caused disappointment in the wake of newly acquired freedoms from European domination. Some parts of Africa, like South Africa, had racist governments that blatantly and legally discriminated against blacks. Opposing the racist policies led to detention and even death. In addition, civil wars in some parts of Africa precipitated immigration into the United States. In view of this and also taking into consideration civil wars in other parts of the world, such as Bosnia, the U.S. Congress reformed its policy towards refugees.

African immigrants benefited from the Refuge Act of 1980 and the immigration Reform and Control Act of 1986. One offered new refugees permanent resident status after one year while the other legalized the status of 31,000 Africans living in the United States since 1982. It could be argued that such a step encouraged African immigrants to stay in the United States. The Temporary Protected Status (TPS) that is part of the Diversity Visa Lottery Act of 1990 also acted as an impetus for African immigration from African countries such as Sudan, Sierra Leone, Liberia, Somalia, and Burundi. The act has a provision that gives temporary refuge status to foreign nationals present in the United States who would be subject to either violence due to armed conflict or environmental disaster if repatriated.

This Diversity Visa Lottery Act of 1990, further, offers immigrant visas to high school graduates in an attempt to increase the low rates of underrepresented nations in the United States. The visa lottery thus became another vehicle through which Africans primarily immigrated to the United States. Some Africans come to the United States to study or on exchange programs and then decide to stay because they have developed love relationships that culminate in marriages. Others come with babies who grow into children and teenagers while parents are attending school. Having raised their children here, they then decide to stay. Their decision is mainly based on their conclusion that their children will find it hard to adapt to their countries of origin. Yet others come to the United States through family reunification programs.

In the 1960s and 1970s most Africans who came to the United States had strong desires to go back and contribute towards their respective countries nation building.

The trend has changed in the last two decades. Recent African voluntary immigrants chose to stay, build a life for their families, and find ways of integrating into the U.S. society – the focus of the next section.

Challenges, and Collective and Multiple Identities

The recent African immigrants are not a monolithic group; they come from various countries in Africa and the Caribbean. Although they speak English, they also speak different languages that are not mutually intelligible. African cultures have as many similarities as they have differences. Ideological diversity also abounds. A case in point is the view of how South Africans should deal with the post-apartheid society, how Nigeria should mediate the corruption in that country, how to raise children in the U.S. culture, and how to best integrate into U.S. society.

In most part Africans will associate and form strong alliances with those who come from the same African countries. You will also find organizations formed along those lines (e.g., you will find an Igbo organization, a Somali organization, South African in the Bay Area, et al.). Organizations formed along African country of origin lines are mostly support system groups designed to strengthen relationships and help one another in times of need. In addition, such communal organizations offer ties with people from respective homes who share a common language. It also important to note that some alliances are formed based on the different regions from the same country (e.g., in the case of South Africans, people from the eastern Cape will feel closer to one another than they would with people from Gauteng), although, survival, the need for community, and fear of isolation often force collective identity based on the country of origin to be stronger and more enduring.

In addition to this collective identity defined by specific countries of origin, Africans from different parts of Africa do share a collective identity based on a continent of origin, the differences notwithstanding. Africans tend to come together to an "African party" to share their respective vibrant cultures and also to discuss difficult issues that they face as immigrants. Some of the challenges that recent African immigrants face are the same as those faced by African Americans. To start with they share some phenotypes, and in the United States discrimination on the basis of how you look persists.

Police brutality (as in the case of the death of Amadou Diallo, an African immigrant who was killed by police) and racial profiling affect them, as does the subtle perception as inferior and less than others. Additionally, Africans accents are described as heavy (although as an African immigrant myself, I never understood that); this tends to invite both intrigue and repulsion from others. I personally have had students' evaluation where one student asked that the school should make me change my accent. I have also had people admire "my heavy accent."

Discussions with some of the immigrants have revealed that they are often told that "you have an accent." To some, to the extent that having an accent suggests ignorance and stupidity, this observation becomes troubling – particularly since we all have accents, a point that most U.S. people miss, in my experience. One immigrant related how a taxi driver attempted to take advantage of her in terms of pricing because he thought that since she "had an accent" her knowledge of the place and the pricing was minimal and therefore she was a prime target for exploitation.

Other problems are presented by men and women's relationships as they try to adapt to the new culture. Domestic violence is a reality in the communities of recent African immigrants. Some men come with their cultural beliefs about women as inferior and subservient. In 2005 professor Uwazie of the Criminal Justice Department at California State University, Sacramento, called a meeting that was triggered by a series of domestic violent acts committed by men on women in the Sacramento area and other parts of the United States. I was asked to be the co-moderator of the discussions.

In one of the Sacramento incidents a Ghanaian man reportedly stabbed his wife 22 times to death, after an argument between the estranged couple. In another case, a Nigerian man drove all the way from Atlanta, Georgia, to stalk his Ondo-born wife living separately in Dallas, Texas. He eventually shot her to death in her car. Also, in August 2005 a Nigerian man used a hammer to murder his Sierra Leonean-born wife at their home in a Dallas suburb. The murder reportedly occurred in front of the couples' seven-year-old daughter. Ben Edokpayi reported on the meeting in the newspaper *Times of Nigeria* in an article entitled "An Elephant in the House." I am going to briefly summarize his report to give you insights into the thinking of recent African immigrants from different countries, both men and women on this issue.

Edokpayi acknowledges the existence of patriarchy and male chauvinism as an epidemic in Africa. He reports that while incidents of domestic violence in African communities in the diaspora are only now coming into the limelight, the problem has long been an entrenched epidemic in African countries where male chauvinism rules. He writes that "the dominant thread that ran through many of the evening's contributions on the subject was the juxtaposition of the African and American cultures and how the two can be effectively combined by recent transplants from across the Atlantic." He goes on to give a sampling of the discussions that reflected the variety of opinions:

"The *support system you have back home doesn't exist here. In order to feel comfortable here we need to know our limitations. The rules of the game are not the same as you might have say in Ghana*," said Ngissah.

A Nigerian auditor who's been married to his wife for 30 years had a different perspective. *"We already know the problem. First of all you can't put old wine into new wine. You can think you can bring your Igbo culture and enforce it here? It just won't work,"* he said, adding rather humorously, *"You go to our African parties and take a look at the face of our women. They look worn out and don't want to dance. Why? Because they spend most of their time cooking, cleaning and taking care of the home all by themselves. That's abuse!"*

Another Nigerian, Sylvester Okonkwo, presented an interesting angle to the clash of cultures and how it frames the issue. *"Let's not make this sound as if it's an African problem,"* he said. *"The African culture has its own pluses and minuses. Most of us studied here and gained employment here. We have a proverb that says when you are in a foreign land, 'learn all the good things there and leave the bad ones alone,'* said Okonkwo.

I agree with Edokpayi's observation that "most participants agreed that it was tough to balance the two cultures, all were in agreement that the African culture was intrinsically sound and could be a good insulation against the pressures of today's microwave world where materialistic pursuits and the hurry for results tend to obfuscate everything else." The discussions offer hope to the extent that the domestic violence is acknowledged, discussed, and the determination to come with solutions salient. In her article "What it means to be an Asian Indian Woman," Y. Lakshmi Malroutu posits that among the recent Asian Indian immigrants, domestic violence is hidden and denied. This should speak well of the recent African immigrants.

Mediating the tension brought by raising children who grow up in the United States also presents paradoxes. An experience of children who grow up in the United States and have minimal to zero experience of Africa is often the discussion of common experiences. Children assume a different identity from their parents and most likely identify as African Americans, proclaiming more of an affinity in cultural experiences to African American children who are descendants of former enslaved Africans than to their parents. Often parents have to decide which behavior should be accepted and which not. In the research that I am currently conducting on this topic, a student from Ethiopia relates how her mother preferred that she and her siblings associate with other recent immigrant children who have better manners than the rest of American kids. It is only recently, she says, that her mother has accepted that they are culturally American and have chosen their identity accordingly.

I have two daughters, too, who grew up here. When I first came one was two weeks old and the other just a year-and-a-half old. They identify with no hesitation as African Americans. We also have different views and perspectives on things in addition to those engendered by generational differences. I would like them to offer people food when they come to visit without asking if they want food or not. People will then reject the food politely afterwards if they choose to, but they constantly remind me that they have to ask since this is "America." Most parents have a variation of these cognitive dissonances to deal with. In most part parents identify with Africa more than their children do. In my research I found that African adults will identify as "Africans in America" and children will identify as African Americans.

Relationships with African Americans

It has also been argued that recent African immigrants perform well in school, have better study habits, and have excellent job performance rates. This behavior pattern parallels that of other immigrants of different continental origin. An assessment of the applicability of Ogbu's theory on voluntary and involuntary minority then becomes relevant here. This assessment should also take into consideration that the late Ogbu was also a recent African immigrant who came to the United States in the 1960s from Nigeria. Ogbu asserts that in understanding the performance of minorities in the United States a distinction between the types of minority status and the different types of cultural differences should be taken into account (Ogbu, 1993).

Voluntary minority refers to immigrants like the recent African immigrants who came to the United States through other reasons than U.S. enslavement. Involuntary minority refers to the status of African Americans who are descendants of enslaved people. Ogbu argues that there is an absence of persistent basic academic difficulties among the voluntary minorities despite the primary cultural differences with the Euro-American culture. Involuntary minorities, on the other hand, Ogbu further posits, have difficulties because of the nature of their responses to their forced incorporation and subsequent persistent mistreatment by the Euro-American power structures. Despite the phenomenal strides that have been made, legacy of sanitized unequal treatment still endures. Ogbu argues that African Americans have thus formed oppositional identity and cultural frame of references that tend to impact performance.

If we are to follow Ogbu's argument, if indeed, recent African immigrants are performing better, than their success could be attributed to the fact that they have a better response to the structural discrimination and unwelcoming school environments. What Ogbu's theory fails to take into consideration is the fact that some Euro-Americans feel more comfortable with recent African immigrants than they do with African Americans. When I first came to the United States as a student, an African American professor at Denison University in Ohio, at an orientation into the U.S. society, explained that in his experience there is less guilt whether subconscious or salient, for Euro-Americans towards recent African immigrants. As a result they tend to be more receptive and friendlier to recent African immigrants. Obviously this friendly attitude has its unfair benefits. The friendly atmosphere contributes towards a learning environment conducive to producing good results, or conversely a friendly working environment. This then becomes a structural and institutional hurdle for others who are not afforded the same courtesy to overcome. I have personally experienced this, as this discussion will later show. The fact that African immigrants enter the country mostly with more than a high school diploma, should also explain their relatively high level of educational attainment.

African immigrants are not immune to the adverse impact of competition for resources that often manifest in xenophobia. They have been looked at as taking away jobs from those already here and have also been victims of hate crimes. The other challenge that they have to face pertains to their relationship with African Americans who are descendants of former enslaved people. Professors Lani Guinier and Henry Louis Gates, Jr., a Harvard law professor and the chairman of Harvard's African and African-American Department, respectively, spoke at the third Black Alumni Weekend of Harvard University, which took place October 3–5, 2003, and drew more than 600 former students. Their comments illustrate the tension and challenge.

According to the Harvard University news of January–February, 2004, university officieals were pleased with an eight percent increase in black students (530) from the 2003 enrollment. However, the celebratory mood of the evening was broken by Professor Guinier, whose mother is white and whose father immigrated from Jamaica, when she advised that Harvard should reconsider its celebration since the majority of the black students were not true African Americans, but West Indian and African immigrants or their children, or to a lesser extent, children of biracial couples. Professor Gates, Jr., supported her assertions and charges (Onyeanyi, 2006).

Such comments by highly visible African Americans continued when Mr. Alan Keyes, a former right-wing Republican presidential candidate, accused Mr. Barack Obama, a senator from Illinois, of not being a true African American since his father was from Kenya. Alan Keyes is quoted in a *New York Times* article of August 27, 2004, titled "'African-American' Becomes a Term for Debate," as saying, "Barack Obama claims an African-American heritage." Mr. Keyes said on the ABC program "This Week" with George Stephanopoulos, "Barack Obama and I have the same race — that is, physical characteristics. We are not from the same heritage."

Yet another prominent African American, an administrator at the University of Columbia, Dr. Bobby Austin, was quoted in the same *New York Times* article of August 27, 2004, saying, "some people feared that black immigrants and their children would snatch up the hard-won opportunities made possible by the civil rights movement." Dr. Austin further said, "We've suffered so much that we're a bit weary and immigration seems like one more hurdle we will have to climb. People are asking: 'Will I have to climb over these immigrants to get to my dream? Will my children have to climb?'" Perceptions and thoughts like this permeate to the other parts of the community. Oftentimes in my classes I will have African American students asking me why do Africans hate them and vice versa. I often tell them that I do not wish to participate in this divide-and-conquer mentality that does not benefit us.

The workplace also fails to help bridge the gap between the two. I am a recent African immigrant, as I have mentioned before. Prior to coming to California State University, Sacramento, I was employed in Washington, in an institution that was predominately Euro-American. For years I was the only faculty of African descent. Efforts to encourage a hire of African Americans were often met with, "but we have you." For years the institution and some of its people felt comfortable with me and did not find it necessary to hire an African American who was born and raised in the United States.

When I discussed my concerns about this with some of my former colleagues and expressed that I felt like a token because of their attitude and refusal to hire African Americans, they would tell me how they did not see me as a token but as a strong, highly opinionated woman. As can be expected, they missed the point.

Their behavior made me fully understand what the professor in Denison meant, that hiring an African American evokes feelings that they would rather not deal with. When they did subsequently hire an African American, they displayed such racist behavior towards her that, among other issues, she was forced out.

Recently, I spoke with one of my former colleagues, Vicki Scannell, who is also a friend from the same institution. She told me that the problem still persists and the excuse that is now being made is that the institution does not pay enough to attract African Americans. The impression created then remains that African Americans will not work for less pay while hardworking Euro-Americans would. Of course, my friend, who is also Euro-American, made a point to remind them that institutional racism, and not pay, accounts for the absence of African American professors.

African Americans, as I mentioned earlier, paved the way for contemporary African immigrants — it would benefit both groups to unite and work together. Students where I am teaching seem to do a better job of bridging the gap. Two years ago they invited me to speak at an event they organized and the thesis was "bridging the gap between people of Africans descent from the continent and the diaspora."

Despite all the challenges that I have mentioned, African immigrants do share a life with their native-born counterparts. There are many intermarriages between them. Their offspring and their unions provide an element of diversity in the United States that should not be ignored since it bridges the gap between the native born and foreign born. Second-generation Africans are commanding leadership roles in arenas large and small throughout the country. Whether members of Congress such as Barack Obama, leaders of black community and student organizations, or even up-and-coming hip-hop artists such as Akon, African second-generation immigrants are wholehearted participants in and even creators of today's African American culture.

Continuously infused with new influences from their own diaspora, Africans are contributing to the fluid adaptability of U.S. dynamic urban culture. In the process of redefining their race and culture in a social order far different from that of their parents, African immigrants are both giving to and taking from African American tradition in a reciprocal and mutually advantageous relationship (Salim Omar Eisa, 2005).

They have embraced the economic opportunities offered by the United States. According to the Schomburg Center for Research in Black Culture, "Some highly educated [African] immigrants, realizing that their limited proficiency in English and their foreign degrees would make it difficult to get the American jobs they coveted, have instead opened their own businesses. This entrepreneurial spirit is deeply ingrained in Africa, where the informal economic sector is particularly dynamic." The Bay Area and Sacramento, like many other U.S. cities, have African restaurants, African hair braiding salons, nightclubs, music stores, and many other entrepreneurial ventures that provide economic stability.

Although there were about 100,000 highly educated African professionals throughout the United States in 1999, many more are also involved in jobs where less education and often less skill may be required. They work as cab drivers, parking lot attendants, airport workers or waiters, waitresses, and cooks in restaurants. Even African women who have traditionally been in the background of most traditional African family structure now find themselves at the forefront of economic opportunities in the United States and thus are playing important economic roles in maintaining the family structure both for the family members who are still in Africa and those in the United States.

References

Africa News Service (1999, November 21).

[The] African Sun Times (2006, February 6).

Daff, Marieme (2002, August 9). Women-migration: Women taking their places in African immigration. *Inter Press services*.

Diouf, Sylviane (2005). The new African diaspora. From *In Motion: The African American Migration Experience* (p. 1). New York: Schomburg Center for Research in Black Culture.

Edokpayi, Ben (2006). *The Times of Nigeria*.

Eissa, Salih Omar (2005). *Diversity and transformation: African Americans and African immigration to the United States*. Immigration Policy Brief.

Halter, Marilyn (1993). *Between race and ethnicity: Cape Verdean American immigrants 1860–1965* (pp. 67–98). Champaign, IL: University of Illinois Press.

Logan, John R., & Deane, Glenn (2003, August 15). *Black diversity in metropolitan America*. Lewis Mumford Center for Comparative Urban and Regional Research, University of Albany, p. 4.

Mosupyoe, Boatamo. *Recent African immigrants in the U.S.*, unpublished manuscript.

Ogbu, John (1993). Difference in cultural frame of references. *International Journal of Behavioral Development, 16*(3), 483–506.

Onyeanyi, Chika A. (2006, February 6). *The African Sun Times*.

Schomburg Center for Research in Black Culture (2005, February). The waves of migration. From *In Motion: The African American Migration Experience*. *www.inmotionaame.org*

Takougang, Joseph. Recent African immigrants to the United States: A historical perspective. *The Western Journal of Black Studies*, 19(1).

U.S. Census, 2000.

Reflection Questions

1. Upon reading this chapter, what do you consider to be legitimate knowledge? (Optional)

2. In your view, when is knowledge only information and when is knowledge a resource? How do you make the distinction? Please offer a brief explanation using two examples to illustrate your point.

3. Who in your view benefits from publishing distorted knowledge? Why do you suppose this knowledge is still used despite its distortion? (Optional)

4. How can you be sure that the knowledge you hold about someone else's racial/ethnic community is not distorted? Please offer a brief explanation using two examples to illustrate your point.

5. How can you be sure that the knowledge that someone holds about you is accurate? (Optional)

Race, Class and Gender

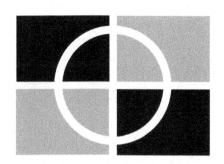

▣ Framing Questions

1. Define the terms *race, class,* and *gender.*

2. Why do you think the authors up to this point have emphasized awareness regarding race, class, and gender? (Optional)

3. In what ways do you see or not see the ways race, class, and gender influence the way you are perceived and/or treated by others? Please offer a brief explanation using two examples to illustrate your point.

4. Are there instances that you can name when race, class, and gender matter most and least? Please offer a brief explanation using two examples to illustrate your point.

5. Why do you suppose race, class, and gender are often discussed as being interlinked as opposed to being discussed individually? (Optional)

Introduction

Boatamo Mosupyoe

The articles in this section *focus* on women and their experiences. The accounts about women and their experiences show women's thinking, knowing, and being manifest in multicentric ways. From these multicentric contexts the articles show (a) women of different descents' relative position in a hierarchy of status, (b) the interactional process that tends to perpetuate inequality, (c) the experience resulting from participating in those interactions, (d) the importance of relations between women and women, men and women, and men and men, in shaping the character of inequality and dominance, (e) the impact of the legacy of the past on the present forms of inequality, (f) the function of internalized sexism, classism and racism, and (g) how raising level of consciousness to the intersection of race, class, generational differences, transformational resistance, physicality, spatial differences, and gender can enhance the understanding and offer hope for reaching solutions. Further, the articles inquire into various social practices, historical processes, and the multiple cultural logics of gender relations.

The intersection of race, class, and gender gives a historical development of thought on the three concepts. The article starts by giving definitions of the terms. The definitions were coined by the dominant group that also benefited from the definitions in real life. Race has been defined as a biological concept when in reality it is a social construct that has functioned to engender systems of inequality that favored groups of Euro descent. Class is described as a system that ranks people according to their relative economic status. Since the top ranking group because of racial classification is the one that controls resources and access, it tends also to be favored by classism. Gender refers to the experiences of women and men, cultural definitions of womanhood and manhood and the interconnections between race, gender, sexual orientation, age, class, and other forms of oppression.

The article cites examples from different communities to illustrate the importance of the intersection of race, class, and gender. The importance of addressing the intersection is emphasized. However, addressing the intersection becomes very difficult since both men of color and women of Euro descent tend to refuse to acknowledge its existence. Men of color, understandably, also face brutality and discrimination from oppressive Euro-male structures. Consequently, they feel that addressing gender inequality as they practice it is a further unfair attack on them.

Similarly, some women of Euro descent find it difficult to acknowledge that they enjoy privilege because of their skin color, because they too are discriminated against by the male Euro-structures.

Lien Tien continues the dialogue of race, class, and gender with an emphasis on how past history perpetuates negative images in the present. Tien also shows how the laws impacted the public's image of Asian women, thereby affecting their relative position in a hierarchy of status. This article "U.S. Attitudes Toward Women of Asian Ancestry: Legislative and Media Perspectives," further examines how the United States immigration laws have been designed to prevent women of Asian descent and their children from entering the United States, even in cases where they were married to U.S. service men stationed in Asian countries. The legacy of exclusion dates to pre-World War II. Through a series of three acts: the Chinese Exclusion Act of 1882, the Immigration Act of 1917, and the National Origins Act of 1924, the United States effectively barred Asians from becoming U.S. citizens. The subsequent laws, despite their attempts at ending exclusion, created images of women of Asian ancestry as "erotic and sexual beings."

Tien references the play *Miss Saigon* as perpetuating the image of Asian women as temporary romantic and sexual partners for U.S. servicemen. That the sentiments about women of Asian descent are unacceptable as marriage partners to U.S. servicemen, and that their children are not U.S. citizens are common, is clearly shown in how the laws have been formulated. Tien argues that the laws also reflect the attitudes and feelings of the U.S. people towards women of Asian descent. Some practices like the "picture bride," which were negating the Euro concept of romance, were not interpreted as different; instead they were used to the advantage of those who were opposed to Japanese immigration. Euro-Americans then interpreted the practice as immoral, a view which underscored the image of Asian women as immoral, debauched, subservient, and depraved.

Tien continues by examining various laws that applied to women of Asian ancestry from different parts of Asia. While laws like the MacCarran-Walter Act passed on June 27, 1952, were designed to eliminate race-based exclusion, the act still contained quotas that favored European immigration and highly disfavored immigration from Asian countries. Even the laws that were formulated to rectify the Vietnamese situation, still had loopholes that ensured the exclusion and sent a message that women of Asian ancestry were not wanted in the United States, Tien contends. The laws functioned to reinforce stereotypic images about women of Asian ancestry. The attitudes contributed towards internalized racists and sexists attitudes in both the dominant and the Asian communities.

Rita Liberti's article, "Beyond Entertainment Value: Understanding the Intersectionality of Race, Gender, Physicality, and Sport," shows that contrary to popular belief, sport is not immune from the impact of the value system of the U.S. society. Indeed, she argues, the intersection of race, class, and gender as it manifests in the cultural space of sport reveals that claims of women's universal experience is a myth. She points out that female athletes of color in the 21st century are still underrepresented with marginalized positions in relation to those of their Euro-American counterparts. In addition, Liberti posits, the media representation of women athletes of color is not only minimal; it also reaffirms their marginal status in sport. In instances where they are represented, she argues, their physicality is constructed as negative and lacking of heterosexual qualities. The latter clearly shows the perpetuation of the normative white, middle-class femininity as standards against which every woman should be judged to qualify as fit to be called a woman. Deviations from these Eurocentric middle-class feminine images render both their "disqualification" as women and their descriptions as leaving much to be desired in feminine grace and refinement. Liberti's article challenges us to examine sport as more than just a treat and innocent diversion, but as a vehicle through which the cultural stereotypes of race, class, gender, physicality, and heterosexism are reproduced and reaffirmed.

Valerie Talavera-Bustillos examines the educational experiences of first generation Chicana students in her article "Chicanas and Transformational Resistance: Analyzing College Aspirations within the Family Context." Talavera-Bustillos shows that there are obvious conflicts engendered by generational differences, educational aspirations, and gender roles that the first generation Chicana college and university students have to mediate. The conflicts among other things are created by contradictory roles that manifest as a negotiation and a refutation of oppressive gender roles. Talavera-Bustillos demonstrates how expressions of transformational resistance strategically enabled this generation to both maintain and achieve their educational goals. Further, Talavera-Bustillos argues, transformational resistance also provided a platform where this generation could redefine traditional gender roles as they enter college with determination to achieve their goals.

In "What It Means to be an Asian Indian Woman," Y. Lakshmi Malroutu shows the diversity of the Asian Indian society but most importantly she discusses how traditional gender roles of the Asian Indian societies have transferred to the Asian Indian immigrant societies in the United States. Examples of these are having arranged marriages and considering the wishes of parents as primary when choosing a spouse, etc. Patriarchy and sexism continue to prevail even in the 21st century among Asian Indian immigrants. Men are still considered the primary immigrants, Lakshmi Malroutu argues, and women enter the country as their dependents. She further posits that the success of woman is still defined by her "ability" to maintain the marriage and keep the family together irrespective of abuse. This kind of attitude valorizes women's suffering by discouraging divorce and encouraging perceptions of single motherhood as detrimental to and unfit for proper child development.

The last article "Is the Glass Ceiling Cracked Yet" reflects that change towards gender equality is possible but you have to go through a process of mediation and tension. The articles trace the challenges and achievements of Rwanda and South Africa on gender equality and compares in some instances to the USA. In terms of representation in government it seems that while Hilary's 18 million votes have delivered some cracks in the glass ceiling Rwanda and South Africa have gone beyond and their reality challenges the gluey floors/glass ceiling dichotomy to include metaphors that reflect the change. Change is possible; the mere fact that cracks were made in the "highest, hardest, glass ceiling" is an indication of a movement towards change. Change is achieved by acknowledgement that informs mechanism to redress and transform. The discourse requires an understanding of paradigms and variables that function to either perpetuate or promote gender equality.

The articles suggest to us how to mediate the tension. They inform us of the importance of a multicentric approach to gender issues. In a multicentric environment parties will have to exercise the ability to move from the center to the margin in a fashion that will include similarities and differences in a lineal, circular, and spiral fashion. They remind us that the coexistence of multiple centers should also be encouraged. The concept of humanity entails differences and similarities. The reduction of humanity to commonalities has historically ended up in genocides and persecution of those who were different and perceived as inhuman, because they were different.

We have to learn to live with differences. The Eurocentric, sexist, classist, and patriarchal approaches have been unable to do that in many ways. The realities of the differences are obvious. Implicit in these articles is an important message: the construction and reconstruction of relationships, whether they are racial, sexual, heterosexist, or based on class, require a multicentric approach that can engender understanding and resolution of the challenges.

The Intersection of Race, Class and Gender

Boatamo Mosupyoe

The Purpose

The purpose of this article is to offer an introductory definition and explanation of what the intersection of race, class and gender means. The article will trace the historical development of thought on the three concepts and briefly analyze their impact on men and women relationships and status.

Much has been written about the impact of racism on people of Asian, African, Mexican, Native American descents. The debate about what is important in gender relations has spanned the discourse for ages. Views have varied from looking at race as the most salient, and class and gender as less salient. As time progresses views changed, in other words views moved from isolating the three to putting them on the same par. Progressive feminists and scholars like bell hooks, (1984) Cornell West (1993) and most recently Cole and Guy-Sheftall (2003) have stressed the importance of an analysis that focuses on the confluence of race, class, and gender in understanding the complexities of communities of color in the U.S. and the challenges that they face. In order to fully understand the impact, the three variables have to be considered. Institutionalized racism, economic injustices, and gender all play a role in the relegation of people to secondary status in societies like the United States.

Explaining the Topic

Historically race has been defined on the basis of how people look. In other words, race has been defined around intrinsic criteria that use phenotypes attributes ascribed by birth to distinguish people from one another. The classifications went a step further to assign and associate certain behavior and skills with certain races. Some scholars of European descent argued that Euro phenotypes reflect highest forms of beauty, in other words people of Euro-descent are the most beautiful of all the people on earth. They are the standards of beauty against which everybody should be measured. Their "fine" hair, sharp noses, "pink skin" which they described and still describe as "white," represented the ultimate forms of beauty. White also came to mean "pure," "innocent," and "less likely to do evil and wrong deeds." Further, it was argued that because of the size of their skulls people of Euro-descent possess superior intellect. The logic centered around the intrinsic nature of the phenotypes, and therefore were presented and explained as biologically determined. Since they are biologically determined, they cannot be changed and have to be accepted as factual and static.

This way of thinking influenced how important political, economic, educational, social, cultural, etc. decisions were made. People of Euro descent were said to be the "norm," the "supreme," the "yard stick," and the "natural." Other people who are not of Euro-descent were not only classified but were also described in comparison with the Euro model in the most unfavorable ways. People were looked upon as inferior precisely because they were not of Euro-descent. Much has been written to dispel the myth of race as a biological construct. Race is a social construct. Although the classification uses obvious physical characteristics to group people, it is very illogical and arbitrary to conclude that the shape of somebody's nose, the color of their skin and the size of their skull give them genetic advantage in terms of intellect, beauty, and behavior over the others.

The definition of race in biological terms was clearly designed to institute and maintain a system of social inequality that ensured and still ensures the preservation of racism. It guaranteed that only people who look a certain way will have access to resources and maintain control. Moreover, this classification influences how people interact with one another. Associating physical characteristics with behavior often leads to discrimination based on race. Joy James in her article "Experience, Reflection, Judgment and Action: Teaching Theory, Talking Community," writes in part:

> "I seem continuously challenged to "prove" that I am qualified. Comparing my work experiences with those of other African American Academics, I notice that in spite of being hired through a highly competitive process, we seemed to be asked more routinely, almost reflectively, if we have Ph.D. We could attribute this and have to our "diminutive" height, youngish appearances, or casual attire. Yet I notice that white women about our height, unsuited, and under sixty seem not to be interrogated as frequently about their qualifications." (D Bell and Klein Radically Speaking, 1996, p 37).

Clearly from this quote Joy James qualifications and credentials are questioned precisely because she is not of Euro descent. In simple terms, the motivation of questioning her qualifications are racist. This explains and indicates the unfair and irrational privilege the color of the skin confers on people of Euro-descent. As much as I want to write about this in the past tense, the fact of the matter is, it still happens today.

Together with race, class can function and has functioned as a form of discrimination. The tendency to socially rank people according to their relative economic system gives rise to classism. The class ranking system, unlike race, is often considered extrinsic to the individual. It is also looked upon as situational and fluid and therefore allows an individual to choose her or his position in the class hierarchy system. This is not necessarily true since class does not happen in a vacuum. It intersects with other variables that influences the status of people in a society. More often than not, in all systems of stratification, the top ranked group controls the economic resources and also enjoys the highest prestige and privilege. Historically, in societies where race has been used to rank people, people who were favored by the race classification as superior, become the people who are also favored by the class system. In societies like the United States and South Africa male of Euro-descent have been the favored group that also defined and determined policies. Policies favored those who looked like them skin wise and gender wise. This favoritism resulted in systems of race and gender inequality that take struggles to penetrate and overcome.

Gender refers to a social construct whereby certain characteristics, behavior, and actions are assigned and associated with people based on their biological sex. "Gender also refers to the experiences of women and men, cultural definitions of womanhood and manhood and the interconnections between race, gender, sexual orientation, age, class, and other oppression." (Cole and Guy-Sheftall, 2003, pxxii). Gender constitutes one of the most salient modes of organizing inequality among the sexes. Vouching for gender as the most quintessential of the three undermines the interconnection of the three, that is, race, class and gender. The three have to be considered in an analysis of discriminatory practices. Experiences of the system and of the intersection of the different systems articulating the actual experiences of inequality, will necessarily be different from man to man, woman to woman, and man to woman. In addition, the experience will be different from one group to another, as well as from groups within a society. Women and men's experiences across class and race have both similarities and differences. It is important not to deny the differences of experiences.

Feminism as a Concept

This section examines the development of the concept of feminism and global feminism from the 1960's onwards. The examination best exemplifies the complexities of the confluence of race, class, and gender. The efforts of the United Nations Commission on the status of women are well known. Despite sometimes fruitless attempts, the Commission was relentless in its efforts to represent women's issues to the United Nations. It's efforts were eventually successful. The advocates of women's rights eventually managed to convince the United Nations General Assembly to declare 1976–1985 the decade of women. In addition, the advocates and women were able to convince the United Nations to fund an International Women's Conference in 1975 in Mexico City. The theme of the conference was "Equality, Development, and Peace." The theme was intended to be inclusive of world's women's issues; however, what it achieved was a clear picture of dissimilarities of women's experiences world wide.[1]

The conference highlighted the differences in thought and experiences between women of Euro-descent, who I will refer to as women of the north and the others, who I will refer to as women of the south.[2] The theme Equality became the focal point of women of Euro descent. Their definition of equality in relation to men formed an important area of focus for them. Other women could not identify with the priorities and the agenda as determined by women of Euro- descent. They looked upon them as, and indeed, they were, part of the oppressive dominant structures that women of the south sought equality from. After all, most of the governing structures where the delegates came from composed of people of Euro-descent. That also meant to most if not all women at the time, women of Euro-descent represented an extension of those oppressive structures. In addition, their priorities were to be liberated from racial oppression and not gender oppression. **At that time,** race and not gender seemed to form the salient variable for women of the south. Of course, later the approach would evolve to recognizing the importance of the intersection of race, class and gender, as this discussion will later illustrate.

Conversations about feminism centered around the definition of the term. To women of the south the term would be irrelevant to their experiences if its translation meant to "be like a man and act like a man." It sounded to women of the south as if women of Euro-descent wanted to be men, in a nutshell. The women of the south did not want to be men; instead they saw an urgent need just to be treated like human beings, to have roofs over their heads, to earn wages that would enable them to feed their children, as priorities. The women of the south's arguments have been articulated outside of the conference by scholars like Lewis (1977). She describes the way in which race is more often a salient feature of oppression in African American women's lives. Lewis **then,** further argued that gender relations in communities of color cannot be interpreted in the Euro-centric terms that reflect the experiences of women of Euro-descent. Historically, African American women have tended to see racial discrimination as a more powerful cause of their subordination. In the 1980's and 1990's scholars like bell hooks also articulate experiences that are similar to those articulated by women of the south at the Mexico conference. In her book *Feminist Theory,* from margin to center (1984), bell hooks writes in part:

> When I participated in feminist groups, I found that white women adopted a condescending attitude towards me and other non-white participants. The condescension they directed at black women was one of the means they employed to remind us that the women's movement was "theirs"—that we were able to participate because they allowed it, even encouraged it, we were needed to legitimate the process. They did not see us as equals. They did not treat us as equals. And though they expected us to provide first hand accounts of black experiences, they felt it was their role to decide if these experiences were authentic. Frequently, college-educated black women (even those from poor and working class backgrounds) were dismissed as mere imitators. Our presence in movement activities did not count (p 11).

Sentiments such as these articulated by hooks, were present in the Mexico conference. The agenda and the access were seen as determined by women of Euro-descent.

These actions clearly indicated and proved to others that women of Euro descent were oppressive. Others in discussing Chicana women's experiences also confirmed the primacy of race in determining an individual's position in the economic order in the United States. Similar experiences by women of Asian descent and Native American women also abound.

The other two themes, Peace and Development, seemed to resonate more with women who were not of European descent. The different themes and the different experiences of women in these contexts then brought into question the universal applicability of the term feminism to women's issues. The visibility of the differences intensified during the mid-decade world conference on women held in Copenhagen in 1980. Women were determined to unite and resolve their differences. The determination, notwithstanding, the difference were present and they needed to be confronted. As part of the solution the intersection of race, gender, together with their implication on access and privilege had to be acknowledged. The discourse and the process proved difficult then as it does today in the 21st century. Cole and Guy-Sheftall (2003) notice the difficulty even today. These two remarkable women have been involved both in the civil rights and women's movements, and have been committed to the elimination of racism, sexism, classism and heterosexism in all of their professional lives. They write in part,

> *We have been engaged in difficult dialogues with white feminists about the importance of understanding the particular experiences of women of color, and the need to take seriously the intersection of race, class and gender in the lives of all women, not only women of color"* (xxviii)

Arguably, most women of Euro-descent refuse or find it difficult to acknowledge the privilege their skin color confers to them in societies like the United States. Much has been debated about the origin or root of the denial. I will posit the views of two Euro-American women, one that I know personally and have interacted with extensively, and the other who I am acquainted with through her work. The first woman Kyzyl-Fenno-Smith is a respected librarian and scholar; she often articulates how as a woman of Euro-descent she recognizes the tremendous effort spent in maintaining the advantage accorded by the 'pink' Euro skin by Euro-American women.

From Fenno-Smith's point of view the unconscious claim reflects one symptom of the concerted effort to maintain the privilege. She succinctly points out that women we are talking about are smart and articulate in ways that demonstrate a deeper level of understanding sexual discrimination, institutionalized and otherwise, what then blinds them to racial discrimination? Fenno-Smith argues that some women of Euro-descent become so skilled in the art of perpetuating their own privilege that they believe it is natural and self perpetuating. What complicates matters is the undeniable fact that women of Euro descent have also been discriminated against by Euro-male dominated structures. However, Fenno-Smith cautions that this should not be confused with or equated to something in the unconscious level. The often uttered phrase "I am doing the best I can," in the discussion of the intersection proves that the domain where the privilege exists is the conscious level. Fenno-Smith also says that it benefits Euro-American women to maintain the privilege, since most of the time Euro-American men, and not women, are blamed for the exclusion and discrimination. It is, she concludes, to the benefit of the women to maintain the status quo.[3]

Peggy Mackintosh in her article "White Privilege, Unpacking the Invisible Knapsack," posits a different view from Fenno-Smith's. Her divergent view is mirrored in her statement:

> *After I realized the extent to which men work from a basis of unacknowledged privilege, I understood that most of their oppressiveness was unconscious. Then I remembered the frequent charges from women of color that white women whom they encounter are oppressive.*

Mackintosh and Fenno-Smith with their divergent views represent those women of Euro-descent who recognize the existence of racism in woman to woman relationship and therefore, offer hope for the achievement of an ideal. Problems of denial or lack of awareness or consciousness resulted in women from the south's reluctance to embrace the term feminism. The problems had linguistic, definition, and substantive implications as well. English constituted the first language of some and not all of the delegates; this impacted the efficacy of translation. The different experiences and agendas impacted the substance of the term.

The controversy surrounding the relevance of the concept feminism to "poor people" precipitated the International Women Tribune Center (IWTC) to hold a forum made up primarily by women from North and South America on "What is Feminism?" These group of women decided that feminism should not be viewed as a list of separate issues, but as a political perspective on women's lives and the problem of domination. Focusing on the problem of domination, then women have to contend with the domination of women of Euro-descent over other women. In the United States, Australia, New Zealand, and South Africa, for example where systems still use skin color to confer privilege, women of Euro-descent had to acknowledge the privilege and its implications. When this is achieved then women can work for a definition with the contribution from everybody. This then eliminates confusion and engenders common ownership of the word.

It is worth mentioning here that it is now ten years since South Africa has been freed from a brutal blatant racist system of apartheid that classified and treated people based on the color of their skin. The progress in South Africa remarkable as it is, it takes more than ten years to transform or even eradicate a system that has been in place for 342 years. Further, Euro-Africans will be super humans to just automatically and miraculously rid themselves of the deeply socialization process that taught them that they are superior because of their race. South Africa and the United States are comparable. In spite of the civil rights movement, the U.S. is still battling different manifestations of racism, classism, and sexism.

Towards the Intersection of Race, Class and Gender

Increasingly, recent scholarship suggests a shift without denying race as one of the important variables in understanding gender and racial relationships. The scholarship has no choice but to shift, since the intersection dates from time immemorial. What has been missing is the acknowledgement of its existence. In the case of the United States like in South Africa, with racist pasts, it became difficult for women and men of color to acknowledge the intersection. Instead, what happened in such situations racial oppression seemed to take primacy over gender oppression. This is true for most communities of color in the United States and elsewhere. Women were faced with a difficult choice, (that should not have been a choice at all), of addressing either gender oppression and risk being labeled collaborators with the Euro enemy or just sticking to addressing racial oppression in the face of patriarchy and sexism from men of color. Anyway, the intersection manifested in various forms. I will first examine the intersection as it found articulation between women and women and then between men and women.

The experiences of Sojourner Truth and Francis Gage best exemplify the intersection that was present in the long history of racial, class, and gender relationships in the United States. Their experiences also prove the complexities of the relationships and the difficulty of assigning hierarchies to oppression. However, I am very much aware that some women of color in the United States will still maintain that in a racially divided society, race and not gender becomes more prominent in creating experiences of discrimination. This paradigm becomes clear in the analysis of Sojourner Truth's experiences in Akron Ohio. At this conference that was attended mostly if not exclusively (except for Sojourner) by Euro-American women and men, men were giving reasons why Euro-American women should not be given the right to vote. One man after the other stood in the podium and justified the exclusion of women from participating in making decisions that affected their daily lives.[4]

Arguments for the exclusion of Euro-American women included the sin of the first mother, Eve was created second and sinned first, that was a powerful reason for the exclusion, one man reasoned. One man referred to the birth of Jesus Christ. Jesus Christ was not a woman; therefore, women should not be given the right to vote. Other arguments pertained to the physical weakness of Euro-American women, since men helped them over puddles of water, opened doors for them, and pulled chairs for them to sit. Arguments about women's inferior intellect were also cited as the reason. After the men made their arguments, Euro-American women were paralyzed into silence, until Sojourner Truth decided to go to the podium to respond. When she stood up, Euro-American women protested, not the men, but the women. They whispered to Francis Gage to stop Ms. Truth from going to the podium because they did not want their course to be mixed up with "the Negro's" course, they declared, very upset.

Francis Gage, an equally remarkable Euro-American woman ignored the Euro-American women's pleas and did not stop Sojourner from going to the podium.

Once on the podium Sojourner addressed every argument that men cited. When she said that Jesus Christ was made by a woman and God, and man had nothing to do with it, there was a thundering applause even from those who had earlier on objected. She continued to even more applause when she addressed the sin of the first mother, by saying that, if one woman was able to turn the world upside down like that, then the women of the north and of the south will be able to turn it back right, if men would allow them.

Perhaps the most applause came when she declared that nobody helped her over puddles of water, and nobody opened doors for her; she could work from sun rise to sun set with somebody, a slave owner, beating her up on her back with a lash; not only that, she also saw most of her children sold into slavery and continued to ask, "And, Aint I a woman?" Sojourner rescued Euro-American women from the men that day in Ohio. Initially, her race as an African American woman, invoked rejection from Euro-American women. To them she was a Negro, period, her gender and her support for their course was irrelevant. Sojourner knew that she would not be part of those who would be granted the right to vote. The struggle for the right to vote at that time was for women of Euro-descent. That notwithstanding, she saw the struggle as that of all women. She and Miss Gage saw the intersection that others failed to see. In this context one would be justified to say that race seem more salient here than gender. Be that as it may, they both exist in the equation.

Rollins (1985), in her ethnographic work on black domestics in the United States, shows a different manifestation of the intersection of race, class and gender between women and women. Aspects of inequality as played out in the relationship between an African American woman employee and her Euro-American woman employer manifest in ways that blends the three variables. Phenotype distinctions, that is, race becomes an instrument that the employer uses to dehumanize her African American employee. The Euro-American employee treated the African American as invisible, as though she does not exist. The employers' skin color translated into a symbol of success, which made it easier for her to achieve with her African American employee than with other women of Euro-descent. Further, gender (female to female) blended together with class (/servant/employee to master/employer) and phenotypes (skin color, etc.) in determining the dynamics of the relationship. The African American employee would exhibit extreme forms of deference to the Euro-American employer, on one hand. On the other hand the Euro-American employer will display condescending maternalism towards her African-American employee. In addition, the employer will feel entitled to intrude into her employee's life.

The invasion served to empower the employer and reaffirmed her self worth as she continued to demean her employee who was under pressure to develop affective bonds. One other dynamic that manifested in this relationship was the need for the African American employee to perpetuate the false notion of their employer's superiority and their (African American) inferiority in their employer's mind. They would not reveal their economic successes to their Euro-American women employers, e.g., children in college, owning a car. They understood the need of their employer to feel superior in the face of the Euro-American male patriarchy and sexism. Similarly, Segura (1994) in her discussion of Chicana' women's triple oppression in the contemporary USA also sees race as playing a decisive role in the access of Chicana women to jobs. Segura sees the confluence as important and like the others she acknowledges that racial discrimination sometimes makes race more salient in determining an individual's position in the economic order in the USA.

The intersection of gender relations is very complex. The complexity increases as it relates to men and women of color relationships, especially in a racially divided society like the United States and South Africa. In their book Gender Talk, Cole and Guy-Sheftall (2003) write:

> "We have also been engaged in difficult dialogues with Black men about their sexism, problematic conceptions of Black manhood, and their own gender privilege, even within a culture that continues to be deeply racist and demonizes them" (xxxii).

Confronting sexism and forms of patriarchy in communities of color has historically posed a challenge. The saliency of race functioned to both preclude and undermine the importance of addressing the forms of patriarchy and sexism as practiced by men of color. Both Chicana and African American women talk about how the men in their communities will label them traitors and collaborators with the Euro system that brutalizes them on the daily basis when they attempted to address sexism as they experienced it from the men of color. The same dynamic also manifested in Asian American communities. Chow in her article "The Development of Feminist Consciousness Among Asian American Women" writes:

> As Asian women became active in their communities, they encountered sexism. Even though many Asian American women realized that they usually occupied subservient positions in the male-dominated organizations within Asian communities, their ethnic pride and loyalty frequently kept them from public revolt. More recently some Asian American women have recognized that these organizations have not been particularly responsive to their needs and concerns as women. They also protested that their intense involvement did not and will not result in equal participation as long as the traditional dominance by men and the gendered division of labor remain (Ngang-Ling Chow, 1987, p288).

The arguments varied. In the video Black is Black Ain't, (1995) bell hooks clearly articulates the presence of gender inequality in the African American communities and the energy that is directed at making it a taboo subject. She recalls an incident where her father unilaterally ordered her mother to leave the house. The incident confused her and conflicted with her perception of marriage as a partnership. In the same video bell hooks continues to take issue with males of color equating the reclamation of the race to the redemption of an emasculated male identity. Ironically, when male identity is defined as such, it encompasses forms of oppressions that marginalize women of color. In the same video Angela Davis also talks about how women subordination in the African American community needs to be addressed, and how African American males should take equal responsibility.

Often men will cite traditional values to justify sexism, even in the U.S. Chicana women will be told that they are betraying La Rasa. Elizabeth Martinez (1998) notes that in situations where Chicano and Chicana are faced with racism, fighting for women's rights is relegated to secondary status. She states "women will feel an impulse towards unity with rather than enmity towards their brothers" p. 183. Confronting sexism in the communities of color also translated for men into the desire by women of color to be like women of Euro-descent, adopting their values and ideals. This was just another way of silencing the women from addressing the sexism and patriarchy in their communities. Examples of instances where women of color are silenced when they try to address sexism within their own communities are many. Women are often told that they should not air dirty linen in public, because the enemy will use it against the race. Again here this quote from Cole and Guy-Sheftall elucidates the issue; *"whatever differences that we have as Black brothers and sisters should and can be worked out behind closed doors, and not be aired in public, as if we need to be validated by whites or the white media."* (xxxii). This was said by an African American male journalist, reacting to statements made by an African American woman about O. J. Simpson and Clarence Thomas.

In the Asian American women's protest against sexism within the community will be criticized as *"weakening of the male ego, dilution of efforts and resources in Asian Communities, destruction of working relationships between Asian men and women, setbacks for the Asian American cause, cooptation into the larger society— in short the affiliation with the feminist movement is perceived is perceived as a threat to solidarity within their own community."* (Ngan-Ling Chow, 1987, p2).

Since there are similarities and also differences in the experience of women of color with South African women, I will in the next section examine the experiences of women in South Africa for comparative purposes.

The South African Case

For a long time indigenous African women in South Africa faced the same dilemma. It became very difficult for women to address the subordination of women within the movements that were fighting against the racist policies of the South African Apartheid Government. Apartheid was the system that divided people based on the color of the skin and treated them accordingly. The indigenous Africans were placed at the bottom of the ladder in the hierarchical structure of oppression hierarchy and relegated to the margins. It was a brutal racist system that treated Africans as secondary citizens with no rights at all. The apartheid racist system was also very sexist. Women were denied many legal rights. At some point African women were legally denied the right to occupy a house if the husband died and the woman did not have a son. An African woman could not purchase anything on credit unless her husband also co-signs. Outside of the apartheid sexist and racist laws, African women were also faced with forms of patriarchy from within their own culture. Much has been debated about the origin of the sexism and patriarchy. Granted some of it was inherited and imposed by the Euro-Africans during colonialism and apartheid era. Be that as it may, it existed and it impacted women's lives. It needed to be addressed.

The preference was to talk about the contributions of women to the liberation struggle, but not to address the gender inequality among the Africans. Often three different views prevailed. One view preferred that the close door or closet resolution of the problem. In other words, if men and women publicly confronted patriarchy and sexism, the evil apartheid agents will use it against them. The second view opted for the problem to be left to individual couples married or single to resolve. The advocates of the view opposed turning the issues into a systemic problem within the movement. The last view saw women's subordination and exclusion as an important but not as an urgent problem; or as unimportant. To them overthrowing the racist regime superceded any kind of struggle.

The then liberation movements in South Africa made efforts and strides in gender issues. Indeed, the African National Congress Women's Charter and the Women's League bear testimony to this. However, on a daily basis, women did face some of the similar difficulties that women in the United States faced. Shahrazad Ali's ideas in her book *The Black Man's Guide to Understanding Black Women* (1990), about the relationship between African American men and women, echoed what African women had to face when they dared address sexism within their own community. Ali posits that men must rule and women must submit to their natural and traditional roles, as well as to the man's will. These ideas are presented as traditional roles. Any woman who was seen to violate these roles was then described as embracing evil Western ideas. In South Africa women faced the same obstacles as well.

What should be understood is, women experience sexism and patriarchy. The experience and not the western ideas prompts their objection to the dictates that put them in the situation. It is common knowledge that I lost a husband and son on the same day, and at the time when I was expecting one of my daughters. During that period I was required to sit in a very hot room with my head bowed to show my grief. I was pained in the most terrible way; I did not need to have my head bowed all the time. I felt I needed to go outside and get some fresh air. I was pregnant and it was very hot. While my mother was very reluctant to go against the dictates of my late husband's mother, and could not bring herself to rescue me, I was fortunate that my sister was there. Mary Grace, my sister would tell everybody that I needed to take a walk and needed fresh air. That caused a lot of tension that my mother avoided, but to my sister my comfort was most important. She knew I was grieving. She could not even comprehend the extent of my grief, because she said to me after the tragedy, "Ati (my name) I am feeling so much pain, and Simmy (my late husband) and Thami (my late son) are just my brother-in-law and nephew, I cannot even imagine what pain you are feeling right now." My sister knew I was grieving whether my head was bowed 24 hour a day or not. A widow then was not allowed to go outside because that would undermine the extent of her grief, while a widower could go about and even sit under a tree, in a shade. If this was tradition, it was a tradition that was oppressing me and I needed it changed. I was experiencing it as oppressive that is why I wanted it changed, not because some Euro-woman told me it was oppressive. I don't need a Euro-woman to tell me about my experience.

In 1996 I was invited to speak to a multiracial audience at University of Witwatersrand on my research that focused on the mediation of patriarchy and sexism by women in South Africa. During the talk I referred to the differential treatment of widows and widowers, and to this experience. While I love my culture very much, I am aware of oppressive tenants in it. At the end of my talk an African man stood up and berated me on embracing Western values and undermining the fundamentals of the African culture. He told me that he would be damned to listen to somebody who has just come from the US to lecture him on sexism. Needless to say, I did not have to respond to this man, because all the women in the audience of all descents and colors responded to him and lectured him on patriarchy and sexism. The only thing that I said at the end was to ask the women if they have been to the U.S. and the answer was no. That was an attempt to silence me. The man was obviously oblivious to the intersection of racial and sexual oppression.

Conclusion

Clearly, attempts to silence existed and still exists when the intersection of race, class, and gender are addressed. This should not be the case. Acknowledging the existence of sexism, patriarchy, and gender inequality will lead us to solutions and better relationships. The call to the recognition of the intersection does not constitute an oblivion to women of Euro-descents' subordination. However, it is important for Euro-American women to recognize the existence of privilege for a true sisterhood and brotherhood to be forged. It is in order here that I conclude by referring to MacKinnon (1996) disturbing claims that really prove her lack of awareness to the intersection of race, class and gender.

MacKinnon fails to understand or see the presence of race when she was given the statistics that African American women are raped twice as Euro-American women by Euro-American men. She asked "when African American women are raped twice as white women are they not raped as women." Her question indicates that she marginalizes the racial component in the whole equation. Her lack of awareness becomes even more apparent when she continues to claim that she views the whole experience as a composite rather than a divided unitary whole. Her line of argument still fails to acknowledge the meaning of the intersection of race, class, and gender. To the extent that patriarchal atrocities sometimes affect other women more than the others, points to different contexts created by multiple factors. Those multiple factors, race and class being the two of them need to be addressed together with sexual inequality. The fact that the tendency is to subject women of color with PhD's to more interrogation than women of Euro-descent to proof their qualifications, the fact that Euro-American women ideas will be embraced quicker, the fact that

African American or Mexican women are raped twice more than Euro-American women, demand the approach that takes race, class, and gender into account.

Men of color too should take responsibility. Addressing sexism and patriarchy does not mean women hate men. I personally love men to death, and that should not stop me from addressing sexism in as much as it should not stop me from addressing racism, classism, and heterosexism and their intersection.

References

Cole, J. B. and Guy-Sheftall 2003, *Gender Talk, The Struggle for Women's Equality in African American Communities,* New York: Random House Publishing Group.

hooks, bell 1984, *Feminist Theory from margin to center,* Boston: South End Press.

Joy James 1996, "Experience, Reflection, Judgment and Action Teaching Theory, Talking Community," in D. Bell and Klein *Radically Speaking: Feminism Reclaimed,* p 37 ed. Australia: Spinifex Press.

MacKinnon, P. 1996, "From Practice to Theory, or What is White Anyway" in Bell, D. and Klein, R. *Radically Speaking: Feminism Reclaimed,* pp 45–54 ed. Australia: Spinifex Press.

MacKintosh, P. 1990, White Privilege: Unpacking the Invisible Knapsack" an excerpt from working papers 189. *White Privilege and Male Privilege: A Personal Account of Coming to See Correspondence through Work in Women's Studies.*

Marlon Riggs et al. 1995, *Black is Back Ain't.* California: California Newsreel.

Martínez E. De Colores Means All of Us Latina Views for a Multi-Colored Century. Cambridge: South End Press.

Mosupyoe, B. 1999, *Women's Multicentric Ways of Knowing, Being, and Thinking, 2nd* Edition. New York: McGraw-Hill Companies, Inc.

Ngan-Ling, E 1987, "The Development of Feminist Consciousness Among Asian American Women" in *Gender and Society, Vol. 1. No. 3 September 1987* 284–289, 1987 Sociology for Women Society.

Segura, D. A. 1994 Working at Motherhood: Chicana and Mexican Immigrant Mothers and Employment. London: Routledge.

Notes

[1]Mosupyoe (1999).

[2]The north and south characterization follows the debate at the United Nations in the 1970's. The intention was to move away from the political and economic valuation of other countries as inferior. People claimed confusion with New Zealand and Australia. They were both regarded as northern and therefore part of the west. The north in this article refers to "western-Euro" and the south to indigenous and/or different from western-Euro."

[3]ibid.

[4]Mosupyoe, (1999).

U.S. Attitudes toward Women of Asian Ancestry: Legislative and Media Perspectives

Liang Tien

The image of women of Asian ancestry as erotic and sexual objects dominated the U.S. entertainment industry for decades. The "exotic Oriental" and her sexual objectification haunted the portrayals of Asian women, from Ah-Choi (the Chinese madam) of the 1880s to the Chinese prostitute in the movie *The World of Suzie Wong* (Mason & Patrick, 1960) and the sultry Indian princess in the movie *Far Pavilions* (Bond, 1984). To what extent does this erotic image of Asian American women portrayed in the media reflect the image and sentiment of the American people?

One method of determining a country's sentiment is to examine its national laws. In a representative government like that of the United States, the process of passing legislation must have popular support, or at least no great opposition. For a bill to become law, there must be a majority of favorable votes in the House of Representatives, the Senate, and acceptance by a president's administration. Legislation both influences and is influenced by the values and attitudes of the American people. To the extent that legislators are elected to represent their constituencies, the laws that they pass can be viewed as an indicator of the sentiment of the majority of the people. To the extent that Americans look to laws for guidance, bills that become law often shape the values and attitudes of the American people. The complex process of lawmaking and the infrequency with which laws are changed result in a relatively stable ideology that can be identified through an examination of U.S. statutes on a particular subject.

To ascertain U.S. sentiment toward women of Asian ancestry, federal legislation on the topic introduced during the past 100-plus years was reviewed. Immigration legislation is one area that has systematically and specifically addressed women of Asian ancestry. Immigration laws govern the admission and exclusion of particular groups of people to the United States. Immigration legislation defines the groups that the United States wishes to include in its citizenry through the granting of and eligibility for immigrant visas. Conversely, immigration legislation also defines those groups that the United States wishes to exclude. Historically, the United States has excluded and kept undesired groups outside of its borders through the denial of legal entry and citizenship and restriction of immigrant status. Consequently, U.S. ideology regarding women of Asian ancestry can be determined through study of its immigration legislation.

This chapter examines federal immigration legislation regarding women of Asian ancestry. Examining U.S. immigration legislation revealed that there have been significant laws addressing Asian women in relationships with U.S. servicemen that defined whether, when, and under what conditions they and their children were allowed to enter the United States.

This review of immigration legislation revealed a continued history of prohibitions against the entry of Asian women, specifically, Asian women who are fiancées or wives of U.S. servicemen stationed overseas and have borne Amerasian (i.e., mixed-race) children. Regardless of the feeling, intent, or wishes of individual servicemen toward the Asian women with whom they became romantically involved, federal legislation established the parameters regarding how they were to behave toward Asian women, and it failed to recognize or legitimatize U.S. servicemen's romantic relationships with women of Asian ancestry. Such exclusionary legislation suggests an American sentiment that Asian women are not acceptable for marriage to U.S. servicemen or that Amerasian children are not American citizens. U.S. laws bar the entry of Asian women and Amerasian children resulting in overseas-duty U.S. servicemen returning to the United States without the product (i.e., fiancée or wife and child or children) of their romantic liaisons with Asian women.

Before World War II: A Legacy of Exclusion

The United States entered World War II with legislative prohibitions against the entry of people of Asian ancestry. Three immigration laws firmly established the exclusion of people of Asian ancestry: (a) the Chinese Exclusion Act of 1882, (b) the Immigration Act of 1917, and (c) the National Origins Act of 1924.

The Chinese Exclusion Act of 1882 prohibited immigration of any person from China and barred from naturalization those Chinese immigrants who were already in the United States. Given the tendency of Chinese men to immigrate first, this in effect excluded the immigration of Chinese women to the United States. The 1800s were a time of widespread prostitution in the American West due to the paucity of women. Prostitutes of every nationality were abundant in California. However, the Chinese, as a group, were singled out as depraved "Orientals," and Chinese women were characterized as sexually subservient. The newspapers of the day described Chinese women as "reared to a life of shame from infancy and that not one virtuous China woman had been brought to this country. They were also accused of disseminating vile disease capable of destroying the very morals, the manhood and the health of our people" (Yung, 1995, p. 32).

The Immigration Act of 1917 perpetuated this image by naming all people from Asia *inadmissible aliens*. It created the "barred zone of the Asia-Pacific triangle" (U.S. Immigration and Naturalization Service, 1996, p. A-1-5). This legislation barred all Asians from immigration from 1917 until World War II. At that time, this legislation primarily affected the Japanese, given the hostile relations between the United States and Japan. After the earlier U.S. exclusion of Chinese immigrants, there was an influx of Japanese immigrants to the West Coast. Beginning in 1885, Japan permitted laborers to emigrate to the United States. The Japanese from drought ridden Japan could find a place and the United States received much needed workers. Japanese women immigrated some years after the peak years of the immigration of Japanese men. The majority of the Japanese women came as "picture brides," that is, women married in Japan by proxy to Japanese men in the United States through family arrangement. The practice of arranged marriages and marriage ceremonies by proxy with a photograph of the spouse was antithetical to the European practice of romantic marriage. Those who opposed Japanese immigration considered the practice of picture marriage as immoral (Glenn, 1986). Picture brides reinforced the existing image of Asian women as subservient, immoral, and depraved.

The National Origins Act of 1924 established an annual quota for each nation based on the percentage of people from that nation already residing in the United States as of 1920 and specified that aliens ineligible for citizenship could not enter as immigrants. The National Origins Act also specified that natives of Western Hemisphere countries were nonquota persons (U.S. Immigration and Naturalization Service [INS], 1996). This was racially discriminatory in that any people from Europe could immigrate to the United States at will, whereas no one from Asia and the Pacific Islands could immigrate and all other had to wait for visas based on country-specific annual quotas.

These three federal acts effectively prohibited Asians already in the United States from becoming U.S. citizens, barred further immigration of people of Asian ancestry, and prohibited Asian wives from joining their husbands who were already in the United States. Asian American men found themselves permanently separated from their wives and relegated to "bachelor communities." To remedy this situation, legislation was introduced in 1935 to allow for the entry of Asian wives. The intent of the Alien Wife Bill was to "extend that privilege [immigration] to alien wives of other races ineligible for citizenship." This legislation died in committee. It was reintroduced in 1937 and again in 1939, with the same result—reflecting the unwillingness of Americans to accept Asian women.

These three pieces of immigration legislation, together with the defeat of the Alien Wife Bill, ensured that the Asian American community existing in the United States would not expand and that no new Asian American communities could be established. No other group of immigrants was ever targeted as such for exclusion.

The anti-Asian sentiment of the United States reflected in these pieces of legislation, including women of Asian ancestry, was clear. The United States considered any person of Asian ancestry not only unfit for U.S. citizenship, but also unacceptable for entry into the United States.

America entered the World War II era with a firmly established tradition of exclusionary immigration legislation against people of Asian ancestry. Immigration legislation regarding women of Asian ancestry was set within the historical context of the exclusion of all Asians.

World War II: Splitting Asian Americans

On December 7, 1941, Japan attacked the U.S. naval base at Pearl Harbor, Hawaii, provoking a U.S. declaration of war against Japan the following day. On December 11, 1941, Germany and Italy declared war on the United States. World War II forced the entry of the United States into the global arena, leading to its evolution as a global superpower. Both during and since World War II, substantial numbers of U.S. military personnel were dispatched around the world, including various countries on the Pacific Basin and Asian continent.

During World War II, U.S. servicemen were stationed in Europe, China, and several countries in the Pacific. There were approximately 1 million World War II war brides, that is, women of various nationalities who married U.S. servicemen stationed abroad. Between 1944 and 1950, 150,000 to 200,000 couples married in Europe, and 50,000 to 100,000 couples married in Asia (Shukert, 1988). No legislation was enacted to exclude women of European ancestry from entering the United States to join their husbands. The differential treatment of European and Asian women illustrates the discriminatory image in the United States of women of Asian ancestry.

China as an Allied Country

The first legislation to address the immigration of Asian women was the repeal of the Chinese Exclusion Act of 1882 in 1943 (Immigration Act of December 17, 1943). During World War II, the enemy on the European front was Germany. On the Asian front, the enemy was Japan, whereas China became an allied nation in 1941. The repeal of the Chinese Exclusion Act, passed in the context of a nation at war, had the effect of splitting Asian groups.

Within the United States, Americans of Japanese ancestry were labeled a potential threat to domestic security and evacuated from the West Coast and imprisoned at alternate locations. This was not done with Americans of German ancestry. Instead of accepting the possibility that security forces were lax on the naval base in Hawaii, the blame for Pearl Harbor was placed on the "otherness" of Asians. Editorial comments like the following expressed the otherness view of Asians held by White Americans:

> *We thought he [the Japanese] was bound by certain Western standards of international conduct. . . . They are not of the West, and have nothing to do with what we think is right. So Secretary Hull cried bitterly of "infamy" but the attack was not infamous. It was the Japanese acting according to their code. What earthly reason ever existed for expecting them to act according to our code? None. . . . The Pacific enemy will not change his nature. (Brier, 1994, p. 9)*

Chinese immigrants, on the other hand, were not imprisoned but hailed as the good Asian. They were cast in a positive light by the newspapers of the day. Appearing daily on the front pages of U.S. newspapers were reports like the following: "*American and Chinese airmen of the United States* [italics added] fourteenth Air Force aided in the victory" (*New York Times,* 1943, p. 5). "Brig. Gen. Edgar Flenn, Chief of Staff of the United States Fourteenth United States Air Force, said . . . *American planes* [italics added] were striking from dawn to dusk *to support the Chinese* [italics added]" (*New York Times,* 1943, p. 5). The Chinese were considered brave soldiers worthy of American support.

Throughout the war, U.S. servicemen traveled to and were stationed in China. Concurrently, Chinese units were traveling to the United States for military training. With the friendly interchange, it became unseemly to exclude the immigration of Chinese people. Two years into the alliance with China, the United States passed the Magnuson Act of December 17, 1943 (Immigration Act of December 17, 1943). The Magnuson Act granted eligibility for naturalization to people of Chinese descent; it effectively repealed the Chinese Exclusion Act of 1882. Chinese people were no longer excluded from immigration by their ineligibility for citizenship. Although the act allowed for the immigration of Chinese people, it set an annual quota of only 105 immigrants. Chinese women who were wives or fiancées of U.S. servicemen stationed in China during the war were included as part of this numerical quota; this very low quota made the immigration of Chinese women negligible. In contrast, England, another allied nation, was allowed more than 40% of the annual quota for all countries. This made it possible for the English to migrate without waiting as the quota was so large. This quota system continued the United States's basic policy of excluding Asian women (Kim, 1992).

Continued Exclusion of Other Asians and Pacific Islanders

During World War II, U.S. servicemen were also stationed in the Philippines and other island countries in the Pacific Ocean. Although the Magnuson Act repealed the exclusion of Chinese immigrants, it let stand the Immigration Act of 1917, that continued to exclude Pacific Islanders and people from other Asian countries from entry into the United States. The romantic relationships that ensued between U.S. servicemen stationed in the Pacific and the women there are depicted in the movie *South Pacific* (Hammerstein & Osborn, 1958). Americans' unwillingness to accept mixed-race relationships legitimized through marriage is well articulated. Despite the large number of U.S. servicemen stationed in the Pacific, no waivers were introduced or passed to allow for the immigration of Pacific Islanders or other Asian women who became involved with U.S. servicemen.

After World War II: Differential Treatment

On May 8, 1945, Germany unconditionally surrendered to the Allies. On September 2, 1945, Japan also surrendered unconditionally. The victorious Allies included Great Britain and the Commonwealth, France, the United States, the Soviet Union, and China. The U.S. military withdrawal from Europe began in August 1945. Troop withdrawal from Europe and the Far East continued through the end of the year. Immediately following the U.S. troop withdrawal the immigration of the women from various nations who married U.S. servicemen began.

After World War II, U.S. military personnel entered Germany and Japan. The United States participated in the postwar occupation of Germany by stationing U.S. military personnel there. Additionally, the United States, the sole occupying power of Japan, stationed a sizable number of military personnel there.

The War Brides Act and the G.I. Financées Act: Preference for European Women

The next piece of legislation reflecting U.S. attitudes toward Asian women was the War Brides Act of 1945. The war in Europe ended in August of 1945. During the fall and winter of 1945, U.S. troops stationed in Europe began returning home. Every day, long lists of servicemen due to land in various ports around the country were published. Newspapers throughout the country published daily a "Schedule of the Arrival of Troops" derived from information provided by Army ports of embarkation in various cities. The schedules appeared as follows:

> *New York—arrivals, due today, due tomorrow, due Sunday, due Monday, due Tuesday. Newport News, VA, arrived, due today. Boston, arrived, due today. San Francisco, due yesterday, due today. Portland, due yesterday. Tacoma, WA due yesterday. Seattle, WA due yesterday. San Diego, CA due yesterday. Los Angeles, due yesterday. (New York Times, 1945, p. 26)*

At the same time, news of European wives trying to join their American husbands were also being reported in the newspapers. The December 10, 1945, *New York Times* ran the following stories:

> *Since Herbert John Lamoureaux, 22-year-old former American soldier, could not swim to his wife, she is determined to sail to him. So said Mrs. Veronica Lamoureaux, attractive brunette English girl, today. . . . "It would have given him great happiness if we could all have been united this Christmas," the former GI's 23-year-old wife said. She added, however, that she was confident she could book passage to the United States. (p. 26)*

Mrs. Yvonne Goppert, 21-year-old Briton, was reunited with her American husband yesterday for the first time in seven months. They were married on May 11 and on May 18 Lieutenant Goppert received orders to go to France on a glider towed by a C-46. Mrs. Goppert hid on the plane in a box eighteen inches high, two feet wide and four and a half feet long. The couple spent two weeks honeymooning. (p. 26)

These reports systematically excluded women of Asian ancestry.

Beside the columns reporting the daily arrival of troops were announcements about the arrival of their wives. *The New York Times* reported the following on December 27, 1945:

War brides of the United States soldiers from the Atlantic area will begin to follow their redeployed husbands in January, according to an official Army announcement today. The brides will embark through Southampton, England, it said. Quotas have not yet been set, but once the movement of brides is started, it will continue until all brides have reached the United States, the War Department orders state. The ship on which brides will sail will be used for this purpose only. (p. 2)

The next day, December 28, 1945, before the first war veterans were barely home from Europe, the United States passed, without committee hearing or floor debate, the War Brides Act. The purpose of the Act was "to expedite the admission to the United States, of alien spouses and alien minor children of citizen members of the United States armed forces . . . provided they are admissible under the immigration laws." The act waived visa requirements and exclusion based on physical or mental defects for women who had married members of the American armed forces. Within months of U.S. servicemen returning to the United States, their British, European, New Zealander, and Australian wives were able to join them, at the expense of U.S. taxpayers. The War Brides Act was passed while European war brides were on their way to the United States.

One year after passage of the War Brides Act, the G.I. Fiancées Act of 1946 was enacted. Like the War Brides Act, this act was passed without committee hearings or floor debate. The purpose of the Fiancées Act was to "facilitate the admission into the US of the alien fiancées of members of the armed forces of the US . . . provided that the alien is not subject to exclusion from the United States under the immigration laws." With the passage of these two acts, all British, European, New Zealander, and Australian wives and fiancées of U.S. servicemen were allowed to enter the United States.

The image of and attitudes toward women from English-speaking and European countries had to have been positive for these two pieces of legislation to go forth with such speed and so little opposition. The policy of inclusion for women of European ancestry is repeated in both the War Brides Act and the Fiancée Act.

This was in marked contrast to the treatment of wives of Asian ancestry. Missing from the newspaper accounts were the stories of U.S. servicemen's wives from the Pacific Islands and China. Also missing were the wives themselves. Typical is the following story of a Chinese woman who married a U.S. serviceman:

> When she married Sam in China forty years ago, she had to keep the marriage secret at first. If the military found out, they would have shipped Sam out and the couple would have been separated. He could even have been court martialed and dishonorably discharged. The U.S. government discouraged its soldiers from taking war brides in foreign countries and did everything to prevent such marriages. Since Kun-yi lived with Sam, though married in fact, she was called a foreign prostitute. (Sung, 1990, p. 92)

The War Brides Act and the Fiancées Act let stand the exclusion of Asians. This allowed for the Kun-yi situation and thus continued the policy of excluding Asians, including Asian wives and fiancées.

Limited Inclusion of Chinese Women: China as an Ally

After World War II, the U.S. withdrew its servicemen from China. Chinese women were still restricted from immigration under the limited 105 persons per year quota. To facilitate the immigration of Asian wives, the Alien Wife Bill was reintroduced, for the third time, in 1939. After the start of World War II, when China became an ally, the same bill was again introduced in 1941, then in 1942. In total, this bill was introduced five times without passage. A restricted version of the bill was finally enacted after the end of World War II. The Immigration Act of August 9, 1946 granted Chinese wives of U.S. citizens nonquota status. The effect of this legislation was the long-awaited entry to the United States of those Chinese women married to U.S. servicemen and civilians stationed in China.

This legislation had limited impact because it affected only the Chinese community. The Immigration Act of 1946 only allowed for American men who served in the armed forces during World War II to return to China, marry a Chinese woman, and bring her back to the United States. The men who took advantage of this were predominantly Chinese Americans. This situation was depicted in the movie *Eat a Bowl of Tea* (Cha & Roscoe, 1989). By providing only for nonquota status for Chinese wives, the bill continued the exclusion of all other wives of Asian ancestry.

Limited Inclusion of Japanese Women: Occupation of Japan

Between 1944 and 1950, 50,000 to 100,000 couples were married in Asia (Shukert, 1988). Unlike British, European, New Zealander, and Australian women, Asian women married to U.S. servicemen were still barred from entry into the United States. During World War II, U.S. servicemen were stationed in large numbers in the Pacific Islands and later in Japan during the occupation. Both the War Brides Act and the Fiancées Act barred women of Asian ancestry from joining their servicemen husbands and fiancées in the United States. The War Brides Act provided that alien wives of U.S. citizens who were serving in the U.S. armed forces and were "admissible under the immigration laws, be admitted to the United States." Likewise, the Fiancées Act also included exclusionary language. It provided for the admission of "alien fiancées of members of the armed forces of the US . . . provided that the alien is not subject to exclusion from the United States under the immigration laws."

U.S. forces have been stationed on Japanese soil since 1945. Not surprisingly, a number of men developed romantic relationships with Japanese women. However, Japanese women, regardless of whether or not they were married to U.S. servicemen, could not immigrate to the United States. In an attempt to address the issue of U.S. servicemen in romantic relationships with Japanese women, the initial Alien Wife Bill was reintroduced in 1947 for the sixth time. In 1947, the bill passed as the Soldier Brides Act. It reflected minimal attempts to counteract exclusion based on race. The Act stipulated that an "alien spouse of an American citizen by marriage occurring before 30 days after the enactment of this Act (July 22, 1947), shall not be considered as inadmissible because of race." These time limitations were later extended, then finally removed.

In contrast to the War Brides Act, no exceptions were made to expedite the speedy immigration of these Japanese wives. Instead, placement of tight time restrictions made immigration almost impossible. Although the time restrictions were later extended, the restrictions echoed the earlier exclusion of women of Asian ancestry.

Differential Treatment and Racial Preference

The differential treatment of women of Asian ancestry compared to women of European ancestry in post–World War II legislation reflected a clear racial preference. The European wives of U.S. servicemen were welcomed and quickly reunited with their husbands in the United States. In contrast, wives of Asian ancestry were initially barred, then later tightly restricted from following their husbands to the United States. The exclusion of women from Asian and Pacific Islander countries resulted in a situation in which servicemen could engage in romantic relationships, even legitimize those relationships with local marriage ceremonies, and still return to the United States without their Asian wives or fiancées. The legislative message about Asian women was that it was acceptable and even expected for servicemen to fraternize with Asian women but not to make them legitimate wives. The legislation protected the overseas servicemen by enabling them to return home unencumbered by their Asian women. This implied that Asian women were acceptable as sexual partners but unacceptable as U.S. citizens or members of U.S. families.

The restrictive legislation regarding women of Asian ancestry perpetuated the myth of the erotic Oriental. The legislation reflected the image of the Asian seductress portrayed in the press and popular media. It relegated Asian women to the images of An-Choi, the Chinese madam of the 1880s; Suzie Wong, the Chinese prostitute in the movie *The World of Suzie Wong* (Mason & Patrick, 1960); and the geisha in the movie *Sayonara* (Mitchner & Osborn, 1957) and the play *The Story of Miss Saigon* (Behr & Steyn, 1989).

The Cold War Years

Elimination of Race-Based Exclusions from Naturalization

With the end of the World War II and the spread of Communism from the Soviet Union to China, the United States was into the Cold War years. The nation's security interest was focused on containment of Communism abroad and eradication of Communist influences within the United States. Internationally, the United States was assuming increasing leadership of the Western nations against the perceived expansionist intentions of its former ally, the Soviet Union. As the Cold War heated up, it brought the United States into a military confrontation with Communist forces in Korea and Vietnam.

Within the United States's new role as a world superpower protecting the world from Communism, the 1952 Immigration and Nationality Act, commonly referred to as the McCarran–Walter Act, was passed on June 27, 1952. The McCarran–Walter Act eliminated race as a bar to naturalization. This allowed those people of Asian ancestry who were residing in the United States to become citizens. The act eliminated previous restrictive legislation that barred immigration based on a person's inability to become a U.S. citizen. The Asian wives of U.S. servicemen were no longer subject to exclusion based on race. In response to the elimination of race-based exclusion from naturalization, Japanese women married to U.S. servicemen were able to immigrate. As a result, 85.9% of the immigrants from Japan between 1952 and 1960 were women (Daniels, 1990).

Although it eliminated race-based naturalization discrimination, the McCarran–Walter Act continued the race-based national quota immigration system. The quotas continued the policy of race-based discrimination. For example, "Ireland had a quota of 17,756 and Germany had a quota of 25,814, while quotas for . . . China (105), Japan (185), the Philippines (100), and the Pacific Islands (100) were negligible" (Kim, 1992, p. 1110).

Elimination of Race-Based Immigration: The Immigration and Nationality Act

Racial equality was in the national spotlight during the 1950s and 1960s. The 1954 U.S. Supreme Court ruling in the case of *Brown v. Board of Education* on the issue of segregation signaled a change in U.S. race relations. Out of this increased focus on civil rights, Congress passed the Immigration and Nationality Act Amendments on October 3, 1965. The 1965 Immigration and Nationality Act eliminated the race-based quotas. For the first time in the history of regulated immigration, each Asian country received the same quota as European countries. Each country received an annual quota of 20,000 immigrant visas, with a ceiling of 170,000 for the Eastern Hemisphere. In addition, immediate relatives of U.S. citizens were not subject to quota restrictions.

With the passage of this Act, there were no longer any legislative restrictions against the immigration of people from Asia, including Asian women. The barriers to Asians established by the Immigration Act of 1917 that created the "barred zone of the Asia-Pacific triangle" were eliminated (Yung, 1995). With the elimination of race-based barriers to naturalization in 1952 and immigration in 1965, Asian wives of U.S. servicemen could not be categorically excluded from immigration into the United States. However, despite the liberal changes in immigration legislation just described, the exclusion of women of Asian ancestry continued in the legislative treatment of wives of U.S. servicemen in the Korean and Vietnam Wars.

Return to Exclusionary Policies for Amerasians: The Korean and Vietnam Wars

The next immigration legislation to address women of Asian ancestry came in response to the Korean and Vietnam Wars. The Immigration Act of 1982, commonly referred to as the Amerasian Act, excluded women of Asian ancestry in their status as mothers of Amerasians. The idea that Asian women were not acceptable as legitimate spouses for U.S. citizens was thereby continued. *Amerasian* is a term first used by Pearl S. Buck in 1966 to refer to individuals of mixed American and Asian parentage, specifically children fathered by American servicemen stationed in Asia. However, the servicemen, by definition, cannot be U.S. citizens of Asian ancestry because U.S. officials "consider the physical appearance" (Pub. L. No. 97-359, § 1698(3)(B)) to determine parentage. Without mixed-race appearance, American lineage is not established for children of Asian women and Asian American servicemen.

On June 27, 1950, President Truman committed U.S. military forces to aid South Korea against a Communist-backed North Korean invasion. Three years later, on July 27, 1953, an armistice was signed that signaled the end to the shooting part of the war. The conflict ended in a military stalemate, not an end to the war. The United States continues to station military personnel in South Korea to protect it from communist North Korea. Large numbers of U.S. troops have been stationed in South Korea since 1950.

Simultaneously, the United States was involved in armed conflict in the southern tip of the Asian continent. In Vietnam, fighting erupted between France and the Communist-backed Viet Minh in 1947. The United States, in its role as the world defender of democratic freedom against Communism, supported the French. By 1953, the United States was providing 80% of the cost of France's war effort. After the French defeat in 1954, the United States assumed responsibility for the fight in Vietnam. Between 1954 and the U.S. withdrawal in 1975, increasing numbers of military personnel were deployed to Vietnam and the former French Indochina countries in Southeast Asia.

With the large number of U.S. military personnel stationed in Korea and Indochina, romantic relationships between U.S. servicemen and Korean and Vietnamese women inevitably developed. Despite the passage of the Alien Wife Bill, the Soldier Brides Act, the McCarran–Walter Act, and the Immigration and Nationality Act of 1965, the United States still found occasion to continue the exclusion of Asian women.

More than 30 years after the United States dispatched servicemen to Korea, it attempted to address the Amerasian question. This was the first legislative recognition of the United States's responsibility for the Amerasian children of U.S. servicemen. On January 9, 1981, the Amerasian Immigration Act was introduced. The intent of the bill was "to amend the Immigration and Nationality Act to provide preferential treatment in the admission of unmarried or married son or daughter of a citizen of the United States if [the son or daughter] was born in Korea, Vietnam, Laos, or Thailand after 1950, and was fathered by an United States citizen who, at the time of the alien's conception, was serving in the Armed Forces of the United States during active duty for the United States or for the United Nations Organization" (H.R. 808, 97th Congress, 1st Session).

The same year that Congress was considering passage of the Amerasian Immigration Act, Vincent Chin, a Chinese American, was beaten to death in Detroit, Michigan. The U.S. auto industry was beset by the import of more fuel-efficient Japanese cars. Detroit's 16% unemployment rate was blamed on Japan. In June 1982, Chin, a native born American of Chinese ancestry, went to a bar to celebrate his upcoming wedding. In the bar, two White autoworkers shouted, "It's because of you motherfuckers that we're out of work." Outside of the bar, the same two autoworkers bludgeoned Chin to death with a baseball bat.

In the interests of job protection, Simpson-Mazzoli introduced the Immigration Reform and Control Act (IRCA) that was passed in 1982. The target of IRCA was to curb, and eventually eliminate, undocumented aliens working in the United States by establishing employer-based monitoring of INS status (Kim, 1992). Along the same vein of blaming others for U.S. troubles, Congress, in committee hearings, questioned the character of Asian women who were mothers of Amerasians. Committee members were concerned that U.S. servicemen were susceptible to being seduced by Asian women who wished to immigrate if the mothers of Amerasian were allowed immigrant status with their Amerasian children.

Public Law No. 97-359, Section 1698, Preferential Treatment in the Admission of Children of U.S. Citizens, commonly referred to as the Amerasian Immigration Act of 1982, was enacted into law on October 22, 1982. The Amerasian Immigration Act established immigration preference for Amerasians. However, it continued to deny, the special relationship of the mothers of Amerasians with the United States through its servicemen. Two conditions under which Amerasian children could immigrate to the United States resulted in the exclusion of women of Asian ancestry. One condition was that only the minor Amerasian child could immigrate, not the Asian mother or other family members. The second condition was that the mother of the Amerasian had to sign an irrevocable release of family rights for the child to immigrate. The release disallowed the mother any future claims on the child. This not only meant forced separation of the Amerasian child from his or her mother, but also no hope of future reunification. Even after reaching adulthood and gaining citizenship, the Amerasian could not sponsor his or her Asian mother as a nonquota relative. Amerasians who immigrated to the United States came essentially as orphans to be fostered by American families.

The proviso of the irrevocable release made clear the United States intent of total dissociation from those Asian women who had relations with U.S. servicemen. Again, this relegated those relationships between Asian women and U.S. servicemen to the status of temporary sexual liaisons. Asian women were acceptable only as temporary romantic partners for the comfort of U.S. servicemen stationed overseas. This time, the added message was that not only were Asian women unacceptable as legitimate wives, but they also were unacceptable as mothers to rear "American" children.

Diplomatic Breakdown and Exclusion Following the Vietnam War

The popular image of women involved with U.S. servicemen in Vietnam is depicted in the play *Miss Saigon* (Behr & Steyn, 1989). This image continues the age-old U.S. concept of Asian women as temporary romantic and sexual partners. The Communist Vietnamese victory in 1975 added an additional incentive for Americans to denigrate Asians and Asian women. The loss of the Vietnam War had profound ramifications for the United States. It was a shock to American self-confidence as a military power and world leader. This resulted in the United States severing all diplomatic relations with Vietnam until 1994, thus preventing Vietnamese Amerasians from immigrating under the Amerasian Immigration Act of 1982.

On August 6, 1987, 12 years after the last U.S. servicemen left Southeast Asia, and under pressure from Vietnam, the Amerasian Homecoming Act (H.R. 3171, 100th Congress, 1st Session) was first introduced in Congress. The purpose of the bill was to permit the immigration of Vietnamese Amerasians to the United States. The bill died in the Committee on the Judiciary. It was introduced again on October 28, 1987, but met the same fate. On December 27, 1987, provisions for the immigration of Vietnamese Amerasians were passed as part the Omnibus Budget Reconciliation Act, the Amerasian Immigration Section.

Under extreme pressure from the Vietnamese government, this proviso specifically included the immigration of Vietnamese families. The Amerasian Immigration Section provided for waivers of numerical limitations on immigration for Amerasians and existing exclusionary policies. The waivers meant that adult Amerasians could immigrate and mothers of Amerasians could accompany their children to the United States. However, administrative interpretation of the legislation initially established a condition under which the Vietnamese mother could be excluded. Those family members eligible for immigration with the Amerasian included the Amerasian's spouse, child, *or* natural mother and her spouse or child. If the accompanying family member was a spouse, then the natural mother "shall not be accorded any right, privilege, or status." Amerasians initially had to choose between their mother and their spouse. Again, there existed a loophole to exclude women of Asian ancestry, once again sending the not-so-subtle message that women of Asian ancestry were not wanted in the United States.

Effects of Lingering Images

As discussed earlier, the persistent image of Asian women as erotic, temporary sexual partners for U.S. servicemen reflects the sentiments of the majority of Americans. In turn, the passage of exclusionary immigration legislation reflects and perpetuates the sexual and erotic image of women of Asian ancestry.

Stereotypic Images

The image reflected in law is not limited to Asian women living in Asia. This image also affects women of Asian ancestry born in the United States. Asian American women are exposed to the sexualized images of themselves. Two Asian American women described examples of this type of exposure.

> On a tour to Niagara Falls, other passengers kept intimating to Calvert that Yi-fong was just a girl he was taking on an extramarital fling. Although he introduced Yi-fong as his wife, they kept referring to her as his girlfriend and made snide remarks about his leaving his wife at home. People are unable to or refuse to grasp the fact that two people from different backgrounds can be married. (Sung, 1990, pp. 88–89)

> Another attitude that seems especially prevalent is the mail-order-bride mentality. Occasionally when I'm with my boyfriend—who is as Anglo as you can get—total strangers walk up and ask him where I'm from, if I speak English. . . . The same mentality is responsible for a certain class of male that seems to think Asian women are easy to please, utterly subservient and desperately clamoring for Anglo husbands. . . . During lunch in the dorm cafeteria, [a White student] sauntered over and said (this is true), "Hello, Me see you here very long time. Me think you very pretty. I don't like American girls. I only like Asian women." (Kim, 1990, p. M4)

Erotic Images

The capitulation to this erotic image of Asian American women by the Asian American community influences the stigmatization of Asian American women in interracial relationships. "Chinese feel that women who married Americans are not decent. This is a stereotype. For me, that hurt a lot because I feel that I had to prove my character" (Sung, 1990, p. 92). "Intermarriage between Whites and Asians has been seen in recent times by some Asian Americans as evidence of racial conquest and cultural genocide rather than social acceptance and success for the Asian minority" (Kim, 1982, p. 92).

Repeated exposure to erotic imagery of oneself can have a profound effect on the development of the psychosexual identity. The incorporation of this erotic image by Asian American women has led some to feel ashamed of and reject their Asian ancestry.

> *Second-class treatment like this (Asian women are easy to please, utterly subservient and desperately clamoring for Anglo husbands) has made a lot of American-born Asians ashamed of their heritage in a way that other Americans aren't. You'll probably never catch one of us with a button reading, "Kiss me, I'm Korean." In fact, there is a heavy burden on us to deny all ethnicity and to prove we're just like everyone else, i.e., real Americans. The results are sometimes pathetic. I used to present my middle name as "Susan" instead of "Suhn."* (Kim, 1990, p. M4)

Identity Issues

Every Asian American woman, at some level, must contend with the image of the erotic being that is not acceptable as a legitimate partner in a long-term relationship. When Asian American women consider their identities as Americans with the elements of race, ethnicity, and gender, they do not encounter a society that encourages them to be self defined. Anti-Asian immigration legislation denigrates their worth, and erotic and sexual images objectify them. During the many years of their exclusion Asian American women were unable to participate in the legislative and political dialogue about themselves. After so many years of forced silence, Asian American women at last can and should engage in a dialogue with the greater population of U.S. citizens through participation in the legislative process so as to shape their own images.

◼️⊕ Conclusion

Federal legislation of the last 100-plus years articulates enduring images of and sentiments toward women of Asian ancestry. The most common image is that women of Asian ancestry are erotic and sexualized beings. The prevalent sentiment is that women of Asian ancestry are acceptable for temporary romantic liaisons but not as wives or mothers of U.S. citizens. This legislative presentation echoes the erotic, sexualized Asian American woman portrayed in the popular media. In looking to legislation for guidance, many Americans not of Asian ancestry may use these attitudes and images as a priori proof that Asian women are not acceptable for marriage or motherhood. Legislation can then, in turn, be used to legitimize and continue the stereotype of Asian women as erotic sex objects.

The images and sentiments presented through immigration legislation continues to be felt by Asian American women and Asian American communities throughout the United States. More positive images of Asian American women need to be articulated in a number of areas. Scientifically, qualitative research is needed on how Asian American women cope with the erotic images reflected in immigration legislation and the media. Research on the actual self-images of Asian American women is clearly needed. Social scientists need to conduct more research on the confluence of racial, ethnic, and gender identity among Asian American women. Models of identity development are necessary to guide research on gender, race, ethnic minorities, and women in the United States. Finally, more research is needed to examine the effects of these negative images of Asian American women on their relationships.

At the community level, dialogues between Asian American communities and the larger community of U.S. citizens are needed to challenge existing images and sentiments and promote new ones. Institutions of higher education need to support their Asian American female academicians and establish curricula for the teaching of Asian American women. Creative writers and makers of popular media need to develop works that truthfully reflect the lives of Asian American women in all of their complexities. Legislatively, the Asian American community needs to lobby for the elimination of legislation that denigrates Asian American women, such as the Amerasian Immigration Act of 1982. And, as citizens of a representative government, we all need to be vigilant against any legislation that either promotes a derogatory image of Asian Americans or discriminates against anyone on the basis of race, ethnicity, or gender.

References

Amerasian Homecoming Act, H.R. 3171, 100th Cong., 1st Sess. (1987).

Amerasian Immigration Act of 1982, Pub. L. No. 97-359, 96 Stat. 1716 (1982).

Amerasian Immigration Section of the Omnibus Budget Reconciliation Act of 1987, Pub. L. No. 100-202, § 584 (1987).

Behr, E., & Steyn, M. (1989). [musical] *The Story of Miss Saigon*. London: Jonathan Cape (1991).

Bond, J. (1984). *Far Pavilions*. [television mini-series] P. Duffel (director). Washington, DC: Acorn Media.

Brier, R. (1994). Looking around. *San Francisco Chronicle*, p. 9.

Brown v. Board of Education, 347 U.S. 483 (1954).

Buck, P. S. H. (with Harris, T. F.) (1966). *For spacious skies: Journey in dialogue*. New York: John Day Co.

Cha, L., & Roscoe, J. (1989). *Eat a Bowl of Tea*. [film] W. Wang (director). Burbank, CA: Columbia Pictures.

Chinese Exclusion Act of 1882, 22 Stat. 58.

Daniels, R. (1990). *Coming to America: A history of immigration and ethnicity in American life*. New York: HarperCollins.

G.I. Fiancées Act, 60 Stat. 416 (1946).

Glenn, E. N. (1986). *Issei, Nisei, war bride: Three generations of Japanese American women in domestic service.* Philadelphia: Temple University Press.

Hammerstein, O., & Osborn, P. (1958). *South Pacific.* [film] J. Logan (director). Hollywood, CA: 20th Century Fox.

Immigration Act of August 9, 1946, 60 Stat. 975. (1946).

Immigration Act of 1917, 39 Stat. 874. (1917).

Immigration Act of 1943, 16 Stat. 682. (1943).

Immigration Act of 1982, 96 Stat. 1716. (1982).

Immigration and Nationality Act Amendments of 1965, 79 Stat. 911. (1965).

Immigration and Nationality Act [McCarran–Walter Act], 66 Stat. 163 (1952).

Immigration Reform and Control Act of 1986, 100 Stat. 3359.

Kim, A. (1990). For the last time, darn it, I am not a mail-order bride. *Los Angeles Times,* p. M4.

Kim, E. (1982). *Asian American literature.* Philadelphia: Temple University Press.

Kim, H. -C. (1992). *Asian Americans and the Supreme Count: A documentary history.* Westport, CT: Greenwood Press.

Mason, R., & Patrick, J. (1960). *The World of Suzie Wong.* [film] R. Quine (director). Hollywood, CA: Worldfilm.

Mitchner, J., & Osborn (1957). *Sayonara.* [film] J. Logan (director). Hollywood, CA: MGM Studios.

National Origins Act of 1924, 43 Stat. 153. (1924).

New York Times. (1943, November 22, p. 5). *Japanese threat to Changsha seen.*

New York Times. (1945, December 10, p. 26). *Chinese press for fleeing Chang Teh.*

New York Times. (1945, December 24, p. 4). *Glider Stowaway here with husband.*

New York Times. (1945, December 24, p. 6). *Former GI tried to swim to them.*

New York Times. (1945, December 27, p. 2). *French brides to begin Sailing for U.S. in month.*

Omnibus Budget Reconciliation Act, 100 Stat. 1329 (1987).

Shukert, E. B. (1988). *The war brides of World War II.* Navato, CA: Predidio Press.

Soldier Brides Act, 61 Stat. 190 (1947).

Sung, B. L. (1990). *Chinese American intermarriage.* New York: Center for Migration Studies.

U.S. Immigration and Naturalization Service. (1996). *Statistical yearbook of the Immigration and Naturalization Service,* 1994. Washington, DC: U.S. Government Printing Office.

War Brides Act of 1945, 59 Stat. 659.

Yung, J. (1995). *Unbound feet: A social history of Chinese women in San Francisco.* Berkeley: University of California Press.

Beyond Entertainment Value: Understanding the Intersectionality of Race, Gender, Physicality, and Sport

Rita Libuti

Introduction

Sport takes up significant cultural space. Whether we consider ourselves fans or not it is difficult to deny the reality that sport surrounds and saturates us. Regardless of one's interest and involvement in sport there is a propensity to conceive of the cultural institution as unconnected from cultural values and norms. As the sport sociologist George Sage (1998)[1] notes, however, "the traditional tendency to separate sport from the rest of society, treating it and its participants as isolated from the rest of the world and as existing in a value-free and ideologically pristine environment is erroneous—it presumes that there are no links between sport and our other social institutions and Liberti cultural practices" (preface, p. xi-xii). Compounding the myth that sport is somehow independent from the broader culture in which it sits is the notion that it is also a meritocracy, where the only inhibitor to an individual's success is her or his will to achieve. Sport is envisioned and presented to us as a level playing field, where we all have equal opportunity to paths that advance our status. In this view, individual agency trumps any structural or social forces that may hinder or prevent our full and unfettered participation in sport. It is little wonder, for example, that Nike's slogan "Just Do It" has become such a central phrase in our language, as we tend to see (and are encouraged to see) sport involvement as simply a matter of lacing up our shoes and just doing it.

This popular view tends to treat sport as an innocent diversion, where we go to escape and simply have fun. While it might be that for some, sport studies scholars argue that it is also a really rich cultural site to examine how norms are reinforced and challenged. Far from mere games and amusement, we can use sport as a lens through which to examine broader issues including those that relate to race and gender for example. Thus, in this essay my specific aim is to examine a portion of the small, yet significant body of academic literature that engages issues about women of color in sport. The discussion is intended to address the following questions: What place do female athletes of color hold in U.S. society in the early 21st century? How are female athletes of color represented to us by the media? How do those images and discourses reinforce or subvert dominant race and gender ideologies? What meanings do women of color bring to their sport experiences and what do their stories offer us in terms of a deeper understanding of the complexities of race and gender as they get played out in sport and the broader culture?

Title IX and Women of Color

If I'd lived prior to the 1980s, it would have been different, because I would have been playing to prove African Americans are equal. Now, I don't necessarily feel I have to play for black people, because obviously they're doing everything in all sports. (Venus Williams)

In the final decades of the 20th century we witnessed incredible growth of organized sport in the United States. From youth athletic leagues to elite, professional activities, sport blossomed into the multibillion dollar industry it is today. Female athletes of color have been a small, yet important part of that revolution, bringing the opportunity to compete to thousands of girls and women as well as fame and notoriety to those at the more elite levels of sport. Tennis stars Venus and Serena Williams, golf great Michelle Wie, and professional basketball players Lisa Leslie and Sheryl Swoopes represent a few women of color whose athletic achievements have earned them a level of recognition beyond their peers of today and female sports' stars of yesterday. The presence of these high profile female athletes as well as the millions more who participate in organized sport of some kind reflects women's entrance into the broader expanse of sport in the final decades of the 20th century. Many observers credit a federal law, Title IX of the Education Amendments of 1972, which prohibits gender discrimination in federally funded programs, with altering the sport landscape by making it more accessible to female athletes. Without question, Title IX has afforded many more girls and women the opportunity to participate in school and college sport, but has it done so for all females? Are African American women and other women of color doing "everything in all sports" as Venus Williams suggests?

The origins of the Title IX legislation are embedded in the resistance movements of the 1960s, notably the civil rights campaign. The law was created to promote equity between men and women within federally funded educational institutions, including graduate and professional schools. In 1972 Title IX advocates saw that the need for the law in the fact that 9 percent of all medical degrees and only 7 percent of all law degrees were awarded to women (*About Title IX,* n.d.).[2] Though few lawmakers, educational leaders, and athletic personnel realized it in 1972, the implications of Title IX on sport would be enormous as expenditures of boys' and men's athletics grossly outweighed money spent on girls' and women's sport. Title IX forced schools to work towards correcting this imbalance in an effort to provide female students with far greater access and opportunity in athletics than they had historically. In public high schools prior to 1972, for example, boys outnumbered girls in sport by 3.7 million to 295,000. Budgetary spending within athletic programs was also inequitable, with boys receiving 99 cents of every dollar spent on high school sport (Coakley, 2007, p. 238).[3] In 2004, 32 years after the passage of Title IX nearly 3 million girls participate in high school sport (along with over 4 million boys). As the sport sociology scholar Mary Jo Kane noted, "girls went [in a generation] from asking 'will there be a team' to 'will I make the team?' " (Media Education Foundation, 2002).[4]

Despite the significant rise in athletic opportunities for girls and women, a closer look at the data reveals that female athletes of color are underrepresented and that their position remains a marginal one in relation to white women. Unfortunately, this reality often gets lost amid much stronger rhetoric of unbelievable growth and opportunity for girls and women in sport since the 1970s. The generic use of "girls" and "women" in this context obscures the realities and experiences of female athletes of color. Mathewson (1996)[5] argues that a "single axis analysis" (p. 242) whose focus remains on gender ignores the unique and important ways in which sexism and racism impact the lives and experiences of women of color. This monolithic view not only privileges white women, but "distracts from the action at the intersection [of race and gender] or the 'function at the junction'" (p. 243)[6] thereby flattening out the complexities surrounding sport involvement, equity, and racial and ethnic identity.

While the sheer number of opportunities to participate in intercollegiate athletics has grown for women of color in the past 35 years, they remain marginalized and underrepresented. On the surface, however, the numbers warrant some optimism. Between 1971 and 2001 the number of women of color participating in intercollegiate sport grew tremendously from 2,137 to 22,541. Female athletes of color represented 15 percent of all women athletes in 2001 as compared to only 7 percent in 1971. However, women of color make up 25 percent of female undergraduates on campuses throughout the United States, thus their participation numbers in sport fall far short in comparison (*Minority Women,* 2003).[7] At the highest level of collegiate competition (National Collegiate Athletic Association, Division I) African American women comprise the largest nonwhite group, but are clustered around two sports, basketball and track, where they make up one-third and one-quarter of the female athletes in those sports respectively. When basketball and track are taken out of the equation, black women represent only 2.7 percent of Division I female college athletes (Suggs, 2005, p. 180).[8] The situation for other women of color is not much better. For example, Asian Americans represented only 1.8 percent of all female athletes at the Division I level and Latinas only 3 percent (Suggs, 2005, p. 181).[9] Tina Sloan Green, director of the Black Women in Sport Foundation and professor of physical education at Temple University claims that "Title IX was for white women. I'm not going to say black women haven't benefited, but they have been left out" (quoted in Suggs, 2001, p. A36).[10]

Part of the answer to the racial and ethnic disparities in the growth of female college athletics lies with the types of activities schools have added to come into compliance with the federal law. The number of soccer and rowing teams added to athletic departments to come into compliance with Title IX outdistanced all other activities, with soccer experiencing a 381 percent gain and rowing a 178 percent increase in a 12-year period beginning in 1986 (Suggs, 2001).[11] As the number of teams grew, so too did opportunities to compete, but not among black women and other women of color as these activities "attract masses of white suburban girls, but very few others" (Suggs, 2001, p. A35).[12] In addition, marked increases in the number of university teams in golf and lacrosse add to the disparity since these activities have historically not drawn women of color in significant numbers (Suggs, 2001). Tonya M. Evans (1998)[13] contends that Title IX will never fulfill its promise because the "continued addition of country club and prep school sports to achieve equity without corresponding programs to introduce such sports to [women of color] at an early age will leave a significant portion of women out of the running for gender equity" (p. 117).[14] With this in mind, we should be mindful of the way the sometimes celebratory rhetoric surrounding Title IX paints "women" with the same broad brush, minimizing and making invisible the position and experiences of women of color in sport.

Representing Female Athletes of Color

Cultural representations found in sport media outlets both produce and reveal who and what matter in this culture. (Kane & Pearce, 2002, p. 69)[15]

Despite the overall gains women have made in sport, their presence in various media has remained negligible. The female athlete of color's status is far more marginal, with very limited coverage, making her media status far more precarious than white women. Believing that media reproduce and sometimes subvert dominant ideas about gender and race, sport studies scholars are interested in the ways that female athletes are represented when they do make inroads into the male preserve of sport. As Pamela Creedon (1994)[16] suggests, "contemporary mass media, like the plays, epic poems, fairy tales, fables, parables and myths before them, preserve, transmit and create important cultural information" (p. 6). Thus our attention to media as a vehicle through which ideas and values about women and race are conveyed becomes crucial.

Messner, Duncan, and Cooky's (2003) study of the amount and quality of televised sports news about female athletics throughout the decade of the 1990s illustrates that little has changed with regard to the insignificant amount of attention paid to women in sport. In 1999, for example, the three network affiliates in their study spent on average a little over 8 percent of all sports news stories on women's athletics – this accounted for very little change from earlier in the decade. Also analyzed by the researchers were 17 hours of airtime from ESPN's SportsCenter, which devoted even less time to female athletics—just 2.2 percent. Even after fairly high profile women's events (1999 World Cup, the WNBA Championship, and the NCAA "Final Four" basketball tournament in March) network affiliates and ESPN SportsCenter did not increase their coverage of female athletics and "returned to business-as-usual coverage of men's sports" (p. 48).[17] This "near silence" (p. 49)[18] serves to reinforce the myth that women don't play sports, because if they did we'd see it on TV, as well as further cements the tendency to see sport as a *natural* place for men to be (and an *unnatural* one for women). Finally, the authors contend, when women are featured as a part of a sports news story their accomplishments are trivialized by a preoccupation with "nonserious, sexualized, and/or humorous women athletes or events" (p. 47).[19] Indeed, the authors of this study note that one of the longest segments devoted to "women's sport" over the course of the many hours they examined was a piece done on a nude female bungee jumper! The framing of female athletes in this way tarnishes what little credibility they may have with the public in addition to promoting a view that they are not to be taken seriously (or as seriously as male athletes and their athletic achievements).

Nonwhite women are pushed even further into the margins of this minimal sports news coverage in print form as well. As one of the nation's top selling sports magazines, *Sports Illustrated* (and its swimsuit issue) has served as a point of departure for scholars interested in how gender and racial ideologies get played out in sport media (Davis, 1997; Bishop, 2003).[20,21] In a study of *Sports Illustrated* covers spanning 35 years, researchers conclude that female athletes appeared on about 6 percent (114) of the 1,835 covers examined. Of the small fraction of covers highlighting female athletes, black women appeared only five times (Williams, 1994).[22] A look beyond the *Sports Illustrated* covers, into the pages of the magazine, confirms the peripheral exposure afforded to black female athletes. In a content analysis of feature articles in *Sports Illustrated* from 1954 to 1987, Lumpkin and Williams (1991)[23] found that of the 3,723 feature articles over the span of the study, women accounted for only 320 pieces. Of this fraction, black women accounted for only 16 feature articles over the course of 33 years in this weekly publication.

In addition to quantitative data, scholars also employ qualitative methods to examine how athletes are talked about and shown to us. While we tend to accept these mediated images and discourses around sport at face value and are not likely to challenge what we see and hear, there is nonetheless a good deal of cultural work occurring. As Coakley (2007)[24] explains, "most of us believe that, when we see a sport event on television, we are seeing it 'the way it is.' We don't usually think that what we are seeing, hearing, and reading is a series of narratives and images selected for particular reasons and grounded in the social worlds and interests of those producing the event, controlling the images, and delivering the commentary" (p. 406). Thus interrogating and analyzing how female athletes of color are represented via various mediums becomes an important project in furthering our understanding of the ways dominant race and gender ideologies get played out in sport and the broader culture. Using as starting points fairly high-profile female athletes of color, including former professional golfer Nancy Lopez and tennis stars Venus and Serena Williams, I'd like to briefly sketch out how media construct particular images of these athletes that ultimately reaffirm and reproduce, rather than eradicate, racial and gendered hierarchies.

Nancy Lopez retired from the Ladies Professional Golf Association (LPGA) in 2002 after a brilliant 25-year career in which she won nearly 50 tournaments. Lopez's identity as a Mexican-American and her working-class roots were often used to promote her "as the ideal, assimilated Mexican woman" (Jamieson, 2000, p. 145),[25] helping to underscore the myth of sport as an equal playing field where anyone, regardless of race, class, and gender can achieve the pinnacle of athletic success. A part of Lopez's widespread appeal and popularity, among mainly middle- and upper-class white golf fans, rests with the way the media "whitened" (Douglas & Jamieson, 2006, p. 122)[26] her identity, making her seem less like a distant other. She was embraced, according to the authors, because "she conducted herself in a manner that made (white) audiences feel comfortable" (p. 126). For example, Lopez's marriage to professional baseball player Ray Knight was one of the levels on which this strategy played itself out. Her marriage to Knight as well as the birth of three children in the first few years on the professional tour "served as a constant reminder of her heterosexuality" (p. 127). The media's effort to promote Lopez's heterosexual identity is not to be understated within a female sporting culture that has long associated athleticism with masculine women and lesbianism. These narratives worked to normalize Lopez, muting ethnic and class difference from the many middle-class, white fans that followed her career. Nancy Lopez's "accommodating" and "gracious" (Douglas & Jamieson, p. 131) demeanor were threads around which her femininity was framed. This helped to promote a non-threatening image of Lopez for her fans who thus conceived of her not as an "exceptional other" [working-class Mexican] but as "every woman" [middle-class and white].

While Nancy Lopez's femininity was not in question, such was not the case for tennis stars Venus and Serena Williams whose muscularity served to perpetuate and reinforce dominant [white] stereotypes of black female physicality. Contemporary understandings of the Williams sisters are linked to historical representations of black women, as beyond the boundaries of white standards and notions of femininity and womanhood (Vertinsky & Captain, 1998).[27] Cultural stereotypes of black women as uncivilized, hypersexual, masculine, and aggressive not only fueled myth but also furthered black female bodies from what they weren't—white. As the sport historian Susan Cahn (1994)[28] astutely writes,

> *African American women's work history as slaves, tenant farmers, domestics, and wageworkers disqualified them from standards of femininity defined around the frail or inactive female body. Their very public presence in the labor force exempted African Americans from ideals of womanhood that rested on the presumed refinement and femininity of a privatized domestic arena. Failing to meet these standards, black women were often represented in the*

dominant culture as masculine females lacking in feminine grace, delicacy, and refinement. (p. 127)

In part, the "decidedly ambivalent and, at times, aggressive reaction toward Venus and Serena [Williams'] accomplishments" rests with perceptions that black women are beyond the bounds of white middle-class femininity (Douglas, 2005, p. 258).[29] The Williams' powerful physiques are constructed and represented to us as far removed from more preferred embodiments of femininity. Women's Tennis Association member and media star, Anna Kournikova remarked in a 2001 interview, "I hate my muscles. I'm not Venus Williams. I'm not Serena Williams. I'm feminine. I don't want to look like they do. I'm not masculine like they are" (quoted in Schultz, 2005, p. 346).[30] Another observer took his comments even further than Kournikova's questioning the Williams' femininity and their status *as women*, "I can't even watch them play anymore. I find it disgusting. I find both of those, what do you want to call them—they're just too muscular. They're boys" (quoted in Schultz, 2005, p. 346).[31] In addition to their bodies, Venus and Serena's tennis outfits as well as their beaded cornrows were used as evidence of their racial and gendered "otherness" (Schultz, 2005; Spencer, 2004).[32] What links the mediated narratives of Nancy Lopez and Venus and Serena Williams are the ways in which each is constructed against the normative standards of white, middle-class femininity. In this way sport serves as an intriguing and highly visible location to examine how dominant notions of gender and race get reaffirmed.

Resisting Representations

. . . [I]t is only when we begin to understand the lived experiences of women of color, rather than fitting them into categorical analyses, that we may articulate the multifaceted encounters of women living at the margins of race, class, gender, and sexuality. (Jamieson, 2003, p. 3)[33]

The preceding discussion of the structural and ideological barriers and stereotypes that women of color face upon entrance into sport is not meant to imply that these athletes are passive recipients of the racism and sexism that surrounds them. Female athletes of color also act as agents in response to the constraints that seek to inhibit their involvement and actions, or those who attempt to speak for or represent them. This "agency" manifests itself in the ways female athletes of color move into athletics and make meaning from their sport experiences. From their stories we are more clearly able to understand how multiple oppressive spaces intersect and how they are challenged. In addition, giving voice to female athletes of color underscores the breadth of experiences rather than a monolithic one, while challenging racial and ethnic stereotypes (Bruening, Armstrong, & Pastore, 2005).[34]

Deemed passive and frail, Asian American girls and women are thus stereotyped as nonathletic, in terms of interest and ability. Amid the dearth of research on the experiences of Asian American female athletes their stories remain invisible and thus these stereotypes remain firmly entrenched. Hanson (2005)[35] suggests, however, that at the high school level, Asian American women . . . are just as likely (if not more likely) to participate in sport as are other groups of women" (p. 304). In contrast to stereotypical images, Asian American families serve as a powerful positive influence upon girls' and women's entrance into sport. Moreover, according to Hanson, the "presence and success of their mothers in the labor force" presents young Asian American girls with compelling female role models to emulate (p. 304).[36] Gender, as a construct, is enacted differently across a range of ethnic and racial identities, foregrounding the very specific and unique ways that Asian American women and other women of color are socialized into sport, understand sport, and experience it.

Similarly, Jamieson (2003)[37] argues for the "relevance of Chicana voices in sports studies" (p. 1) because these perspectives force us away from the shallowness of stereotypes as well as illuminate the various levels of resistance employed in and through sport by female athletes of color. The narratives of Latina college softball players reveal the "middle space" many occupy as they move into sport and articulate the ways they resist dominant notions of who and what they should be in contrast to their own conceptualizations of self. Latina athletes construct various levels of "oppositional consciousness . . . as they navigated shifting identities and subjectivities" (p. 7).[38] In doing so Latina athletes use sport as a place to challenge the assumptions others have of them as women of color. For instance, one player, self-identified as black and Mexican, described her interaction with teammates in which she unsettles the finite and mutually exclusive racial categories on which they rest their assumptions. She notes, "white players will watch what they say around you and not tell you certain jokes. Because I'm black and Mexican they don't know which way to go" (quotes in Jamieson, 2003, p. 12).[39] This interaction, within a sport setting, sheds light on the ways Latinas and other women of color have engaged with various strategies to resist categorization by others and reclaim some agency in the process as they work toward defining themselves and their experiences.

Concluding Remarks

My hope is that this essay encourages readers to (re)examine the cultural space that sport inhabits. Amid the games and competitive contests are negotiations for cultural power. Like other social institutions, sport is an arena where cultural values and norms are being reproduced and challenged. Thus, sport, as our lens onto the social world, deserves our critical attention. In this essay we saw that universal claims of "women's experience" in sport should be viewed with caution and critical interrogation. As Hall (1996)[40] notes, "black sportswomen [and other women of color] are not simply subjected to more disadvantages than their white counterparts; their oppression, because of racism, is qualitatively different in kind" (p. 44).[39] Examining the place and status of women of color in sport forces us to think beyond the narrow contours of white, middle-class, and male identity. Representations, as well as the experiences, of female athletes of color are shaped by the dynamics of racism and sexism but are not necessarily destined by those forces. Women of color have a long history of enacting tools and strategies to combat the social forces of racism and sexism. Sport provides us with an excellent location to study this process.

Notes

[1]Sage, G. H. (1998). *Power and ideology in American sport: A critical perspective.* Champaign, IL.: Human Kinetics.

[2]*About Title IX.* (n.d.). Retrieved July 20, 2006, from http://bailiwick.lib.uiowa. edu/ge/aboutRE.html/pdfciteRE.html

[3,24]Coakley, J. (2007). *Sports in society: Issues and controversies.* Boston: McGraw Hill.

[4]Media Education Foundation. (2002). *Playing unfair: The media image of the female athlete* [video recording]. Northampton, MA.: Media Education Foundation.

[5,6]Mathewson, A. D. (1996). Black women, gender equity and the function at the junction. *Marquette Sports Law Journal, 6,* 239–266.

[7]Minority women still underrepresented in college sports. (July 11, 2003). *Chronicle of Higher Education,* p. A31.

[8]Suggs, W. (2005). *A place on the team: The triumph and tragedy of Title IX.* Princeton, NJ: Princeton University Press.

[9,10,11,12]Suggs, W. (2001, November 30). Left behind: Title IX has done little for minority female athletes because of socioeconomic and cultural factors, and indifference. *Chronicle of Higher Education,* pp. A1, A35–A37.

[13,14]Evans, T. M. (1998). In the Title IX race toward gender equity, the black female athlete is left to finish last: The lack of access for the "Invisible Woman." *Howard Law Journal, 42,* 105–128.

[15]Kane, M. J. & Pearce, K. D. (2002). Representations of female athletes in young adult sports fiction: Issues and intersections of race and gender. In M. Gatz, M. A. Messner, & S. J. Ball-Rokeach (Eds.), *Paradoxes of Youth and Sport* (pp. 69–91). Albany, NY: State University of New York Press.

[16]Creedon, P. J. (1994). *Women, media, and sport: Challenging gender values.* Thousand Oaks, CA.: Sage.

[17,18,19]Messner, M., Duncan, M. C., & Cooky, C. (2003). Silence, sports bras, and wrestling porn: Women in televised sports news and highlights shows. *Journal of Sport and Social Issues, 27,* 38–51.

[20]Davis, L. R. (1997). *The swimsuit issue and sport: Hegemonic masculinity in* Sports Illustrated. Albany, NY: State University of New York Press.

[21]Bishop, R. (2003). Missing in action: Feature coverage of women's sports in *Sports Illustrated, 27,* 184–194.

[22]Williams, L. D. (1994). Sportswomen in black and white: Sports history from an Afro-American perspective. In P. J. Creedon (Eds.), *Women, media, and sport: Challenging gender values* (pp. 45–66). Thousand Oaks, CA.: Sage.

[23]Lumpkin, A. & Williams, L. D. (1991). An analysis of *Sports Illustrated* featured articles, 1954–1987. *Sociology of Sport Journal, 8,* 16–32.

[25]Jamieson, K. M. (2000). Reading Nancy Lopez: Decoding representations of race, class, and sexuality. In S. Birrell & M. G. McDonald (Eds.), *Reading sport: Critical essays on power and representation* (pp. 144–165). Boston: Northeastern University Press.

[26]Douglas, D. D. & Jamieson, K. M. (2006). A farewell to remember: Interrogating the Nancy Lopez farewell tour. *Sociology of Sport Journal, 23,* 117–141.

[27]Vertinsky, P. & Captain, G. (1998). More myth than history: American culture and representations of the black female's athletic ability. *Journal of Sport History, 25,* 532–561.

[28]Cahn, S. K. (1994). *Coming on strong: Gender and sexuality in twentieth-century women's sport.* Cambridge, MA: Harvard University Press.

[29]Douglas, D. D. (2005). Venus, Serena, and the women's tennis association: When and where "race" enters. *Sociology of Sport Journal, 22,* 256–282.

[30,31]Schultz, J. (2005). Reading the catsuit: Serena Williams and the production of blackness at the 2002 U.S. Open. *Journal of Sport and Social Issues, 29,* 338–357.

[32]Spencer, N. E. (2004). Sister Act VI: Venus and Serena Williams at Indian Wells:"Sincere fictions" and white racism. *Journal of Sport and Social Issues, 28,* 115–135.

[33,37,38,39]Jamieson, K. M. (2003). Occupying a middle space: Toward a Mestiza sport studies. *Sociology of Sport Journal, 20,* 1–16.

[34]Bruening, J. E., Armstrong, K. L., & Pastore, D. L. (2005). Listening to the voices: The experiences of African American female student athletes. *Research Quarterly for Exercise and Sport, 76,* 82–100.

[35,36]Hanson, S. L. (2005). Hidden dragons: Asian American women and sport. *Journal of Sport and Social Issues, 29,* 279–312.

[40]Hall, M. A. (1996). *Feminism and sporting bodies: Essays on theory and practice.* Champaign, IL.: Human Kinetics.

What It Means to Be an Asian Indian Woman

Y. Lakshmi Malroutu

"India émigré Indra Nooyi named first female CEO of PepsiCo" read headlines in the business section of major newspapers. On August 14, 2006, Nooyi became the first Asian Indian woman CEO of a Fortune 500 company joining a small but elite group of 11 women CEOs of Fortune 500 companies. Does this appointment symbolize the emergence of a new era and a chink in the corporate glass ceiling that many feel hinders ambitious Asian Indians from landing the top jobs in corporate America? According to some news reports, Nooyi landed the top job because she is a leader who is capable of leading a conglomerate in a global society and not because of her gender or ethnicity. So we are left grappling with the question of where Asian Indians stand in mainstream America and among other Asian groups. Why do we remain an overlooked minority despite our significant contributions in the fields of technology, science, and business? What do these sporadic moments in the sun mean for the Asian Indian group as a whole? While we celebrate the achievements of our successes, we seem to be at a loss to collectively confront issues facing us as a group especially when confronted with questions about our identity and inclusion in the Asian society.

To consider how Asian Indian immigrants are faring in the United States, I refer back to an essay that I wrote nearly 10 years ago, highlighting my experiences as a first-generation immigrant. Revisiting the topic of what it means to be an Asian Indian woman in the United States, I go over some of my experiences in this narrative. Although some experiences in the narrative continue to be the same, some things have changed; some are positive while others are not so rosy. Since the narrative expounds my personal experiences and perspective, it is not possible to use this essay as a representation of the Asian Indian group experience. Even though the challenges that I face are unique to my situation there is a thread of universality in the echoes of our voices.

Contemporary Demographic Portrait of Asian Indians

First and foremost, I expound the issue of identity and representation in the context of the Asian milieu. This narrative is an attempt to extricate the term "Asian Indian" from "Asian" and focus specifically on that group, a group that is not often recognized nor represented. The Census 2000 reports that more than 1.6 million Asian Indians and nearly 1.9 million Asian Indians in combination with at least one other race make their home in the United States (Reeves & Bennett, 2004). Even though they are the third largest Asian group, Asian Indians do not seem to benefit from the largeness of their group. The significant increase in numbers has not helped the group leave its footprints within the Asian context as they still remain on the periphery mostly obscured or omitted when stories of Asians are narrated. Even in the 21st century, Asian Indians remain the forgotten Asians and their experiences in the United States receive minimal consideration.

To understand the identity of Asian Indians one has to recognize the makeup of the group and the ambiguity that they experience regarding their multiple identities. Most Americans tend to perceive Asian Indian immigrants as a homogenous group. This perception is prevalent in the studies on Asian Indians where group differences are not adequately identified and discussed. In reality, Asian Indian immigrants have more subgroup differences than any other Asian immigrant group. While the term "Asian Indians" refers to people from India, the prevalent term used often is "South Asian," which encompasses people who trace their heritage to India, Pakistan, Bangladesh, Nepal, Sri Lanka, and other places on the Indian subcontinent. The broader term South Asians acknowledges common interests of the group while allowing for intragroup differences.

As South Asian people from the Indian subcontinent increasingly started participating in the complex and often heated debates about race and ethnicity in the United States, they confronted questions about naming and claiming an identity that designates their group in this country. Claiming any single identity omits the significant political, historical, economic, and religious differences between their countries of origin. This construction process parallels the gradual recognition of the term "Asian American" for peoples of East and Southeast Asian ancestry.

The Heterogeneity of the Asian Indian Society

The Asian Indian society is very diverse with linguistic, regional, caste, class, and religious differences. The subethnic division based on regional and linguistic differences follow a long legacy of regional and linguistic movements in India. While differences such as place of origin, caste, and language do not play a determining role within small groups of Asian Indians living in towns in the United States, these factors do play a decisive role in bigger cities such as New York City, Jersey City, Chicago, and San Jose and others, where organizations are formed based along these lines. Also evident among the Asian Indian groups are religious differences and tensions.

In Corvallis, Oregon, where I attended graduate school there were about 25 families of Indian origin. The families came from several states in India and religious, state, and caste differences were evident within the group. Because of the small numbers there was limited possibility of forming separate organizations in Corvallis and the families were forced to congregate as a whole and form social friendships. However, the friendships were out of necessity and underneath the friendly façade I could sometimes experience the aggressive and fragmented nature of Indian subcultures. Since I grew up in Calcutta, a busy metropolis of India, I was unaccustomed to dealing with the nuances of the subethnic differences. Growing up, the class distinction was very much in place in India. I attended private schools and had little or no contact with people beneath my socioeconomic status. The household help who assisted with chores at home and the chauffeur who drove us to and from our school and around were part of the household makeup, but my siblings and I did not have much contact with their children.

Interestingly, subgroup identity was a strong presence in New York City. After completing my graduate studies in Oregon, I moved to New York City in 1992, where I started my university teaching career at Queens College, City University of New York. There were dozens of Indian organizations based on religion, class, and region. Indian and South Asian immigrants transplanted three major non-Christian religions – Hinduism, Sikhism, and Islam, and several minor religions such as Jainism, Buddhism, and Zoroastrianism. Because of the distinctiveness of their cultures and religions, Asian Indians seem to have multiple identities. The majority of my Indian friends in New York belonged to several organizations based on religious and regional differences and most of them were comfortable in their multiple identities.

The Immigration of Asian Indians

The first wave of South Asian immigration occurred at the tail end of the 1800s from an India still under British colonial rule. Scientists and technocrats comprised most of the second wave, who came to the United States after the relaxing of the immigration policies in 1965. In early 1900s when Asian immigrants were not eligible for U.S. citizenship, Indian leaders organized the "citizenship movement" to get Indian immigrants considered Caucasian and thus eligible for citizenship. However, when the U.S. Census Bureau classified Indian as white in 1970, Indian community leaders lobbied the U.S. government to reclassify them as Asian Indians. They wanted Indians to be classified separately as a minority group partly because minority groups were entitled to a number of benefits in the post-civil rights era. The U.S. Census Bureau has classified Asian Indians as one of the Asian and Pacific Islander groups since 1980. Although Indians and other South Asians culturally and physically differ from other Asian groups, the governmental classification of Indians and other South Asians into the Asian and Pacific Islander category has influenced their ethnic and panethnic identities.

The Recent Asian Indians

The former Immigration and Naturalization Service (INS), now called the U.S. Citizenship and Immigration Services, radically structured the homogeneity of the community as it consciously selected technically trained and English educated individuals from South Asia. The rapid financial success that this group achieved in the United States is now a matter of undisputed record. In 1999, the median family income of Asian Indians was the second highest of all Asian groups at $70,708, slightly less than the Japanese median family income (Reeves & Bennett, 2004). Along with its quest for financial stability, the community also became preoccupied with maintaining its cultural integrity and consequently, established numerous linguistically and regionally specific "cultural" associations.

It was only in the 1980s and with the help of the Family Reunification Act that the community demographics started to turn heterogeneous. Individuals who were kin to the first group or were displaced from other regions of the world such as Africa began migrating to the United States. Vocationally, the later immigrants moved into blue-collar work and local businesses as shopkeepers, taxi drivers, and motel owners. During this time, the Asian Indian community became divided by a chasm that was formed along class lines based on education, occupation, and economics.

In recent years, in response to the events in India and in this country, the Asian Indian community has segued into two major platforms with thrusts towards being "South Asian" and "pan-Hindu." The first group is more inclusive and has a secular and multicultural view of India. They focus on the similarities of South Asians and the issues facing them, especially in the aftermath of 9/11 terrorist attacks. On the other hand, the pan-Hindu group focuses on India and its culture, and feels strongly in the exclusion of other South Asian communities because they do not share the same history.

Gender Expectations for Asian Indian Women

The second area that I will develop to help understand Asian Indian immigrants is the expectations that the group sets for itself: expectations for their women and expectations for success. Being an Asian Indian has certain advantages; for example, one's life is clearly laid out. All one has to do is just follow the red brick road and he or she is rewarded with approval and acceptance. One is expected to follow the few identified status professions – doctor, engineer, or computer scientist.

As a freshmen orientation advisor, I meet many first- and second-generation Asian Indians and their parents to assist with scheduling of courses. Parents with single-minded determination steer their children into completing premedicine, preengineering, and computer science or natural science degrees at the exclusion of the arts and the humanities. In many instances, the son or daughter do not have much say in selecting a major – they just follow the expectations laid down by their parents and the society.

I am single, and much of my life revolves around my career and this makes me an oddity among most Asian Indians. Though most Indians will not say outright that I have chosen to live an unconventional life by remaining single, they say as much through their unspoken words. Marriage provides a woman with her primary identity and in India, as in many other South Asian cultures, marriage and mother-hood provide women with their primary identities (Malroutu, 1999).[1]

Marriage is undoubtedly the central priority in the Asian Indian's social life, and is the end toward which all girls are conditioned to achieve. The fact of my life is that as a single, professional woman I command more awe than understanding, more questions than solutions, more isolation than inclusion. It is not just a social disconnect that I experience; it is an emotional one as well because most Asian Indians have yet to accept or even comprehend the possibility of someone, especially a woman, being both single and content.

The concept of marrying for love is still foreign to most Asian Indians. Most of my friends had arranged marriages. Relatives or friends would suggest a suitable match or a man's family would inquire about a young woman after spotting her at a social function. Some of my friends selected their own spouses, but they usually chose someone who was from the same region, caste, and socioeconomic background, out of deference to their parents' wishes and social pressures. Another determining factor in mate selection is the color of one's skin. It is an exasperating yet amusing experience to read matrimonial advertisements in Indian newspapers and websites. In the ads, the gradations of color quoted include "white," "very fair," "wheat," and "dark wheat" (Malroutu, 1999).[2]

Even on the celluloid screen, the paradigm of woman/wife/mother remains monotonously unchanged from the 20th century. Despite the spirited and uncon-ventional carrying-ons before marriage, once married, the leading lady suddenly transforms herself into a conventional wife draped in a "sari" or "salwar-kameez" and an epitome of goodness, sweetness, and virtue. The deeper message within the film remains the same, that is, the unshakable conviction that this is the way a good wife or daughter-in-law behaves.

My female friends, those who had arranged marriages and those who chose their partners, generally seem to fall into the category of good wife and mother. Even though all of them have graduate degrees and hold professional careers, their home lives seem to follow a predictable pattern of making sure that the meals are prepared on time, dishes washed, parties organized, and the other humdrum of life. On the surface, my Asian Indian friends have an ideal family – a successful hus-band, their own careers, nice children, and a nice home in a nice neighborhood, but I feel the frustration and disappointment that some experience in their marriage. But they are hesitant to elaborate on their problems lest they upset the façade of blissful life. Divorces and separations are few and far between and I personally know of only a handful of women who are divorced. An Indian acquaintance of mine ran away with a Caucasian because her husband did not measure up to her expectations but sadly found that the other man did not either.

In addition to their commitment to retaining cultural identity, Asian Indian community leaders become strongly engaged in upholding an impeccable image of the community and thus deny the existence of social problems such as sexual assault, mental illness, homelessness, intergenerational conflict, unemployment, and delinquency. Absorbed in affirming group cohesion, all social problems are relegated to the periphery. Although the community turns a blind eye to many troublesome issues, it denies abuse of women in particular, because it presumes that being away from the structural oppressions of extended families and strict gender hierarchies prevalent in South Asian countries, women's independence and liberation are heightened in the United States. However, not all is well within the women's community.

In the South Asian community, men are the primary immigrants, whereas women enter the country as their dependents: wives, daughters, or on a few occasions, mothers and sisters. The women's community that congregate in the United States, educationally and financially have more in common with the later immigrants than the more prosperous early group. For instance, according to Census 2000, although 54 percent of Asian Indian women over 16 years old worked outside their families, the annual median earnings was $35,173, an amount that was significantly lower than the median earnings of men in the community ($51,904) (Reeves & Bennett, 2004).[3] However, it is more than financial dependency that plagues South Asian women in the United States. Underneath the veneer of the placid and companionable family, domestic violence lurks silently taking its toll on South Asian women.

A woman is judged to have failed in her role if she cannot maintain her marriage and provide her children with a father, regardless of his conduct. An encouragement to keep one's family intact comes from the belief that being a single mother is detrimental to her children's proper development. Divorce is still unacceptable in the Asian Indian community and the percentage of divorced couples in the United States (2.4%) is indicative of this conviction (Reeves & Bennett, 2004).[4] Thus, the main burden of keeping the family intact primarily rests on women. An added incentive to keep the family together at all costs comes also from the cultural glorification of women's suffering. South Asian societies tend to extol women who endure violence for the sake of their families' togetherness.

In addition, the pervasive notion of "karma" plays a crucial role in intensifying women's tolerance of domestic violence. Many South Asian women tend to believe in "karma," one's predestination or fate. Thus, they may feel that their situation in an abusive relationship is their destiny. Several of these barriers interacting in complex ways make South Asian women feel helpless to change their situations and accept abuse as inevitable. My involvement with Sakhi, an organization that assists South Asian women escape domestic violence in New York City, opened my eyes to the horrors that women were forced to endure by their husbands. At one of their annual fundraisers, I heard the testimony of a woman who survived burns to 60 percent of her body and face when her husband poured kerosene, threw a match on her, locked their apartment door from the outside, and left her to die because he had found another woman and did not want to stay married. While women are held to higher standards in keeping their families intact, men have more latitude in deciding whether they want to remain in the marriage.

Acculturation Problems of Elderly Women

Another group of Asian Indians that has not received much attention is the elderly, especially elderly women. I conducted an exploratory research study on the acculturation problems and service needs of Asian Indian elderly in New York City in 1997 to gather data on key issues associated with the adjustment and coping mechanisms of elderly Asian Indian immigrants. In 2000, nearly 4 percent of the Asian Indian population in the United States was 60 years or older (Reeves & Bennett, 2004). Because the Asian Indian elderly come to this country with different cultural expectation, they face many problems because of differences in their expectations and the treatment they receive.

Individual problems for the Asian Indian elderly in this country include the psychological and emotional conflict between retaining their position in the family and society and loss of identity and power. The majority of elderly, more than half, are married or widowed women, live with their adult children, and experience overcrowding, lack of privacy, the emotional strain of three generations residing in a two- or three-bedroom apartment or house, and further dilution of financial resources (Malroutu, 1999a).[5] Social problems involve the older person's interaction with the social environment, such as language barriers, illiteracy, isolation, and immobility. In the study, it was found that elderly, especially women, have limited access to the outside world because of their fear to venture outside on their own in their traditional clothes. Besides overcrowding, lack of language fluency is a major problem for the majority of elderly women (Malroutu, 2001).[6]

The number of new older immigrants who are entering the United States as dependents do not demonstrate a proficiency in English and are dependent on family members to act as interpreters of both language and culture. In the absence of familial help, the elderly (mostly women) feel isolated and lonely even when they live in neighborhoods predominantly occupied by Asian Indians. Many elderly women have immigrated as dependents of their professional adult children and as caregivers of grandchildren, while some immigrated for financial and medical reasons. In contrast to recent immigrants, Asian Indian elderly who have worked in the United States are fluent in English and have access to health and other social services (Malroutu, 2001).[7]

The elderly immigrant women frequently talk about their relatives, friends, and social networks in India, returning home to India, and in general, feel lonely and depressed. This group is reluctant to develop close associations with neighbors unless they have similar linguistic and religious beliefs. So even when the elderly women find themselves among others of their own kind, they still experience loneliness and isolation (Malroutu, 1999b).[8]

Institutional problems include inadequate knowledge of social services, poverty, immigration status, and lack of culturally sensitive social services. The addition of the elderly immigrants into the household results in financial strain on families that may already be strapped for money (Malroutu, 1999a).[9] Many elderly women feel a debt of gratitude to their children who they feel have made sacrifices to help them immigrate, and are reticent to complain or seek assistance if their families are unable to adequately provide for them. The Welfare Reform Act also plays a significant role in limiting access to health care for recent immigrants.

This narrative is an attempt to highlight the Asian Indian dilemma within the Asian context. Asian Indians are frequently subjected to and subject themselves to the model-minority thesis with the belief that they are a financially successful group with no or few problems. Marginalization of individuals and families who do not fit the mold is common with limited recourse to addressing the issues.

References

Malroutu, Y. L. (1999). The balancing act. In P. G. Min & R. Kim, (Eds.), *Struggle for ethnic identity*. Walnut Creek, CA: AltaMira Press, Sage Publications.

Malroutu, Y. L. (1999a). Factors affecting retirement income sources and financial dependency of Asian Indian elderly in New York City. In G. Olson (Ed.), *Proceedings of Asian Consumer and Family Economics Association,* 17–22.

Malroutu, Y. L. (1999b). Acculturation problems and service needs of Asian Indian elderly in New York City: Executive summary. Unpublished report.

Malroutu, Y. L. (2001). Predictors of elderly Asian Indians' dependence on informal support systems. In J. Fan and L. Malroutu (Eds.), *Proceedings of Asian Consumer and Family Economics Association,* 163–171.

Reeves, T. J., & Bennett, C. E. (2004). We the people: Asians in the United States. Washington, DC: U.S. Census Bureau.

Y. Lakshmi Malroutu, Ph.D. is a Professor in the Department of Family and Consumer Sciences, California State University, Sacramento. Her research interests include Financial Adequacy for Retirement, Money Attitudes and Behaviors of College Students, and Asian-Indian Elderly.

Chicanas and Transformational Resistance: Analyzing College Aspirations within the Family Context

Valerie Talavera-Bustillos

They [Chicanas] create and live a range of non-stereotypical expressions of Chicana womanhood.

—(En)Countering Domestic Violence, Complicity and Definitions of Chicana Womanhood, Russel y Rodriguez

There is a misconception that the Chicano family and within it, female gender roles, are traditional and unchanged. However, as Mendoza (2005) notes, "there is no typical Chicano family." For example, if we look at Chicana(o) families there are diverse perspectives, values and gender roles. One way to understand this diversity is to analyze how they view one of their own female family members entering college. The act of obtaining a college degree signifies a variety of differences she will have compared to her parents and family in general, such as the college experience: attending classes, interacting with faculty, researchers, and other students, completing research papers and final exams; after she graduates she will have increased opportunities that come with the advantages of obtaining a college degree, such as increased social and economic mobility, economic independence, and improved occupational opportunities. These experiences and characteristics oppose stereotypical ideas of a typical Chicana woman. For example, Russel y Rodriguez (1997)[1] provides an example of traditional gender roles from a research participant in her study, ". . . Patricia Pena understood her identity mostly as 'mother/wife/family woman' " (p. 121).[1] This illustrates how women's traditional gender roles continue to be centrally connected to the family.

This research project will address how family members view the changing gender roles within their family when a young Chicana pursues a college degree. It is important to note that this research deconstructs the notion of family: instead of perceiving them as sharing the same ideas, beliefs, and gender roles, these individuals will be identified specifically as parents, brothers/sisters, grandparents, uncles/aunts, and cousins to bring attention to the family not as one agreeable unit, but one made up of individuals with varying perspectives, goals, and values. The main objective is to examine the lived experiences of first-generation Chicana college students within the context of the family. My study is guided by two research questions: 1) How do family members respond to Chicana college aspirations? and 2) How do Chicana students respond to challenges to their college aspirations?

Chicana and Chicano scholars characterize the Chicana(o) family as a critical support system that assists and promotes family and individual success (Baca Zinn, 1975; Griswold del Castillo, 1984; Sanchez, 1993; Zavella, 1987).[2] In this paper I will illustrate the diverse perspectives of individuals within Chicana(o) families to examine how they view the changing gender roles in their family when a young female pursues a higher education. I utilize resistance theory (Giroux, 1983) with Solórzano and Delgado Bernal's (2001) definition of transformational resistance[1] to identify examples in my study and document how these students respond to challenges in their quest for a college education. Their personal narratives are analyzed to identify: individual family members' response to the plans to attend college and under what conditions they get challenged, and finally, whether these student reactions constitute resistant behavior.

Patricia Hill Collins (1998) highlights the importance of understanding dynamics within families. For example, she explains, "Just as the traditional family ideal provides a rich site for understanding intersectional inequalities, *reclaiming notions of family that reject hierarchical thinking may provide an intriguing and important site of resistance* [italics added]" (p. 77).[3] These insights by Hill Collins allow us to view the family as a place not only where traditional gender roles are prescribed, but also where they can be redefined. As Ortiz and Elrod (2002) state, ". . . family becomes a focal point of and incubator for antisubordination discourse and practice" (p. 268–269).[4] In other words, the family can be a site where change occurs and in the case of this study it can be a place where young daughters begin to rebel against traditional gender roles and construct their own idea of what their roles as women will become. Villenas and Moreno (2001) also state that "[a]lthough Chicana/Latina daughters listen to women in their families evoke discourses of Latino patriarchy about *honor y verguenza,* mothers and daughters also learn to negotiate and refute oppressive gender ideologies" (p. 685).[5] Mothers provide daughters with tools, practices, concepts, and critiques that can be utilized to combat gender subordination. My research utilizes resistance theory as a framework to examine how Chicanas "negotiate and refute oppressive gender ideologies" they encounter with family members in their desire to attend college.

There are many messages given to young daughters, some that are contradictory to traditional gender roles. This can provide a contradictory view of Chicana womanhood and may become a way for them to understand the complexities of what it means to be a Chicana. These alternative views of Chicana womanhood allow women to choose alternative gender roles. One alternative to becoming a wife and mother is to attend college. An examination of how college aspirations are viewed, accepted, or refuted may be one way to measure the Chicana(o) family's adaptability to a shift in gender roles. Villenas and Moreno (2001) illustrated that "[f]or Latinas/Chicanas, these contradictory gender teachings often involve knowing how to be *una mujer de hogar* (a woman of the home), while at the same time knowing how to be self-reliant (*valerse por si misma*)" (p. 673).[6] Being self-reliant counters gender subordination, and it signals a transformational shift that liberates women from traditional restricted gender roles. Villenas and Moreno (2001) state,

> ... *teachings between mothers and daughters ... are the interruptive spaces of possibility. ....daughters are subversively taught to dream possibilities beyond their mothers' lives ... [and] alternative ways of being mujer in community, family and beyond nation. (p. 675)*[7]

This research allow us to see how mothers offer their daughters wide-ranging versions of Chicana womanhood that at times can counter traditional gender roles. I will document how Chicanas who have their parents' support of their college aspirations can and do "dream possibilities beyond their mother's lives." In the subsequent accounts, I will illustrate how these Chicanas use resistance to make their college aspirations a reality.

Resistance Theory: The Possibilities of Transformation

Resistance theory[2] explains how resistant behaviors are both responses to social inequalities and attempts to improve social status (Giroux 1983, 2001).[8] The general family unit follows traditional gender roles, where women are expected to be wife/mother/ family woman. In this study, I analyze the family as a site where traditional gender roles are expected and reinforced. Figure 1-A illustrates how the family follows a cyclical pattern to reinforce traditional gender roles for women. It is within the family that certain standards and expectations serve to maintain the status quo of women's defined roles attached to family life.

Although there are many forms of resistance (Foley, 1977; Willis, 1976),[9] I apply Solórzano & Delgado Bernal's (2001) concept of transformational resistance which is,

> *a form of student behavior that is accompanied with a critique of domination and a desire for self or social liberation. In other words, the student must hold an awareness and critique of her/his oppressive conditions and structures of domination and the student must be motivated by a sense of social justice. (p. 319)*[10]

Figure 1-A. **Traditional Gender Roles and College Aspirations.** Cyclical pattern of the status quo, Chicana gender subordination, traditional gender roles of women solely as wife and mother. Student's college aspirations break cycle of traditional gender roles with parent support for higher education and self-reliance. With parental support and their college aspirations, students break the cycle to become women who achieve social and economic mobility and independence.

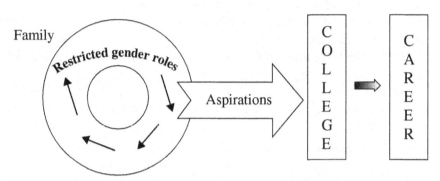

This concept is a tool to understand individual actions within a particular social context that allows us to see the intent to change, to transform one's situation, at the individual and/or collective level. I propose that despite parental support for the college plans, individuals within the family respond to the Chicana students' college plans by questioning their decision to attend college. It is in these conversations that the notion of Chicanas as wives and mothers becomes prescribed and enforced. What is critical to understand is that the student's college aspirations conflict with individual family member's expectations of women being wives and mothers. Yet even more significant is how these Chicanas respond to challenges to their college aspirations.

In my research, the analysis of data reveals 33 different expressions of transformational resistance (Figure 2). In Solórzano and Bernal (2001) they present a new concept of transformational resistance. Here I provide examples of this behavior and define them. I present specific types of transformational resistance: Desire to Prove Others Wrong, Goal Affirmation, Ignoring, and Avoidance.

The Study

In this research I examine the college aspirations of first-generation college students. What emerges from the personal interviews is who does and does not support student college aspirations. Of the 30 research participants, less than half (13) did not face any challenges to their college aspirations. The experiences of the 17 women who did are the foundation for my analysis. The ethnographic nature of this study enables the participants'[3] voice to shape my analysis of the educational experiences of these Chicana students.

Sample and Methodology

Due to the qualitative methodology of this research project, the sample size was relatively small and not generalizable; therefore, qualitative data is used to describe the participants of the study. I incorporated three key areas of research from ethnography, Chicano studies, and Chicana feminism as a foundation for my methodology. First, Strauss and Corbin's (1990) concept of "theoretical sensitivity" helped guide my analysis of data (pp. 41–42). Paraphrasing Solórzano (1997), the sources include: (a) pertinent literature on education and resistance; (b) one's personal and professional experiences with education and resistance; and (c) the analytic process of conducting research on Chicana educational experiences and resistance. Hence, my own training as a scholar with my theoretical sensitivity as a first-generation working-class Chicana college student inform my analysis.

Second, research in the field of Chicano studies also shaped how and why I analyze the research data. For example, the salient work of Angie Chabram (1990) illustrates the importance of the Chicana(o) intellectual's role. She explained how within Chicana discourse, " . . . decolonizing anthropology from a Chicano perspective meant critically reviewing culture and the institutional construction of culture: interrogating 'ethnographic authority' . . . But most importantly it meant scrutinizing the official anthropological culture . . ." (p. 239).[11] I incorporated decolonial social science techniques such as decolonizing educational ethnographic research when I challenged the myth of static, traditional gender roles within the Chicano family to really "see" how Chicanas were living and creating a variety of gender roles. Another way my analysis was formed was through important concepts put forth by Chicana theorist Dolores Delgado Bernal (2000). Her work on Chicana feminist epistemology highlighted the way in which I read and understood the data. As with other Chicana ethnographies (Davalos, 2003) that follow Maxine Baca Zinn's (1975) ideal of cultural responsibility and reciprocity, participants received compensation[4] for their contributions to this study.

I focused on two samples of first-year college students who had enrolled either in a four-year university or a community college. The two student samples have four important characteristics that served as criteria for the samples. The subjects are: (1) Chicana[5]; (2) first-generation in college; (3) low socioeconomic status (SES); and (4) recent high school graduates. Only those who graduated from a public or private Los Angeles County high school in June of 1997 participated in this research project. Both samples are taken from Los Angeles County, which contained the largest concentration of Chicanas in California and the nation (Bureau of Census, 2000; Statistical Record of Hispanics, 1995).[12]

The research began with data collection in August 1997. Potential subjects who fit the criteria were identified and chosen for each sample, for a total of 30 women.

Individual interviews were conducted before fall 1997 classes began. The focus group was scheduled after the first interviews were completed. After the focus group, the second interview was conducted to include any unanswered questions. Data collection was completed in December 1997. Data analysis began in January 1998 and continued until March 1998.

Results: Analysis of Transformational Resistance

In this study, 13 out of the 30 participants received only praise, encouragement, and support for their college aspirations and are able to enroll in a college or university without situations where their aspirations are challenged. However, the remaining 17 had their college aspirations questioned. Figure 1-B illustrates how some family members question, challenge, or doubt college plans of the young Chicanas in their family. By doing so, these family members attempt to reinforce their own ideas of the role young females should take in their family. It is important to note that of the 30 participants, all but two received support, motivation, or information to attend college from one or both of their parents.

This research focuses on the experiences of the 17 women whose college aspirations were challenged by family members. Despite strong parental support, certain family members see these Chicanas as rejecting the prescribed gender roles of the larger family unit (see Figure 1-B). By challenging the student's college aspirations, individual family members reinforce expectations based on their gender towards roles of wife and mother family woman.

Figure 1-B **Attempts at Maintaining Traditional Gender Roles.** Some family members question and doubt college plans, with expectations of traditional gender roles.

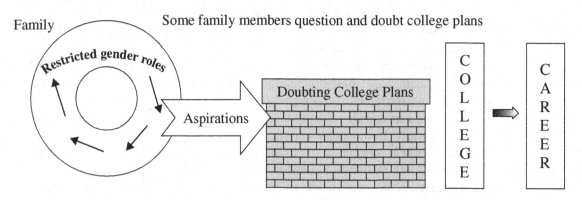

Types of Transformational Resistance

Students exhibited a variety of expressions of transformational resistance. The following will detail their experiences with their family member who contested their college aspirations and provide them as examples of transformational resistance. The expressions are: Desire to Prove Others Wrong, Ignoring, and Avoidance (Figure 2).

Desire to Prove Others Wrong. Some students resist those individuals who doubt they will attend college expressing a desire to "prove them wrong" (see Yosso, 2001).[13] Susan's mother strongly supports her college plans. Susan, who was a stellar student in high school, whose dream it is to attend a highly competitive university, and who is a university student, remembers one encounter vividly:

> *Yes, one of my brothers . . . the one that's nearest to my age, I don't know, he just said it . . . it got to me a lot. [He said] "Why are you going to school if you're going to end up pregnant and married anyways?" . . . You know it's not true, you know it's not necessarily going to work that way . . . Maybe he didn't think much of it, but I did. I really took it seriously; I took it to the heart. At that time, I think I had . . . I had sent my application already for the [university], and I'm, like, this is the school I had my heart set on, so when he told me that, I was, like, "Damn!" you know. It was a hard time. It was like one little comment can really hurt you. Yeah, I told him . . . "You don't know! I am going to finish high school and go to college." (Interview, September 3, 1997)*

Despite knowing she excels in school and her focus on academics, her brother still expects she will become pregnant and leave college. For him, the family pattern of women as wives and mothers allows him to focus only on her gender and

Figure 2 New Forms of Transformational Resistance.

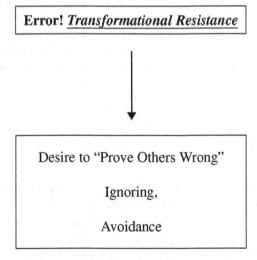

dismiss her educational goal of college attendance. Susan resists and confronts her brother's limited educational expectations of her and expresses her determination to attend college and prove him wrong.

Ignoring. I found that some students resist by ignoring those who either question or do not support their college aspirations. Dora, a community college student shared her experience:

Well, yeah, they [my cousins, neighbors] are like, "Oh, you're not going to make it [in college]. Why are you going to go? Just go here [high school]" . . . I don't pay attention to them, I don't want to! I don't want to end up like a typical Mexican housewife with a husband that beats on them. Well, I see the people around me, and I don't want to end up like them. I don't want to end up like a housewife. I want to make something of myself I want to have a career. (Interview, September 9, 1997)

Dora resists the expectations of her peers by ignoring their unsupportive comments. The women in her family formulate her understanding of what a woman is and does, when she refers to a "typical Mexican housewife." Her cousins and friends discourage her college aspirations, yet her desire is to be a different kind of woman.

Avoidance. Students demonstrate resistance by avoiding individuals who are not supportive of their college plans. For example, Esperanza states:

I stayed away from my mom's side of the family. . . .It was like they thought they were "all that" [better than everybody]. We lived in South Central [Los Angeles] and . . . they just assumed that I was going to be involved in gangs . . . be pregnant. . . . [they said] "Wow, you're going to graduate from high school!" [I said] "No, I am going to go to college." [There were] rumors . . . "There's no way she's going to make it. I don't even think she'll graduate from high school. Her and her brother, I know they are in gangs, . . . and I was, like, "You know?" It was, like, I lived in that area, and because I was a girl . . . [they'd think] "She can't possibly graduate high school; she's going to get pregnant." And if I would talk to them . . . [they would ask] "Do you have a boyfriend?" [I'd say] "Well, no," and they . . . [would say] "Are you sure you don't?" [They thought] I had to have a boyfriend, I had to have sex and I was going to get pregnant sooner or later. It was like something that had to happen; it was my destiny. It was around my 10th- or 11th- grade year that I, like, [had] no communication [with them]. . . .[I thought] forget it, . . .They just couldn't understand that, you could go to school on that side of town and also make it. (Interview, September 3, 1997)

Esperanza resists her family's low expectations of her, based on her neighborhood environment and the stereotype of early teen pregnancy. She avoids them and remains committed to her college aspirations. Despite being from the same family, ideas of success are tied to her neighborhood. In this example, being from a poor area plagued with crime and poverty, ideas of class come to define who can and

Figure 1-C **Transformational Resistance.** When family members challenge student's college plans. Students face challenges to their college aspirations and maintain them with acts of transformational resistance. Transformational resistance allows students to continue to college for an education and professional career to achieve their goal to be self-reliant.

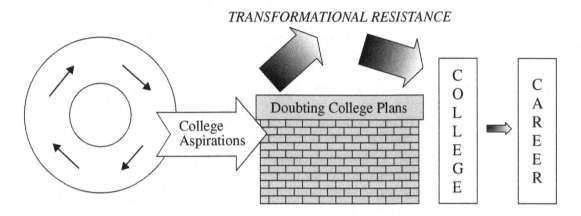

TRANSFORMATIONAL RESISTANCE

cannot become a college student. However, she exhibits transformational resistance through her college aspirations.

The majority of research participants encountered challenges to their college aspirations that triggered transformational resistance (Figure 1C). These Chicanas consciously struggle with the restricted gender roles prescribed by some members of the family and yet with transformational resistance, they remain focused on their college aspirations. This is transformational resistance: the ability for these young Chicanas to resist traditional gender role expectations and hold fast to their dreams of college education. Their desire to be self-reliant and the parental support they received seems to be connected to their acts of transformational resistance.

Discussion: Negotiating Gender Roles with Resistance

Interviews and focus groups provide evidence of how students resist gender roles as they attempt to improve their social status by obtaining a college education. Some students mention they would use their education to acquire better occupational opportunities and financial success. Moreover, for some of the students in this study, they resist ideas based on traditional gender roles within the family because it stands as a barrier to their college aspirations. Most importantly, how Chicanas respond to traditional familial expectations of traditional gender roles enables them to challenge and redefine their role as women.

Of the 30 women, 17 Chicanas in this study express transformational resistance. Most expressions are initiated by the pressure or expectation to conform to their family traditional gender roles. All of these college students are the first in their families to attend college; hence, they are the first to change their families' patterns of limited education and career opportunities. As a result, having a college education or a professional career expands the traditional role of women within the family. Some of the students specifically mention that they want to be able to leave their husband or mate and not be forced to stay in a situation solely for financial reasons, and did not want to be in the role of a passive, dependent female. As women they understand the importance of financial security and the independence a college education allows. Here again we see the identification of traditional gender roles of Chicana women as wives and mothers. The students' desire is to be self-reliant, *valerse por si misma*. Based on their family experiences, they challenge traditional gender roles by becoming college students.

An important finding was how some family members view college attendance and being a wife and mother as mutually exclusive. These students have family expectations of marriage *instead of* a college degree; yet these women describe how they desire both—children and a career. This is a reflection of how Chicana mothers provide messages of both the traditional and the actual roles of women. These young Chicanas can see both family and career as viable options; thus they understand and practice the complexity of Chicana gender roles. For example, some of these students express their desire to put their educational career before any plans of marriage or children, while some other women said they wanted to have a marriage, family, and career, and still others did not want to get married or have children. All of these students begin the process of rethinking the role of women in the family with their entrance into college.

My research documents parental support for Chicana college aspirations and my analysis reveals Chicano families can be both a source of support and challenges for young Chicana students. Of the 30 women in this study, all but 2 received parental support for their college aspirations. Specifically, parental support and their family situations are central to how the young women see themselves as Chicanas. Parental support illustrates they are encouraging their daughters to attain an education rather than follow the traditional gender role of wife/mother. This research illustrates for these women, the patriarchal notion of women solely as mothers and wives is a traditional gender role that is just one of many roles Chicana choose.

Chicana resistance has been and continues to be part of our culture, our identity. For example, Russel y Rodriguez explains, " . . . while the stereotype of the submissive Chicana wife-mother may be wielded as a cultural "ideal," Chicanas' challenges to that role are also *equally culturally valid and real*. . . . Consequently, we must understand that the continual effort to create the cultural stereotype of the submissive Chicana mother-wife *co-exists* [italics added] with equally powerful expressions of Chicana agency (p. 128).[14] As Russel y Rodriguez points out, research documents the voices and lived experiences of mujeres, both inside and outside of traditional gender roles or a mixture of both. It informs how we think about these traditional gender roles and how we live, contest, and reformulate them through our actions, and in the case of this research, through educational advancement.

Summary

This research focuses on the educational experiences of first-generation Chicana students. This study offers a glimpse into the complexity of resistance theory by extending the significant research of Solórzano and Delgado Bernal (2001) and applying it within the context of the Chicana(o) family. I highlight how expressions of transformational resistance are crucial to the educational advancement of the first-generation college students in this study.

These community college and university students expressed transformational resistance in various manners in their pursuit of a college education. As I examine the personal narratives of the research participants, I find they utilize transformational resistance as a strategy to maintain their college aspirations and achieve their goal of college. More important, it reveals how the traditional gender role of women as wife and mother is redefined with their entrance into college.

References

Arellano & Padilla. (1996). Academic invulnerability among a select group of Latina university students. *Hispanic Journal of Behavioral Sciences, 18*(4) 485–506.

Baca Zinn, M. (1975). Field research in minority communities: Political, ethnical and methodological observations by an insider." *Social Problems, 27*(2) pp. 216–233.

Baca Zinn, M. (1977). Political familism: Toward sex role equality in Chicano families. *Aztlan: Chicano Journal of the Social Sciences and the Arts, 6* (Winter), 13–26.

Bourdieu, P. (1977). Cultural reproduction and social reproduction. In J. Karable & H. Halsey (Eds.), *Power and ideology in education* (pp. 487–511). New York: Oxford University Press.

California Postsecondary Education Commission (2005). *Are they going? University enrollment and eligibility for African Americans and Latinos.* March, Fact sheet 05-03. Retrieved from www.cpec.ca.gov/eligibility

Chabram, A. (1990). Chicana(o) studies ss oppositional ethnography. *Cultural Studies, 4* (3). 228–247.

Clarricotes, K. (1981). The experiences of patriarchal schooling. *Interchange*, (12).

Cuadraz Holguin, G. (1993). *Meritocracy (un)challenged: The making of a Chicano and Chicana professoriate and professional class* (Dissertation) UMI Dissertation Services: A Bell & Howell Company.

Davalos, K. M. (2003). La quinceniera: Making gender and ethnic identities. In Alicia Gaspar De Alba (Ed.), *Velvet barrios: Popular culture and chicana/o sexualities.* New York: Palgrave MacMillian.

Delgadillo, T. (1998). Forms of Chicana feminist resistance: Hybrid spirituality in Ana Castillo's so far from God. *MFS Modern Fiction Studies, 44*(4) 888–916.

Delgado Bernal, D. (1997). *Chicana school resistance and grassroots leadership: Providing alternative history of the 1968 East Los Angeles blowouts.* Unpublished doctoral dissertation, University of California, Los Angeles.

Delgado Bernal, D. (1998). Chicana feminist epistemology in educational research. *Harvard Educational Review, 68*(4), 555–582.

Delgado Bernal, D. (2001) Learning and living pedagogies of the home: The Mestiza consciousness of Chicana students. *Qualitative Studies in Education, 14*(5), 623–639.

Delgado Bernal, D, & Solórzano, G. (1997). Academic Language and Chicana(o) activist scholars: Balancing the academy and the communities one hopes to serve. *International Journal of Educational Reform, 6*(2), 226–231.

Escobedo, T. (1990). Are Hispanic women in higher education the nonexistent minority? *Educational Researcher, 9*(9), 7–12.

Fernandes, J. V. (1988). From the theories of social and cultural reproduction to resistance theory. *British Journal of Sociology of Education,* 9(2).

Fordham, S. (1988). Racelessness as a factor in black students' school success: Pragmatic strategy or Pyrrhic victory?" *Harvard Educational Review, 58*(1).

Gándara, P. (1993) Passing through the eye of the needle: High achieving Chicanas. *Hispanic Journal of Behavioral Sciences, 4,* 167–179.

Gándara, P. (1995). *Over the ivy walls.* Albany, New York: State of New York Press.

Gibson, M. A. (1991). Ethnicity, gender, and social class: The school adaptation patterns of West Indian Youths. In M. A. Gibson & J. U. Ogbu (Eds.), *Minority status and schooling: A comparative study of immigrant and involuntary minorities.* New York: Garland.

Gibson, M. A. & Bhachu, P. (1991). The dynamics of educational decision making: A comparative study of Sikhs in Britain and the U.S In M. A. Gibson & J. U. Ogbu (Eds.), *Minority status and schooling: A comparative study of immigrant and involuntary minorities.* New York: Garland.

Giroux, H. (1983). Theories of reproduction and resistance in the new sociology of education: A critical analysis. *Harvard Educational Review, 53*(3).

Giroux, H. (2001). *Theory and resistance in education: Towards a pedagogy for the opposition* (2nd ed.). Westport, CT.: Bergin & Garvey.

Griswold del Castillo, R. (1984). *La familia: Chicano families in the urban Southwest, 1848 to present.* Indiana: University of Notre Dame Press.

Hayes-Bautista, D. E., Hsu, P., Perez, A., & Kharamanian, M. I. (2003). *The Latino majority has emerged: Los Angeles.* Center for the Study of Latino Health and Culture.

Horvat, E. (1996). *African-American students and college choice decision making in social context.* Unpublished doctoral dissertation, University of California, Los Angeles.

Hill Collins, P. (1998). It's all in the family: Intersections of gender, race and nation. *Hypatia, 13*(3).

Latina Feminist Group. (2001). *Telling to live: Latina feminist testimonios.* Durham, SC: Duke University Press.

Marsiglia, F., & Holleran, L. (1999). I've learned so much from my mother: Narratives from a group of Chicana high school students. *Social Work in Education, 21*(4), 220–237.

McDonough, P. (1997). *Choosing colleges: How social class and schools structure opportunity.* New York: State University of New York Press.

McRobbie, A (1978). Working class girls and the culture of femininity. In *Centre for Contemporary Cultural Studies Women's Group. Women Take Issue.* Hutchinson: London.

Mendoza, R. (2006). Chicanos in the United States: Statistical and cultural considerations. In N. Porras-Hein & J. Stokes (Eds.) *La familia Chicana.* Dubuque, IA:. Kendall Hunt.

Ohrn, E., (1993). Gender influences and resistance in school. *British Journal of Sociology of Education,* 14, 2147–2158.

Olivos, E. (2004). Tensions, contradictions, and resistance: An activist's reflection of the struggles of Latino parents in the public school system. *High School Journal, 87*(4), 25–36.

Ortiz, F. I., & Gonzalez, G. (1996). The preparation of Latino high school youth for university eligibility. In Hurtado, Figueroa, & Garcia (Eds.), *Strategic intervention in education: Expanding the Latina/Latino pipeline.* (UC eligibility Study) University of California, Santa Cruz.

Ortiz, V., & Elrod, J.. (2002). Construction project: Color me queer (+) Color me family-Camilo's story. In Francisco Valdes, Jerome McCristal Culp, & Angela P. Harris (Eds.), *Crossroads, direction and a new critical race theory* Philadelphia: Temple University Press.

Pizarro, M. (2005). *Chicanas and Chicanos in school: Racial profiling, identity battles and empowerment.* Austin, TX: University of Texas Press.

Revilla, A. (2004). Muxerista pedagogy. *High School Journal, 87*(4).

Russel y Rodriguez, M. (1997) "(En)Countering domestic violence, complicity, and definitions of Chicana womanhood. *Voces: A Journal of Chicana/Latina Studies,* (2), 104–141.

Sanchez, G. (1993) *Becoming Mexican American: Ethnicity, culture and identity in Chicano Los Angeles, 1900–1945.* Oxford University Press: London.

Segura, D., & Pierce, J. L. (1993) Chicana/o family structure and gender personality: Chodorow, familism and psychoanalytic sociology revisited. *Signs: Journal of Women and Culture and Society, 19*(1), 62–91.

Solórzano, D., & Solórzano, R. (1995) "The Chicano educational experience: A proposed framework for effective schools in Chicano communities." *Educational Policy, 9*, 293–314.

Solórzano, D., & Villalpando, O. (1998). Critical race theory, marginality and the experiences of students of color in higher education. In Carlos Alberto Torres & Theodore R. Mitchell (Eds.), *Sociology of education: Emerging perspectives.* Albany, NY: State University Press.

Solórzano, D., & Delgado Bernal, D. (2001) A critical race and Lat Crit theory framework: Chicana and Chicano students in an urban context. *Urban Education, 36*, 300–342.

Talavera-Bustillos, V. (1998) Chicana college choice and resistance: An exploratory study of first generation college students. Unpublished doctoral dissertation, University of California, Los Angeles.

United States Bureau of the Census, 2000. (2000). Washington DC: United States Government Printing Office.

Urahn, S. K. (1989) Student and parent attitudes about financing education: Effects on postsecondary attendance and choice for blacks, whites and Hispanics.*Dissertation Abstract International,* A50 (08): 2404.

Valencia, R. (2004). *Chicano school failure and success* (2nd Ed.). New York: Routledge Falmer.

Vasquez, M. J. (1992). Confronting barriers to the participation of Mexican American women in higher education. *Hispanic Journal of Behavioral Sciences, 4*(2), 147–165.

Villenas, S., & Deyhle, D. (1999). Critical race theory and ethnographies challenging the stereotypes: Latino families, schooling, resilience and resistance. *Curriculum Inquiry, 29*(4), 413–444.

Villenas, S., & Moreno, M. (2001) To valerse por si misma between race, capitalism, and patriarchy: Latina mother-daughter pedagogies in North Carolina *International Journal of Qualitative Studies in Education, 14*(5), 671–687.

Willis, P. (1997). *Learning to labor.* Lexington, MA.: D.C. Health.

Yosso, T. (2000). A critical race and Lat Crit approach to medial literacy: Chicana/o resistance in visual microagressions. Unpublished doctoral dissertation, University of California, Los Angeles.

Yosso, T. (2006). *Critical race counterstories along the Chicana/Chicano educational pipeline.* New York: Routledge.

Zavella, P. (1987). *Women's work and Chicano Families: Canner workers of Santa Clara Valley.* New York: Teacher's College Press.

Zine, J. (2000). Redefining resistance: Towards an Islamic subculture in schools. *Race, Ethnicity and Education, 3*(3).

Notes

[1] In their work, they define multiple forms of resistance, Self-Defeating, Reactionary, Conformist and Transformative. Daniel Solórzano and Dolores Delgado Bernal, "A Critical Race and Lat Crit Theory Framework: Chicana and Chicano Students in an Urban Context." *Urban Education* 36, (2001): 318.

[2] Resistance theory builds on and is similar to both social and cultural reproduction theories, see Bowles and Ginits, 1976; Bourdeui, 1977.

[3] I utilize pseudonyms for purposes of confidentiality. In place of their actual names, I chose to use the names of women in my life who display and live transformational resistance.

[4] Students were given a small stipend and attended a college information session and received a listing of contacts, in particular, the community college students received brochures and information on the transfer process.

[5] I define Chicana to denote any female who is of Mexican ancestry.

Is the Glass Ceiling Cracked Yet? Women in Rwanda, South Africa and the United States, 1994–2010

Boatamo Mosupyoe

> *"Making gender equality a reality is a core commitment of UNDP. As a cross-cutting issue, gender must be addressed in everything the organisation does. Why? Because equality between women and men is just, fair and right—it is a worthy goal in and of itself, one that lies at the heart of human development and human rights; and because gender inequality is an obstacle to progress, a road-block on the path of human development. When development is not 'en-gendered' it is 'endangered'.... There are two complementary approaches to achieving gender equality: mainstreaming gender and promoting women's empowerment. Both are critical." (United Nations Development Programme, 2002)*

We are in the 21st century and the issue of gender equality remains salient in global education, economic, political, scientific, cultural, academic, and other discourses and agendas. As recent as in 2008 when Hillary Clinton lost to Barack Obama she remarked that although the effort to shatter the glass ceiling failed, it, however, culminated with 18 million cracks (Milbank 2008). Her failure to reach the highest office in the United States of America indicates the strength and formidability of the glass ceiling, even in a country that perceives itself as the leader of the world. Hillary's 18 million votes failed to break the glass ceiling, prompting Mosupyoe to assert "one area in which the USA has failed to lead is in having a person other than a male of European descent to its highest office. It is also worth mentioning that the second office, that of the Vice President has suffered the same fate" (2008: v). The glass ceiling refers to the challenge women face to achieve equal and fair representation with men in senior executive positions in the workplace. Berry and Frank (2010) define the glass ceiling as an invisible obstruction that stands in the way of women's ability to occupy the highest executive jobs.

This invisible obstruction mutually operates with the problematic sticky floors that locate women at the bottom of the economic pyramid. In variable forms the obscured glass ceiling is discernable in different parts of the world, manifesting in and informed by different contexts. Equally true, cracks have been made to the ceiling, to borrow Hillary Clinton's words, in different ways. Turning to Africa, this paper examines how two African countries, Rwanda and South Africa, have negotiated and attempt to synthesize the tripartite and mutually constitutive paradigms: glass ceilings, sticky floors, and cracks. The analysis also makes few comparisons with the United States. The question remains, have Rwanda and South Africa delivered a crack or completely crumbled the imperceptible stubborn configurations of women's inequality? Have the two countries advanced beyond the metaphorical glass ceiling, cracks, and sticky floor variables to new realities and emblematic formations that will offer novel descriptions?

An analysis of the following can help us formulate our understanding: (1) a brief historical background of the events of 1994 that led to self-determination in both countries; (2) post-conflict approaches to gender equality and men's and women's participation in the reconstruction; (3) the pronouncement of the constitutions of both countries on the status of women, (4) the function of the dual legislative/electoral voluntary/involuntary allocation of percentages to gender shared governance, and (5) the representation of women in government, informal, and private sector. Both countries have made a concerted effort to address gender equality. Akin to the UNDP statement on gender, in principle both countries seem to understand that "when development is not `en-gendered' it is `endangered.'" In development transformation is achieved by an acknowledgment that informs mechanisms to redress inequalities. The discourse requires an understanding of paradigms and variables that function to either perpetuate gender inequality or promote gender equality. To give context to Rwanda and South Africa's achievements and challenges on gender equality, a brief history is in order.

A juxtaposition of the 1990 events of the two countries reveals that at the end of April while South Africa celebrated its independence from centuries of discrimination of indigenous people by a white minority, Rwanda experienced genocide that culminated in the death of almost a million Tutsis. It could even be argued that the attention of the world on the "miraculous" transformation in South Africa contributed toward the diverted focus from the inhumane genocide in Rwanda. Nevertheless, the Rwandan Patriotic Front (RPF) managed to gain military victory in July 1994. The post-conflict reconstruction in both countries assumed forms and approaches that included security, justice and reconciliation, individual healing, governance, etc. In an effort to bridge the divide engendered by race, class, ethnicity, gender, etc., the two countries established somewhat similar administrative processes. The processes' main intent was to build consensus and avoid further division among the citizens of the respective countries.

The 1994–2003 Rwandese Broad Based Government of National Unity mirrors in principle and intent the 1994–1997 South African provision for a Government of National Unity. In the South African election of April 27, 1994, the African National Congress obtained the majority of seats in the National Assembly, and together with the other parties, including those that supported and perpetuated the racist apartheid system, formed a Government of National Unity. Clause 88 of the interim Constitution of South Africa made a provision for broad participation of political parties. Any party with 20 or more seats in the National Assembly was entitled to one or more cabinet portfolios as membership in the government. More pertinent to the theme of my analysis, both the interim and final constitution states in part that "The Republic of South Africa is one sovereign democratic state founded on the value of Non-Racialism and non-sexism" (Mosupyoe 1999: 53). Furthermore, the part of the Constitution on Commission on Gender Equality states:

> *(1) There shall be a Commission on Gender Equality, which shall consist of a chairperson and such number of members as may be determined by an Act of Parliament. (2) The Commission shall consist of persons who are fit and proper for appointment, South African citizens and broadly representative of the South African community. (3) The object of the Commission shall be to promote gender equality and to advise and to make recommendations to Parliament or any other legislature with regard to any laws or proposed legislation which affects gender equality and the status of women. (Constitution of the Republic of South Africa Act 200 of 1993, repealed by Constitution of the Republic of South Africa, [No. 108 of 1996], G 17678, December 18, 1996)*

An examination of the processes of Rwanda reveals the same spirit of commitment to gender equality. According to http://www.gov.rw/ page.php, the official website of the government of Rwanda, on July, 19, 1994, the RPF established the Government of National Unity with four political parties: the Liberal Party (PL), the Social Democratic Party (PSD), the Christian Democratic Party (PDC), and the Republican Democratic Movement (MDR). Subsequently a 70-member Transitional National Assembly consisting of representatives of the RPF, the four other original parties plus three other smaller parties—namely, the Islamic Party (PDI), the Socialist Party (PSR), and the Democratic Union for Rwandese People (UDPR)—as well as six representatives of the Rwandese Patriotic Army (RPA) came into being. Here again relevant to the thesis of my investigation, the 2003 Rwandan Constitution adopted on May 2003 clearly and unequivocally pronounces gender equality as follows:

> *"Reaffirming our adherence to the principles of human rights enshrined in the United Nations Charter of 26 June 1945, the Convention on the Prevention and Punishment of the crime of Genocide of 9 December 1948, the Universal Declaration of Human Rights of 10 December 1948, the International Convention on the Elimination of All Forms of Racial Discrimination of 21 December 1965, the International Convention on Civil and Political Rights of 19 December 1966, the International Covenant on Economic, Social and Cultural Rights of 19 December 1966, the Convention on the Elimination of all Forms of Discrimination against Women of 1 May 1980, the African Charter of Human and Peoples' Committed to ensuring equal rights between Rwandans and between women and men without prejudice to the principles of gender equality and complementarity in national development." (http://www.rwandahope.com/ constitution.pdf)*

In addition, Article 9 of the Rwanda Constitution obligates 30% of posts for women in decision-making bodies and Article 82 reserves 30% of seats in the Senate for women. Rwanda's legislative milestone also reflects in the bills aimed at ending domestic violence and child abuse. Thus, while Rwanda's constitution has a constitutional involuntary gender-shared governance allocation, South Africa does not. However, both countries have clear and precise constitutional pronouncements on gender equality and the status of women, but approach shared governance allocation differently.

The notion of gender-based shared governance percentage allocation in Africa has been common since the 1990s. Kandawasvika-Nhundu (2009) notes that the desire for visible impact of women's contribution necessitates the practice. The efficacy of the constitutional mandate becomes evident with an analysis of Rwanda's achievements. Rwanda occupies the highest position in the world, with its highest number of women parliamentarians, also leading Europe, North America, and Asia. Women constitute 56.3% of parliamentarians in the Lower House and 34.6% in the Senate. The latter is an improvement from 48.8% and 30%, respectively, before the 2008 elections. The South African constitution, unlike the Rwandese constitution, does not mandate a percentage of gender-shared representation for elected public officials. Even in the absence of such a provision South Africa in terms of numbers has made strides. The representation of women in the local government has improved from 19% after 1995 to 40% after the 2007 elections (Letsholo & Nkwinika 2006: 21; Chikulo & Mbao 2006: 54); and from 27.5% in 1994 to 43% in the National Assembly in 2009. Compared to the United States, both countries, with Rwanda leading, possess a decisive numerical strength of women representation in parliament. As of October 2010, of the 100 members of the U.S. Senate only 17 are women, while the 111th United States Congress consists of 541 elected officials, only 75 are women. Furthermore, in the U.S. federal government, women occupy 44.1% of available positions but only hold a mere 13% of Senior Executive Service (SES) positions (Annual Report on the Federal Workforce, 2009). In this area it is safe to say that Rwanda and South Africa have delivered a much more powerful blow to the ceiling than the United States, with Rwanda's glass ceiling at a more advanced stage of destruction. The glass might be cracked, but sticky floors remain, as persistent gender inequalities can still be traced to other areas in government. Both Rwanda and South Africa have not had a woman occupying the highest office of the presidency. However, South Africa has had two women Vice Presidents, and three women Speakers of the House. Rwanda has a woman as the Speaker of the House, and of course the United States also has a woman as a speaker of the house. While change is evident, it would be premature to declare a total destruction of the glass ceiling with its complimentary opposite sticky floors.

The South Africa ruling party, the African National Congress (ANC), has adopted a voluntary gendered shared governance to negotiate the sticky floors. This is done on the party and not the government level. The results of the 2008 census underscored the need. The 2008 census reveals that while women outnumber men across all salary levels in government at 54.76%, men still hold 67.8% of senior management positions. The census also shows that in the private sector the employment of women in executive positions has slightly improved but leaves a lot to be desired. The other area to measure achievements and challenges is the informal economy sector. The informal economy sector is "the part of economic activity that is neither taxed nor monitored by government, and it is not included in government's Gross National Product (GNP); as opposed to a formal economy" (Phalane 2009: 2). South African women make up 40.4% of the street traders according to the 2007 national estimates (Phalane 2009: 43; Braude 2004: 7; StatsSA 2007: 33).

The informal economy sector also offers a clear indication of persistent inequalities that still demand a consideration of the intersectionality of race and class 16 years after South African indigenous people freed themselves from white oppression. In this sector low wages and lack of benefits locate women at the bottom of the economic ladder. African (black) women make up 50% of people employed in the informal economy sector, domestic sector, and subsistence agriculture. These statistics—11.4% of African women work as domestic workers as compared to 7.7% of Colourdes, .03% of Indians, and 0.2% of white women (Phalane 2009: 45)—remind us that aftermaths of white privilege accorded to white women during apartheid remain part of the discourse and tension to be negotiated. The ANC purposeful 50/50 2005 Get the Balance Right campaign produces visible impact on government gender equity; the informal economic sector and the private sector need more attention, perhaps a gendered campaign that also takes the intersectionality into consideration.

As in South Africa, in Rwanda women also constitute the majority in the informal sector. Inter Press Service News Agency (2010) reports that the Rwandan government aims to register 900,000 informal businesses to increase tax revenue. To that effect they have embarked on registering the informal sector businesses through an agency called Rwanda Development Board. One of its tasks is "the sensitisation and mobilisation of women to invest in doing business" (http://ipsnews .net/africa/nota.asp?idnews=51756).

Rwandese women also form cooperatives that allow them to sell their goods to stores like Macy's in the United States. The famous peace basket has improved how women conduct business and has allowed them to get loans through the Women's Guarantee Fund. Some rural women have complained about the efficacy of the program but that notwithstanding Rwanda has made progress in the informal sector and through legislation it has repealed laws that prevented women from inheriting land, and thus improving economic growth and freedom for Rwanda's women. The new laws also allow them to sign for bank loans.

The discussions show that although gender inequalities persist, the gluey floors/ glass ceiling dichotomy experienced a shift that calls for new definitions of the degree and intensity of formidability. The transformation in Rwandan and South African governments defy the crack allegory because of the visible gaping holes in some places. The application of the metaphor should not obscure areas where gender parity exists as a result of transformation. In countries where women's involvement with knowledge production and construction transcends party affiliation and engagement with the media intensified to provide a gender sensitivity lens, the glass ceiling metaphor demands a definition that highlights the achievements of gender parity in areas where it has occurred. In conclusion, one must acknowledge that the glass ceiling/gluey floor dichotomy works with patriarchal traditions that also need mediation as they contribute to the slow progression of women into senior-level positions. The latter include society's social expectations of women entering traditionally male-dominated positions (Gherardi & Poggio 2001) and internalized sexism where women locate themselves at the bottom of the hierarchy (Conrad et al. 2010). This personal orientation regarding the hierarchical structure may affect the chances of women advancing more so than the glass ceiling. Conrad et al. (2010) state that anything that is perceived as real is real in all of its consequences.

References

Aimable Twahirwa and Kudzai Makombe 2010 *Inter Press Service News Agency*, "Women Win by Formalising Businesses.

Annual Report on the Federal Workforce. 2009. http://www1.eeoc.gov//federal/reports/fsp2009/ index.cfm?renderforprint=1, accessed October 2010.

Berry, P. & Franks, T. 2010. Women in the world of corporate business: Looking at the glass ceiling. *Contemporary Issues in Education Research*, 3(2), 1–9. Retrieved May 19, 2010 from EBSCOhost database.

Braude, W. 2004. *South African Country Analysis, A Naledi Global Poverty Network Workforce Development Study*. South Africa: Naledi.

Chikulo, B., and Mbao, M. 2006. North West: Gender. In *EISA Election Update: South Africa*.

Conrad, P., Carr, P., Knight, S., Renfrew, M. R., Dunn, M. B., and Pololi, L. 2010.

Hierarchy as a Barrier to Advancement for Women in Academic Medicine. *Journal of Women's Health 19*(4): 799–805.

Constitution of the Republic of Rwanda, http://www.rwandahope.com/constitution .pdf, accessed July 2010.

Constitution of the Republic of South Africa Act 200 of 1993, repealed by Constitution of the Republic of South Africa, [No. 108 of 1996], G 17678, 18 December 1996, http://www.info.gov.za/documents/constitution/ index.htm, accessed July 2010.

Gherardi, S., and Poggio, B. 2001. Creating and recreating gender order in organizations. *Journal of World Business 36*: 245–259.

Kandawasvika, Nhundu, R. 2010. Expert Opinion: Strategies and Legislation Adopted in Africa that Call for the 30% Quota, http://www.iknowpolitics.org/en/node/9289.

Letsholo, S., and Nkwinika, T. 2006. Gauteng Gender Issues. In *EISA Election Update: South Africa*.

Milbank, D. 2008, June 8. A Thank-You for 18 million cracks in the glass ceiling. *Washington Post*, p. 1.

Mosupyoe, Boatamo. 1999. *Women's Multicentric Way of Knowing, Being, and Thinking.* New York: McGraw-Hill.

Mosupyoe, Boatamo. 2008. Introduction. In Rita Cameron-Wedding and Y. Boatamo (Eds.), *Institutions, Ideologies, and Individuals,* eds. Dubuque, IA: Kendall/ Hunt.

Phalane, Manthiba, M. 2009. *Gender, Structural Adjustment and Informal Economic Sector Trade in Africa: A Case Study of Women Workers in the Informal Sector of North West Province, South Africa.* PhD dissertation, University of the North.

Statistics South Africa (Stats SA) 2007: 33.

The UN Development Programme (UNDP). 2002. Gender Equality Practice Note. New York: United Nations Development Programme.

Reflection Questions

1. What do these readings reveal about what it means to be a woman and woman of color? (Optional)

2. What are the similarities and differences between each of the readings? (Optional)

3. Some of the authors shared their early childhood memories related to womanhood. Do you have any early childhood memories that brought awareness about what it meant to be a woman or how women are viewed? Please offer a brief explanation using two examples to illustrate your point.

4. What are the social, political, and economic systems that frame the experience and identity of being a woman of color? (Optional)

5. In what ways did the readings extend or enrich your understanding regarding being a woman of color in the United States? Please offer a brief explanation using two examples to illustrate your point.

Identity and Institutions

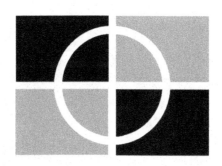

◈ Framing Questions

1. What do you think is the relationship between identity and institutions? (Optional)

2. In what ways, can you apply the theme of identity and institutions? What are the institutions that shape your identity?

3. Are the practices of institutions always visible when they shape our identity? If not, why would some practices be visible and others live out their existence in a covert manner?

4. In your own life, if you participate in more than one institution which institution impacts your life the most? Has this changed over time? (Optional)

Introduction

Brian Baker

This section includes selected readings that address themes and issues that relate to the relationship between *identity* and *institutions.* While this book itself has been divided into five sections, it is necessary to emphasize the fact that any discussion or understanding of *identity* and *institutions* in reality cannot and should not be viewed as being distinct from the "perspectives" and "history" sections, and the readings so far should serve as a basis for understanding the processes and circumstances that influence how racial and ethnic groups come to define and understand their identities, as well as how the identities of "group" form in ways to either reflect or contradict the political, cultural, and social institutions of American society.

What is identity? Does the identity held by a racial-ethnic group remain the same over time or does it change? If identity does change over time, how does identity become transformed? To what extent do larger social, political, and cultural circumstances foster a transformation in racial-ethnic identity? Identity has to do with processes and circumstances that are both internal and external to a specific group, and how a group will define itself on its own terms as well as how it is also defined by another group. A common theme of the readings in this section has to do with how identity as a process is immersed within social institutions, such as law, politics, education, and even the media as popular and public culture. More importantly, many of the readings are rooted somewhere in a perspective relating to *institutional discrimination* as "the denial of opportunities and equal rights to individuals and groups that results from the normal operations of society."[1] In terms of the normal workings of society, racial and ethnic minorities as powerless groups exist in a variety of situations where the dominant society imposes its values and ideas in ways that have powerful and overwhelming effects on a group and how it manages to maintain its identity. At other times, given the structures of society, racial and ethnic minority groups pursue active strategies to assert or reclaim their identity as a process counter to assimilation.

This section begins with "Kill the Indian, Save the Child" by Debra Barker. The purpose of this article is to provide you with an awareness concerning the role of education in the cultural assimilation of American Indian children in the late 19th and early 20th centuries. The American government designed the *Indian boarding school* as an institution to inflict a program of forced assimilation on American Indian children. The fact that this educational program was founded on the ethnocentric philosophical principle *kill the Indian* is very telling due to the fact that Indian children were removed from their families and communities, and once under the control of the boarding school as a total institution, children were stripped of their racial-ethnic identities. In the process of learning how to read and write, Indian children were severely punished for doing anything associated with being Indian. Stories about violence and abuse experienced by American Indians are still remembered and told today, and Barker argues that the main purpose of the Indian boarding school as an institution had little to do with education and more to do with a program of *cultural genocide* implemented toward American Indians by the American government.

In a selection from his book originally published in 1937, Richard Wright provides us with a provocative firsthand account of his life experience with institutionalized racism in "The Ethics of Living Jim Crow." During the process of growing up and becoming increasingly aware of a world rooted in racism, Richard Wright learns how to negotiate his everyday experiences in reference to the rigid rules that elevate whites over blacks. The institutions designed under the Jim Crow era were based on a series of extremely explicit formalized rules, as in the case laws pertaining to where people sat on a bus or where parents sent their children to school based on race, as well as informal rules of protocol, such as eye contact and basic manners. Because all of the rules powerfully reflected race relations and functioned to keep people in their place based on race, Richard Wright speaks to his *Jim Crow education* and strategies of survival.

Extending on the idea of racial formation the social construction of race is "Life on the Color Line," where writer Gregory Williams discusses the ambiguous nature of racial categories. As an individual of mixed racial decent, whose physical appearance in terms of race is actually more white than black, the manner in which Williams perceives his own sense of identity is connected to the institutional arrangements of society and how he is immersed in them. Possessing a sense of identity and affinity with his uncle as African American, he is taken aback when he is described by a white man as "the whitest colored boy" one day. Given the social institutions of the time, Williams is put into one racial category despite the fact that he does not neatly fit into it, and while he is not wholly black, those same institutions will not allow him to be defined as white. This reading calls into question the very idea of race as well as the ambiguous nature of racial categories.

As an extension of gender and identity, Andrea O'Reilly presents an argument on mothering and motherhood in "Ain't That Love?" Given the nature and workings of social institutions, O'Reilly argues that certain strategies related to mothering and motherhood are actually tied to the cultures of racial-ethnic groups as well as the larger system of class stratification. Due to the normal operations of society and normative perceptions of mothering, the strategies and patterns of motherhood for some ethnic minority groups and the working poor are effectively marginalized and delegitimized. O'Reilly makes an argument rooted in a perspective of *antiracism* where other modes and strategies of motherhood are viewed as pathological.

Interestingly, *colors* have been associated with categories of race, and in the history of these associations, the colors themselves have had important connotations. American Indians *are* red; African Americans *are* black; Mexican Americans *are* brown; and, European Americans *are* white. In this color-coded world, Asian Americans *are* yellow. The reality is that while these colors are associated with and inferred over peoples who occupy specific racial-ethnic categories, the reality is the peoples within them are not really those colors. Gary Okihiro plays with these categories and poses the question which is the title of article, "Is Yellow Black or White?" In trying to fit Asian Americans into a category of identities, and in reference to the idea of the *model minority,* Okihiro discusses and relates Asian Americans in reference to African Americans and European Americans. While the dominant perceptions regarding Asian Americans are that they are either "near whites" or "just like blacks," Okihiro makes the argument "yellow" is neither "black" nor "white."

In the last reading of this section, "Imaginary Indians," Brian Baker presents an overview of stereotypes as strategic inventions central to constructing and relegating American Indians to the status of *the other* in American society. The cultural inventions and ideas created in public and popular culture have been so powerful and effectively institutionalized that American Indians continue to experience what they view as obvious forms of institutional discrimination. Yet, given the workings of society's social institutions, which have normalized racism towards American Indians, Americans in general either refuse or possess the inability to acknowledge this fact. Baker discusses many aspects of popular and public culture, including the inventions of Indians as *children* who *roamed* over the land prone to being *wild* and *dancing* savages with an inherent ability to be *warriors.* All of these ideas have been effectively imposed over and associated with Indians, and given a complex system of institutionalized discrimination, not only have American Indians been relegated to the status of mascots in the world of American sports, the very racist notion of *redskin* has been made to appear as not being offensive.

All of the readings in this section are included to force students to critically examine the relationship between institutions and identity, and to understand how identity is a complex process that is central to race and ethnicity. Through time, and in various ways, racial-ethnic groups have had to struggle with identity especially in terms of powerful institutions which have attempted to alter or erase their identity, as in the case of the Indian boarding schools and cultural genocide, or within those institutions in which they are immersed where they either assert or alter some aspect of their identity as in the situations described by Wright in terms of his experience with Jim Crow institutions or the women who attempted to be recognized as Spanish instead of Mexican. All of the readings in the section speak to the importance of identity, and at both the level of the individual and group, people attempt to protect or refashion their identities in terms of how they are immersed in the social, political, and cultural institutions of society.

Notes

[1]Quoted from *Racial and Ethnic Groups* (9th ed.), Richard T. Schaefer, page 77 (Pearson/Prentice Hall, 2004). See chapter titled "Discrimination" (pages 72–102).

[2]Michael Omi and Howard Winant, *Racial Formations in the United States*. New York: Routeledge. 1994.

Kill the Indian, Save the Child: Cultural Genocide and the Boarding School

Debra K. S. Barker

You, who are wise must know that different Nations have different Conceptions of things and you will therefore not take it amiss, if our Ideas of this kind of Education happen not to be the same as yours.

—Canassatego,
Leader of the Six Nations,
Lancaster, Pennsylvania, 1744

If you are familiar with the centrality of the oral tradition within American Indian cultures, you will understand how carefully we listen to the stories of our parents and relatives. As they tell us stories about their lives, they bequeath to us a living text of memory to help us structure our understanding of who we are and how we fit into the larger, more encompassing story of our tribe and culture. You will understand, also, that an integral part of the oral tradition is the voices of those offering testimony from their wisdom and experience.

The voices and testimony that follow speak to the family stories a good number of us have heard from our parents, grandparents, and elders; especially, they recall the story of their unwilling participation in the federal government's effort to re-educate on a massive scale thousands of American Indian children. Of course, education is valuable and empowering. Of course, education—in its most positive aspect—can afford all of us the skills and knowledge to help us realize whatever type of success we can imagine, whether we are talking about a conventional Western education or an education grounded in traditional, tribal ways. The key is that the education be undertaken with respect for the dignity of the students and be designed to empower them, not to diminish them. The process of education that I will be discussing here is one that has emotionally and spiritually devastated generations of American Indian people, setting in motion a concatenation of repercussions, including cultural genocide and generations of family pain.

In recent years documentaries and studies on Indian history only briefly touch on the boarding school system, contextualizing it with a host of other oppressive measures taken by the federal government to destroy the cultures of the people who stood in the way of progress. With one exception, however, studies have relied less on the testimony of Indian witnesses than on the published research of white historians. Indian voices, for the most part, have gone unheard. Given the fact that in the last century Indian education became a national political issue, involving Congress, the War Department, and the Department of the Interior, I wanted to counterpoint Native voices with those of the politicians and policymakers whose philosophical positions and decisions so profoundly affected the lives of our ancestors.

Like so many other experiments and policies implemented by the federal government during the past few hundred years in its attempt to deal with "the Indian problem," the boarding school system ultimately did more harm than good. Understanding the point, Fuchs and Havighurst assert that this federal policy, "rooted in forced assimilation, paradoxically grounded in white humanitarianism . . . left a legacy of unpleasant memories that affect attitudes and policies today" (225). This legacy bequeathed more than simply "unpleasant memories" for generations to come, however. Although it appeared to be the solution the federal government had sought to the Indian problem, it became an instrument that emotionally scarred generations of innocent children, leaving them and their children, as well, victims of institutionalized cultural genocide.

If one were to ask those people who endured, fled, or simply survived boarding school about their memories of their teachers and their education, one might hear some surprising answers. John Lame Deer, a Lakota medicine man, relates in his 1972 autobiography that the Catholic mission boarding school he attended on the Rosebud reservation in South Dakota was run like a prison. My own Aunt Margaret, who attended the same school, loved the bread the students made in the bakery and enjoyed the Saturday night movies, especially *King Kong*. Feeling persecuted by the nuns, however, dreading their unceasing unkindness, she made a successful escape to Aunt Mary Cordier's house in St. Francis, never returning to earn her diploma. My mother, an alumna of 1952, also felt quite bitter about her experiences. She recalled constant hunger, incidents of physical abuse, and traumatic public humiliations for even minor infractions of rules. A particularly vivid memory she shared with me was that of one of the youngest girls at school being punished for wetting her bed. Determined to teach her a lesson, one of the nuns wrapped the child up in her wet sheets and threw her down the outdoor fire escape tunnel. Years later, my mother would still recall the child's terrified screams.

In her 1990 autobiography, *Lakota Woman,* Mary Crow Dog compares children who survived Indian boarding schools to "victims of Nazi concentration camps trying to tell average, middle-class Americans what their experience had been like" (28). As a child, I listened to my mother's stories of her own bleak, joyless childhood. Feeling helpless to comfort her, I could not even comprehend what it must have been like to be without one's family and utterly powerless in the hands of a group of people committed to not only controlling one completely, but also to erasing one's personal and tribal identity. Mary Crow Dog is indeed correct in her analogy.

Extermination by Civilization: Some American History

Indian education in America had been undertaken initially during the colonial period. One of the more successful efforts was that of the Society for Propagation of the Gospel in New England, a London organization which funded the establishment of an Indian college at Harvard during the 1650s. This group also underwrote the expense of books and of Bibles translated into Algonquian, as well as ministers and teachers to convert and educate the "heathen." Yet, as historian Christine Bolt points out, the Native-peoples "were able to educate the whites in the ways of the wilderness without making comparable demands on them and preferred the newcomers' material goods to their culture" (210). Later, in 1701, another English missionary organization, the Society for the Propagation of the Gospel in Foreign Parts, established 170 missions in the colonies (210), inciting a tide of missionization and education that gained momentum as the numbers of Euramericans grew and encroached relentlessly upon Indian land. Even as early as 1744, however, tribal leaders recognized that the curricula and objectives of a Euramerican education were irrelevant to the Indian graduates returning home. Furthermore, colonial educational practices compromised graduates' chances of even surviving in their native environment. Respectfully declining the Euramericans' request to inculcate any more of their young people, the sachems of the Iroquois Confederacy explained:

> Several of our young people were formerly brought up at the colleges of the Northern Provinces; they were instructed in all your science; but when they came back to us, they were bad runners; ignorant of every means of living in the woods; unable to bear either cold or hunger; knew neither how to build a cabin, take a deer, or kill an enemy; spoke our language imperfectly; were therefore neither fit for hunters, warriors, or counselors; they were totally good for nothing. We are, however, not the less obliged by your kind offer, though we decline accepting it; and to show our grateful sense of it, if the gentlemen of Virginia will send us a dozen of their sons, we will take great care of their education, instruct them in all we know, and make men of them. (Qtd. in Franklin 98)

Bolt supports the chiefs' objections and suggests yet another reason why a Euramerican education afforded Indians little benefit in the white world: "Patronized and coerced, required to undertake irksome and sometimes unintelligible tasks and finally offered no secure place in the white world if they wanted, the lot of the small number of educated Indians was an unenviable one" (211).

The federal government and the American public as a whole registered ambivalence when it came to solutions to the Indian problem. In 1792, Benjamin Lincoln, politician and former Revolutionary War general, expressed his hope that Indians would be treated fairly and humanely. Nevertheless, he called for a plan to defoliate the land, thus starving out the "beasts of the forest upon which the unciv-ilized principally depend for support" (qtd. in Pearce 68). The Trail of Tears, which followed as a result of President Andrew Jackson's deliberate enforcement of the unconstitutional Indian Removal Act of 1830, evoked sympathy among many of those who learned of the death march that claimed thousands of Indian lives as they walked the thousand miles between their homes in the Southeast and Oklahoma. Ironically, the tribes immediately involved, the Five Civilized Tribes, were friendly and "civilized" by Euramerican standards. The Cherokee, for instance, had estab-lished their own schools for their children and were printing books and a newspa-per in their own language. According to Fuchs and Havighurst, the Choctaw, another of the "Civilized" tribes, had established "a comprehensive school system of their own with twelve schoolhouses and non-Indian teachers, supported by tribal, missionary, and federal funds" (223).

Yet another factor that inflamed public sentiment regarding "the Indian prob-lem" was the phenomenal popularity of the captivity narrative. This was a genre of popular literature which disseminated to the general public the melodramatic im-age of the Indian as "the consummate villain, the beast who hatcheted fathers, smashed the skulls of infants, and carried off mothers to make them into squaws" (Pearce 58). In accepting this representation, people easily viewed Native people as sub-human and, therefore, undeserving of the same sympathy they might extend to people of their own race. Politicians and philanthropic organizations devoted to the cause of saving this inevitably "vanishing" people would finally conclude that Indians must either conform entirely to the values, religious beliefs, and vocations of white Americans or they would become extinct. As David Adams points out, "The option to maintain a separate cultural identity simply did not exist" (36). Henry Price, the Commissioner of Indian Affairs in 1881, established the position of the federal government in no uncertain terms:

> There is no one who has been a close observer of Indian history and the effect of contact of Indians with civilization, who is not well satisfied that one of two things must eventually take place, to wit, either civilization or extermination of the Indian. Savage and civilized life cannot live and prosper on the same ground. (Qtd. in David Adams 1–2)

In the wake of post-Civil War westward expansion, the growth of the railroad, and Manifest Destiny—the credo buoying up pioneers and entrepreneurs westward in quest of gold and land—the Indian problem became a national issue. Clearly, philanthropists working in behalf of Indian interests would not tolerate all-out ex-termination; as historian Robert M. Utley points out, "public sentiment over-whelmingly favored destruction by civilization rather than by killing" (35).

A federally controlled policy of civilization through education and aggressive missionization appeared to be the most promising avenue of endeavor. After all, ac-cording to one Indian agent's report to Congress, the Brule Sioux, my ancestors, had shown potential to be civilized. Pointing out that, although in the past they had been "splendid animals, having but few human hopes, and much more of the animal than intellectual in their composition," they had begun to live in log cabins (qtd. in David Adams 40). What modern people might not realize, however, was that the Brule Sioux—like other tribes—were given no other choice. The federal government had ordered them to surrender themselves so they could be assigned to reservations.

Indian agents noted in their reports to Congress, however, the apparent futility of civilizing Native children who continued to live within families that persisted in practicing their traditional religion and language. Thomas Morgan, Commissioner of Indian Affairs from 1889 to 1893, warned that if Native children were allowed to grow up within their parents' homes, they would become corrupted by "fathers who are degraded and mothers who are debased." Rather than embrace white Christian values, Indian children would inevitably come to "love the unlovely and to rejoice in the unclean." In Morgan's view, the only way children could "escape the awful doom" of savagery was "for the strong arm of the Nation to reach out, take them in their infancy and place them in its fostering schools . . ." (qtd. in Prucha, *Americanizing the American Indian* 243).

The education of thousands of Indian children became not only a monumental undertaking, but an expensive one, as well. A solution to the problem was offered by Captain Richard Pratt, a former overseer of the Ft. Marion Indian prisoner-of-war camp in Florida and self-styled expert on rehabilitating Indians. His solution was to convert abandoned military forts into boarding schools and then implement an educational program based on a military model. Like others who felt they had special insight into Indian cultures, he thought that Indian people valued neither punctuality nor respect for government authority, clearly hallmarks of "civilized" behavior. The structure and discipline of military training seemed to be the answer to the problem, provided that schools could work with pupils young enough to be successfully indoctrinated.

His first project, the Carlisle Indian School, was established in 1878 in Carlisle, Pennsylvania, and would provide the model upon which federal and mission boarding schools, as well as reservation day schools, based their programs. By 1902, there were ninety reservation boarding schools in existence (David Adams 65), all essentially operating with the ideology espoused by Richard Pratt in an 1881 letter to Senator Henry Dawes. Acknowledging the price the Indian child would have to pay in order to gain the privilege of assimilating into mainstream American life, the Indian would be forced to

> *lose his identity as such, to give up his tribal relations and to be made to feel that he is an American citizen. If I am correct in this supposition, then the sooner all tribal relations are broken up; the sooner the Indian loses all his Indian ways, even his language, the better it will be for him and for the government. . . . (Pratt 266)*

In an address to a Baptist convention in 1883, Pratt elaborated upon the philosophy of education that guided his work with Indian children: "In Indian civilization I am a Baptist, because I believe in immersing the Indians in our civilization and when we get them under holding them there until they are thoroughly soaked" (Pratt 335).

Even as the ideological groundwork was laid for the detribalization of indigenous nations, no one thought to consult Indian people about the prospect of their cultures being eradicated. In fact, policymakers could not understand why Indians were not eager to embrace "civilization." Bolt suggests the paternalistic ethnocentrism that prompted white policymakers to view their culture as clearly superior to any other, observing that whites quite naturally viewed their "home environment" to be more wholesome than those of African Americans and Indians. Because their "home environment" was "held by whites to be the cause of the 'inferiority' of the two races, educators assumed that they would gratefully abandon their values and institutions when prompted to do so by their 'superiors' " (217). Unfortunately, the time soon came when many parents were given no choices regarding their children's education or even their religious training.

Having no ready pupils for his experiment, Pratt embarked on a recruiting mission that took him to my family's reservation in South Dakota, where he persuaded reluctant parents to hand their children over into his care. Pratt, whom historian Robert M. Utley deems wrongheaded but well-meaning, at least gave Indian parents the choice of rejecting his offer. From 1879 to 1918, the Carlisle Industrial School represented a successful model of Indian education that other schools in the United States and Canada would emulate. According to Utley, "During his twenty-four-year tenure the school educated, in all, 4,903 Indian boys and girls from seventy-seven tribes" (xiii).

What made possible the realization of the Carlisle school, as well as that of other federal boarding schools, reservation day schools, and mission schools, was the intrinsic nature of the reservation system itself. Advocates such as Francis Walker, Commissioner of Indian Affairs in 1872, argued that policymakers needed to be hardheaded when it came to "the treatment of savages by a civilized power." As Walker observed, reservations were necessary to bring "the wild beasts [the Indians] to the condition of supplicants for charity" (qtd. in Thomas 60–61). Assigned to reservations, designated wards of the government, and forced into complete economic dependency, Indians were at the mercy of government attempts to control and coerce them into compliancy. Having conquered them militarily, the federal government could then undertake a well-planned campaign to exterminate Indian cultures, resulting in "devastating cultural implications" for the human beings involved (Utley xvii).

In the years to come, Indian agents, serving on reservations as representatives of the federal government, condoned any means necessary to fill boarding schools, lending new significance to the term, "compulsory education." In fact, Congress enacted legislation in 1892 formally empowering government officials to use force when Native parents balked at the prospect of their children being taken from them, herded onto trains, and transported hundreds of miles away to boarding schools. David Adams notes that not until 1904 were officials required to obtain parental consent to remove their children to non-reservation boarding schools (89).

To enforce compliance with the new compulsory attendance law, Indian agents used whatever means necessary. For example, at the Yankton Agency in South Dakota, the home reservation of my great-grandfather, John Cordier, agents withheld rations to reluctant parents (David Adams 202). Consequently, children at the Pine Ridge agency knew that if they played truant, their parents might starve. J. B. Harrison, of the Indian Rights Association, reported: "When a child was absent from school without a good reason, the rations of the whole family were cut off til he returned" (qtd. in David Adams 203).

During the autumn, agents often supervised what were essentially kidnapping raids. Agency police were ordered to hunt down and seize bodily children who were-hiding or had been hidden by their parents. Fletcher J. Cowart, agent of the Mescolero Agency in New Mexico, described in his annual report for 1886 the cries and "lamentations" of Indian mothers and the stark terror of small, uncomprehending children about to be taken away by impatient strangers, perhaps never seeing their parents again (199). After witnessing such a particularly wrenching scene, one agent understated a dimension of Indian culture that he had observed, noting in his annual report to the Commissioner of Indian Affairs, "I have been impressed with the great fondness Indians have for their children. This may be one cause why they do not like to part from them" (qtd. in David Adams 205). A remarkably empathetic agent, W. D. C. Gibson, reported in 1887,

> It is really a pitiful sight to witness their distress and sorrow at times when they come to talk about the children and ask how many 'moons' before they come home, while their appearance indicates that they had passed a restless night, or perhaps not slept any. (163)

In comparison with the tone and tenor of other agents' reports, this agent appears to be one of the few who viewed Indians as human beings, rather than as obstinate and godless savages.

One of the most dramatic accounts of parents' resisting the kidnapping of their children comes from an annual report filed by an agent at the Yakima agency. In his 1885 report, Agent R. H. Milroy explained that he was forced to arrest and lock up Cotiahan, a Yakima tribal leader who refused to reveal where he had hidden his child. Making an example of him to the other band members, Milroy chained the father's leg and "put him to sawing wood, and told him if he refused to work, he would be tied to a tree and whipped" (200).

Had the children and parents been able to foresee the humiliation, anguish, and deprivation that constituted their children's "education" in these boarding schools, they might have resisted the agents' overtures even more aggressively than they did. As he was being led onto the train bound for Carlisle, Luther Standing Bear recalls thinking at the time that he was being taken away to be killed. "I could think of no reason why white people wanted Indian boys and girls except to kill them, and not having the remotest idea of what a school was, I thought we were going East to die," he writes (*Land of the Spotted Eagle* 230–31).

⬦ Barbed Wire and the Bible

In one sense those children would "die," passing from one life to another: stripped naked of the clothes their mothers had made for them, renamed with the names of American Civil War heroes and famous Indian fighters, and re-educated to adopt the "civilized" values of the race that had conquered them. In a quite literal sense, however, hundreds of children died. Neglect, hunger, disease, homesickness—even suicide—left the testimony of acres of little tombstones at boarding schools all over the United States. Luther Standing Bear tells us that "In the graveyard at Carlisle most of the graves are those of little ones" (*Land of the Spotted Eagle* 234). Chief Standing Bear goes on to say that by the third year Carlisle Indian School was in operation, almost one-half of the Plains children had died. Sadly, anxious parents back home might never be notified that their children were ill, much less dead and buried. Too often, rather than deal with the questions and tears of bereft parents, Indian agents would leave telegrams and letters to gather dust on their desks (*My People, the Sioux* 162–63). Ojibwa scholar Basil Johnston recalls a particularly virulent epidemic at his boarding school that claimed "between thirty to fifty boys at a time: chicken pox, measles and mumps . . ." (82). Not surprisingly, John Cook, Indian agent at the Rosebud reservation, warned that given "the large percentage of deaths among the scholars" at Carlisle, parents would not allow their children to be taken away (*Annual Report* 1881, 52).

When military and prison systems induct a new member into their respective institutions, their first step is to dismantle the individual's identity. Boarding school inductions followed similar lines. When Basil Johnston first met his new class-mates at Peter Claver's Residential School, he was struck by the fact that they all had been shaven bald. In a 1900 article she published in *The Atlantic Monthly*, Dakota writer Zitkala-Ša (Gertrude Bonnin) describes being dragged screaming into a chair, where she was tied and her hair cut. (A shocked student once asked me, "Did they do the same thing to white girls who went away to school?") Zitkala-Ša explained to her readers that in Dakota culture, to have one's hair cut meant two things, both momentous. Either one had been publicly exposed as a coward or one was in the throes of grief at the loss of a dear one. Along with the haircut, the children were then subjected to a further humiliation—delousing—a practice that persisted until the 1960s, according to Mary Crow Dog. An alumna of my mother's school, who attended in the late 1960s, Crow Dog reports in the chapter of her autobiography entitled "Civilize Them with a Stick" that the nuns would "dump the children into tubs of alcohol, a sort of rubbing alcohol, 'to get the germs off' " (35).

Stripped of their clothes, which were usually burned, children were issued uniforms that distinguished them as inmates, so to speak. In the last century, girls were given dresses which were close-fitting and to Zitkala-Ša's thinking, immodest. Boys were issued little military uniforms, which they later learned to sew for themselves and their classmates. Betty Eadie writes in her 1992 memoir that after the haircut and delousing, girls were issued "two dresses each, one color for one week, the other for the following week. These uniforms would help identify runaways" (7).

Just as children were stripped of all outward marks of identity, they were threatened, bullied, and beaten to conform to their teachers' expectations of what constituted civilized behavior. When Congress considered enacting legislation banning corporal punishment in boarding schools, Captain Richard Pratt was incensed, insisting that such a ban "would mean the end of Indian schools" (qtd. in Hyde, *A Sioux Chronicle* 57). Children received a spectrum of punishments for speaking their own language, for instance. Marcella La Beau remembers that children caught speaking Lakota would have their mouths washed out with soap before they were punished (qtd. in Josephy 436). A Klamath man recalls that older boys were forced to walk around a tree stump for an hour, carrying a fence rail on their backs (David Adams 125). One of the most dramatic incidents of punishment is recounted by a Blackfoot student, Lone Wolf, who witnessed the event. Angered at hearing a boy speaking his Native language, a white supervisor threw the boy across a room, breaking his collarbone (qtd. in Josephy 435).

Because the constitutional right of freedom of religion was denied to Indians, Indian children were forced to practice the religion of whatever Christian denomination prevailed at their school. Children were also punished for not worshipping with the zeal the teachers demanded of them. Mary Crow Dog's grandmother told her a story that happened when she was very young and caught by the nuns playing jacks instead of praying. As a punishment, she was locked in a tiny cell in an attic, in the dark, and fed only bread and water for a week (Crow Dog 32). Betty Eadie recalls, "My sister Thelma was often beaten by [the nuns] with a little hose and was then forced to thank the Sister who had done it or be beaten again" (9).

Unable to bear the regimentation, spoiled food, bleak living conditions, and utter lack of emotional support, many children ran away. Consequently, one agent at Cheyenne and Arapaho Agency felt compelled to place bars on the dormitory windows and padlock the doors to prevent children from escaping (David Adams 127). Even in this century, according to Betty Eadie, children were locked in their rooms at night (8). Punishment for running away was usually severe. As Mary Crow Dog explains, her grandmother and her fellow inmates were made examples to other children after they were found and returned to school: "The nuns stripped them naked and whipped them. They used a horse buggy whip on my grandmother. Then she was put back into the attic—for two weeks" (32). One particularly incensed school principal hunted down a group of escaped Ute students, drove them back at gunpoint "like wolves," then threatened to hang them (David Adams 219). Luckily, my Aunt Margaret was never caught. Just last summer, while we were at Rosebud, she pointed out to me the route she took to escape what had become an intensely miserable period of her life.

As I look at old photographs of my mother and Aunt Margaret's school grounds, as well as those of other schools, I am struck by two images that recur with frequency: the barbed wire fences and the rows of little children behind those fences, identically dressed, staring warily into the camera. From all the accounts I have read and heard, from the 1880s to the 1960s, the typical boarding school operated on a daily basis like a military prison for children. Basil Johnston and his classmates objected to the absolute lack of privacy, of having every hour of day scheduled: "The boys resented the never ending surveillance that began in the morning and ended only late at night, after they had all fallen asleep; a surveillance that went on day after day, week after week, month after month, year after year" (137). My mother recalls having only two hours of free time a week outdoors—on Sunday afternoon. She said that boys and girls could mingle and talk on the grounds, but everyone had to remain standing for that time; no one was allowed to sit on the ground, unless the person had a telephone book to sit on. (My mother would later laugh about the irrationality of this stipulation: "Where on earth were we going to get telephone books?") Apparently, the nuns were concerned that students might engage in sexual activity on the school grounds in full sight of everyone. "They treated us like we were savages," my mother said.

Children awoke each morning to reveille and fell asleep to taps. Medicine man John Lame Deer remembers falling in for roll call four times each day. He recalls, "We had to stand at attention, or march in step" (25). His grandson Archie Lame Deer, who is my mother's age and perhaps a classmate of hers at St. Francis, tells us that a priest would order the boys to march around the playground holding sticks as if they were rifles. "If we'd had blond hair and blue eyes," he jokes, "you might have taken us for Hitler youth in Nazi Germany" (49).

Even girls were not exempt from the military regimentation. In her book *Oglala Women,* Marla N. Powers presents testimony from a woman who attended Rapid City Indian School, recounting the bugles and bells that dictated when they awakened, ate, worked, had inspections, and slept. The girls marched, too: "We fell into formations. We had officers for each company . . . a captain and a major. . . . We knew every drill there was to be known, right flank, left flank, forward march, and double time" (111). Thomson Highway adds that he knew of girls getting their heads shaved for "minor infractions" of rules (*War against the Indians*).

The education and training most children received was equally regimented, culturally irrelevant, and ultimately a waste of time, according to a number of disillusioned graduates. Understanding nothing about Indian people, teachers assumed that the children were unfeeling and impervious to humiliation. Charles Eastman, who earned his M.D. at Boston College, writes in his autobiography *From the Deep Woods to Civilization* of the humiliation of class recitation at Dr. Alfred Riggs Santee Training School: "For a whole week we youthful warriors were held up and harassed with words of three letters . . . rat, cat, and so forth . . . until not a semblance of our native dignity and self-respect was left" (46). To make the learning process even more fraught with anxiety, students reciting their lessons were asked to do so "taking the position of a soldier at attention" (Pratt 244).

Christine Bolt notes that in both white and Indian cultures children learned by memorization. However, the rote learning by which Indian children were inculcated with the religion and values of the dominant culture must have been not only tortuous, but bewildering as well. Bolt explains,

> *The Indian mission children were asked to memorize hymns and passages from Scripture which they frequently did not understand and which contradicted all their own learned traditions. Incomprehension was compounded by the fact that pupils of every degree of attainment were at first taught together. . . . (213)*

The ninth-grade students at Pierre Indian School in South Dakota must certainly have puzzled over the usefulness and relevance of *Julius Caesar* and *Lady of the Lake* to the lives they would lead as they adapted to their dramatically changing world. Indeed, how could Shakespeare help a Cheyenne person negotiate the cultural transition from tribal values to those of the American West? No doubt Paiute children in Nevada prior to 1931 were equally mystified by the following lines they were forced to memorize and recite:

> *What do we plant*
> *When we plant the tree?*
> *We plant the ship*
> *That sails the sea. . . . (Qtd. in Szasz 33)*

My aunt Margaret never did have an occasion to use the Latin she was taught after she learned to speak English, although she did point out that Mass and prayers were in Latin, hence the necessity of the hours spent memorizing all those Latin verb conjugations. Studying secretarial skills as a part of her curriculum, my mother at least received an education that would theoretically prepare her to survive and earn economic independence in the white world.

Going on to earn an Associate's Degree from Haskell Institute, a former boarding school which is today a university, my mother managed to surpass the expectations non-Indian teachers and administrators usually had of Indian students. From the inception of the boarding school idea, however, federal officials generally held very low expectations of what Indian students might achieve professionally after they completed school. Secretary of the Interior Henry Teller had articulated a philosophy of education that had been adopted not only by Richard Pratt at Carlisle, but also by boarding schools everywhere up until the middle of this century. Within the curriculum of these schools, Teller declared, "more attention should be paid to teaching them to labor than to read" (qtd. in Prucha, *American Indian Policy* 271).

Students were expected to become laborers or domestic servants. In fact, policymakers envisioned Native people leaving their reservations to join the ranks of what was viewed at that time as a permanent underclass in white society. Captain Pratt's vision was that eventually tribal people would be swallowed up into the melting pot of immigrants that had become mainstream Euramerican culture. What he probably did not foresee, however, was that his philosophy would defeat the aspirations of some Indian people to use their education to secure more fulfilling professions than those in manual labor or domestic service.

Chief Standing Bear's situation is a case in point. Like so many others at the mercy of a paternalistic boarding school, he had little say in determining his own future. Standing Bear had wanted to spend his entire day in the classroom getting an education, rather than devote half of it working in the tinshop learning a profession that would be useless back at Rosebud. Eventually, after pointing out that the government was supplying his reservation with an abundance of tinware, he asked Captain Pratt if he could learn carpentry instead. Pratt refused his request. Standing Bear writes, "What worried me was the thought that I might not be able to work at the trade after I returned home. But Captain Pratt could not understand why I wanted to make a change, and so the matter was dropped" (*My People, the Sioux* 176). In this century, white educators' expectations of their Indian students clearly have not changed. In his 1992 autobiography, *The Gift of Power,* medicine man Archie Lame Deer states that his boarding school teachers held the opinion that "we Indians were only good at menial jobs. They did not prepare us to become teachers, lawyers, or doctors" (49).

According to the testimony of Native people and historians, boarding school students were essentially trained, then treated as indentured servants, not as scholars—a fact that students' parents were unaware of. Making the best of a difficult situation, parents such as those of Luther Standing Bear and Stay at Home Spotted Tail hoped that their sons' white education would afford them both professions and the knowledge they would need to protect and defend both personal and tribal interests. Unfortunately, this was not the case for Chief Spotted Tail's son. Visiting his son at Carlisle in 1880, Spotted Tail talked with the Lakota boys from Rosebud, learning that they were all generally "miserable and homesick" (Hyde 322). However, when he discovered that his son was working at harness making, rather than learning to read, write, and speak English, "the thunder began to roll," George Hyde explains, noting that ordinarily Spotted Tail's son would be back home at Rosebud, "training to become a chief," not a farmhand (322).

Although the students were there ostensibly to earn an education, child labor was vitally important to support the expense of maintaining the boarding school. Indeed, one-half of the pupils' day was devoted to the maintenance and upkeep of their prison, including farming, cooking, sewing their own uniforms, and making their own shoes. In his memoir, *Battlefield and Classroom,* Richard Pratt explains that even children too young to be put to work had to ". . . witness the productions of the older ones in harness making, tin ware, boots and shoes, clothing, blacksmith and wagon making . . ." (259). The prized jobs at his school were those in the kitchen, recalls Basil Johnston, because there students could eat the leftover food from their teachers' plates and at least satisfy their incessant hunger (49). Johnston's recollection of hunger echoes the testimony of students over a range of residential institutions. Not until the publication of the Meriam Report in 1928 and the subsequent investigations of the Red Cross was it widely known that children had to survive on "a diet that was the equivalent of slow starvation" (Szasz 19). The Meriam Report criticized the boarding school system on another charge, as well—

the failure to demonstrate the practices they taught. Girls in home economics classes were lectured on the elements of proper nutrition and meal planning; yet, the schools themselves rarely provided milk, fruit, or vegetables in the children's diets (351).

A cruel irony, of course, was that graduates returning to the reservation might not find an opportunity to use the education or vocational training they received in these institutions. Robert Utley points out that "with the spoils system ascendant, the few government jobs available rarely went to Indians, and few Carlisle graduates found any occupation to utilize their newly learned talents" (xvi). As in the case of Standing Bear, who found no use for his training as a tinsmith, other students, such as those trained as hatmakers and tailors, found few opportunities to become independent and self-supporting once they returned home.

On the other hand, Indian graduates were not always successful in finding a place in the white world, either. My grandfather, Levi Prue, who graduated from Haskell Institute with a degree in accounting, could find only occasional, short-term employment at home—or within a Bureau of Indian Affairs office or other Indian agencies. After finding that white employers in Omaha were not anxious to hire an educated Indian, my grandfather, who loved to read and disliked the mind-numbing tedium of sheer manual labor, went to work in a cold storage company, then a sheet metal plant, before finally trading in his dreams for a bottle. On the advice of Uncle Moses Red Owl, who feared that she would not find a BIA (Bureau of Indian Affairs) job on the reservation, my mother decided not to return to Rosebud to look for work. Instead, she moved to a succession of white towns looking for some kind of meaningful employment. Unfortunately, she never had the opportunity to exercise her college degree or her shorthand skills (taking dictation at 120 words a minute). During the 1950s, racism against Indians had not abated much since my grandfather's day, so my mother also resigned herself to factory work.

At least my mother and grandfather did not have to face the type of racial discrimination that prevented them from securing a residence in the white world. In *My People, the Sioux,* Luther Standing Bear writes of his discouragement at facing racial discrimination in Philadelphia, where he wanted to work as a clerk in Wanamaker's Store. He explains, "I was to prove to all people that the Indians could learn and work as well as the white people . . ." (179). Unfortunately, he was denied the opportunity to prove his equality—white landlords refused to rent a room to him. Chief Standing Bear explains, "When I would find something that seemed suitable, and the people discovered my nationality, they would look at me in a surprised sort of way, and say that they had no place for an Indian boy" (189).

Sadly, many graduates returned to the reservation finding they did not belong there, either. A white education was an acquisition of dubious value for young people returning home expecting to reintegrate into their communities, earn a living, and move on with their lives. As Robert Utley points out, "The result was that they either existed in a shadow world neither Indian nor white, with acceptance denied by both worlds, or they cast off the veneer of Carlisle and again became Indians" (xvi). Commenting upon this predicament from a Native perspective, John Lame Deer writes, "When we enter the school, we at least know that we are Indians. We come out half red and half white, not knowing what we are" (27). For Sun Elk, a Taos Pueblo graduate, his homecoming would be a heartbreaking one. Soon after his arrival, tribal elders came to his parents' home, and, completely ignoring him, made the following pronouncement to his father:

> *Your son who calls himself Rafael has lived with the white men. He has been far away. . . . He has not . . . learned the things that Indian boys should learn. He has no hair. . . . He cannot even speak our language. He is not one of us. (Qtd. in Josephy 436)*

Alienated from home and family, culturally as well as emotionally, some Indian people have struggled with their ambivalence about claiming a relation to the people of whom they had been taught to be ashamed. Inculcated with white values and taught the Euramerican version of American history, Pequot minister William Apess, for instance, before he went on to work as an Indian rights activist, grew up "terrified" of Indians. LaVonne Brown Ruoff explains that "whites had filled him with stereotypical stories about Indian cruelty but never told him how cruelly they treated Indians" (1781). Albert White Hat, now a professor at Sinte Glеśka University and spiritual leader at Rosebud, recalls having grown so alienated from his cultural roots that when he and his friends would watch western movies, "we cheered for the cavalry" (Beasley 41).

The emotional cost of the boarding school experience upon generations of Native families has been incalculable. When I was a child I would watch my mother brood for hours, chain smoking over memories that intruded insistently upon the present. Passed around from relative to relative, from orphanage to boarding school, she—like so many other Indian children—had to bear the consequences of her parents' shattered lives. Her life story and those of other boarding school survivors remind me of Basil Johnston's description of the youngest children at his boarding school, "the babies":

> *They were a sad lot, this little crowd of babies; they seldom laughed or smiled and often cried and whimpered during the day and at night. . . . [T]hey were hunched in their wretchedness and misery in a corner of the recreation hall, their outsized boots dangling several inches above the asphalt floor. And though Paul Migwanabe and Joe Thompson and other carvers made toys for them, the babies didn't play with their cars and boats; they just held on to them, hugged them and took them to bed at night, for that was all they had in the world when the lights went out, and they dared not let it go. (60)*

Given such testimony, we must ask: What was to be the destiny of children like these? What were the experiences of children who grew up never feeling the nurturing of parents, who emerged from an institution without knowing how to function within a family, without possessing a sense of belonging to a particular group, of sharing a particular history, or of feeling pride in their ancestors? Whom were these individuals allowed to feel proud of? The Pilgrims? Christopher Columbus? These are the queries of the academic researcher, of course. Yet, they are also questions posed with bitterness by those who recognize that their own cultural heroes and tribal identities have been erased out of history by the Colonizers. We have been spiritually dispossessed with that erasure, bereft of our language and our pride in being Indian, diminished by the loss of the cultural knowledge that constitutes the psychic infrastructure of a people. My ancestors made this point more emphatically: A people without a history is like wind across the buffalo grass. A history, after all, is a narrative, a story. And the boarding school robbed generations of Indian children of the stories of their families and tribes, stories that would have otherwise empowered them with knowledge, wisdom, survival skills, and a spiritual foundation.

Aside from being an instrument of cultural genocide, another insidious effect of the boarding school system has been its effectiveness in eroding the foundation of tribal culture, the family. Since the inception of the boarding school system in the last century up to the present, Indian families all over the United States have struggled and are still struggling with healing the pain of generations of family dysfunction. The documentaries, *The War Against the Indians* and *The Native Americans,* both present testimony from Native people explaining that the years of institutionalizing did not foster in children the nurturing skills they would need to be parents. One of the producers of another well-known documentary on boarding schools, *In the White Man's Image,* Matthew "Sitting Bear" Jones, explains how the boarding schools have perpetuated generations of dysfunction within families: "They didn't teach us to be parents at the schools and we didn't have parents to teach us to be parents. When we had children we didn't know how to raise them" ("Boarding Schools" B2).

Healing Our Hoop

My approach to the subject of the boarding school system, as I have noted, grows out of my desire that the voices of adult children survivors be heard, and that the audiences which listen will understand how this important dimension of Indian history fits into the larger context of factors that have played a role in the attempted cultural genocide of the first Americans. For Indian audiences, I hope that this testimony will bring the kind of healing shock I experienced after reading an interview with Carol Anne Heart Looking Horse in Sandy Johnson's *The Book of Elders.* Her story and those of others have helped me to construct the narrative of my family, as I hope they will for other people.

In her interview, Looking Horse discusses the "historical grief" we bear and its relation to not only the attempted eradication of our culture, but also the trauma our parents experienced as they were forced through this process. As tribal nations regain control over the education of their own children, she observes, Indian teachers have been able to teach our young people about the relationship between this history and our parents' personal experience. In doing so, we are able to help young people to make strides in recovering their culture, learning a history of America that does not demonize their ancestors, and regaining pride in tribal heritage.

An important key to this recovery lies in the tribal college. In sites such as Sinte Gleśka University on the Rosebud reservation, for instance, students have the opportunity to learn from Indian professors and to complete a core curriculum of Lakota studies that includes language, history, and traditional knowledge. At the same time, students can remain in proximity to their families and communities, sustaining the family bonds that have been so cherished within traditional families. A major challenge that tribal colleges all over the United States face, however, is financial. As always, the destinies of Native people have been subject to the seemingly capricious decisions of the federal government. For instance, although Congress had at one time authorized financial support of amounts up to $6,000 for each student attending college, the Reagan administration made cuts in allocations. By 1989 a student might receive only $1,900 of the funds Congress had originally allocated (Wright and Tierney 17). Even now, Congress continues to slash appropriations once promised to Indian tribes—funds which would enable Native people to pursue their dreams of economic independence and self-determination. Thankfully, a handful of tribal communities—not all—are experiencing an economic and cultural renaissance, due to gaming revenues that enable tribes to build new schools and hire qualified teachers to help bring the next generation proudly into the coming century. And, they will be proud, for they will have the choices our parents and grandparents were denied: to walk in either world, in the tracks and in the image not of the Colonizers, but of the ancestors.

Works Cited

Adams, David Wallace. *The Federal Indian Boarding School: A Study of Environment and Response, 1879–1918*. Diss. Indiana University, 1975.

Adams, Evelyn C. *American Indian Education, Government Schools and Economic Progress*. New York: King's Crown Press, 1941.

Annual Report of the Secretary of the Interior. Washington: GPO, 1879–1895.

Beasley, Conger, Jr. "The Return of the Lakota: An Indian People Thrive 500 Years After Columbus." *The Environmental Magazine* Sept.–Oct. 1992: 38+.

"Boarding Schools Likened to Concentration Camps." *Indian Country Today (Lakota Times)* 5 Oct. 1994: B2.

Bolt, Christine. *American Indian Policy and American Reform: Case Studies of the Campaign to Assimilate the American Indians*. London: Allen & Unwin, 1987.

Cowart, Fletcher J. "Reports of Agents in New Mexico." Secretary of the Interior. *Annual Report of the Secretary of the Interior.* Washington: GPO, 1886.

Crow Dog, Mary, and Richard Erdoes. *Lakota Woman.* New York: Harper Perennial, 1990.

Eadie, Betty J. *Embraced by the Light.* New York: Bantam Books, 1992.

Eastman, Charles. *From the Deep Woods to Civilization: Chapters in the Autobiography of an Indian.* 1916. Lincoln: U of Nebraska P, 1977.

Franklin, Benjamin. "Remarks Concerning the Savages of North America." *The Writings of Benjamin Franklin.* Ed. Albert Henry Smyth. Vol. 10. New York: Macmillan, 1907. 10 vols.

Fuchs, Estelle, and Robert J. Havighurst. *To Live on This Earth: American Indian Education.* New York: Doubleday, 1972.

Gibson, W. D. C. "Reports of Agents in Nevada." Secretary of the Interior. *Annual Report of the Secretary of the Interior.* Washington: GPO, 1887.

Hyde, George E. *A Sioux Chronicle.* Norman: U of Oklahoma P, 1956.

———. *Spotted Tail's Folk: A History of the Brule Sioux.* Norman: U of Oklahoma P, 1961.

In the White Man's Image. Prod. Christine Lesiak and Matthew Jones. Videocassette. PBS Video. 1991.

Indian Removal Act of 1830.28 May 1830, c. 148, 4 stat. 411.

Johnson, Sandy. *The Book of Elders: The Life Stories of Great American Indians as Told to Sandy Johnson.* San Francisco: Harper Collins, 1994.

Johnston, Basil H. *Indian School Days.* Norman: U of Oklahoma P, 1988.

Josephy, Alvin M. *500 Nations: An Illustrated History of North American Indians.* New York: Alfred A. Knopf, 1994.

King Kong. Dir. Ernest B. Schoedsack. Perf. Fay Wray, Bruce Cabot, Robert Armstrong. Universal, 1933.

Lame Deer, Archie, and Richard Erdoes. *The Gift of Power: The Life and Teachings of a Lakota Medicine Man.* Santa Fe: Bear & Company, 1992.

Lame Deer, John (Fire), and Richard Erdoes. *Lame Deer, Seeker of Visions.* New York: Pocket Books, 1972.

Meriam, Lewis, et al. *The Problem of Indian Administration.* 1928. Introd. Frank C. Miller. New York: Johnson Reprint Corporation, 1971.

Milroy, R. H. "Reports of Agents in Washington Territory." Secretary of the Interior. *Annual Report of the Secretary of the Interior.* Washington: GPO, 1885.

The Native Americans. Narr. Joy Harjo. 3 episodes. TBS Productions. 1992.

Pearce, Roy Harvey. *The Savages of America: A Study of the Indian and the Idea of Civilization.* Baltimore: Johns Hopkins UP, 1953.

Powers, Marla N. *Oglala Women: Myth, Ritual, and Reality.* Chicago: U of Chicago P, 1986.

Pratt, Richard Henry. *Battlefield and Classroom: Four Decades with the American Indian, 1867–1904.* Ed. Robert M. Utley. Lincoln: U of Nebraska P, 1964.

Prucha, Francis Paul. *American Indian Policy in Crisis: Christian Reformers and the Indian, 1865–1900*. Norman: U of Oklahoma P, 1976.

———, ed. *Americanizing the American Indians: Writings by the "Friends of the Indian," 1800–1900*. Cambridge: Harvard UP, 1973.

Ruoff, A. LaVonne Brown. "William Apess." *The Health Anthology of American Literature*. Ed. Paul Lauter. Vol. 1, 2nd ed. Lexington, MA: D. C. Heath, 1994. 1780–81.

Standing Bear, Luther. *Land of the Spotted Eagle*. Lincoln: U of Nebraska P, 1933.

———. *My People, the Sioux*. Lincoln: U of Nebraska P, 1975.

Szasz, Margaret Connell. *Education and the American Indian: The Road to Self-Determination Since 1928*. 2nd ed. Albuquerque: U of New Mexico P, 1974.

Thomas, Robert K. "On an Indian Reservation: How Colonialism Works." *The Way: An Anthology of American Indian Literature*. Eds. Shirley Hill Witt and Stan Steiner. New York: Alfred A. Knopf, 1972. 60–68.

Utley, Robert M. Introduction. *Battlefield and Classroom: Four Decades with the American Indian, 1867–1904*. Ed. Robert M. Utley. Lincoln: U of Nebraska P, 1964. ix–xix.

The War against the Indians. Narr. Harry Rasky. Canada Broadcasting Corporation. 1992.

Witt, Shirley Hill, and Stan Steiner, eds. *The Way: An Anthology of American Indian Literature*. New York: Alfred A. Knopf, 1972.

Wright, Bobby, and William G. Tierney. "American Indians in Higher Education." *Change*. March–April 1991: 11–18.

Zitkala-Ša. (Gertrude Bonnin). "The School Days of an Indian Girl." *Atlantic Monthly* Feb. 1900: 185–94. Rpt. in *American Indian Stories*. Washington: Hayworth Publishing House, 1921. 52–56.

The Ethics of Living Jim Crow: An Autobiographical Sketch

Richard Wright

 I

My first lesson in how to live as a Negro came when I was quite small. We were living in Arkansas. Our house stood behind the railroad tracks. Its skimpy yard was paved with black cinders. Nothing green ever grew in that yard. The only touch of green we could see was far away, beyond the tracks, over where the white folks lived. But cinders were good enough for me and I never missed the green growing things. And anyhow cinders were fine weapons. You could always have a nice hot war with huge black cinders. All you had to do was crouch behind the brick pillars of a house with your hands full of gritty ammunition. And the first woolly black head you saw pop out from behind another row of pillars was your target. You tried your very best to knock it off. It was great fun.

I never fully realized the appalling disadvantages of a cinder environment till one day the gang to which I belonged found itself engaged in a war with the white boys who lived beyond the tracks. As usual we laid down our cinder barrage, thinking that this would wipe the white boys out. But they replied with a steady bombardment of broken bottles. We doubled our cinder barrage, but they hid behind trees, hedges, and the sloping embankments of their lawns. Having no such fortifications, we retreated to the brick pillars of our homes. During the retreat a broken milk bottle caught me behind the ear, opening a deep gash which bled profusely. The sight of blood pouring over my face completely demoralized our ranks. My fellow-combatants left me standing paralyzed in the center of the yard, and scurried for their homes. A kind neighbor saw me and rushed me to a doctor, who took three stitches in my neck.

I sat brooding on my front steps, nursing my wound and waiting for my mother to come from work. I felt that a grave injustice had been done me. It was all right to throw cinders. The greatest harm a cinder could do was leave a bruise. But broken bottles were dangerous; they left you cut, bleeding, and helpless.

When night fell, my mother came from the white folks' kitchen. I raced down the street to meet her. I could just feel in my bones that she would understand. I knew she would tell me exactly what to do next time. I grabbed her hand and babbled out the whole story. She examined my wound, then slapped me.

"How come yuh didn't hide?" she asked me. "How come yuh awways fightin'?"

I was outraged, and bawled. Between sobs I told her that I didn't have any trees or hedges to hide behind. There wasn't a thing I could have used as a trench. And you couldn't throw very far when you were hiding behind the brick pillars of a house. She grabbed a barrel stave, dragged me home, stripped me naked, and beat me till I had a fever of one hundred and two. She would smack my rump with the stave, and, while the skin was still smarting, impart to me gems of Jim Crow wisdom. I was never to throw cinders any more. I was never to fight any more wars. I was never, never, under any conditions, to fight *white* folks again. And they were absolutely right in clouting me with the broken milk bottle. Didn't I know she was working hard every day in the hot kitchens of the white folks to make money to take care of me? When was I ever going to learn to be a good boy? She couldn't be bothered with my fights. She finished by telling me that I ought to be thankful to God as long as I lived that they didn't kill me.

All that night I was delirious and could not sleep. Each time I closed my eyes I saw monstrous white faces suspended from the ceiling, leering at me.

From that time on, the charm of my cinder yard was gone. The green trees, the trimmed hedges, the cropped lawns grew very meaningful, became a symbol. Even today when I think of white folks, the hard, sharp outlines of white houses surrounded by trees, lawns, and hedges are present somewhere in the background of my mind. Through the years they grew into an overreaching symbol of fear.

It was a long time before I came in close contact with white folks again. We moved from Arkansas to Mississippi. Here we had the good fortune not to live behind the railroad tracks, or close to white neighborhoods. We lived in the very heart of the local Black Belt. There were black churches and black preachers; there were black schools and black teachers; black groceries and black clerks. In fact, everything was so solidly black that for a long time I did not even think of white folks, save in remote and vague terms. But this could not last forever. As one grows older one eats more. One's clothing costs more. When I finished grammar school I had to go to work. My mother could no longer feed and clothe me on her cooking job.

There is but one place where a black boy who knows no trade can get a job, and that's where the houses and faces are white, where the trees, lawns, and hedges are green. My first job was with an optical company in Jackson, Mississippi. The morning I applied I stood straight and neat before the boss, answering all his questions with sharp yessirs and nosirs. I was very careful to pronounce my *sirs* distinctly, in order that he might know that I was polite, that I knew where I was, and that I knew he was a *white* man. I wanted that job badly.

He looked me over as though he were examining a prize poodle. He questioned me closely about my schooling, being particularly insistent about how much mathematics I had had. He seemed very pleased when I told him I had had two years of algebra.

"Boy, how would you like to try to learn something around here?" he asked me.

"I'd like it fine, sir," I said, happy. I had visions of "working my way up." Even Negroes have those visions.

"All right," he said. "Come on."

I followed him to the small factory.

"Pease," he said to a white man of about thirty-five, "this is Richard. He's going to work for us."

Pease looked at me and nodded.

I was then taken to a white boy of about seventeen.

"Morrie, this is Richard, who's going to work for us."

"Whut yuh sayin' there, boy!" Morrie boomed at me.

"Fine!" I answered.

The boss instructed these two to help me, teach me, give me jobs to do, and let me learn what I could in my spare time.

My wages were five dollars a week.

I worked hard, trying to please. For the first month I got along O. K. Both Pease and Morrie seemed to like me. But one thing was missing. And I kept thinking about it. I was not learning anything and nobody was volunteering to help me. Thinking they had forgotten that I was to learn something about the mechanics of grinding lenses, I asked Morrie one day to tell me about the work. He grew red.

"Whut yuh tryin' t' do, nigger, get smart?" he asked.

"Naw; I ain' tryin' t' git smart," I said.

"Well, don't, if yuh know whut's good for yuh!"

I was puzzled. Maybe he just doesn't want to help me, I thought. I went to Pease.

"Say, are yuh crazy, you black bastard?" Pease asked me, his gray eyes growing hard.

I spoke out, reminding him that the boss had said I was to be given a chance to learn something.

"Nigger, you think you're *white,* don't you?"

"Naw, sir!"

"Well, you're acting mighty like it!"

"But, Mr. Pease, the boss said. . . ."

Pease shook his fist in my face.

"This is a *white* man's work around here, and you better watch yourself!"

From then on they changed toward me. They said good-morning no more. When I was just a bit slow in performing some duty, I was called a lazy black son-of-a-bitch.

Once I thought of reporting all this to the boss. But the mere idea of what would happen to me if Pease and Morrie should learn that I had "snitched" stopped me. And after all the boss was a white man, too. What was the use?

The climax came at noon one summer day. Pease called me to his work-bench. To get to him I had to go between two narrow benches and stand with my back against a wall.

"Yes, sir," I said.

"Richard, I want to ask you something," Pease began pleasantly, not looking up from his work.

"Yes, sir," I said again.

Morrie came over, blocking the narrow passage between the benches. He folded his arms, staring at me solemnly.

I looked from one to the other, sensing that something was coming.

"Yes, sir," I said for the third time.

Pease looked up and spoke very slowly.

"Richard, *Mr.* Morrie here tells me you called me *Pease.*"

I stiffened. A void seemed to open up in me. I knew this was the show-down.

He meant that I had failed to call him Mr. Pease. I looked at Morrie. He was gripping a steel bar in his hands. I opened my mouth to speak, to protest, to assure Pease that I had never called him simply *Pease,* and that I had never had any intentions of doing so, when Morrie grabbed me by the collar, ramming my head against the wall.

"Now, be careful, nigger!" snarled Morrie, baring his teeth. "*I* heard yuh call 'im *Pease!* 'N' if yuh say yuh didn't, yuh're callin' me a *lie,* see?" He waved the steel bar threateningly.

If I had said: No, sir Mr. Pease, I never called you *Pease,* I would have been automatically calling Morrie a liar. And if I had said: Yes, sir, Mr. Pease, I called you *Pease,* I would have been pleading guilty to having uttered the worst insult that a Negro can utter to a southern white man. I stood hesitating, trying to frame a neutral reply.

"Richard, I asked you a question!" said Pease. Anger was creeping into his voice.

"I don't remember calling you *Pease,* Mr. Pease," I said cautiously. "And if I did, I sure didn't mean. . . ."

"You black son-of-a-bitch! You called me *Pease,* then!" he spat, slapping me till I bent sideways over a bench. Morrie was on top of me, demanding:

"Didn't yuh call 'im *Pease?* If yuh say yuh didn't, I'll rip yo' gut string loose with this bar, yuh black granny dodger! Yuh can't call a white man a lie 'n' git erway with it, you black son-of-a-bitch!"

I wilted. I begged them not to bother me. I knew what they wanted. They wanted me to leave.

"I'll leave," I promised. "I'll leave right *now.*"

They gave me a minute to get out of the factory. I was warned not to show up again, or tell the boss.

I went.

When I told the folks at home what had happened, they called me a fool. They told me that I must never again attempt to exceed my boundaries. When you are working for white folks, they said, you got to "stay in your place" if you want to keep working.

II

My Jim Crow education continued on my next job, which was portering in a clothing store. One morning, while polishing brass out front, the boss and his twenty-year-old son got out of their car and half dragged and half kicked a Negro woman into the store. A policeman standing at the corner looked on, twirling his night-stick. I watched out of the corner of my eye, never slackening the strokes of my chamois upon the brass. After a few minutes, I heard shrill screams coming from the rear of the store. Later the woman stumbled out, bleeding, crying, and holding her stomach. When she reached the end of the block, the policeman grabbed her and accused her of being drunk. Silently, I watched him throw her into a patrol wagon.

When I went to the rear of the store, the boss and his son were washing their hands at the sink. They were chuckling. The floor was bloody and strewn with wisps of hair and clothing. No doubt I must have appeared pretty shocked, for the boss slapped me reassuringly on the back.

"Boy, that's what we do to niggers when they don't want to pay their bills," he said, laughing.

His son looked at me and grinned.

"Here, hava cigarette," he said.

Not knowing what to do, I took it. He lit his and held the match for me. This was a gesture of kindness, indicating that even if they had beaten the poor old woman, they would not beat me if I knew enough to keep my mouth shut.

"Yes, sir," I said, and asked no questions.

After they had gone, I sat on the edge of a packing box and stared at the bloody floor till the cigarette went out.

That day at noon, while eating in a hamburger joint, I told my fellow Negro porters what had happened. No one seemed surprised. One fellow, after swallowing a huge bite, turned to me and asked:

"Huh! Is tha' all they did t' her?"

"Yeah. Wasn't tha' enough?" I asked.

"Shucks! Man, she's a lucky bitch!" he said, burying his lips deep into a juicy hamburger. "Hell, it's a wonder they didn't lay her when they got through."

III

I was learning fast, but not quite fast enough. One day, while I was delivering packages in the suburbs, my bicycle tire was punctured. I walked along the hot, dusty road, sweating and leading my bicycle by the handle-bars.

A car slowed at my side.

"What's the matter, boy?" a white man called.

I told him my bicycle was broken and I was walking back to town.

"That's too bad," he said, "Hop on the running board."

He stopped the car. I clutched hard at my bicycle with one hand and clung to the side of the car with the other.

"All set?"

"Yes, sir," I answered. The car started.

It was full of young white men. They were drinking. I watched the flask pass from mouth to mouth.

"Wanna drink, boy?" one asked.

I laughed as the wind whipped my face. Instinctively obeying the freshly planted precepts of my mother, I said:

"Oh, no!"

The words were hardly out of my mouth before I felt something hard and cold smash me between the eyes. It was an empty whisky bottle. I saw stars, and fell backwards from the speeding car into the dust of the road, my feet becoming entangled in the steel spokes of my bicycle. The white men piled out and stood over me.

"Nigger, ain' yuh learned no better sense'n tha' yet?" asked the man who hit me. "Ain't yuh learned t' say *sir* t' a white man yet?"

Dazed, I pulled to my feet. My elbows and legs were bleeding. Fists doubled, the white man advanced, kicking my bicycle out of the way.

"Aw, leave the bastard alone. He's got enough," said one.

They stood looking at me. I rubbed my shins, trying to stop the flow of blood. No doubt they felt a sort of contemptuous pity, for one asked:

"Yuh wanna ride t' town now, nigger? Yuh reckon yuh know enough t' ride now?"

"I wanna walk," I said, simply.

Maybe it sounded funny. They laughed.

"Well, walk, yuh black son-of-a-bitch!"

When they left they comforted me with:

"Nigger, yuh sho better be damn glad it wuz us yuh talked t' tha' way. Yuh're a lucky bastard, 'cause if yuh'd said tha' t' somebody else, yuh might've been a dead nigger now."

IV

Negroes who have lived South know the dread of being caught alone upon the streets in white neighborhoods after the sun has set. In such a simple situation as this the plight of the Negro in America is graphically symbolized. While white strangers may be in these neighborhoods trying to get home, they can pass unmolested. But the color of a Negro's skin makes him easily recognizable, makes him suspect, converts him into a defenseless target.

Late one Saturday night I made some deliveries in a white neighborhood. I was pedaling my bicycle back to the store as fast as I could, when a police car, swerving toward me, jammed me into the curbing.

"Get down and put up your hands!" the policemen ordered.

I did. They climbed out of the car, guns drawn, faces set, and advanced slowly.

"Keep still!" they ordered.

I reached my hands higher. They searched my pockets and packages. They seemed dissatisfied when they could find nothing incriminating. Finally, one of them said:

"Boy, tell your boss not to send you out in white neighborhoods after sundown."

As usual, I said:

"Yes, sir."

 V

My next job was a hall-boy in a hotel. Here my Jim Crow education broadened and deepened. When the bell-boys were busy, I was often called to assist them. As many of the rooms in the hotel were occupied by prostitutes, I was constantly called to carry them liquor and cigarettes. These women were nude most of the time. They did not bother about clothing, even for bell-boys. When you went into their rooms, you were supposed to take their nakedness for granted, as though it startled you no more than a blue vase or a red rug. Your presence awoke in them no sense of shame, for you were not regarded as human. If they were alone, you cold steal sidelong glimpses at them. But if they were receiving men, not a flicker of your eyelids could show. I remember one incident vividly. A new woman, a huge, snowy-skinned blonde, took a room on my floor. I was sent to wait upon her. She was in bed with a thick-set man; both were nude and uncovered. She said she wanted some liquor and slid out of bed and waddled across the floor to get her money from a dresser drawer. I watched her.

"Nigger, what in hell you looking at?" the white man asked me, raising himself upon his elbows.

"Nothing," I answered, looking miles deep into the blank wall of the room.

"Keep your eyes where they belong, if you want to be healthy!" he said.

"Yes, sir."

VI

One of the bell-boys I knew in this hotel was keeping steady company with one of the Negro maids. Out of a clear sky the police descended upon his home and arrested him, accusing him of bastardy. The poor boy swore he had had no intimate relations with the girl. Nevertheless, they forced him to marry her. When the child arrived, it was found to be much lighter in complexion than either of the two supposedly legal parents. The white men around the hotel made a great joke of it. They spread the rumor that some white cow must have scared the poor girl while she was carrying the baby. If you were in their presence when this explanation was offered, you were supposed to laugh.

VII

One of the bell-boys was caught in bed with a white prostitute. He was castrated and run out of town. Immediately after this all the bell-boys and hall-boys were called together and warned. We were given to understand that the boy who had been castrated was a "mighty, mighty lucky bastard." We were impressed with the fact that next time the management of the hotel would not be responsible for the lives of "trouble-makin' niggers." We were silent.

VIII

One night, just as I was about to go home, I met one of the Negro maids. She lived in my direction, and we fell in to walk part of the way home together. As we passed the white night-watchman, he slapped the maid on her buttock. I turned around, amazed. The watchman looked at me with a long, hard, fixed-under stare. Suddenly he pulled his gun and asked:

"Nigger, don't yuh like it?"

I hesitated.

"I asked yuh don't yuh like it?" he asked again, stepping forward.

"Yes, sir," I mumbled.

"Talk like it, then!"

"Oh, yes sir!" I said with as much heartiness as I could muster.

Outside, I walked ahead of the girl, ashamed to face her. She caught up with me and said:

"Don't be a fool! Yuh couldn't help it!"

This watchman boasted of having killed two Negroes in self-defense.

Yet, in spite of all this, the life of the hotel ran with an amazing smoothness. It would have been impossible for a stranger to detect anything. The maids, the hall-boys, and the bell-boys were all smiles. They had to be.

IX

I had learned my Jim Crow lessons so thoroughly that I kept the hotel job till I left Jackson for Memphis. It so happened that while in Memphis I applied for a job at a branch of the optical company. I was hired. And for some reason, as long as I worked there, they never brought my past against me.

Here my Jim Crow education assumed quite a different form. It was no longer brutally cruel, but subtly cruel. Here I learned to lie, to steal, to dissemble. I learned to play that dual role which every Negro must play if he wants to eat and live.

For example, it was almost impossible to get a book to read. It was assumed that after a Negro had imbibed what scanty schooling the state furnished he had no further need for books. I was always borrowing books from men on the job. One day I mustered enough courage to ask one of the men to let me get books from the library in his name. Surprisingly, he consented. I cannot help but think that he consented because he was a Roman Catholic and felt a vague sympathy for Negroes, being himself an object of hatred. Armed with a library card, I obtained books in the following manner: I would write a note to the librarian, saying: "Please let this nigger boy have the following books." I would then sign it with the white man's name.

When I went to the library, I would stand at the desk, hat in hand, looking as unbookish as possible. When I received the books desired I would take them home. If the books listed in the note happened to be out, I would sneak into the lobby and forge a new one. I never took any chances guessing with the white librarian about what the fictitious white man would want to read. No doubt if any of the white patrons had suspected that some of the volumes they enjoyed had been in the home of a Negro, they would not have tolerated it for an instant.

The factory force of the optical company in Memphis was much larger than that in Jackson, and more urbanized. At least they liked to talk, and would engage the Negro help in conversation whenever possible. By this means I found that many subjects were taboo from the white man's point of view. Among the topics they did not like to discuss with Negroes were the following: American white women; the Ku Klux Klan; France, and how Negro soldiers fared while there; French women; Jack Johnson; the entire northern part of the United States; the Civil War; Abraham Lincoln; U.S. Grant; General Sherman; Catholics; the Pope; Jews; the Republican Party; slavery; social equality; Communism; Socialism; the 13th and 14th Amendments to the Constitution; or any topic calling for positive knowledge or manly self-assertion on the part of the Negro. The most accepted topics were sex and religion.

There were many times when I had to exercise a great deal of ingenuity to keep out of trouble. It is a southern custom that all men must take off their hats when they enter an elevator. And especially did this apply to us blacks with rigid force. One day I stepped into an elevator with my arms full of packages. I was forced to ride with my hat on. Two white men stared at me coldly. Then one of them very kindly lifted my hat and placed it upon my armful of packages. Now the most accepted response for a Negro to make under such circumstances is to look at the white man out of the corner of his eye and grin. To have said: "Thank you!" would have made the white man *think* that you *thought* you were receiving from him a personal service. For such an act I have seen Negroes take a blow in the mouth. Finding the first alternative distasteful, and the second dangerous, I hit upon an acceptable course of action which fell safely between these two poles. I immediately—no sooner than my hat was lifted—pretended that my packages were about to spill, and appeared deeply distressed with keeping them in my arms. In this fashion I evaded having to acknowledge his service, and, in spite of adverse circumstances, salvaged a slender shred of personal pride.

How do Negroes feel about the way they have to live? How do they discuss it when alone amongst themselves? I think this question can be answered in a single sentence. A friend of mine who ran an elevator once told me:

"Lawd, man! Ef it wuzn't fer them polices 'n' them ol' lynch-mobs, there wouldn't be nothin' but uproar down here!"

Life on the Color Line: The True Story of a White Boy Who Discovered He Was Black

Gregory Howard Williams

That first Friday, Uncle Jim picked me up at lunchtime. We stopped at every small-town diner between Muncie and Albany dumping rotten meat, fruit, potato rinds, and all types of stinking garbage into large oil drums lashed on the back of his truck. I tried to brace the cans as we raced over the country roads. It all went smoothly until Uncle Jim plunged pell-mell down a dip, sending me a foot in the air. I managed to keep the drums in place, but was drenched with slimy garbage.

Uncle Jim had an extra work shirt in the cab, but by late afternoon when we arrived at a small-town café, I was reeking of garbage. While I wrestled a can to the alley, a middle-aged white man appeared at the rear door. From his long, casual chat with Uncle Jim I guessed he was the owner. My body tensed when I heard the man ask: "Who's that white boy?"

Uncle Jim said I was his nephew.

"He's the whitest colored boy I ever seen. Are you sure he wasn't just caught in the wrong net?" The owner chuckled.

I wanted to smash his face with the can when I lugged it back to the diner, and caught him gaping at me. His sharply pressed long white apron reminded me of the Ku Klux Klan leader I saw on Uncle Osco's new television following the 1954 Supreme Court decision outlawing segregated schools. [*Brown v. Board of Education,* 347 U.S. 483 (1954)—Ed.] That beefy-faced, white-robed Klansman stood in front of a burning cross, railing against black and white children learning together. He claimed that the Supreme Court was encouraging "race-mixing" and the only result would be the "bestial mongrel mulatto, the dreg of human society." In the refuge of Uncle Osco's sitting room, I had laughed at the pale, jowly southerner. In a white sheet and pointed hat, he looked more like the "dreg of society" than anybody I knew. Yet his nasal repetition of "mongrel mulatto" finally hit like a thunderbolt. He was talking about me. I was the Klan's worst nightmare. I was what the violence directed against integration was all about. I was what they hated and wanted to destroy. And that was the biggest puzzle in the world to me because I had absolutely nothing.

The café owner had a different idea. He didn't want to destroy me, he wanted to exhibit me. While I lugged garbage from his rear door, he hovered there beckoning me inside. There were people he wanted me to meet, he coaxed. He tried to engage me in conversation. "Gonna be a pig farmer like your uncle?" he asked with a chuckle.

"I'm gonna be a lawyer," I quipped.

His face reddened with laughter. "You gonna have to shovel a lot of shit to make that happen. Come on, these folks really want to see you. We all wanna see Muncie's first colored lawyer. I even got a piece of pie for you."

I knew he was insulting me, but I was tempted by the pie. When I noticed Uncle Jim frowning, I mumbled "No thanks." Soon the café owner was miles behind, and I was overcome by feelings of self-pity, confusion, and anger. As Uncle Jim turned down a gravel lane, I concentrated more on keeping the garbage off me than on fantasizing about dumping it on the man who had ridiculed my dream.

As the truck slowed, a strange form sprouted on the horizon. Uncle Jim pulled to a stop, and I realized it was the unfinished foundation of a house protruding three feet above the ground. The black tar paper sides and top gave it a sinister aura. It was Uncle Jim's home.

"Boy, I'm sorry about that ol' white man," he said as we carried groceries to the house. "He don't know shit. I learned a long time ago that you just have to laugh at white folks or they'll drive you crazy. Forgit 'bout him. We gonna have us a helluva dinner."

"Ain't That Love?": Antiracism and Racial Constructions of Motherhood

Andrea O'Reilly

Dominant ideologies and discourses of mothering and motherhood are racialized and racist; that is, they represent only one experience of mothering, that of white middle-class women, and position this experience as the real, natural and universal one. Any discussion of mothers and antiracism must, therefore, begin with an understanding of how discourses of motherhood become racially codified and constructed. This essay explores how the development and dissemination of one normative discourse of motherhood—that of so-called sensitive mothering— causes other experiences of mothering—working class, ethnic—to be marginalized and delegitimized.

Motherhood is a cultural construction that varies with time and place; there is no one essential or universal experience of motherhood. However, the diverse meanings and experiences of mothering become marginalized and erased through the construction of an official definition of motherhood. Through a complex process of intersecting forces—economics, politics, cultural institutions (what Teresa de Lauretis would call social technologies)—the dominant definition of motherhood is codified as the official and only meaning of motherhood.[1] Alternative meanings of mothering are marginalized and rendered illegitimate. The dominant definition is able to suppress its own construction as an ideology and thus naturalizes its specific construction of motherhood as the universal, real, natural maternal experience.

The dominant discourse of motherhood is, however, historically determined and thus variable. In the Victorian era, for example, the ideology of moral motherhood that saw mothers as naturally pure, pious and chaste emerged as the dominant discourse. This ideology, however, was race- and class-specific: Only white and middle-class women could wear the halo of the madonna and transform the world through their moral influence and social housekeeping. Slave mothers, in contrast, were defined as breeders, placed not on a pedestal, as white women were, but on the auction block.

After World War II, the discourse of the happy homemaker made the "stay-at-home mom and apple pie" mode of mothering the normal and natural motherhood experience. Again, only white and middle-class women could, in fact, experience what discursively was inscribed as natural and universal. In the 1970s, the era in which many baby boomers became parents, a new hegemonic discourse of motherhood began to take shape, one that authors Valerie Walkerdine and Helen Lucey appropriately term "sensitive mothering" in their landmark book *Democracy in the Kitchen: Regulating Mothers and Socializing Daughters.*

Walkerdine and Lucey examine how the maternal behavior of the middle-class became culturally constructed and codified as the real, normal and natural way to mother. Natural mothering begins with the ideological presupposition that children have needs that are met by the mother. To mother, therefore, is to be sensitive to the needs of children, that is, to engage in sensitive mothering. The first characteristic of the sensitive mother, Walkerdine and Lucey explain,

> *is that her domestic life is centred around her children and not around her housework. The boundaries between this work and children's play have to be blurred . . . While the mother is being sensitive to the child's needs, she is not doing any housework. She has to be available and ready to meet demands, and those household tasks which she undertakes have to become pedagogic tasks . . . The second feature of the sensitive mother is the way she regulates her children. Essentially there should be no overt regulation; regulation should go underground; no power battles, no insensitive sanctions as these would interfere with the child's illusion that she is the source of her wishes, that she has "free will."[2]*

This mode of mothering is drawn from the parenting styles of the so-called baby-boom generation. Today good mothering is defined as child-centered and is characterized by flexibility, spontaneity, democracy, affection, nurturance and playfulness. This mode of mothering is contrasted to the earlier stern, rigid, authoritative, "a child should be seen and not heard" variety of parenting. Today's ideal mother is not only expected to be "at home" with her children—as her mother was with her in the fifties—she is also required to spend, in the language of eighties' parenting books, "quality time" with her children. While the fifties mom would put her children in the pram or playpen to tend to her household chores, today's mom is to "be with" her child at all times physically and, most importantly, psychologically. Whether the activity is one of the numerous structured moms-and-tots programs—swimming, kindergym, dance—or an at-home activity—reading, gardening, cooking, playing—the mother's day is to revolve around the child, not her housework as it was in the fifties, and is to be centered upon the child's educational development. The child is to be involved in any domestic labor performed and the chore at hand is be transformed into a learning experience for the child.

Working-class mothers, Walkerdine and Lucey emphasize, do not practice so-called sensitive mothering; work does not become play nor do power and conflict go underground. Working-class mothers, in the authors' study, do play with their children but only after domestic chores have been tended to. In working-class households, the boundaries between mothering and domestic labor are maintained and the very real work of domestic labor is not transformed—or trivialized—into a game for the child's benefit. Nor does the mother abdicate her power and authority to create the illusion of a family democracy. This type of mothering, however, becomes pathologized as deficiency and deviance because the middle-class style of sensitive mothering has been codified, both socially and discursively, as natural. Working-class mothering is, thus, not simply different, it is deemed unnatural, and working-class mothers are deemed unfit mothers in need of regulation. In other words, "there is something wrong with working-class mothering which should be put right by making it more middle-class."[3]

Lucey and Walkerdine do not specifically look at African-American mothering in their book. The research that has been done on black mothering, however, does suggest that Lucey and Walkerdine's observations may be applied to black women's experiences of mothering, at least among working-class families.[4] Patricia Hill Collins, for example, argues, in her many works on black mothering, that there is a distinct African-American experience of mothering. African-American mothering, what she calls mother-work, is about "maintain[ing] family life in the face of forces that undermine family integrity" while "recognizing that individual survival, empowerment, and identity require group survival, empowerment, and identity."[5] Central concerns of "racial ethnic" (Collins's term) mothers include keeping the children born to you, the physical survival of those children, teaching the children resistance and how to survive in a racist world, giving to those children their racial/cultural history and identity, and a social activism and communal mothering on behalf of all the community's children. What the research on black mothering suggests is that sensitive mothering is not valued or practiced by African-American mothers, particularly if the family in question is urban and working-class.

In her brilliant book *Maternal Thinking,* Sara Ruddick argues that the first duty of mothers is to protect and preserve their children: "to keep safe whatever is vulnerable and valuable in a child."[6] "Preserving the lives of children," Ruddick writes, "is the central constitutive, invariant aim of maternal practice."[7] "To be committed to meeting children's demand for preservation," Ruddick continues, "does not require enthusiasm or even love; it simply means to see vulnerability and to respond to it with care rather than abuse, indifference, or flight."[8] Though maternal practice is composed of two other demands—nurturance and training—this first demand, what Ruddick calls preservative love, is what describes much of economically disadvantaged African-American women's mother-work. For many African-American women, securing food, shelter and clothing, building safe neighborhoods, and fighting a racist world is what defines both the meaning and experience of their mother-work and mother-love. However, because sensitive mothering has been naturalized as the universal normal experience of motherhood, preservative love is not regarded as real, legitimate or "good enough" mothering.

In the mothering of my children and in my teaching on motherhood, I seek to challenge the normative discourse of sensitive mothering by inscribing mothering as a culturally determined experience. I bring to this struggle the experience of being raised in a white, middle-class family by a working-class mother. The stories my mother tells me of my early childhood indicate that my mother's mode of mothering was clearly that of working-class 1950s culture. She used to "air" me on the front porch in the pram and, later, in the playpen each morning—summers and winters—as she tended to her housework and the caring of my infant sister. It was the early 1960s, and my mother had an eight-year-old daughter from her first marriage and three children under the age of three from her second marriage.

My mother grew up poor in a working-class family from, what was called in my hometown of Hamilton, Ontario, the "wrong side of the tracks." In the 1950s she found herself divorced with a young baby to raise. At twenty-eight she married my father, a man from an established middle-class family, and moved to middle-class suburbia. My mother has often told me she never really felt she was a part of the suburban culture of young motherhood—the morning coffees in each other's kitchens, afternoons in the park, recipe sharing, and the borrowing of that cup of sugar.

Having had my children in graduate school with no one to share young motherhood with, I envied my mother and could not understand why she kept herself apart from what I imagined to be a feminist utopia of female solidarity. Only recently have I been able to see my mother's experience for what it was: It was the 1950s, and she was an older divorcee with a young daughter, from a poor, working-class family, among young, newly married women from "good" middle-class families. I can only imagine the culture shock she must have experienced and speculate upon how she was received by those "good" middle-class neighbors of hers. The memories of my later childhood reveal that my mother eventually became part of that middle-class culture and practiced, at least occasionally, the so-called sensitive mothering Walkerdine and Lucey discuss.

The struggles of my mother were replayed when I became a mother thirty years later at the relatively young age of twenty-three. While my class affiliation was middle-class, my spouse was working-class; and though we were educated—both of us were pursuing graduate degrees at the time—we were also very poor. At that time, though, my energies were focused on challenging the oppressiveness of motherhood as a patriarchal institution. As a student of women's studies, my perspective was decidedly feminist, and I sought to imagine and achieve an experience of mothering that was empowering or, at the very least, not oppressive to me or my children. What I had not considered in my feminist practice of mothering was how the philosophy of so-called sensitive mothering to which I subscribed was a regulatory discourse as oppressive as the patriarchal one with which I was familiar.

I became conscious of the class and racial dimensions of discourses on mothering only upon reading *Democracy in the Kitchen* and Toni Morrison's novel *Sula* midway through my early mothering years.[9] What these readings forced me to recognize is that although so-called sensitive mothering is neither real nor universal, it results in the regulation of middle-class mothers and the pathologizing of working-class mothering.

I planned to use the novel *Sula* in my teaching as a way to talk about racist constructions of motherhood and to arrive at an antiracist perspective in the way we perceive and practice mothering. I became more and more convinced that any attempt at teaching antiracism to children and students was doomed to failure as long as our perceptions and practices of mothering were racialized and racist. How can a white middle-class woman who sees her sensitive mothering as more real—and hence superior—possibly teach antiracism to her child? In turn, how can a black mother empower her child to resist racism when that child is encouraged to see her own mother's mode of mothering as insufficient? With these questions in mind I set to work.

I presented a lecture on *Sula* at the conclusion of a first-year humanities course entitled "Concepts of the Male and Female in Western Culture" in March 1995, a class made up mostly of mature and returning students. The perspective of the course was thoroughly feminist and issues of race and racism had been discussed in the classroom. My audience was, thus, a highly informed and, for the most part, receptive one.

I spoke with much passion on how the mother's preservative love in the novel had been pathologized by the critics because it did not fit the bill of sensitive mothering. I stressed the need to deconstruct the hegemony of sensitive mothering so that other expressions of mothering are given legitimacy and validity. With this lecture I hoped to generate discussion on the ways in which black and working-class women's mothering is often delegitimized and how white middle-class women are regulated in trying to achieve this sensitive mothering. Instead, what I got was a hazy fog of incomprehension, bewilderment and indifference.

Interestingly, when I moved from the topic of mothering to other themes in *Sula*—women's friendship, growing up female—I could feel—almost see—a shift in the students' response to my lecture: Suddenly there was connection, interest and understanding. I also observed, though could not account for, a noticeable change in the emotional climate of the lecture hall. Inexplicably, during the first part of my lecture on motherhood the atmosphere was serious and noticeably tense, yet in the latter section the mood was lighthearted and relaxed. When we talked about the lecture and text later in tutorial, the students, much to my dismay, replicated the patronizing stance of the critics regarding Eva's mothering—we can't be too hard on her, it wasn't her fault, she would have done it differently had she had the choice and so on. They had missed the whole point of my lecture.

I was troubled, dismayed and perplexed by my students' misunderstanding/incomprehension; eventually though I attributed it to a weak lecture. Not until I started working on this essay did I think about the experience again and see it from a different perspective. At the same time, a Caribbean student in a course I was teaching told the class about her family experience. This student's mother, like many Caribbean women, came to Canada in the early 1970s to secure work and left her children back home with her parents in the hope of creating a better life for them. The mother sent her earnings home, visited her children on holidays, and several years later, when she had good, permanent work, had her children join her in Canada. The eldest sister had great difficulty adjusting to this change and blamed her mother for being absent all those years. Good mothers, the daughter told her mother, don't leave their children for a day, let alone for many years. Good mothers, like those of her Canadian friends, did things with their kids, were not always so tired and away so much working. What the daughter was saying is: Why can't you be more like other mothers? Why can't you be normal?

Hearing this student's story I began to make sense of my former students' reaction to my lecture. Though sensitive mothering is a recent ideological construction of motherhood—having been around only two decades—it has very successfully taken up residence in the dominant culture. (It reminds one of the aliens in *The Invasion of the Body Snatchers* who enter and take over, en masse, the human population.) Good mothers read to their children, enroll them in ballet and piano lessons, enrich them with theatre, art and culture; they are patient, nurturing, spontaneous, sensitive and—most importantly—child-centered, transforming even the most mundane task into an entertaining and educational experience for their children.

Now no mother can actually live the ideological script of sensitive mothering, though all mothers are judged by it and many mothers seek to achieve it. And most children, very much cultural creatures, interpret their own mother's mothering from the discourse of sensitive mothering. On several occasions my children have responded to my behavior or comments with the statement: Mothers don't do, or say, that. We have embraced so completely this discourse of mothering that we see it as the best, ideal, normal and, ultimately, only way to mother. Hence my students' confusion: Why would I problematize something so good, so natural? Why wouldn't I want the characters in this book to partake in such mothering, given how good it is? And why shouldn't we help others to achieve the same experience of sensitive mothering? Why not indeed?

With my own children I struggle to make conscious to them the ways in which mothering is overdetermined and regulated by cultural discourses, such as sensitive mothering. Discussions about racism and antiracism have always been part of our children's upbringing. What is more difficult to work through with our growing children is, I think, how practices of mothering are racialized and class-specific. After all, kids don't see mothering as a practice. I strive to challenge that perception in my mothering. What I seek to emphasize to my children, both in word and deed, is that my experience of mothering and their experience of being mothered are culturally determined. I want them to know that children are mothered differently and that one way is not any more real, natural or legitimate than any other way.

When my kids respond to something I have said or done with the line "Mothers don't do that" or, conversely, "All the other mothers are . . . so why can't you?" I remind them that there is no one way to mother or be mothered. As I seek to free myself from the regulation of sensitive mothering, I share with my children my critique of this discourse by giving concrete examples of how this discourse is oppressive to me—and by implication to them—and how it results in the "putting down" of other mothers.

In my critique of sensitive mothering I am not suggesting that I am against reading to your child or playing, every now and then, "let's wash the floors" to make enjoyable an otherwise tedious chore. However, what I do find deeply disturbing is the codification of this discourse as the official and only way to mother. Walkerdine and Lucey argue that sensitive mothering is ultimately bad for both mother and child: It trivializes women's domestic labor, causes the mother's workday to be never-ending and compels her to be manipulative with her children—to make them believe that her wishes are really their own—so as to avoid authoritarianism and conflict. It causes the child to confuse work with play and to see the self as completely in control of circumstances—somewhat problematic lessons, particularly for black and working-class kids in a racist and capitalist world. While I agree with Lucey and Walkerdine's observations, I am less interested in debating the pros and cons of sensitive mothering than in deconstructing any normative discourse of mothering that pathologizes difference and seeks to regulate it.

What has this to do with mothers acting against racism? My students' incomprehension at my lecture and my student's moving story have brought home to me the intricate relationship between mothering and racism; mothering and antiracism. If that mother could have told her daughter that her survivalist type of mother-love—mothering as separation—*was* an expression of mothering, as good as, if not better than, the dominant mode, perhaps there would have been less blame and more understanding between mother and daughter. With my own lecture I would have been able to talk about an antiracist perspective with respect to mothering far more effectively had the students not been so thoroughly identified with the dominant discourse of mothering.

Adrienne Rich in her ovarian work *Of Woman Born* discusses how motherhood is an institution that is defined and controlled by patriarchy. I would add that ideologies of mothering, and the institutions they create, are also thoroughly racialized and racist. I believe that the teaching and practice of antiracism through mothering can happen if, and only if, the dominant mode of mothering is identified and challenged as racist. It does not help to build an antiracist household on foundations that are racist.

⬛◉ Notes

[1]Teresa de Lauretis, "The Technology of Gender," in *Technologies of Gender* (Bloomington: Indiana University Press, 1987), 1–30.

[2]Valerie Walkerdine and Helen Lucey, *Democracy in the Kitchen: Regulating Mothers and Socializing Daughters* (London: Virago Press, 1989) 20, 23–24.

[3]Ibid., taken from the back cover.

[4]See, for example: Valora Washington, "The Black Mother in the United States: History, Theory, Research, and Issues," in *The Different Faces of Motherhood,* ed. Beverly Birns and Dale F. Hay (New York: Plenum Press, 1988), 185–213; Filomina Chioma Steady, ed., *The Black Woman Cross-Culturally* (Rochester, VT: Schenkman Books, 1981); Patricia Bell-Scott et al., *Double Stitch: Black Women Write About Mothers and Daughters* (New York: HarperPerennial, 1991); Carol B. Stack, *All Our Kin: Strategies for Survival in a Black Community* (New York: Harper & Row, 1974); Patricia Hill Collins, *Black Feminist Thought: Knowledge, Consciousness and the Politics of Empowerment* (New York: Unwin Hyman, 1990); bell hooks, "Revolutionary Parenting" in *Feminist Theory: From Margin to Center* (Boston: South End Press, 1984), 133–46, and "Homeplace" in *Yearning: Race, Gender, and Cultural Politics* (Boston: South End Press, 1990), 41–49.

[5]Patricia Hill Collins, "Shifting the Center: Race, Class, and Feminist Theorizing About Motherhood" in *Mothering: Ideology, Experience, and Agency,* ed. Evelyn Nakano Glenn, Grace Chang and Linda Rennie Forcey (New York: Routledge, 1994), 47.

[6]Sara Ruddick, *Maternal Thinking: Toward a Politics of Peace* (Boston: Beacon, 1989), 80.

[7]Ibid., 19.

[8]Ibid.

[9]Toni Morrison, *Sula* (New York: New American Library, 1973). The contemporary critical responses to a dialogue in the novel brought home to me how thoroughly identified our culture is with the discourse of sensitive mothering. In this novel, Eva, the mother, is left by her husband in 1895 with "$1.65, five eggs, three beets" and three children to feed. After her baby son nearly dies from constipation Eva leaves her children in the care of a neighbor, saying she will be back the next day, only to return eighteen months later with money and one of her legs gone. It was rumored that Eva placed her leg under a train in order to collect insurance money to support her children. Years later, her now adult daughter, Hannah, asks her mother if "[She] ever love[d] us?" The mother responds: "You settin' here with your healthy-ass self and ax me did I love you? Them big old eyes in your head would a been two holes full of maggots if I hadn't." The daughter then asks: "Did you ever, you know, play with us?" Eva replies: "Play? Wasn't nobody playin' in 1895. Just 'cause you got it good now you think it was always this good? 1895 was a killer, girl. Things was bad. Niggers was dying like flies . . . Don't that count? Ain't that love? You want me to tinkle you under the jaw and forget 'bout them sores in your mouth?" (67–69). Many readers of the novel question, with Hannah, whether Eva did in fact mother her children. Her mothering has been called unnatural and untraditional. The words unnatural and untraditional, however, accrue meaning only if both the speaker (writer) and listener (reader) know what is meant by their opposites, the normative terms—in this instance, natural and traditional. When a critic, like Dayle Delancy, laments that Eva has "no time to lavish traditional displays of affection upon her children" or that "she has to work for the survival of her offspring at the expense of having fun with them" ["Motherlove Is a Killer" in *Sage* 8 (fall 1990): 15–18] she is working from a very specific discourse of what constitutes good mothering—namely that of sensitive mothering.

Is Yellow Black or White?

Gary Y. Okihiro

Between 1985 and 1990 in New York City, there were three major protests against Korean storeowners in African communities, while in Los Angeles, as one boycott ended in the summer of 1991, another began, and within a six-month period, five Korean grocery stores were fire-bombed. In a Los Angeles courtroom, the television monitors showed fifteen-year-old Latasha Harlins punch Soon Ja Du and turn to leave the store, when Du lifts a gun and fires pointblank at Harlin's head, killing her. On December 15, 1991, Yong Tae Park died of bullet wounds received during a robbery on his liquor store the previous day; Park was the seventh Korean storeowner killed in Los Angeles by African male suspects that year. "Black Power. No Justice, No Peace! Boycott Korean Stores! The Battle for Brooklyn," the poster read. "Crack, the 'housing crisis,' and Korean merchants is a conspiracy to destabilizing our community. . . . The Korean merchants are agents of the U.S. government in their conspiracy to destabilize the economy of our community. They are rewarded by the government and financed by big business."[1] In south central Los Angeles in April and May 1992, following the acquittal of police officers in the beating of African American Rodney G. King, Koreatown was besieged, eighteen-year-old Edward Song Lee died in a hail of bullets, nearly fifty Korean merchants were injured, and damage to about 2,000 Korean stores topped $400 million. Parts of Japantown were also hit, and losses to Japanese businesses exceeded $3 million. Is Yellow black or white?

In laying the intellectual foundation for what we now call the model minority stereotype, social scientists William Caudill and George De Vos stated their hypothesis: "there seems to be a significant compatibility (but by no means identity) between the value systems found in the culture of Japan and the value systems found in American middle class culture." That compatibility, they cautioned, did not mean similarity but rather a sharing of certain values and adaptive mechanisms, such that "when they [Japanese and white middle-class Americans] meet under conditions favorable for acculturation . . . Japanese Americans, acting in terms of their Japanese values and personality, will behave in ways that are favorably evaluated by middle class Americans."[2] Although Caudill and De Vos tried to distinguish between identity and compatibility, similarity and sharing, subsequent variations on the theme depicted Asians as "just like whites." And so, is yellow black or white?

The question is multilayered. Is yellow black or white? is a question of Asian American identity. Is yellow black or white? is a question of Third World identity, or the relationships among people of color. Is yellow black or white? is a question of American identity, or the nature of America's racial formation.[3] Implicit within the question is a construct of American society that defines race relations as bipolar—between black and white—and that locates Asians (and American Indians and Latinos) somewhere along the divide between black and white. Asians, thus, are "near-whites" or "just like blacks."[4] The construct is historicized, within the progressive tradition of American history, to show the evolution of Asians from minority to majority status, or "from hardship and discrimination to become a model of self-respect and achievement in today's America."[5] "Scratch a Japanese-American," social scientist Harry Kitano was quoted as saying, "and you find a Wasp," and Asians have been bestowed the highest accolade of having "outwhited the Whites."[6] The construct, importantly, is not mere ideology but is a social practice that assigns to Asian Americans, and indeed to all minorities, places within the social formation. Further, the designations, the roles, and the relationships function to institute and perpetuate a repression that begets and maintains privilege. Asian Americans have served the master class, whether as "near blacks" in the past or as "near-whites" in the present or as "marginal men" in both the past and the present. Yellow is emphatically neither white nor black; but insofar as Asians and Africans share subordinate position to the master class, yellow is a shade of black, and black, a shade of yellow.

We are a kindred people, African and Asian Americans. We share a history of migration, interaction and cultural sharing and commerce and trade. We share a history of European colonization, decolonization, and independence under neocolonization and dependency. We share a history of oppression in the United States, successively serving as slave and cheap labor, as peoples excluded and absorbed, as victims of mob rule and Jim Crow. We share a history of struggle for freedom and the democratization of America, of demands for equality and human dignity, of insistence on making real the promise that all men and women are created equal. We are a kindred people, forged in the fire of white supremacy and struggle, but how can we recall that kinship when our memories have been massaged by white hands, and how can we remember the past when our storytellers have been whispering, amid the din of Western civilization and Anglo-conformity?

We know each other well, Africans and Asians. Some of the first inhabitants of South and Southeast Asia were a people called "Negrito," who were gatherers and hunters and slash-and-burn cultivators. They may have been absorbed or expelled by the Veddoids, a later group of immigrants to the Indian subcontinent, but remnants survive today as the Semang of the Malay Peninsula, the Mincopies of the Andaman Islands, and the Negritos of the Philippines. One branch of the Dravidians, who arrived in South Asia probably after 1000 B.C.E., were black people, who at first apparently intermarried with the lighter-skinned Indo-Aryan branch of Dravidians, but who were later denigrated in the caste system that evolved on the Gangetic plains.[7]

Trade, if not migration, between Africa and Asia predated the arrival of Portuguese ships in the Indian Ocean by at least a thousand years. African ambergris, tortoiseshell, rhinoceros horns, and especially ivory left African ports for Arabia, India, Indonesia, and China. The *Periplus of the Erythraean Sea,* a handbook compiled by a Greek-Egyptian sailor sometime during the first three centuries C.E., described Indonesian food crops, such as coconuts, and cultural items, such as sewn boats, along the East African coast perhaps as far south as Mozambique, and historians believe that Indonesians may have settled on Madagascar in the early centuries C.E., but after the time of the *Periplus.*[8] The Chinese Ch'engshih Tuan, in his *Yu-yang-tsa-tsu* written in the ninth century C.E., described East Africa, or the "land of Po-pa-li," where the women were "clean and well-behaved" and where the trade products were ivory and ambergris.[9]

From the eighth through twelfth centuries, the Hindu kingdom of Sri Vijaya, centered on Sumatra, was the dominant mercantile power in the Indian Ocean; it controlled the sea routes between India and China and likely traded directly with people along the East African coast. About the same time, the Chola kingdom in southeast India sent traders to East Africa, where their cowrie currency, system of weights, and trade beads became standard and widespread. By the thirteenth century, both Sri Vijaya and the Chola kingdom fell into decline, and the west Indian Ocean became an Islamic sphere. Still, the Ming dynasty, which gained control of China in 1368, sent a fleet to East Africa in 1417 and again in 1421, and Ming porcelain has been found in abundance among the ruins of mosques, tombs, houses, and palaces on the islands and on the mainland along the East African coast. Fei-Hsin, a junior officer on the 1417 expedition, described the townspeople of Mogadishu: "the men wear their hair in rolls which hang down all round and wrap cotton cloths round their waists" and the women "apply a yellow varnish to their shaven crowns and hang several strings of disks from their ears and wear silver rings round their necks."[10]

Besides the trade in goods, Africans and Asians engaged in a slave trade that was "probably a constant factor" in the Indian Ocean from the tenth to the thirteenth centuries.[11] Much of that trade was conducted by Africanized Muslims, who sent African slaves to the shores of the Persian Gulf, to India, and to China. In the year 1119, "most of the wealthy in Canton possessed negro slaves," and East African slave soldiers were used extensively by the Sassanian kings of Persia during the seventh century and by the Bahmanid kings of the Deccan in India during the fourteenth and fifteenth centuries.[12] Africans in Asia sometimes rose from the ranks of slaves to become military and political leaders, such as Malik Sarvar of Delhi, who became the sultan's deputy in 1389, was appointed governor of the eastern province, and eventually ruled as an independent king. Perhaps most influential was

Malik Ambar, who was born in Ethiopia around 1550, sold into slavery in India, and rose to become a commander and ruler in the Decan. Ferista, a contemporary Arab historian, called Ambar "the most enlightened financier of whom we read in Indian history," and he reported that "the justice and wisdom of the government of Mullik Ambar have become proverbial in the Deccan."[13] The East African slave trade remained small in volume until the nineteenth century, when European colonies in the Americas and the Indian Ocean opened a larger market for slaves.[14]

The creation of that global system of labor and the conjunction of Africans, Asians, and Europeans began long before the nineteenth century. African and Asian civilizations contributed much to the dawning of European civilization in the Greek city-states. The armies of the Islamic Almoravids ranged across the Sudan and North Africa to Carthage and the Iberian Peninsula, and the Mongol armies of Chingiz Khan penetrated the European heartland. The invaders brought not only devastation but also religion, culture, and science. That intimacy would later be denied by the Europeans, who, after crusades to expel the "infidels" from Christendom and after the rise of nationalism and mercantile capitalism, conceived an ideology that justified their expansion and appropriation of land, labor, and resources in Africa, Asia, and the Americas. That ideology, in the name of religion and science, posited the purity and superiority of European peoples and cultures, unsullied by the anti-Christian, uncivilized non-Europeans—the Other—and found expression in European colonization of the Third World.

Seeking first the kingdom of gold, Europeans set sail for Asia down the African coast and around the Cape of Good Hope to India and China, and later west across the Atlantic Ocean to India, where instead they stumbled into the landmass they named the Americas. Colonization followed trade just as surely as capital required labor. European plantations in the Americas devoured the native inhabitants and, unstated, demanded African laborers from across the Atlantic in the miserable system of human bondage that supplied an outlet for European manufacturers and produced the agricultural products that enriched the metropole. The reciprocal of European development was Third World underdevelopment, and the web spun by European capitalism crisscrossed and captured the globe, creating a world-system in which capital and labor flowed as naturally as the ocean currents that circled the Atlantic and Pacific.

Some of the earliest Asians in the Americas came by way of the Spanish galleon trade between Manila and Acapulco in the early seventeenth century. Chinese and Filipino crew members and servants on those Spanish ships settled in Mexico, and Filipino "Manilamen" found their way to Louisiana, where, in 1763, they created the oldest continuous Asian American communities in North America.[15] The Filipinos named their fishing and shrimping settlements Manila Village, St. Malo, Leon Rojas, Bayou Cholas, and Bassa Bassa. But the main body of Asian migration to the Americas came after the termination of the African slave trade in the nineteenth century and the consequent need for a new source of labor for the plantations, mines, and public works in Central and South America, Africa, and the islands of the Pacific and Caribbean.

A forerunner of the nineteenth-century coolie trade and the successor of the earlier East African slave trade was the use of Asian and African slaves on board European ships in the Indian Ocean and a European carrying trade that took Asian slaves from Bengal, southern India and Sri Lanka, the Indonesian archipelago, the Philippines, and Japan to Dutch and Portuguese possessions in Asia and Africa. Beginning in the early sixteenth century, largely because of the debilitating effects of disease upon European sailors, Arab, South Asian, Malay, and African slaves frequently made up the majority of the crews on Portuguese vessels plying Indian Ocean waters.[16] Asian slaves were joined by Africans taken from Madagascar and East Africa and were brought to the Dutch settlement at the Cape of Good Hope after 1658. By 1795, there were 16,839 slaves in the colony, and in 1834, the year slavery was abolished at the Cape, there were approximately 34,000 slaves.[17] The slaves produced mixed offspring with the indigenous San and Khoikhoi and with whites, forming the group the Europeans called the Cape Coloured. South Asians arrived on the East Coast of eighteenth-century America as indentured workers and slaves. Brought to Massachusetts and Pennsylvania on board English and American trade vessels possibly during the 1780s and 1790s, South Asians with Anglicized names such as James Dunn, John Ballay, Joseph Green, George Jimor, and Thomas Robinson served indentures, were sold and bought as slaves, likely married African American women, and became members of the local African American communities.[18]

In 1833, slavery was formally abolished in the British Empire, but during the period of transition, slaves over six years of age served apprenticeships from four to six years as unpaid and later as paid labor. Apprenticeships ended in the British colonies in 1838, leading to the claim by sugar planters of a chronic labor shortage and a determination "to make us, as far as possible, independent of our negro population," according to John Gladstone, father of Robert and William Gladstone and one of the largest slaveholders and proprietors of estates in British Guiana.[19] Slavery, as pointed out by historian Hugh Tinker, produced both "a system and attitude of mind" that enabled a new system of slavery—coolieism—that incorporated many of the same oppressive features of the old.[20]

White planters saw the "new slaves" as subhuman and mere units of production. In 1836, anticipating the end of African slave apprenticeships, John Gladstone inquired about purchasing a hundred coolies from Gillanders, Arbuthnot & Company, who had supplied thousands of South Asians to Mauritius. The firm assured Gladstone that the Dhangars, or "hill coolies" of India, were "always spoken of as more akin to the monkey than the man. They have no religion, no education, and in their present state no wants beyond eating, drinking and sleeping: and to procure which they are willing to labour."[21] In May 1838, the first contingent of what would become a veritable stream of indentured labor arrived in British Guiana. The 396 Asian Indians were contracted to work nine to ten hours a day (as compared with seven and a half hours daily under apprenticeships) for sixteen cents (compared with thirty-two cents for free workers). In addition to economic exploitation, the indentured laborers were subject to disease and harsh treatment, particularly during the "seasoning," or breaking-in, period, resulting in numerous runaways and high mortality rates. From May 1845 to December 1849, 11,437 Asian Indians were indentured on sugar estates in British Guiana. Of that total as of December 1849, 11,437 Asian Indians were indentured on sugar estates in British Guiana. Of that total as of December 1849, only 6,417 still remained on the estates, whereas 643 were listed as sick, vagrants, paupers, or children 2,218 had died on the estates in jails and hospitals or were found dead elsewhere, and 2,259 were unaccounted for, of whom more than half were probably dead. Even those who had served their period of contract were left to wander "about the roads and streets, or lie down, sicken and die" or were castigated as "vagrants" who were stereotyped as "eating every species of garbage . . . filthy in (their) habits, lazy and addicted to pilfering."[23] Little wonder that Asian Indian indentures composed and sang this song as they sailed for Trinidad:

What kind plate,
What kind cup,
With a ticket to cut
in Trinidad,
O people of India
We are going to die there.[24]

Chinese and Asian Indian "coolies" were sold and indentured to European and American ship captains in a barter called by the Chinese "the buying and selling of pigs." The Chinese coolies, or "pigs," were restrained in "pigpens", one such barracoon on Amoy in 1852 was described in a British report "the coolies were penned up in numbers from 10 to 12 in a wooden shed, like a slave barracoon, nearly naked, very filthy, and room only sufficient to lie; the space 220 by 24 feet with a bamboo floor near the roof; the number in all about 500."[25] On the shore, the coolies were strapped naked and on their chests were painted the letters C (California), P (Peru), or S (Sandwich Islands), denoting their destinations. Once on board the ship, they were placed below deck in the hold, where they were usually confined for the duration of the transpacific passage. Overcrowding and a short supply of food and water led to revolts, suicides, and murders. Fearing a revolt, the crew of an American ship, the *Waverly,* drove the Chinese coolies below deck and cosed the hatch on October 27, 1855: "on opening them some twelve or fourteen hours afterwards it was found that nearly three hundred of the unfortunate beings had perished by suffocation."[26] Chao-ch'un Li and 165 other coolies petitioned the Cuba Commission about ill-treatment and abuse: "When quitting Macao," they testified, "we proceeded to sea, we were confined in the hold below; some were even shut up in bamboo cages, or chained to iron posts, and a few were indiscriminately selected and flogged as a means of intimidating all others; while we cannot estimate the deaths that, in all, took place, from sickness, blows, hunger, thirst, or from suicide by leaping into the sea."[27] As many as a third of the coolies died during the journey across the Pacific on board ships bound for the Americas. During the years 1860 to 1863, for example, of the 7,884 Chinese coolies shipped to Peru, 2,400 or 30.4 percent, died en route.[28] The African slave and Asian coolie were kinsmen and kinswomen in that world created by European masters.

Between 1848 and 1874, 124,813 Chinese coolies reached Cuba from Macao, Amoy, Canton, Hong Kong, Swatow, Saigon, and Manila. Within Cuba's plantation system, wrote historian Franklin W. Knight, the Chinese became "coinheritors with the Negroes of the lowliness of caste, the abuse, the ruthless exploitation. . . . Chinese labor in cuba in the nineteenth century was slavery in every social aspect except the name."[29] Coolies were sold in the open market, following advertisements that appeared in the local newspapers. Prospective buyers inspected the human merchandise, lined up on a platform, before the bargaining began, and the Asians were "virtually sold to the planters."[30] Conditions on Cuba's plantations were desperate. Chien T'ang, Chao Chang, A-chao Wen, and about three hundred of their compatriots in labor testified that they worked daily from between 2 and 4 a.m. until midnight, including Sundays, and others described the harsh treatment they received at the hands of overseers and masters. Confinement, shackling with chains, flogging, and cutting off fingers, ears, an limbs were methods employed to ensure docility and productivity in the workplace. A-pa Ho reported that for making a cigarette, "I was flogged with a rattan rod so severely that my flesh was lacerated and the bones became visible." A-chen Lu stated: "I have seen men beaten to death, the bodies being afterwards buried, and no report being made to the authorities"; A-sheng Hsieh told of Chen and Liang, who committed suicide after having been severely beaten. "The administrator accused them of cutting grass slowly," testified Hsieh, "and directing four men to hold them in a prostrate position, inflicted with a whip, a flogging which almost killed them. The first afterwards hanged himself, and the second drowned himself."[30]

In the United States, white planters similarly saw Chinese laborers as the "coinheritors with the Negroes of the lowliness of caste, the abuse, the ruthless exploitation." Before the Civil War, southern planters saw African slaves as a counter to immigration to their region by, in the words of Edmund Ruffin, "the hordes of immigrants now flowing from Europe." After the war, the planters saw free blacks as a troublesome presence and sought to deport and colonize them outside the United States and to replace them with Europeans and Asians.[31] In 1869, Godfrey Barnsley, a Georgia planter and New Orleans factory predicted that Mississippi Valley planters would recruit "large numbers of Chinese to take the place of negroes as they are said to be better laborers[,] more intelligent and can be had for $12 to $13 per month and rations." William M. Lawton, chair of the Committee on Chinese Immigrants for the South Carolina Agricultural and Mechanical Society, put it more bluntly: "I look upon the introduction of Chinese on our Rice lands, & especially on the unhealthy cotton lands as new and essential machines in the room of others that have been destroyed [or are] wearing out, year by year."[32] Africans and Asians, according to that point of view, were mere fodder for the fields and factories of the master class.

Africans and Asians, however, were not the same. After the Civil War, southern employers viewed African Americans not only as essential laborers but also as political liabilities insofar as they voted and voted Republican.[33] The problem, thus, was how to maintain white political supremacy while employing cheap and efficient "colored" workers, thereby ensuring white economic supremacy. William M. Burwell, in an essay published in the July 1869 issue of *De Bow's Review,* described the challenge: "We will state the problem for consideration. It is: To retain in the hands of the whites the control and direction of social and political action, without impairing the content of the labor capacity of the colored race." Asian migrant workers, it seemed to some southerners, provided the ideal solution to the problem in that they were productive laborers and noncitizens who could not vote. Further, Asian workers would be used to discipline African workers and depress wages. On June 30, 1869, the *Vicksburg Times,* a proponent of Asian migration, editorialized: "Emancipation has spoiled the negro, and carried him away from fields of agriculture." The *Times* went on to exult at the impending arrival of several hundred Chinese coolies: "Our colored friends who have left the farm for politics and plunder, should go down to the *Great Republic* today and look at the new laborer who is destined to crowd the negro from the American farm." Arkansas Reconstruction governor Powell Clayton observed: "Undoubtedly the underlying motive for this effort to bring in Chinese laborers was to punish the negro for having abandoned the control of his old master, and to regulate the conditions of his employment and the scale of wages to be paid him."[34]

African and Asian workers, nonetheless, were related insofar as they were both essential for the maintenance of white supremacy, they were both members of an oppressed class of "colored" laborers, and they were both tied historically to the global network of labor migration as slaves and coolies. As anthropologist Lucy M. Cohen has shown, the planters in the American South were members of a Caribbean plantation complex, and the plans they formulated for Chinese migration drew from their cultural bonds with West Indian societies.[35] For example, during the 1850s, Daniel Lee of the *Southern Cultivator* and J. D. B. De Bow of *De Bow's Review,* despite their preference for African slaves, informed their readers about the growing use of Asian coolie labor in the plantations of the West Indies, and after the Civil War in October 1865, John Little Smith, an eminent jurist, reported in several southern newspapers that, according to an American ship captain who had taken Chinese coolies to Cuba, the Chinese were the "best and cheapest labor in the world" and would make good plantation workers and unparalleled servants.[36]

Despite their interest in Asian coolies, southern planters were stymied by the 1862 act of Congress that had prohibited American involvement in the coolie trade. To skirt federal restrictions on the importation of Asian workers, the planters and labor contractors crafted a distinction between coolies, who were involuntary and bonded labor, and Asian migrants, who were voluntary and free labor. That distinction, they noted, enabled the comparatively easy entry of Chinese into California, and when a shipload of Chinese from Cuba was impounded in 1867 at the port of New Orleans, planter Bradish Johnson argued: "What if the government should forbid the employment of the thousands of Chinese who have worked on the railroads, on the mines, and agriculture of California? No reason had been found for their exclusion and they were valuable for that country. The cultivators of cane and cotton would not be made an exception."[37] Johnson won his point, and the case was discontinued. Meanwhile, planters held Chinese labor conventions, such as the 1869 Memphis convention that drew delegates from Alabama, Arkansas, Georgia, Kentucky, Louisiana, Mississippi, Missouri, South Carolina, Tennessee, and California, representing agricultural, railroad, and other business interests, and formed immigration committees and companies, and labor agents continued to bring Chinese workers, under contract, to the South, procuring them from Cuba, California, and China. After 1877, when white supremacist Democrats had broken the grip of Reconstruction through fraud and violence, southern planters reverted to a preference for African American workers, and interest in Asians declined and vanished.[38]

Although advocates of Chinese labor in the South learned to distinguish slave from coolie, and coolie from migrant, the migration of Asians to America cannot be divorced from the African slave trade, or from the coolie trade that followed in its wake. Both trades were systems of bonded labor, and both trades formed the contexts and reasons for the entry of Asians into America. Contract labor was the means by which Chinese and Japanese migrated to the Hawaiian kingdom and the American South, whereas the credit-ticket system was the means by which many Chinese gained admittance into California. But a system that advanced credit to laborers and constrained those workers to a term of service until the debt was paid was a scant advance over the earlier forms of coolie and contract labor,[39] and, perhaps more importantly, all of the successive systems of labor—from slave to coolie to contract to credit-ticket—were varieties of migrant labor and functioned to sustain a global order of supremacy and subordination.[40] The lines that directed Africans and Asians to America's shore converge at that point, and the impetus for that intersection came from the economic requirement and advantage of bonded labor buttressed by the relief in the centrality of whiteness and the marginality of its negation—nonwhiteness.

African Americans recognized early on the wide embrace of racism and equated racism directed at Asians with racism directed at Africans. Frederick Douglass pointedly declared that the southern planters' scheme to displace African with Asian labor was stimulated by the same economic and racist motives that supported the edifice of African slavery. The white oligarchy of the South, he stated, "believed in slavery and they believe in it still." During the late 1870s and early 1880s, when a Chinese exclusion bill was being debated in the Congress, Blanche K. Bruce of Mississippi, the lone African American senator, spoke out and voted against the discriminatory legislation, and the *Christian Recorder,* an African American newspaper in Boston, editorialized: "Only a few years ago the cry was, not 'The Chinese must go,' but 'The niggers must go' and it came from the same strata of society. There is not a man to-day who rails out against the yellow man from China but would equally rail out against the black man if opportunity only afforded."[41]

In his *Observations Concerning the Increase of Mankind,* published in 1751, Benjamin Franklin divided humankind along the color line of white and nonwhite. The number of "purely white people," he noted with regret, was greatly exceeded by the number of blacks and "Tawneys," who inhabited Africa, Asia, and the Americas. Whites had cleared America of its forests and thereby made it "reflect a brighter light"; therefore, argued Franklin, "why should we . . . darken its people? Why increase the sons of Africa, by planting them in America, where we have so fair an opportunity, by excluding all Blacks and Tawneys, of increasing the lovely White. . . .?"[42] According to historian Alexander Saxton, the same racism that sought to increase the "lovely White" and that justified the expulsion and extermination of American Indians and the enslavement of Africans was carried, like so much baggage, west across the American continent, where it was applied to Asians, the majority of whom resided along the Pacific coast.[43]

Franklin's binary racial hierarchy found expression in a book written by Hinton R. Helper of North Carolina, who would become a chief Republican antislavery polemicist. Describing his visit to California in his *The Land of Gold,* published in 1855, Helper wrote of the inhabitants of a small coastal town north of San Francisco: "Bodega contains not more than four hundred inhabitants, including 'Digger' Indians, 'niggers,' and dogs, the last by far the most useful and decent of the concern." Of the Chinese, Helper charged that the "semibarbarians" had no more right to be in California than "flocks of blackbirds have in a wheat field," and he offered his view of American race relations: "No inferior race of men can exist in these United States without becoming subordinate to the will of the Anglo-Americans. . . . It is so with the Negroes in the South; it is so with the Irish in the North; it is so with the Indians in New England; and it will be so with the Chinese in California."[44] Within months after the end of the Civil War, the *New York Times* warned of allied dangers: "We have four millions of degraded negroes in the South . . . and if there were to be a flood-tide of Chinese population—a population befouled with all the social vices, with no knowledge or appreciation of free institutions or constitutional liberty, with heathenish souls and heathenish propensities . . . we should be prepared to bid farewell to republicanism."[45] In popular culture, the stereotype character of the "heathen chinee" made its debut in American theater by way of the blackface minstrel shows, and Chinese were paired with black sambos in Wild West melodramas.[46]

The institutionalization of Africans and Asians as the Other, as nonwhites, was embraced in American law and proposed legislation. California's state assembly passed two companion bills excluding from the state both Chinese and African Americans, modeled on the black codes of midwestern states.[47] In 1854, Justice Charles J. Murray delivered the California Supreme Court's ruling on *The People v. George W. Hall,* in which Hall, a white man, was convicted of murder based upon the testimony of Chinese witnesses. Murray outlined the precedents that established that "no black or mulatto person, or Indian, shall be allowed to give evidence in favor of, or against a white man," and he considered the generic meaning of the terms "black" and "white." The words, Murray contended, were oppositional, and "black" meant "nonwhite," and "white" excluded all persons of color. In addition, the intent of the law was to shield white men "from the testimony of the degraded and demoralized caste" and to protect the very foundations of the state from the "actual and present danger" of "a race of people whom nature has marked as inferior, and who are incapable of progress or intellectual development beyond a certain point . . . differing in language, opinions, color, and physical conformation; between whom and ourselves nature has placed an impassable difference."[48] The Chinese testimony thus was inadmissible, and Hall's conviction was reversed.

Like exclusion, antimiscegenation laws helped to maintain the boundary between white and nonwhite. Virginia banned interracial marriages in 1691.[49] Besides withholding state sanction of interracial cohabitation, antimiscegenation laws sought to prevent race mixing and the creation of "hybrid races" and the "contamination" and lowering of the superior by the inferior race. The issue of Chinese and white parents, predicted John F. Miller at California's 1878 constitutional convention, would be "a hybrid of the most despicable, a mongrel of the most detestable that has ever afflicted the earth." California enacted its antimiscegenation law two years later, prohibiting marriages between whites and nonwhites, "negro, mulatto, or Mongolian."[50] Based on the same reasons for antimiscegenation laws, African, Asian, and American Indian children were excluded in 1860 from California's public schools designated for whites, and the state's superintendent of public instruction had the power to deny state funds to schools that violated the law. Nonwhite children attended separate schools established at public expense.[51]

Asian laborers might have been ideal replacements for African slaves because they were productive and incapable of becoming citizens, but they were also useful in that they were neither white nor black. Although some believed that the addition of yet another group of people to society would only add to the complexity and hence difficulty of race relations, others saw the entrance of Asians as a way to insulate whites from blacks. Asians were simultaneously members of the nonwhite Other, despite their sometime official classification as white, and an intermediate group between white and black. The foundations of that social hierarchy can be found in the economic relations of the plantation system. Franklin Knight informs us that in nineteenth-century Cuba, Asians were classified as whites, yet "their conditions of labor tended to be identical to those of slaves," and on plantations with a mixed labor force, Asians "bridged the gap between black and white," assisting slaves in the fields and factories but, unlike slaves, performing simple semiskilled tasks and handling machines.[52]

In Louisiana before the 1870 census, Chinese were counted as whites in the absence of a separate category for people who were neither white nor black.[53] Despite that classification, whites perceived Asians as belonging to the economic, if not social, caste assigned to Africans. In 1927, taking up a Chinese American challenge by Gong Lum to Mississippi's Jim Crow schools, the U.S. Supreme Court, citing its 1896 landmark decision *Plessy v. Ferguson,* which set forth the "separate but equal" doctrine, affirmed the state supreme court's ruling that Chinese were non-white and hence "colored" and thus could be barred from schools reserved for whites. A Chinese man who married an African American woman during the 1930s recalled: "Before 1942, the Chinese had no status in Mississippi whatever. They were considered on the same status as the Negro. If a Chinese man *did* have a woman, it *had* to be a Negro." Mississippi planter William Alexander Percy described Delta society in his autobiography, *Lanterns on the Levee,* published in 1941: "Small Chinese storekeepers are almost as ubiquitous as in the South Seas. Barred from social intercourse with the whites, they smuggle through wives from China or, more frequently, breed lawfully or otherwise with the Negro."[54]

The Chinese, however, occupied an ambiguous position racially, as reflected in Louisiana's census. In 1860, Chinese were classified as whites; in 1870, they were listed as Chinese; in 1880, children of Chinese men and non-Chinese women were classed as Chinese; but in 1900, all of those children were reclassified as blacks or whites and only those born in China or with two Chinese parents were listed as Chinese.[55] In Mississippi, according to sociologist James W. Loewen, the Chinese were initially assigned "a near-Negro position" with no more legal rights or political power, but neither whites nor blacks "quite thought of them *as* Negroes," and they later served in some respects "as middlemen between white and black."[56] In fact, that function both mediated and advanced the prevailing social relations.

In 1925, two months after the founding of A. Philip Randolph's Brotherhood of Sleeping Car Porters, the Pullman Company hired Filipinos to serve on its private cars as attendants, cooks, and busboys. African Americans, who had for more than fifty years worked in those capacities, were henceforth relegated to the position of porter and denied mobility to easier, more-lucrative positions. At first, the Brotherhood called Filipinos "scab labor" and sought their elimination from Pullman lines; however, during its most desperate years, the 1930s, the Brotherhood, unlike the racist American Federation of Labor that had excluded both Africans and Asians, recognized the hand of capital in dividing workers and saw the common plight of black and yellow: "We wish it understood," explained a policy statement, "that the Brotherhood has nothing against Filipinos. They have been used against the unionization of Pullman porters just as Negroes have been used against the unionization of white workers . . . We will take in Filipinos as members . . . We want our Filipino brothers to understand that it is necessary for them to join the Brotherhood in order to help secure conditions and wages which they too will benefit from."[57]

Amid such examples of solidarity, African Americans were severely tested by the capitalist system, which deliberately pitted African against Asian workers, whereby Asians were used to discipline African workers and to depress their wages. The root cause of African and Asian American oppression was further clouded by mutual ethnocentrism and prejudice that frequently devolved from the ideas and practices of the master class. It is not surprising, therefore, that some African Americans, like Howard University professor Kelly Miller, saw a danger in linking the claims of African and Asian Americans. "The Negro is an American citizen whose American residence and citizenry reach further back than the great majority of the white race," wrote Miller. "He has from the beginning contributed a full share of the glory and grandeur of America and his claims to patrimony are his just and rightful due. The Japanese, on the other hand, is the eleventh hour comer, and is claiming the privilege of those who have borne the heat and burden of the day."[58]

What is surprising, instead, was the extent and degree of solidarity felt by African Americans toward Asian Americans. The *Chicago Defender* explained that Chinese and Japanese learned from racist America, having been "taught to scorn the Race or lose the little footing they may now boast," and Mary Church Terrell believed that Japanese shunned African Americans in an attempt to avoid the stigma of inferiority that whites had placed upon blacks.[59] And despite dismay over Asian American ethnocentrism, African Americans steadfastly realized that the enemy was white supremacy and that anti-Asianism was anti-Africanism in another guise. Thus, in 1906 and 1907, when the San Francisco school board ruled that Japanese children had to attend "Oriental schools" and when President Theodore Roosevelt intervened to avoid an international incident, the *Colored American Magazine* declared: "We are with the President in the California muddle, for as California would treat the Japanese she would also treat the Negroes. It is not that we desire to attend schools with the whites at all, per se, but the principle involved in the attempt to classify us as inferiors—not because we are necessarily inferior, but on the grounds of color—forms the crux of our protest."[60]

The Philippine-American war, like many of America's imperialist wars, provided an extraordinary test for American minorities. The late nineteenth century, America's period of manifest destiny and expansionism overseas, was a time of severe repression at home for African Americans. Shouldering the white man's burden was an opportunity for making domestic claims and gains, but at the expense of peoples of color with whom African Americans identified: the Cubans, Puerto Ricans, and Filipinos. Bishop Henry M. Turner of the African Methodist Episcopal church characterized the U.S. presence in the Philippiaes as "an unholy war of conquest" against "a feeble band of sable patriots," and Frederick L. McGhee, a founder of the Niagara Movement, observed that America was out "to rule earth's inferior races, and if they object make war upon them," and thus concluded that African Americans could not support the war against the Filipinos.[62] From the Philippines, an African American soldier wrote home to Milwaukee, where his letter was published in the Wisconsin Weekly Advocate on May 17, 1900:

> *I have mingled freely with the natives and have had talks with American colored men here in business and who have lived here for years, in order to learn of them the cause of their (Filipino) dissatisfaction and the reason for this insurrection, and I must confess they have a just grievance. . . . (Americans) began to apply home treatment for colored peoples: cursed them as damned niggers, steal (from) and ravish them, rob them on the street of their small change, take from the fruit vendors whatever suited their fancy, and kick the*

poor unfortunate if he complained, desecrate their church property, and after fighting began, looted everything in sight, burning, robbing the graves.

I have seen with my own eyes carcasses lying bare in the boiling sun, the results of raids on receptacles for the dead in search of diamonds. The white' troops, thinking we would be proud to emulate their conduct . . . One fellow . . . told me how some fellows he knew had cut off a native woman's arm in order to get a fine inlaid bracelet. . . . They talked with impunity of "niggers" to our soldiers, never once thinking that they were talking to home "niggers" and should they be brought to remember that at home this is the same vile epithet they hurl at us, they beg pardon and make some elfiminate (sic) excuse about what the Filipino is called.

I want to say right here that if it were not for the sake of the 10,000,000 black people in the United Sates, God alone knows on which side of the subject I would be.

General Robert P. Hughes, a commander in the Philippines, entertained some doubt over "which side of the subject " African American troops fell when he reported: "The darkey troops . . . mixed with the natives at once. Whenever they came together they became great friends." And according to a contemporary report, white troops deserted because they found the Army irksome, whereas black troops deserted "for the purpose of joining the insurgents," whose cause they saw as the struggle of all colored people against white domination. Perhaps the most famous African American deserter was David Eagan of the Twenty-fourth Infantry, who joined the Filipino freedom fighters and fought the Yankee imperialists for two years.[63] After the war—the war in which General "Howlin' Jake" Smith ordered his men to "kill and burn, kill and burn, the more you kill and the more you burn the more you please me" and the war that cost over 600,000 Filipino lives for the sake of "civilizing" those who remained—about 500 African Americans, many of whom had married Filipino women, chose to stay in the Philippines.[64]

Asians, like African Americans, resisted their exploitation and subjugation, and in the shared struggle for equality secured the blessings of democracy for all peoples. On this point we must be clear. Inclusion, human dignity, and civil rights are not "black issues" nor are they gains for one group made at the expense of another. Likewise, the democratization of America fought for by African and Asian Americans was advantageous for both groups. The "separate but equal" doctrine of *Plessy v. Ferguson,* for instance, was a basis for the 1927 case Gong *Lum v. Rice,* and both were cited as precedents in the *1954 Brown v. Board of Education* decision.[65] In addition to those parallel and conjoining struggles for freedom, African and Asian American lives converge like rivers through time. In full knowledge of intergroup conflicts and hatreds among America's minorities and their sources and functions, I will recall here only acts of antiracialism and solidarity between Asian and African Americans.[66]

During the late 1840s and early 1850s, African Americans gathered with Chinese and whites at San Francisco's Washerwoman's Bay to wash clothes, and relations between Chinese and Africans were apparently friendly. William Newby, a prominent African American leader in the city, reported to Frederick Douglass "that the Chinese were the most mistreated group in the state and that blacks were the only people who did not abuse them." Both shared with Indians, Newby pointed out, the "same civil rights disabilities," insofar as they were denied the franchise and debarred from the courts." In 1869, the first Japanese settlers arrived in California and established the Wakamatsu Tea and Silk Farm Colony near Sacramento. The colony failed, but among that group of adventurers was Masumizu Kuninosuke, who married an African American woman, had three daughters and a son, and operated a fish store in Sacramento for many years. Sacramento Chinese shared their church with African Americans for some time during the nineteenth century, and in San Francisco, Jean Ng, an African American married to a Chinese American, was buried in a Chinese cemetery. In 1913, Charley Sing, a Mobile, Alabama, Chinese laundryman, tried to get permission to marry Lillie Lambert, an African American. A Filipino band made sweet music under the baton of its African American conductor, Walter Loving, at the San Francisco Panama-Pacific International Exposition in 1915, and touring African American musicians sometimes stayed at Chinese-owned lodging houses in San Francisco. In 1927, Lemon Lee Sing, a sixty-eight-year-old Chinese laundryman in New York City, sought permission to adopt Firman Smith, an abandoned African American child he had found sleeping in a hallway. Sing fed and clothed Firman, enrolled him in school, and ultimately won from the courts custody of the child. Sam Lee, a Chinese restaurant owner in Washington, D.C., refused to fire one of his African American employees, despite threats on his life, while in Chicago, in 1929, a Chinese restaurant was dynamited for serving African Americans.

Many of us, Asian and Pacific Americans, several generations native-born, came of age during America's imperialist war in Vietnam and the African American freedom struggle of the 1960s. Many of us found our identity by reading Franz Fanon and Malcolm X, Cheikh Anta Diop and W.E.B. Du Bois, Leopold Senghor and Langston Hughes. Many more of us, however, have migrated to the United States since 1965; we came of age in Reagan's America, the era of yuppies and yappies, and wasn't that the time when history came to an end?—announced, significantly, by an Asian American. During fall semester 1990, I asked my Asian American students with whom they felt a closer kinship: African or European Americans? They almost universally expressed affinity with whites, and I recalled how in 1944, amid strident, anti-Japanese wartime propaganda and concentration camps for Japanese Americans, the *Negro Digest* conducted a poll among its readers. To the question, "Should negroes discriminate against Japanese?" 66 percent in the North and West and 53 percent in the South answered "No." During spring semester 1991, I asked my Asian American students the same question, and all of them claimed kinship with African Americans, and I recalled how in 1960, Yuri Kochiyama, born in San Pedro, California, and interned during the war at the Jerome concentration camp in Arkansas, and her husband, a veteran of World War II, enrolled in the Harlem Freedom School established by Malcolm X to learn African American history and to engage in the struggle for civil rights."

We are a kindred people, African and Asian Americans. We share a history of migration, cultural interaction, and trade. We share a history of colonization, oppression and exploitation, and parallel and mutual struggles for freedom. We are a kindred people, forged in the fire of white supremacy and tempered in the water of resistance. Yet that kinship has been obscured from our range of vision, and that common cause, turned into a competition for access and resources. We have not yet realized the full meaning of Du Bois's poetic insight: "The stars of dark Andromeda belong up there in the great heaven that hangs above this tortured world. Despite the crude and cruel motives behind her shame and exposure, her degradation and enchaining, the fire and freedom of black Africa, with the uncurbed might of her consort Asia, are indispensable to the fertilizing of the universal soil of mankind, which Europe alone never would nor could give this aching world."

Is yellow black or white? In 1914, Takao Ozawa, a Japanese national, filed for naturalization on the basis of his over twenty-eight-year residence in the United States and the degree of his "Americanization." Further, Ozawa contended, Asians were not specifically excluded under the naturalization laws, and thus he should be considered a "free white person." The U.S. Supreme Court rendered its decision on November 13, 1922, rejecting Ozawa's application and claim. Only whites and Africans were accorded the privilege of naturalization, wrote Associate Justice George Sutherland, and although the founding fathers might not have contemplated Asians within the meaning of either black or white, it was evident that they were not included within the category of "free white persons." Ruled Sutherland: "the appellant is clearly of a race which is not Caucasian, and therefore belongs entirely outside the zone on the negative side."[76] The marginalization of Asians—"entirely outside the zone"—was accompanied by their negation as "nonwhites"—"on the negative side"—in this institutionalization of the racial state. Yellow is not white.

But yellow is not black either, and the question posed is, in a real sense, a false and mystifying proposition. The question is only valid within the meanings given to and played out in the American racial formation, relations that have been posited as a black and white dyad. There are other options. Whites considered Asians "as blacks" or, at the very last, as replacements for blacks in the post-Civil War South, but whites imported Chinese precisely because they were not blacks and were thus perpetual aliens, who could never vote. Similarly, whites upheld Asians as "near-whites" or "whiter than whites" in the model minority stereotype, and yet Asians experienced and continue to face white racism "like blacks" in educational and occupational barriers and ceilings and in anti-Asian abuse and physical violence. Further, in both instances, Asians were used to "discipline" African Americans (and other minorities according to the model minority stereotype). That marginalization of Asians, in fact, within a black and white racial formation, "disciplines" both Africans and Asians and constitutes the essential site of Asian American oppression. By seeing only black and white, the presence and absence of all color, whites render Asians, American Indians, and Latinos invisible, ignoring the gradations and complexities of the full spectrum between the racial poles. At the same time,

Asians share with Africans the status and repression of nonwhites—as the Other—and therein lies the debilitating aspect of Asian-African antipathy and the liberating nature of African-Asian unity.

On November 27, 1991, about 1,200 people gathered outside Los Angeles City Hall to participate in a prayer vigil sponsored by the African-Korean American Christian Alliance, a group formed the previous month. A newspaper reporter described the "almost surreal" scene:

> Elderly Korean American women twirling and dancing with homeless men in front of the podium. Koreans and street people in a human chain, holding hands but not looking at each other. Shoes and clothing ruined by cow manure, which had been freshly spread over the rally grounds in an unfortunate oversight. Alliance co-chair Rev. Hee Min Park startled rally-goers when he began quoting from Marther Luther King's famous "I have a dream" speech. Black homeless people listened in stunned silence at first, as the pastor's voice with a heavy immigrant accent filled the slain black minister's familiar words. Then a few began chanting "Amen" in response to Park's litany.[77]

Park's articulation of King's dream reminds me of Maxine Hong Kingston's version of the story of Ts'ai Yen, a Han poetess kidnapped by "barbarians," in her book *The Woman Warrior.* Although she had lived among them for twelve years, Ts'ai Yen still considered the people primitive, until one evening, while inside her tent, she heard "music tremble and rise like desert wind." Night after night the barbarians blew on their flutes, and try as she Africans were apparently friendly. William Newby, a prominent African American leader in the city, reported to Frederick Douglass "that the Chinese were the most mistreated group in the state and that blacks were the only people who did not abuse them." Both shared with Indians, Newby pointed out, the "same civil rights disabilities," insofar as they were denied the franchise and debarred from the courts.[66] In 1869, the first Japanese settlers arrived in California and established the Wakamatsu Tea and Silk Farm Colony near Sacramento. The colony failed, but among that group of adventurers was Masumizu Kuninosuke, who married an African American woman, had three daughters and a son, and operated a fish store in Sacramento for many years.[67] Sacramento Chinese shared their church with African Americans for some time during the nineteenth century, and in San Francisco, Jean Ng, an African American married to a Chinese American, was buried in a Chinese cemetery. In 1913, Charley Sing, a Mobile, Alabama, Chinese laundryman, tried to get permission to marry Lilie Lambert, an African American.[68] A Filipino band made sweet music under the baton of its African American conductor, Walter Loving, at the San Francisco Panama-Pacific International Exposition in 1915, and touring African American musicians sometimes stayed at Chinese-owned lodging houses in San Francisco.[69] In 1927, Lemon Lee Sing, a sixty-eight-year-old Chinese laundryman in New York City, sought permission to adopt Firman Smith, an abandoned African American child he had found sleeping in a hallway. Sing fed and clothed Firman, enrolled him in school, and ultimately won from the courts custody of the child.[70] Sam Lee, a Chinese restaurant owner in Washington, D.C., refused to fire one of his African American employees, despite threats on his life, while in Chicago, in 1929, a Chinese restaurant was dynamited for serving African Americans.[71]

Many of us, Asian and Pacific Americans, several generations native-born, came of age during America's imperialist war in Vietnam and the African American freedom struggle of the 1960s. Many of us found our identity by reading Franz Fanon and Malcom X, Cheikh Anta Diop and W. E. B. Du Bois, Leopold Senghor and Langston Hughes. Many more of us, however, have migrated to the United States since 1965; we came of age in Reagan's America, the era of yuppies and yappies, and wasn't that the time when history came to an end?—announced, significantly, by an Asian American.[72] During fall semester 1990, I asked my Asian American students with whom they felt a closer kinship: African or European Americans? They almost universally expressed affinity with whites, and I recall how in 1944, amid strident, anti-Japanese wartime propaganda and concentration camps for Japanese Americans, the *Negro Digest* conducted a poll among its readers. To the question, "Should negroes discriminate against Japanese?" 66 percent in the North and West and 53 percent in the South answered "No."[73] During spring semester 1991, I asked my Asian American students the same question, and all of them claimed kinship with African Americans, and I recalled how in 1960, Yuri Kochiyama, born in San Pedro, California, and interned during the war at the Jerome concentration camp in Arkansas, and her husband, a veteran of World War II, enrolled in the Harlem Freedom School established by Malcom X to learn African American history and to engage in the struggle for civil rights.[74]

Notes

[1]Poster of the December 12th Movement, Brooklyn Chapter, 1990.

[2]William Caudill and George De Vos, "Achievement, Culture and Personality: The Case of the Japanese Americans," *American Anthropologist* 58 (1956): 1107.

[3]For a definition of racial formation, see Michael Omi and Howard Winant, *Racial Formation in the United States: From the 1960s to the 1980s* (New York: Routledge & Kegan Paul, 1986), pp. 57–86.

[4]See, e.g., James W. Loewen, *The Mississippi Chinese: Between Black and White* (Cambridge: Harvard University Press, 1971).

[5]*U.S. News & World Report,* December 26, 1966. See also Dan Caldwell, "The Negroization of the Chinese Stereotype in California," *Southern California Quarterly 53* (June 1971): 123–31, on the convergence of the Chinese and African American physiognomy; and Dennis M. Ogawa, *From Japs to Japanese: The Evolution of Japanese-American Stereotypes* (Berkeley: McCutchan Publishing, 1971), on the progression of Japanese American stereotypes.

[6]"Success Story: Outwhiting the Whites," *Newsweek,* June 21, 1971.

[7]Hugh Tinker, *South Asia: A Short History* (Honolulu: University of Hawaii Press, 1990), pp. 1–5.

[8]J. E. G. Sutton, *The East African Coast: An Historical and Archaeological Review* (Dar es Salaam: East African Publishing House, 1966), p. 8.

[9]G. S. P. Freeman-Grenville, ed., *The East African Coast: Select Documents from the First to the Earlier Nineteenth Century* (London: Oxford University Press, 1962), p. 8.

[10]Gervase Mathew, "The East African Coast until the Coming of the Portuguese," in *History of East Africa*, ed. Roland Oliver and Gervase Mathew (London: Oxford University Press, 1963), 1:116, 120–21.

[11]Ibid., p. 106.

[12]Ibid, pp. 101, 108, 121.

[13]Joseph E. Harris, *The African Presence in Asia: Consequences of the East African Slave Trade* (Evanston: Northwestern University Press, 1971), pp. 78–79, 91–98.

[14]Ibid., pp. 7–10; and Edward A. Alpers, *The East African Slave Trade* (Dar es Salaam: East African Publishing House, 1967), pp. 4–5.

[15]Marina E. Espina, *Filipinos in Louisiana* (New Orleans: A. F. Laborde & Sons, 1988), p. 1.

[16]Arnold Rubin, *Black Nanban: Africans in Japan during the Sixteenth Century* (Bloomington: African Studies Program, Indiana University, 1974), pp. 1–2, 9.

[17]R. L. Watson, *The Slave Question: Liberty and Property in South Africa* (Hanover: Weslyan University Press, 1990), pp. 9–10; and Robert Ross, *Cape of Torments: Slavery and Resistance in South Africa* (London: Routledge & Kegan Paul, 1983), pp. 11, 13.

[18]Joan M. Jensen, *Passage from India: Asian Indian Immigrants in North America* (New Haven: Yale University Press, 1988), pp. 12–13.

[19]Alan H. Adamson, *Sugar without Slaves: The Political Economy of British Guiana, 1838–1904* (New Haven: Yale University Press, 1972), pp. 31, 41.

[20]Hugh Tinker, *A New System of Slavery: The Export of Indian Labour Overseas, 1830–1920* (London: Oxford University Press, 1974), p. 19. For overviews of Asian Indian and Chinese migration and indentureship in the Caribbean, see K. O. Laurence, *Immigration into the West Indies in the 19th Century* (Mona, West Indies: Caribbean Universities Press, 1971); and William A. Green, *British Slave Emancipation: The Sugar Colonies and the Great Experiment, 1830–1865* (London: Oxford University Press, 1976), pp. 276–86, 289–93.

[21]Tinker, *New System of Slavery,* p. 63.

[22]Adamson, *Sugar without Slaves,* p. 48. Asian Indian and Chinese indentured laborers inherited, in the minds of the white planters, the alleged vices of African slaves in Trinidad. See David Vincent Trotman, *Crime in Trinidad: Conflict and Control in a Plantation Society, 1838–1900* (Knoxville: University of Tennessee Press, 1986), pp. 69, 87–88.

[23]Noor Kumar Mahabir, *The Still Cry: Personal Accounts of East Indians in Trinidad and Tobago during Indentureship (1845–1917)* (Tacarigua, Trinidad: Calaloux Publications, 1985), p. 41. For life on the sugar estates, see Adamson, *Sugar without Slaves,* pp. 104–59; and Judith Ann Weller, *The East Indian Indenture in Trinidad* (Rio Piedras, P.R.: Institute of Caribbean Studies, University of Puerto Rico, 1968).

[24]Cited in Ching-Hwang Yen, *Coolies and Mandarins: China's Protection of Overseas Chinese during the Late Ch'ing Period (1851–1911)* (Singapore: Singapore University Press, 1985), p. 59.

[25]Shih-shan H. Tsai, "American Involvement in the Coolie Trade," *American Studies* 6, nos. 3 and 4 (December 1976): 54. For a more detailed account of U.S. involvement in the coolie trade and coolie resistance, see Robert J. Schwendinger, *Ocean of Bitter Dreams: Maritime Relations between China and the United States, 1850–1915* (Tucson: Westernlore Press, 1988), pp. 18–62.

[26]Yen, *Coolies and Mandarins,* pp. 61–62.

[27]Persia C. Campbell, *Chinese Coolie Emigration to Countries within the British Empire* (London: P. S. King & Son, 1923), p. 95; and Watt Stewart, *Chinese Bondage in Peru* (Durham: Duke University Press, 1951), pp. 62, 66, 97. See also Yen, *Coolies and Mandarins,* p. 62.

[28]Franklin W. Knight, *Slave Society in Cuba during the Nineteenth Century* (Madison: University of Wisconsin Press, 1970), p. 119. African slavery in Cuba, of course, was governed by slave codes

that differed significantly from the institutions that regulated the coolie system. On the complementarity and distinctions between African slavery and Chinese indentured labor, see Rebecca J. Scott, *Slave Emancipation in Cuba: The Transition to Free Labor, 1860–1899* (Princeton: Princeton University Press, 1985), pp. 29–35, 109–10.

[29]Yen, *Coolies and Mandarins,* p. 63; and Knight, *Slave Society,* p. 116.

[30]Yen, *Coolies and Mandarins* pp. 64, 66–68. For a comparison, see Jan Breman, *Taming the Coolie Beast: Plantation Society and the Colonial Order in Southeast Asia* (Delhi: Oxford University Press, 1989); and Wing Yung, *My Life in China and America* (New York: Henry Holt, 1909), p. 195, on Chinese coolies in Peru.

[31]James L. Roark, *Masters without Slaves: Southern Planters in the Civil War and Reconstruction* (New York: W. W. Norton, 1977), p. 165. See also Rowland T. Berthoff, "Southern Attitudes toward Immigration, 1865–1914," *Journal of Southern History* 17, no. 3 (August 1951): 328–60; and George E. Pozzetta, "Foreigners in Florida: A Study of Immigration Promotion, 1865–1910," *Florida Historical Quarterly* 53, no.2 (October 1974): 164–80.

[32]Roark, *Masters without Slaves* p. 167.

[33]Loewen, *Mississippi Chinese,* pp. 21–24.

[34]Ibid., p. 23.

[35]Lucy M. Cohen, *Chinese in the Post-Civil War South: A People without a History* (Baton Rouge: Louisiana State University Press, 1984); idem, "Entry of Chinese to the Lower South from 1865 to 1879: Policy Dilemmas," *Southern Studies* 17, no. 1 (Spring, 1978): 5–37; and idem, "Early Arrivals," *Southern Exposure,* July/August 1984, pp. 24–30.

[36]Cohen, "Entry of Chinese," pp. 8–12.

[37]Ibid., p. 20.

[38]Loewen, *Mississippi Chinese,* p. 26.

[39]Cohen, *Chinese in the Post–Civil War South,* p. 44; and Gunther Barth, *Bitter Strength: A History of the Chinese in the United States, 1850–1870* (Cambridge: Harvard University Press, 1964), p. 67. See also Shih-shan Henry Tsai, *The Chinese Experience in America* (Bloomington: Indiana University Press, 1986), pp. 3–7; idem, "American Involvement"; Roger Daniels, *Asian America: Chinese and Japanese in the United States since 1850* (Seattle: University of Washington Press, 1988), pp. 13–15; and Sucheng Chan, *This Bitter-Sweet Soil: The Chinese in California Agriculture, 1860–1910* (Berkeley and Los Angeles: University of California Press, 1986), pp. 21, 26.

[40]June Mei, "Socioeconomic Origins of Emigration: Guangdong to California, 1850 to 1882," in *Labor Immigration under Capitalism: Asian Workers in the United States before World War II,* ed. Lucie Cheng and Edna Bonacich (Berkeley and Los Angeles: University of California Press, 1984), p. 220; and Sucheng Chan, *Asian Americans: An Interpretive History* (Boston: Twayne Publishers, 1991), p. 4.

[41]David J. Hellwig, "Black Reactions to Chinese Immigration and the Anti-Chinese Movement: 1850–1910," *Amerasia Journal* 6, no. 2 (1979): 27, 30, 31. See also Philip S. Foner, "Reverend George Washington Woodbey: Early Twentieth Century California Black Socialist," *Journal of Negro History* 6, no. 2 (April 1976): 149–50. In their 1943 struggle for repeal of the exclusion laws, Chinese Americans recognized a common cause with African Americans in their quest for equality. Renqiu Yu, "Little Heard Voices: The Chinese Hand Laundry Alliance and the *China Daily News'* Appeal for Repeal of the Chinese Exclusion Act in 1943," in *Chinese America: History and Perspectives, 1990,* ed. Marlon K. Hom et al. (San Francisco: Chinese Historical Society of America, 1990), pp. 28–29, 31–32.

[42]Quoted in Takaki, *Iron Cages,* p. 14.

[43]Alexander Saxton, *The Indispensable Enemy: Labor and the Anti-Chinese Movement in California* (Berkeley and Los Angeles: University of California Press, 1971), pp. 19–45; and idem, *The Rise and Fall of the White Republic: Class Politics and Mass Culture in Nineteenth Century America* (London: Verso, 1990). See also Luther W. Spoehr, "Sambo and the Heathen Chinese: Californians' Racial Stereotypes in the Late 1870s," *Pacific Historical Review* 42, no. 2 (May 1973): 185–204; and Miller, *Unwelcome Immigrant.*

[45]Saxton, *Indispensable Enemy,* p. 18; and Caldwell, "Negroization of the Chinese Stereotype," p. 127.

[46]Cited in Ronad Takaki, *Strangers from a Different Shore: A History of Asian Americans* (Boston: Little, Brown & Co., 1989), pp. 100–101.

[47]Saxton, *Indispensable Enemy,* p. 20.

[48]Ibid., p. 19–20. For comparision of Chinese and African American intelligence, see U.S. Congress, Senate, *Report of the Joint Special Committee to Investigate Chinese Immigration,* 44th Cong., 2d sess., 1877, pp. 942, 1133–34.

[48]Quoted in Wu, *"Chink!"* pp. 36–43.

[49]George M. Fredrickson, *The Arrogance of Race: Historical Perspectives on Slavery, Racism, and Social Inequality* (Middletown: Wesleyan University Press, 1988), p. 196. Cf. Takaki, *Strangers from a Different Shore,* p. 101, who, like Winthrop Jordan, claims that a 1664 Maryland law that discouraged the marriage of "Negro slaves" with "freeborne English women" by imposing a penalty requiring such women and their children to be consigned into slavery should be viewed as ban on interracial marriage. Fredrickson, however, argues that before the 1690s, bans of interracial unions were largely class as opposed to race-based.

[50]Takaki, *Strangers from a Different Shore,* pp. 101–2.

[51]Elmer Clarence Sandmeyer, *The Anti-Chinese Movement in California* (Urbana: University of Illinois Press, 1973), p. 50; Victor Low, *The Unimpressible Race: A Century of Educational Struggle by the Chinese in San Francisco* (San Francisco: East/West Publishing Co., 1982), pp., 6–37: and Charles M. Wollenberg, *All Deliberate Speed: Segregation and Exclusion in California Schools, 1855–1975* (Berkeley and Los Angeles: University of California Press, 1976), pp. 30, 31, 39–43.

[52]Knight, *Slave Society,* p. 71.

[53]Cohen, *Chinese in the Post-Civil War South,* p. 167.

[54]Loewen, *Mississippi Chinese,* pp. 59, 61, 66–68.

[55]Cohen, *Chinese in the Post-Civil War South,* pp. 167–68. Sociologists Omi and Winant point out that racial classification is "an intensely political process" and is not a mere academic exercise but denies or provides access to resources and opportunities (Omi and Winant, *Racial Formation,* pp. 3–4).

[56]Loewen, *Mississippi Chinese,* p. 60. Similarly, the biracial offspring of Africans, Europeans, and American Indians occupied an ambiguous social and legal position in the South. See Adele Logan Alexander, *Ambiguous Lives: Free Women of Color in Rural Georgia, 1789–1879* (Fayetteville: University of Arkansas Press, 1991).

[57]Barbara M. Posadas, "The Hierarchy of Color and Psychological Adjustment in an Industrial Environment: Filipinos, the Pullman Company, and the Brotherhood of Sleeping Car Porters," *Labor History* 23, no. 3 (1982): 363.

[58]Kelly Miller, *The Everlasting Stain* (Washington, D.C.; Associated Publishers, 1924), p. 163.

[59]David J. Hellwig, "Afro-American Reactions to the Japanese and the Anti-Japanese Movement, 1906–1924," *Phylon* 38, no. 1 (March 1977: 103.

[60]*The Colored American Magazine* 12, no. 3 (March 1907): 169.

[61]Willard B. Gatewood, Jr,. *"Smoked Yankees" and the Struggle for Empire: Letters from Negro Soldiers, 1898–1902* (Urbana: University of Illinois Press, 1971), p. 13; and William Loren Katz, *The Black West* (Seattle: Open Hand Publishing, 1987), pp. 323–24. On African American soldiers and the Vietnam War, see Byron G. Fiman, Jonathan F. Borus, and M. Duncan Stanton, "Black-White and American-Vietnamese Relations among Soldiers in Vietnam," *Journal of Social Issues* 31, no.4 (1975): 39–48.

[62]Gatewood, *"Smoked Yankees,"* pp. 14, 15.

[63]Luzviminda Francisco, "The First Vietnam: The Philippine-American War, 1899–1902," *in Letters in Exile: An Introductory Reader on the History of Philipinos in America,* ed. Jesse Quinsaat (Los Angeles: UCLA Asian American Studies Center, 1976), pp. 15, 19; and Gatewood, *"Smoked Yankees,"* p. 15.

[64]Richard Kluger, *Simple Justice: The History of* Brown v. Broad of Education *and Black America's Struggle for Equality* (New York: Vintage Books, 1975), pp. 120–22, 191, 423, 448, 554, 565–66, 670, 703–4.

[65]On African and Asian American conflicts, see Arnold Shankman's three publications: " 'Asiatic Ogre' or 'Desirable Citizen'? The Image of Japanese Americans in the Afro-American Press, 1867–1933," *Pacific Historical Review* 46, no. 4 (November 1977): 567–87; "Black on Yellow: Afro-Americans View Chinese-Americans," *Phylon* 39, no. 1 (Spring 1978): 1–17; and *Ambivalent Friends: Afro-Americans View the Immigrant* (Westport: Greenwood Press, 1982).

[66]Rudolph M. Lapp, *Blacks in Gold Rush California* (New Haven: Yale University Press, 1977), pp. 104–5.

[67]Bill Hosokawa, *Nisei: The Quiet Americans* (New York: William Morrow, 1969), pp. 31–33.

[68]Lapp, *Blacks in Gold Rush California,* pp. 104–5, 109–10; Douglas Daniels, *Pioneer Urbanites: A Social and Cultural History of Black San Francisco* (Philadelphia: Temple University Press, 1980), p. 97; and Shankman, *Ambivalent Friends,* pp. 31–32. On marriages between Africans and Asians in the South, see Loewen, *Mississippi Chinese,* pp. 135–53; Cohen, *Chinese in the Post-Civil War South,* pp. 149–72; and Doris Black, "The Black Chinese," *Sepia,* December 1975, pp. 19–24.

[69]Kenneth G. Goode, *California's Black Pioneers: A Brief Historical Survey* (Santa Barbara: McNally & Loftin, 1974), p. 110; and Shankman, *Ambivalent Friends,* p. 30.

[70]Shankman, "Black on Yellow," pp. 15–16.

[71]Ibid., p. 16.

[72]Francis Fukuyama, "The End of History?" *National Interest* 16 (Summer 1989): 3–18. The symbol of a man of color, particularly a man of Japanese ancestry, schooled in the West proclaiming "the triumph of the West" added substance to the finality of that "triumph," especially to those dubbed by Allan Bloom "we faithful defenders of the Western Alliance" (Allan Bloom, "Responses to Fukuyama," *National Interest* 16 [Summer 1989]: 19).

[73]*Negro Digest,* September 1944, p. 66.

[74]Yuri Kochiyama, "Because Movement Work is Contagious," *Gidra,* 1990, pp. 6, 10.

[75]W. E. B. Du Bois, *The World and Africa, An Inquiry into the Part Which Africa Has Played in World History* (New York: International Publishers, 1965), p. 260.

[76]Frank F. Chuman, *The Bamboo People: The Law and Japanese-Americans* (Del Mar, Calif.: Publisher's Inc., 1976), pp. 70–71. See also Yuji Ichioka, *The Issei: The World of the First Generation Japanese Immigrants, 1885–1924* (New York: Free Press, 1988), pp. 210–26.

77*Korea Times,* December 9, 1991. In Los Angeles, after meeting between the Korean American Grocers Association and several African American gang leaders on May 25, 1992, the merchants announced plans to hire gang members, and a participant in the negotiations reported a "total bond between the two groups," which included the widely feared gangs the Bloods and the Crips (*Asian Week,* May 29, 1992; and *Korea Times,* June 8, 1992).

78Maxine Hong Kingston, *The Woman Warrier: Memories of a Girlhood among Ghosts* (New York: Alfred A. Knopf, 1976), pp. 241–43.

Is Yellow Black or White? ▶ **357**

Imaginary Indians: Invoking Invented Ideas in Popular and Public Culture

Brian Baker

Introduction

This paper will provide an analysis relating to *imaginary Indians* based on ideas invented by members of dominant American culture that functioned to set Indians apart from society as *the other.* I will begin with a brief discussion of the relevance of being relegated to the status of *other,* especially as it relates to public and popular culture. Second, I will argue that in order to understand the idea of *imaginary Indians,* one must decolonize the mind (*think outside of the box*). After presenting a short discussion of *the other* and challenging conventional thinking, I will present an overview of four interrelated dimensions of *imaginary Indians:* (1) Indians roaming on the land; (2) Indians as children; (3) wild and dancing Indians; and (4) Indians as redskins and warriors. In terms of public culture and Indians roaming the land, I will introduce an experience where I encountered a sign in a national park that strategically misrepresented Indians and continues to remain as an official representation of Indian history in Sequoia/Kings Canyon National Park located in California. In terms of Indians as children, as well as in the case of wild and dancing Indians, I relate instances of imaginary Indians in popular culture to real historical circumstances in which the imagined ideas about Indians had far-reaching and real consequences. I will end with a discussion of how Indians continue to be relegated to a status of otherness via mascots in the culture of American sports, especially when it comes to imaginary Indians as redskins and warriors. In a contemporary world that espouses diversity and respect in the context of multicultural awareness, not only do Indians continue to be exploited as the other in this context, ironically Americans continue in their efforts to normalize *redskins* and *wahoo* as socially and politically acceptable.

⬥ To Be Imagined as "Other"

In recent years, scholars writing in the fields of Ethnic and Cultural Studies have increasingly used *other* as a way to reference and describe the position of racial and ethnic minorities in American society. In reference to his own lived experience as a Mexican American individual, Arturo Madrid wrote about experiencing life as *the other* in American society. A minority group is relegated to the status of other when it is set apart and distinguished by the majority group as not only being different, but in a very powerful way where observed racial and cultural differences of a minority group are distorted or magnified in their translation by the majority group. The groups who come to occupy the niche of other in American political, economic and cultural institutions, then experience *invisibility* and *visibility* in their daily lives. At times, the other is invisible due to the fact that the other is ignored and unnoticed, while at other times the other is very visible due to the fact that ideas and stereotypes that are crucial to existing as the other are highlighted. In both situations, the ideas that are invented and invoked play a key role in how individuals within a racial ethnic minority group experience their lived status as the other, despite the fact that invented ideas are rooted in an imaginary world. However, while imaginary in their content, the ideas invented and invoked are powerful products created by the majority group due to the fact that those ideas have an inherent and real impact on how a minority group will experience the world as *the other.*[1]

I will develop this perspective about the other in reference to the ideas about American Indians that were invented and invoked by Americans to not only rationalize and justify colonialism, but how those ideas continue to have an integral existence in American popular and public culture. Despite the fact that American Indians continue to challenge images imposed over them, Americans fully immersed in dominant culture continue to resist as they desire to keep American Indians within the category of otherness when it comes to popular and public culture.

⬥ Ideas Shape Imagination and Worldview

To begin to understand the idea of *imaginary Indians,* one must start by decolonizing the mind. In terms understanding the powerful reality of colonialism and institutional racism, we must deconstruct and examine our basic ideas that we have been socialized into accepting uncritically. At the beginning of the semester in my Native American Experience course, I make the statement that when Columbus (*who was lost and did not know where he was*) discovered America (*it was already here*), there were not any *Indians* in the New World (*technically at the time it was already very old*).[2] So, if there were no *Indians* here prior to the day in 1492 when Columbus lost his way to its shores, who were the people here? Students struggle for ways to answer, and the ideas they come up with actually reflect something about a colonial perspective deeply ingrained within a politically loaded American imagination that has passed through the minds of generations since time immemorial. Some of the answers to surface are what they view as the possibly more appropriate labels like *Native Americans* or *North American indigenous people*. This is a good way to begin the course, as I point out that these ideas are also rooted in the political and cultural categories of a western, hence an American, definition of the world. I highlight the fact that in North America alone there are *Native Canadians* and *Native Mexicans* in addition to *Native Americans* and that these categories of *indigenous* are associated with the geopolitical boundaries that cut through the landscape. These boundaries as political inventions have nothing to do with the peoples already here the night before Columbus planted his lost souls on the land. For most students, this is the first time that they have ever made this distinction and acknowledged the idea of native people in other countries.

While *North American indigenous people* may possibly be a good way to think about and understand who lived here the night before Columbus lost his way over the big water, I still find it necessary to force them to think about indigenous people at a level outside of a colonial framework that they have been socialized into accepting. First, they need to think outside of the conventional continental thinking itself as it is a problem rooted in a western scientific conceptualization of the world. The people here did not view North America as a distinct continent separate from South America. In fact, to those indigenous to the area that has been labeled as Mesoamerica did not view themselves as somewhere amid two continents. Second, while *indigenous people* may be the more accurate way to conceptualize people already here, I find it necessary to encourage students to take this one step further. Rather than a people, there were (*and continue to be*) many distinct *peoples* with specific cultural ways of knowing organized under unique political systems interconnected in various ways across what some indigenous peoples defined as *Turtle Island*.³

After getting them to re-imagine the landscape of indigenous peoples on the back of a turtle in the water, I then ask them a second question. Today, there are *Indians* in America, so where did they come from? From time immemorial and over the generations, as direct descendents of hundreds of peoples who defined themselves in indigenous ways (such as *Annishinabe, Dine, Haudenosaunee,* or *Lakota*), at some point in the colonial history that gave rise to America they did in some way become *Indian* once they began to emphasize larger commonalities and ideas shared as indigenous peoples who came together under this dimension of identity linked to the American political system.⁴ While the indigenous peoples re-imagined themselves through history, and actively pursued strategies to either preserve or adapt their political and cultural frameworks between the geopolitical lines that define American colonial rule, the Americans also invented ideas about imaginary Indians as a way to explain and validate the effective ways in which they subjugated the indigenous peoples who became American Indians.

Indians Roaming on the Land

While it is possible to challenge the ideas that were invented about Indians by Americans, it is especially difficult to change them because they have become so effectively institutionalized within the frameworks of public culture and ingrained in the American imagination. I recall confronting one idea about Indians during a camping trip to Sequoia/Kings Canyon National Park located in California. While we saw and participated in the wonders of the landscape by hiking on the trails among the largest trees in the world, swam in the cold rivers of early spring and lounged on their riverbanks, we experienced something so powerful and striking that it stood out in such a way that it came to characterize the entire trip. This was something created by Americans and imposed over the landscape, and while seemingly innocent in terms of ignorance, it was something not only connected to ideas about Indians, it also reflected how such ideas have become so effectively institutionalized that most Americans accept them unquestionably.

We hiked to the top of Moro Rock, a part of the landscape existing above the trees, and because it was in fact a huge rock, the view of the peaks that define the Great Western Divide was spectacular. It was wonderful, and we spent much time talking about scenery and, like many people who climb their way up, we took pictures. Despite our memory of this spectacular view from the top of Moro Rock, there is one that is of greater importance when you experience this as Native people. Before the final trek to the top of Moro Rock stands one of those placards that you read as a tourist. This particular placard provided two brief histories of Moro Rock, one having to do with its own geological history and another having to do with its associated human history.

It was the officiated version of human history through inscription on the landmark created by the National Park Service that left of us in jaw-dropping awe. In terms of this placard being a product attached to public culture, the human history for this majestic place began with the declaration *Indians roamed here for several thousand years.* What? Were they lost? Were they ignorant savages who never knew where they were for thousands of years? As both Indians and academics, we were especially aware of the fact that the idea of the *roaming* or *wandering* Indian was conveniently invented and invoked during Manifest Destiny. This *imaginary Indian* wandering aimlessly over the land was a powerful political philosophy and arrogant cultural perspective central to Manifest Destiny in that it validated the idea that Indians did not *settle* on the land because they *roamed* over it. In the process of colonialism, white American law makers and officials in the Bureau of Indian Affairs exploited *roam* and *wander* in reference to *Indians* in order to justify how the United States would deal with the *Indian problem.* Eventually, it became necessary to constrain the *roaming Indians* and limit their human existence on the landscape by drawing reservation boundaries around them in order to enclose and isolate them from American society. Once relegated to an inhumane existence on reservations where it was not possible to support their families, the *roaming Indians* no longer existed as obstacles to Americans who were provided with the opportunity to settle and bring civilization to the landscape.

Here in this public place in the wilderness and within the boundaries that define America, we had just experienced *institutionalized racism* toward and as Indians. To write into metal that *Indians roamed here for thousands of years* is indeed a powerful action related to the invention of imaginary Indians connected to a history of American racism. But, this seemingly innocent inscription was followed by yet another invention – *Neither sign nor record indicate they considered Moro Rock a special place.* What? Were those damn Indians blind too? Did they roam endlessly around and around Moro Rock for thousands of years and never realize that it was there? Despite the fact that National Park Service has maintained a Native village as one of the tourist attractions within the immediate vicinity that it has memorialized as *ancient,* the colonizers who inscribed their racism onto the placard have gone out of their way to ignore the village as evidence about residence by invoking the idea of the roaming Indian. The fact that Indians did not feel a need to post a sign nor leave a record on the rock is only evidence that Indians had a different cultural understanding and awareness, and that there was not a need to leave an inscription. To ignore the village in this case is more than ignorance as the ideas being communicated were intentionally designed to devalue Indians as those who *roamed* over the landscape *for several thousand years.*[5]

In a convenient way, the National Park Service inscription to Moro Rock reinforces dominant ideas and stereotypes about Native Americans, conveniently writing them out of the official human history and Moro Rock only becomes recognized for its unique geological significance once white people discover it, and in no way did they *roam* their way there. The next line is very telling – *Indians led Hale Tharp, the first white man to the rock in 1858.* How could the Indians have *led* the white man with a funny name to this place when they simply *roamed* in the area and seemed to be unaware of it? Why would *Indians lead* this colonizer to this place if they did not regard it as special? Was it because they were indeed showing the man with a funny name a truly majestic place and that it was necessary for him see it? In any event, the fact that Hale Tharp climbed the rock three years later is memorialized as an important event in the human history, the area in which the Indians roamed was discovered, named, and climbed by the colonizer.

Before leaving this place, in front of the placard acting as an obstacle to the entry to the way up to the top of Moro Rock, we (as Chippewa, Wintu, and Abenaki people) mimicked the idea of *roaming Indians* who were not aware of their surroundings. We took pictures to memorialize our own Indian ignorance. The non-Indians working for the National Park Service viewed our actions as inappropriate and disrespectful to non-Indian hikers who accepted the idea of the *roaming Indians* and to the white man with a funny name acknowledged for bringing history to Moro Rock, and our questions about the sign were relegated to being trivial nonsense. We disagreed, because if it were trivial nonsense it would be easy to change the language on the sign, and for what it's worth, the placard with its inscribed Indian imagery would not have been bolted there as a permanent political and cultural fixture in the first place.

◆ Indians as "Children"

The Americans invented strategic images pertaining to Indians to fuel the colonial machine driven by them across the land, and like bumps and potholes in the road, they understood that there was an unrelenting *Indian problem.*[6] To even conceptualize *Indians as a problem* reflects the fact that Americans viewed Indians as not having a place in the emerging political and cultural institutions that were coming to define the landscape, because Americans regarded Indians as *blood-thirsty savages* who, due to their natural tendency towards *laziness,* were unable to care for their own interests and needs. In fact, throughout the course of the 19th century, American political officials increasingly described Indians as *children* who needed to be looked after. Rooted in a combination of various acts of legislation passed by Congress and legal rulings proclaimed by the U.S. Supreme Court, the federal government successfully elevated itself to the position of *guardian* with an inherent authority and necessary obligation to look out for the Indian *ward.* In a literal sense, Indians were legally defined and relegated to the status of *children* under the tutelage of the U.S. government as the *parent.*[7] Through its self-appointed position of guardian looking out for the wards under its care, the American government created the idea of the *Great Father* who cared for the *red children* who, due to their inherent *cultural inferiority,* required constant American paternalistic guidance.

Once the lines were drawn, the lives of Indians who were defined as red children who roamed over the land were confined to an existence on the landscape enclosed by reservation boundaries. Near the latter part of the 19th century, indigenous peoples who at one time possessed the ability and means to sustain their own livelihoods were now blamed for the fact that they could not even feed or clothe themselves, which only served to strengthen the idea that Indians were like children. While they continued to possess a sense of being indigenous to the land, Americans began to see America's red children as *indigents* on the land and it became necessary for the *Great Father* to feed them. In a picture taken at Pine Ridge in 1891, a photographer captured a number of Indians standing in line on *ration day.* Instead of paying attention to the political and cultural circumstances associated with geographic isolation, the fact that indigenous economies were turned upside down and inside out, or American racism towards Indians as the more important and powerful factors which precluded the Indians in the photograph from making a living on their own terms altogether, the accepted explanation invented stated that these Indians were *lazy* and due to the own *cultural inferiority,* they were responsible for the poverty and starvation that came to define their lives. The Great Father realized that this was the natural and inevitable outcome when you leave children to fend for themselves without a pair of paternalistic hands to guide them. Because it translated into official evidence pertaining to lazy Indians living on the government dole, the photograph was easily exploited as a means to insert this image of Indians into the American mindset by the federal government. To equate Indians with *cultural inferiority* and to regard them as *children* was rooted in the *social Darwinism,* a theory of human evolution and societies that was directly connected to Manifest Destiny.

While the representation of Indians as *children* appeared in many aspects of early 20th century popular culture, I will direct attention to an ad for *Boston Baked Beans* from this period. In this ad, we are confronted by a strategically designed political image where a benevolent Uncle Sam is holding a spoonful of baked beans for an apparently starving Indian who stands on his tip-toes in order to greedily reach up and gobble down the beans that are being provided. The fact that Uncle Sam is intentionally created as being much taller and is holding the spoon for a shorter Indian invokes the basic idea of a parent spoon-feeding a young child; the Great Father dressed up in his red, white, and blue outfit going out of his way to provide for the Indian child draped in nothing but a rag; and finally, the mindful guardian acting in the best interest of the ward.

Despite the ideas about the imaginary Indian already mentioned about the Great Father as the guardian caring for the Indian children as wards, this image itself is based on an inherent contradiction. The Indian being presented in this ad is portrayed as being so inferior and childlike that he will gobble anything and it appears that good old Uncle Sam as an icon of American political culture is actually feeding him a second can of *Boston Baked Beans.* Sometimes I joke with students about this image, and suggest that I would hate to be sitting next this Indian around the campfire after he consumed two cans of baked beans because it could be a potentially explosive situation. But, there is a point to be made here about contradiction. While a second can of baked beans could not at all be very good to the indigent Indian child consuming them, Uncle Sam as the Great Father is feeding him a second can because the child will devour them. In terms of the Indians standing in the ration line at Pine Ridge in 1891, the food being provided by the Great Father to the red children was not at all that good in quality nor healthy in terms of diet, and Indians devised ways to eat rations that consisted of basic staples such as flour, salt, coffee, and lard. In terms of the oral histories and stories that I have heard, elders have spoken to the fact that sometimes the only thing to eat was either lard on bread, or fry-bread.

It had nothing to do with cultural inferiority and childlike qualities invented by Americans invoked over Indians; rather the Indians in the ration line at Pine Ridge in 1891 were just trying to survive in the same way as the Indian in the ad. In both cases, in the real photo and invented image in the ad, despite the positive portrayal of the Great Father and Uncle Sam providing food to the red children, the reality of the situation in both images is that the Indians as children were being provided with a diet that was substandard, and in terms of obligations when it came for the Great Father to care for the Indian children, it really did not matter because they were *only Indians.* What really mattered was the imaginary Indian as a public and popular idea in itself, and the appearance that the Great Father cared for the Indian children.

Wild and Dancing Indians

At this point, I want to reference a presentation that I once did at a museum having to do with representations of Indians in 19th century American art. I began the presentation with a recent (*as opposed to an old*) picture of a group of grade school non-Indian children dressed up like and mimicking their idea of the *imaginary Indian*. Some were sitting "Indian style" and a few of them were pounding on their "tom-toms." Others were standing, some were standing with one hand being held up as if they were an Indian saying "how," and others had a hand that appeared to be clapping over their mouths while screeching "woo woo woo." They all wore paper feathers glued to headbands worn on their heads. What I found to be the most offensive and revealing aspect of these *imaginary Indian* children was that it was clear that they were immersed in a classroom setting and two white teachers were also present. While it appeared that they just completed a unit where they learned about Indians, the fact that stereotypes pertaining to the imaginary Indian predominated in how the children posed for picture in the presence of their teachers is evidence that they really did not learn anything. Non-Indian children have been playing Indian for well over a century, and the images included in the photo have been passed from one generation to the next and they continue to be necessary components to how children become imagine Indians even in an educational context.

Because these children emulated the *wild* and *dancing* Indian images that were key elements of the Hollywood "cowboy and Indian" movies, it is obvious that the children are making progress in terms of being socialized into accepting the imaginary Indian. They will continue to be bombarded by invented ideas that relegate Indians to the status of other in American society and simply equate Indian with deviant behavior. Here, I will draw on a scene from an American film classic, *It's a Wonderful Life,* and an episode of *The Andy Griffith Show.* As texts loaded with powerful ideas about Indians, neither had any thing directly to do with Indians and there are no Indian characters. Instead, as products of popular culture, both associate good and moral with white Americans on the one hand while simultaneously equating bad and immoral with imaginary Indians on the other. Because there are no Indians present in these two pieces of Americana, these examples are important because they illustrate that illicit ideas about imaginary Indians only need to be inferred and the outcome is that powerfully negative images are communicated to an American audience. Symbolically, both texts manipulate and rely on the symbol of an *Indian head* adorned with a plains-style feathered headdress.

Originally shown American theatres in 1946, *It's a Wonderful Life* has had a life span of six decades in American popular culture as it continues to appear countless times on television during the Christmas season. In one of the final scenes, George Bailey is shown what it would have been like if he had not existed, an opportunity provided to him by an angel named Clarence. The angel is sent by God to help George Bailey, a good Christian and outstanding American, at a time when he is contemplating suicide and wishing that he had not been born. The good and moral town of *Bedford Falls,* is now *Pottersville,* defined by evil and illicit activities, because George Bailey is seeing what the world would have been like without him. Running down the main street, George Bailey passes pawn shops, burlesque shows, taverns, and pool halls, establishments that did not exist before. At the end of the street, he stops where the *Bailey Building & Loan* used to be, and it is now *Dime a Dance* where immoral women are employed. In this scene, when he as a good, moral human being faces the decadent context of *Pottersville* and the former location of his family business, there is a lighted Indian head flashing above George Bailey. It is the sign for the *Indian Club.* This Indian head becomes the symbol that defines the negative context of the scene, where the drinking and debauchery that characterizes the town is associated with Indians, and the once moral people are now *wild* and *dancing,* hence acting like Indians. While very subtle and only for a few minutes, viewers are reminded of the imaginary Indian that exists in American popular culture and accept it uncritically.[8]

This imaginary Indian who was *wild* and prone to savage *dancing* played a crucial role subverting Indian religions in a country founded on the principle of religious freedom. In fact, through law and policy Americans interfered with the many dances and ceremonies that were important to Indian religious systems because they viewed such things as either immoral or threatening. While law and policy relating to Indians were the legitimate and legal ways in which Americans precluded Indians from practicing their religions, what happened to the Wiyot Indians in 1860 California is a powerful example of how Americans regarded their *wild* and *dancing* Indian neighbors. Given their religious worldview, the Wiyot Indians of the Humboldt Bay area traveled to Indian Island every year to hold their *World Renewal Ceremony.* In order for this one group of Indians to remain as Wiyot people, and in order for the world to continue as they knew it, it was necessary for them to perform the *World Renewal Ceremony* as part of the annual cycle. If they did not perform this ceremony, the world as they understood it would cease to exist. The residents of Eureka, California, equated the *World Renewal Ceremony* of the Wiyot with *wild* Indians *dancing* uncontrollably in reference to what had been inserted into the American imagination – *Indians on the warpath.* Late one night during the time period when the Wiyot people were involved in their religious ceremony to make the world go around, some white men from Eureka traveled out to Indian Island, and with their hatchets and machetes, they killed most of the sleeping Wiyot people. While residents of Eureka heard the screams of the Wiyot being killed that night, they were no longer threatened by *wild* and *dancing* Indians out on the island. In the years that followed, the Wiyot were not allowed to practice the *World Renewal Ceremony,* and the world, as they knew it, did come to an end.

At the end of *It's a Wonderful Life,* viewers are reminded about the imaginary Indian prone to being *wild* and *dancing,* and in this case the context has to do with alcohol as another dimension of the imaginary Indian in the context of American popular culture. In 1963, an episode of *The Andy Griffith Show* aired that was titled

Aunt Bea's Medicine Man, which not only plays on the image of Indians associated with *firewater,* but also invokes the image of Indians as *evil* and *cunning.* The episode also degrades the basic idea of a *medicine man* as a medical and spiritual healer in Indian communities. The opening scene of this episode makes it clear that no resident of the quaint white American town of Mayberry has ever seen or known a *real Indian.* Images about Indians are invoked by a product being peddled by a traveling salesman, who is selling an *Indian Elixir* to the good white residents of Mayberry. Similar to the Indian head flashing above George Bailey is an Indian head on the label of the *Indian Elixir* bottle. Despite the fact that the non-Indian *medicine man* passing through town equates Indians (*i.e., Pawnees*) with devils, ironically the good and moral Aunt Bea equates the *Indian Elixir* with her own "baptism" after she drinks it. In the end, Aunt Bea and the women's church group become *wild* and out of control after drinking the *Indian Elixir.* Because Aunt Bea and the women's church group were *singing* and *dancing* uncontrollably after becoming intoxicated from the *Indian Elixir,* they are arrested by Andy and Barney. Once in jail, and after they sober up, they realize that were they tricked by the devil as the content of the *medicine* they purchased is 85% alcohol. Like Aunt Bea and the women from the church group, the audience associates their *drinking* and *wild* behavior with Indians.[9]

Like Aunt Bea and George Bailey, in addition to the moral white residents in the imaginary worlds of Mayberry and Bedford Falls, the white children in the visual described above have a good sense of who Indians are despite not having any direct experience with real Indian people. They are all aware of the *imaginary Indian* as the other, and the children in the photo are simply being taught to mimic a history of negative images invented by Americans and associated with Indians. Just like the Indian head on Aunt Bea's *Indian Elixir* bottle and the Indian head on the *Indian Club* sign flashing above George Bailey, the imaginary Indians created by the children posing for a picture are rooted in an historical context where it is clear that the images are designed to create a dimension of otherness when it comes to Indians. In the same way that it was presented to George Bailey in 1946 and Aunt Bea in 1963, the children playing Indian in decades later in the 21st century continue to equate *Indian* with acting *wild* and *dancing* while having feathers on their heads.

Indians as Redskins and Warriors

During a time period when Americans imposed many constraints over Indians that prevented them from practicing their religions and speaking their languages, or asserting important dimensions of their indigenous Indian identities, Americans became more fascinated with, and began to play Indian in reference to, their imaginary world of cultural ideas and political inventions relating to Indians.[10]

Within the American imagination, there has always been something special about American Indians in terms of ideas and symbolism, especially when it comes to playing Indian. Since the 1700s, the literal collecting and wearing of cultural artifacts, either as authentic or fake, to play Indian has reflected dominant cultural interpretations and ideas about Indians. When the symbolic dimensions of Indian are invoked in reference to the material objects associated with the idea of Indian, the assumption is that one passes through racial and ethnic boundaries to become Indian. The ability to play Indian by members of the dominant society in the context of popular culture is intimately tied to the invented ideas that reflect American racism towards Indians. For example, consider a scene from *Annie Get Your Gun* (1951), where Betty Hutton, playing Annie Oakley, sings *I'm an Indian Too* after being adopted by the Indians with whom she performs in the Buffalo Bill Show. The way in which this scene unfolds not only demonstrates how simple and ordinary it is for one to pass through a cultural boundary in order to *become Indian,* the scene reduces *becoming Indian* to simple material objects in a way that devalues Indians. Simply, one needs to collect and arrange material objects associated with the imaginary Indian that exists in the dominant culture regardless of how Indians define those same things. Following the placement of a necklace made out of the "teeth of many bear" around her neck and the enactment of what popular culture views as ritualistic Indian behavior, Chief Sitting Bull finally plunks a red feather in her hair and proclaims *Now!* From a dominant cultural perspective, what passes for Indian-sounding music and chanting begins, and in her robust voice, the star sings her own becoming Indian song. In terms of the appropriation of material and symbolic culture, she declares:

> Just like the Sem-i-nole, the Nav-a-ho, the Kick-a-poo!
> Like those Indians, I'm an Indian too!
> A Sioux, ooh-ooh! A Sioux, ooh-ooh![11]

The problem with this scene is that the very important and relevant distinctions that differentiate these three Nations of Indians mentioned are effectively erased or strategically ignored because they are irrelevant to the American *imaginary Indian* that resides in the invented world of popular culture. Instead of becoming a tribally specific Indian person within a unique cultural context, she simply becomes *Indian* devoid of any specific cultural content because in this imaginary world all Indians are basically the same. What becomes especially relevant here is that she becomes *Indian* based on the ideas of dominant culture. *I'm an Indian too* as a text is grounded on ideas and material objects that one needs to collect in order to be or act like an Indian, and such items as *to-tem poles, tom-o-hawks,* and even a *small pa-poose* are all referenced. While all the Indian chiefs continue to appear to be wild as they dance around during her *becoming Indian ceremony,* she pounds on a drum and grunts in an ape-like manner.

In essence, to become or play Indian as it is portrayed in *Annie Get Your Gun* is rooted in a history of racism towards Indians and continues to be the foundation of how children play and act on their idea of Indian. The imaginary Indian has also been invented as a *mascot* and *team name* in American sports and has been successfully institutionalized in terms of being a larger, more visible dimension of popular culture. In this imaginary world, Indians are conceptualized as *fierce heathen warriors* inherently prone to being *cold-blooded* and *cunning* in the ability to *fight* and *kill*. The fact that Indians have been referenced as *wagon-burners, wahoos,* and *redskins,* in addition to a litany of other derogatory names, in history by Americans reflects how Indians were set apart as the other in popular culture. For example, in California during the gold rush, the Native peoples were called *diggers,* which reflected how Americans, especially in their quest for wealth, relegated the Native peoples of California to a position of inferiority as the other. Amid the gold rush, incidents of genocide have been widely recorded, and while the Native Californian population was 150,000 in 1840 before the gold rush, by 1870 there were less than 30,000 Native peoples in California.[12] Today, *Chief Wahoo* of the Cleveland Indians and the *Washington Redskins* are just two obvious examples of the imaginary Indian existing within the parameters of contemporary American popular culture. Like the idea of *digger* and its consequences to Californian Indians, the fact that Americans referenced and viewed Indians as *wahoos* and *redskins* have had powerful consequences for real Indians.

In recent decades, and still throughout the country today, there have been a number of heated debates at the levels of local high school (e.g.., *Kelseyville Indians* in Kelseyville, California), state (e.g.., *Fighting Illini/Chief Illiniwek,* at the University of Illinois, Champaign-Urbana) and national (e.g., *Washington Redskins*) politics regarding the exploitation of American Indians for team names and as mascots. Debates and controversies themselves reflect something complex about ideas and meanings, especially as the responses by members of the dominant society and the extent to which individuals have internalized the basic ideas about the imaginary Indian articulate a perspective that the mascots in and of themselves are a way in which they respect and honor American Indians. Many American Indians view the use of their histories and identities in the context of stereotyping firmly entrenched in a history of American racism towards Indians.[13] While many American Indians object to being misused and reduced to mascots and team names in the world of sports, their voices are not heard and their perspectives are ignored. One problem has to do with the fact that American Indians have historically been and continue to be a very small percentage of the overall American population, and because of this, they have been a minority in terms of being a racial/ethnic minority population when it comes to visibility and political power. In terms of national politics and issues, this has compelled Susan Harjo and other Indian activists to file a lawsuit against the *Washington Redskins* as a strategy to tear down structures of racism towards Indians.[14] While the very concept and name *redskin* is directly connected to American racism towards Indians, team owners and many Americans choose to ignore and hide behind ignorance in their refusal to acknowledge this fact.

The most popular image invoked and exploited relating to Indians in the context of sports has to do with popular cultural notions of an *Indian chief,* and the symbol created to reflect team identity is an Indian head wearing a full-feathered headdress, an image widely and visibly apparent throughout the United States. The image has become so prolific and powerfully one-dimensional that it has become the imaginary Indian, and as such, it has effectively erased real Indians from historical and contemporary contexts. An example from northern California comes to mind, the *Kelseyville Indians.* In this context, with the generic Indian head, non-Indians view themselves as Indian when they compete in sports with opposing teams. They become and play Indian based on their ideas, and any connection or affinity that they may feel to local Indians is a complete fabrication.

The Indian head, as symbol representing the *imaginary Indian* flashing on the sign above George Bailey when he faces immoral people and on the bottle disguised as a medicine that tricks Aunt Bea into getting drunk, is also the symbol for the *Kelseyville Indians.* In the same way that the presence of the Indian head is only necessary to communicate an idea about Indians and has nothing to do with George Bailey and Aunt Bea, the Indian head for the *Kelseyville Indians* has nothing to do with history or culture of Indians from the area, as its purpose is only meant to represent some aspect of the *Imaginary Indian.* In fact, the very idea of the *Kelseyville Indians* is oxymoronic in itself. As a community founded in the vicinity of Clear Lake, the town is named after one of the first successful Americans in the area, Andrew Kelsey. Arriving in 1847, Kelsey and his partner, as colonizers, exploited the Pomo Indians of the area through conditions of enslavement. In 1849, Kelsey forced many Pomos to help in mines during the gold rush, and eventually he was killed by two Pomo men. In retaliation and months later, Americans responded to what was described as a Pomo rebellion against good and moral citizens and sent troops to Badonnapoti, an island located in Clear Lake and a home to Pomo people. In the aftermath of an attack, over 150 Pomo people were killed with hatches and axes, and today the Pomo people remember this as *Bloody Island,* a massacre connected to their enslavement and exploitation by Andrew Kelsey, who is revered by having a town named after him. It is an insult to the local Indian people of the area, the Pomo, to have the *Kelseyville Indians,* an idea invented to whitewash history of the area and write Pomo people out of the imagination of popular culture. Today, the debate surrounding the politics of the *Kelseyville Indians* is still taking place, as non-Indians in Kelseyville are hesitant to give up *their Indian identity.*

◀◆▶ Conclusion

While it is possible to challenge the *imaginary Indian* invented by Americans, the fact of the matter is that it is extremely difficult to change ideas associated with it because the reality is that those ideas have been effectively institutionalized within the frameworks of public culture and ingrained in the American imagination. Children today, in terms of their understanding of how to play Indian, still act on a legacy of stereotypes invented about Indians in a history of colonialism. While the ideas pertaining to the *imaginary Indian* as represented in *It's a Wonderful Life, Aunt Bea's Medicine Man,* and *Annie Get Your Gun* may exist in the context of the middle decades of the 20th century, the ideas pertaining to the imaginary Indian in the early years of the 21st century remain relatively unchanged. The ideas pertaining to the imaginary Indian are still visible and enacted when it comes to the *imaginary Indian* in the world of sports, where Indians are reduced to mascots and team names because they are still being defined as *the other.* Today, and nearly four years later, one small yet very powerful instance of *institutionalized racism* towards Indians still stands out – *Indians roamed here for several thousand years. Neither sign nor record indicate they considered Moro Rock a special place.* This idea is connected to *Indians as children,* an invention related to the idea of *wild and dancing Indians.* In the end, and as long as the *imaginary Indian* continues to have an existence in American popular and public culture as a *redskin warrior,* Indians in America will continue to experience *institutionalized racism* due to their colonial imposed status as *the other.*

Notes

[1] Artruro Madrid. *Being "The Other": Ethnic Identity in a Changing Society.* Pages 505–511 in *Down to Earth Sociology (The Free Press, 1997).* Also see *We Talk, You Listen* (MacMillan, 1970), by the late Lakota scholar Vine Deloria, Jr.

[2] The very idea that Columbus "discovered" America is a perspective grounded in the worldview of western culture. Despite arguments that reflect the "doctrine of discovery" many Indians dispute this idea and continue to question the idea of recognizing "Columbus Day" as an American holiday.

[3] While there are a variety of ways in which the indigenous peoples viewed and conceptualized the land, some viewed the *turtle* as a central player in creation. In the case of the *Haudenosaunee* (a confederacy of Seneca, Cayuga, Onondoga, Oneida, and Mohawk Nations), more generally known as Iroquois, viewed *Turtle Island* as the place where *Sky Woman* came to after she fell out of the sky. See *Encyclopedia of the Haudenosaunee,* edited by Bruce Johansen and Barbara Mann (Greenwood Press, 2000).

[4] See Joane Nagel, *American Indian Ethnic Renewal.*

[5] The intent was to construct the idea that Indians did not know where they were, despite the fact that they were quite knowledgeable about the landscape in terms of its geography.

[6] For a discussion of what has become defined as "the Indian problem" and how it was written into history, see Stephen Cornell, pages 33–50, in *The Return of the Native* (Oxford University Press, 1988).

[7] See Francis Paul Prucha, *The Great Father: The United States Government and the American Indians* (University of Nebraska Press, 1984). This legal relationship is rooted in *Cherokee Nation v. Georgia* (1831) and *Worcester v. Georgia* (1832) where the U.S. Supreme Court determined that federal government to the "guardian" over Indians who were its "wards" (see pages 208–213).

[8] *It's a Wonderful Life* (Republic Pictures, 2001), starring Jimmy Stewart as George Bailey was originally released in 1946. The title of the scene is "Pottersville" and it takes place near the end of the film. It is interesting to note that a picture from this scene with the Indian head on the sign is used as the background for the "Chapter Selection" section on the DVD.

[9]*Aunt Bea's Medicine Man* originally aired on March 11, 1963. In this episode of *The Andy Griffith Show,* Aunt Bea, played by Frances Bavier, is upset about her health and a recent visit to the doctor. Because she is concerned about her health and is feeling troubled, she buys two bottles of the "Indian Elixir" from a traveling salesman.

[10]See Philip Deloria, *Playing Indian* (Yale University Press, 1999).

[11]Quoted from *Annie Get Your Gun* (Warner Home Video, 2000).

[12]See James R. Rawls, *Indians of California: The Changing Image* (University of Oklahoma Press, 1984). Rawls does provide many different reference to the emergence of *diggers* as it was applied to California Indians, he also devotes one chapter, "Extermination" (pages 171–202), to the genocide and the depopulation of Native California.

[13]See *Team Spirits: The Native American Mascot Controversy,* edited by C. Richard King and Charles Springwood (University of Nebraska Press, 2001).

[14]*Ibid.* See Suzan J. Harjo, *Fighting Name-Calling: Challenging "Redskins" in Court* (pages 189–207).

Reflection Questions

1. How were institutions used to shape the identity of Native Americans, Asians, and Chicanos?

2. In what ways, do you think those responsible for changing the identities of the populations in question 1 had their identities impacted? (Optional)

3. What role do some of these readings play to challenge or surface your own assumptions, stereotypes, or misunderstandings of how we see difference or similarity? (Optional)

4. Does individual freedom exist ideally or actually exist given the readings? (Optional)

5. When you look at films and television, how do they portray different racial/ethnic communities? Provide a brief explanation by offering two examples in your discussion.

Response and Responsibility

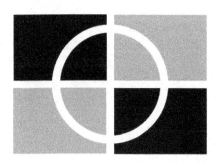

Framing Questions

1. What are some dominant themes that lead you either to believe race relations may or may not change? Please provide some examples as to why you think change will or will not happen.

2. Given the previous readings, why do you think this section is called "Response and Responsibility"? (Optional)

3. How would you define the term *response* given the previous readings and comparing that with your own experience? What inspires you to respond to a situation versus not responding at all? (Optional)

4. How would you define the term *responsibility* given the previous readings and comparing them with your own experience? What inspires you to take responsibility and when are you not inspired to take responsibility? Please offer a brief explanation using two examples to illustrate your point.

Introduction

Eric Vega

Ethnic Studies concerns itself with both abstract ideas and social justice. It presents historical and sociological information regarding race, ethnicity, gender and class. At the same time Ethnic Studies also discusses strategies for confronting unequal social relations in our community and nation. These discussions and dialogs offer us a chance to think critically about how others have confronted questions of power and privilege. This is both tricky and complex because the subject matter of inequality is not purely abstract or academic.

The specific struggles of women and people of color for liberation and respect are in themselves political controversies. Simply raising the issue of race or ethnicity is for many people an unsettling political terrain. But this is exactly the world of ideas and social struggle that informs this book. Both parts are integral to Ethnic Studies research and both parts continue to reanimate our lectures and study. In other words, this book is not just a data dump of terms and abstract ideas to memorize for the teacher. That is because the subject consistently breaks the bounds of objective analysis. The data and terms raise uncomfortable questions regarding response and responsibility.

A few years ago our Department of Ethnic Studies received racially motivated death threats. The caller felt deeply threatened by the intersection of people of color analyzing questions of race and ethnicity. This immersion in political controversy is not likely to be found in the Geology or Math departments. That is not to suggest Ethnic Studies has the "truth" or even complete answers to the difficult questions that surround us. It is more true to say our readings and our study are precisely about going deeper and learning how we can use language and ideas to inform our strategies for making the world a better place. As an example, this book asks the reader to move away from shallow or simplistic responses to racism. In our classes it is not enough to observe that the Ku Klux Klan makes you feel bad or sad. It is more important to ask questions regarding the historical and ideological context for white supremacist organizations. How do you respond to hate organizations when they work to insert themselves into popular consciousness? When you move beyond their cartoon like imagery, to what extent are their ideas accepted? These are difficult questions rooted in both theory and practice.

On the theoretical side, there are many explanations for the recurring controversies and issues connected to racial and ethnic relations. One way of approaching this topic is to examine identity. Who are we? Do we socially construct ourselves? What is the history of identity and what is its connection to the order of the nation? Historically, in the social sciences, intellectuals have formulated classic questions to help us examine popular ideas regarding identity. People like Freud, Marx and Nietzche have argued that we must examine the subconscious, money relations or the will to power if we want to honestly examine how people see themselves and relate to others. Ethnic Studies continues this tradition of observation and questioning. It asks the following kinds of questions. How have racial and ethnic groups been silenced or marginalized? What is the relationship of identity to power? In what ways do we have a fixed identity? What are the consequences of a constructed identity? As we work our way through these complex questions we rely on basic terms and theories. Stereotypes, ethnocentrism, assimilation and theories of prejudice and discrimination are the building blocks for examining questions related to racial and ethnic identity. But again it is critical to acknowledge that these words and ideas arise out of the struggles of historically subjugated peoples. That is not to suggest that social struggles are limited to problems associated with oppression and victimization. It is instead to say that our ideas about ourselves and about the world around us are fundamentally connected to the actual struggles of people. This means that an accurate description of the ethnic experience in this country must include an examination of social movements, political demands, styles of organizing, legal information and strategies that people of color have used historically to achieve their objectives.

This section of the book offers examples of how scholars, activists and communities have responded to the challenge of identify and power relations. Overt, popularly supported violence, segregation and discrimination are an important part of this nation's history of race relations. Subsequent attempts at comity have resulted in important legislative and judicial reforms that we think of as civil rights. But how much has changed? Has the werewolf face of white supremacy been replaced with a smiley face that disguises deeper problems? In *Facing the Demon Head On,* Manning Marable asks us to consider the racial implications of an emergent prison/punishment industry. With an estimated two million people incarcerated, he examines the "civil death" that is the consequence of this oppressive institution. The 1954 Supreme Court decision, *Brown v Board of Education of Topeka Kansas* has often been touted as the turning point in U.S. race relations. The popular opinion holds that the post-Brown era is all about tolerance, institutional neutrality and desegregation. Professor Scott provides a critical assessment of this view. As a matter of history, racial and ethnic minorities have placed great emphasis on education as a cornerstone for upward mobility and equal treatment. Despite tremendous opposition they voiced support for civil rights laws and integration of the public school system. But the resources and political will to see educational opportunity become a reality has not occurred over the last fifty years. Instead resegregation and mass incarceration are increasingly the norm. Professor Scott examines this lack of progress and the absence of a mass movement demanding racial justice in schools. He concludes his article by analyzing strategies and viewpoints that focus on educating African American children.

Emerging out of the Black Power Movement, Pan African Studies has grown over the last forty years to create a body of knowledge that reflects the experience of the African diaspora. In *Voyage of Discovery: Sacramento and the Politics of Ordinary Black People*, Professor Covin describes the evolution of Black Studies and its connection to the Sacramento community. Issues of identity and power are not simply the story of politicians and elites. As discussed in this article, Pan African Studies must also be the history of how working class people have negotiated with power in their everyday lives to create political space and unity.

Response and resistance to forms of abusive power do not follow a straight line. Sometimes it involves negotiation at other times it involves open challenges and disruptions to the prevailing order. As an example, over a long period of time many people negotiated their way through slavery but ultimately it was not reformed but abolished. Today an emerging political movement is beginning to challenge assumptions regarding the inhumane treatment of undocumented workers in this country. In her article, *Arizona: Ground Zero for the War on Immigrants and Latinos(as)* Professor Ramirez discusses the recent history of punitive anti-immigrant laws passed in the state of Arizona. These laws, including efforts to restrict Ethnic Studies courses have generated a swift and enduring movement of activists willing to challenge traditional law enforcement perspectives on immigration. To date, an energetic Latino(a) based civil rights movement has successfully used marches, political rallies and boycotts to challenge racial profiling and institutionalized discrimination. This article asks us to think about "illegality" as a framing device for popularly supported inequality.

The final article in this section looks at how the Ethnic Studies Department at Sacramento State has worked with Will C. Wood Middle School and Hiram Johnson High School to address issues raised by the parents and students in those communities. In *Community Psychology and Social Change: The 65th Street Corridor Community Collaborative Project*, Kim-Ju, Lucas and Mark highlight some of the theory and practice that has informed this successful program. A growing body of evidence shows that community mobilizations based on collaborative research and action can increase college access and retention rates. Relying on a team of CSUS faculty and students and rooted in theories of community psychology, this project continues to provide tutor/mentor assistance, college preparation, and leadership training and parent partnership programs.

Facing the Demon Head On: Race and the Prison Industrial Complex

Manning Marable

We know through painful experience that freedom is never voluntarily given by the oppressor; it must be demanded by the oppressed.

—Martin Luther King, Jr.

"Letter from Birmingham Jail," April 16, 1963

 I

When I was a child, the only two prisons I had ever heard about were Alcatraz and Sing Sing. Alcatraz was the formidable, stone citadel, perched on a small island in the middle of the San Francisco Bay. I saw *The Birdman of Alcatraz* starring Burt Lancaster, and the film left a deep impression about prison life. I suppose my knowledge of Sing Sing was acquired in a similar fashion. My images of crime and punishment were derived from Edgar G. Robinson, or perhaps some obscure character actors who were usually cast as hoodlums. Somehow, though, I knew that the phrase "to send him up the river" meant a one-way trip along the Hudson River to the infamous Sing Sing Prison.

Nothing I have seen or experienced prepared me for the reality of Sing Sing. The prison itself seems literally carved out of the side of a massive cliff that hovers just above the Hudson River. Parking is usually difficult to find near the prison, so you have to walk a good distance before you come to the outer gate, the first of a series of razor sharp barriers. The main entrance looks remarkably small, compared to the vast size of the prison. Entering the front door, you find yourself in a relatively small room, with several guards and a walk-through metal detector. Your clothing and other personal items are carefully checked. Permission to go inside the prison is severely restricted, and you must be approved through a review process well before your visit.

From *The Meaning of Race in America* by Manning Marable. Reprinted by permission of the author.

On the other side of the entrance area, shielded by rows of steel bars, is a hallway that is lined with wooden benches on either side. It is here that inmates wait before being summoned to their hearings to determine whether they have merited early release. During my first time visiting Sing Sing, there were about a half dozen young males, all African Americans and mostly in their twenties, who were sitting nervously on the benches. Most would be forced to wait for hours in order to have fifteen minutes before the parole board. In fifteen short minutes, they would learn whether they would be released, or ordered to serve another term of years behind bars. You could see clearly the hopeful anxiety in each man's face, trying to anticipate the queries of their inquisitors. The right answer at the right moment could bring their suffering to an end.

The prisoners also know that the parole board's decisions are directly influenced by authorities in political power. Under former Governor Mario Cuomo, for instance, approximately 54 percent of violent offenders received parole on their first appearance before a parole board. Since 1995 under Governor George Pataki, only one-third of violent offenders were granted parole after their first review. As Robert Gangi, the director of the Correctional Association of New York, observed, "Given the practice of the parole board, there are more and more long-termers that no matter how well they behave, no matter how many programs they complete, the parole board is not going to let them out."

As you walk through the prison, you go down a series of hallways, separated by small containments that have two sets of steel bars on either side, and secured by a prison guard. Only one set of doors opens at a time. The guard must lock and secure the first door before you're permitted to walk through the second door. Because the prison was constructed on a side of a cliff, there are also a series of steps that must be climbed to go from one area to another.

At the end of one hallway is the infamous, seventy-year-old structure, Cell Block B. The guards informed me, with considerable pride, that Cell Block B was one of the largest enclosed incarceration areas of its kind in the world. One must first walk through a series of double barred steel doors separated by a small interlocking security chamber. Once passing through the second door, one enters a vast open space, surrounded by massive concrete walls and ceiling. In the center of this chamber, filling up nearly the entire space, is a solid iron cage, five stories high. Every story or tier contains 68 separate prison cells, front and back, for a total of 136 cells on each level. Each tier is separated by small-railed catwalks and narrow stairwells.

Each cell is a tiny confined space, with barely enough room for a prisoner's toilet, sink, and bed. Prisoners are not allowed to place any clothing or items covering the front of their cells, except when using their toilets. In effect, personal privacy is nonexistent. The massive metal structure is like a huge iron and steel echo chamber, where every sound from tier to tier resonates and can be easily heard. The whole oppressive environment—the pungent smells of sweat and human waste, the absence of fresh air, the lack of privacy, the close quarters of men who have been condemned to live much of their natural lives in tiny steel cages—

is so horrific that I find it even now impossible to express in words its awesome reality. Perhaps the only word for it is evil.

Ted Conover, the author of *Newjack: Guarding Sing Sing,* who worked for nine months as a correctional officer at the prison, had a similar experience when he spent his first day on the job in Cell Block B. Conover was immediately overwhelmed by the constant level of noise, the demands of his supervisors, and the general chaos. "Being a new face," Conover noted, "was like being a substitute teacher. They test you. They defy you. And your job is to get them to comply." Conover questioned the ability of anyone to withstand the psychological stresses and physical levels of brutality that permeated the entire character of life in Sing Sing. "Every day is terrifying," Conover observed. "From the first minute, you're presented with challenges no one prepared you for. It's like working in an explosives factory. You think you're going to get killed. But you have to put it out of your mind."

Violence against prisoners is a daily occurrence. Conover described the process of carrying out a "shakedown" of solitary confinement cells. The guards go from cell to cell, demanding that each individual prisoner strip, turn around, raise his arms, and permit himself to be body searched. For prisoners who refused to be humiliated by this demeaning procedure, a group of guards pushed their way into their cells and forcibly carried out body searches. It was months after Conover was working in Sing Sing, however, that he realized that prisoners who resisted being physically searched were trying to hold on to some element of self-respect, to refuse to participate in their own violation. "If enough people did that together," Conover recognized, "the correctional system would come tumbling down."

In this man-made hell-on-earth, something within the human spirit nevertheless flourishes. About two decades ago, the prisoners of Cell Block B somehow managed to overwhelm their guards, protesting their inhumane conditions. For several days seventeen correctional officers were held as hostages. But in the end, the prisoners recognized that escape was impossible, and that this act of resistance was more symbolic than anything else. To demand to be treated as a human being in an inhumane environment is to be a revolutionary.

Seven years ago I received an invitation to visit Sing Sing from the Reverend George William ("Bill") Webber, who in 1982 had started the master's degree program at New York Theological Seminary (NYTS). When Bill began visiting Sing Sing on a regular basis, he observed that there were a small but highly motivated number of prisoners who had finished their bachelor's degrees and wanted to take more advanced courses. NYTS began to offer a graduate program designed for long-term prisoners at the facility. As the NYTS program developed, inmates at various correctional facilities throughout New York State were selected for admission and then transferred to Sing Sing. About fourteen to sixteen men were selected every year, with a waiting list of one or more years.

I was escorted to the rear quarters of the prison, which consist of religious quarters and chapels of different denominations. At the bottom of a stairwell was the entrance to a classroom. The students were already waiting there and were eager to introduce themselves. There was Louis, a twenty-nine-year-old man of Puerto Rican descent, who had already spent twelve years of his brief life inside penal institutions; Kevin, a middle-aged African-American man, articulate and serious, who had been in Sing Sing for nineteen years, and who was now actively involved in AIDS awareness and antiviolence programs within the inmate population; "Doc," a thirteen-year prisoner who planned to be a counselor; Paul, a seventeen-year inmate interested in working with teenagers and young adults after his release; and Felipe, a prisoner for nineteen years, who was preparing himself for the ministry.

The NYTS program is basically designed to prepare these men for community service. There is a rigorous academic program, where lectures and classroom discussions are held three hours a day, five days a week. Forty-two credit hours must be taken to complete the degree. Inmates are also required to perform an additional fifteen credit hours of field service within the prison, which can range from working in the AIDS ward to tutoring other prisoners. Since the program was established, more than 200 men have graduated with master's degrees. Only 5 percent of those inmates who have completed the program and were released were subsequently returned to prison.

The NYTS program is exceptional, in part, because so few educational programs of its type exist in U.S. prisons. In 1995, only one-third of all U.S. prisons provided college course work, and fewer than one in four prisoners were enrolled in some kind of educational or tutorial program behind bars. There are only about 11,000 paid teachers who are currently employed by penal institutions, or about one teacher per ninety-three prisoners.

One can only imagine the personal courage and determination of these men, most of whom entered prison without a high-school diploma or GED. From the first day of their sentences inside Sing Sing, they experienced what the NYTS 1994 program graduates accurately described as "social death": "We are told what we can eat, when we can eat it, and how we must eat it. We are told what type of clothing we can wear, when to wear it, and where we can wear it; when we can sleep and when we cannot sleep; where we can walk and where we cannot walk; when we can show affection to our families and when we cannot show affection; where we can sit and where we cannot sit; where we can stand and where we cannot stand." Despite the hostility of many prison guards, most of whom come from the same oppressed classes of those whom they are employed to guard, the men involved in the program withstand the daily abuse and harassment. In their own words, "We see ourselves as agents of change."

II

For a variety of reasons, rates of violent crime, including murder, rape, and robbery, increased dramatically in the 1960s and 1970s. Much of this increase occurred in urban areas. By the late 1970s, nearly one-half of all Americans were afraid to walk within a mile of their homes at night, and 90 percent responded in surveys that the U.S. criminal-justice system was not dealing harshly enough with criminals. Politicians like Richard M. Nixon, George Wallace, and Ronald Reagan began to campaign successfully on the theme of law and order. The death penalty, which was briefly outlawed by the Supreme Court, was reinstated. Local, state, and federal expenditures for law enforcement rose sharply. Behind much of anticrime rhetoric was a not-too-subtle racial dimension, the projection of crude stereotypes about the link between criminality and black people. Rarely did these politicians observe that minority and poor people, not the white middle class, were statistically much more likely to experience violent crimes of all kinds. The argument was made that law-enforcement officers should be given much greater latitude in suppressing crime, that sentences should be lengthened and made mandatory, and that prisons should be designed not for the purpose of rehabilitation, but punishment.

Consequently, there was a rapid expansion in the personnel of the criminal-justice system, as well as the construction of new prisons. What occurred in New York State, for example, was typical of what happened nationally. From 1817 to 1981, New York had opened thirty-three state prisons. From 1982 to 1999, another thirty-eight state prisons were constructed. The state's prison population at the time of the Attica prison revolt in September 1971 was about 12,500. By 1999, there were more than 71,000 prisoners in New York State correctional facilities.

In 1974, the number of Americans incarcerated in all state prisons stood at 187,500. By 1991, the number had reached 711,700. Nearly two-thirds of all state prisoners in 1991 had less than a high-school education. One-third of all prisoners were unemployed at the time of their arrests. Incarceration rates by the end of the 1980s had soared to unprecedented rates, especially for black Americans. As of December 1989, the total U.S. prison population, including federal institutions, exceeded 1 million for the first time in history, an incarceration rate of the general population of 1 out of every 250 citizens. For African Americans, the rate was over 700 per 100,000, or about seven times higher than for whites. About one-half of all prisoners were black. Twenty-three percent of all black males in their twenties were either in prison, on parole, on probation, or awaiting trial. The rate of incarceration of black Americans in 1989 had even surpassed that experienced by blacks who still lived under the apartheid regime of South Africa.

By the early 1990s, rates for all types of violent crime began to plummet. But the laws sending offenders to prison were made even more severe. Children were increasingly viewed in courts as adults and subjected to harsher penalties. Laws like California's "three strikes and you're out" eliminated the possibility of parole for repeat offenders. The vast majority of these new prisoners were nonviolent offenders, and many of these were convicted of drug offenses that carried long prison terms. In New York, African Americans and Latinos make up 25 percent of the total population, but by 1999 they represented 83 percent of all state prisoners and 94 percent of all individuals convicted on drug offenses. The pattern of racial bias in these statistics is confirmed by the research of the U.S. Commission on Civil Rights, which found that while African Americans today constitute only

14 percent of all drug users nationally, they account for 35 percent of all drug arrests, 55 percent of all drug convictions, and 75 percent of all prison admissions for drug offenses. Currently, the racial proportions of those under some type of correctional supervision, including parole and probation, are one in fifteen for young white males, one in ten for young Latino males, and one in three for young African-American males. Statistically today, more than eight out of every ten African-American males will be arrested at some point in their lifetime.

Structural racism is so difficult to dismantle in our nation today, in part, because political leaders in both major parties have deliberately redirected billions of our tax dollars away from investments in public education into the construction of what many scholars now describe as a prison industrial complex. This is the terrible connection between education and incarceration.

A 1998 study produced by the Correctional Association of New York and the Washington, D.C.–based Justice Policy Institute illustrated that in New York State hundreds of millions of dollars have been reallocated from the budgets of public universities to prison construction. The report stated: "Since fiscal year 1988, New York's public universities have seen their operating budgets plummet by 29 percent while funding for prisons has increased by 76 percent. In actual dollars, there has nearly been an equal trade-off, with the Department of Correctional Services receiving a $761 million increase during that time while state funding for New York's city and state university systems has declined by $615 million." By 1998, New York State was spending nearly twice what it had allocated to run its prison system a decade ago. To pay for that massive expansion, tuitions and fees for students at the State University of New York (SUNY) and the City University of New York (CUNY) had to be dramatically hiked.

For black and Latino young adults, these shifts have made it much more difficult to attend college than in the past, but much easier to go to prison. The New York State study found: "There are more blacks (34,809) and Hispanics (22,421) locked up in prison than there are attending the State University of New York, where there are 27,925 black and Hispanic students. Since 1989, there have been more blacks entering the prison system for drug offenses each year than there were graduating from SUNY with undergraduate, masters, and doctoral degrees—combined."

The devastating pattern of schools versus prisons in New York exists throughout our country. In California, thousands of black and Latino young adults were denied access to state universities because of the passage of Proposition 209, which destroyed affirmative action. Thousands more have been driven out by the steadily growing cost of tuition and cutbacks in student loans. Meanwhile, hundreds of millions of dollars have been siphoned away from the state's education budget and spent on building prisons.

In 1977, California had 19,600 inmates in its state prison system. By 2000, the number of that state's prisoners exceeded 163,000. In the past two decades of the twentieth century, California has constructed one new state university, but twenty-one new prisons. California's prison system "holds more inmates in its jails and prisons than do France, Great Britain, Germany, Japan, Singapore, and the Netherlands combined." And future trends are worse. The California Department of Corrections estimated in 2000 that it would need to spend $6.1 billion over the coming decade just to maintain the present prison population. There are more employees at work in the American prison industry than in any Fortune 500 corporation, with the one exception of General Motors.

Instead of funding more teachers, we are hiring extra prison guards. Instead of building new classrooms, we are constructing new jails. Instead of books, we now have bars everywhere.

III

The latest innovation in American corrections is termed "special housing units" (SHUs), but which prisoners also generally refer to as The Box. SHUs are uniquely designed solitary confinement cells in which prisoners are locked down for twenty-three hours a day for months or even years at a time. SHU cell blocks are electronically monitored, prefabricated structures of concrete and steel, about 14 feet long and 8 1/2 feet wide, amounting to 120 square feet of space. The two inmates who are confined in each cell, however, actually have only about 60 square feet of usable space, or 30 square feet per person. All meals are served to prisoners through a thin slot cut into the steel door. The toilet unit, sink, and shower are all located in the cell. Prisoners are permitted one hour "exercise time" each day in a small concrete balcony, surrounded by heavy security wire, directly connected with their SHU cells. Educational and rehabilitation programs for SHU prisoners are prohibited.

As of 1998, New York State had confined 5,700 state prisoners in SHUs, about 8 percent of its total inmate population. Currently under construction in Upstate New York is a new 750-cell maximum-security SHU facility that will cost state taxpayers $180 million. Although Amnesty International and human-rights groups in the United States have widely condemned SHUs, claiming that such forms of imprisonment constitute the definition of torture under international law, other states have followed New York's example. As of 1998, California had constructed 2,942 SHU beds, followed by Mississippi (1,756), Arizona (1,728), Virginia (1,267), Texas (1,229), Louisiana (1,048), and Florida (1,000). Solitary confinement, which historically had been defined even by corrections officials as an extreme disciplinary measure, is becoming increasingly the norm.

The introduction of SHUs reflects a general mood in the country that the growing penal population is essentially beyond redemption. If convicted felons cease to be viewed as human beings, why should they be treated with any humanity? This punitive spirit was behind the Republican-controlled Congress and President Clinton's decision in 1995 to eliminate inmate eligibility for federal Pell Grant awards for higher education. As of 1994, 23,000 prisoners throughout the United States had received Pell Grants, averaging about $1,500 per award. The total amount of educational support granted prisoners, $35 million, represented only 0.6 percent of all Pell Grant funding nationally. Many studies have found that prisoners who participate in higher education programs, and especially those who complete college degrees, have significantly lower rates of recidivism. For all prison inmates, for example, recidivism averages between 50 percent and 70 percent. Federal parolees have a recidivism rate of 40 percent. Prisoners with a college education have recidivism rates of only 5 to 10 percent. Given the high success ratio of prisoners who complete advanced degree work and the relatively low cost of public investment, such educational programs should make sense. But following the federal government's lead, many states have also ended their tuition benefits programs for state prisoners.

The economic consequences of the vast expansion of our prison industrial complex are profound. According to criminal-justice scholar David Barlow at the University of Wisconsin at Milwaukee, between 1980 and 2000 the combined expenditures of federal, state, and local governments on police have increased about 400 percent. Corrections expenditures for building new prisons, upgrading existing facilities, hiring more guards, and related costs increased approximately 1,000 percent. Although it currently costs about $70,000 to construct a typical prison cell, and about $25,000 annually to supervise and maintain each prisoner, the United States is still building hundreds of new prison beds every week.

The driving ideological and cultural force that rationalizes and justifies mass incarceration is the white American public's stereotypical perceptions about race and crime. As Andrew Hacker perceptively noted in 1995, "Quite clearly, 'black crime' does not make people think about tax evasion or embezzling from brokerage firms. Rather, the offenses generally associated with blacks are those . . . involving violence." A number of researchers have found that racial stereotypes of African Americans—as "violent," "aggressive," "hostile," and "short-tempered"— greatly influence whites' judgments about crime. Generally, most whites are inclined to give black and Latino defendants more severe judgments of guilt and lengthier prison sentences than whites who commit identical crimes. Racial bias has been well established, especially in capital cases, where killers of white victims are much more likely to receive the death penalty than those who murder African Americans.

The greatest victims of these racialized processes of unequal justice, of course, are African-American and Latino young people. In April 2000, utilizing national and state data compiled by the FBI, the Justice Department and six leading foundations issued a comprehensive study that documented vast racial disparities at every level of the juvenile justice process. African Americans under age eighteen constitute 15 percent of their national age group, yet they currently represent 26 percent of all those who are arrested. After entering the criminal-justice system, white and black juveniles with the same records are treated in radically different ways. According to the Justice Department's study, among white youth offenders, 66 percent are referred to juvenile courts, while only 31 percent of the African-American youth are taken there. Blacks make up 44 percent of those detained in juvenile jails, 46 percent of all those tried in adult criminal courts, as well as 58 percent of all juveniles who are warehoused in adult prison. In practical terms, this means that young African Americans who are arrested and charged with a crime are more than six times more likely to be assigned to prison than white youth offenders.

For those young people who have never been to prison before, African Americans are nine times more likely than whites to be sentenced to juvenile prisons. For youths charged with drug offenses, blacks are forty-eight times more likely than whites to be sentenced to juvenile prison. White youths charged with violent offenses are incarcerated on average for 193 days after trial; by contrast, African-American youths are held 254 days, and Latino youths are incarcerated 305 days.

Even outside of the prison walls, the black community's parameters are largely defined by the agents of state and private power. There are now approximately 600,000 police officers and 1.5 million private security guards in the United States. Increasingly, however, black and poor communities are being "policed" by special paramilitary units, often called SWAT (Special Weapons and Tactics) teams. Researcher Christian Parenti cited studies indicating that "the nation has more than 30,000 such heavily armed, military trained police units." SWAT-team mobilizations, or "call outs," increased 400 percent between 1980 and 1995, with a 34 percent increase in the incidents of deadly force recorded by SWAT teams from 1995 to 1998.

What are the practical political consequences for regulating black and brown bodies through the coercive institutional space of our correctional facilities? Perhaps the greatest impact is on the process of black voting. According to the statistical data of the Sentencing Project, a non-profit research center in Washington, D.C., forty-eight states and the District of Columbia bar prisoners who have been convicted of a felony from voting. Thirty-two states bar ex-felons who are currently on parole from voting. Twenty-eight states even prohibit adults from voting if they are felony probationers. There are eight states that deny voting rights to former prisoners who had been serving time for felonies, even after they have completed their sentences: Alabama, Florida, Iowa, Kentucky, Mississippi, Nevada, Virginia, and Wyoming. In Arizona, ex-felons are disfranchised for life if they are convicted of a second felony. Delaware disfranchises some ex-felons for five years after they finish their sentences, and Maryland bars them from voting for an additional three years.

The net result to democracy is devastating. The Sentencing Project released these statistics in 2002:

- An estimated 3.9 million Americans, or one in fifty adults, have currently or permanently lost their voting rights as a result of a felony conviction.
- 1.4 million African-American men, or 13 percent of black men, are disfranchised, a rate seven times the national average.
- More than 2 million white Americans (Hispanic and non-Hispanic) are disfranchised.

- Over half a million women have lost their right to vote.
- In seven states that deny the vote to ex-offenders, one in four black men is *permanently* disfranchised.
- Given current rates of incarceration, three in ten of the next generation of black men can expect to be disfranchised at some point in their lifetime. In states that disfranchise ex-offenders, as many as 40 percent of black men may permanently lose their right to vote.
- 1.4 million disfranchised persons are ex-offenders who have completed their sentences. The state of Florida had at least 200,000 ex-felons who were unable to vote in the 2000 presidential elections.

The Sentencing Project adds that "the scale of felony voting disenfranchisement is far greater than in any other nation and has serious implications for democratic processes and racial inclusion." In effect, the Voting Rights Act of 1965, which guaranteed millions of African Americans the right to the electoral franchise, is being gradually repealed by state restrictions on voting for ex-felons. A people who are imprisoned in disproportionately higher numbers, and then systematically denied the right to vote, can in no way claim to live under a democracy.

The consequence of such widespread disfranchisement is what can be called "civil death." The individual who has been convicted of a felony, serves time, and successfully completes parole nevertheless continues to be penalized at every turn. He/she is penalized in the labor force, being denied certain jobs because of a criminal record. He/she has little direct access or influence on the decision-making processes of the political system. He/she may be employed and pay taxes, assuming all of the normal responsibilities of other citizens, yet may be temporarily or permanently barred from the one activity that defines citizenship itself—voting. Individuals who are penalized in this way have little incentive to participate in the normal public activities defining civic life because they exercise no voice in public decision making. Ex-prisoners on parole are also frequently discouraged from participation in public demonstrations or political meetings because of parole restrictions. For many ex-prisoners, there is a retreat from individual political activity; a sense of alienation and frustration easily leads to apathy. Those who experience civic death largely cease to view themselves as "civic actors," as people who possess the independent capacity to make important changes within society and within governmental policies.

Criminal-justice scholars have described prison as a metaphor for the most oppressive and socially destructive conditions of structural racism in America. As Alvin J. Bronstein observed in the *Prisoners' Rights Sourcebook* (1981), edited by Ira Robbins:

> In a very real sense, the prison is the outside world, squeezed into a very small space. The total and largely self-contained society that is prison contains all of the evils of that outside world, only much more concentrated. . . . Hence, militancy is especially great in prison, not because of a few agitators, but because

the repression—whether justified or not—is harsh and undiluted. Because prison is one of the most severe sanctions in our society, the subjects of that sanction include the most alienated and the most aggressive members of society. And since the sense of injustice is most developed where the penalties are the greatest, the resentment and bitterness . . . [are] deep and pervasive.

Many women and men who do manage to survive incarceration often acquire critical insights about the nature of the legal process and the criminal-justice system that could provide important and powerful lessons for young people in racialized minority communities. Like Frederick Douglass and Fannie Lou Hamer before them, they frequently do not have formal educational credentials or middle-class privileges. Yet from theorizing about their practical day-to-day experiences within the prison system, they come to a richer understanding of how that system actually works and how to develop innovative and creative ways to subvert it. As Bronstein noted, "It is no coincidence that many of the classics of black literature, such as those by Malcolm X, Eldridge Cleaver, Bobby Seale, and George Jackson, are prison memoirs, in whole or in part." Paradoxically, such strong personalities, who were able to survive the system, found ways to learn its lessons and to become empowered in the process. An essential step in transforming this system is in "reproducing" leaders like Malcolm X. The site of the most extreme oppression could have the greatest potential for creating the most effective leadership.

IV

It is absolutely clear that a new leviathan of racial inequality has been constructed across our country. It lacks the brutal simplicity of the old Jim Crow system, with its omnipresent "white" and "colored" signs. Yet it is in many respects potentially far more brutalizing, because it presents itself to the world as a correctional system that is theoretically fair and essentially color-blind. The Black Freedom Movement of the 1960s was successful largely because it convinced a majority of white middle-class Americans that racial segregation was economically inefficient and that politically it could neither be sustained nor justified. The movement utilized the power of creative disruption, making it impossible for the old system of white prejudice, power, and privilege to function in the same old ways it had for nearly a century. How can Americans who still believe in racial equality and social justice stand silently while millions of our fellow citizens are being destroyed all around us?

It is abundantly clear that the political demand for mass incarceration and the draconian termination of voting rights to ex-felons will only contribute toward a more dangerous society. No walls can be constructed high enough, and no electronic surveillance cameras and alarms sophisticated enough, to protect white middle- and upper-class American families from the consequences of these policies. Keep in mind that approximately 600,000 people are released from prison every year; that about one-sixth of all reentering ex-prisoners, 100,000 people, are being released without any form of community correctional supervision; that about 75 percent of reentering prisoners have substance abuse histories; and that an estimated 16 percent suffer from mental illness. Nearly two-thirds of this reentering prison population will be arrested again within three years. The madness of our penal policies and of the criminal-justice system places the entire society at risk. Dismantling the prison industrial complex represents the great moral assignment and political challenge of our time.

During my last visit to Sing Sing, I noticed something new. The prison's correctional officials had erected a large, bright yellow sign over the door at the prison's public entrance. The colorful sign reads: "Through these doors pass some of the finest corrections professionals in the world."

I stood frozen for a second, immediately recalling the chillingly brutal sign posted above the entrance gate at Auschwitz and other concentration camps: *Arbeit Macht Frei* ("Work Makes Us Free"). I later asked Bill Webber and a few prisoners what they thought about the new sign. Bill thought a moment, then said simply, "demonic." One of the M.A. students, a thirty-five-year-old Latino named Tony, agreed with Bill's blunt assessment. But Tony added, "Let us face the demon head on." With more than 2 million Americans who are now incarcerated, it is time to face the demon head on.

Challenging the Dilemma of *Brown v. Topeka Board of Education:* And the Rush Toward Resegregation

Otis L. Scott

Introduction

It has been more than six years since this nation took a brief time out to reflect on the significance of the 1954 landmark Supreme Court decision, <u>Brown vs. Topeka Board of Education</u>. Across the nation countless events were staged in commemoration of the path breaking Court decision. Most of these events hailed the significant role <u>Brown</u> played in dismantling the walls of *de jure* Jim Crow segregation enclosing public schools in southern and border states of this nation. Not nearly enough attention was given to the fact of public school regegregation occurring in the post <u>Brown</u> era.

This article is a general examination of the pre- and post-<u>Brown</u> eras with critical attention given to the extent to which the Court decision addressed the dreams of proponents of public school desegregation. I contend that the effects of <u>Brown</u> must be understood within a heuristic model that demands we critically examine the responses of American society – especially its formal governing institutions – and secondly, its citizenry, to policies and practices of desegregation. In raising these concerns I also raise up the need for a critical examination of the concept of integration which has, and to a diminishing extent today, still serves as the norm driving the discourse around public school desegregation. The core of my discussion turns on the phenomena of public school resegregation which has rendered hollow the promises of the Warren Court's ruling in this important case.

Historical Context

The United States prior to the <u>Brown v. Board</u> decision of 1954 was for all intents and purposes an apartheid society. Policies and practices separating African Americans from white Americans was a defining feature of this nation beginning in the seventeenth century. Segregation practices long existing by habits of custom and heart were engrained into the nation's social formations and subsequently canonized in local, state and national laws.

Given this fact of history the United States was created with what the historian W.E.B. DuBois called the color line (DuBois 1903). The line has divided Black and whites into two distinct societies; separate and unequal. The metaphorical line is as much an issue today as it was at the dawn of the 20th century following the 1896 Supreme Court decision in Plessy v. Ferguson. This decision established in legal concrete, that the races – particularly African descended people and white people – were to be kept separate in public spaces, thus limiting social contact. This decision also had negative implications for other people racialized as a *minority* in the United States. Again, following habits of heart and mind in matters of race long in force in this nation, Plessy articulated this nation's policy on race. Namely, the separation of African people from white people was right, just and proper in order to maintain domestic tranquility and most importantly, white supremacy.

There were few spaces in public life in the United States where the operation of what became known as the "Jim Crow" doctrine of racial separation was more pronounced and more destructive than in public education. And so where were the practices of the pronouncement more destructive than when used to deny African American children living in border and southern states a quality education and the life enhancing opportunities expected from receiving a quality education.

Jim Crow's Children

This nation's dereliction in providing any form of a meaningful education for African Americans long predates the 1896 Plessy decision. The Virginia legislature as early as 1680 passed a law prohibiting Africans from gathering together for any reason. Doing so was punishable by "Twenty Lashes on the Bare Back well laid on" (Irons 2002).

The intent of such severe legislation was to discourage slaves from forming their own schools and from meeting to conjure up plans to overthrow their masters. If Africans in colonial America received any form of education it was one heavily doused with biblical teachings counseling the virtues of obedience, supplication, faith in the deliverance of God and the benevolence of white people. Throughout the antebellum south any efforts at providing a quality education (primarily teaching literacy skills) for African men, women and children were typically clandestine. Such efforts were almost always illegal. Slave owners feared that any form of literacy would lead to insurrection. One defender of this position asked in 1895, "Is there any great moral reason why we should incur the tremendous risk of having our wives and children slaughtered in consequence of our slaves being taught to read incendiary publications?" (Irons 2002).

The first institutionalized efforts to educate African Americans were made after the Civil War by the Reconstruction Congress. There is clear evidence that African Americans took advantage of the opportunity to learn to read and write (Bullock 1967).

If one reviews the policy positions taken by African Americans elected and appointed to office during the brief period of Reconstruction (1865-1876), it will be revealed the extent to which newly freed African Americans expressed an unflagging desire for an education for both adults and especially for children. Reconstruction efforts were brought to a screeching halt after 1876 by virtue of the grand betrayal brokered between the political forces supporting the Republican, Rutherford B. Hayes and those supporting Democrat, Samuel B. Tilden. After receiving sufficient electoral votes to be declared president of the United States in 1877, Hayes, honoring his promises to Southern politicos, began dismantling the fledgling and fragile political – legal infrastructure crafted by African Americans and their white allies for including freed men and "free men" into the civic culture of this nation. In effect, Hayes sabotaged efforts by African Americans to become citizens by re-creating the ante bellum conditions for racists in both the north and the south to again get the upper hand in determining the racial etiquette of the south and the nation as a whole. For African Americans this meant a return to the abject status of racial pariah. This status was assured by the by the 1896 Supreme Court ruling in <u>Plessy v. Ferguson.</u>

❖ <u>Plessy</u> as Prologue for <u>Brown</u>

Typical of the educational environment for African Americans living in the post <u>Plessy</u> south is described by James T. Patterson (2001),

> *Schools for black people were especially bad-indeed primitive . . . .*
>
> *Sunflower County, Mississippi, a cotton plantation region, had no high schools for Blacks. In the elementary grades of the county's*
>
> *Black schools, many of the teachers worked primarily as cooks or domestics on the plantations. Most had no more than a fourth grade education (10).*

Continuing, he notes that,

> *In the 1948–49 school year, the average investment per pupil in Atlanta public school facilities was $228.05 for Blacks and $570.00 for whites. In 1949-50 there was an average of 36.2 Black children per classroom, compared to an average of 22.6 among whites (11).*

By the early 1950s just as in the preceding decades after the civil war, racial segregation was the hallmark of American apartheid. Public schools in the south and border states were the parade ground where Jim Crow marched and drummed out his message of separation, inequality and inferiority. Schools for African American children were the by products of systematic and institutionalized racism.

Chinks in the armor of Jim Crow began to appear in the decades of the 1940s primarily due to the activism of the National Association for the Advancement of Colored People (NAACP). The NAACP had won some important cases before the U.S. Supreme Court in controversies involving all white primary elections (*Smith v. Allwright* 1944) and segregated law schools (*Sweatt v. Painter,* 1950).

The belated initiatives by presidents Franklin D. Roosevelt to open the nation's war industries to African American workers and Harry Truman's Executive Order (E.O. 9981, July 26, 1948) desegregating the armed forces as the decade of the 1940s closed, at least gave notice that the Executive Branch was willing to address America's race dilemma.

The <u>Brown</u> Case

When the 1950s began Linda Brown had just turned six years old. In some respects she typified the thousands of African American children attending segregated public schools. She lived within walking distance, or a short car ride, of a white school in or near her Topeka, Kansas neighborhood. In Linda's case there was a bit of an irony. She lived in an integrated neighborhood and regularly played with white school children. On occasion her white playmates even stayed overnight in her parent's home. Yet, she could not attend the white elementary school just a few blocks from her house. Instead she had to rise early each school morning, walk through a dangerous train switch yard, which was usually a hang out place for some of the town's derelicts and transients, catch a bus which took her to an all Black elementary school some two miles from her house.

Fed up with the color line and the indignities of public school segregation, Oliver Brown, Linda's father, challenged Topeka, Kansas' Jim Crow school system. The challenge came after his being refused to register his daughter in the white school near his house. Typically a mild mannered man – not having a record of activism –Oliver Brown sought out the assistance of the local branch of the NAACP headed by McKinley Burnett (Kluger 1976). Burnett is often times acknowledged as the understated and real hero of the Brown saga. It was he who developed the strategy, organized parents, pulled together the resources necessary to challenge the Topeka School Board's segregation policies (Irons 2002). It was McKinley Burnett who convinced the national NAACP to take on the Topeka case as part of a growing number of school segregation cases the national office was seriously considering.

The Brown case was initially heard before the District Court for the District of Kansas on February 28th, 1951. Robert L. Carter, an able and respected attorney with the NAACP Legal and Defense Fund argued for an injunction forbidding Topeka's public schools from segregating African American elementary school children from white children. By all accounts Carter's presentation was masterfully structured and convincingly presented to the District judges. Indeed, the judges of the District Court were moved to register their empathy for African American children deprived of the higher quality education typically provided to white children. On this point the Court noted, "Segregation of white and colored children in public schools has a detrimental effect on colored children" (Kluger 2002). But the judges refused to issue an injunction, resting their decision instead on the fact that the provisions of the 1896 <u>Plessy</u> decision which decreed that public schools were to be "separate but equal" was still the law of the land.

On October first of the same year, the Brown case was joined with other law suits from South Carolina, Delaware, Virginia, and the District of Columbia challenging public school segregation. While the end results of the Brown case are well-known and certainly represent a sea change in the application of the 14th amendment's equal protection clause to African American children, it was not the first challenge to segregated public schools. In 1849 a similar challenge in the Sarah Roberts case (Roberts v. City of Boston) was filed in Boston, Massachusetts. In 1947, seven years before the Brown decision, The California State Supreme Court declared that the segregated public school system in Orange County, in southern California, was discriminatory towards Mexican American elementary school children (Mendez v. Westminster School District). In Kansas between 1881 and 1949 some eleven cases were filed challenging segregated schools. At the time Brown was argued before the U.S. Supreme Court, the racially segregated public school system was the norm in a good part of the nation. It was legally sanctioned or permitted in twenty four states.

The legal strategy leading to the cases comprising Brown deserves more attention than is the subject of this article. It is important to point out that the assault against public school segregation was well-strategized in advance by some of the best legal minds – Black and white – associated with the NAACP. The plans were underway earnestly in the 1930s with legal challenges being considered against segregation in graduate and professional schools, voting rights and housing (Greenberg 1994).

The chief architect of the desegregation strategy was Charles Hamilton Houston, who was the dean of the Howard University Law School while he was also taking the lead in orchestrating a response to public school segregation. The core of the strategy was its focus on graduate and professional education institutions rather than elementary education. Houston's thinking was that by drawing on the "equal" provisions of Plessy and forcing states to build professional and graduate schools *equal* in all aspects to the white graduate and professional schools, he would overwhelm their ability to support two separate systems of graduate and professional education. Using this strategy he won a landmark decision in 1936 when the Maryland Supreme Court ordered the University of Maryland's law school to admit Donald Murray, a Black student, rather than send him to an out of state law school. (Murray v. Maryland). He won a similar case before the U.S. Supreme Court in 1938 (Missouri ex rel Gaines v. Canada). The Supreme Court in this case found that the University of Missouri, though it did create a separate law school for Black students, the facility-in a building shared with a hotel and a movie theatre-provided a "privilege . . . for white students" which it did not provide for Black students.

In 1939 Houston's prize student, Thurgood Marshall, took over as the chief counsel for the NAACP and established the NAACP Legal Defense and Education Fund. By the late 1940s Marshall was of a mind that the "validity" of the segregation statutes which the NAACP had left unchallenged with its "equalization" strategy was insufficient as a strategy for dismantling segregation laws. At the time the elementary school cases were accepted by the NAACP, the organization's strategy was focused on proving that public school segregation imposed restrictions on African American school children which denied them equal protection of the laws as prescribed by the 14th amendment to the U.S. Constitution. Interestingly, Marshall and his brilliant team of colleagues drew from the research studies by social and behavioral scientists in making their case. In particular the doll studies by Professors Kenneth Clark and his wife, Mamie, were instrumental. Using black and white dolls the Clark's demonstrated that the behaviors of African American children choosing white dolls in a testing situation, and attributing to the dolls positive characteristics, displayed the extent to which segregation had diminished the children's sense of identity and self esteem. Their studies, while controversial, were sufficient to convincing the Justices of the destructive effects racial segregation can have on children.

Significance of <u>Brown</u>

To assert that the unanimous decision rendered by the Court on May 17, 1954 was of landmark proportions is now well-supported. Given its message and the times, the ruling was tantamount to the earth tilting a few degrees off its normal axis. The Court's pronouncement that "separate educational facilities are inherently unequal," and thus constituting a denial of the equal protection clause of the 14th amendment, was for its day a profound rebuke of the long standing provisions of the 1896 <u>Plessy</u> decision. In effect the Court said that African American children deserved to receive an opportunity for an education which constitutionally should be on par with that provided to most white children living in the South.

Because of many questions and uncertainties as how to implement the provisions of the decision, the Supreme Court delivered a <u>Brown II</u> decision a year later. This decision did not provide necessary direction to southern school boards or establish the standards they were to follow in desegregating their public schools. Instead, the Court established the vague principle that desegregation should proceed "with all deliberate speed." This limp edict allowed southern states, their school boards and their public officials – elected and appointed – an escape route from implementing fourteenth amendment provisions of the first <u>Brown</u> decision.

Limitations of <u>Brown II</u>

<u>Brown II</u> was a failure. It failed to give sufficient guidance and direction to the federal courts in desegregation cases. As such, it did not hold states or courts accountable for implementing 14th amendment protections for African American public school children in the south. Thus, only the most courageous judges would venture on their own and rule in the favor of fourteenth amendment protections for African American school children. <u>Brown II</u> was also a failure in that it succumbed to the deeply entrenched belief of white supremacy and separation of the races

subscribed to by the great majority of white southerners and no few northerners. The Warren Court, notwithstanding its unanimous decision in Brown I, was not about the business of transforming southern racial values and practices. It had spoken loudly in extending the 14th amendment a new to African American children, but it was not about to take on – head to head – the ideology of white supremacy. The court had gone as far as it cared on the issue of state sponsored school desegregation.

And because of this the "with all deliberate speed" clause allowed southern politicians, policy makers of various stripes and the ordinary white citizens to dodge school desegregation. As noted above, the Supreme Court should have stepped in and ordered compliance with its ruling. It took no such action. As a result racial segregation in southern school districts changed very little between 1955 and 1964 (Patterson 2001). Regarding the glacial movement of desegregation in the south, James T. Patterson notes, "By early 1964, only 1.2 percent of black children in the eleven southern states attended school with whites" (Patterson, 2001). Similarly, northern schools were virtually untouched by desegregation until the mid 1970s. The major point here is that the adherents of Brown were unable to muster the political or moral might necessary to transforming the decision into a national social/political strategy. The object of which would have been to desegregate this nation's public schools.

The fact that this was not done is more of a comment on the unwillingness of this nation's leadership communities to advance desegregation than it is a negative comment on the failings of the U.S. Supreme Court. It is more a critical comment on the lack of a national will; a will undergirded by the moral premise that it is fundamentally wrong, intolerable and unacceptable for any of this nation's children to have to attend schools – especially those segregated by race – where they will predictably receive an inferior education. An education which will also predictably, close doors of opportunity in their faces.

While there were many millions of Americans of all ethnicities and social economic classes in agreement that African American children and children of color should have an opportunity for a quality education, there was never a national consensus of commitment to bringing about the radical changes in how this nation conducted the business of public school education. To wit, there was never a national will to make Brown other than the symbolization of an education norm. That this is the case is disturbingly illustrated by the strident and racist oppositional voices generated by both Brown decisions.

Resistance to the Brown Decisions

To state that the Supreme Court's desegregation decision caused severe undulations in the social, political and legal fabric of the south is to speak to the obvious. This was not a decision that most southerners were expecting although for decades there were growing signs of African American impatience with Jim Crow.

In the main, resistance to the Brown decisions was the order of the day in the south. While there was some reluctant compliance in states, e.g., Arkansas and Tennessee, in the main, resistance was fierce and unrelenting. Typically such resistance took three forms: litigation, privatization and terror. Most southern states challenged desegregation orders through the courts; thus, dragging out implementation. Privatization of public schools was a second form of resistance. White parents, with the aid of school officials and politicians, formed private academies and other institutions, often times using public funds as a way of evading desegregation. The third form of resistance was well known: the use of terror. White segregationists formed hate groups like White Citizen's Councils which became vehicles for transporting hate speech and acts of terrorism against African Americans and anyone else, or anything, presumed to be a threat to segregation.

The most effective assault against the idealistic, albeit vague, mandates of the Supreme Court was launched by presidents Richard Nixon, Ronald Reagan and the two presidents Bush. All four presidents were hostile to desegregation and especially when the federal courts ordered bussing to implement desegregation. Nixon, sought to change what he and his administration believed was an overly active federal judiciary (with particular criticism aimed at the decisions by the Warren Court). Attempting to mitigate this activism he began appointing conservative judges to the federal judiciary and to the Supreme Court. Appointees to the federal judiciary in the decades of the 70s and 80s were made by presidents committed to shaping a more conservative federal judiciary with judges having no zeal for enforcing civil rights laws. It is perversely ironical to note that during this era of redemption, President Ronald Reagan, with inarguably mean spirited intentions, nominated Clarence Thomas, no ally of civil rights activists and the second African American to serve on the U.S. Supreme Court, to replace Thurgood Marshall.

In a series of Supreme Court decisions beginning in 1974 and extending into the mid nineties, the conservative voices on the Court and elsewhere in the federal judiciary essentially rendered a moribund Brown, dead. Examples of key decisions during this period were Milliken v Bradley (1974); Board of Education of Oklahoma City v. Dowell (1991); Freeman v. Pitts (1992); Missouri v. Jenkins (1995).

In Milliken, a Detroit, Michigan case, the Court made Brown all but irrelevant for most northern cities by not approving desegregation plans combining city and suburban schools. In the Board of Education of Oklahoma City v. Dowell the Court ruled that school districts could be released from desegregation orders if they created "unitary" – meaning racially mixed – schools. In the Freeman case the Court provided that a school district could dismantle its desegregation plans without having to desegregate its faculty or provide students equal access to its programs. In Missouri v. Jenkins, the Court prohibited efforts to attract white suburban and private school students voluntarily into city schools by using strong academic programs. Adding an additional nail in the coffin of school and parent-based initiatives to achieve racial balance in public schools, the Supreme Court in 2007 ruled in two cases: Parents Involved in Community Schools v. Seattle School District, No.1 and Crystal Meredith v. Jefferson County Board of Education, that attempts to mitigate segregation by using race based formulas to create more classroom diversity were unconstitutional.

Today for all intents and purposes the idealistic provisions of <u>Brown</u> are memories of a failed future. This is because of the factors previously mentioned: a combination of a weak commitment by policy makers at all levels to enforce desegregation; a Supreme Court's unwillingness to pursue enforcement of its mandates; an intense backlash by both southerners and northerners against court ordered desegregation; no national will to undo segregated schools; the general inability of the African American civil rights community and allies to mount an effective response to the loop hole language in the "with all deliberate speed" clause.

Post <u>Brown</u> and Public School Resegregation

In a 2009 report, "Reviving the Goal of an Integrated Society: A 21st Century Challenge," authored by Gary Orfield, we are given a fresh and disturbing look at the consequences of no meaningful implementation and enforcement of the 1954 Court decision. A telling conclusion of Orfield's study is that this nation's public schools are predominately racially segregated – separate and unequal. The nation has rushed back to the past.

Several scholarly retrospectives of the decades since <u>Brown</u>, (Frankenberg and Lee, 2002; Orwell and Eaton, 1996; Dawkins and Braddock 1994), have noted that since the mid 1980s African American and Latino students have become increasingly more segregated in public schools. Again, the significant problematic here is – not that increasing racial isolation is underway – to be sure this is a concern – but the fact that the schools attended by African American and Latino students are more closely associated with "low parental involvement, lack of resources, less experienced and credentialed teachers, and higher teacher turnover all of which in combination exacerbate educational inequality for mostly minority students" (Frankenberg and Lee 2002; Kozol 2005; Darling-Hammond 2010).

Contemporary racial segregation results from a complicated web of economic, political, social and legal issues not directly related the past *de jure* race based proscriptions separating social and education interaction. A post civil rights economy from which white Americans benefitted allowing them upward mobility out of central cities to suburbs and exurbs where their children attended quality schools, to a large extent has accounted for today's school segregation. But this factor alone cannot be left unexamined. We also must understand, as previously argued, this nation has never made a serious and sustained commitment to providing a quality education to Black and Brown children. And for that matter, poor white children suffer similarly from inferior education opportunities. Resulting from this are the millions of children left behind in squalid teaching and learning environments.

The trend toward resegregation is occurring in every region of the U.S. Indeed, more Black students attended segregated school at the beginning of the 21st century than the decade after <u>Brown.</u> Linda Darling-Hammond informs us that by the year 2000, 72 percent of Black students attend predominantly minority schools. This compares to 68 percent in 1980. (Darling-Hammond 2010) In the Northeast nearly four of five Black students attend schools where they and other students of color are the majority of the school population.

Nearly half of Black students in the Northeast and the Midwest attend schools defined as intensely segregated. In these schools 90–100 percent of their students are people of color. One in six Black students attend schools defined as hyper segregated – that is – nearly 100 percent of their peers are students of color.

The fact that public school resegregation is occurring is a cause for attention by public policy makers, community leaders, parents and others professing a belief in values and practices of multicultural and diversity teaching-learning practices. For there is something to be said for schooling which brings students from diverse racial, ethnic, religious, economic backgrounds together in a classroom. One could persuasively argue that doing so prepares them for optimally functioning in a diverse nation and global community. Such learning occasions can be a humanizing experience for all-including teachers and administrators.

As normatively optimistic and desirable as public school desegregation and a quality education are, it is trumped by what I consider to be the most significant threat to African American students posed by public school resegregation. Compelling studies inform us of abiding features of segregated and hyper segregated attended by Black students. About 50 percent of these students attend schools where 75 percent of the students are impoverished. By way of contrast, only five percent of white students attend similar schools. In schools where poverty is extreme–meaning – schools where 90–100 percent of students are poor, 80 percent of these students are Black and Latino (Orfield and Lee 2005).

An increased number of African Americans are themselves impoverished and attending schools where they are joined by an increasing number of Black, Latino, and to a lesser extent, Asian and White students. In too many urban areas of the U.S. poor Black students are 70–100 percent of all poor students of color. Their education experiences tend to be circumscribed by a series of institutionalized limitations and deficiencies.

We are informed by researchers (Orfield and Lee 2005; Hochschild, 1984; Darling-Hammond 2010) that academic achievement is in many instances related to poverty. Schools attended by Black students tend to be plagued by fewer qualified/credentialed teachers and administrators, fewer instructional resources and materials, low performance on standardized tests, fewer AP and college preparation courses, high exposure to gangs, violence and crime. These schools are described as "drop out factories."

(*NY Times,* May 17, 2009). It is true that not all schools attended by poor students of color are composites of the litany of dysfunction previously described. There are examples of schooling where teachers and administrators, parents, community members, and students are crafting and experiencing first rate public school educations. These schools should be celebrated and supported (Ogletree 2004). But these exemplars are a typical – not the rule. Too many African American students are attending segregated public schools where their education experiences are preparing them for a 21st century caste existence similar to that visited upon previous generation of the children of Jim Crow.

◉ What Is to Be Done?

The reality of social formation in this nation is that its history of discrimination, the *minoritizing* and marginalizing of cultural groups is deeply institutionalized in the social formation of this nation. We cannot escape who we are. No matter the feel good fluffy escapist attempts by popular culture outlets to portray contemporary America society as post racial. The color line remains as a defining feature of who we are. Yet, as a nation we remain hopelessly deluded, believing that the race based sins of the past are in the past.

This is clearly evident when one looks at the state of public school education for African American children. These are children attending urban schools where they are not being prepared to take advantage of opportunities for social, economic, and education mobility. The central education issue for the African American community is not one framed by *who the child sits next to in a classroom, but whether or not the child is receiving a quality education at the school she/he is attending.* The compelling social/education/political challenge for the African American community is not desegregation, but access to *quality education.* There is compelling and disturbing evidence that African Americans in too many of this nation's urban public schools are being drastically shortchanged by poor quality education.

◉ Responding to the Challenge

The question at this point then becomes how does one respond to the fact that the promises of <u>Brown</u> have not been realized. The question becomes paramount especially being that the nation has clearly lost its interest in public school desegregation as a desired public policy outcome. In the main, I believe the responses should be framed, or at least influenced, by what have been the responses to efforts to effect public school desegregation. Indeed, there are salient lessons to be learned from this history. For example, one of the important lessons learned from <u>Brown</u> is that, at least for the foreseeable future, there is neither the national will nor leadership to reshape public schools around policies and practices of racial desegregation. That is, there exists no national discourse focused on reshaping schools around resource allocation practices designed to insure that all children have an opportunity to receive a high quality education experience. Another clearly delivered lesson from <u>Brown</u> is that the parents of children attending quality public schools in suburbs and exurbs are adamantly against any desegregation schemes which take their children from neighborhood schools. Parents are also only tepid to any in-bussing efforts bringing urban children into suburban schools and neighborhoods. Still another lesson learned and which must be heeded is that the African American civil rights and the progressive elements of the nation's education communities have been unable to develop the strategies needed to excite and sustain the interest of a nation in the benefits of a high quality public school education for all children.

Given these and other lessons gained from the post-<u>Brown</u> era and the predictable lack of appetite for more substantive approaches to institutional change in this nation, this writer is not surprised that the typical small "l" liberal approaches to addressing the shortcomings of the nation's response to public school desegregation. Contemporarily the strategies offered and righteously defended include the following in various iterations:

- Mounting a national campaign to educate Americans regarding the inequalities of education provided to urban dwelling African Americans and other people of color and the dire implications of this.
- Energizing civil rights organizations to take more aggressive lobbying tactics on behalf of access to quality education for all public school students.
- Filing law suits on behalf of aggrieved students of color.
- Energizing and holding public policy makers accountable for passing legislation designed to close education gaps and holding school officials accountable for implementing the expectations.

These strategies are in and of themselves reasonable. They lay claims on this nation's advocacy organizations, policy making and education leadership to do the right thing on behalf of public school children. Indeed, noble intentions. But, unfortunately, these pronouncements fail to take into account the history of responses this nation has made to the social justice claims by people of color. If the past is prologue, one cannot simply put blind faith in the likelihood that these approaches-even if adopted – would have the desired effect. The strategies place too much stock in normalistic and gradualistic approaches to social change. Such approaches have historically inadequately met the social objectives of people of color. These approaches too often rest on the presumptive belief that decision making processes are basically fair, equally accessible to prince and pauper alike, and are fundamentally committed to the concept and practices of a quality education for all children. The evidence supporting these beliefs is tragically thin.

Given the gravity of the challenges facing African American children and given the responses by this nation to desegregation efforts along with the lessons learned from <u>Brown</u>, it is time for African Americans to give serious attention to other strategies. The social and cultural costs for not doing so are too horrifying to disregard. Simply stated, consider the life chances for a young person graduating from high school today without the critical thinking skills, numeracy skills, reading skills and experiences with information technology. Consider the life chances of young Black males and females who have dropped out of school before graduating.

I am recommending that African American parents, community members and leaders develop education strategies based on a fundamental proposition emanating from the social history of African descended people in this nation. The proposition is this. African Americans, and any allies gained along the way, must first and foremost take the responsibility for educating African American children.

The proposition is neither defeatist (likely to be alleged) nor cynical. Its truth is based in the truth of the social experiences of African Americans. This truth demonstrates that there have been only two instances in nearly four centuries of the African presence in this part of the diaspora where the federal government has willfully committed resources to educate African people.

The first was during the Reconstruction Era after the Civil War with the formation of the Freedmen's Bureau. According to historian, John Hope Franklin, the Bureau's most significant impact was providing education opportunities for newly freed slaves. The Bureau established and helped to administer an array of educational institutions from day schools to colleges (1966). The second instance of a federal commitment to addressing and repairing social damage done to African Americans due to institutionalized and individual discrimination was during the administration of President Lyndon B. Johnson. The Johnson administration's advocacy of civil rights and equal opportunity legislation set the tone for improvements in education programs benefiting African American and poor children and for opening access to colleges and universities. Unfortunately, both periods were short-lived and existed within the maelstrom of challenge and resistance, especially from white southerners.

Specific Prescriptions

Against this backdrop and given what we know about the nation's responses to the concept and practice of desegregation and given the grave consequences now facing African American students in too many inner city schools, I strongly recommend two other courses of action. Both can be undertaken simultaneously.

First, African American must reorganize institutional resources, e.g., families, churches, civic and social organizations, etc., around another fundamental proposition. Namely, educating children is the primary responsibility of African Americans. Any one wishing to assist in this effort should be considered, but the primary responsibility rests with African Americans. Institutionalizing this proposition can take several delivery forms, among these are:

- Private schools-secular or sectarian
- Charter schools
- Gendered schools-all male or all female
- Charter magnet schools

These institutions would be open to all students, but the emphasis would be on providing African American students a high quality culturally relevant education experience. The considerable wealth (more than 800 billion dollars in annual spending power) and talent from such sectors in the African American community such as: education, business, entertainment, churches, professional athletics and ordinary citizens must be marshaled and focused on providing education alternatives to

African Americans. The ability to do this exists. The will to do so must be cultivated, bolstered and sustained. In short, African Americans must themselves take on this imperative project.

This is a much needed and long overdue approach to addressing the fact that this nation has not taken the education interests of African American and most children of color seriously. Again, this step towards education independence and self-reliance is dictated by the African American's social history. As pointed out above, this history is replete with incidences of betrayal and subterfuge by the institutions charged with protecting the rights of African Americans (Bell 2002). It seems foolhardy, and in fact, is culturally suicidal, to continue to depend on extant institutions of education to prepare African American children to compete on equal footing with others in this nation. Lessons from African American history speak to the need for a drastically different education paradigm. The stakes for not doing so are much too high. A people simply cannot advance socially, economically, politically or culturally, if their children and subsequently, their adults, are miseducated at worst, and poorly educated at best.

Secondly, most segregated public schools attended by Black students are institutions of education malpractice. These are not redeeming, freeing institutions committed to preparing students for the challenges of making a living in an increasingly interconnected world of work. Students have little or no transferable skills, experiences or knowledge bases which can be used in either the legitimate domestic or international marketplaces. Deprived of a quality education, Black students are not able to compete with better educated students for access to colleges and universities, vocational training or workforce employment in other than dead end entry level low wage jobs. Tragically, students fitting this profile live lives that are swift, brutish and short; too many of them are destined to fill jails, prisons and cemeteries.

And because the stakes are so terribly high, public policy makers, parents, community members, the faith community and all other civic, social organizations must be held accountable. The Black community – its leadership and parents must take the lead in the response. This tragic situation threatens to continue creating and institutionalizing a caste of people having nothing to contribute to the progress of Black people or anyone else. They will constitute what the historian Carter G. Woodson forewarned as a casualties of a destructive education system, a new category of slaves (Woodson 1990).

To the point. Time has long past for Black leadership to do the organizing, discovery work and litigation necessary for pressing class action law suits on behalf of Black students receiving low quality public school education. This situation must be as aggressively pursued as was the strategy developed and implemented by Charles Hamilton Houston and those brave men and women who joined him in the decades long struggle against *de jure* public school segregation.

The schools attended by Black students are supported by tax dollars. Those tax dollars are used by public officials–both elected and appointed – to craft and serve up teaching and learning experiences known and proven to be inferior to the quality of education provided to students attending more affluent schools. It is known and documented that Black, Latino and poor white students, if they do graduate from high school, have received an education that is – with few exceptions – inferior to that received by their counterparts graduating from better supported and resourced school systems. The differential education experience ill prepares Black students to compete on par with students having a stronger public school learning experience (Kozol 2005).

I do not argue here that all public school students must have the *same* public school learning experience. I do argue that all public school students must have an opportunity to receive a *quality* education. Absent the element of *quality*, Black students are denied opportunities to compete for access higher education and training, rewarding workforce employment and in short, lose out on opportunities to fully develop their human potential.

Herein rests the basis for class action law suits. The core argument rests on the proposition that a low quality education, fueled and supported by public tax dollars, effectively deprives Black students of the provisions of the equal protection clause of the 14th amendment of the U.S. Constitution. The class action suits should allege that local, state and national systems of public supported education, using tax dollars, plan and implement curricula, hire teachers, administrators and others, intimately involved in the delivery of an inferior education experience for students.

The critically important organizing and research strategies needed as a prerequisite to launching the litigation urged here are outside the scope of this discussion. I recommend that the seed can be planted by parents, community leaders, lawyers and others committed to striking out on a more aggressive path to resolve, what I consider the paramount civil rights issue of this day. Namely, providing a high quality education to Black children and by extension to all children. I am not arguing against the reformist approaches previously noted in this discussion. They are also necessary. But they have their limitations. They don't fundamentally restructure how public education is delivered in this nation. Successful class action suits will have that affect. Tax dollars will have to be used in ways assuring that a quality education for all students is the objective and desired outcome.

It seems foolhardy and indeed, culturally destructive, to continue depending on the extant education processes to educate Black students. At the risk of overusing a clichè, a paradigm shift is in order. The stakes for not doing so are much too high. For the last three decades we have borne witness to the destruction of miseducated and poorly educated Black youth. A people cannot advance socially, politically, economically or culturally, if their children are poorly educated-giving rise to a poorly educated, vulnerable and otherwise subjugated generation of adults.

There is a long enduring historical lesson which bears serious and steadfast attention. History is not kind to a people who deliver up their children to a society's institutions of education when these institutions, like the others comprising the social order, have been implicated in the historical oppression of the people.

Selected Sources

1. Bullock, H. (1967). <u>A History of Negro Education in the South.</u> Cambridge, Massachusetts: Harvard University Press.

2. Bell, D. (2004). <u>Silent Covenants.</u> New York, New York: Oxford University Press.

3. Darling-Hammond, L. (2010). <u>The Flat World and Education.</u> New York, New York: Teacher's College Press.

4. Dawkins, M.P. and Braddock, J.H. (1994). *The continuing significance of desegregation: School racial composition and African American inclusion in American society.* <u>Journal of Negro Education.</u> 63(3), 394–405.

5. DuBois, W. E.B. (1953). <u>The Souls of Black Folk.</u> New York, New York: Blue Heron.

6. Frankenberg, E. and Lee, C. (2002). <u>Race in American Public Schools: Rapidly Resegregating School Districts.</u> Cambridge, Massachusetts: The Civil Rights Project Harvard University.

7. Franklin, J.H. (1966). <u>From Slavery to Freedom.</u> New York, New York: Vintage Books.

8. Greenberg, J. (1994). <u>Crusaders in the Courts: How a Dedicated Band of Lawyers Fought for the Civil Rights Revolution.</u> New York, New York: Basic Books.

9. Hochschild, J. (1984). <u>The New American Dilemma: Liberal Democracy and School Desegregation.</u> New Haven, Connecticut: Yale University.

10. Irons, P. (2002). <u>Jim Crow's Children</u>. New York, New York: Penguin Books.

11. Kluger, R. (1976). <u>Simple Justice: The History of Brown v. Board of Education and Black Americans' Struggle for Equality.</u> New York, New York: Alfred P. Knopf.

12. Kozol, J. (2005). <u>The Shame of a Nation.</u> New York: Crown.

13. Orfield, G. and Eaton, S. (1996). <u>Dismantling Desegregation: The Quiet Reversal of Brown v. Board of Education.</u> New York, New York: The New Press.

14. Orfield, G. and Lee, C. (2005). <u>Why Segregation Matters: Poverty and Educational Inequality</u>. Cambridge, MA.: The Civil Rights Project.

15. Patterson, J. (2001). <u>Brown v. Board of Education: A Civil Rights Milestone and its Troubled Legacy</u>. New York, New York: Oxford University Press.

16. Woodson, C.G. (1990). <u>The Miseducation of the Negro.</u> Nashville, TN.: Winston-Derek.

Legacies of War: The United States' Obligation Toward Amerasians

Robin S. Levi

The U.S. Government's Attitude Toward Relationships with Asian Women

A. Vietnam

In contrast to the popular perception held in Vietnam and the United States (and reinforced by *Miss Saigon*), most Amerasian children came from long-term relationships between servicemen and Vietnamese women who were not bargirls. These women usually worked around military bases as launderers, hotel clerks, or menial laborers in other occupations.

Soldiers in Vietnam frequently felt the need to find solace in women and liquor. The U.S. military encouraged this behavior with a tacit "bread and circuses" attitude. The government encouraged "R & R" as a way to escape from the rigors of jungle warfare. But while the military flew married men to meet their wives in Hawaii, it sent single men to other exotic cities. Unmarried servicemen were sent to Asian locales, which led them to believe the U.S. government expected them to conduct their "R & R" with Asian women.

The U.S. military also facilitated the use of local prostitutes. For example, after monthly trips to town resulted in chaos, Marine commanders at Danan decided to restrict their men's sexual activity to areas surrounding the base. Military brothels could be found within the perimeter of at least three U.S. base camps. The military brothels were set up by military commanders and were under the direct operational control of a brigade commander with the rank of colonel. Further, the military periodically checked the health of the prostitutes to curtail the spread of sexually transmitted diseases. The military also regulated prices. If women requested more than a certain price, the military would declare their brothel off-limits.

From 29 *Stanford Journal of International Law* 459 (1993) by Robin S. Levi. Copyright © 1993 by Board of Trustees of the Leland Stanford Junior University. Reprinted by permission.

The U.S. Army officially disapproved of U.S. servicemen living with Vietnamese women, and at times the military police sanctioned soldiers. But unofficially, the U.S. Army allowed many of these living situations (which the soldiers called "liv[ing] on the economy with a national") to continue in order to preserve the soldiers' morale.

Once a serviceman completed his tour of duty, the military's disapproval of his relationship with a Vietnamese woman resurfaced. It was incredibly difficult for servicemen to maneuver through the U.S. bureaucracy to bring their children, girl-friends, or wives back to the United States. Some servicemen tried for many years to get their children out of Vietnam, while others gave up before they left. Some were so busy preparing to end their "year abroad" that they forgot to try to return with those who had been their families there. Some men did not care, and some did not know that they had children. Regardless of what stood in the serviceman's way (government, bureaucracy, confusion, or indifference), the result remained the same: tens of thousands of children left in Vietnam after 1975, rejected by Vietnamese society and dreaming of their unknown father and his land.

B. South Korea and the Philippines

The relationships in South Korea and the Philippines are fairly similar to those that existed in Vietnam. In South Korea the troops are now on one-year tours similar to those soldiers had in Vietnam and the Philippines. Most of the men come through for short stays while their ships are repaired. About eighteen thousand registered women work in the bar or club areas near U.S. bases in South Korea. Registered women have identification cards and are the only ones allowed to work in the clubs. In order to get an ID card, a woman must have a chest X ray and blood test every six months and an AIDS test every three months. In addition, the women are tested every week for sexually transmitted diseases [STDs]. The Korean police conduct spot checks to ensure that all women have proper ID cards; women without cards can receive jail sentences of up to twelve months. Furthermore, the clubs themselves are checked for cleanliness and STD rates among the women.

The bases in the Philippines had a similar system of registering sex workers. Fifteen thousand to seventeen thousand sex workers were employed around Subic Bay, approximately nine thousand of whom were registered. As in South Korea, unregistered sex workers could be jailed. The U.S. military provided medicine and technical assistance to the clinics. Here, as in South Korea, the military deemed a club "off-limits" for U.S. servicemen if too many women tested positive for sexually transmitted diseases. Most of the U.S. servicemen did not take responsibility for the children born from their relationships, whether short- or long-term, with sex workers. Furthermore, the U.S. government failed to instruct its servicemen regarding possible parental responsibility. Instead, the government focused on teaching servicemen to avoid venereal disease.

◄ The Lives of Amerasians

A. Amerasians in Vietnam

Vietnam does not accept Amerasians either legally or socially and subjects them to mistreatment that leads to severe emotional trauma. Because nationality, race, and personal identity derive from the father in Vietnamese society, the Vietnamese government considers Amerasians U.S. nationals. In Vietnam the father registers the birth in the family registry, claims paternity, registers the child for school, and procures employment for the child. Without a father to perform these essential functions (at times a stepfather has assisted the Amerasian), a child in Vietnam will have difficulty becoming a functioning part of Vietnamese society. Amerasians are told they are not Vietnamese, although the person who is supposed to give them their identity is not present. The fact that Vietnamese social and legal institutions make it difficult for Amerasians to establish an identity intensifies the identity crisis that mixed race children inherently face.

Vietnam has a Confucian, patriarchal family system, where a person's identity is derived more from the family group, including both the living members and ancestors, than from the individual self. Therefore, an Amerasian child lacks not only a father but also a father's family and ancestors. A child in Vietnam without a supporting familial group is seen as something less than a full person, which increases the Amerasians' lack of identity.

Another factor that contributes to discrimination against Amerasians in Vietnam is homogeneity. Mixed racial ancestry is easily noticed, and Vietnamese society considers people with mixed ancestry as contributing to "racial impurity in the nation." An official from Ho Chi Minh City's Department of Social Welfare stated, "Our society does not need these bad elements."[1]

The final factor contributing to the ostracism of Vietnamese Amerasians is that they are living reminders of the foreign occupation of Vietnam. For some of them, even their names, given by their families, *My Lai* (American half-breed) or *My Phuong* (Vietnamese American), are insults. Vietnamese society faults Amerasians' mothers for consorting with the enemy and considers the mothers prostitutes. Amerasians are considered the children of the enemy: "It was not unusual for an Amerasian child to be singled out by a teacher or a police officer as the offspring of the enemy who had bombed the village."[2] Because communist education emphasizes the evils of the United States, it is very difficult for Amerasians to attend school. Students are taunted in school and by the public and are sometimes told to go back to their "country." Many Amerasians quickly drop out of school; thus a large number of them are illiterate. Amerasian children's identity crises are often intensified by the fact that many mothers destroyed all mementos of their relationships with their children's fathers so that the government would not send them to reeducation camps as punishment for fraternizing with the enemy.

Regardless of the destruction of documentary evidence linking Amerasians to their American fathers, their non-Asian features frequently betray the children's mixed heritage. Some mothers try to disguise the children's American features by putting shoe polish in their hair and powder on their skin. The Amerasians who have experienced the greatest discrimination and whose identities have been the most difficult to hide are the children of African American servicemen. One example is the story of a young black Amerasian: "Vinh Doan came to expect rejection. His father was a black serviceman whom he never met. His Vietnamese mother spent years telling him he was ugly because he looked like his father, then gave him to a neighbor when he was seven years old."[3] Black Amerasians are lowest in the hierarchy of Vietnamese society due to the traditional prejudice against dark skin found in all Asian societies, as well as racial prejudice brought by the European and American presence.

Although the Vietnamese government officially denies discriminating against Amerasians, it prevents many mothers from participating in certain government programs. Mothers of Amerasians are often rejected by their families due to the humiliation the mother has caused the family. A significant percentage of mothers, refusing to live under these conditions, give up their children for adoption, sell their children for their potential value as a ticket to the United States, or simply abandon them. Many Amerasians have ended up in orphanages. Since Vietnamese orphanages are often run badly and have severe overcrowding problems, most Amerasian children have ended up on the streets, and many have turned to prostitution.

B. Amerasians in South Korea

South Korea is also a homogenous and Confucian nation with a strict class hierarchy. A more dramatic disparity between the upper and lower classes exists there than in Vietnam, and it is very difficult to be successful unless one attends one of the top universities, which are expensive and exclusive. As in Vietnam, the father is the cornerstone of family life and the conduit to public life. Without a father, it is impossible to carry out the traditional responsibilities of ancestor worship. While the religious importance of ancestor worship has decreased with modernization, some symbolic value remains, and the Amerasian who is not able to conduct ancestor worship naturally will be viewed as "different." In recent years, nationalism and cultural pride, along with economic clout, have increased in South Korea. Koreans equate citizenship with their homogenous racial ancestry. Thus, Amerasians remain only marginal members of Korea's society, because without fathers they are prevented from fully participating in Korean culture and religion.

Official discrimination against Amerasians is formally outlawed in South Korea, but covert discrimination continues. The most egregious example is that Amerasians are not allowed to serve in the Korean military. In a nation that considers itself consistently on the brink of war, exclusion from military service serves as a serious obstacle to being accepted by the society and obtaining a good job. Further, most Amerasians cannot afford to go to the better universities. The cumulative effect of not having fathers, military service capability, education credentials, and economic power relegates Amerasians to the lower classes of Korean society.

The degree to which Korean Amerasians encounter discrimination depends on the race of the father. If the father was black, racial discrimination is more blatant. If the father was white, the Amerasian child has a better chance of adoption by society. Nonetheless, all Amerasians are taunted for their American-looking features and are immediately branded as children of imperialists and prostitutes.

Although it should be acknowledged that the U.S. and South Korean governments have taken some financial responsibility for the few registered Amerasians in South Korea, Korean Amerasians have lives similar to Vietnamese Amerasians, filled with poverty, discrimination, and solitude. It is unlikely that financial support from the United States or South Korea will continue once the U.S. military leaves.

C. Amerasians in the Philippines

Filipino Amerasians were excluded from previous Amerasian immigration laws because of the perception that Filipino Amerasians did not experience discrimination at significant levels. This perception could have been generated by the belief that the Philippines support a very diverse population and therefore mixed race children would be easily accepted. Indeed, Amerasians are capable of being accepted and succeeding in the Filipino society; for example, the mayor of Olongapo, Richard Gordon, is a white Amerasian. Some white Amerasians have become big performing stars in the Philippines, prized for their light skin.

Nevertheless, Filipinos consider themselves a homogenous population, despite their history of intermarriages over the centuries. They also have a strong belief in kinship relations. Because most Filipino Amerasians are interracial children from single-parent households, they are left at a disadvantage with regard to both of these traditions.

The most significant obstacle to Filipino Amerasians is that they are often judged by the circumstances of their birth. Amerasians from certain parts of the Philippines are immediately assumed to be the children of prostitutes and U.S. servicemen, and they are treated as such. Therefore, even though in the past Amerasians have been functioning members of society, Amerasians with U.S. servicemen for fathers are not so lucky. Further, because most are born into a life of poverty next to the bases, many end up working in the bar system that facilitated their birth. Others are sold by their mothers or abandoned. Amerasians in the Philippines experience discrimination and hardship remarkably similar to that experienced by the Amerasians discussed above. Most struggle to survive in the bar scene near the base.

Since the U.S. military withdrew, these children have become subject to increased anti-American sentiment. The closing of the bases also removed the main source of health services and income for the Amerasians and their mothers. Like

Vietnamese Amerasians, Filipino Amerasians are now the remaining traces of U.S. intervention in the Philippines. Any residual resentment against the U.S. presence in the Philippines can easily be vented against Filipino Amerasians. They are without resources and discriminated against in a country that is itself poor.

VI. The U.S. Government's Treatment of Amerasians

A. Amerasians under U.S. Immigration Law

A child born in the United States can elect U.S. citizenship regardless of the nationality of her parents. Attaining citizenship is more difficult when the child is born outside the United States. A child born outside the United States to married parents can be a U.S. citizen if one parent is a U.S. citizen who has fulfilled certain age and residency requirements. However, children born out of wedlock, like most Amerasian children, face significantly more stringent citizenship requirements. This factor has made it unlikely that more than a small percentage of Amerasians could receive U.S. citizenship through their parents.

Amerasian children are in the lowest preference category for emigration to the United States because they are usually unable to prove officially that they are related to any U.S. citizen. Rarely can they find U.S. citizens to sponsor them.

B. Statutes Assisting Amerasians

1. Orderly Departure Program

The first U.S. effort to help Amerasians began inadvertently, after the government became concerned with the plight of the boat people fleeing Vietnam. The media attention given to the Vietnamese refugees in rickety boats on unsafe seas, and their subsequent unpleasant treatment by unwelcoming Southeast Asian countries, led the U.S. government in 1979 to develop the Orderly Departure Program (ODP) under the auspices of the United Nations.[4] The United Nations designed the ODP to give people a safe method of exit from Vietnam. Vietnam agreed to grant exit visas, and the UN High Commissioner for Refugees (UNHCR) agreed to be the processor.

Under the ODP, Vietnamese Amerasians are in a better position to immigrate to the United States than they were under the conventional immigration regulations. Amerasians must fill out applications to participate in the ODP, but the U.S. government no longer requires supporting documents from them. Further, President [Ronald] Reagan accorded priority status to Amerasians by including them in one of three categories of refugees given priority for orderly departure.

Nevertheless, the ODP as it relates to Amerasians has several problems. First, since the United States government and Vietnam do not have diplomatic relations, the United States has been hampered by not having a processing office in Ho Chi

Minh City. Moreover, Amerasians often do not have the knowledge necessary to successfully apply. Many of them, living in the streets, may not even have heard about the ODP. Second, because the ODP classifies recipients as refugees, the Vietnamese government does not think Amerasians should be included; it considers them U.S. citizens. Thus their exclusion from official services, according to the Vietnamese government, does not constitute discrimination.

2. The Refugee Act of 1980

The 1980 Refugee Act, implementing the 1951 [United Nations] Convention Relating to the Status of Refugees and its updated Protocol,[5] did little to help Amerasians. The Refugee Act characterized a refugee as a person fleeing a country "because of persecution or a well-founded fear of persecution on account of race, religion, nationality, [or] membership in a particular social group." . . . However, the U.S. government did not direct this legislation specifically at Amerasians, and it has several proof requirements and forms. The act is likely to benefit mainly the more educated Asians who are able to fulfill the specific requirements and successfully complete the forms and interviews. . . . In the case of South Korea and the Philippines, the U.S. government tends to be unwilling to grant Amerasians refugee status, as they are from countries with governments friendly to the United States. Therefore, the Refugee Act is rarely used by Amerasians.

3. 1982 Amerasian Amendments

The United States' next effort to assist Amerasians was the enactment of the 1982 Amerasian Amendments.[6] These amendments were the result of a concerted effort by some legislators—who saw the Amerasians as the United States' responsibility—to help those children. The amendments cover Amerasian children from Korea, Vietnam, Laos, Cambodia, and Thailand. They put qualified children into the highest preference category for immigration. In order to qualify, children must petition the Attorney General and give [his or] her reason to believe that they were fathered by a U.S. citizen and were born between 1950 and October 22, 1982. The physical appearance of the Amerasian is to be considered, along with documentary proof. By expanding coverage to Amerasians in some nations, the amendments have helped the non-Vietnamese Amerasians who did not benefit under the ODP. Also, the amendments expand eligibility to those born as late as 1982, taking account of the fact that not all Amerasians are born during military conflicts.

Several problems remain. First, the amendments still force Amerasians to emigrate alone, often leaving loved ones behind. In addition, although Amerasians from several countries can take advantage of the amendments, the strict provisions of the amendments and the lack of diplomatic relations between the United States and Vietnam combine to make it particularly difficult for Vietnamese Amerasians to qualify. Moreover, the amendments do not cover the many Amerasians in the Philippines, and the 1982 cutoff date eliminates Amerasians who were subsequently born in Asia. Finally, the financial sponsor requirements are difficult to fulfill and defy the obligation of the United States to take responsibility for Amerasians.

4. 1984 Amerasian Initiative

President Reagan attempted to ameliorate some of the damaging effects of the 1982 amendments on Vietnamese Amerasians through the 1984 Amerasian Initiative. In contrast to earlier policy, the Initiative allows Vietnamese Amerasians using the ODP to emigrate with qualifying family members. This provision has encouraged more Amerasians to emigrate, because they need not leave their families behind. It has also increased their chances of building successful lives in the United States, because they will have familial support with them.

Unfortunately, the U.S. government offended Vietnam by claiming that the Vietnamese government was using the ODP to facilitate emigration of ethnic Chinese rather than Vietnamese Amerasians, and that as a result the quotas set by the Initiative for Vietnamese Amerasians remained unfilled. Vietnam claimed that the United States was trying to make the Vietnamese government the "bad guy." As a result, Vietnam suspended the ODP program to the United States in 1986 but resurrected it eighteen months later after a sharp increase in the number of people trying to escape Vietnam by boat. Thus the Initiative suffered from both poor United States–Vietnam relations and its limited scope.

◉ The Homecoming Act

The most recent and comprehensive legislation concerning Amerasians is the Indochinese Refugee Resettlement and Protection Act of 1987 (Homecoming Act).[7] The purpose of the Homecoming Act was to fulfill the United States' legal and moral obligations to Vietnamese Amerasians. . . .

The Homecoming Act, enacted in March 1988, stated that all Amerasian children born in Vietnam between January 1, 1962, and January 1, 1976, could emigrate to the United States, accompanied by either immediate family, guardians, or a spouse. The act set a deadline of two years for all Amerasians to arrive in the United States and exempted them from immigration quotas. Congress included the two-year deadline to speed the processing of Amerasian immigrants, because processing under the ODP had been so slow. The State Department claimed that the deadline was too stringent to allow for adequate processing of all Amerasians. Nonetheless, comparing the speed of processing under the Homecoming Act with the speed under previous acts shows that the deadline did accelerate processing.

In 1990, Congress indefinitely extended the deadline for allowing Amerasians into the United States and removed the provision that had forced them to choose between spouse and family for immediate immigration. The act's original budget and timetable were based on an estimate of twelve thousand to fourteen thousand Amerasians remaining in Vietnam, but this estimate was later revised to forty thousand.

Finally, the act did not characterize Amerasians as refugees, which appeased the Vietnamese government.

After Congress passed the Homecoming Act, [its two Congressional co-sponsors—Ed.] traveled to Vietnam to reach an agreement with Vietnamese Foreign Minister Nguyen Co Thach. The agreement stated that the Vietnamese government would allow the Amerasians to emigrate to the United States. This new spirit of cooperation stems from Vietnam's desire for the U.S. government to end its trade embargo, as Vietnam is willing to make the necessary efforts to improve its relationship with the United States. Vietnam has also tried to assist the U.S. government in processing Amerasians by transporting them from outlying areas to Ho Chi Minh City and by increasing the number of carriers that are permitted to fly emigrants out of Vietnam.

B. Problems Faced by Amerasians in the United States: Squawking like a Chicken

In Asia, most Amerasians lived in the street, frequently surviving through criminal means and having little education and limited familial support. As a result of their background and lack of identity, Amerasian immigrants are at higher risk for problems such as drug use, crime, and suicide than previous Indochinese immigrants.

Although many other refugee groups have similar problems, these problems are more acute among Amerasians. One important reason is that upon arrival in the United States, Amerasians are, on average, eighteen years old, much older and less adaptable than French Eurasians who emigrate to France. Amerasians in the United States have a saying: "I was born like a duck but lived with the chickens. Now I live with the ducks but I squawk like a chicken."

Many Amerasians thought that once they arrived in the United States they would find their fathers and their identities. They also thought that they would be welcomed by their fathers, like lost children finally finding their way home. In short, Amerasians hoped to find the answers to all their problems in the United States.

The Amerasian dream least likely to be fulfilled is that of finding one's American father in the United States. Very few Amerasians have clear identifying information about their fathers; most just have names and hometowns. The U.S. government has led Amerasians to believe that it will help them contact their fathers and give the fathers the option of caring for their children. But due to a combination of domestic privacy laws and government inactivity, that help has not materialized.

As a result of the Freedom of Information Act and a British case concerning children fathered by U.S. soldiers in Great Britain, the U.S. government must allow limited access to records about U.S. servicemen. Other organizations, such as the Red Cross, the Amerasian Registry, and the Buck Foundation, use that information to assist Amerasians searching for their fathers. However, this information is frequently too limited to be useful. Even if Amerasians do find their fathers, often the fathers do not want them or the reunions otherwise fail to work out. Amerasians find such rejections devastating because they expected their fathers to help them find their identities and fill the role Vietnamese fathers play. Although there have been some success stories, many workers at volunteer agencies do not think they make up for the countless other rejections. In fact, some mothers have tried to prevent their children from even beginning the search for their fathers.

The presence of racism in the United States also surprises Amerasians, especially black Amerasians. Further, the Vietnamese community that rejected them in Vietnam continues to reject them in the United States, although the rejection is less severe. As one unemployed Amerasian said, "[I]f the discrimination in Vietnam was 100, the discrimination here is about 50." Many examples exist of Amerasians trying to talk with Vietnamese people in Vietnamese and being snubbed. These rejections increase the Amerasians' sense of alienation; even though they are in the United States, the old problem of discrimination continues to plague them.

Another problem that many Vietnamese Amerasians face is not having attended school in Vietnam. Many stopped attending school as a result of taunts from their schoolmates and teachers. Most are illiterate in Vietnamese and unaccustomed to school, which makes it difficult for them to learn in the United States. Further, as a result of their Vietnamese illiteracy, it is very difficult for them to learn to read and write English.

The street is an environment with which most Amerasians are familiar. [M]any survived by living on the street; they robbed, prostituted themselves, and participated in other illegal activities. In Asia, they supported themselves on the street without any help from the government. When Amerasians in the United States begin having problems in school, finding jobs, or living on welfare, some of them revert to the familiar methods of street survival. This leaves Amerasians at a high risk for becoming criminals and suffering the consequences of criminal activity.

All of the problems discussed above are easily noticed and measured. Less quantifiable, but just as serious, is the general feeling of depression and alienation that affects many Amerasians, leaving them at high risk for suicide. Unfortunately, not nearly enough counselors are available to talk with them about their emotional problems.

Conclusion and Recommendations

The problems facing Amerasians are daunting but not insurmountable. The settlement of Vietnamese Amerasians in the United States has been fairly effective and can provide guidance for programs to assist other groups of Amerasians. The federal government and volunteer organizations have worked as partners and have shown that the government, when willing, can rectify its wrongs. Based on its international obligations, however, the United States still has a long way to go in helping Amerasians.

Notes

[1] Marilyn T. Trautfield, Note, *America's Responsibility to Amerasian Children: Too Little Too Late,* 10 Brooklyn Journal of International Law 55, 61 (1984).

[2] *See* Anne Keegan, *Children of Vietnam Find Few Fathers at U.S. Doors,* Chicago Tribune, May 13, 1987, at C1.

[3] Lisa Belkin, *Children of Two Lands in Search of Home,* New York Times, May 19, 1988, at A20. . . .

[4] *See* Marykim DeMonaco, Note, *Disorderly Departure: An Analysis of the United States Policy toward Amerasian Immigration,* 15 Brooklyn Journal of International Law 641, 653–57 (1989).

[5] [United Nations] Convention Relating to Status of Refugees, July 28, 1951, 189 U.N.T.S. 137; [United Nations] Protocol Relating to the Status of Refugees, *entered into force,* January 31, 1967, 19 U.S.T. 6223.

[6] 8 U.S.C. § 1154 (1988).

[7] Indochinese Refugee Resettlement and Protection Act, Pub. L. No. 100–202, 101 Stat. 1329–40 (1987).

Asian Americans and Debates about Affirmative Action

L. Ling-Chi Wang

In the past two years, both proponents and opponents have written extensively on the topic of affirmative action. But a national dialogue has yet to take place because both sides are locked in intractable positions, unwilling and unable to listen to and understand each other. Since the beginning of 1995, the national debate has become increasingly acrimonious and polarized. The July 20, 1995 decision of the Regents of the University of California to abolish its long standing affirmative action policy on admissions, faculty and staff hiring, and contracts, as well as the anti-affirmative action California initiative, known as the California Civil Rights Initiative (CCRI), to be placed on the November 1996 ballot, have contributed to the polarization of the national debate. The recent Republican victory in the 1994 elections and several U.S. Supreme Court decisions have greatly strengthened the forces opposed to affirmative action. Despite clear demographic and political shifts in the past three decades, there is a conspicuous absence of any critical, yet constructive, appraisal of the policy.

As one who has supported and worked on issues related to affirmative action during the past 28 years in the Asian American community, I would like to share my understanding and appraisal of the policy and the position I think Asian Americans should take in the national debate. While Asian Americans have slowly become more visible in the political debate, both proponents and opponents of affirmative action have largely misrepresented and marginalized the perspectives and positions of Asian Americans. I shall begin by briefly placing affirmative action in historical and political perspectives, at the risk of being redundant, since misinformation and confusion over both the intents and objectives of affirmative action policy still exist. I shall then outline where Asian Americans are situated in the unfolding national debate. Finally, I shall conclude with a critique of affirmative action as it has been practiced in the past thirty years and what Asian Americans can do to help reconfigure affirmative action within the context of a re-envisioned multiracial America. Asian Americans are central to this debate and play a vital role in shaping its outcome.

⊕ Affirmative Action in Perspective

The issue of fairness and justice in the distribution of scarce resources in our race- and class-conscious society lies at the heart of the current debate over affirmative action. Scarcity invariably creates competition and conflict. In this competition, political and economic elites have the power to define universalistic and meritocratic criteria for distributing scarce resources. For example, access to a University of California (UC) education is considered a scarce resource—in 1993, only 20,413 out of 272,800 high school graduates, which is less than ten percent, were admitted into the nine-campus system. The criteria established by the Regents of the University—grade point average (GPA) and standardized test scores—are assumed to be both fair and reliable and, therefore, universal.

The Johnson administration introduced affirmative action policies, pursuant to Executive Order 11246 in 1965, to help dismantle entrenched segregation and discrimination based on race and gender and to promote racial equality and integration. Opponents of affirmative action argue that it is unfair because it subverts meritocracy, condones mediocrity, promotes group rights, racial quotas, reverse discrimination, and above all, invites big government intrusion. Following the logic of the US Supreme Court decision in *Bakke v. the University of California* (1978), they argue that affirmative action in college admissions is morally wrong and un-American, despite its good intentions, because it grants *group rights* based on race and gender at the expense of *individual rights and merits*.

The July 20, 1995, decision by the UC Regents illustrates the argument against affirmative action policies in college admissions. Writing in defense of his anti-affirmative action resolution, UC Regent Ward Connerly declared,

> We have not "killed" or "scrapped" affirmative action. We have not adopted an academic meritocracy. Instead, the regents have eliminated what amounts to a racial Monopoly board in which students are allowed to proceed with their college educations on the basis of their color or the origin of their ancestors. . . . The University of California still has the "welcome mat" out for students of all races. We cherish our diversity and want more of it; we just want to achieve it *naturally* rather *than* artificially.

Likewise, explaining his anti-affirmative action position, UC Regent Stephen Nakashima wrote,

> The Regents' decision to terminate the discriminatory preference accorded to "minority" persons in hiring and contracting resulted from an increasing awareness that discrimination should not beget discrimination. The history books are full of tragedies born of what someone sincerely thought was justified to correct some prior wrong or to enhance the position of some groups. . . .

In the popular vernacular, *"the playing field has been leveled" after years of requiring only Asians and white males to bear the burden of a tilted field.*

The arguments of Connerly and Nakashima are based on the following major assumptions: (1) the US is and should be a *naturally* color-blind society; (2) granting group rights or privileges based on race or gender in the distribution of scarce resource(s) is *artificial* and discriminatory to Asian Americans and whites and, therefore, illegal and wrong; (3) affirmative action policies condone mediocrity and sacrifice merit and excellence; and (4) the sole criteria for the distribution of scarce resources are those based on individual merits and rights.

All four assumptions are flawed. The US has never existed *naturally* as a color-blind society. From the framing of its Constitution to its past and present policies for women and communities of color, the US has created *artificial* social barriers and relied on institutionalized segregation based on race and gender. For example, Harvard University denied admissions to qualified women and minorities for the first 328 years of its 358 year history, artificially protecting and perpetuating the group rights and privileges of white male gentiles. Its policy of excluding women and minorities can be characterized as affirmative action for white males or a policy that condoned mediocrity. Harvard invoked the concept of individual merit only when its protected privileged status for the white male group was challenged in the 1960s. Thus, throughout US history, artificial group rights or privileges have been used to favor white males at the expense of minorities and women.

Under intense pressure from the civil rights movement, universities reluctantly adopted affirmative action policies for minorities and women in the late 1960s as a token concession. Thus, affirmative action was introduced as a device to lend Harvard and other universities an appearance of fairness and integration. Harvard redefined "merit" by adding an "ethnic docket" to its list of other dockets, including wealthy alumni, athletes, and graduates of preparatory schools, in the admission process. This policy was never intended to promote substantive equality or integration; rather, it was designed to allow a small number of token minorities and women into white male dominated universities and work places.

Consequently, under the guise of affirmative action, elite universities like Harvard and the University of California admit more children of well-connected alumni than underrepresented minorities under "affirmative action." It seems that benefactors of "affirmative action" include *all* students admitted by non-competitive criteria, such as legacy, leadership qualities, athletic ability, disability, and historical racial or gender discrimination.

After 30 years of affirmative action, the racial divide in the US remains as wide and deep as that identified by President Johnson's Commission on Civil Disorder in the wake of urban riots in 1967. The Commission concluded in 1968,

What white Americans have never fully understood—but what the Negro can never forget—is that white society is deeply implicated in the ghetto. White institutions created it, white institutions maintain it, and white society condones it.

That was in 1968. Today, "white Americans" still do not understand the racial divide. Despite federal measures to abolish racial discrimination, such as the 1954 *Brown v. Board of Education* decision and the Civil Rights Act of 1964, the US has not succeeded in eliminating racial fissures. Yet many continue to believe that the US is a color-blind society. The opponents of affirmative action rest their case on this presumption of color-blindness and demand that public policies be carried out without distinction of race, gender, color, or national origin.

Asian Americans in the Affirmative Action Discourse

I will now discuss how opposing sides view and treat Asian Americans and then offer a more inclusive and multiracial vision of the US. Asian Americans have become a major focus of the national debate as both sides of the affirmative action issue use Asian Americans to advance their respective arguments. These arguments point to the complexity of race relations in the US and the need to rethink race and race relations. Among the examples of unfairness cited most frequently by opponents of affirmative action is the policy's adverse impact on Asian Americans. For example, in the 1980s, the opponents of affirmative action seized Asian American complaints of discriminatory admission policies in several top research universities as a means to dismantle affirmative action. More recently, the opponents of affirmative action have cited the lawsuit against San Francisco Unified School District action, the *Brian Ho* case, as an example of injustice engendered by affirmative action. Opponents exploit the "model minority" myth, in which Asian Americans are portrayed as highly motivated and hardworking people, by depicting them as victims of an unfair policy that favors group rights over individual merits.

Anti-affirmative action arguments rely on three major flawed assumptions. First, they assume that Asian Americans are a homogeneous group, ignoring the diverse composition of the group—which ranges from recent refugees from Southeast Asia to descendants of California's Chinese pioneers. Secondly, they assume that a legacy of historical and institutional racism against Asian Americans does not exist. They assume that Asian Americans are intergrated into the mainstream and do not face discrimination nor experience anti-Asian sentiment. Lastly, they assume that Asian Americans no longer need affirmative action programs to overcome past injustice and racial discrimination. Thus, they assume that Asian Americans, in departure from the past, no longer constitute a racial minority and are fully integrated into the white majority.

Defenders of affirmative action also view Asian Americans as a model minority; two perspectives have emerged from them. Some claim that Asian Americans no longer need or deserve to be included in affirmative action programs. With good intention, supporters use the "success of Asian Americans" as an argument for reserving affirmative action for other minorities. They argue that, while Asian Americans once experienced discrimination, they now compete on a level-playing field because of affirmative action and, therefore, no longer need affirmative action programs. In other words, affirmative action has become a sound, temporary public policy which can outlive its usefulness once those who have experienced discrimination in the past have achieved success.

Other proponents of affirmative action presume that all Asian Americans oppose affirmative action since they are already a "model minority." They see the Asian American presence in the debate as a monkey wrench in their "black-versus-white" paradigm of racial discourse. In their view, there is no room for an Asian American presence in both their theories and public policy formulations. In short, they want to exclude Asian Americans from racial discourse, even in times of backlash against affirmative action. They marginalize, if not exclude, those Asian Americans who strongly support affirmative action in public forums and protest rallies. In my opinion, their exclusionary posture aids and abets opponents of affirmative action.

Thus, while opponents of affirmative action divide the Asian American communities by national origin and class and pit Asian Americans against other minorities, a tactic which is both divisive and racist, supporters of affirmative action also deliberately exclude and marginalize Asian Americans in a fashion just as divisive and racist. Both sides incorrectly view Asian Americans as a model minority and erroneously assume their homogeneity and uniform success. While about half of the Asian American population is successful according to educational, occupational, and income measures, the other half—many of whom are non-English-speaking recent immigrants and refugees—is not and needs public assistance and affirmative action. Nonetheless, both halves need affirmative action—they are equally susceptible to racism and discrimination which pose a constant threat to their lives, human dignity, and basic rights.

Asian Americans should not allow themselves to be used or marginalized in intellectual discourses, policy formulations, and political debates over affirmative action. They need to speak out against these misrepresentations promoted by both sides of the debate and articulate their positions forcefully. Their presence is essential for understanding the complexity of current race relations in the US and to re-thinking race and race relations in the 21st century.

⬦ Re-Envisioning Multiracial America

The nation is at a critical juncture in its history. After five hundred years of racial oppression and exclusion, fundamental questions remain. What kind of society should historically oppressed communities seek for themselves and their children? What should be the vision for the US as a whole in the 21st century?

The social progress made through integration and affirmative action, including the creation of a sizable black middle class, has fallen far short of the substantive changes necessary to create a truly equal society which is free of racism and sexism. As much as one-half to two-thirds of African Americans still live in near or dire poverty. For millions of Americans of all races, the dream of racial equality and economic justice remains unfulfilled.

The integrationist paradigm and strategy used in the past three decades failed for five important reasons. First, affirmative action, in the final analysis, is a token concession which was granted under tremendous political pressure during the height of the civil rights movement. It promotes integration for some and alienation for most, including poor whites. It is a temporary and discretionary policy of political expediency which can be taken back at any time. Second by adopting the terms and conditions of integration, affirmative action is judged as fair and universal when it ensures advantages to white males. Furthermore, beneficiaries of affirmative action are deemed less qualified and undeserving, even if they are fully qualified. For these reasons, affirmative action, in its current form, is denounced as a program that unfairly privileges minorities and women at the expense of white males. Third, by adopting the terms and conditions of integration, affirmative action also requires women and minority groups to fight for their own shares of the token concession. Built into these terms is a self-defeating, divide-and-conquer strategy based largely on identity politics in which minorities and women are pitted against each other in a contest to determine which group faces greater discrimination and victimization. While identity politics and victimology are necessary and empowering, they pose limits and present pitfalls. Fourth, the dominant race relations paradigm assumes a black versus white dichotomy which marginalizes other racial minorities. Under this bipolar paradigm, civil rights is a black issue, relegating the civil rights issues of Asian Americans, Chicanos/Latinos, Native Americans, and women to the fringe. This paradigm prevents a multiracial vision of America from emerging, promotes inter- and intra-minority conflict, and, above all, undermines solidarity among racial minorities, women, and poor whites in their efforts to combat racism, sexism, and economic injustice. Last but not least, the race-based policy obscures the significance of class within each racial group, especially within the Asian American communities. As a result, class interests are frequently confused with or manipulated as race-based interests and vice versa. For these five reasons, it is important to re-think race relations and civil rights. It is time to reformulate affirmative action and to re-envision America as a multiracial democracy.

The political backlash which began during the Nixon era has now become a tsunami sweeping across the nation. The backlash has been greatly reinforced by a growing sense of vulnerability among the predominantly white population as the US loses its dominant position in the global economy and its population becomes increasingly multiracial through immigration from Asia and Latin America. This backlash is particularly evident in California, as exemplified by legislative strategies such as Proposition 187, the English-only proposition, and gerrymandering reapportionment.

There is, however, a legacy of the 1960s that has long been forgotten which deserves our attention and support. I am referring to the Third World legacy which united racial minority and white students in the fight against racial oppression and created the ethnic studies departments now found in various universities across the nation. For the first and only time in US history, racial minority groups joined hands with whites in a common cause to transform institutions of higher education. They steadfastly refused to be divided and conquered. The concept of Third World may be passé but the vision of multiracial democracy and the idea of solidarity among oppressed groups are more urgent than ever if the US is to transform itself.

Racial minorities and women in California have an opportunity and an obligation to build a new society for the US. This is especially true in multiracial cities like Los Angeles and San Francisco, where racial minorities and women are clearly in the majority. But, it is also in these cities that they are hopelessly divided and against each other, compelled by the current power structure to accept and live with political domination and economic injustice. This situation must be reversed. It must, however, also go beyond simply chipping away power and privilege from the white males and striving for group gains, and in turn, using the same power and privileges to exclude and oppress others. I hope for a new society and new government which will not repeat the same mistakes and atrocities of the past.

Toward this end, America needs a bold new vision for itself. I suggest a critical re-examination of affirmative action, especially its limits, and an attempt to learn from past mistakes. It is certainly important to build a united force of minorities, women, and white males to defeat the racially motivated backlash against affirmative action and other progressive programs. I cannot overemphasize the importance of coalition building. The backlash, however, cannot be defeated simply to return to business as usual. The nation should return to the promise of equality and justice embodied in the Declaration of Independence and mandated in our Constitution. America must re-envision itself and become a political and economic democracy that is truly multiracial, what historian Harold Cruse called "democratic ethnic pluralism." This means that the US identity is not simply conceptualized as black and white, but as multicolor, including Asian Americans, Chicanos/Latinos, Native Americans, women, and gay of all colors and classes.

The anti-affirmative action forces issue a rare challenge for Asian Americans. They occupy a unique position in meeting this challenge and can help break the deadlock between the opposing sides of the affirmative action debate. Asian Americans could not have asked for a better opportunity and vehicle to take up this challenge. To take full advantage of this opportunity, they must have the courage to critically examine their past actions as well as their successes and failures. They must avoid repeating past mistakes and be prepared to modify past policies, including affirmative action policy. To achieve a multiracial political and economic democracy, a multiracial vision and coalition is needed. Asian Americans must join with others who share this vision to defeat the forces of reaction and to re-envision, transform, and rebuild America.

⊕ Further Reading

Aguilar-San Juan, Karin, ed. *The State of Asian America: Activism and Resistance in the 1990s* (1994).

Asian Women United of California, ed. *Making Waves: An Anthology of Writings by and About Asian American Women* (1989).

Eng, David, and Alice Hom, eds. *Q & A: Queer in Asian America* (1998).

Gee, Emma, et al., eds. *Counterpoint: Perspectives on Asian America* (1976).

Ho, Fred. *Legacy to Liberation: Politics and Culture of Revolutionary Asian/Pacific America* (2000).

Hune, Shirley. "Opening the American Mind and Body: The Role of Asian American Studies," *Change* 21, no. 6 (November/December 1989): 56–63.

Kibria, Nazli. "The Racial Gap: South Asian American Racial Identity and the Asian American Movement," in *A Part Yet Apart: South Asians in Asian America,* ed. Lavina Dhingra Shankar and Rajini Srikanth (1998), 69–78.

Kondo, Dorinne. "Art, Activism, Asia, and Asian Americans," in *About Face: Performing Race in Fashion and Theater (1997),* 227–260.

Leadership Education for Asian Pacifics: Asian Pacific American Public Policy, *The State of Asian Pacific America: Policy Issues to the Year 2020* (1993).

Lee, Wen Ho, with Helen Zia, *My Country Versus Me* (2000).

Leong, Russell, ed. *Asian American Sexualities: Dimensions of the Gay and Lesbian Experience* (1996).

Lim-Hing, Shirley, ed. *The Very Inside: An Anthology of Writing by Asian and Pacific Island Lesbian and Bisexual Women* (1994).

Ling, Susie. "The Mountain Movers: Asian American Women's Movement in Los Angeles," *Amerasia Journal* 15, no. 1 (1989): 51–67.

Morales, Royal F., *Makibaka, the Pilipino American Struggle* (1974).

Nakanishi, Don. "Linkages and Boundaries: Twenty-Five Years of Asian American Studies," *Amerasia Journal* 21, no. 3 (1995/96): xvii–xxv.

National Asian Pacific American Legal Consortium, *Selected Incidents of Anti-Asian Violence in 1993* (1993).

Ong, Paul, ed. *The State of Asian Pacific America: Economic Diversity, Issues and Policies* (1994).

Root, Maria P. P., ed. *The Multiracial Experience: Racial Borders as the New Frontier* (1996).

———. *Racially Mixed People in America* (1992).

Shah, Sonia, ed *Dragon Ladies: Asian American Feminists Breath Fire* (1997).

Stober, Dan, and Ian Hoffman. *A Convenient Spy: Wen Ho Lee and the Politics of Nuclear Espionage* (2001).

Tachiki, Amy, et al., eds. *Roots: An Asian American Reader* (1971).

Takagi, Dana Y. *Retreat from Race: Asian-American Admissions Policies and Racial Politics* (1992).

Trask, Haunani-Kay. *From a Native Daughter: Colonialism and Sovereignty in Hawaii* (1993).

Umemoto, Karen. "On Strike': San Francisco State College Strike 1968–69: The Role of Asian American Students," *Amerasia Journal* 15, no. 1 (1989), 3–41.

Wei, William. *The Asian American Movement* (1993).

Yamamoto, Eric. *Interracial Justice: Conflict and Reconciliation in Post-Civil Rights America* (1999).

Zia, Helen. *American Dreams: The Emergence of an American People* (2001).

A Voyage of Discovery: Sacramento and the Politics of Ordinary Black People

David Covin

Good Afternoon,

Thank you for the introduction.

I am honored and humbled to be invited to speak at the 40th Anniversary of Ethnic Studies at Sacramento State University. It is a singular honor to be invited to speak at the university where I taught for 35 years, to be invited by my home department, and my home program of Pan African Studies within that department, to be invited by my colleagues. This honor is enhanced by the distinction of the department. This Ethnic Studies department is one of the most outstanding in the country. An indicator of that reality is that one of its past chairs, Dr. Otis Scott, is the only person ever elected to two consecutive terms as President of the National Association of Ethnic Studies. Another indicator is the distinction of each of the separate programs which constitute it: Asian-American Studies, Latino/Chicano Studies, Native American Studies, and Pan African Studies. My program, Pan African Studies, as currently constituted, is one of the strongest in the country. It has a sterling legacy of teachers, scholars, activists, and mentors. As a continuation of that legacy, its current composition, consisting of nationally and internationally renowned faculty members, places it in the first rank in the United States, and in the world.

Sac State's Ethnic Studies Department has a quadruple legacy of scholarship, teaching, activism, and mentoring. It is built – and operates – to serve students and to serve the community. There is no *link* between the department and the community. There is a *commonality*. That is represented, for example, by Cooper-Woodson College – which unites students, faculty, and community residents in a mentoring and support system. In the whole country there is no counterpart.

To be chosen to speak by such an illustrious group of colleagues is, indeed, a humbling honor.

This afternoon I'm going to talk about a Voyage of Discovery that has taken place over the past 40 years. It is the voyage of my discipline, Pan African Studies. By extension, it represents the voyage made by every aspect of the Ethnic Studies department. My focus is specifically on Pan African Studies. In the course of the discussion I will use one of my books as an illustration of how a particular work contributes to the voyage.

Pan African Studies, as the field is named on this campus, and Black Studies, as it is more widely known, elsewhere is also designated as Africana Studies, Africology, Afro-American Studies, and various and sundry other appellations.

By whatever name, 40 years ago, it was virtually non-existent as an academic discipline. Beginning at San Francisco State, in 1966, the first Black Studies departments and programs were established. In 1968 and 1969 there was an explosion in their number following the assassination of Dr. Martin Luther King, Jr. The program here began as part of the broader program of Ethnic Studies, in the academic year, 1969-70. The Black Studies programs and departments established in those early years were not academic disciplines. They were part of a social movement – the Black Movement, more popularly known as the Black Power Movement.

They were not academic disciplines because there were no academic Black Studies departments or programs to produce the scholars who would populate them. If we look at the early incumbents of Black Studies positions on this campus, for example, we find Dr. William Gibson, who was a historian; Dr. Maxwell Owusu, who was an anthropologist; Dr. Addison Somerville, who was a Psychologist; Jesse McClure, who had an MSW; Dr. Fannie Canson, who was an Educational administrator; Mugo-Mugo Gatheru, who was an author and a historian; Gabriel Bannerman-Richter, who was an English teacher and writer; Dr. Allan Gordon, who was an Art Historian. Not one of them was the product of a Black Studies Department. In the cohort I came in with in 1970, there were two of us who were political scientists, an artist, a dramatist, a fine arts graduate who was a poet, and a social worker. No graduates of Black Studies departments. There weren't any.

Black Studies, as an academic discipline, had to be created. The job of early Black Studies departments was to do precisely that: *Create* Black Studies.

It did not have to be done out of whole-cloth because there was a rich tradition of Black scholarship which could be drawn on. But that tradition was academically diffuse. There was the incomparable and path-breaking work of Dr. W.E.B. DuBois, the historical work of Dr. Carter G. Woodson, and Dr. John Hope Franklin. There were the pioneering studies of John Henrick Clark, C.L.R. James. There was Dr. Anna Julia Cooper, the Harlem Renaissance writers, scholars, artists, musicians. There was the Negritude movement. The work of sociologists like Dr. C. Eric Lincoln and anthropologists like Dr. Sinclair Drake. The political scientist, Dr. Ralph Bunche. Dancer/scholars like Katherine Dunham. There was a rich history of scholarly investigation and artistic creativity. But there was no academic discipline devoted, particularly, to mining and developing that treasure trove.

The people I've mentioned were stars – luminaries – but there were very few foot-soldiers dedicated to this work. Most Black people who had come to maturity before the 1950s, were not high-school graduates. Those who were hired to teach Black Studies in the 1960s and 70s had to figure out the parameters, the dimensions, of this new field. That work was both driven and complicated by the reality that the field had emerged out of a social movement.

One of the constants of the human condition is that if you get two people together, they will disagree with each other – on just about anything. Add to that people who are fired up about a social movement – extremely opinionated – and others steeped in the tradition of objective academic rigor, and you have a very explosive mix indeed. Figuring out what this new discipline was going to be – the very first step in creating Black Studies – was no walk down a garden path.

Combined with this was the condition that a lot of these new faculty members were practicing "learning as you go." They hadn't read Ida B. Wells, Mary McCleod Bethune, David Diop, Paul Lawrence Dunbar, Phyllis Wheatley, Marcus Garvey. These people weren't covered in any classes taught in the colleges and universities they'd attended. The new teachers had to learn them on their own. And for several years that's what most Black Studies consisted of - drawing on the rich seed-bed of scholarship and artistic accomplishment that earlier generations of Black people had produced – but which had enjoyed a very narrow audience, accomplishment that was almost entirely excluded from traditional academia.

How do all these disparate people, doing their own basic learning, in the throes of a social movement, figure out what their discipline is going to be? They were learning almost everything as they went along. I'll use what happened here to illustrate some of what that means.

Does Black Studies (Afro-American Studies) – as many people thought, believed, and argued – mean the study of Black people in the United States? Here – on this campus – almost half the people teaching Black Studies were from Africa: Maxwell Owusu, Mugo-Mugo Gatheru, Gabriel Bannerman-Richter, John Shoka. It didn't make sense for Black Studies to be restricted to the United States. As people educated themselves they increasingly became exposed to the African *diaspora* – a term many had never even heard before they began their careers as Black Studies professors. The African *diaspora* – Black people in the United States, but also in the Caribbean, Central America, South America, even Canada for heaven's sake – for starters. How does one convey that the field encompasses all these African peoples? On this campus, the faculty said, Let's make it clear, explicit, that Black Studies means the study of African people – *wherever they are*. Let's call ourselves Pan African Studies. They changed the program's name from Black Studies to Pan African Studies. Its mission – was to join with others – across the world – to create an academic discipline of a new type.

Let me lay out what that means. Despite the remarkable work done by pioneering Black scholars and artists, by comparison with other works produced, those by or about people of African descent were negligible. In the discipline I was trained in, political science, for example, in the two major journals of the discipline, from 1886–1990, a period of 104 years, a total of 6,157 articles were published. Fifty-four of those were focused on Black politics. 6,103 were not. Of the 54 articles on Black politics – 17 were really not on Black politics at all, but were about slavery, the politics of slavery. In reality, then, only 37 articles focused on Black politics after the Civil War. Approximately one-half of one percent of all the articles. That's what I mean by negligible. 99.5 percent of the articles were not about Black politics. Plainly and simply, that means for most people who wanted to study Black politics, there was nothing to study.

The task that fell to these new scholars was – creating a literature, a subject matter, a body of knowledge for their discipline – even as they were trying to figure out its parameters.

How did they do?

We'll use Pan African Studies at Sac State as an indicator. CSU Sacramento is not a Research I institution. That means its primary mission, the mission of its faculty, is not research, but teaching. Community service is also a major responsibility of this university – a responsibility greatly heightened for Pan African Studies. In California, research is primarily the mission of the U.C. system. It is funded to support research. The workload of its faculty is based around research. That is not true here. Research in the CSU system, has to be torn out of faculty members' hides.

Given all that, how did the Pan African Studies faculty – who were not paid to do original research, to produce subject matter – but to disseminate it – how did they do?

Faculty members associated with Pan African Studies at Sac State since its inception have written 64 books, almost 700 articles, book chapters, book reviews, and short stories. They have produced major works of art – which have been hung, played, and performed in galleries, theaters, and concert halls all over the world. They have been consultants on projects of every kind all over the planet. They have produced films, CDs, radio and television programs. They have produced web-sites and blogs. They have created and edited journals. They have appeared in radio, television, newspaper, journal, and magazine interviews. They have had articles, even books, written about *them*.

Now, let us compare their production of Black articles over 40 years, to that of another academic discipline, political science, for the whole country: over 104 years. All of Political Science over 104 years: 37 articles. Pan African Studies at Sac State over 40 years: 700.

This is one program, in a non-Research I institution. Can you imagine the total amount of work produced by Black Studies scholars in colleges and universities of every description, including Research I institutions, throughout this region, throughout this state, throughout this country, and throughout the world over these 40 years? It is . . . staggering. It is an academic achievement of colossal magnitude. And it is recognized . . . by almost no one. That is why this anniversary needs to be celebrated and broadcast – to every village and hamlet.

This discipline has been sailing on an unprecedented Voyage of Discovery.

I'm going to use my book, *Black Politics After the Civil Rights Movement: Sacramento, 1970–2000,* as an illustration of the kinds of places this voyage has taken us, the kind of discovery such research produces. By the way, that title is the publisher's title. I call the book, *The Politics of Ordinary Black People.*

It took me 40 years to write it. So you can see I was not working on a publish or perish schedule. I would have perished.

The objective of academic research is to produce new knowledge, at the very least, to produce promising and likely speculations. Most of us produce the latter: promising and likely speculations.

I liken the conduct of original research to taking voyages of discovery. Their objectives are the same. What is "original" research but going somewhere no one's ever been? If somebody's already been there, it's not original.

Christopher Columbus undertook voyages of discovery. But he wasn't looking for someplace new. He was looking for some place old – the Indies, the Orient, the East. He was looking for a new "passage" to the Indies. That's what he was trying to discover. He didn't "discover" the new passage. He didn't know there was a whole hemisphere between Europe and the East. Going for the East – he ended up in the West.

That's what doing original research is like. You don't know where you're going. You often end up at a different place than you thought you would. You are often surprised, and often don't know where you are once you've arrived. You may even think you're some place you're not. Columbus thought he was in the Indies. He ended up somewhere he didn't even know existed.

That's original research. Every time you begin it, you are entering the unknown.

In the 40 years since the advent of Black Studies, Black Political scientists have produced a tremendous amount of research. Bearing witness to their productivity is that unlike the U.S.A., the American Political Science Association, the APSA, has had three Black presidents during that period, one of them a woman (the three followed by some forty-five years the Presidency of Ralph Bunche in 1954). Presidents of the APSA are elected on the basis of their leading role in the discipline. So the three Black presidents speak to the quality of Black scholarship over the past four decades. Political Science, nevertheless, remains a backwards discipline on questions of race, despite the prodigious output of Black scholars, because white scholars and *all* non-Black scholars produce articles on Black politics at about the same rate they always have.

Despite the many discoveries of my colleagues in the field of Black politics, there were a number of unanswered or even unaddressed questions I wanted to explore. That's why I did the research that produced this book.

Most political studies deal with officeholders, appointed officials, bureaucracies, organizations, social movements, individual actors – variations across class, gender, age, race, public opinion, as well as connections among these variables – at the local, state, national, and international levels. I wanted to understand how ordinary Black people – who held no political office – fit into that complex aggregation of structures, activities, and orientations.

One of the salient findings of most of the major studies was that the Black politics of the 30 years between 1970 and 2000, usually referred to in the literature as the Post-Civil Rights Era, had not been worthy successors of the Civil Rights and

Black Power epoch. Black politics had become increasingly dysfunctional. Some scholars also identified a declining significance of race, identified in politics, as deracialization.

Some preliminary studies I had done raised questions about these findings. While it was incontestable – as other studies showed that after the late 1970s the Civil Rights and Black Power Movements had ended, it was equally incontestable that ferocious opposition to those gains persisted. Yet my work showed, and no serious work really contradicted it, that the gains of the Civil Rights and Black Power movements continued, and in most instances had been enhanced. How could that be, I wondered, if Black politics had become increasingly dysfunctional.

I used Sacramento as a universe to explore these questions. A 2002 edition of *Time* magazine unintentionally validated the academic viability of the project by identifying Sacramento as the city most representative of the diversity of the national population.

Focusing on Sacramento I was able to look in much more detail at Black organizations, residential patterns, social networking, social movements, officeholders, political campaigns, and three critical elements derived from social movement research: social spaces, social narrative, and social memory, than I would have been able to do looking at the country at large, or even at a very big city.

I was also able to identify national Black political efforts which were present in Sacramento, such as the War on Poverty, the Harold Washington Mayoral campaign, the Jesse Jackson Presidential campaigns, and the Million Man March. In them I could examine the relationships between national and even international political efforts and local ones.

I divided the analysis by decades, in order both to make it manageable and to enable the identification of changes, trends, and continuities over time.

Let me highlight some of my principal findings:

1. The emergence of a significant Black middle class in Sacramento, beginning in the mid 1960's, and increasing rapidly in each subsequent decade.
2. A fluid Black population, with births, deaths, and people moving in and out of the area.
3. A tendency of Black people to identify certain governmental programs, governmental offices, and geographical areas as "theirs" regardless of demographic characteristics.
4. A tendency of other population groups to acquiesce to such Black claims.
5. Affronts to Black people served as powerful incentives for mobilizing Black people, with the police department most frequently the source of the affronts.
6. A high level of organization among the Black population, characterized over time by a significant decrease in the number of working class organizations and an almost geometric expansion in the number of mixed and middle-class organizations.

7. An almost total absence of organization of the Black underclass, except the Nation of Islam, and a very small number of secular organizations during the 90s.

8. A consistent increase in the total number of Black organizations and in the number of organizations intentionally founded to be specifically Black, despite widely disseminated notions of a declining significance of race.

9. No support for the proposition that for Black people, between 1970 and 2000, there was a decline in the significance of race. If anything, the data showed an *increase* in the significance of race.

10. A general and consistent lack of political involvement by Black churches throughout the whole period.

11. The Nation of Islam bucked the trend of Black religious detachment from politics from 1984 on.

12. The cathartic and empowering effect of the appeal for Black Unity.

I'll talk about a few of these findings to illustrate their explanatory power.

The tendency of Black people to identify certain social spaces as their own, and to take them over, is related to Black use of social narratives and social memory. Black people, more than any other similarly oppressed or exploited group, were empowered and mobilized by the Civil Rights and Black Power Movements. As a result, the War on Poverty, closely connected to those movements, was claimed by Black people when it came to Sacramento. For the most part, they captured it, though most poor people in Sacramento were not Black, they were white. Yet in every target area where there was a significant Black population, Black people ended up running the poverty organization whether the majority or plurality was white or Latino, because in no case was the majority or plurality Black. This is one instance of the tendency of Black people to identify certain social spaces as their own and take them over.

Another avenue that opened up such possibilities for Black people arose when the Sacramento City Council went to a district system of election, Black activists worked hard to develop two Black-influence districts. Each of those 2 districts, council district 2 and council district 5, had white super majorities. Yet Black people, using Black narrative to dominate political spaces, claimed those districts as their own and twice elected Black people in district 2, and once got a Black person appointed. In district 5 they elected 1 Black person, got another appointed, and later elected a Black person to consecutive terms. Still later, in District 8, where the plurality population was white, but in which Black people had mobilized to have boundaries drawn to make it a Black influence district, Black people elected a councilman to two consecutive terms, and when he died, elected his wife to the seat. In every single one of these electoral instances, white, Latino, and Asian populations deferred to Black assertions.

The significance of the cathartic and empowering impact of the appeal to Black Unity was revealed in the distinction between organizing and mobilizing.

There is a persistent, perpetual, and relentless appeal for Black Unity that emerges from African peoples. It is an appeal which makes no rational sense. Within the United States the Black population is too large, too dispersed, too varied, too complex, and too conflicted for Black Unity to have any possibility of being realized organizationally. Yet the appeal to Black Unity has a powerful effect as a mobilizing tool.

Black people in the aggregate crave racial unity. That's why metaphors such as house slaves, field slaves, uncle Toms, Aunt Gemimas, oreos, and handkerchief heads are so effective. That's why Clarence Thomas, Wardell Connerly, and Condoleeza Rice are such anathemas. They accent disunity, the fractured condition of the Black population.

The irony is that contested figures such as Shelby Steele and Alan Keyes accurately reflect the reality that the Black population is not monolithic. Most Black people wish it were, because they believe – if it were, they would be much more effective in achieving their collective aspirations. This is all wishful thinking, but it is powerful wishful thinking with profound implications for Black political life. It "keeps hope alive" – and raises the prospect of realizing *"The Impossible Dream."* The appeal to Black Unity can *mobilize* the Black underclass without the need to *organize* it. Whereas only the underclass has shown the ability *to organize* itself, it rarely does, and then – except for religious purposes and gangs – only for short periods of time. Appeals to Black unity, however, issued by the Black working class and the Black middle class can and do effectively *mobilize* the Black underclass.

Which brings me to . . . Barak Hussein Obama. He is . . . the manifestation . . . of the impossible dream. How did he occur? To answer that question, one must first understand the role of the Black electorate in the Presidential election – particularly in the Democratic primaries. That means not concentrating on polling numbers, the party platform, who Ted and Caroline Kennedy endorsed, what Pfloufe's and Axelrod's strategies were. It doesn't even mean examining the effects of the Congressional Black Caucus. It means scrutinizing the deep work of ordinary Black people. The census is misleading. In the election of Harold Washington in Chicago, the Jesse Jackson Presidential campaigns, Obama's primary victories on Super Tuesday – deep Black organizational work and appeals to Black unity resulted in Black mobilizations which by all conventional measures, were impossible, because they actually seemed – to increase the size of the Black population.

How did the realization of *the impossible dream*, the election of Barak Hussein Obama to the presidency of the United States of America, occur?

A rigorous analysis of the political work of ordinary Black people in Sacramento over a thirty-year period provides critical clues for us. How did Robbie Robertson, elected in a Sacramento City Council district with an overwhelming white majority, occur?

How did Dan Thompson, elected in a Sacramento City Council district with an overwhelming white majority, occur?

How did Grantland Johnson, a product of this program at Sac State, elected in a Sacramento City Council district with an overwhelming white majority, occur?

How did Lauren Hammond, also a product of this program, elected in a Sacramento City Council district with an overwhelming white majority – for four consecutive terms, occur?

How did Sam Pannell, elected to the Sacramento City Council from a white plurality district for two consecutive terms, occur?

How did Bonnie Pannell, elected in the same City Council district for three consecutive terms, occur?

How did Grantland Johnson, elected to the County Board of Supervisors in a district with not only a white super majority, but with a Black population as a negligible minority, occur?

What this study shows is an extraordinary, day-to-day organizational life of ordinary Black people – organizing and mobilizing at a far greater intensity than any other population group, and across a broader spectrum of political issues, creating a dense and networked organizational infrastructure, which is effective at seizing and dominating public spaces and selected social narratives. It shows a driven, emergent Black middle class; cross-class, cross-gender, cross-sectional, cross-national mobilizations in an effort to achieve the chimera of Black Unity. All this comes from a demeaned part of the population, woefully bereft of material resources, and tremendously outnumbered – who, against all odds, assert claims to office, create a narrative to give their claims authenticity, and hyper-mobilize in a transcendent search for unity.

This study shows us that ordinary Black people do what other ordinary people do: They participate in their children's school and after school activities. They are in the PTO, or PTA, as the case might be. They coach little league, are soccer moms, referee Pop Warner football leagues. They join professional associations, hold offices in labor unions, join environmental organizations, women's organizations, and volunteer in raising funds for cancer survivors. They populate recreational leagues for softball, basketball, bowling and golf. They join the VFW and the American Legion. They are active participants in the Democratic and Republican parties. They do what everybody else does. And then – they create – in addition, a wholly alternative world. Of women's and men's organizations, health organizations, educational organizations, professional organizations, civil rights organizations, PACs, voter registration efforts, health advocacies, legal ventures, political education webs, blogs, newsletters, magazines, whole cultural venues – all of which are Black. They invest themselves – fully – in two entirely different worlds.

I mentioned the APSA. There is also the National Conference of Black Political Scientists. Black political scientists belong to, and are active in both. There is the American Sociological Association. There is also the Association of Black Sociologists. There is the American Medical Association. There is also the National Medical Association (which is Black). There is the American Bar Association.

There is also the National Bar Association (which is Black). In every arena of life in this country – black people are engaged in the dominant organizations and in counterpart organizations which are Black. They also engage in Black organizations for which there are no dominant counterparts. This research shows that these tendencies have not stopped. They have not diminished. On the contrary, they increased - dramatically – between 1970 and 2000. This is an extraordinary expenditure of effort – of resources, both human and material – that goes far beyond the norm. It speaks to a felt need, because if people didn't feel an urgency for such exertions – a need for them – they certainly wouldn't engage in them.

Sometimes . . . it works. Not only in this city, and this county. But in the person of the President of the United States of America – becoming the living embodiment of *the impossible dream.*

This is where we need the microscope – a kind of biological chemistry, if you will. We can't get at the root of the mysteries abiding in the continual realization of *impossible dreams* by looking only at the big people. We have to look at the little people. And to do that we have to approach research questions from outside the dominant paradigm. We must rely less, as it were, on our understandings of musculature, and develop our understandings of chemical interactions. We must have a reliable vision of the micro as well as the macro. That's how we can produce – in this arena – new knowledge, or at the very least, promising and likely speculations.

We cannot begin to understand these phenomena without the very specific scholarship Pan African Studies brings to the table.

These – are the Voyages of Discovery – on which our scholars and our students – set sail.

Arizona: Ground Zero for the War on Immigrants and Latinos(as)

Elvia Ramirez

Introduction

Few issues today elicit as much controversy and debate as undocumented immigration. Recent immigration laws passed by the Arizona legislature – most notably SB 1070 – have catapulted immigration issues to the national spotlight. Claiming that the federal government has failed to uphold its responsibility of securing our national borders (particularly the one shared with Mexico), politicians in Arizona have passed a series of laws targeting undocumented immigrants. In this article, I review the politics of immigration as they have unfolded in the state of Arizona. Based on an analysis of newspaper articles and social science research, I examine the debate surrounding the passage of SB 1070, one of the most punitive anti-immigrant laws ever passed by any state legislature in recent U.S. history. First, I explain what SB 1070 is and discuss why it generated much controversy and debate. I then document resistance strategies employed by opponents of SB 1070, followed by a review of subsequent bills introduced by Arizona politicians that target immigrants and their children, immigrant teachers, and Ethnic Studies programs. I conclude with an analysis of factors explaining the current anti-immigrant and anti-Latino(a) climate present in the state of Arizona.

What Is SB 1070?

On April 23, 2010, Governor Jan Brewer from Arizona signed the Support Our Law Enforcement and Safe Neighborhoods Act – also known as SB 1070 – into law. Introduced by Republican state Senator Russell Pierce and drafted by the private prison industry (which would stand to benefit financially from the imprisonment of immigrants), SB 1070 seeks to criminalize undocumented immigrants by defining their presence in the U.S. as "trespassing." Under federal law, unlawful presence is considered a civil infraction (rather than a crime) and can result in deportation (Guskin & Wilson, 2007). Under SB 1070, however, it would be a state crime to be in the country illegally, and immigrants would be forced to carry proper immigration paperwork at all times (Garcia & Chandler, 2010; Rentería, 2010). Failing to carry papers would be considered a misdemeanor, punishable by up to six months of jail and a $2,500 fine before deportation (Riccardi, 2010a). This law would thus make Arizona the first state in the nation to criminalize undocumented immigrants (Rentería, 2010). Furthermore, under SB 1070, police officers would be required to question someone's immigration status if they had "reasonable suspicion" that person was undocumented. Police officers would thus be required to function as immigration agents and arrest anyone who could not produce documents proving their legal status (Garcia & Chandler, 2010). SB 1070 would also make seeking work illegal for day laborers, and would make transporting and employing undocumented immigrants a crime (Garcia & Chandler, 2010; Riccardi, 2010a). The law was set to take effect on July 29, 2010.

SB 1070 and the Institutionalization of Racial Profiling

The signing of SB 1070 into law generated a flurry of criticism and reaction throughout the country. Immigrant rights activists, civil rights leaders, politicians, religious leaders, and ordinary citizens interpreted SB 1070 as a racist attempt by the Arizona legislature to terrorize immigrant communities and institutionalize racial profiling. In particular, many felt the law's provision that police officers question individuals suspected of being undocumented would lead to the unfair targeting of Mexicans/Latinos(as). As Alfredo Gutierrez, a Mexican American former state senator from Arizona, observed, "'Reasonable suspicion' in Arizona isn't going to be someone who looks like a Canadian, whatever a Canadian looks like, it's going to be someone who looks like my family" (as cited in Hing, 2010a, para. 4). Indeed, though the overwhelming majority of Mexicans in this country are U.S. citizens or legal immigrants, "Mexicanness" is often a basis for suspecting "illegality" under immigration law, and Mexicans/Latinos(as) who speak Spanish and have brown skin color are generally subjected to greater levels of surveillance and harassment by immigration enforcement personnel (Johnson, 2000; Romero, 2006). Civil rights leaders thus feared that Latinos(as) who are U.S. citizens or legal residents would also be negatively impacted by this law. Alessandra Soler Meetze, president of the ACLU of Arizona, for example, commented, "A lot of U.S. citizens are going to be swept up in the application of this law for something as simple as having an accent and leaving their wallet at home" (as cited in Riccardi, 2010a, p. 2). Interestingly, law enforcement agencies were not entirely supportive of SB 1070 either, particularly because they feared it would lead to racial profiling and loss of the public's trust (Riccardi, 2010a; Wood, 2010a). In short, many felt SB 1070 would promote racial profiling by subjecting people of color, particularly Latinos(as), to increased surveillance and harassment by law enforcement agencies.

The fears of racial profiling articulated by critics of SB 1070 are certainly not unfounded. Research finds that police officers *do* engage in racial profiling when they are entrusted with immigration enforcement duties. Since 1995, Section 287(g) of the Immigration and Nationality Act (INA) has allowed Immigration and Customs Enforcement (ICE) to enter into partnership agreements with local law enforcement agencies that grant a limited set of immigration enforcement powers to police officers. (The use of police officers as immigration agents is thus not unprecedented; in fact, the 287(g) program served as an inspiration for the architects of SB 1070). A study by the U.S. Inspector General evaluating the 287(g) program found that police officers participating in this program receive an inadequate amount of training and supervision by ICE and often engage in racial profiling (Immigration Policy Center, 2010). Many other studies have reached similar conclusions. A report by the ACLU of Georgia, for example, argues that police officers deputized as immigration agents through the 287(g) program in Gwinnet County, Georgia engaged in racial profiling insofar as they "disproportionately target[ed] people of color for pretextual stops, investigations, and enforcement" (ACLU of Georgia, 2010, p. 5). The report notes that although racial profiling was a problem in Gwinnet County before the implementation of the 287(g) program, racial profiling only got worse after the county participated in the program, with Latinos(as) suffering the brunt of law enforcement harassment.

Perhaps the most egregious case of racial profiling and harassment of Latinos(as) by local police deputized as immigration agents under the 287(g) program is that of the notorious Sheriff from Maricopa County in Arizona, Joe Arpaio. Joe Arpaio led the largest 287(g) operation in the country, essentially turning his police department into a de facto immigration-enforcement agency (Immigration Policy Center, 2010; Sterling, 2010). An overzealous, xenophobic anti-immigrant crusader, Arpaio would have his deputies raid Latino(a) neighborhoods and workplaces in search of undocumented immigrants (Sterling, 2010). Moreover, under his supervision, prisoners were housed in tent cities under the blazing Arizona desert sun, made to wear pink underwear, were served spoiled food, and were reportedly physically assaulted as well (Hing, 2010c). Given his abuses of power, the Obama administration revoked his 287(g) agreement in 2009, though this has not stopped Arpaio from continuing his immigration sweeps in predominantly Latino(a) neighborhoods. Arpaio has also been under federal civil rights investigation into whether his department systematically violated the rights of Latinos(as) and engaged in racial profiling while enforcing federal immigration laws (Riccardi, 2010b). Recently, he was sued by the U.S. Justice Department for refusing to cooperate with this federal civil rights investigation (Medrano, 2010a).

The case of Joe Arpaio clearly illustrates the potential for racial profiling and other abuses when local police are granted immigration enforcement duties. In fact, this is a major reason that civil rights groups and activists have called for the repeal of 287(g) programs. According to the Immigration Policy Center, 287(g) programs are also problematic because they result in mistakes by police officers. For example, in 2007, Pedro Guzman, a Latino male who is a U.S. citizen and is developmentally disabled, was wrongly identified as an undocumented immigrant by local police participating in a 287(g) program. Guzman was then transferred to an ICE detention center and deported to Mexico (Immigration Policy Center, 2010). Clearly, even when police officers are trained in immigration law, they engage in racial profiling and make costly mistakes as a result. Significantly, the potential for racial profiling is even greater under SB 1070 than under the 287(g) program, given that SB 1070 does not provide for the training of police officers in immigration law.

Shortly after being introduced, SB 1070 was amended to bar police officers from using race/ethnicity as grounds for questioning individuals – a move interpreted by critics as a mere "cosmetic" change that made SB 1070 "minimally less racist" (Hing, 2010b). Opponents of SB 1070 thus continued to mobilize against the measure.

Resistance Strategies

Opponents of SB 1070 challenged the measure in three major ways, including: (1) organizing marches and protests; (2) calling for boycotts of Arizona; and (3) filing lawsuits challenging the constitutionality of the measure. For example, on May 1, 2010, as part of the yearly worldwide march commemorating International Workers' Day, thousands of people marched in San Francisco's Mission District to denounce SB 1070 and to demand immigration reform (Berton, 2010). Many also gathered that same day in downtown Sacramento to press for similar demands. Furthermore, in mid May of 2010, immigrant rights activists gathered at Sun Life Stadium in South Florida to protest before the game between the Arizona Diamondbacks and the Florida Marlins (Chardy, 2010). Also, up to 200,000 people took to the streets in Phoenix, Arizona in June 2010, in what was the second largest march in Arizona's history (Fernandez, 2010b). Marches and protests were also held in many other parts of the country.

The second major strategy used by opponents of SB 1070 was the use of the boycott. This strategy had been effectively used in the 1990's against Arizona when politicians there had voted against a holiday honoring Dr. Martin Luther King Jr.'s birthday (Wood, 2010b). Many critics of SB 1070 hoped that a boycott of Arizona would constitute a "wake-up" call to citizens of Arizona and would dissuade other states from enacting similar legislation (Wood, 2010b). California Senate leader Darrel Steinberg, for example, petitioned Governor Arnold Schwarzenegger "to 'deliver an unequivocal message' of disgust by tearing up the state's contracts with Arizona businesses and government agencies" (Theriault, 2010, para. 1). Many cities throughout the country, including Sacramento, thus approved boycotts of Arizona. Furthermore, several civil rights groups and unions, such as the Service Employees International Union, the National Council of La Raza, Asian American Justice Center, and League of United Latin American Citizens, announced travel boycotts of Arizona. Academic organizations, such as the American Educational Research Association (AERA), American Anthropological Association (AAA), Mujeres Activas en Letras y Cambio Social (MALCS), and the Southwestern Anthropological Association, also announced they would not be holding their annual meetings in Arizona.

Musicians and other celebrities also joined in on the boycott of Arizona. Led by Zack Rocha from Rage Against the Machine, a coalition of artists formed a group called "The Sound Strike" in order to raise awareness about SB 1070. These artists promised to skip Arizona on concert tours until SB 1070 was repealed (Michaels, 2010). "Fans of our music, our stories, our films and our words can be pulled over and harassed every day because they are brown or black, or for the way they speak, or for the music they listen to," explained Zack de la Rocha (as cited in Michaels, 2010, para. 3). Zack de la Rocha also expressed fears that other states in the nation would follow Arizona's lead, a pattern portending disastrous consequences for immigrants and people of color. "If other states follow the direction of Arizona," de la Rocha remarked, "we could be headed towards a pre-Civil Rights era reality" (as cited in Michaels, 2010, para. 7).

Other musicians and celebrities also joined the effort. Eugene Rodriguez from the U.S.-based group Los Cenzontles, for example, wrote a *corrido* (a popular ballad) titled "State of Shame" denouncing SB 1070 (Frontera Norte Sur, 2010). Furthermore, in Mexico City, a concert starring Latin American musical groups Jaguares, Maldita Vecindad, and Molotov was held to publicly protest the passage of SB 1070. Sports teams also joined in on the protest against SB 1070. Arizona's professional basketball team, the Phoenix Suns, for example, wore jerseys that said "Los Suns" in order to express solidarity with Latinos(as) and others opposing SB 1070 (Lewis, 2010).

The third major strategy used by opponents of SB 1070 was filing lawsuits challenging the constitutionality of the measure. Some of the groups filing lawsuits include the American Civil Liberties Union (ACLU), Mexican American Legal Defense and Education Fund (MALDEF), and the National Association for the Advancement of Colored People (NAACP). These groups labeled SB 1070 as "extreme" because it "invites the racial profiling of people of color, violates the First Amendment and interferes with federal law" (Chardy, 2010, para. 10). A Phoenix police officer, Officer Martin Escobar, also filed a lawsuit against the measure, arguing that it would force him to violate Latinos(as)' civil rights and would subject him to disciplinary action if he failed to enforce the law and legal action if he did (Duda, 2010). On July 6, 2010, the U.S. Department of Justice also filed a lawsuit against the bill because it felt the measure intruded into areas (immigration and border security) of authority reserved only for the federal government (Richey, 2010).

Current Status of SB 1070

Just hours before it was to go into effect, a federal judge halted the implementation of most of SB 1070's provisions. U.S District Judge Susan Bolton issued a temporary injunction against the most controversial elements of the bill, including the requirement that police officers check a person's immigration status while enforcing other laws, the requirement that immigrants carry their paperwork at all times, and the provision that made it unlawful for undocumented immigrants to seek employment in public places. The judge also blocked police officers from making warrantless arrests of suspected undocumented immigrants. Provisions of the law that did go into effect included the law's prohibition on stopping a motor vehicle to pick up day laborers, knowingly employing undocumented workers, and a provision striking down sanctuary city policies (Cattan, 2010). Attorneys for Governor Jan Brewer immediately appealed the decision. On April 11, 2011, the Ninth Circuit Court of Appeals in San Francisco, California, struck down Governor Brewer's appeal and upheld Judge Susan Bolton's ban on the most controversial sections of SB 1070 (Riccardi, 2011). It is possible the case may now go before the Supreme Court.

The Saga Continues

The fact that most of SB 1070 has been declared illegal by U.S. District Judge Susan Bolton and the Ninth Circuit Court of Appeals has not deterred politicians in Arizona and elsewhere from pursuing laws similar to SB 1070 as well as other measures that are even more anti-immigrant and patently unconstitutional. According to a report released by Immigration Works USA, more than twenty-five states may try to pass laws similar to SB 1070 when their state legislatures convene in 2011 (Goodwin, 2010). There is indeed strong support for this measure throughout the country, with polls showing a 60 percent voter approval rating for the measure (Carcamo, 2010). SB 1070 may also come to California, the state with the largest share of immigrants. In November 2010, the California secretary of state's office authorized a signature drive by a tea party activist to put a similar law as Arizona's before California voters. If it gathers enough signatures, the proposal, dubbed "Support Federal Immigration Law Act," will go before California voters during the 2012 election cycle (Lagos, 2010). If this measure were to go before California voters, there is a strong possibility it would be approved. A poll conducted by USC/Los Angeles Times in May 2010 found that half of California voters approve of Arizona's immigration measure, though support for this measure is divided along racial/ethnic, age, and party lines: Whites, older voters, males, and Republicans are largely in favor of it, while most Latinos (71%) and Asians (57%) oppose it (Wu, 2010). All the contentious and bitter politics associated with the immigration controversy in Arizona may thus come to (or, more accurately stated, *return* to) California in the near future.

Politicians in Arizona, led by Russell Pearce, have also challenged birthright citizenship for the U.S.-born children of undocumented immigrants. Anti-immigrant advocates like to refer to these children as "anchor babies," suggesting that undocumented immigrant parents use their U.S.-born children to establish themselves in this country (Guskin & Wilson, 2007). Yet, as Guskin & Wilson (2007) note, having a U.S.-born child does not provide a path for legalization for undocumented immigrants nor does it protect them from deportation. Nonetheless, Arizona Republicans were pushing for bills (SB 1308 and SB 1309) that would have eliminated the right of U.S.-born children of undocumented immigrants to automatically become U.S. citizens. Legislators in at least a dozen other states agreed to push for similar legislation (Vock, 2010).

As critics note, the push to deny citizenship for the U.S.-born children of undocumented immigrants is patently unconstitutional. The Supreme Court has previously ruled, in the 1898 case of *United States v. Wong*, that children born in the U.S. are automatically U.S. citizens, regardless of their parents' immigration status (Hing, 2011b). Critics thus interpret the push to end birthright citizenship as mere spectacle. "This is political theater, not a serious effort to create a legal test. . . . It strikes me as unwise, un-American, and unconstitutional" commented Gabriel J. Chin, a law professor at the University of Arizona (as cited in Lacey, 2011a, p. 2). Such a proposal also represents a huge step back in regards to civil rights for immigrants and people of color. As Karen Narasaki from the Asian American Justice Center insightfully observes, proponents of this measure "would drag us back to a time when minorities were not considered equal to whites nor worthy of being citizens . . . While their language is more carefully chosen than that used a century ago, their motives are no less clear" (as cited in Hing, 2011a, para. 12).

Arizona politicians also introduced a measure (SB 1405) that would have forced hospitals to check a person's immigration status before rendering non-emergency medical care (Hing, 2011b). This measure would have thus forced medical professionals to function as immigration agents – a move medical professionals and many others critiqued for endangering the lives of immigrants and their children, as well as placing the public's health at risk (since immigrants with contagious diseases would fear seeking medical help).

Senator Russell Pearce also introduced SB 1611, an "omnibus bill" that is even more punitive towards immigrants than SB 1070. This measure would: (a) bar children from K-12 schools if they cannot produce a U.S.-issued birth certificate or naturalization document; (b) prohibit undocumented immigrants from attending community colleges and universities in Arizona; (c) cut off undocumented immigrants from emergency medical care; (d) require individuals filing for a marriage license to show their immigration papers; (e) require individuals buying or operating a vehicle to show proof of legal residence; and (f) require businesses to use E-verify, the federal immigration database (Hing, 2011b). Like previous bills, this measure included provisions that are unconstitutional. For example, it goes against legal precedent established by the 1982 Supreme Court case of *Plyler v. Doe*, which established children's rights to K-12 public education regardless of their parents' immigration status.

In mid-March 2011, the Arizona Senate voted down all these anti-immigrant bills (i.e. SB 1308, SB 1309, SB 1405, SB 1611). It also rejected SB 1407, a bill which would have required schools to gather information about the immigration status of their students (Hing, 2011c). The Senate's repudiation of these bills was reportedly the result of pressure from the business community, which was concerned about the "unintended consequences" of such anti-immigrant legislation.

In a letter addressed to Senator Pearce and signed by the Greater Phoenix Chamber of Commerce and sixty CEO's from Arizona-based businesses, business leaders articulated concerns about the impact of boycotts on Arizona businesses (Hing, 2011c). "It is an undeniable fact that each of our companies and our employees were impacted by the boycotts and the coincident negative image," wrote the business leaders (as cited in Hing, 2011c, para. 16). Immigrant rights activists rejoiced over the Senate's rejection of these bills. "These are major wins for the fight for a better Arizona," remarked Jennifer Allen, executive director of Border Action Network (Hing, 2011, para. 8). It is likely, however, that the Senate's vote represents a mere temporary break in anti-immigrant bashing rather than a fundamental shift in Arizona's stance on immigration. These anti-immigrant measures may in fact resurface later in the Arizona legislature or as ballot propositions (Barr, 2011).

Arizona's Attack on Ethnic Studies and Immigrant Teachers

In addition to passing a suite of anti-immigrant measures, politicians in Arizona have attacked Ethnic Studies programs and immigrant teachers. Less than three weeks after signing SB 1070 into law, Governor Jan Brewer approved House Bill 2281, a measure targeting Ethnic Studies courses in public (K-12) schools. The brainchild of Tom Horne, then-superintendent of public instruction, HB 2281 bans courses that "promote resentment toward one race; that are designed for students of one race; that promote ethnic solidarity 'instead of treating students as individuals'; or that encourage 'the overthrow of the United States government'" (Richardson, 2010, para. 2). School districts that do not comply with the law stand to lose ten percent of state funding (Llanos, 2010). The law was set to go into effect December 31, 2010.

HB 2281 was aimed specifically at the Tucson Unified School District's Mexican American Studies program, which, according to Tom Horne, was promoting "ethnic chauvinism" (Reyes, 2010; Richardson, 2010). TUSD's program reportedly first came to Horne's attention in April 2006 when Dolores Huerta, co-founder of the United Farm Workers (UFW) and a prominent civil rights activist and leader, told students at a high school there that "Republicans hate Latinos" (Richardson, 2010). Horne (a Republican) subsequently sent his top aide, Margaret Garcia-Dugan, to speak to students and offer an alternative (i.e., Republican) perspective, but students walked out during her speech (Grado, 2010). Horne has also been critical of the program's curriculum, particularly its use of the books *Occupied America* by Rodolfo Acuña and *Pedagogy of the Oppressed* by Paolo Freire. According to Horne, these books are "inappropriate" because they teach Latino students that they are "mistreated" (Lacey 2011b).

The passage of SB 2281 unleashed a firestorm of controversy, criticism, and debate (though not nearly as much as did SB 1070). Human rights experts from the United Nations condemned the measure for violating Arizona's obligation to promote a culture and climate that is respectful of diversity (Richardson, 2010). Critics also noted that HB 2281 stifles free speech, perpetuates the exclusion of people of color from the curriculum, and whitewashes (and thus distorts) history. David Rodriguez, a professor of Chicano(a) Studies at California State University, Northridge, for example, remarked, "This law stifles free speech, it stifles critical information and the expression of a community that has experienced discrimination of all sorts" (as cited in Llanos, 2010, para. 11). Similarly, Myla Vicenti Carpio, an Assistant Professor of American Indian Studies at the University of Arizona, stated, "This is another way of silencing others' history . . . For them to say we don't want ethnic studies, it means that these specific histories aren't important and that they are threatening this narrative that America is great and doesn't do anything wrong" (as cited in Fernandez, 2010a, para. 14).

On his last day as the state superintendent of public instruction, and before assuming his new position as the state's Attorney General, Tom Horne declared that TUSD's Mexican American Studies program was in violation of all four provisions of HB 2281. However, the district's other ethnic studies programs (e.g. Native American Studies, Asian American Studies, and African American Studies) were not deemed to be in violation of HB 2281 and could thus continue (Lacey, 2011b). Thus, only the district's Chicano(a) Studies program was ordered shut down – a decision interpreted by critics as a clear sign that Arizona's bigotry and racism is fixated on Mexicans/Latinos(as) (Tobar, 2011). Teachers from the Tucson Unified School District have filed a lawsuit in federal court challenging the legality of HB 2281 (Lacey, 2011b). The teachers' lawyer, Richard M. Martinez, says the challenge will argue that HB 2281 violates the First and Fourteenth Amendments of the U.S. Constitution because it targets just one district (TUSD) and one group of people (Mexican Americans) (Zehr, 2010).

State officials in Arizona have also launched attacks against immigrant teachers. A few months after SB 1070 and HB 2281 were signed into law, Arizona's Department of Education implemented a policy barring teachers with "accents" from teaching English-language learner classes. Like other anti-immigrant measures, this policy had a disproportionate impact on Latinos(as). During the 1990s, Arizona had hired hundreds of teachers whose native language was Spanish to teach in bilingual education programs (Jordan, 2010). In 2000, however, Arizona voters approved a ballot measure banning bilingual education, and these teachers were subsequently switched to English-language courses. The racist and nativist climate in Arizona has undoubtedly emboldened state education officials to also target these immigrant teachers (Jordan, 2010).

How Arizona Became Ground Zero for the War on Immigrants and Latinos(as)

How did Arizona become ground zero for the war on immigrants and Latinos(as)? In other words, why is Arizona the epicenter of the nation's contemporary anti-immigrant and anti-Latino(a) backlash? According to some immigration experts, the immigration controversy in Arizona has its roots in immigration enforcement policies enacted in the 1990s by then-President Bill Clinton. During this period, California was experiencing an intense wave of anti-immigrant xenophobia, much like Arizona is experiencing today. For example, in 1994, California voters (most of whom were white) approved Proposition 187, an initiative that would have restricted the rights of undocumented immigrants to access education and non-emergency healthcare (Reese & Ramirez, 2002). As a way of shielding himself from the anti-immigrant backlash emerging principally in California, Clinton began spending an unprecedented amount of money on border enforcement – especially on those segments of the border (e.g., El Paso, TX and San Diego, CA) most used by undocumented immigrants coming in from Mexico (Cornelius, 2005). The policies he enacted to fortify the border included Operation Hold the Line in El Paso, Texas (1993), Operation Gatekeeper in San Diego, CA (1994), Operation Safeguard in Arizona (1995), and Operation Rio Grande in southeast Texas (1997) (Cornelius, 2005). According to Douglass Massey, a professor of sociology and public affairs at Princeton University, these border enforcement operations had the effect of diverting immigration flows "through the Sonoran desert into Arizona, which until then, had been a quiet backwater both with respect to border crossings and immigration settlement" (as cited in Wood, 2010c, para. 4). The Tucson sector is now the leading corridor for undocumented entry, making the state of Arizona the main gateway for undocumented immigrants coming in through Mexico (Cornelius, 2005). The flow of undocumented immigrants into Arizona has been unsettling for many in the state, particularly for the older, conservative white population, which is often hostile to immigrants and fearful of increasing diversity and multiculturalism.

Other researchers point to the long history of conservative politics in Arizona. For example, Jack Pitney, a political scientist at Claremont McKenna College, notes that Arizona is, after all, the home of U.S. Senator Barry Goldwater (i.e., "Mr. Conservative"), a politician often credited for reviving conservative politics during the 1960s (Wood, 2010c). Concomitantly, Pitney notes that "Arizona has always had a contrarian, cantankerous streak," which he attributes to older whites' fears of changing demographics in the state of Arizona – particularly the increasing presence of Latinos(as) (Wood, 2010c, para. 10). Furthermore, Amy Goodman notes that Arizona was the only Western state that seceded from the U.S. and joined the Confederacy during the Civil War; a century later, it also opposed the recognition of a Martin Luther King Jr. federal holiday (Goodman, 2010). Conservative, anti-immigrant, and racist politics are thus long established traditions in Arizona.

Still other scholars, such as Deborah Kang, a postdoctoral fellow at UC Berkeley, notes that the current focus on Arizona is myopic, reflecting an ignorance of history. Kang states, "What always surprises me about these debates is how quickly we forget . . . Some in the media have reported that SB 1070 marks a new high-water mark for anti-Mexican sentiment in the United States and a new precedent in the history of American immigration law" (as cited in Wood, 2010c, para. 12).

Yet, Mexican immigrants, she notes, have been repeatedly scapegoated for this nation's economic troubles. For example, during the 1920s, 1930s, and 1950s, Mexicans (including undocumented immigrants, legal residents, and U.S. citizens) were forcibly deported from the U.S. in deportation campaigns – all in the midst of a national economic downturn (Wood, 2010c). Indeed, when times get tough, politicians strategically direct people's anger towards immigrants (and other disenfranchised populations) and away from politicians and employers (Reese & Ramirez, 2002). The current economic crisis in this country thus makes the conditions ripe for nativism and racism. Unfortunately, immigrants and the Latino(a) community have become the convenient scapegoats for our society's current social and economic ills.

Conclusion

This chapter examined the politics of immigration in Arizona and critically reviewed the series of laws being passed by the Arizona legislature targeting immigrants and the larger Latino(a) community. Reputedly distressed over the federal government's 'unwillingness' to secure our national borders, politicians in Arizona passed SB 1070 and introduced other bills aimed at deterring undocumented immigrants from entering and settling in the state of Arizona. Although these anti-immigrant bills have been popular with the larger (particularly older, conservative White) public in Arizona and throughout the country, they do nothing to address the root causes of migration and are thus ineffective in stemming the flow of undocumented immigrants into the country. Instead, these policies only perpetuate racial profiling and lead to the political, economic, and social disenfranchisement of the immigrant community in general, and of the Mexican/Latino(a) community in particular. Politicians in Arizona have also launched attacks on Ethnic Studies programs, particularly Chicano(a) Studies, and on immigrant teachers. As social justice advocates note, HB 2281, along with SB 1070, threatens to transform Arizona into a "new South" – that is, a state notorious for its institutionalized discrimination against racial/ethnic minorities (Medrano, 2010b).

Civil rights leaders and immigrant rights activists have vehemently critiqued the racist policies being proposed and enacted in Arizona and have effectively mounted resistance to these measures via marches and protests, boycotts, and lawsuits. These resistance strategies have been largely successful; most of SB 1070 has been declared illegal by the courts, and politicians in Arizona have abandoned (at least for now) other draconian anti-immigrant measures (e.g., SB 1308 and SB 1309). The struggle for immigrant and human rights is far from over, however. Many other states are proposing similar anti-immigrant legislation as Arizona, and it is possible that Arizona's attack on Ethnic Studies programs may also spill over into other states. It is thus critical that we all become engaged in the struggle for social justice and help challenge the repressive and intolerant climate that exists in Arizona and in many other parts of the country. *La lucha sigue!*

References

American Civil Liberties Union (ACLU) of Georgia (2010, March). The persistence of racial profiling in Gwinnett: Time for accountability, transparency, and an end to 287(g). Retrieved from http://www.acluga.org

Barr, A. (2011, March 18). Ariz. rejects immigration crackdowns. *Politico*. Retrieved from http://www.politico.com

Berton, J. (2010, May 2). Thousands protest new Arizona law. *San Francisco Chronicle*, pp. C1.

Carcamo, C. (2010, June 2). Poll: Californians narrowly support immigration law. *Orange County Register*, pp. A.

Cattan, N. (2010, July 29). Arizona immigration law 2010: As SB 1070 takes effect, Mexicans say 'Adios, Arizona'; Arizona immigration law targeting immigrants has already encouraged Mexicans to begin returning home, even as a U.S. judge halted key portions of SB 1070 from taking effect. The Mexico government is boosting legal services in Arizona, and shelters in Sonora state are preparing for an influx. *Christian Science Monitor*. Retrieved from http://www.csmonitor.com

Chardy, A. (2010, May 18). Arizona immigration law protested at Florida Marlins game. *Miami Herald,* pp. B3.

Cornelius, W. (2005). Controlling 'unwanted' immigration: Lessons from the United States, 1993–2004. *Journal of Ethnic and Migration Studies, 31*(4), 775–794.

Duda, J. (2010, August 13). Arizona and Maricopa county election officials investigate Arpaio TV ads. *Arizona Capitol Times*. Retrieved from http://azcapitoltimes.com

Fernandez, V. (2010a, May 28). Arizona's ban on ethnic studies worries more than Latinos. *La Prensa – San Diego*. Retrieved from http://www.laprensa-sandiego.org

Fernandez, V. (2010b, June 4). Thousands protest SB 1070 in Phoenix rally. *La Prensa - San Diego*. Retrieved from http://www.laprensa-sandiego.org

Frontera Norte-Sur (2010, May 21). The Arizona prairie fire spreads. *La Prensa – San Diego*. Retrieved from http://www.laprensa-sandiego.org

Garcia, A., & Chandler, B. (2010, May 20). Has Arizona replaced Mississippi as the most racist state? *Jackson Advocate*, pp. 4A.

Goodman, A. (2010, April 29). Arizona's immigration law: An open invitation to racial profiling. *The Oregonian*. Retrieved from http://www.oregonlive.com

Goodwin, L. (2010, October 28). Report: 25 states considering Arizona-style immigration laws. *Yahoo! News*. Retrieved from http://news.yahoo.com

Grado, G. (2010, November 15). Culture war brewing over ethnic studies in Tucson schools. *Arizona Capitol Times*. Retrieved from http://azcapitoltimes.com

Guskin, J., & Wilson, D. L. (2007). *The politics of immigration: Questions and answers.* New York: Monthly Review Press.

Hing, J. (2010a, April 23). Arizona legalizes racial profiling with SB 1070, says advocates. *Colorlines: News for action*. Retrieved from http://colorlines.com

Hing, J. (2010b, April 30). AZ tweaks SB 1070, now minimally less racist, still just as dangerous. *Colorlines: News for action*. Retrieved from http://colorlines.com

Hing, J. (2010c, September 23). Joe Arpaio accused of misusing $80 million in tax-payer funds. *Colorlines: News for action*. Retrieved from http://colorlines.com

Hing, J. (2011a, January 5). Lawmakers in 14 states coordinate birthright citizenship attack. *Colorlines: News for action*. Retrieved from http://colorlines.com

Hing, J. (2011b, February 23). Arizona's suite of new anti-immigrant bills moves to Senate. *Colorlines: News for action*. Retrieved from http://colorlines.com

Hing, J. (2011c, March 18). Arizona may finally be ready to 'take a time out' on immigrant bashing." *Colorlines: News for action*. Retrieved from http://colorlines.com

Immigration Policy Center (2010, April 2). Local enforcement of immigration laws through the 287(g) program: Time, money, and resources don't add up to community safety. Retrieved from http://www.immigrationpolicy.org

Johnson, K. (2000). The case against race profiling in immigration enforcement. *Washington University Law Quarterly, 78*(3), 676–736.

Jordan, M. (2010, April 30). Arizona grades teachers on fluency. *Wall Street Journal*. Retrieved From http://online.wsj.com

Lacey, M. (2011a, January 4). Birthright citizenship looms as next immigration battle. *New York Times*. Retrieved from http://www.nytimes.com

Lacey, M. (2011b, January 8). Citing 'brainwashing,' Arizona declares a Latino class illegal. *New York Times*, pp. A1.

Lagos, M. (2010, November 24). State Ok's anti-illegals ballot initiative petition. *San Francisco Chronicle*, pp. C4.

Lewis, C. (2010, May 13). Arizona bans ethnic studies in schools; Debate over Latino influence heightened. *National Post*, pp. A13.

Llanos, C. (2010, May 12). Arizona ethnic studies ban condemned. *Pasadena Star – News*. Retrieved from http://www.pasadenastarnews.com

Medrano, L. (2010a, September 2). Joe Arpaio: Why is Obama administration suing an outspoken Arizona sheriff?; The Justice Department said Thursday that Sheriff Joe Arpaio of Arizona's Maricopa County is not cooperating in an investigation into whether his department has used racial profiling in sweeps to catch illegal im-migrants. *Christian Science Monitor*. Retrieved from http://www.csmonitor.com

Medrano, L. (2010b, December 31). Ethnic studies classes illegal in Arizona pub-lic schools as of Jan. 1; Much of the controversial Arizona immigration law re-mains tied up in court, but a law banning ethnic studies in Arizona is set to take effect Saturday. A Tucson school district vows to fight it. *Christian Science Monitor*. Retrieved from http://www.csmonitor.com

Michaels, S. (2010, May 27). Rage Against the Machine leads Arizona boycott. *Guardian Unlimited*. Retrieved from http://www.guardian.co.uk

Morning Star (2010, July 8). World – Obama sues over Arizona's racist law.

Reese, E. & Ramirez, E. (2002). The new ethnic politics of welfare: Struggles over legal immigrants' rights to welfare in California. *Journal of Poverty, 6(3), 29–62.*

Rentería, M. (2010, July 15). A look at the SB 1070 law. *San Antonio Express-News*, pp. 16CX.

Reyes, R. A. (2010, June 3). The other Arizona battle: A new law makes ethnic studies classes illegal; Since when is it bad to learn about different cultures? *Christian Science Monitor*. Retrieved from http://www.csmonitor.com

Riccardi, N. (2010a, April 13). Arizona passes strict illegal immigration act. *Los Angeles Times*. Retrieved from http://articles.latimes.com

Riccardi, N. (2010b, September 18). Internal memo accuses Arpaio's office of misdeeds; The sheriff's No. 2 man allegedly headed improper inquiries and surveillance. *Los Angeles Times*. Retrieved from http://articles.latimes.com

Riccardi, N. (2011, April 12). Court upholds ban on Arizona immigration law. *Los Angeles Times*. Retrieved from http://articles.latimes.com

Richardson, V. (2010, May 13). Arizona governor now targeting ethnic studies; law infuriates liberals again. *Washington Times,* pp. A1.

Richey, W. (2010, July 29). SB 1070: appeal seeks to reinstate all parts of Arizona law; The toughest provisions of SB 1070, the Arizona law about illegal immigration, were blocked Wednesday by a judge. Arizona Gov. Jan Brewer said Thursday she is appealing the decision. *Christian Science Monitor*. Retrieved from http://www.csmonitor.com

Romero, M. (2006). Racial profiling and immigration law enforcement: Rounding up of usual suspects in the Latino community. *Critical Sociology, 32*(2–3), 447–473.

Sterling, T. G. (2010). *Illegal: Life and death in Arizona's immigration war zone.* Guilford, CT: Lyons Press.

Theriault, D. C. (2010, April 28). California Senate leader: Tear up contracts with Arizona over immigration law. *Contra Costa Times*. Retrieved from http://www.contracostatimes.com

Tobar, H. (2011, January 14). Offended at being dragged into Arizona controversy; Ethnic studies foes cite professors' Mexican American history book. *Los Angeles Times*. Retrieved from http://articles.latimes.com

Vock, D. C. (2010, December 20). Arizona lawmakers fight 'birthright citizenship.' *Sacramento Bee*, pp. A1, A13.

Wood, D. B. (2010a, April 26). Arizona immigration law puts police in 'impossible situation'; A new Arizona anti-illegal immigration law asks police to perform tasks that are often contradictory, critics say – enforcing immigration law and criminal law. *Christian Science Monitor*. Retrieved from http://www.csmonitor.com

Wood, D. B. (2010b, April 28). Arizona immigration law: California leads call for boycotts; the new Arizona immigration law spurred California officials to call for boycotts of its eastern neighbor, and the effects to image and industry could be both symbolic and substantial. *Christian Science Monitor*. Retrieved from http://www.csmonitor.com

Wood, D. B. (2010c, August 3). How Arizona became ground zero for immigration reform; Arizona didn't turn into a pressure cooker for immigration reform overnight, historians say. *Christian Science Monitor*. Retrieved from http://www.csmonitor.com

Wu, Suzanne (2010, June 1). Immigration law divides California voters. *USC College News*. Retrieved from http://dornsife.usc.edu

Zehr, M. A. (2010, September 22). Tucson students aren't deterred by ethnic studies controversy. *Education Week*. Retrieved from http://www.edweek.org

Community Psychology and Social Change: The 65th Street Corridor Community Collaborative Project

Greg M. Kim-Ju, Joyia Lucas & Gregory Yee Mark

Introduction

Data from the Organization for Economic Co-operation and Development (OECD) show declining educational attainment rates in the United States, where its high school graduation ranking has fallen from 1st in the 1970s to 13th in the 2000s and its college dropout rate is the highest among industrialized nations (Pathways to Prosperity, 2011). These rates are especially strong for traditionally underserved populations who have lower graduation rates and generally take longer to receive their degrees. For example, data on educational attainment by ethnicity show that a higher percentage of African Americans and Latinos, compared to White Americans, drop out of high school and do not receive a Bachelor's degree (U.S. Census Bureau, 2005). Furthermore, data on first-generation college students show that they are more likely to face greater obstacles to their success on campus, from less academic preparation and leadership skills, to lack of knowledge about study habits and college finances, to lower educational aspirations, compared to their non-first-generation cohorts (Schmidt, 2003; Thayer, 2000). The implications of educational attainment are evident for economic outcomes, especially earnings, where full-time, year-round workers who are high school dropouts may on average earn $23,400 annually whereas those with professional degrees may earn on average $109,600 annually (Cheeseman Day & Newburger, 2002). Add to this, the 40-year synthetic work-life earnings estimates (i.e., expected earnings amount over a 40-year work period) for full-time, year-round workers average $1 million for high school dropouts and $2.1 million for those with professional degrees (Cheeseman Day & Newburger, 2002). Furthermore, there are a host of potentially harmful social and psychological (e.g., lower sense of control and less social support) and health (e.g., greater health risk behaviors such as smoking) outcomes that are directly or indirectly related to lower educational attainment (American Psychological Association, Task Force on

Socioeconomic Status, 2007; Ross & Wu, 1995). Recent data from OECD (2010) illustrate this point elegantly where a positive relationship exists between educational attainment and self-reported good health, political interest, and interpersonal trust. Specifically, those individuals with lower educational attainment reported poorer health, less political interest, and less trust of others. Given these concerns with disparities in college access and completion rates, as well as their implications across multiple domains of life, President Obama, in his 2009 State of the Union Address, set a goal for the U.S. to have the world's highest college completion rates by 2020 (Lederman, 2009). He later announced a $12 billion community-college initiative as part of his efforts to support this goal (Kellog & Tomsho, 2009).

For higher education institutions, there is a growing recognition that community-based learning and research can serve to increase college access and retention and that prevention and intervention efforts during the K-12 pipeline can improve both chances of entering and graduating from higher education. There have been a number of efforts, from university-driven initiatives to grass-roots ones, to develop and implement programs to meet social, academic, health, and educational needs across the U.S. (Reardon, 1998; Sobredo, Kim-Ju, Figueroa, Mark, & Fabionar, 2008). This chapter examines a community-mobilization effort in Sacramento, California that started in 2002 to initially address academic issues but later developed into a comprehensive effort aimed at improving academic performance, reducing violence and problem behaviors, and providing educational pathways for underrepresented groups. We first turn to a discussion of community mobilization, focusing on community psychology, the framework utilized to guide our work in Sacramento.

Community Mobilization

Community mobilization is defined as people organizing and taking action in response to specific community issues (Fawcett et al., 2000; Kim-Ju, Mark, Cohen, Garcia-Santiago & Nguyen, 2008). Although a number of community mobilization approaches that focus on specific strategies and issues and emphasize particular relationships between researchers and communities exist in the social sciences, they all utilize collective efforts to improve social, educational, and health outcomes. In the past few decades, the field of psychology has witnessed the emergence of several community-based approaches to social change in the international and domestic arenas. Within the U.S., community psychology has developed a rich tradition that can be traced to several intellectual trends and pragmatic concerns such as the growth of mental health issues and the rise of clinical psychology in the 1960s, as well as the social and political reforms of that period (Nelson & Prilleltensky, 2010).

The impetus for community-based approaches such as community psychology to foster social change has largely been in response to the inability of mainstream psychology rooted in Western values of individualism to satisfy the demands of social change in diverse cultural settings. In particular, the traditional focus on the individual in areas such as personality, social psychology, and clinical psychology had, at the very least, relegated the role of real-world contexts to secondary status and, at worst, blinded researchers from acknowledging and understanding the impact of real-world contexts on human behavior. This could be seen in social psychology with its traditional emphasis on the concept of attitude in understanding social behavior (Allport, 1935) and in clinical psychology where individual-centered approaches afforded greater roles of testing and psychotherapy (Nelson & Prilleltensky, 2010). Furthermore, as mainstream psychology focused more on the individual and face-to-face dyads, the study of human behavior increasingly relied on artificial settings (e.g., psychological labs). The analysis of social change in mainstream psychology had essentially been reduced to the study of individual participants in artificially induced interventions in labs (Banuazizi, 1996). One important implication of this development was that theorizing about human behavior and issues often favored ahistorical, apolitical, and acultural individual-level explanations that failed to acknowledge the role of social structure in social change. As such, issues being understood and characterized in terms of the individual without attention to context often resulted in pathological interpretations or "blaming the victim" (Ryan, 1971). In contrast, community psychology, with its holistic, ecological, and prevention-focused approach, gained momentum in psychology in efforts to address social, educational, and health issues for culturally diverse, especially marginalized, groups.

The field of community psychology, with its roots in the 1960s, seeks to bring about social change and enhance the lives of individuals and their communities through a collaborative process of research and action between researchers and communities (Dalton, Elias & Wandersmann, 2001). Several themes are critical to community psychology: its ecological nature, the importance of cultural diversity, and its emphasis on social change (Nelson & Prilleltensky, 2010). Trickett (1996) uses the metaphor of an eco-system to examine the "transactions" and relationships between people and their environments. This is in contrast to the reductionistic metaphor used in mainstream psychology which tends to focus on basic processes such as cognition and perception. This ecology metaphor allows researchers to contextualize issues and problems faced by individuals. In particular, through their collaborative relationships with community members, researchers become involved in an "authentic exploration of social processes in the setting" and arrive at a more nuanced understanding of individuals and their settings (Trickett, 1996, p. 214). Thus, the emphasis on context is important in that it allows researchers to critically examine and separate cultural values shaping people's behavior and social structure impinging on their response and to create interventions that are locally relevant.

Community psychology is furthermore a value-driven form of inquiry and intervention that highlights the role of advocacy and collaborative relationships between researchers and community members (Rappaport, 1990). Rather than intervening after problems have been identified to reduce issues and problem behaviors, community psychology emphasizes prevention and promotion by focusing on assets and resources within communities—rather than deficits and problems—and leverages them to foster social action and change (Cowen, 1994). As Prilleltensky and Nelson

(2009) state, highlighting prevention and assets reflects the emphasis on health—in preventing psychosocial problems and promoting the well-being of individuals.

Although community can be defined in different ways, from the physical to the psychological, community psychology seeks to create a psychological sense of community by providing connection and support for individuals (Nelson & Prilleltensky, 2010). This sense of community is related to people's values of caring, compassion and support for their communities, and involves community psychologists who must work with, not for, disadvantaged groups and other stakeholders to facilitate a greater sense of control and determination in developing prevention and intervention programs (Rappaport, 1981). As this sense of community grows, individuals feel greater control in their lives and actively participate in their communities. With their active participation, people feel empowered and included, believing they have greater ownership of their lives and environment. The balance of this article describes a community mobilization effort that draws on many of the principles of community psychology in its effort to address social and academic outcomes.

The 65th Street Corridor Community Collaborative Project

The 65th Street Corridor Community Collaborative (Collaborative) at California State University, Sacramento (Sacramento State) is a community mobilization effort that draws on many of the principles of community psychology to increase academic achievement, foster leadership skills, reduce violence and problem behaviors, and create pathways to and improve retention in higher education for students from low-income families, for first-generation college students and for those from underrepresented groups. The Collaborative serves 7th through 12th grade students at two schools, Will C. Wood Middle School (WW) and Hiram Johnson High School (HJ), located along Sacramento's 65th Street Corridor, a low-income and diverse community adjacent to Sacramento State, as well as university students. It includes three established programmatic components, a Tutoring and Mentoring program, a Student Bridge program, a Parent Partnership program for low-income 7th–12th grade students at the aforementioned schools, and a developing Leadership Program for college students at Sacramento State. The work of the Collaborative has been extremely successful in past years, utilizing effective outreach and community service opportunities to create academic pathways from grades seven through twelve to higher education for disadvantaged groups in Sacramento.

Background

WW and HJ are located in ethnically diverse, multilingual communities, with a high representation of working class individuals (Sobredo, Kim-Ju, Figueroa, Mark & Fabionar, 2008). In 2006, White Americans represented 51 percent of Sacramento's population, followed by Latinos at 24 percent, Asian Americans and Pacific Islanders, 18.6 percent, African Americans, 14 percent, and American Indians, 1.3 percent

(U.S. Census Bureau, 2006). Thirty-five percent of those residing in Sacramento reported to be bilingual. As Table 1 shows, the student body population at HJ and WW mirrors this ethnic and linguistic diversity. In academic year 2009–2010 at WW, 41 percent of the student body of 754 included Latinos, 39 percent, Asian Americans and Pacific Islanders, 14 percent, African Americans, and 5 percent, White Americans. English Learners made up 38 percent of the student body (SCUSD Will C. Wood Accountability Report, 2010). Nearly 80 percent of the students were socioeconomically disadvantaged, defined as students participating in a free or reduced-price meal program or whose parents did not receive a high school diploma. Similarly, at HJ, the student body population of 2,153 included a large percentage of Latinos (39%) and Asian Americans and Pacific Islanders (30%), and a smaller percentage of African Americans (15%) and White Americans (10%). Thirty-three percent of its student body was English Learners and 70 percent of the students were socioeconomically disadvantaged (SCUSD Hiram Johnson Accountability Report, 2010).

A substantial portion of the students from both schools struggle academically. As Table 2 indicates, a large percentage of WW students were not proficient in English Language Arts, Mathematics, History-Social Science, and Science in the 2009–2010 academic year. With the exception of Science, WW students underperformed compared to their District and State counterparts. The percentage of students who scored in the 'Proficient' or 'Advanced' level in these subjects was even lower at HJ. Seventy-five percent or greater of HJ students were not proficient in English Language Arts, Mathematics, History-Social Science, and Science in the 2009–2010 academic year. The proficiency rates for HJ students were substantially lower in these subjects compared to their District and State high school counterparts. In academic year 2008–2009, the four-year graduation rate was 64 percent (vs. 81 percent for District and 83 percent for State) and the one-year dropout rate was 12 percent (vs. six percent for District and four percent for State). Sixteen percent of graduates from the class of 2009 had completed all courses required for admission to the University of California

TABLE 4-1 Demographic Characteristics of Will C. Wood Middle School and Hiram Johnson High School		
Demographic Characteristics	**WW[a] (N = 754)**	**HJ[b] (N = 2153)**
Ethnicity		
African Americans	14%	15%
AAPI[c]	39%	30%
Latinos	41%	39%
White Americans	5%	10%
English Learners	38%	33%
Socioeconomically Disadvantaged	80%	70%

Notes: [a]Will C. Wood Middle School; [b]Hiram Johnson High School; [c]Asian Americans and Pacific Islanders.

TABLE 4-2 Proficiency or Advanced Level of Will C. Wood Middle School and Hiram Johnson High School Students Compared to District and State Students

Proficiency or Advanced	WW[a]	Middle Schools - District	Middle Schools - State	HJ[b]	High Schools - District	High Schools - State
English Language Arts	38%	48%	52%	24%	48%	52%
Mathematics	40%	46%	48%	11%	46%	48%
History-Social Science	32%	41%	44%	18%	41%	44%
Science	53%	46%	54%	23%	46%	54%

Notes: [a]Will C. Wood Middle School; [b]Hiram Johnson High School.

or California State University systems (vs. 46 percent for District and 37 percent for State), with only nine percent going on to four-year universities, though 44 percent attended community colleges.

In addition to poor academic performance, WW and HJ have higher suspension rates compared to the other schools in their District and State. In academic year 2009–2010, for instance, there were 443 suspension incidents at WW, a ratio of 59 such incidents for every 100 students. This is nearly three times the average rate of the District (vs. 23 incidents / 100 students) and State (vs. 20 incidents / 100 students). HJ reported 724 suspension incidents in the same year, a rate of 34 incidents per 100 students (vs. 24 incidents / 100 students for District and 16 incidents / 100 students for State).

Given these academic and social issues affecting students and their families residing in the 65th Street Corridor area, researchers and community members designed several prevention and intervention programs to address these emerging issues and to create an environment where social, academic, and educational alternatives and pathways would be available for these students and families. Much of this work started in 2002 and has been sustained by a cadre of faculty members and students at Sacramento State and committed students, teachers and administration at WW and HJ who have leveraged their resources to develop both research and service programs to address the aforementioned issues. Central to this work is the community psychology approach described above which has provided a framework from which to develop, implement, and sustain partnerships with and programs in these schools. The model has allowed the researchers involved in this Collaborative to better understand the realities of urban education, including the social, political, and economic conditions impacting the lives and education of urban children and their families.

Mission

The work of the 65th Street Corridor Community Collaborative Project is aimed at increasing student academic achievement, fostering student leadership, reducing violence and problem behaviors, and creating educational pathways for disadvantaged students living in neighborhoods where a lack of access to educational and economic resources create a need for innovative, community-based strategies. It also aims to improve retention of low-income, first-generation college students at Sacramento State by providing greater human and social capital to navigate their college experience. This work is an ongoing interaction between Sacramento State and the 65th Street Corridor and creates a venue for community concerns to be voiced and addressed at the grassroots level and in a systematic fashion. The following sections outline the Collaborative's programs.

WW and HJ Tutoring and Mentoring Program

The Tutoring and Mentoring program at WW and HJ was developed to address the schools' low standardized test scores and poor academic performance. This program provides opportunities for the 7th -12th grade students to receive direct tutoring in math, English and science classes from Sacramento State students. University students serve as tutors/mentors and must attend orientation and training sessions to learn about the history of the program in the 65th Street Corridor as well as tutoring and mentoring skills in the 7th -12th grade classrooms. In fall 2010, the program recruited 50 tutors/mentors to serve 800 7th-12th grade students. The Collaborative averages 50 tutors/mentors each semester but works to increase the number of tutors/mentors in the classrooms, with the aim to provide tutoring to improve standardized test scores at the two schools and to provide mentoring to discourage problem behaviors and encourage prosocial behaviors. WW and HJ students receive mentoring from their tutors/mentors during class periods about being good students and citizens and are encouraged to ask questions about higher education.

Our assessment data of academic achievement indicate this program's direct impact on improving test scores. For example, API scores for WW have steadily increased each year this program has been in place, from 546 in 2002 to 705 in 2009–2010. This represents a 30 percent increase over that time period, nearly double compared to the next highest middle school in Sacramento City Unified School District. Although not as substantial, API scores at HJ have increased from 585 in 2004-2005 to 611 in 2009–2010. Furthermore, teachers and staff at WW and HJ have praised tutors/mentors for being role models for their students and encouraging positive behaviors and providing alternative pathways for academic and educational success.

Student Bridge Program

The Student Bridge program was developed to provide more information about college preparation and increase access for first-generation, low-income, and traditionally underrepresented students. Through a series of field trips over the academic school year, students gain an understanding of a "college-going culture" in this program. Our preliminary data on past student field trips show that interest in attending college significantly increased for many of the students who participated in the field trips and that they were significantly more knowledgeable about college information items (e.g., SAT/ACT requirements, college application process, financial aid) after their participation in the field trip. In the past year, this program served over 200 students who participated in field trips. In our most recent 12th grade field trip in 2009–2010, 53 out of the 83 students who attended and were eligible for college applied to Sacramento State. With this program, Sacramento State faculty and students coordinate with WW and HJ with respect to the number of field trips. With the assistance of student coordinators who aid in planning and execution, there are separate field trips for HJ 9th, HJ 10th, and HJ 12th grade students in the fall semester and WW 7th and 8th grade students and HJ 11th grade students in spring semester.

Parent Partnership Program

In the Parent Partnership program, we work with school staff over the academic year to identify a number of parents who wish to receive more information about being involved in their children's education and to play an active role by participating in field trips and workshops. The program invites parents to spend a day at our university campus in order to demystify the college experience and to learn about topics ranging from financial aid to student campus experiences. Translation services are provided in several languages (e.g., Spanish, Hmong, and Mien) for those parents who need them. In addition, a small set of parents learn strategies and receive educational materials to help their children improve their academic achievement and consider best practices and pathways to higher education through two Parent Education Workshops over the academic year. With this program, faculty plan for and invite 70 to 80 parents from each school partner, totaling two parent field trips during the academic year. At WW, 30 to 40 parents are identified and asked to participate in two Parent Education Workshops over the academic year. Furthermore, at the end of the school year, a Family Literacy Night is organized and opened to a larger set of parents at WW where they have the opportunity to read with their children and to see "million word readers" recognized by staff. Preliminary data for this program indicate that parents become more motivated and knowledgeable about preparing their children for higher education and continue to stay interested while they participate in field trips and workshops. At the past two Family Literacy Night events at WW, over 300 students, staff, parents, and community members celebrated the academic success of WW students.

Leadership Program

The leadership program focuses on assisting first-generation college students, many of whom come from low-income families, with their campus experience during their first year. We are currently piloting a semester-long course to improve student persistence and resilience and offering community service opportunities. A faculty member teaches a course designed for migrant students new to university life, form and functions, and focuses on assisting students with making a successful transition to the university. Seventy-five students are currently enrolled in the pilot course, with 20 of them participating as tutors/mentors. In this program, with the guidance of faculty and a student coordinator, one section of this course each semester is offered and additional resiliency and community service workshops to first-year College Assistance Migrant Program (CAMP) students and other first-generation students at Sacramento State are provided. Students reflect on their first-year experience and have opportunities to participate in the aforementioned programs to integrate themselves in the university and surrounding communities. A group of university students moves on to leadership positions as coordinators in the Mentoring and Tutoring, Student Bridge, and Parent Field Trip programs. These university students lead orientation and training sessions and hold reflection sessions for tutors/mentors at the beginning and end of each semester. This program aims to foster leadership skills in college students from low-income, underrepresented groups by offering them opportunities to participate as service learners and coordinators in all of the programs.

Evaluation

Sacramento State students and faculty through the Collaborative have conducted various levels of assessment (K-12 students, university students, programs) in past years. The past two years, for instance, we have conducted annual focus groups and administered surveys with students and parents (in four languages – Mien, Hmong, Spanish, and English) to identify issues of concern for students and families, assess available resources, tailor programs to meet emerging needs, and evaluate the effectiveness of programs. We assess and evaluate all programs and the overall project in relation to the goals and objectives discussed above. Assessment and evaluation occur with participants at all schools (WW, HJ, Sacramento State) to compare the effectiveness of our programs across time points (semester 1 vs. semester 2) and between groups (experimental—direct services received vs. control—no direct services).

Sustainability

The Collaborative, as well as CEC, have received a strong reception and support from Sacramento City Unified School District and Sacramento State, having been recognized as valuable assets to the school partners, to the District, and to Sacramento State. The Collaborative continues to have the support of the College of Social Sciences and Interdisciplinary Studies as well as the Provost Office and the Office of the President at Sacramento State. Our activities are consistent with Sacramento State's *Destination 2010 Academic Strategic Plan* which emphasizes the development of positive relations with the surrounding community, especially the objectives of creating active educational partnerships with school districts in the Sacramento region and providing significant services to the community.

A key to providing sustainability of programs is to build the capacity of the institution to support and deliver programs. In addition to providing assistance with risk management support for university students, CEC serves to institutionalize community service as a pedagogical approach. Another key component to sustainability is the continued creation of new partnerships, both on campus and in the Sacramento area. We continue to partner with other faculty and departments at Sacramento State to expand community service opportunities to meet the emerging needs of our community partners. For example, faculty members and students from a number of disciplines, including but not limited to Ethnic Studies, Psychology, Math, Teacher Education, Bilingual/Multicultural Education, Liberal Studies, Child Development, and Women's Studies have participated in the Collaborative. In the future, we anticipate our programs to be absorbed and supported by the university and school partners. For example, we anticipate that the class for the Leadership Program will eventually be supported by the Educational Opportunity Program at our university. Furthermore, our community partners have shared costs involved with past programs. HJ, for instance, incorporated a community service project designed for high school seniors that the Collaborative had developed in 2006. Finally, we share best practices with other schools and interested parties as we disseminate effective practices via reports and publications.

Conclusion

There are a number of social, educational, and health issues facing adolescents and young adults in the U.S. today. Psychologists and other social scientists have employed different strategies and approaches to address these issues. This chapter focused on community psychology as a guiding framework to not only address the issues described above but also to recognize the sociocultural conditions of students and families from HJ and WW to better inform the practices, activities, and programs of the Collaborative. While these issues can be addressed using a number of approaches in the social sciences, community psychology confers several advantages given its emphasis on ecology, cultural diversity, and social change. HJ and WW represent exciting cases where faculty and students from Sacramento State in partnership with HJ and WW staff and community members have been able to forge a sense of community and collaboratively design and shape exciting programs that foster social change in the spirit of community psychology.

Author Note

Greg M. Kim-Ju, Department of Psychology; Joyia Lucas, Department of Psychology & Gregory Yee Mark, Department of Ethnic Studies, California State University, Sacramento.

We are thankful for the generous support from the Sacramento Regional Community Foundation. We wish to thank the editors of this book for their encouragement and Linda Rickards-Ito for her comments on earlier drafts of this chapter.

Correspondence concerning this article should be addressed to Greg M. Kim-Ju, Department of Psychology, California State University, Sacramento, 6000 J Street, Sacramento, CA 95819-6007. Electronic mail may be sent to kimju@csus.edu.

References

Allport, G. W. (1935). Attitudes. In C. Murchison (Ed.), *Handbook of social psychology* (pp. 798-884). Worchester, MA: Clark University Press.

American Psychological Association, Task Force on Socioeconomic Status. (2007). *Report of the APA Task Force on Socioeconomic Status.* Washington, DC: American Psychological Association.

Banuazizi, A. (1996). Psychology, the distant other, and the dialectics of change. In M.B. Lykes, A. Banuazizi, R. Liem, & M. Morris, M. (Eds.), *Myths about the powerless contesting social inequalities* (pp. 179–200). Philadelphia, PA: Temple University Press.

Cheeseman Day, J., & Newburger, E. C. (2002). *The big payoff: Educational attainment and synthetic estimates of work-life earnings.* Washington, DC: United States Census Bureau. Retrieved from http://www.census.gov/prod/2002pubs/p23–210.pdf

Cowen, E. L. (1994). The wooing of primary prevention. *American Journal of Community Psychology, 8,* 258–284.

Dalton, J., Elias, M., & Wandersmann, A. (2001). *Community psychology: Linking individuals and communities.* Belmont, CA: Wadsworth.

Fawcett, S. B., Francisco V. T., Hyra D., Paine-Andrews, A., Schultz, J. A., Russos, S., Fisher, J. L., & Evensen, P. (2000). Building healthy communities. In A. R Tarlov, R. F. St. Peter (Eds.), *The society and population health reader: A state and community perspective* (pp. 75–93). New York: New Press.

Kellog, A. P., & Tomsho, R. (2009, July 14). Obama plans community-college initiative. *The Wall Street Journal.* Retrieved from *http://online.wsj.com/article/SB124753606193236373.html*

Kim-Ju, G. M., Mark, G., Cohen, R., Garcia-Santiago, O., & Nguyen, P. (2008). Community mobilization and its application to youth violence prevention. *American Journal of Preventive Medicine, 34,* S5–S12.

Lederman, D. (2009, February 25). College for all. *Inside Higher Ed.* Retrieved from *http://www.insidehighered.com/news/2009/02/25/obama*

Nelson, G., & Prilleltensky, I. (Eds.). (2010). *Community psychology: In pursuit of liberation and well-being.* (2nd ed.). New York: Palgrave Macmillan.

Organization for Economic Co-operation and Development. (2010). *Education at a Glance 2010: OECD Indicators.* OECD Publishing.

Pathways to prosperity: Meeting the challenge of preparing young Americans for the 21st Century. (2011). Retrieved from Harvard University, Graduate School of Education   http://www.gse.harvard.edu/news_events/features/2011/Pathways_to_Prosperity_Feb2011.pdf

Prilleltensky, I & Nelson, G. (2009). Community psychology: Advancing social justice. In D. Fox, I. Prilleltensky, & S. Austin (Eds.), *Critical psychology: An introduction.* London: Sage.

Rappaport, J. (1981). In praise of paradox: A social policy of empowerment over prevention. *American Journal of Community Psychology, 9,* 1–25.

Rappaport, J. (1990). Research methods and the empowerment social agenda. In P. Tolan, C. Keys, F. Chertok, & L. Jason (Eds.), *Researching community psychology: Issues of theory and methods.* Washington, DC: American Psychological Association.

Reardon, K. (1998). Enhancing the development capacity of East St. Louis' community Organizations. *Journal of Planning Education and Research, 17 (4),* 323–333.

Ross, C. E., & Wu, C. (1995). The links between education and health. *American Sociological Review, 60,* 719–745.

Ryan, W. (1971). *Blaming the victim.* New York: Random House

Sacramento City Unified School District (2010). *Hiram W. Johnson High School Accountability Report Card 2009–2010.* Retrieved from *http://sacramentocity.school- wisepress.com/home/site.aspx?entity=20589&year=2010&lo* cale=en-US

Sacramento City Unified School District (2010). *Will C. Wood Middle School Accountability Report Card 2009–2010.* Retrieved from *http://sacramentocity .schoolwisepress.com/home/site.aspx?entity=20392&year=2010&lo* cale=en-US

Schmidt, P. (2003). Academe's Hispanic Future: The nation's largest minority group faces big obstacles in higher education, and colleges struggle to find the right ways to help. *The Chronicle of Higher Education, 50(14),* A8.

Sobredo, J., Kim-Ju, G. M., Figueroa, J, Mark, G., & Fabionar, J. (2008). An ethnic studies model of community mobilization: Collaborative partnership with a high risk public high school. *American Journal of Preventive Medicine, 34,* S82–S88.

Thayer, P. B. 2000. Retention of students from first generation and low income backgrounds. *Opportunity Outlook,* 2–8.

Trickett, E. J. (1996). A future for community psychology: The contexts of diversity and the diversity of contexts. *American Journal of Community Psychology, 24,* 209–226.

U.S. Census Bureau (2005). American Community Survey 2005. Available from U.S. Census Bureau Web site, http://www.census.gov.

U.S. Census Bureau (2006). American Community Survey 2006. Available from U.S. Census Bureau Web site, http://www.census.gov.

Reflection Questions

1. In your view, how much do context and politics define the human condition? (Optional)

2. To what degree do you believe these readings demonstrate a response and/or responsibility? (Optional)

3. Of the readings in this section, was there one reading in particular that you believed to be most effective in demonstrating response and responsibility given your own background? Please identify the reading and provide a brief explanation for your selection.

4. What are your personal examples that illustrate your own response and responsibility? (Optional)

5. Given the readings, what kind of person does it take to be responsive and responsible when it comes to creating positive race relations? Please offer a brief explanation using two examples to illustrate your point.